BUSINESS AND GOVERNMENT IN AMERICA SINCE 1870

A Twelve-Volume Anthology
of Scholarly Articles

Series Editor
ROBERT F. HIMMELBERG
Fordham University

A GARLAND SERIES

SERIES CONTENTS

VOLUME

11

REGULATORY ISSUES SINCE 1964

THE RISE OF THE DEREGULATION MOVEMENT

Edited with introductions by

ROBERT F. HIMMELBERG

GARLAND PUBLISHING, INC.
New York & London
1994

Library of Congress Cataloging-in-Publication Data

Regulatory issues since 1964 : the rise of the deregulation movement / edited with introductions by Robert F. Himmelberg.
        p.   cm. — (Business and government in America since
1870 ; v. 11)
        ISBN 0–8153–1413–2 (alk. paper)
        1.Deregulation—United States—History—20th century.
2. Industry and state—United States—History—20th century.
3. Competition—United States—History—20th century.
4. Business and politics—United States—History—20th
century.   I. Himmelberg, Robert F.   II. Series.
HD3616.U46R433   1994
338.973—dc20   93–47533
                                                              CIP

Printed on acid-free, 250-year-life paper
Manufactured in the United States of America

CONTENTS

SERIES INTRODUCTION

This compilation of articles provides a very broad and representative selection of the scholarly literature found in learned journals on the subject of government-business relations in the age of industry, the period since 1870. The scope of this collection is wide, covering all the arenas of business-government interaction. Sectorially, the focus is on manufacturing and transportation, upon whose rapid expansion after the Civil War the modern industrial economy was founded.

For the volumes covering the years from 1870 to 1965 (Volumes I through IX) it has been possible, while exercising selectivity, to include a very high proportion of everything published within the past thirty years. This literature is found largely in historical journals. More selectivity had to be employed for Volumes X through XII, which cover the period since 1965. Historians have not yet trodden much on the ground of the very recent past but social scientists and legal scholars have offered abundant materials, so abundant as to require a relatively severe selectivity. By choosing articles that appear to have a long-term analytical value and by excluding those too narrow in scope, too preoccupied with methodological questions or otherwise unsuitable for a non-specialized audience, an extensive and accessible body of writing has, however, been assembled for the post-1965 period, mainly from economics and legal periodicals.

The volumes are designed to contain articles relating to a particular period and to one or more topics within a period. The literature of business-government relations has four logically distinct major topics: antitrust, regulation, promotion, and cooperation. These topics define distinctive aspects of the relationship. Yet, the distinctions sometimes in practice blur, the ostensible, publicly proclaimed purposes of policy sometimes differing from the actually intended purposes or the actual outcomes.

Antitrust policy emerges in Volume I, which covers the era 1870–1900 when big business appeared, and figures prominently throughout the series. Several volumes are devoted entirely to it. Uniquely American, at least until relatively recently, antitrust policy has a complex history and much of what scholars have discovered about its origin and evolution is recorded only in the articles gathered in this collection. The literature reproduced here makes clear that the intent and impact of antitrust policy has varied enormously during its one-hundred-year history, which dates from the Sherman Act of 1890. Tension between competing objectives has existed from the outset. Should the "trusts" be broken up on the grounds that super-corporations inevitably conflict with democratic government and entrepreneurial opportunity? Or should only "bad trusts", those guilty of crushing competitors through unfair methods, suffer dissolution? Is cartelistic behavior always an illegal restraint of trade, or should it sometimes be tolerated if it helps small business to survive? Put most broadly, should the aim of antitrust policy be simply promoting competition, or should other conflicting social and economic values be recognized?

Business regulation also arose during the early stages of industrialization, appearing at the federal level with the enactment of the Interstate Commerce Act in 1887. The term "regulation" is used here to denote government policies intended, not to promote or restore competition, but to require specific behavior from business. The classic justification for regulation was the argument that in some situations the public interest could be served only through governmental prescription, that in some instances a remedy simply could not be obtained through the workings of the marketplace. Theoretically there are two such instances. The first occurs in the case of "natural monopoly," market situations in which competition would be wasteful and competing firms do not and should not exist. Railroads and public utilities were early identified as industries of this sort and were the first targets of government regulation. Would-be regulators early discovered a second justification for applying the regulatory approach, the situation in which competition fails to provide rival firms with incentives to avoid methods that may injure public health or well being. The argument found early expression in regulation of the meat-packing industry and has over the course of the twentieth century created a remarkable body of federal regulatory practices. The history of regulation, however, has not unfolded, any more than the history of antitrust, according to the logic of theory. It has been determined by the interplay between many factors, including the ideas of reformers, the complaints of those who have felt injured, policy rivalries among businessmen themselves, and the capacity or incapacity of government to execute planned reform. A major focus of recent literature on regulation, and to an extent on antitrust also, is the thesis of capture, the notion that regulatory efforts have often fallen captive to the interests they were intended to oppose.

The third theme of relations between government and business, promotion and encouragement, also emerged during the initial stages of the industrial era. Railroad subsidies abounded during the age of building the transcontinentals, of course, and protective tariffs were almost as old as the Republic itself. In the early twentieth century government support of trade expansion abroad enlarged and gradually became a major thread of government policy. Resembling promotion but logically distinct in many respects is the fourth category of business-government interaction, the area of cooperative relationships. Few scholars, even those who believe ongoing conflict has chiefly characterized business-government relations, would deny that cooperation has occurred at certain points, as during American participation in the major wars of the twentieth century. But in recent years many writers who conceive of business-government relations as taking place within a "corporatist" framework have perceived the scope and continuity of cooperative tendencies as very broad.

These four categories describe the subjects or topics around which scholarly investigation of business-government relations has revolved. There is, however, another approach to analyzing the literature of this relationship, one in which we ask about a writer's interpretive perspective, the conceptualizations the writer brings to the subject. All historians and social scientists, including those who created the literature collected here, adopt an interpretive standpoint from which to view society and its workings. An interpretive standpoint is a way of understanding the structure of society and the way those structural elements relate and interact; in other words, it is a "model" of society. Several rival models have competed for acceptance among scholars in recent times. Readers will be better equipped for informed reading of the literature assembled in these volumes if they are knowledgeable about these interpretive standpoints and the aim here therefore is to define the most important of these and give them appropriate labels.

Until the 1950s the prevailing interpretation of business-government relations—indeed, of American history generally— was the progressive viewpoint. The term progressive refers in the first place to the reform ideology and activity of the early twentieth century, the period before World War I. The perspective of the progressive generation continued for many years to dominate historical writing, not only on the period itself but on the whole of American history. According to the progressive perspective, the rise of big business during the late nineteenth and early twentieth centuries created a radical shift in the balance of economic and political power in America in favor of concentrated wealth. The rise of the "trusts", the powerful firms that came to predominate in many industries in the years after 1880, and the creation of cartels and other arrangements for suppressing competition, threatened independent capitalists and consumers with raw economic exploitation. This concentration of economic power threatened to utterly suborn representative political institutions as well and reduce American democracy to a plutocracy. In the progressive view the predominating tone of business-government relations was therefore necessarily antagonistic and conflictual.

The progressive paradigm became deeply embedded in the American consciousness. Reformist politicians have often reverted to it in shaping their ideological and rhetorical appeals. Franklin D. Roosevelt's attack in the campaign of 1936 upon "economic royalists" and John Kennedy's denunciation in 1962 of Big Steel during the controversy over price guidelines as "utterly contemptuous of the public interest" are vivid examples. The progressive outlook is evidently a persistent element in the popular historical consciousness. The power of the progressive conception of American history is in fact readily confirmed by reference to the way twentieth-century history is periodized, in textbooks and popular histories, into epochs of reform (the Progressive, New Deal, Fair Deal and Great Society periods) and of reaction (the Twenties, the Eisenhower and Reagan eras).

But if the progressive interpretation of business government relations retains some force among some historians and in the consciousness of liberal opinion makers and the public, its hold on much of the academic mind has long since weakened. A reaction among historians and other academics against the progressive paradigm emerged soon after the end of the Second World War and gathered force during the 1950s. The reaction was especially sharp among historians writing business history. Writing at a time when a reinvigorated American economy appeared to have overcome the doldrums of the 1930s and to be demonstrating the superiority of capitalism over other systems, energetic business and economic historians completely revised the progressive interpretation of the founders of American big business. The revisionists interpreted the founders not as greedy robber barons but as heroes of the entrepreneurial spirit, the spirit of enterprise and productivity. This revisionist interpretation proved too one-dimensional and celebratory to be maintained without modification. Revisionism, however, did succeed in thoroughly discrediting the progressive point of view. This circumstance, together with the impact of interpretive concepts emanating from post-war social science, moved historians to replace the progressive paradigm with a new and more sophisticated framework for understanding American political economy, the pluralist framework.

Pluralism as the dominant interpretive mode replaced progressivism in the 1950s and 60s. Speaking broadly, the pluralist model understands public policy as the result of struggle between economic and social groups. A major by-product of industrialization is the sharpening of differences between groups playing distinctive economic roles and a heightened articulation of self-interested goals and purposes on the part of such groups. Thus, government-business relations, that is, the shape of government policies towards business, are the result of rivalries among the major interest groups, business, labor, consumers, and so on. But the nature of the struggle is complex because the major groups are themselves divided into more or less rivalrous sub-groups. Business itself is divided; both intra- and inter-industry rivalries exist, sometimes in acute forms. Government policy is not merely the result of nonbusiness groups seeking to shape that policy but also of some business interests seeking to impose their own wishes on others.

During the 1960s pluralist interpretation became more complex. One important source of this heightened complexity was what some commentators have called the "organizational" outlook. Again influenced by currents in American social science, this time sociology, practitioners employing the organizational perspective are struck by the ever-increasing importance of large bureaucratic organizations in American life since the onset of industrialization. Business has continuously evolved in terms of an ever larger role for the large corporation, but other spheres, including government and the professions, also are organized in terms of large hierarchical bureaucracies. Borrowing from Weberian sociological traditions, writers impressed by the organizational perspective have explored the thesis that large bureaucracies wherever situated have similar requirements and tend to develop in those who manage them similar values and expectations. Thus, this brand of pluralism stresses the extent to which group leaders, including the managers and technicians who run the large corporations, developed accommodative as well as merely self-seeking motives. Business leaders, many of them at least, came to share certain values, such as respect for stability in the overall economy, which leads them to seek harmonious and cooperative relationships between interest groups and between them and the government. Government is assigned the role, in this construct, of facilitating and stimulating cooperative modes of behavior and umpiring conflicts. In the literature on business and government, figures who have advocated this kind of polity are often dubbed "corporatists" or "corporate liberals." Broadly defined, corporatism is the practice of cooperation between government and the corporate world to resolve economic issues. The existence and the importance of corporatist relationships has been one of the major emphases of recent scholarship but there is much disagreement as to the intentions of its practitioners and its impact. Some scholars have interpreted corporatism in a more or less positive light, as an ideology and a practice entailing cooperation rather than conflict between government and business, as an alternative to an adversarial relationship, a way of obtaining desirable economic performance from business without resorting to governmental coercion.

But others, especially but not only those writing in the vein of the "New Left", have argued that members of the corporate elite have frequently pursued their own narrow interests under the cover of ostensibly cooperative endeavors. The New Leftists emerged in the 1960s, expounding a more radical criticism of business than the progressive-liberal historians had advanced. The New Leftists doubted or denied outright that the American system was pluralist at all in any meaningful sense. Control of public policy might appear as a contest between social groups, but in fact one group, or rather class, those who controlled big business, enjoyed such lopsided power that the contest was apparently not real. Behind the facade of political infighting over government policy toward business, the masters of the corporate world quietly steered events toward outcomes which cemented in place control of the economy by monopoly capital.

These four conceptualizations, the progressive, the pluralist, the corporatist, and the New Leftist, are essentially theories of the structure and process of American political economy. However, rarely are researchers slavishly devoted to a theoretical perspective. Thus, those who see, in the progressive vein, an ongoing conflictual relationship between the people and business sometimes argue against the reformers and in favor of the businessmen. Even more significant and widespread is the conclusion of many writers using the pluralist or corporatist modes of interpretation, that regulation has not fostered equity and economic progress but rather has hardened the economy's vital arteries. Pluralists initially assumed that policies arising from a political arena to which all organized interests have access will inevitably achieve benign results, that the policy outputs will construct a system of "countervailing power" among organized interest groups. The assumption of acceptable outcomes is still prevalent, but a skeptical version of the results of interest group rivalries became manifest in the late

1960s, holding that both in origin and ongoing impact, business regulation was too often subject to "capture." In this view, regulatory measures and agencies and other policies seeking to guide business behavior toward balanced and generally acceptable outcomes readily fall under the control of the very interests they were intended to regulate.

There has emerged in recent years still another approach to the origin and process of social-economic policy that has been applied to the business-government connection. In this interpretation of the connection, a few examples of which will be found in articles collected here, emphasis is placed on the relative autonomy of government administrators and regulators. Seen by the pluralists as merely the creatures of the organizational struggles that result in public policies, in this new view regulators are seen as possessing substantial room for independent action. Thus the state is not merely to be seen as a passive receptor and executor of outcomes that social forces determine but as having a partially autonomous role which the officers of the state presumably will use to extend their own interests rather than the interests articulated by social groups.

These categories, progressivism, pluralism, corporatism, Leftism and the "autonomous officialdom" viewpoint, represent the major schools of thought and interpretation that readers will discover in the literature reproduced in these volumes. Writers investigating specific historical incidents, trends or problems have, in most cases, written through the framework provided by one or another of these interpretive models. As an alert reader will discover, most writers do have certain assumptions about the structure and dynamics of social relationships, and these assumptions stem from one of the models that have been described.

Interpretation of the relationship between business and government in the age of industry has given rise to a literature that is large and complex. It presents a stimulating intellectual challenge and is certainly relevant for anyone seeking understanding of contemporary business-government relations and endeavoring to predict, or to shape, their future course.

INTRODUCTION

Deregulation is the policy of restricting the scope of traditional regulatory activities intended to correct market malfunction caused by monopoly or other kinds of marketplace defects and returning regulated industries to the discipline of the competitive market. The movement for deregulation appeared in the late 1960s and came to fruition in the late 70s, its theoretical basis resting on three propositions: that regulatory agencies often were "captured" by the interests they were supposed to regulate; that regulation had sometimes been imposed without good reason, sometimes because an industry wanted to escape the competitive regimen; and finally, that technological change now made possible returning to a competitive status industries that before needed to be regulated.

Enthusiasm for deregulation blossomed amid political circumstances often hostile to big business. The tendency among students, academics and other intellectuals during the great controversy of the 1960s and early 70s over the Vietnam War was to adopt the theory of the "military-industrial complex" and to assume that most of what government did was at the behest of big business. The "capture" theory came into its own in these years and the traditional regulatory activities of the Interstate Commerce Commission, the Civil Aeronautics Board, the Federal Communications Commission, and many other regulatory agencies now came under severe criticism as too friendly toward, or as controlled by, the very interests the commissions were intended to regulate in the public interest. But partisans of the New Left neither initiated nor acted as the only force demanding deregulation. Deregulation, the returning of industry to the marketplace, appealed to many conservatives and to many people who had no strong ideological bent. Indeed, the initial, and much of the continuing, undermining of regulation performed by economists and other academic students of regulation was based on theoretical and empirical considerations rather than on ideology. Peaking during the presidency of Jimmy Carter, and continuing into the 1980s, deregulation was premised upon a wide-spread revulsion, in social and political circles, against much of traditional regulatory activity. The result was reform of the traditional regulatory agencies and actual dismantling of regulation for trucking, the airlines, and other industries. These now were to be subject to the vicissitudes of the marketplace.

The articles included in this volume provide insight into deregulation from several perspectives. The articles by Frank L. Barton and Byron Nupp, and D.L. Kaserman, for example, are helpful concerning the skepticism about transportation regulation that arose among academic theoreticians during the 1960s and 1970s. Several articles discuss, and endeavor to test, the proposition that regulation retards economic growth or creates other economic problems, such as undue profits. (See the articles by Frank L. Barton and Byron Nupp and by Gregory B. Christainsen and Robert H. Haveman.) Still another issue, the results of deregulation, is analyzed by another set of articles, including those by Michael Fix and George Eads, by Alexander L. Morton and by Richard H.K. Vietor.

Regulatory
Issues
Since 1964

REGULATION AND ECONOMIC PERFORMANCE IN TRANSPORTATION

Frank L. Barton* and Byron Nupp**

Regulation of transportation is one of our older economic policies, following perhaps only the tariff and public land policies in importance to American history. Public policy in economics may have two objectives, not necessarily separate: economic development and balancing conflicting interests. Regulation is considered primarily in terms of its balancing function, but it has also certain imputed or explicit developmental goals. Actually economic performance may require both economic and political balance. The economist senses this in his concept of equilibrium, for where the concentration of economic forces sets aside the classic equilibrium, the balance is restored through political means; hence regulation.

Perhaps the fundamental basis of economic conflict is the constant struggle between producers and consumers. In transportation the producers are represented by the common carrier systems; the consumers by the shippers of goods and other user groups. Some would equate the user interest with the general public interest. However, such an equation is not accurate. Transportation is usually an intermediate process in the production of final consumer satisfactions. Users of transportation are most often themselves powerful producer interests fighting for a share of the distribution of income. They will not only try to maximize their profit from the ultimate consumer but will also seek savings from their intermediate suppliers, including transportation. Similarly, transportation producers will try the same tactic on their consumers, and thus the need for a balancing mechanism arises. Where the free market fails (and it often has failed), public policy takes over.

Public attitude toward this conflict has been rather one-sided. The public often sees the carrier or other public service industry as the exploiter and identifies the public interest with transportation users. This unfortunate misunderstanding derives from historical circumstances. The first incursion of public policy in this field was against

* Deputy Under Secretary for Transportation, Department of Commerce. LL.B. Georgetown University Law School.

** Chief, Land Transportation Staff, Office of the Under Secretary for Transportation, Department of Commerce.

the carriers and attempted in the early Granger laws[1] and the original Act to Regulate Commerce of 1887[2] to redress the balance in favor of the shippers against the railroads. While this purpose was predominant, especially during the early part of this century with the strengthening amendments in the Hepburn[3] and Mann-Elkins[4] acts among others, carrier protection against shippers had a place. The predatory wars of the Standard Oil Trust against the carriers are well known, as are the former practices of rebates and preferential rates exacted from the carriers by powerful economic interests.

Law itself was not very helpful in the early years in bringing about a more accurate understanding of the true balancing role of regulation. The prevailing laissez-faire mystique sought a rationalization of the need for public policy. Such a rationalization was found in *Munn v. Illinois*[5] and similar pronouncements concerning industries "affected with a public interest," twisting the honorable English doctrine of "common callings"[6] into an injunction against natural monopolies. The public readily accepted this rationalization that a common carrier was a sort of misbegotten child whose naturally mischievous tendencies required permanent parole under a regulatory commission.

Thanks to *Nebbia v. New York*[7] and greater public sophistication in economics, there has been a gradual return toward the original English concept of "common callings." However, there is continuing need to vest some industries with public interest status, and nature does not accomplish this. To vest an industry with public interest status is a conscious decision of public policy. It implies a two-way obligation; namely, to protect the users against exploitation and to maintain the integrity of the service itself to the extent necessary.

Transportation regulation has evolved in such a way as to illustrate the wider interest in the regulatory process. The economic pendulum has swung away from the monopolistic carrier in favor of the

---

[1] The Granger laws were a series of state statutes sponsored by the Granger organizations in the various states. Generally, these statutes dealt with the storage and shipment of grain and other agricultural produce. See, e.g., Munn v. Illinois, 94 U.S. 113 (1876).

[2] 24 Stat. 379 (1887).

[3] 34 Stat. 584 (1906).

[4] 36 Stat. 539 (1910).

[5] 94 U.S. 113 (1876). The background of this case is discussed in H. Smith, Government and Business 129-33 (1958), based on Commons, Legal Foundations of Capitalism (1924).

[6] See discussion in Munn v. Illinois, supra note 5, at 125-30.

[7] 291 U.S. 502 (1934).

shipper. The nature of the market itself has been a fundamental force here. Alternative forms of transportation developed, giving the shipper choices which he was quick to exploit. Common carriage in new forms such as trucking, air, and barge sought regulation against the shipper's demand for excessive competition. The shipper's advantage was pressed in another direction. The new forms permitted *private* transportation which grew rapidly and exceeded the size of common carriage in each of the newer modes. But the user interest was not content. It sought the reinforcement of public policy itself through wide exemptions from common carrier status, in such areas as agricultural marketing or bulk commodity movements.[8] The government as a shipper took up the idea and added one of its own: special rates from regulated common carriers.[9]

It would seem, given the advantages now possessed by the shipper interest, that some new balance should be struck in favor of the common carrier. A greater share of income should go to the latter so that he can renew his plant and improve his service policy. Moreover, common carriage should be allowed to grow at a rate at least equal to the growth rate of the economy as a whole. Growth should be stimulated by restricting the present possibilities of incursion into the common carrier market by equalizing exemptions and eliminating abuse of private privileges in transportation. Such a redressing of the economic balance also would have developmental ends. It would increase the efficiency and economy of common carrier service and widen the economic opportunity of other shipper groups.

While the common carrier has extra costs imposed by his public obligation, he can offset these costs in part through his service to a

---

[8] Agricultural exemption, section 203(b)(4b), Motor Carrier Act of 1935, 49 Stat. 545 (1935), 49 U.S.C. § 303(b)(5) (1958), exempts motor vehicles controlled and operated by a cooperative association as defined in the Agricultural Marketing Act, and section 203(b)(6), Motor Carrier Act of 1935, 49 Stat. 545 (1935), 49 U.S.C. § 303(b)(6) (1958), exempts motor vehicles used in carrying ordinary livestock, fish, or agricultural commodities but not including manufactured products thereof. The Transportation Act of 1958, 72 Stat. 568 (1958), 49 U.S.C. §§ 1231, 1232 (1958), added an interesting amendment to this latter exemption specifically naming commodities no longer subject to the exemption.

Bulk commodity exemptions apply only to water transportation and are contained in section 303 of the Interstate Commerce Act, 54 Stat. 931 (1940), as amended, 49 U.S.C. § 903 (1958). All liquid bulk commodities carried in tank vessels are exempt. Dry bulk commodities that were in the water trades on June 1, 1939 are exempt so long as not more than three commodities are carried in a tow or vessel, or the tow or vessel has no commodities under regulation.

[9] Section 22 of the Interstate Commerce Act, 24 Stat. 387 (1887), as amended, 49 U.S.C. § 22 (1958), providing for "free or reduced" transportation, is the outstanding example. Alaska, Hawaii, and other non-contiguous water trades are permitted to quote special governmental rates under the Intercoastal Shipping Act, 47 Stat. 1427 (1933), 46 U.S.C. §§ 843-48 (1958).

greater number of shippers. He obtains a wider sampling of traffic than does a private carrier, and some operating economies are undoubtedly inherent in this wider market. It is in the public interest that this operating economy accrue to the common carrier and not be dissipated through a skimming by private interests. A large volume of the transportation service in the nation is provided by small independent operators who, all too frequently, do not provide regularly scheduled services and responsible accounting because they are exempted from regulation. The availability of this traffic to responsible common carriers would do much to increase economy and efficiency and help significantly to maintain the integrity of carrier services.[10]

What can public policy do here? Laws governing exemptions from regulation can be more nearly equal and more specific in defining the exemption intended. In some cases the exemption can be made a part of the regulatory process itself by basing it on regulatory determination rather than absolute legislative license. The present commercial zone exemption in the Motor Carrier Act[11] is an example of a conditional exemption based on the regulatory process itself. In the case of the private carrier, the exemption should be limited as much as possible to the shipper's private interest in his own traffic. An exemption should stand on its own merits only and not be in competition with public interests.

What are the public benefits that flow from a system of regulated common carrier service? Essentially, the public interest is fostered by the general availability of service to all on an equal basis, a factor considered essential to the preservation and advancement of economic opportunity. Thus, to the extent that equality of economic opportunity increases industrial efficiency and promotes economic growth, the operation of a common carrier system becomes a vehicle for promoting both economic and sociological good. To this extent the maintenance of a sound common carrier service is a developmental policy of importance to the whole economy.

This factor is well illustrated by the controversy over regulation of pipelines.[12] Pipelines grew up as an essentially private transporta-

---

10 The Doyle Report, Staff of Senate Committee on Interstate and Foreign Commerce, 87th Cong., 1st Sess., Report on National Transportation Policy (Comm. Print 1961), gives an extensive background on exempt and illegal transportation, particularly by motor carrier, at 515-46.
11 49 Stat. 545 (1935), 49 U.S.C. § 303(b)(8) (1958).
12 Hepburn Act, 34 Stat. 584 (1906). A thorough discussion of the pipeline problem is found in H.R. Rep. No. 27, 86th Cong., 1st Sess. (1959).

tion service and came to be used as a means of promoting economic concentration in the oil industry. In declaring pipelines common carriers, the Hepburn Act intended to open up economic opportunity to shippers outside the restrictions of the larger oil companies. In other forms of transportation this factor, though possibly not so dramatic, is present nevertheless.

Thus economic performance is one of the elements involved in regulation, even though oriented in form toward a public policy of balance between producer and user interests in transportation. The public is interested in maintaining the integrity of both interests.

The integrity of a common carrier service or indeed any other public service industry cannot be taken for granted. Day by day, week by week, year in and year out, service on the best possible terms is a necessity. Integrity must be maintained. The public service corporation must be made accountable for its own corporate and financial integrity. Experience has shown that the free play of economic forces has not always been successful in this regard. To maintain such integrity, and to promote the most efficient use of capital, public intervention has been necessary.

There are several reasons why public policy must supplement the normal workings of a free economy for maximum economic efficiency in transportation service. Discontinuous investment destroys the market as a completely effective arbiter of the integrity of some transportation firms. The railroads provide a good example.[13] A single railroad line provides an enormous capacity. The history of cut-throat rivalry in the industry indicates that there is always the temptation to price so as to use the full capacity. In fact there is often a cycle of cut-throat rivalry followed by intervals of high stable rates as the few competitors learn to live for awhile in harmony. Rate regulation is necessary to provide a reasonable return on capital under these conditions. Recently, with the introduction of jet transports, the airline industry may have developed into an industry with an ever-present danger of ruinous undermining of the price structure. This is the classic picture of oligopoly or imperfect competition described by economists.

At the other extreme is the danger of a capital structure representing perfect continuity of investment profile.[14] Here the danger

---

[13] An excellent discussion is found in Locklin, Economics of Transportation 137-66 (1954). An extensive bibliography gives the development of the theoretical literature in this field.

[14] A perfect continuity of investment would mean ideally that investment could

is a ruinous over-capacity of investment through the free entry of small operators. The trucking industry in the depression period was such an industry. The perfect continuity of investment discouraged the development of a reliable service or any kind of rate structure reasonably related to the true cost of doing business. Regulation providing for control of entry and control of rates was enacted to correct this cause of economic inefficiency.

Competition between transportation industries with widely differing cost structures is another area where the free market force may not be entirely adequate. Some regulatory separation of rate structures may be necessary, although this does not condone the umbrella theory of ratemaking.[15] As the Transportation Act of 1958 apparently intended, the public is entitled to the inherent cost and service advantages of each mode.[16] It is assumed that where there is a unit cost disadvantage there must be a service advantage to offset it. Thus low rail or water costs are accompanied by high minimum volumes which hamper the flexibility of the shipper. Higher truck costs are accompanied by flexible service which is worth the premium paid.

The danger is that rate and service advantages will be used to spot special rates on individual movements or points, and not be related to a genuine common carrier service policy reflecting a cost advantage. Rate structures should be widely applicable to serve entire trades or sectors of the economy on equitable terms and not merely particularly favored stations or shippers. The implication is that there

---

be adjusted immediately to the demands for service through small increments. Such continuity would not work practically because the small increments, represented in highway transportation by motor trucks, can be acquired by an infinite number of entrepreneurs. The lack of knowledge of the state of the investment in the industry would result in irrationalities in the investment pattern at given points in time. Such a pattern is not always conducive to the best service. There is thus a clear choice of policy; continuity of investment can be achieved either through the direct response of many free entrepreneurs or by the actions of a limited number of concerns who would add to their investment to meet a given level of business. Most authorities on motor carrier regulation imply that restriction of entry and controls of rates are necessary in the interests of maintaining an acceptable standard of service.

15 The umbrella theory of ratemaking is a protective device whereby the rates of a low-cost carrier are made higher by a regulatory agency so that the rates of a high-cost carrier will be competitive.

16 Exact meanings of the amendments to section 15a of the Interstate Commerce Act provided in the Transportation Act of 1958, 72 Stat. 572 (1958), 49 U.S.C. § 15a (1958), ultimately will be the result of ICC and court decisions. While prohibiting the holding of rates to a given level to protect the traffic of any given mode of transportation, the legislation also requires that such rates take into account the objectives of the National Transportation Policy in the act, 54 Stat. 899 (1940), 49 U.S.C. preceding § 1 (1958).

must be a service policy of the common carrier industry to go hand-in-hand with a rate policy.

Some of the obstacles to a complete market orientation of service policy by the transportation industry have been noted. Not only is regulation necessary to overcome these imperfections, but private initiative itself will tend to be a matter of conscious policy as much as automatic reactions to market or other free economic forces. Business policy has supplemented the invisible hand of Adam Smith and is an indispensable part of a public service such as transportation. Rates, terms of service, and new investment policies are developed in the first instance through the initiative of management. Regulatory impacts, while decisive in shaping the direction of policy, are sketchy and deal with only a part of the total spectrum of activity in a public service business. Often regulatory decisions merely ratify a policy that has been worked out in detail by industry or some contending part of it.

It is important to remember, however, that business policy is a conscious endeavor. Like all human activities it has its uses and abuses. Where business policy degenerates into corporate manipulation, the public interest will not be served. The large corporation, with its diverse sources of funds with varying priorities on income and ambiguous relationships among security holders and management, is an artificial economic entity that does not conform to the classic concept of the entrepreneur. Not every element of management or ownership will be interested in the long-run advantage of the firm. Some may find it possible to discover their own profit in the corporation's disadvantage or even downfall.

A limited amount of pulling and hauling within the corporate family may be tolerated, if not excused, in business generally. In public service industries intra-corporate abuses cannot be tolerated. It is not surprising, therefore, that public regulation has moved into the details of corporative transactions in public service enterprises. Too often this occurred after the corporate horse had been stolen; witness the Public Utility Holding Company Act which brought about the reform of the financial structure of the utility industry.[17] Free-wheeling transactions in transportation and utility stocks and

---

[17] 49 Stat. 803 (1935), 15 U.S.C. §§ 79-79z-6 (1958). The most spectacular feature of this act was the "death sentence" clause, 49 Stat. 820 (1935), 15 U.S.C. §§ 79k(b) (1), (2), which allowed the Securities and Exchange Commission to rearrange the corporate structures of the holding company empires in the utility field. See Koontz & Gable, Public Control of Economic Enterprise (1956).

bonds work directly against economic performance. This fact can be attested to by more than a century's observations—from Jay Gould's rusty Erie tracks to the present plight of the New Haven.

Regulation, therefore, has the economic objective of keeping out gross business policy abuses and fostering sound management standards. Upon a foundation of sound management, business policy can move on to creative opportunities to improve transportation service in the public interest.

Certainly regulation can shore up and promote economic efficiency through direct controls. In other respects the direct application of regulation works as a disadvantage.

The regulatory agency cannot have as intimate a knowledge of men and events as those working daily in the transportation field. Market conditions change constantly, new techniques and technologies arise, and better management methods are discovered. Not only is a business management closer to its problems, but also it must deal in greater detail with the involvement of greater numbers of persons. There is always the danger that regulatory standards will not be entirely suitable for the most efficient operation of a transportation enterprise.

Here is a dilemma. The regulatory authorities must be informed adequately of corporate activities in the services they regulate. This information must come to them in a standard form so that it can be used to yield an accurate picture of events. Yet the heart of the problem concerning management standards is that the standards promulgated by a commission may not be the best from the standpoint of economic efficiency. Such standards as safety, accounting, and statistics are cases in point.

Safety standards involve every type of operation. As techniques improve, old safety standards become out of date. The detailed requirements of the Ash Pan Act[18] for coal burning locomotives are amusing today. Accounting and statistical standards similarly become outmoded as progress goes on. The accounting profession has complained frequently about the outmoded accounting enforced upon regulated enterprises.[19] The cost standards of the Interstate Commerce Commission have been attacked as being of very limited usefulness in managing a railroad.[20] It is not known whether every

---

[18] 35 Stat. 476 (1908), 45 U.S.C. §§ 17–21 (1958).

[19] A particularly good statement of this issue appears in 36 Harv. Bus. Rev., May-June, 1958, pp. 115-24.

[20] Meyers, Competition in the Transportation Industries (1959).

statistical table obtained from the carriers is useful either to the regulator or the carrier.

This serious dilemma is not close to resolution. Is it possible for the public to be informed about the public service industries through standards that are most useful to management and which are constantly evolving? Does the normal regulatory prescription fit this need, or can other approaches be used? If there are other approaches, how wide can be their application to such affairs of public service industries as safety, accounting, financing, service policies, and ratemaking?

An approach toward this problem may be to utilize the resources of business policy in close conjunction with regulatory policy. In other words, in some areas of regulatory requirements, methods might be devised whereby well-considered business policies and standards might be adopted by the regulatory bodies as suitable for their information. For example, the various branches of the industry, through periodic committees or conferences, might recommend revisions of safety standards to reflect the latest advances. The commissions would have the option of adopting or modifying them in the public interest. Accounting and cost standards also might be developed in this way.

Such an approach is not alien to government-business relationships. Ratemaking is essentially left to the carriers, although frequent regulatory actions, sometimes quite detailed, set basic direction to policy. Outside regulation, the process of promulgating industrial standards is similar to the one described. The Bureau of Standards in the Department of Commerce serves as the secretariat to an elaborate series of industrial committees. These committees, reflecting the current experience of industry, recommend standards which are studied and tested in the Bureau's laboratories and then, if accepted, are promulgated as standards for the operation of industry. A similar process takes place in the Commodity Standards Division of the Department of Commerce with respect to consumer goods, and so agricultural standards are evolved in a similar way through the Department of Agriculture.

Greater attention should be given to the possibilities of adopting means whereby progressive business policies of transportation industries can be reflected in official regulatory policies. Regulation should become less concerned with detailed matters and more with basic policies and trends. Regulation thus freed could have a creative role in the economic development of transportation. This role could be increased greatly without in any way becoming involved in the detailed workings of the industry.

Inherent in the regulatory process is the recognition of the public interest in common carriers. This interest requires protection of the shippers and protection of transportation from the predaciousness of the shippers.

Naturally the present regulatory process, evolving through the years, has many shortcomings. Not only is it too detailed and meddlesome in what are really non-essentials, but it leaves great gaps of public interest unprotected. These gaps not only affect the common carrier system adversely but hamper the work of the commissions themselves through the many loopholes and ambiguities provided.

Recently all of the regulatory commissions have taken steps to improve their own internal management. Backlogs of cases have become a national problem. Through the delegation of detailed matters to employee boards or other less formal procedures, it is hoped that the time of the responsible members can be conserved to engage in policy making. The next step, obviously, is to bring many higher rated employees into the policy-making process by freeing regulation of cumbersome and time-consuming detail which may hamper the determination or establishment of effective business policy for transportation service.

But even when this step has been taken, it will have only cleared the way for the really creative role of regulatory policy—the revision and keeping up to date of the statutes themselves, and the use of ex parte authority to guide the policies of transportation service industries. The aim would be to bring common carriers fully into the stream of economic progress and to promote economic development policies through effective common carrier services.

Much must be learned about orderly revisions of our regulatory statutes. There appears to be a school of thought which regards the regulatory statutes as sacred texts to be amended only after a painful process analogous to an amendment to the Constitution. Another school appears to feel the whole regulatory set-up is so hopeless that it should be reformed in one fell swoop once and for all. Still another group feels that the statutes should be amended with a very light touch and only after obtaining broad consensus among carriers and other economic interests. There is an element of merit in all these positions, but none represents fully the kind of approach that is needed.

The regulatory statutes should be dealt with neither gently nor harshly, but systematically and periodically and through authoritative channels. For example, the executive branch and the committees of Congress should make periodic reviews of regulatory performance and be able to present, possibly in each session of Congress, a program of revisions. Such a systematic approach is lacking today, although there have been extensive reviews and some amendments in recent years.

A regulatory law must steer a middle course between two extremes if it is to be an effective instrument of economic policy. It must get away from detailed prescription similar to the legislative ratemaking of former years. It also must provide sufficient policy guidance to hold the commissions to explicit standards. Generally speaking, our regulatory statutes have kept to the middle course reasonably well. If they have erred, it has been on the side of generality. As the Doyle Report points out, a law should be specific enough so that the courts and administrative agencies are not free to "rattle around" in very general provisions.[21] Possibly more systematic revisions of future regulatory laws should provide explicit policy guides and standards for the regulatory bodies. Such a practice exists in Canada where the periodic Royal Commissions provide policy reviews for the benefit of the regulatory tribunals of that country.

Given a law to administer which is periodically reviewed and adjusted to the needs of the times, what should the members of the commissions themselves do? The regulatory commissions should be essentially policy-making bodies, conducting studies and investigations on their own motion, and promulgating guidelines on specific subjects for the benefit of the commissions' employees who should make practically all detailed determinations. Regulation here has scored some successes, but there has been too much immersion in detail. Even many *ex parte* investigations have dragged on for years, wallowed in massive detail, and failed to come to the clear understanding of policy which such an investigation is intended to produce.

Public regulation is no place to allow policy to be made by default. Programs should not be made to depend on the cases which happen to arise. Regulation is a dynamic process which seeks out public interests and needs. Regulation is not incompatible with economic

---

[21] The Doyle Report, supra note 10, at 446-48.

performance. Conducted properly, it can be an instrument to increase the economic performance of the common carrier industry. It can be a primary means of attaining economic goals for our society.

To be most effective in this regard some changes in process and procedure are necessary. Authoritative and systematic review of regulatory laws and objectives is needed. The tribunals themselves must continue to alter their management of the subject matter before them, first by delegating more detail, then by exploring better means of enlisting the knowledge and skills of the carriers, and finally and most importantly, by transforming the responsible members into policy-making officials seeking new and better directions.

The Making of Forest Policy in Pulp and Paper Trade Associations, 1878–1986

by Willard S. Bromley

The Paper Industry's Early Indifference to Forestry

Records of the American Paper Institute in New York City show that until the end of the last century, the pulp and paper industry in the United States had no reason to be seriously concerned over "forest policy." Until then there was no need to be interested in the social and economic aims underlying forest management and forestry development. Forest products were not successfully used on a commercial scale to make paper until after the 1860s, when the groundwood process was developed to make newsprint.[1]

For the making of finer grades of paper, rags—mostly imported—and cotton were still the major sources of raw materials even in the 1880s. The early trade associations were thus more concerned with supplies of rags from abroad than with domestic wood supplies. In 1878 several product and regional groups of paper manufacturers organized their first national organization, the American Paper Makers Association, the APMA, with William Whiting of the

Whiting Paper Company as president. At the association's eighth annual meeting in July 1885, the principal item of business was "the supply of rags for paper making. . . . Cholera had broken out abroad and therefore, importation of rags from infected areas was severely restricted. Prices went up to such an extent that those branches of the industry dependent upon rags for raw material became completely demoralized."[2]

Forestry and Pulpwood Issues Taken Up By Papermakers

It was not until the annual meeting in 1891 that committee agendas of the APMA even made reference to "forest depletion."[3] Wood was gaining in importance as the basic raw material for paper. The development of chemical pulping processes (soda, sulfite, and sulfate, in that order) accelerated the demand for wood and expanded the scope of species to be used. To the industry, however, wood was a readily available and inexpensive raw material in these early years. The association discussed "forest depletion" more to demonstrate its concern publicly than because it really feared a shortage.

Eleven years after the pulp and paper

industry set up its own association, the name was changed to the "American Paper and Pulp Association" and H. J. Chisholm was elected president. Members at that time paid a one-time-only admission charge of $10.00. In 1905 the association established its first permanent headquarters, in New York City, but it did not create any standing bodies to deal with wood supply or forest policy until fifteen years later.

In 1920, the APPA created a "Woodlands Section" devoted to "problems connected with pulpwood supply." The first two meetings, both in 1921, discussed tractors for harvesting pulpwood, forest maps for managing timber and taxation, slash disposal, reforestation, woods wages and employment conditions, and the general application of forestry methods to pulpwood operations. Up to 1926, the secretary of the section was O. M. Porter, and then D. A. Crocker was secretary-forester for a few years. The section created its first standing committees on pulpwood trade customs and on forestry. At the seventh annual meeting of the section, in 1927, primary speakers were the directors of the Department of Agriculture's Northeast, Lake States, and Appalachian forest experiment stations: respectively, Samuel T. Dana, Raphael Zon, and Earl H. Frothingham. According to the agenda, each man discussed for his region the topic, "Is practical forest management for the continuous production of pulpwood possible?" Just before his retirement early in 1928, O. M. Porter initiated a monthly mimeographed publication entitled "Pulpwood."

In 1929, Charles W. Boyce, acting secretary of the APPA, presented to the "Cost Convention" at Wausau, Wisconsin, a paper entitled "Pulpwood Costs as Affected

---

1. Ann M. Carlton, *Handbook of Pulp and Paper Technology*, 2nd edition (New York: Van Nostrand Reinhold Company, 1970), p. 709. Dard Hunter claimed that the first groundwood pulp mill in the United States was built in Curtisville, Massachusetts, in 1867 (*Papermaking—The History and Technique of an Ancient Craft* [New York, Alfred A. Knopf Inc., 1943], p. XX), although other sources have given that honor to slightly older plants in New York State or Maine (see David C. Smith, "Pulp and Paper Industry," *Encyclopedia of American Forest and Conservation History* [New York: Macmillan Publishing Company for the Forest History Society, 1983], p. 551).

2. *New Horizons: A History of Seventy-five Years of the American Paper and Pulp Association* (New York: APPA, 1952), p. 8.

3. Titles of papers and other information about the early policies of the APMA and APPA are based on the minutes of meetings and copies of letters and publications bound in volumes by years and filed in the library of the American Paper Institute, New York, 1887–1982. Unfortunately, the texts of the papers are not in the API files.

14

Figure 1.
Key dates in Pulp and Paper
Organizations and Policy

1878	APMA (American Paper Makers Association) organized.
1897	APPA (American Paper and Pulp Association) replaced APMA.
1905	First permanent headquarters of APPA established in New York City.
1920	APPA Woodlands Section and Forest Policy Committee set up.
1934	APA (American Pulpwood Association) established.
1954	APPA dropped Woodlands Section and Forest Policy Committee, to rely on APA for pulpwood issues.
1967	API (American Paper Institute) replaced APPA, by consolidating some fourteen separate associations of the paper industry.

Figure 2.
Key Dates in Coordinating Forest Policy
with all Forest Product Groups Nationally

1943	FIC (Forest Industries Council) organized.
1959	ECFI (Economic Council of the Forest Industries) initiated.
1965	NFPA (National Forest Products Association) consolidated major regional and forest product associations and replaced NLMA.
1966	FIC expanded representation to include about a half-dozen major regional and forest groups.
1968	AFI (American Forest Institute) replaced AFPI.
1970	ECFI includes leaders of pulp and paper for first time.
1977	FIAC (Forest Industries Advisory Council) replaced ECFI.
1985	FIAC & FIC are placed on a standby basis, not to meet unless significant major issues arise which justify calling a meeting.
1986	AFI is reorganized as AFC (American Forest Council).

by Regional Competition."[4] In this paper Boyce stressed the need for sound long-term investment in forests by pulp and paper companies. He urged companies to take their initial steps in practicing forestry on lands close to their mills.

Beyond these early presentations and publications, a careful scrutiny of the records for formal actions taken by the national association of the industry in its first fifty years does not show much concern or action in national-level forest policy. On

4. Cost Association of the Paper Industry, "Pulp and Paper Profits 1924–1932," manuscript in the Library of the American Paper Institute, New York.

the other hand, the elected leaders of the APPA thought forestry important enough to hire technically trained foresters as the first four full-time staff executives (with the title of executive secretary) of the association: Hugh P. Baker (Yale 1904), O. M. Porter (Yale 1915), Charles W. Boyce (University of Michigan 1914), and E. W. Tinker (Yale 1915). Their combined service from 1920 to 1956 carried the APPA "Woodlands Section" forward during a period when the industry was gradually coming to see pulpwood as its basic raw material.

The American Pulpwood Association was organized in 1934, partly to develop

Figure 3.
Industrial Organizations Dealing with Forest Policy (1985)

Forest Industries Advisory Council (FIAC)
Committee of Past Chairmen

Forest Industries Council (FIC)
Operations Committee (chief staff executives of FIC member associations)

FIC Member Associations

American Forest Institute

American Paper Institute

American Plywood Association

American Pulpwood Association

American Wood Council

Industrial Forestry Association

National Forest Products Association

Southern Forest Products Association

Western Wood Products Association

Forest Industries Committee on Timber Valuation and Taxation

FIC Issues Committees
(active only as needed)

- Safety and Health
- Transportation
- Communications
- Energy
- Company Executives and Forestry Deans
- API/NFPA Environmental Council

American Forest Institute
(secretariat of FIC)

- Provides information and education
- Supports tree farm system
- Southern Forest Institute

PULP AND PAPER   193

15

an industry code of operation under the National Industrial Recovery Act.[5] Although the Paper Industry Authority created to administer the code lasted only until 1935,[6] it represented a new level of policy cooperation among users and consumers of pulp and pulpwood. From its founding to the present the APA has represented dealers and producers of wood and wood chips such as chip mills, sawmills, and veneer mills, as well as the paper and pulp manufacturers. Suppliers who are completely independent of the pulp mills have always provided the latter with more than half their total annual wood requirements. Given the mills' dependence on wood from lands not controlled by the pulp and paper companies, a single association representing the entire production process has made good economic and political sense.

A major portion of the expenses of APA was always covered by assessments on the "consumer" members, representing more than fifty pulp companies by 1985. Also by the 1980s, the supplier and "associate" members represented close to 100,000 independent business operations concerned with pulpwood or equipment used in processing pulpwood. Many of them supported APA programs although they were not full members. The association could therefore bring these businesses' support into wider associations representing the entire forest products sector, as well as to the legislative, forest policy, and public education programs of the APA itself.

The Forest Industries Council, 1943–60

The Forest Industries Council (FIC) was initiated in 1943 to meet the urgent need for a policy-coordinating committee to represent the forest industries as a whole. At the beginning of World War II the forest industries were frequently in conflict with each other as they dealt with Congress, the War Department, and other government agencies. Wilson Compton, secretary-manager of the NLMA (National Lumber Manufacturers Association), E. W. Tinker, newly appointed executive secretary of the APPA (American Paper and Pulp Associa-

tion), and several of the top leaders in the forest industries, such as F. K. Weyerhaeuser of Weyerhaeuser Sales Co., S. B. Copeland of Northwest Paper Co., and A. B. Hansen of Northern Paper Mills, all saw the need for coordination. This was accomplished by having the elected and paid staff officers of the major forest industry associations meet — as the FIC — at least annually and as needed to determine policies and plans of action. The major associations then representing paper (APPA) and pulpwood (APA) were located in New York City, and the lumber association (NLMA) had its headquarters in Washington, D.C. From its inception the FIC functioned without a staff, office, or budget of its own. One of the member associations provided secretarial services.

It was not easy for these different segments of the forest industries to set aside some of their basic differences. The solid wood (lumber and plywood) segment required heavy logging equipment, usually in large camp operations, and relied upon national forests and other government forest reserves primarily in the western United States for its raw material. The fiber wood (pulpwood and pulp) segment required very small logging equipment and small crews and relied almost entirely on small timber purchased from farmers and woodlot owners in the South and North, east of the Rocky Mountains.

As representatives of the two groups met in 1943 and subsequent years, however, they discovered common goals and soon saw the advantage of working together. They strove to coordinate their responses to a series of challenges:[7]

1. Concerted and continued efforts to extend federal control over private forestry enterprise through regulation of cutting practices. In 1942 Congress had received and approved in principle committee recommendations that the states adopt "minimum forestry practices" that met the standards of the federal government. The congressional action implied further that the federal government would step in to enforce its

own standards in any state that did not do so on its own initiative.
2. Increased taxes on forest operations. Some owners in all forest regions cited high property taxes as their major reasons for clearcutting and liquidating or selling their timber. The forest industries pressed vigorously for recognition of the long-term investments required for sound forest management. Although property taxes as such were levied by state governments, tax relief arrived from another direction when Congress amended the federal income tax law in 1944, applying the new capital gains provision to reduce materially taxes on timber holdings cut or sold after being held for six months or more. Many timber owners ploughed the resulting tax savings back into a tremendous expansion of tree planting and other forest improvements.
3. The constantly expanding government ownership of forest resources, which industry representatives saw as constantly shrinking their room to maneuver. By 1953 the federal government had 153 national forests, with a total 181 million acres of forestland. Of that, 21 million were in Alaska and 19 million had been purchased primarily in eastern states. Public ownership of forestland by other federal agencies and state governments in most forested states was increasing rapidly in the late 1950s and early 1960s, reducing the forestland available for commercial operations, increasing the cost of forest harvesting, and raising the prices of forest products to consumers.

The second annual meeting of the FIC on 5 December 1944 produced several structural and policy changes. Membership was reconstituted to include:

5 representatives from NLMA
3 representatives from APPA
1 representative from APA
1 representative from SPCA (the Southern Pulpwood Conservation Association)

The staff managers of these associations were to serve as ex officio members of the council.

At this same meeting the council adopted a general forest policy statement that it referred to member associations for approval and application to their respective programs. With minor exceptions, the industry's trade associations used this 1944 statement as a firm foundation for decision making and action over the next forty years. It expressed "faith that private enter-

---

5. Information on forest policies of the APA is based on the minutes of meetings of the members, board of directors, and executive committee of the American Pulpwood Association, Washington, D.C., 1934–82.

6. David C. Smith, *History of Papermaking in the United States, 1791–1969* (New York: Lockwood Publishing Company, 1970), pp. 448–49.

7. From a statement prepared by H. P. Newson of the National Forest Products Association for the 1981 meeting of the Forest Industries Advisory Council. The last half of this article quotes and draws heavily from his text with his permission. As general references, see also the articles on the various associations and institutes in the *Encyclopedia of American Forest and Conservation History*, including that by Newson on the "Forest Industries Council."

16

prise and initiative can provide the most effective management, use, and renewal of our nation's forests." The overall statement emphasized protection from fire, insects, and disease; adoption of improved forest practices; more complete utilization of forest products; equalization of state and local taxes; and adequate support of state forestry organizations.

On the controversial subjects of regulation and ownership, the council agreed to support "public regulation when necessary or desirable, to be administered under state law"; to encourage "the sale and exchange of public lands in order to restore desirable lands to private ownership as well as to consolidate public holdings"; and to encourage "public ownership and practical management of forest lands which are incapable of producing sufficient wood to maintain profitable private ownership."

New Structures and Coordination, 1945–70

The early meetings of the Forest Industries Council were sporadic. Some years the council met only once or not at all. It was understood, however, that the paid staff officers of each member associations were free to, and expected to, call for a full meeting of the council if needed. Frequently just the staff officers or their alternates met as the "Operations Committee" when a legislative, governmental, or policy problem justified getting together.

Another measure taken to permit swift or continuous action on important issues was to make some committees completely independent. For example, American Forest Products Industries, Inc., had been created officially in 1932 as part of the NLMA, but it was reactivated under the FIC to serve the industry's need for public education and public relations work. Charles Gillett served as AFPI's staff director from 1948 until the 1960s. In 1968 the AFPI was reorganized as the American Forest Institute, AFI. The AFI also served as the secretariat for the Forest Industries Council. In 1963 the FIC committee on taxation also became independent and was renamed the Forest Industries Committee on Timber Valuation and Taxation, with Earl Tanner as chairman. Each independent committee broadened its base of financial support to include individual companies in the fiber as well as the solid wood industries.

Member companies of the paper industry's trade associations individually supported and helped finance the programs of the AFPI, which kept the general public informed of the actions and views of the

pulp, paper, and all other forest-based industries. The AFPI, in contrast to other association committees and councils, did not engage in direct lobbying. The paper and pulp associations also maintained separate structures to represent their most direct interests. The APPA was reorganized in 1966 as the American Paper Institute, API, and maintained its own Committee on Public Affairs to act on legislation and regulations affecting pulp and paper. The API dealt directly with the manufacture and sale of pulp and paper, and relied on the APA (American Pulpwood Association) to keep the pulp and paper and the pulpwood industries informed and to act on policies and legislation specifically affecting pulpwood production.

In some cases, the FIC gave one association the authority to address a specific problem on behalf of all its members. The NLMA and its successor, the National Forest Products Association (NFPA), had the most funds and staff to deal with forestry and forestland problems and usually provided leadership in these fields. With its small budget and staff the leading role of the APA was limited to issues affecting safety, costs, and working conditions in the logging of pulpwood and related forest products. The APPA initially was concerned primarily with foreign trade and transportation issues, although it and its successor, the API, later represented the pulp and paper industry's interest in debates over air and water pollution.

Another important industry group, the Forest Industries Advisory Council, brought together a select group of about one hundred of the chief and senior executive officers of the major forest corporations in the country for annual meetings from 1959 to 1985 to consider broadly defined common concerns and to recommend specific industry policies. The FIAC actually grew out of the Economic Council of the Forest Industries, initiated by and for the lumber industry in 1959. Its scope and interests broadened when pulp and paper executives were invited to participate in 1970, after which the annual meeting of executives was institutionalized as the Forest Industries Advisory Council, to draft policy recommendations for all forest-based industries. These were summarized in the report from each annual meeting.

New FIC Members and Challenges in the 1970s

In the late 1960s the representation of the Forest Industries Council itself grew to include major regional and product orga-

nizations already within the NFPA federation. This included the American Plywood Association, the Southern Forest Products Association, and the Western Wood Products Association. Later the American Forest Institute, the American Wood Council, and the Forest Industries Committee on Timber Valuation and Taxation also acquired FIC representation.

These changes were effected by 1970, when the pulp and paper industry executives were for the first time specifically invited to participate in the annual Economic Council of the Forest Industries. The 1970 meeting faced what council members saw as two grave and closely related problems: 1) a new environmental awareness critical of the entire industry was spreading rapidly and gaining momentum; 2) the existing structure did not represent the industry to the government and the public satisfactorily, especially in the face of this new situation.

To meet these challenges the economic council asked the Forest Industries Council to redirect the public educational and relations work of the American Forest Institute and to devote more funds to communications programs over the next two to three years. One of the steps taken was to have the members of the FIC to serve as the board of trustees of the AFI.

The first industrywide effort to meet the environmentalist challenge began immediately after the economic council meeting. Within five weeks a combination of FIC member groups prepared and distributed throughout the entire industry a "Handbook on Environmental Information for the Forest Industry." This booklet, issued in time for effective use by industry spokespeople on the first "Earth Day," provided a digest of past and current positive achievements by the industry, to counter the negative images of the industry disseminated by Earth Day activists.

There followed a sustained series of joint efforts by the forest industries to deal with their common problems. The public relations work of the API and the AFI, and lobbying by more focused association committees (such as the FIC Environment and Health Council), contributed directly to the following results:

1. The development and adoption of standards in the Clean Water Act (1977) that were more acceptable to the industry than those that had been initially proposed to Congress.
2. The development of national logging safety standards (1971) later adopted officially by the Occupational Safety and Health Administration (OSHA).

3. The defeat of a solid waste disposal tax (1976) proposed in Congress.
4. A congressional compromise on the National Forest Management Act (1976), which permitted clearcutting in the national forests under some circumstances. This act modified the 1897 Organic Act, which a 1973 federal court decision (the famous Monongahela case) had interpreted as forbidding clearcutting altogether.
5. An intensive FIC "Forest Productivity Report" (1980) that provided the industry with more current and complete information on the status of forest resources in the major forested states; the study also recommended specific actions by industry and government to make these resources fully productive in the future.
6. Retention and improvement of the timber capital gains and other federal tax savings for forest owners and operators introduced in the 1944 tax law (and which the Forest Industry Committee on Timber Valuation and Taxation of the FIC successfully defended from the 1960s to the present).[8]

Although each of the above achievements might have been accomplished by a single organization working alone or with one or two others, it is unlikely that all of these tasks could have been performed as effectively or as economically without concerted action by an industrywide organization.

Trade Associations and Forest Policy in the 1980s

After 1970 the API and NFPA coordinated their efforts more and more closely both in forest and in broader environmental policy making and litigation (filing briefs as "friends of the court" in cases involving the forest industries). The API moved its environmental personnel to Washington, into the building already occupied by the NFPA. For day-to-day programs and administration the two organizations essentially shared a single staff working on environmental issues, particularly those raised by the Environmental Protection Agency. Similar joint staffs were established

The American Forest Products Industries, Inc. provided classroom teachers with materials explaining forest management and the manufacturing of wood and paper products. As of 1986, the AFPI became the American Forest Council (AFC). AFPI photo.

for government affairs and communications with the general public.

The depressed economic conditions of the forest products industries in the 1980s also encouraged trade associations to consolidate their operations and thereby to cut their expenses. By 1985 many industry executives were looking critically at the costs of annual meetings of the FIAC and even of the FIC. In recent years the major associations and their leaders had begun to cooperate much more closely and directly than they had in the past. As a result of these considerations the FIC agreed at its meeting on 8 May 1985 that "future meetings of the FIAC should be deferred indefinitely. The FIAC could be convened, in the future, at the discretion of the FIC. " The FIC itself thus reverted, in the words of the minutes, "to standby status—meeting only at the call of the Chairman, or if requested by the members."[9]

The Forest Industries Council functioned for more than forty years on behalf of the forest products industry. The need for policy coordination will recur in the future as it has in the past, and surely will

be met by some cooperative or associative body, if not by the FIC itself.[10]

T he overall thrust of this presentation has been to show how forest policy has been developed in the national trade associations that have spoken on behalf of the pulp and paper industry since the 1880s, in close cooperation with the solid wood industries since the formation of the Forest Industries Council in 1943. The FIC and the other organizations it has spawned have permitted its member associations, individual companies, and forest owners themselves to coordinate their positions and actions on issues of common interest. The pulp and paper industry as represented by the American Paper Institute (and previously by the APPA) and the pulpwood industry as represented by the American Pulpwood Association have been and are fully involved in that process. The pulpwood-based industries have come a long way from complete indifference to forest policy over one hundred years ago to their current active participation in forest policies and action on its own and through wider forest products organizations. ▲

8. As of June 1986, the tax reform bills passed by the House and Senate eliminated or reduced the tax benefits for logging and timber sales enacted in the 1940s. The final law may thus end the era of preferential income tax treatment for timberlands.

9. From the minutes of the 8 May 1985 meeting of the Forest Industries Council (Chicago), transmitted to members by Laurence Wiseman, secretary, on 25 June 1985.

10. As of April 1986, the AFI was reorganized and renamed the American Forest Council; along with the NFPA, it moved from the original shared building to new, smaller quarters elsewhere in Washington, D.C.

Public Regulations and the Slowdown in Productivity Growth

By GREGORY B. CHRISTAINSEN AND ROBERT H. HAVEMAN*

Since 1965, indices of labor productivity have had a disappointing and largely unexplained performance. Not only is the rate of productivity growth over the post-1965 period lower than in preceding postwar years, but its upward trend has been broken at least twice. Since 1978, productivity growth has been effectively zero. If the trend of labor productivity from 1946–65 had continued until 1980, the current index would be about 15 percent above its actual level. Table 1 summarizes the postwar behavior of four alternative measures of productivity.

While productivity growth has slowed in nearly all sectors, there is a large variance in the distribution of post-1965 sectoral productivity growth rates. The most dramatic slowdowns have been recorded for the mining, utilities, and construction sectors. The manufacturing sector has experienced a much milder slowdown, and since 1967 its productivity index has risen over 12 percentage points more than that for the entire nonfarm sector.

Many phenomena have contributed to poor productivity performance. They range from subtle changes in worker motivation to the propensity to innovate in both products and processes to exogenous shocks to the production process (due, for example, to unexpected energy price changes) to alterations in output mix, the demographic characteristics of the labor force, or the ratio of labor to capital to the nature and intensity of regulatory policy. Not only are these effects numerous, but they interact in complex and dynamic ways. Numerous assertions

*Assistant professor of economics, Colby College, and professor of economics, University of Wisconsin-Madison, respectively. Helpful comments on an earlier draft by John Bishop, Laurits Christensen, Sheldon Danziger, Donald Nichols, Eugene Smolensky, and Barbara Wolfe are gratefully acknowledged.

have been made regarding the contribution of each of these factors, and studies seeking to identify their relative contributions have been undertaken. At present, the contribution of public regulations to both the productivity slowdown and to poor economic performance generally is both widely debated and little understood. It is this relationship that is the focus of this paper. In Sections I and II, the direct and indirect ways in which regulations can adversely affect productivity are distinguished, and the existing studies of this relationship are described. Sections III and IV describe our attempts to model and estimate the contribution of regulation to the slowdown. Some preliminary results are presented.

I. Public Regulations as a Source of the Productivity Slowdown

By definition, public regulations are interventions into market processes. Because of them, the utility and profit-maximizing decisions of individual decision makers are altered. In a smoothly functioning market economy (without externalities), such interventions ensure deviation from the private sector production frontier. Holding output composition constant, this deviation means that additional inputs are required to produce any given level of output. Under these conditions, increases in the intensity of public regulations will be associated with larger deviations from the private output frontier, and equivalently, reduced rates of growth of output per unit of input—productivity. In a dynamic setting, increased regulatory intensity, through its alteration of private optimizing decisions, is likely to induce reductions in the measured rate of productivity growth.

The channels by which public regulations are likely to affect either the output numera-

TABLE 1–POSTWAR ANNUAL PRODUCTIVITY GROWTH RATES IN THE UNITED STATES,
VARIOUS MEASURES OF PRODUCTIVITY
(Shown in Percent per Year)

	Output per Person-Hour, Private Sector	Output per Person-Hour, Nonfarm Private Sector	Nonresidential Business Income per Person Employed	Total Factor Productivity in Domestic Private Business
1947-66	3.44	2.83	2.9	2.9[a]
1966-73	2.15	1.87	1.3	1.4[b]
1973-78	1.15	1.02	− .1	−
1979	− .9	− 1.2	−	−

Source: Figures for output per person-hour, private sector and output per person-hour, nonfarm private sector were taken from Jerome Mark, p. 486. Figures for nonresidential business income per person employed were taken from Denison (1979c), p. 21. Figures for total factor productivity in domestic private business were taken from Kendrick, p. 511.

[a] For years 1948-66.
[b] For years 1966-76.

tor or input denominator of productivity indices are complex. Each channel involves some aspect of policy-induced business behavior entailing a reduction in the ratio of output to input. To illustrate these channels, we will deal with environmental regulations; analogous channels of impact exist for other forms of regulation.

By their nature, environmental regulations require investments to reduce residual flows. To the extent that these investments compete with standard plant and equipment investments, the ratio of labor to conventional capital will be increased. Moreover, because these regulations are typically based on engineering standards, the activities which they generate tend to be excessively capital intensive. Because these regulations fall especially heavily on new pollution sources, incentive is given for uneconomic retention of existing—and lower productivity—plant and equipment. These regulations have also tended to be more heavily imposed on sectors with high postwar rates of productivity growth (for example, utilities), and in low pollution regions attractive for plant location. And, because pollution control equipment requires manpower to operate it, employment levels rise with no addition to marketable output. Finally, complying with these regulations requires the information-gathering, administrative, and legal activities which require inputs

yielding no saleable output. Meeting these requirements may also require time — causing delay in expansion and modernization plans and the stretching-out of construction periods.

II. Public regulations and the Productivity Slowdown: Some Estimates

No comprehensive study of the effect of public regulations on the slowdown in productivity growth has been undertaken. A few studies of the contribution of environmental and health/safety regulations have been made, however.

The most influential of these is that of Edward Denison (1979a, b, c) who uses his growth accounting framework to derive an estimate of the contribution of these regulations to the retardation of growth in his productivity measure—final output valued at factor cost per unit of labor, capital, and land inputs. Denison's index suggests that the average annual impact of post-1967 environmental regulations on the rate of productivity growth was .05 percentage points from 1967–69, .1 percentage points from 1969–73, .22 percentage points from 1973–75, and .08 percentage points from 1975–78. Robert Crandall has also studied the environmental regulation-productivity interaction, using both cross-section and time-series regression approaches. While the results from these estimates vary substantially, he finds that the index of manufacturing in 1976 is about 1.5 percent below what it would be in the absence of mandated pollution control expenditures, and that those manufacturing sectors heavily impacted by environmental regulations showed a greater slowdown in productivity growth after 1970 than manufacturing as a whole. Finally, Robin Siegel has attempted to account for the slowdown in the private nonfarm labor productivity trend by regressing this quarterly time-series variable on variables designed to account for changes in output due to the business cycle, output and labor force composition, relative energy prices, pollution control expenditures, and capital investment, among other potential factors. Pollution control expenditures were estimated to have caused a 0.5 percentage-point reduction in the rate of productivity growth from 1965–73, but no significant effect after 1975.

These studies have focused on pollution control (as opposed to the full set of public) regulations. They have not been based on a rigorous theoretical or estimation framework, and omitted variable and other data and statistical problems plague the estimates. Elsewhere, we have critiqued these and other studies and the estimates which they have yielded, concluding that between 8–12 percent of the post–1973 slowdown in the growth rate of labor productivity is attributable to environmental regulations (see our paper with Frank Gollop).

III. The Productivity Impact of Regulation: An Empirical Framework

To provide a preliminary evaluation of the contribution of public regulations to the slowdown in productivity growth, we employ a simple time-series regression model for the *U.S.* manufacturing sector. We assume that there is a differentiable aggregate production function underlying economic activity in the manufacturing sector which relates the flow of output (Q) to the flow of total factor input (TFI). The function shifts over time (T) and also in response to what we refer to as "regulatory intensity" (R).

Assuming constant returns to scale, a simple first-order form is

$$(1) \qquad Q = A(TFI) \cdot e^{\alpha R + \beta T}$$

where A, α, and β are parameters. Taking the natural logarithm of both sides of (1):

$$(2) \qquad \ln Q = \ln A + \ln(TFI) + \alpha R + \beta T$$

If $\ln(TFI)$ is subtracted from both sides of (2), an equation for the level of total factor productivity (TFP) is obtained:

$$(3) \qquad \ln(TFP) = \ln A + \alpha R + \beta T$$

That is, to the extent that economic activity follows the hypothesized production function, the level of total factor productivity is a function of a constant, regulatory intensity, and time.

We assume that production in the *U.S.* manufacturing sector can be approximated by (1) except during periods in which the sector is "shocked" by business-cycle effects. Accordingly, in addition to an additive disturbance term (v), we add two terms to (3) designed to capture cyclical effects on total factor productivity. Following William Nordhaus, who has justified this procedure in a more rigorous setting, the additional variables are current and lagged values of $\ln(Q/Q^*)$, where Q is actual output and Q^* is a measure of the level of output which would have been produced in the absence of cyclical influences.[1]

Thus, our equation for the level of total factor productivity is

$$(4) \quad \ln(TFP) = \ln A + \alpha R + \beta T + \gamma \ln\left(\frac{Q}{Q^*}\right)$$
$$+ \delta \ln\left(\frac{Q}{Q^*}\right)_{-1} + v$$

---

[1] Assume that the actual level of output (Q) depends on the level of demand which, in turn, depends on a constant, the price level of sector output relative to the general price level, the deviation of the actual from the "natural" rate of unemployment ($U - U^*$), and "natural" real GNP (GNP^*). The Q^* is estimated by regressing Q on its determinants and imputing values of Q assuming $U = U^*$. (The U^* and GNP^* are from Robert Gordon.)

where γ and δ are parameters, and R enters the equation with an as yet unspecified lag distribution. As is well known, TFP differs from *labor* productivity by a factor reflecting the influence of the ratio of nonlabor to labor inputs (K/L).

We have estimated (4) for the U.S. manufacturing sector from 1958–77 using unpublished annual data on the quantities and proportions of total cost accounted for by labor, capital, energy, and materials, and price and quantity data pertaining to output.[2] In order to reduce the presence of multicollinearity, these inputs were combined into a measure of TFI by using their respective shares in total cost as weights. Because of this comprehensive set of inputs, the effect of some factors often assigned responsibility for the productivity slowdown (for example, the energy crisis) is filtered out of the TFI measure.

"Regulatory intensity" is a difficult concept to define, let alone quantify. As noted, our definition of this concept is based on the view that public regulatory agencies distort optimizing private sector decisions which would, *ceteris paribus*, maximize the measured rate of productivity growth. We have constructed three alternative indices of this variable for the postwar period. The first is based on an estimate of the cumulative number of "major" pieces of regulatory legislation in effect during any of the years in question (R_1).[3] The second and third indices are based on the volume of real federal expenditures on regulatory activities for the years in question (R_2) and the number of full-time federal personnel engaged in regulatory activities (R_3).[4] For our measures, that portion of each agency's activities devoted to the manufacturing sector was

the average of the judgments of several recognized students of regulation.[5] Though crude proxies for regulatory intensity, we believe these indices provide a reasonable characterization of postwar trends in the regulation of the manufacturing sector; indeed, the only characterization available without a major research effort.

Each of the R indices imply only a gradual increase in regulatory intensity until the mid-1960s. Then, all three measures accelerate, with R_2 increasing at a more rapid rate than R_3 which in turn shows a greater acceleration than R_1. All of the measures show a further acceleration during the 1970's, though the acceleration is again least pronounced in the case of R_1. Setting each index equal to 100 in 1947, R_1 attains a level of 402.88 in 1977, while R_2 and R_3 read 1003.77 and 668.03 respectively. While there are exceptions, the indices generally imply a monotonic increase in regulatory intensity during the 1947–77 period.

Alternative estimates of equation (4) were obtained using R_1, R_2, and R_3, with lag specifications chosen on the basis of the Bayesian estimation criterion proposed by John Geweke and Richard Meese. A simple one-year lag was chosen for R_2 and R_3; two-years for R_1. So lagged, the simple correlation coefficients among the alternative measures are: .85 (R_1, R_2), .86 (R_1, R_3), and .94 (R_2, R_3). Pseudo-generalized least squares estimates of the equation were made by using Takeshi Amemiya's procedure for prefiltering the data.

IV. The Productivity Impact of Regulation: Preliminary Results

Combining our regression estimates with estimates of the impact of K/L accounted for by differences in the growth rates of TFP and labor productivity, we obtain the results in Table 2.

---

[2]We wish to thank J. R. Norsworthy and Michael Harper of the U.S. Bureau of Labor Statistics for these data.

[3]This series was calculated from data presented in Center for the Study of American Business.

[4]R_2 and R_3 were estimated from agency data published in the *Budget of the United States Government*. For large, diverse agencies such as the Environmental Protection Agency, data on regulatory functions are separable from other agency functions. For smaller regulatory agencies, we have used expenditure and staffing data for the agency as a whole.

[5]Each individual was asked to estimate the percentage of each agency's activities which are devoted to the manufacturing sector, and how this percentage had changed over time. In each case, the highest and lowest estimates were discarded, and the mean of the remaining estimates was used in constructing these indices.

TABLE 2—CONTRIBUTIONS TO THE RATE OF GROWTH OF LABOR PRODUCTIVITY
IN *U.S.* MANUFACTURING, 1958–77: PRELIMINARY RESULTS

Source	Contribution during:		
	1958-65	1965-73	1973-77
R	0 to −.1	−.1 to −.3	−.2 to −.3
T	.9 to 1.0	.9 to 1.0	.9 to 1.0
Q/Q^*	0 to .1	0	0 to −.1
Unexplained	.4 to .5	−.1 to −.2	−.3 to −.4
Average Growth Rate of Total Factor Productivity	1.4	.6	.3
K/L	1.6	1.9	1.4
Average Growth Rate of Labor Productivity	3.0	2.5	1.7

These numbers are derived by simply taking the parameter estimates for equation (4) and then multiplying them by the average annual changes in the associated variables. In the case of R, the estimated regression coefficients for α are .011 (R_1), .005 (R_2), and .006 (R_3). Lagged appropriately, the average annual changes in R for the three periods of Table 2 are 6.66, 13.48, and 20.44 (R_1), 6.09, 65.90, and 61.32 (R_2), and 5.05, 33.61, and 49.80 (R_3). The average percentage point contributions of regulation to the rate of growth of total factor productivity are then calculated to be $-.073$, $-.148$, and $-.224$ (R_1), $-.030$, $-.330$, and $-.301$ (R_2), and $-.030$, $-.202$, and $-.299$ (R_3).

Neither R_1 nor R_3 was statistically significant at either a .01 or a .05 level, but both were significant at a .10 level. The estimated coefficient for R_2 was significant at the .05 level. In all cases, neither the estimated coefficient on the lagged cyclical variable nor an interaction term for R and T were significant at the .10 level. The same was true of an interaction term for R and K/L in an equation for the level of labor productivity. All other estimated coefficients were significant at the .05 level.

The ranges indicated in Table 2 thus stem from the alternative measures of R. Of the alternatives, R_2 (which shows the greatest acceleration in regulatory intensity over time) implies the most negative impact on the rate of productivity growth. It also implies the greatest rate of "technical change" and the smallest average cyclical impact. These conclusions are reversed for R_1, with those for R_3 being intermediate to the other two.

V. Summary and Caveats

These results suggest that federal regulations are responsible for from 12 to 21 percent of the slowdown in the growth of labor productivity in *U.S.* manufacturing during 1973–77 as compared to 1958–65.[6] They are consistent with previous research noted in section II. Reductions in the ratio of nonlabor to labor inputs (K/L) are responsible for about 15 percent of the slowdown. The contribution of the average cyclical impact could fall anywhere in the 0–15 percent range. The unexplained portion of the slowdown in the rate of productivity growth —often attributed to changes in labor force composition, R&D expenditures, or sectoral output shifts—remains substantial.

These results on the impact of regulation are, in certain important respects, sensitive to the manner in which the model is specified. For example, with alternative lag specifications, estimated coefficients for R may be insignificant. Also, if a separate trend variable for each of the three periods in Table 2 is entered into the model, or if time enters in second-order form, multicollinearity among the explanatory variables causes the coefficients for both regulatory intensity and time to be insignificant. Moreover, the R variables may be capturing other exogenous forces inducing contemporaneous productivity growth reductions, in

[6] This conclusion is derived by taking the difference between the percentage point contributions of each regulatory intensity variable during 1958–65 and 1973–77, and dividing this difference by the difference between the rates of growth of labor productivity during the two periods. These values are all shown in Table 2.

which case improved specifications may reduce the estimated R impacts. While we believe that our 12–21 percent estimated contribution of regulatory intensity to the slowdown in the growth of labor productivity will prove to be robust with respect to improved data and more sophisticated models,[7] we recognize the uncertainties surrounding this estimate caused by less-than-ideal data and the possible recent impact on productivity growth of many other factors —factors which may be difficult to measure or capture in any simple model. It should be noted, however, that the procedure employed is more robust with respect to assumptions than those used in widely quoted studies which estimate the response of investment spending to taxation, private savings to Social Security wealth, or productivity growth to $R\&D$ spending.

Finally, our study focuses on the contribution of public regulations to *measured* productivity. Such regulations are typically undertaken in the belief that they will yield contributions to economic welfare not fully reflected in measured output (for example, improved health and safety; an improved environment). If such gains are forthcoming, growth in "true" economic productivity would exceed its measured counterpart. Our results have little implication for the contribution of public regulations to true productivity growth.

[7]The impact of R was also estimated using 1947–71 data on prices, quantities, and proportions of total cost accounted for by labor, capital energy, and materials compiled by Ernst Berndt and David Wood. This series was extended to 1977 by applying estimated percentage changes in each variable indicated by the *BLS* data, and normalizing cost shares. Because the variable definitions in the two data sets are not identical this exercise, taken by itself, would be of dubious value. This estimation implied an impact on *BLS*-defined labor productivity in the 12–25 percent range, however.

REFERENCES

T. Amemiya, "Generalized Least-Squares with an Estimated Autocovariance Martix," *Econometrica*, July 1973, *41*, 723–32.

E. R. Berndt and D. O. Wood, "Technology, Prices, and the Derived Demand for Energy," *Rev. Econ. Statist.*, Aug. 1975, *62*, 259–68.

G. Christainsen, F. Gollop, and R. Haveman, "Environmental and Health-Safety Regulations, Productivity Growth, and Economic Performance: An Assessment," Joint Economic Committee, U.S. Congress, 1980.

R. Crandall, "Pollution Controls and Productivity Growth in Basic Industries," in Thomas G. Cowing and Rodney Stevenson, eds., *Productivity Measurements in Regulated Industries*, New York forthcoming.

Edward F. Denison, (1979a) "Pollution Abatement Programs: Estimates of Their Effect Upon Output Per Unit of Input, 1975–1978," *Surv. Curr. Bus., Part I*, Aug. 1979, *59*, 58–59.

_____, (1979b) "Explanations of Declining Productivity Growth," *Surv. Curr. Bus., Part II*, Aug. 1979, *59*, 1–24.

_____, (1979c) *Accounting for Slower Economic Growth*, Washington 1979.

J. Geweke and R. Meese, "Estimating Regression Models of Finite But Unknown Order," SSRI Paper no. 7925, Univ. Wisconsin-Madison, 1979.

Robert J. Gordon, *Macroeconomics*, Boston 1978.

J. Kendrick, Testimony before the Congressional Joint Economic Committee, in *Special Study on Economic Change: Hearings before the Joint Economic Committee, Congress of the United States*, Part 2, Washington 1978, 616–36.

J. Mark, Testimony before the Congressional Joint Economic Committee, in *Special Study on Economic Change: Hearings before the Joint Economic Committee, Congress of the United States*, Part 2, Washington 1978, 476–86.

W. O. Nordhaus, "The Recent Productivity Slowdown," *Brookings Papers*, Washington 1972, *3*, 473–546.

R. Siegel, "Why Has Productivity Slowed Down?," *Data Resources Rev.*, Mar. 1979, *1*, 1.59–1.65.

Center for the Study of American Business, *Directory of Federal Agencies*, Formal Publication No. 31, St. Louis 1980.

What Price Sustained Yield?
The Forest Service,
Community Stability, and Timber Monopoly
Under the 1944 Sustained-Yield Act
by David A. Clary

It is recognized that setting up of cooperative sustained yield units involves a certain degree of monopoly. This is unavoidable, and this fact was made clearly evident in the Congressional hearings on this measure. It is my belief, however, that this kind of monopoly, if properly regulated as it is under our cooperative agreements, is of the benevolent type and definitely provides benefits greatly outweighing any disadvantage.

Lyle Watts, Chief, U.S. Forest Service, 1947

The Sustained-Yield Forest Management Act became law on 29 March 1944. Largely the work of David T. Mason and Edward T. Allen of the Western Forestry and Conservation Association, the act expressed Mason's vision of sustained yield as a system of forest management designed to stabilize forest industries so that they could harvest continuously in a given locality rather than exhaust the resource in one area and move on to the next. This interpretation of sustained yield differed from that of the Forest Service, which aimed at sustaining the productive capacity of the forests rather than the well-being of the forest user, although in practice the two philosophies were not incompatible. Nevertheless, the Sustained-Yield Act was the fruit of industrial support in Congress with little encouragement from the Forest Service.

The 1944 legislation, recognizing that public and private timberlands were intermingled in the West, and that a number of timber companies needed new sources of raw material, authorized two types of sustained-yield units, cooperative and federal. Cooperative units would merge the management of national forests and adjacent private timberlands to form "catchment areas" large enough to allow continuous harvesting of timber (by the time the last plot was harvested, the next timber crop would be mature on the first plot). The federal units would achieve the same end in another way, by reserving national forest timber in a given area for exclusive use by local operators. The objective of both kinds of units was community stability—permanent communities of forest workers who would not

have to move on when the local timber supply gave out. Both kinds of units stabilized local economies by giving favored private companies a monopoly over the national forest timber in their area, whether by integrating some private lands into management plans for public forests, or by giving certain private operators exclusive access to public timber.[1]

The Forest Service held two (or more) opinions about this law. On the one hand, cooperative management offered federal foresters new powers to require conservation on lands bordering national forests. On the other hand, the service's top leaders were bent on regulation, not cooperation, and doubted that the industry would ever adopt the service's principles of sustained yield. Cooperative units might backfire, giving private companies as much or more of a voice in national forest management as the Forest

Abbreviations in footnotes The National Archives and Records Service regional depositories are cited as NARS-D for Denver, NARS-LN for Laguna Niguel, and NARS-FW for Fort Worth. Record numbers for these regional collections are cited as accession number/record number (e.g., 54-A-111/59858). Records held in the National Archives in Washington, D.C., are identified by NA record group and box number (e.g., RG95/1369). Abbreviations for frequently cited individual files are explained in the first citations to such files.

1. Sustained-Yield Forest Management Act of 1944, 58 Stat. 132; Harold K. Steen, *The U.S. Forest Service: A History* (Seattle: University of Washington Press, 1976), pp. 251–52; Roy O. Hoover, "Public Law 273 Comes to Shelton: Implementing the Sustained-Yield Forest Management Act of 1944," *Journal of Forest History* 22 (April 1978): 86–101.

As assistant chief of the U.S. Forest Service, Christopher M. Granger favored the sustained-yield program. Forest Service photo.

E. E. Carter, assistant chief of the Forest Service, who counseled caution in creating sustained-yield units in the late 1940s. Forest History Society photo.

Service would acquire in decisions about the private lands. Finally, both types of sustained-yield units sanctioned monopolies, a kind of economic organization that the Forest Service had historically opposed. The service's first reaction was accordingly cautious.[2]

Most federal foresters favored management by short-term sales rather than long-term agreements with the private sector. It was not even clear that the cooperative units would necessarily reward only operators who practiced good forestry—Chief Lyle Watts said "of course" but could not give a "categorical yes." When Watts said that cooperative agreements would favor and perpetuate "responsible private ownership," one regional official, Charles L. Tebbe, ventured that "a number of applicants for cooperative sustained yield units definitely had in mind to eventually turn their holdings over to Government."[3]

At the end of 1944 the Division of Timber Management determined that each region should develop "at least one tentative sustained yield unit plan for preliminary review," although "no final plans or formal hearings" were "anticipated during 1945." By March 1945 seven of the nine regions had complied, suggesting a total of sixty-four possible cooperative units and at least sixty-one federal units. The Forest Service had received actual applications for sixty cooperative units and sixteen federal units.[4]

Opinion in the Forest Service's Washington office divided sharply over the law, although the conflict was not aired in public. Assistant Chief E. E. Carter, for example, thought that it was time to "raise rather sharply the question of whether we mean it when we talk about the stabilization of communities within or close to a National Forest." Discussing the proposed Big Valley federal unit in California, he pointed out that although it would protect a nearby town, "it would also block other possible purchasers who might wish to reach into this working circle [the basic Forest Service planning unit] or become established in it, but that is inherent in the basic idea of the Federal unit and the stabilization of the community on the sustained yield basis." In that particular case, he thought that cooperation with the largest timber owner in the area was impossible. Meanwhile, Assistant Chief Christopher M. Granger was urging the Southeast Region to pursue a possible agreement with the Mansfield Hardwood Lumber Company.[5]

The watchword for the Forest Service as a whole was still caution. When a group including a congressman approached Chief Watts with a proposal for a cooperative unit in the Rogue River area of Oregon, he showed some favor to the proposition, but advised that even an acceptable application would require time to prepare for public hearings. He had no intention of holding such hearings while the war was still on.[6]

After reviewing cases in California, E. E. Carter advised the regional forester in San Francisco "to remember that the justification of a case must include a clear showing of

---

2. Hoover, "Public Law 273," p. 88; "Policy and Instructions Governing the Establishment of Sustained Yield Units," 21 July 1944, "S, PLANS, TM, Federal Units 1936–1949," Region 2, 56-A-144/62230, NARS-D.

3. Charles L. Tebbe to the files, 12 August 1944, "S, PLANS, TM, Federal Units 1936–1949," Region 2, 56-A-144/62230, NARS-D.

4. "Division of Timber Management 1945 Program of Work (Items To Be Stressed)," 21 December 1944; Ira J. Mason to the files, 29 March 1945; both in Division of Timber Management Reading File, NA RG95/1369 (reading files for the Division of Timber Management are held by the National Archives and are hereafter cited simply as DTM with record group and box number).

5. E. E. Carter to the files, 11 April 1945; Christopher Granger to regional forester, Atlanta, 10 May 1945; both in DTM, RG95/1369.

6. Ira J. Mason to regional forester, Portland, 23 June 1945, DTM, RG95/1369.

Left to right: three of the national forests involved in sustained-yield units (Forest Service maps): The Olympic National Forest in Washington.

The Coconino National Forest in Arizona.

public interest due to a danger to an established community that can be given permanence by the proposed action, and that the giving of permanence to that community, and contrasted with the possible use of the timber to support any other or others, is a logical and desirable thing from the viewpoint of public interest."[7]

Carter believed that it would become more urgent to respond to applications for cooperative units "as the war period passes." Meanwhile, Watts objected to a proposed cooperative unit in Oregon because it was in an area where the Forest Service "had contemplated, for the time being at least, continuation of sales on a competitive basis rather than the establishment of . . . sustained yield units." He advised the applying industries to continue their plans for expansion without a hard commitment of federal timber. "Efficient mills established at those locations should be in a reasonably good position to obtain an equitable part of the available timber supply."[8]

The Washington office might look askance at the cooperative sustained-yield program, but some of the regional

offices were downright hostile to the whole idea. Granger scolded the regional forester in Portland for giving "a rather strong impression that you are distinctly cold on the idea of setting up Federal units." He advised tempering "what at this distance appears to be an overly negative attitude on the part of the Region."[9]

Not everyone in Washington shared Granger's enthusiasm for the program, however. E. E. Carter argued for "thinking in terms of obligation to the community . . . rather than our obligation to operating concerns." At the very least he wanted to wait until after the war before considering any such ventures. He agreed that opportunities for cooperative units should be kept open, but his heart obviously was not in the idea. He told a regional forester that the act's primary objective was community stability, "not . . . the relief of cut out lumber manufacturing companies. Probably unnecessarily, I urge that these ideas be kept prominent in the thought of the Forest Service about the application of this law."[10]

7. Carter to regional forester, San Francisco, 4 July 1945, DTM, RG95/1369.

8. Lyle F. Watts to Glenn L. Jackson, USAAF, 16 July 1945, DTM, RG95/1369.

9. Granger to regional forester, Portland, 18 July 1945, DTM, RG95/1369.

10. Granger to regional forester, Missoula, 27 July 1945; A. W. Greeley to the files, 31 July 1945; Carter to regional forester, Portland, 1 August 1945; all in DTM, RG95/1369.

NEW MEXICO

The Carson National Forest in New Mexico.

The official establishment of the Shelton Sustained-Yield Unit in Washington State, on 12 December 1946: from left to right, assistant chief Christopher M. Granger, chief Lyle F. Watts, and L. S. Gross of the Timber Management Division. Forest History Society photo.

The Shelton Unit:
The Lone Attempt at Federal-Private Cooperation

The war was not a lame excuse for delayed implementation of the Sustained-Yield Act. Manpower shortages in the Forest Service were a genuine obstacle to new initiatives. Yet Watts felt called upon to make some effort at establishing sustained-yield units, despite this problem. He selected one—the application of Simpson Logging Company for lands around Shelton, Washington, submitted two days after the law was passed. The Shelton proposal appeared to offer the best possibility of meeting the purposes of the act because Simpson Logging had already "demonstrated a sincere interest in working out arrangements for cooperative sustained yield forest management."[11] A year of negotiations and drafts produced a cooperative agreement and management and operating

plans for the linked federal and private lands. The two parties entered a hundred-year contract, planning to harvest 100 million board feet per year until 1956, after which the cut would be reduced to the "allowable sustained yield of the combined ownerships." The objects were better utilization of the forest, higher local employment, manufacturing capacity matched to the available resources, and an end to fluctuations in population and payrolls.[12]

When the proposal was presented to a public hearing in September 1946 it unleashed a storm of controversy. People in the communities immediately affected by the proposed unit generally supported the idea. Those elsewhere did not. In granting Simpson a monopoly on federal timber, the Forest Service closed the area to others. Farmers, organized labor, small logging operators, and competing companies and communities howled in pain. Small operators would be eliminated, they said. The competitive free market would be destroyed, timber would be diverted from the Puget Sound market, and land uses other than timbering would be restricted. The Grays Harbor communities believed themselves especially ill-used, on the grounds that

11. "Hearing Record, Shelton Cooperative Sustained Unit, Hearing, 19 September 1946," Timber Management Office Permanent Files, Pacific Northwest Region (these files hereafter cited as TMO and listed with the U.S. Forest Service regional office that holds them). Except as otherwise indicated, the account of the establishment of the Shelton unit follows Hoover, "Public Law 273."

12. "Hearing Record," ibid.

29

The 1957 Forest Service caption for this photograph pointed out that the town of Shelton, Washington, was "dependent upon forest industries, and much of the wood used by its mills comes from the nearby Olympic National Forest." Forest Service photo.

their economy was imperiled by unfair competition from Simpson and its newly protected resource base around Shelton—a resource now closed to Grays Harbor enterprises. Nearly all opponents asked for a reduction in the proposed annual cut. The local grange objected bitterly to the federal government's establishing monopolistic power.[13]

With some minor revisions the Shelton Cooperative Sustained-Yield Unit became active on 12 December 1946. The Grays Harbor region would not be won over, however. When its representatives prevailed upon Senator Warren G. Magnuson to ask for an adjustment in the unit boundary to leave timber for Grays Harbor, Watts refused to budge, insisting that the boundaries as established were "needed to insure sufficient annual cut under sustained yield to stabilize Shelton and McCleary." As for landowners and operators outside the unit boundaries, Watts said that Simpson Logging Company was free to purchase timber outside the unit "if it so desires."[14]

Christopher Granger was the chief sponsor of the cooperative unit idea in the Washington office. His memo to the regional foresters (dated 23 December 1946) called the Shelton Unit a "Christmas present" and outlined the next steps to be taken: "Now that the ice is broken and as soon as the financial situation clears up we hope that each Region will make real progress in evaluating possibilities for sustained yield units and acting on each pending case."[15]

The Forest Service hierarchy maintained before the

public its dedication to stabilizing communities dependent upon national forests. As Watts put it in 1947: "In establishing the boundaries of national forest working circles, whether or not subject to cooperative sustained yield management, we are emphasizing consideration of community aspects wherever it is possible to do so. We hope to have milling or logging communities so located with respect to the merchantable timber so that woodworkers will have an opportunity to live at home in permanent communities and to commute to and from work."[16]

The Forest Service had been painting that same lovely picture for several decades. But in actual practice community stability sometimes took a back seat to timber management. Local opponents of the Shelton Unit had claimed that stabilizing Shelton's economy threatened their own livelihoods. Watts brushed that off, parrying every Grays Harbor objection by citing the praise of people in the Shelton community. He apparently had decided that cooperative units were a way of achieving his objectives for the national forests and private resources alike. When one critic suggested that the program was inconsistent with Forest Service history, he replied coldly, "Neither the Department nor the Forest Service takes the position that it has had any unwelcome mandate thrust upon it. . . . The Forest Service promoted the adoption of this measure over a long period and believes that its enactment and its wise application are definitely in the public interest."[17]

To Watts, support from the immediate community was enough to justify a cooperative unit. Having decided that opponents could be ignored or dismissed as favoring their own narrow interests over the public interest, he advised regional foresters to enlist local support for cooperative units. It was not to be, however. The Forest Service at-

---

13. Besides Hoover's excellent summary of the hundreds of pages of testimony and statements of the record, see the extensive file in TMO, Pacific Northwest Region. See also Watts to the record, 10 December 1946; Watts to Representative Walt Noran, 11 December 1946; Watts to Noran, 11 December 1946; all in DTM, RG95/1368.

14. Watts to Magnuson, DTM, RG95/1368.

15. Granger to regional foresters, 23 December 1946, DTM, RG95/1368. Hoover attributes this memorandum to Watts in "Public Law 273," p. 101.

16. Watts to George H. Cecil, 16 January 1947, DTM, RG95/1368.

17. Watts to Ellery Foster, International Woodworkers of America, 22 January 1947, DTM, RG95/1367.

30

tempted to form additional units at Libby, Montana, and Quincy, California, but quickly ran into a storm of opposition from small operators, organized labor, and communities adversely affected. Overriding everything were objections, from self-interest and on legal and ethical principles, to the monopolistic nature of cooperative units, favoring one to the exclusion of all others. In the end, the Shelton Unit was the only cooperative program established under the 1944 legislation. Local opposition scuttled even the Department of the Interior's attempt at cooperative sustained yield on its lands in Oregon.[18]

The Retreat From Cooperative to Federal Units

Frustrated in its attempts to establish more cooperative units, the Forest Service turned to establishing units more within its power—the federal sustained-yield units involving only national forest land.[19] Federal units were not to come easily either. They involved intervention in local economies that troubled some people in the Forest Service. Worse, in many minds, were the possible enemies who could be generated for the whole sustained-yield unit program. Reviewing a plan for the Sitgreaves National Forest in Arizona, even Christopher Granger was bothered about how the service could stabilize any community without destabilizing its neighbors: "In addition to considering whether such an obligation would be worth the additional community benefits, we should also consider whether the additional benefits to Heber would more offset the disruption of established community values at Safford, where the Company's finishing facilities are now located. If Safford is a better place to live than Heber, should we force the Company to move its employees now residing at Safford?"[20]

The line between promoting community stability and high-handed manipulation of private affairs was indeed a thin one, and that made development of sustained-yield units more difficult. The Forest Service managed to create only five federal sustained-yield units, each a perpetual source of frustration and complaint, reserving 1.7 million acres of national forest land in Arizona, California, New Mexico, Oregon, and Washington.[21]

The Grays Harbor Federal Sustained-Yield Unit in Washington reflected the service's retreat. The Forest Service first proposed a cooperative unit for Grays Harbor, in response to that area's outrage over the Shelton cooperative unit. William B. Greeley, former chief of the U.S. Forest Service and at that time head of the West Coast Lumbermen's Association, lobbied for the proposal among community leaders. Despite his good offices, the Forest Service could not come to terms with local industries. Ultimately, the best the service could offer was a wholly federal unit intended to supply local needs and encourage both reforestation and native manufacturing industries. The unit became active in November 1949. Nearly a year later the Lakeview Federal Sustained-Yield Unit in Oregon came into being in similar circumstances.[22] Another federal unit at Big Valley, California, endured for years on paper, but never operated successfully.[23]

The Vallecitos Sustained-Yield Unit, on sixty-five thousand acres of the Carson National Forest in northern New Mexico, began as a social engineering project with some peculiarly scattered purposes—range improvement, community stabilization, and timber sales. The cutting level was low on the forest after World War II, and the regional forester wanted to raise it starting in 1947. The Forest Service came up with a plan to support a sawmill and a box and stock factory near the town of Vallecitos to use the timber and "raise the economic well-being of these small farm-stock owners." Its main purpose, however, was to provide compensating employment income to subsistence-level graziers whose federal grazing allotments were about to be reduced. Sustained-yield forestry, in other words, masked a plan to improve grazing lands.[24]

In assuming charge of the national forests of northern New Mexico, the Forest Service brought technically trained resource managers face to face with an entrenched, deeply traditional, and extremely poor rural population that

18. Watts to Region 1, 13 March 1947, DTM, RG95/1367; Hoover, "Public Law 273," p. 101; Steen, *U.S. Forest Service*, p. 252. There is a lot of correspondence related to the futile attempts to establish cooperative sustained-yield units in RG95/1367 and RG95/1368, most of which indicates utter lack of support in the communities to be blessed, as well as opposition from almost every conceivable type of person and organization. The Forest Service response was almost uniformly to blame opposition on "a lot of misinformation" (a frequent phrase). The Washington office repeatedly urged the regions to beat the bushes in the affected communities for support. The Department of the Interior received authority to institute cooperative sustained-yield units on lands under its jurisdiction in the late 1930s, but was never able to establish any.
19. Watts to regional foresters, 11 April 1946, DTM, RG95/1368.
20. Granger to regional forester, Albuquerque, 15 May 1946, DTM, RG95/1369.
21. Steen, *U.S. Forest Service*, p. 252.

22. Granger to the record, 21 January 1947, DTM, RG95/1368; H. J. Andrews to regional foresters, all regions, 28 June 1949, "S, PLANS, TM, Federal Units 1936–1949," Region 2, 56-A-144/62230, NARS-D. Sinclair A. Wilson, "A Preliminary Statement of Facts Bearing upon Forest Industries in the Grays Harbor Area, State of Washington," 16 February 1948; Walter H. Lund to chief, 26 April 1949; Watts to Region 6, 24 May 1949; and Forest Service, "Sustained Yield Timber Unit in Grays Harbor and Jefferson Counties" (typescript, transcript of hearings 2 August 1949); all in File 2410, "Plans," TMO, Pacific Northwest Region.
23. "Establishment of the Proposed Big Valley Federal Sustained Yield Unit, Public Hearings, Alturas, California, 19 October 1949"; A. A. Hesel, "Amendment to Management Plan, Big Valley Working Circle," 15 November 1949; Harvey B. Mack, "A Study of the Big Valley Federal Unit, Modoc National Forest, 1950–1958"; all in File 2410, "Plans," TMO, California Region. Burton Clark and W. G. Charter, "A Study of the Big Valley Federal Unit," 15 August 1949, "S, PLANS, TM, Federal Units 1936–1949," Region 2, 56-A-144/62230, NARS-D.
24. David O. Scott to regional forester, 18 September 1946; Duncan M. Lang to forest supervisor, Carson National Forest, 26 September 1946; Scott, "Sustained Yield Case Study: Vallecitos Working Circle," 20 March 1947; L. W. Darby to chief, 28 November 1953; all in File 2410, "Plans," TMO, Vallecitos Federal Sustained Yield Unit, Southwest Region (hereafter cited as Vallecitos File 2410).

SUSTAINED YIELD 9

A view of the Carson National Forest in New Mexico in 1939; the Vallecitos Sustained-Yield Unit established in 1948 involved this forest. Forest Service photo.

depended on its herds of livestock for subsistence. Peonage had not been abolished in New Mexico until 1867, and even in the mid-twentieth century the economy and social arrangements in some rural areas were almost medieval. Foresters interested in restoring overused rangeland inevitably threatened the very survival of people in the region. The Forest Service was not insensitive to the problems it created, but was determined to have its way.[25]

When the Forest Service reduced grazing allotments in 1947, Pedro Martinez told the regional forester that the agency did not have the interests of the "poor people" at heart. Nor did he have any confidence in the proposed sustained-yield unit. "Strangers" would come from other states, he predicted. They would say, "The hell with the poor people of Vallecitos, Petaca, and Cañon Plaza. We got the money and we are going to drive them out." He predicted the end of his people's way of life, "as you have taken away from us the rights of our predecessors who were permitted 25 head on a free permit and 60 free sticks of wood for our own use. And where are they? Dead."[26]

It remained to be seen whether technicians trained to manage timber and grass could manage people adeptly, especially people who were so different from the tech-

nicians themselves. It also remained to be seen whether a federal sustained-yield unit would be an effective tool of people management (or community stabilization, as it was called). The process did not start smoothly. Shortly before the unit was activated, the firm that was to develop the sawmill and stock plant pulled out, and the Forest Service had to search for a replacement.

On 21 January 1948, Chief Watts established the Vallecitos Federal Sustained Yield Unit, that same day amending its policy to include the communities of Petaca and Cañon Plaza along with Vallecitos. The policy provided that local people could purchase the locally produced lumber, "but we have no basis for requiring that such sales be made at any specified price."[27] Thus the service could not guarantee that Martinez and his neighbors could afford to buy the lumber, even if they had a legal right to do so.

Vallecitos was the first federal sustained-yield unit established under the 1944 legislation, and the smallest, with an average annual cut of 1.5 million feet. The management plan called for selling unit timber to maintain steady employment for local resident labor and to provide lumber for local requirements. The Vallecitos Lumber Company was established and designated as the "approved respon-

25. See for example Ronald B. Hartzer, *Half a Century in Forest Conservation: A Biography and Oral History of Edward P. Cliff* (Bloomington, Indiana: David A. Clary & Associates, 1981), pp. 142–144. In the 1960s northern New Mexico saw an uprising of Spanish-Americans resentful about several things, among them Forest Service [?]

26. Martinez to regional forester, 21 November 19[??], [??] File 2410.

27. DJK [Dahl J. Kirkpatrick] to [C.] Otto [Lindh], n.d. [1948], Vallecitos File 2410; Ira J. Mason to Region 3, 21 January 1948, and Watts to Region 3, 21 January 1948, DTM, RG95/1367. In explaining why the Vallecitos unit was established, the Forest Service told a senator, "This unit . . . is for the purpose of improving living conditions of a small and remote community of Spanish Americans" (E. I. Kotok to Senator Henry C. Dworshak, 10 August 1948, DTM, RG95/1366).

sible operator," charged with installing, maintaining, and operating a "primary manufacturing plant including planer" at or within a mile of the village of Vallecitos. Ninety percent of the employees were to live within ten miles of the plant. The company's designation soon was terminated for "noncooperation" with this clause of the agreement, and in 1952 the designation went to Jackson Lumber Company of Vallecitos.[28]

Operations in the unit suffered labor-management difficulties arising from cultural conflicts, divergent priorities, and poor relations between the designated operator and the Forest Service. Only five men showed up to operate the mill in the fall of 1952, and the Carson National Forest's timber staff officer investigated. Two storekeepers told him that "the fault was probably with the employees not wishing to work in cold weather, wanting to cut wood for their homes, and possibly wishing to be released to go on relief." Another added that the crews believed that they were not being paid properly for the volume harvested. In addition, the employees preferred to cut only pine, but the company wanted mixed conifer production. A year later, however, the regional office's curiously flat and terse response was that "the advantages to the community are clearly evident."[29]

Meanwhile relations between the operator and the Forest Service deteriorated. In 1955 Jackson Lumber Company engaged a former Forest Service man as "consulting forester" to work with the Forest Service in "planning and supervising the woods operation." He soon complained about the "feeling of continual antagonism and bickering which prevails between the Forest Service and Jackson Lumber Company at Vallecitos." He accused Forest Service personnel of finagling on the scaling of logs and thus cheating the firm, "inciting unrest or dissatisfaction among the workmen," meeting with the people of Vallecitos "to stir up dissent against the Company," and arbitrarily threatening to shut operations down. The Forest Service dismissed his complaints as merely the spite of a disgruntled former employee.[30]

The company failed to meet its quota of 90 percent local employment; about half the labor was imported, and local people complained. The Forest Service proposed new guidelines, extending the labor pool to eight communities and "adjacent rural areas," but somehow in the process

making residents of El Rito ineligible.[31] Jackson Lumber appealed, and the Department of Agriculture held public hearings. Testimony revealed that the ten-mile radius for the labor pool ran through the middle of the community of Ojo Caliente, many of whose residents worked for Jackson. Furthermore, Jackson and its employees fell out over piecework versus hourly payment for work in nonfederal timber, and the workers tried to establish a union to demand an hourly wage. The company fired some of them and brought in workers from Texas.[32]

The main point of dispute was whether Ojo Caliente was a community that ought to be included within the labor-pool boundary; if it were, the company would have no difficulty in reaching the 90 percent local-employment level. Ojo Caliente was an old colonial land grant that had evolved into a succession of smallholdings extending ten miles down a valley. The Anglo foresters saw it as not a community but a rural area. The company and the Forest Service fell into a series of arguments and appeals over the drawing of the ten-mile boundary. Finally, in 1956 the Forest Service agreed to "consider persons residing within the Ojo Caliente Land Grant to qualify as local laborers for purposes of complying with the terms of the two noncompetitive timber sale contracts."[33]

That did not end matters. The sustained-yield exercise in people management was going nowhere, so the Forest Service held hearings on whether to discontinue the unit. Residents of six villages asked that if the unit were to be continued, the 90 percent local-employment policy (that is, exclusion of Ojo Caliente) be enforced.[34] The hearings became so tense that Jackson Lumber Company chose to make no presentation and instead, later submitted a statement for the record. Early in January 1957 the chief of the Forest Service noted that the people generally favored continuing the sustained-yield unit, but not with Jackson Lumber Company. So he appointed an advisory board to offer recommendations on the labor question.[35]

31. Buford H. Starky to Jackson Lumber Company, 2 April 1955; Graves to Jackson Lumber Company, 30 March and 18 August 1955; Fred H. Kennedy to the chief, 5 April 1956; Kirkpatrick, "Guide Lines to be Used in Determining Compliance with Local Labor Requirements Imposed in the Harvest and Manufacture of National Forest Timber from the Vallecitos Federal Sustained Yield Unit," 22 April 1955; all in Vallecitos File 2410.

32. Thomas M. Smith to Kennedy, 9 December 1955, Vallecitos File 2410.

33. Kirkpatrick to Carson National Forest, 9 February 1956; Kirkpatrick to J. L. Jackson, 9 February 1956; Kennedy to the chief, 17 February and 5 April 1956; L. A. Wall to the files, 23 February 1956; Senator Dennis Chavez to Ezra Taft Benson, 27 March 1956; Kennedy to the chief, 6 April 1956; McArdle to Jackson Lumber Company, 20 April 1956; all in Vallecitos File 2410.

34. Vallecitos Sustained-Yield Unit Hearing Record, petitions dated 20 August 1956, Vallecitos File 2410.

35. Catron & Catron to Sidney Williams, USDA, 18 October 1956; Richard E. McArdle, "Decision on·Continuation of Vallecitos Federal Sustained Yield Unit, Carson NF, N. Mex.," 3 January 1957; both in Vallecitos File 2410.

28. Plan submitted by P. V. Woodhead to chief, 26 January 1948, with revisions and amendments; Richard E. McArdle to O. D. Connery, Vallecitos Lumber Company, 17 September 1948; McCardle to Jackson Lumber Company, 8 October 1952; all in Vallecitos File 2410. Watts to Connery, 31 March 1948; McArdle to Connery, 17 September 1948; both in DTM, RG95/1366 and RG95/1367.

29. L. A. Wall to the files, 23 November 1952; Darby to the chief, 20 November 1953; both in Vallecitos File 2410.

30. J. L. Jackson to C. Otto Lindh, 14 January 1955; Dahl J. Kirkpatrick to the files, 1 April 1955; Vernon Bostick to Walter L. Graves (supervisor, Carson National Forest), 25 April 1955; all in Vallecitos File 2410.

The Carpenters and Joiners Union bombarded the Forest Service with complaints that Jackson Lumber imported workers from elsewhere. Senator Dennis Chavez tried to work out a compromise formula, but the union claimed the company would not conform even to that. The Forest Service developed a clause for timber sale contracts requiring local employment on the agency's terms, but the company insisted that it must have the right to say whether sufficient local labor was "available." On 2 May 1957, a Forest Service delegation went to Vallecitos to tell J. L. Jackson, owner of Jackson Lumber, that the clause would stand. Jackson "said that if it had to be that way he was through — that he could not sign a contract with that clause in it." Jackson's mill burned to the ground that night. Three days later the company refused to work under the labor restrictions, and on May 23 the Forest Service revoked Jackson Lumber's designation for the sustained-yield unit.[36]

The Vallecitos Federal Sustained-Yield Unit managed to stay on the books, with little effect on the ground. Another operator was eventually located, but its mill burned down in 1963. In 1966 an inspection report said that the unit had "failed conspicuously to meet its objective" and recommended termination, with a caution about the "delicate public relations situation involved." The question became critical the next year when a fire on the Carson National Forest left a lot of timber to be salvaged. The timber had to be put on open sale because the unit was not functioning.[37]

The Washington office wondered "what to do about an inoperative unit which is obstructing use of National Forest land for benefit of local communities." It was known that the people of Vallecitos would not take termination of the unit lightly. Another local operator, Duke City Lumber Company, was pleading by 1969 for the government to modify or terminate the unit to make the timber available to other firms.[38] Duke City Lumber had a mill operating in Vallecitos, and had been buying national forest timber in regular sales since 1962. It needed access to the unit's timber, but the people of Vallecitos would not budge. The answer was to bring them together. Duke City Lumber applied for designation as the "approved responsible operator." A public meeting in Vallecitos consented, and on 4 April 1972, Duke City Lumber became the sustained-yield unit's operator. Yet this solution too was short-lived — the Duke City sawmill burned down in 1977.[39]

The Vallecitos unit was a dismal failure. By the time the Forest Service acknowledged the mistake, it proved impossible to correct it; local people simply would not go along with termination, for whatever reason. As an exercise in sustained-yield timber management, the unit dedicated to oft-burning, usually idle mills actually inhibited systematic management of the timber on the national forest.

Much of the error lay in the unit's vague and conflicting purposes. The national forest's immediate concern was reduction of livestock grazing by people who could not afford to give up a single calf. The federal managers of the forest were unhappy because of its low timber sales. Superficially the postwar sustained-yield unit movement appeared to offer an answer to both concerns. It did not because sustained-yield management turned less on matters of economics or forestry than on the sentiments of people. People can be cantankerous, and they certainly were at Vallecitos. The problems to be solved there were not the sort that foresters were trained to handle. Even the ageless magic of "sustained yield" proved wanting in the real world. Slogans and labels could not force national forests to be managed the way foresters thought they should be rather than the way the public wanted them managed. The original conceivers of the sustained-yield unit walked into northern New Mexico with their eyes shut to this reality, and as a result their unit never stood a chance.

The Flagstaff Unit — A Subsidized Monopoly

The last federal unit established under the 1944 legislation — the Flagstaff Unit on the Coconino National Forest in Arizona, created in 1949 — came to a better end than the Vallecitos unit. It was terminated.

The Forest Service estimated in 1939 that half the population of Flagstaff depended upon the two sawmills drawing on the Flagstaff working circle: Southwest Lumber Mills, Inc., and the Saginaw-Manistee Lumber Company. As early as 1943, Assistant Chief E. E. Carter suggested that the Flagstaff region might be a good candidate for a sustained-yield unit. An application had been received and a study was underway by 1946. The locally stationed federal foresters favored the proposal as the best way to defeat two basic threats to Flagstaff's economic stability: competition among local mills, and competition between local mills and companies based elsewhere. The first threat arose when previously close cooperation between the two largest local firms — collusion promoted by the Forest Service for several years — threatened to come apart. Forest Service officials saw a sustained-yield unit as a way to stabilize the community and regulate industrial harvesting. Mostly, it appears that Acting Forest Supervisor Roland Rotty was thoroughly enamored of the idea for a sustained-

36. Kirkpatrick to the files, 1 May 1957; Edward C. Groesbeck to the files, 21 May 1957; Kirkpatrick to the files, 7 May 1957; McArdle to J. L. Jackson, 23 May 1957; all in Vallecitos File 2410.

37. M. M. Nelson to R-3, 29 July 1966, "1440 INSPECTION; GFI Timber Management, Mason Bruce, 11–29 October 1965," 75-135/231179, NARS-LN; William D. Hurst to the files, 9 August 1967, "2410-Plans," Box C-07-073-3-6, NARS-FW.

38. B. H. Payne to regional forester, Albuquerque, 10 August 1967; Don D. Seaman to regional forester, Albuquerque, 13 March 1968; T. W. Koskella to forest supervisor, Carson National Forest, 27 May 1969; M. J. Hassell to regional forester, Albuquerque, 15 May 1969; Koskella to William D. Hurst, 31 October 1968; Yale Weinstein, Duke City Lumber Company, to Hassell, 18 April 1969; all in file "2400-Plans," C-07-073-3-6, and "2400-Timber, FY 69," E-27-036-2-4, NARS-FW.

39. Hurst to the chief, 14 February 1972; Edward P. Cliff to Weinstein, Duke City Lumber Company, 4 April 1972; Weinstein to Hassell, 22 July 1977; Vallecitos File 2410.

The Coconino National Forest in Arizona, 1959; the Flagstaff Sustained-Yield Unit controlled timber from this forest. Forest Service photo.

yield unit. The regional forester, in contrast, regarded the whole thing as an unwarranted gift to the two local companies.[40]

The staff of the national forest wanted to stabilize the two firms by giving them a hundred-year exclusive contract for timber from the Coconino National Forest. The foresters hoped that their own management plan would then allow them to divert the companies from railroad logging to highway transport, and above all to avoid the introduction of seasonal logging camps by smaller operators who could undercut the established firms' bids. However, the regional office turned down the proposed hundred-year lease, and the Washington office decided that Flagstaff did not qualify under the Sustained-Yield Act. By 1947 the applicants had enlisted political assistance, and the Forest Service was discovering that the true degree of the community's dependence upon timber could not easily be measured. The locally stationed federal foresters kept promoting the idea, but the Washington office was increasingly sensitive to the plan's monopolistic aspects.[41]

Suddenly in 1948 the Washington office turned around and told the region to go ahead with public hearings on a sustained-yield unit, offering suggestions on how to load the hearings with favorable witnesses. Meanwhile, Forest Service arbitration had produced a formal and approximately equal division of the unit's timber between the two large concerns. The service's twenty-year plan covered the two large companies and one small door and sash mill (the owner of which was soon eager to sell out to the large combine for a good price). This plan gave the big industries a nearly permanent resource that they could exploit over the counter in a number of imaginative ways. Roland Rotty was not worried: "Once I was much concerned about this," he said, "because I did not see why any private citizen should profit by dealing in something that belongs to all the people. Since then I have come to realize that this is the case throughout the entire business world. . . . I see no reason to get excited about this. We should go ahead and conduct our timber management business without trying to prevent somebody making a profit by selling out."[42]

The Washington office was very concerned about public

40. USDA Forest Service, *Coconino National Forest, Arizona*, p. 12. A. A. McCutchen to the chief, 9 September 1947 (citing Carter of 12 May 1943); Lang to the files, 9 July 1946; James G. McNary to regional forester, Albuquerque, 16 September 1946 (application for sustained-yield unit); Lindh to regional forester, Albuquerque, 23 October 1946; "A Case Study of the Flagstaff Federal Sustained Yield Unit," approved 9 September 1947; and Roland Rotty to regional forester, Albuquerque, 17 February 1947; all in File 2410, "Plans," TMO, Southwest Region.

41. Lindh to Rotty, 19 February 1947; R. W. Hussey to Timber Management, 8 August 1947; "A Case Study of the Flagstaff Federal Sustained Yield Unit," approved 9 September 1947; McNary to Clinton P. Anderson, secretary of agriculture, 18 September 1947; Anderson to McNary, 26 September 1947; Watts to secretary of agriculture, 17 October 1947; Granger to Region 3, 20 October 1947; Rotty to regional forester, Albuquerque, 29 October 1947; all in File 2410, "Plans," TMO, Southwest Region. L. S. Gross to Mason, 30 October 1947, (quotation), DTM, RG95/1367.

42. H. E. Ochsner to Region 3, 1 January 1948; Watts to Region 3, 5 April 1948; Gross to the record, 23 April 1948; all in DTM, RG95/1366. Forest Service, "In the Matter of Federal Sustained Yield Unit, Coconino National Forest, Memorandum of Southwest Lumber Mills, re: Allocation of Timber Resources," received 10 February 1948; McNary, "Memorandum of Southwest Lumber Mills, Inc., re: Allocation of Timber Resources," received 10 February 1948; Woodhead to the chief, 5 April 1948; Granger to Region 3, 5 April 1948; Woodhead to G. R. Birklund and to McNary, (two letters) 7 April 1948; Rotty to regional forester, Albuquerque, 7 April 1948; Woodhead to the chief, 8 April 1948; Gross to the record, 23 April 1948; Granger to Region 3, 29 April 1948; Rotty to regional forester, Albuquerque, 7 May 1948; Woodhead to the chief, 10 May 1948; Granger to Region 3, 4 June 1948; G. R. Birklund to Woodhead, 29 June 1948; Rotty to regional forester, Albuquerque, 7 May 1948 (quotation); all in File 2410, "Plans," TMO, Southwest Region.

opposition to the proposed unit, however. Christopher Granger gave the regional office advice on how to handle possible opposition at the hearings. He warned the regional staff to "anticipate" the appearance of opponents at the hearing "and be prepared so far as possible to have them counteracted." He did not want another fiasco like the recent outcry that had killed a proposed unit in California. Granger explained "our position . . . that it is the Forest Service responsibility to make sure that everyone has a good understanding of the proposal but not to engage in public debate at the meeting." The solution was to line up supporting witnesses in advance.[43]

Public sentiment favoring open competition was one major threat to the service's plans for Flagstaff. The current timber plan called for competitive bidding, and the regional office feared that high bidders might take federal timber to mills elsewhere. Establishment of the sustained-yield unit would prevent that. In the interim, the region promised its industrial clients in Flagstaff that "we will continue to supply stumpage to established plants dependent on national-forest timber such as those at Flagstaff. This can be done under war power acts, as long as prospective purchasers bid the OPA [Office of Price Administration] ceiling prices."[44]

During the more than a year that the Flagstaff sustained-yield unit had been under discussion, high-level enthusiasm for the program had swept away any misgivings in the Forest Service. On 25 October 1948, Chief Watts approved the proposed unit. His only real concern was public opposition, which he told the regional forester to defuse. "When you are convinced," he said, "that the proposal will be actively supported locally, you are authorized to proceed" with public hearings.[45] Watts feared the public's "strong sentiment for making all Federal Units competitive." He underscored his belief that the two mills at Flagstaff could not operate year-round if they had to face competitors. He wanted it clearly explained, however, that 15 percent of the allowable annual cut would be set aside for competitive bidding by other purchasers.[46]

Charges that the Forest Service was promoting monopolies clearly worried Watts, and he grasped for responses. "One of the strongest arguments," he said, "is that the two large sawmills offer an opportunity for local laborers to have a choice of employer. Flagstaff is not at all a one company town." Considering that the two mills operated essentially as a combine, and that the Forest Service plan required them to do so, that was a remarkable suggestion. Watts believed that "community stability" depended upon "maintaining the equivalent of the manufacturing facilities

now in operation." That meant no more as well as no less.[47]

As Watts was coming to support the Flagstaff unit in Washington, the southwestern regional office was doing its spadework in Arizona: it prepared an elaborate booklet justifying the sustained-yield unit, sent officials out to make speeches, and obtained favorable comment in the press. But the Forest Service did not win everyone over. One of its supporters praised the Forest Service for trying to eliminate the small mills that "nibble at the flanks of the pine forest," but the Western Forest Industries Association, a group of small operators opposed to the unit, responded that "fundamentally . . . government agencies should be concerned only with the stability of wood using communities and not with that of individual operators." Nine small operators banded together as the Coconino Small Mills Association — belying the assumption that the timber industry of Flagstaff was represented by two large firms and one small — and bought a full-page advertisement in the Flagstaff newspaper under the headline, "Sustained Yield or Sustained Grab?" The stage was set for the public hearing.[48]

The meeting finally took place in Flagstaff on 2 February 1949. A parade of civic leaders, bankers, organized labor, and others came forward to promote the sustained-yield unit. Their chief argument was that stabilizing the two large mills by guaranteeing their timber supply and protecting them from competition would attract development capital and permit them to grow. Small operators, understandably, bemoaned the plans to shut them out of the national forest and predicted the death of their businesses. Afterward, the regional forester suggested increasing the amount of the annual cut to be set aside for competitive sale, but Watts turned that down. Small operators were told that they would receive somewhat more timber than they had taken in recent years and should console themselves with the thought that the two big Flagstaff concerns would not be allowed to bid against them. When one of the two giants tried to buy out a small operator, the Forest Service stopped the action as violating the unit plan.[49]

The Flagstaff Federal Sustained-Yield Unit set aside a perpetual timber supply, free of competition from other firms, for Southwest Lumber and Saginaw-Manistee, who divided the resource between them. The arrangement

43. Granger to Region 3, 26 July 1948, DTM, RG95/95.

44. Lang, "Flagstaff Sustained Yield Unit under Public Law 273," 23 October 1946; Woodhead to the files, 25 October 1946; both in File 2410, "Plans," TMO, Southwest Region.

45. Watts to regional forester, Albuquerque, 25 October 1948, DTM, RG95/1366.

46. Watts to regional foresters, 1 November 1948, DTM, RG95/1366. Watts was generally willing to give in to public sentiment on this issue, but he maintained that Flagstaff was an exception.

47. Watts to Region 6, 23 November 1948, Flagstaff File 2410.

48. "Resume of the Arguments for the Establishment of the Federal Sustained Yield Unit at Flagstaff," received 14 December 1948; Arizona Daily Sun (Flagstaff). 1 December 1948; Arizona Labor Journal, 6 January 1949; Arizona Farmer, 8 January 1949; R. T. Titus, Western Forest Industries Association, to Woodhead, 24 January 1949; C. J. Warren, Southwest Lumber Mills, Inc., to Lindh, 26 January 1949; Arizona Daily Sun, 27 January 1949; Winslow [Arizona] Mail, 20 January 1949; all in File 2410. "Plans," TMO, Southwest Region.

49. "Transcript of Proceedings, In re: Flagstaff Sustained Yield Unit, Public Hearing, Flagstaff, Arizona, February 2, 1949"; Woodhead by Lindh to the chief, 22 March 1949; Watts to Region 3, 11 April 1949; Woodhead by George W. Kimball to Titus, 17 January 1949; Kenneth A. Keeney to regional forester, Albuquerque, 24 May 1950; Kirkpatrick by Lang to Coconino National Forest, 29 May 1950; all in File 2410, "Plans," TMO, Flagstaff Federal Sustained Yield Unit, Southwest Region (hereafter cited as Flagstaff File 2410).

worked well enough, in the Forest Service's opinion. As the regional office reported in 1953,

> The establishment of the Flagstaff Unit has permitted the community to maintain itself so far as the lumber industry is concerned on a comparatively even keel. Whether this would have been possible without the Unit is open to considerable question since the timber now being sold is competitively available to plants at other locations. We cannot claim, therefore, that conditions have been improved as a result of the Federal Unit program but they have not deteriorated as they might have without it.[50]

Conditions in Flagstaff may have been stabilized from one point of view, but economic changes beyond the control of the Forest Service continued to keep the foresters on their toes. For example, Watts had answered charges of monopoly by saying that two colluding operations were preferable to one. That justification went out the window in 1954 when Southwest Lumber Mills bought out Saginaw-Manistee, and the Forest Service made the new giant the sole "approved responsible operator" for the Flagstaff unit. The company embarked on an expansion program.[51]

Sentiment soon emerged nationally for repeal of the Sustained-Yield Forest Management Act, which was increasingly regarded as socialistic, and bills were introduced in Congress. The Forest Service repeatedly had to review the few existing units. In 1956 it reported that it was "impossible to demonstrate" that the Flagstaff unit had produced "any effect upon community developments or expansion. Improvements have occurred but no basis exists for attributing them to the existence of the Federal Unit." That seemed to be no reason to discontinue it, however. Despite the report, the unit did seem to have affected the structure of the local economy: by the next year the number of small operators in the area had dwindled to four (from the original nine).[52]

Southwest Lumber Mills was certainly doing well. In 1957 it received a thirty-year pulpwood contract involving about 6 million cords, to be harvested beginning 1962. By 1960 the company had attracted $40 million in capital to finance its expansion, the financial commitments contingent upon the continued availability of the sustained-yield unit. Meanwhile, the Forest Service tried to attract a newsprint plant to Flagstaff to support "community stability" further by providing a customer for Southwest's pulpwood.[53]

In 1962 the Forest Service granted its burgeoning "approved operator," by then renamed Southwest Forest Industries, Inc., authority to bid on all competitive sales offered within or without the Flagstaff Federal Sustained-Yield Unit, until further notice. Thus ended the reservation of 15 percent of the annual cut for smaller competitors, who thereafter faced direct competition from a very profitable giant, which could now gobble them up.[54]

Southwest Forest Industries clearly enjoyed significant advantages from its monopoly on the sustained-yield unit's future timber. Its profits guaranteed, it dominated the forest industry in a region extending beyond the Flagstaff unit (the corporate headquarters, in fact, were in Phoenix). Relations with the Forest Service were very close. Southwest bought out the Kaibab Lumber Company, one of the few remaining small companies, in 1965 and received permission to transfer that company's national forest timber purchases to itself.[55] The Coconino National Forest staff met with corporation officials to map out how to break the news to the public. The foresters advised explaining that the purchase of Kaibab had been approved "in order to bring local mill capacity in line with available timber."[56]

Throughout the early 1960s, the Flagstaff Federal Sustained-Yield Unit helped Southwest Forest Industries to build a veritable economic empire. By the later years of that decade, however, the political times and Forest Service personnel in the region had changed. The approved operator, jealous of its prerogatives, began to face more serious competition. In 1968 the C. T. Bunger Lumber Company reconstructed an old sawmill, and Passalacqua Lumber Company erected a new facility (both in or near Flagstaff). When these two firms petitioned for exclusion of Southwest from the 15 percent of annual cut formerly reserved for small operators, Regional Forester William D. Hurst agreed. Southwest hit the roof. It claimed that it had "paid

50. Lindh by Darby to the chief, 20 November 1953, Flagstaff File 2410.
51. J. B. Edens, Southwest Lumber Mills (drafted by Kirkpatrick) to forest supervisor, Coconino National Forest, 11 January 1954; Lindh by Kirkpatrick to Edens, 16 February 1954; Mason to Region 3, 11 February 1954; *Arizona Daily Sun* (Flagstaff), 2 June 1954; James M. Potter, Coconino Pulp and Paper, to Keeney, 26 March 1956; McArdle to Coconino Pulp and Paper, 30 March 1956; Irving A. Jennings, Arizona Pulp and Paper, to McArdle, 22 June 1956; McArdle to Arizona Pulp and Paper, 22 June 1956; Clare Hendee for Cliff to E. H. Weig, Ponderosa Paper Products, 14 October 1964; Greeley to Ponderosa Paper Products, 5 August 1968; all in Flagstaff File 2410. In 1956 another "approved responsible operator" was designated for pulpwood, and that designation was bought and sold repeatedly thereafter.
52. Kirkpatrick to the chief, 9 November 1956, letter and enclosures; Kennedy by Kirkpatrick to the chief, 14 February 1957; Kirkpatrick to the files, 24 July 1957; all in Flagstaff File 2410.

53. Southwest Lumber Mills, Inc., *Annual Report for the Year Ended April 30, 1957*; Kennedy by Kirkpatrick to the chief, to attention of Mason, 22 October 1957; R. W. Crawford to Potter, 15 January 1960; Kennedy by Kirkpatrick to M. E. Halffey, Arizona Development Board, 2 February 1960; McArdle by Cliff to regional forester, Albuquerque, 15 March 1960; Weinstein to John T. Utley (N.B., correspondence to this individual was addressed variously to John T. Utley, Jack Uttley, and Jack T. Utley; citations use the exact form that appears on the correspondence), 9 November 1977; all in Flagstaff File 2410.
54. J. Morgan Smith to Southwest Forest Industries, 13 August 1962, Flagstaff File 2410.
55. M. C. Galbraith to Kaibab Lumber Company, 15 July 1965; statement, F. L. Quirk, vice-president, Southwest Forest Industries, 30 September 1965; both in Flagstaff File 2410.
56. R. M. Housley to regional forester, 19 July 1965, Flagstaff File 2410.

dearly" for Kaibab Lumber in order to institute two shifts at its main plant. It was also building a large particleboard plant at Flagstaff to increase timber utilization, and claimed that loss of even 15 percent of the sustained-yield unit's annual cut would be "economically disastrous." To Southwest, its new competitors were "a haphazard and inefficient operation capable of cutting only three to four million feet per year."[57]

The regional forester denied Southwest's appeal on the grounds that the company had never been told it could count on maintaining two shifts indefinitely. Allowable cuts might rise or fall in future years, Hurst said. "For this reason we have not encouraged industry to build beyond the capacity of the Unit to sustain. In past years members of your company have discussed overcutting on the Unit to permit two full-time shifts in the mill with the realization that after a few years the allowable cut would drop to a one shift basis," he told the firm's vice-president. Hurst apparently believed that the Forest Service had created a monster he could no longer control. He hinted that a complete review of the sustained-yield unit could be required if the company insisted—a veiled threat that Flagstaff might no longer qualify under the original legislation.[58]

The extent to which forest officers had previously assisted the designated operator in the name of community stabilization came to light in 1969 after a public complaint led to an internal audit. At Flagstaff the Forest Service had consistently adjusted destination calculations in timber appraisals to keep those in the sustained-yield unit lower than those in competitive sales. The Washington office expressed a "strong belief that there is nothing in the Sustained Yield Forest Management Act which either requires or permits timber in the Sustained Yield Units, either Federal or Cooperative, to be appraised any differently than if it were not in a unit." Furthermore, it was a "false premise" that community stability was to be promoted "by assuring a supply of timber to dependent communities but by a price concession as well. This . . . simply can't be read into the Act." Competing timber industries had justifiably complained about the lower appraisals in the sustained-yield unit. "The effect of appraising this timber to Flagstaff is to give Southwest . . . a price concession as well as providing protection against competition," conceded the regional office. "Our job is to establish fair market value, not sell at reduced prices." Advising Washington on corrective measures, the region admitted that it had "drifted into [its] present position without considering all of the complications." The Coconino National Forest was ordered to correct its appraisal concessions in the sustained-yield unit, but accusations of unfair pricing continued.[59]

The national forest also had to reevaluate its policy on sales to small operators in the 15 percent set aside for them. The regional office declared that the intent of the set-aside "was to afford protection of the small operators who were operating on the Coconino in 1949." However, all such operators had "passed out of the picture with one exception" by 1969 because the Forest Service had refused to allocate timber to small operators. "The whole intent of the Act was to stabilize communities and not individual operators except as a device contributing to community stabilization," Watts said in 1949. It was questionable that the intent of the legislation had been observed at Flagstaff, where Southwest had driven out the small operators in the past and was resisting attempts of new ones to reclaim their 15 percent. Nevertheless, in 1969 (as it had in 1962) the region decided to allow operators of all sizes to bid for the timber on the 15 percent.[60]

When the Forest Service restudied the Flagstaff unit in 1970, it concluded only that "it is difficult to assess what competition would be if the Unit did not exist." Certainly there was little competition visible at the time; only three small competitors of Southwest were working the reopened 15 percent set-aside in 1970. Moreover, the justification for the unit as protecting Flagstaff's economy had also dwindled; Flagstaff was only about one-fifth dependent on forest products industries by this time. Nonetheless, the report recommended continuing the unit because it "has been successful in fulfilling all of its objectives and the purpose for which it exists." F. Leroy Bond in the regional office disagreed, however, pointing out that the timber industry was no longer the "key to economic stability" in Flagstaff.[61]

The unit continued for several more years, despite periodic revisions of the management plan and growing public complaints. When critics again proposed closing the unit down in 1977, Southwest predictably promised "disaster" and "disruption." J. D. Porter, president of the Western Pine Industries Association, had another opinion:

of General Counsel, to the chief, 23 October 1963; Ralph F. Koebel, Assistant General Counsel, to the chief, 3 May 1962; Washington office of the U.S. Forest Service (no date or signature) to Region 3, 10 March 1969; Don D. Seamon to regional forester, 21 March 1969; F. Leroy Bond to Chief, 28 March 1969; Homer J. Hixon to Nelson, 29 April 1969; Payne to Greeley and Cliff, 9 May 1969; MMN [Nelson] to Cliff and Greeley, 12 May 1969; J. D. Porter, Western Pine Industries, to Richard Worthington, 26 March 1975; D. D. Westbury for Worthington to Porter, 4 April 1975; W. L. Evans to Porter, 20 February 1975; Worthington to Joseph D. Cummings, Office of General Counsel, 18 July 1975; Division of Timber Management to regional foresters, Region 1 through Region 10; Porter to Jack Uttley, n.d. [December 1975]; William L. Holmes to Porter, 6 February 1976; all in Flagstaff File 2410.

60. Bond to the files, 17 September 1969, citing memoranda from Region 3 to the chief, 22 March 1949, and the chief to the region, 11 April 1949; Hurst to the chief, 22 September 1969; Hixon to regional forester, Albuquerque, 5 November 1969; all in Flagstaff File 2410.

61. "Periodic Reanalysis, Flagstaff Federal Sustained Yield Unit," 19 November 1970; Bond to the files, 17 September 1969; both in Flagstaff File 2410.

57. C. T. Bunger to Forest Service, 18 April 1968; Phil Passalaqua Lumber Company to Forest Service, received 16 April 1968; W. B. Finley to regional forester, Albuquerque, 7 June 1968; A. T. Hildman, Southwest Forest Industries, to Hurst, 10 April 1969; Hurst to Hildman, 22 April 1969; all in Flagstaff File 2410.

58. Hurst to Hildman, 22 April 1969, Flagstaff File 2410.

59. Koskella for Hurst to forest supervisor, Flagstaff National Forest, 10 March 1969; Rawleigh L. Tremain, Department of Agriculture, Office

We oppose the continuing of the sustained yield unit on the grounds that it favors big business and puts the sustained yield operation at a definite economic advantage over the "outside the unit" operators. This economic, non-competitive advantage gives them unfair advantages at other sales on other forests where they, then, compete at open biddings, having the negotiated or non-bidding value of timber to support their bidding advantage on other forests.[62]

Supervisor Michael A. Kerrick of the Coconino National Forest directed the preparation of a "white paper" on the Flagstaff unit late in 1977. The paper tentatively concluded that "it might be that eliminating the designated operator would serve to promote open and fair competition" and suggested that alternatives should be submitted to the public. In transmitting the paper to Washington early in 1978, the regional office advised that at least one firm was considering challenging the Flagstaff unit in court, and predicted that the Western Forest Industries Association would join any such suit. "There is a possibility that the Unit could be challenged successfully," said the regional forester, "for not meeting the intent of the law; specifically that portion that speaks to following the usual procedures in selling timber."[63]

Opponents of the unit went to work, and the Forest Service began to hear from members of Congress in 1978. The resulting review concluded that "the Unit discriminates against other communities, businesses, and citizens of adjacent communities," and ought to be abolished. Public response to the review included such phrases as "enough is enough," and "Fidelity to SFI [Southwest Forest Industries] is like 'DCS' (Damned Chrysler Syndrome)," the latter a reference to the contemporary public bail-out of the failing Chrysler Corporation. The unit's days were numbered.[64]

Public hearings on the future of the Flagstaff Unit were held in January 1980. Southwest Forest Industries and its friends tried their best to guard its privileges.[65] It was to no avail, however, for public sentiment would no longer tolerate unseemly governmental interest in the care and feeding

of a thoroughly prosperous firm, especially when such federal action disadvantaged others. In May 1980 Forest Service chief Max Peterson told the region, "We concur with your recommendation that the Unit be dissolved." The region's press release said that opinion at the public hearing on this recommendation had been about "equally divided," but with Flagstaff no longer "primarily dependent on the sale of national forest timber," Southwest's monopoly could not be justified.[66]

A revised policy statement for the Coconino National Forest brought it back into the Forest Service mainstream on timber sales, emphasizing advertised, competitive bidding. Southwest Forest Industries' current contracts continued, but timber produced under them could now be taken away from Flagstaff for primary manufacture. Eighty-five percent of the forest's timber would be offered to the highest bidder, without preferential treatment for any category, but was to be manufactured in the Flagstaff region. The remainder of the timber would be sold under Small Business Administration rules to the highest-bidding small firms. Southwest Forest Industries' attempt to save the unit was tossed out of court.[67]

From the start the Flagstaff Federal Sustained-Yield Unit's compliance with the intent of the 1944 federal law was dubious. It became a sore embarrassment to the Forest Service long before it was discontinued. Even the service's own studies in the late 1940s questioned whether Flagstaff's survival depended upon a sustained-yield unit, let alone the peculiar construction that actually emerged.

Well before the unit was established, the Coconino National Forest had been encouraging dominant timber firms at the expense of competition. Thus the arrangement that served Southwest Forest Industries fit into a kind of local "tradition." Local forest officers had a long-standing interest in stabilizing both the economy and the practices of the local timber industry and perceived cooperative large operators as more conducive to that end than small or seasonal operations. During the 1920s and 1930s the forest was divided into exclusive territories for major purchasers. The sustained-yield unit, handing 85 percent of the entire forest to a single combine, was a logical continuation of these previous developments.

The Flagstaff unit, however, was definitely not the kind of arrangement that the framers of the 1944 legislation had foreseen. They had wanted to support communities by stabilizing the flow of natural resources to dependent industries. The Flagstaff program involved the Forest Service in large-scale social and economic engineering—

62. Worthington to regional foresters, 5 September 1975, Timber Sales Office Files, Coconino National Forest. James L. Matson, Kaibab Industries, to John T. Utley, 27 October 1977; Gary F. Tucker, Southwest Forest Industries, to Jack T. Utley, 3 January 1978; Weinstein to Utley, 9 November 1977; Porter to Coconino National Forest, 27 October 1977; all in Flagstaff File 2410.

63. Hassell by Gary E. Cargill to the chief, 27 January 1978, Flagstaff File 2410. Deposition of Michael A. Kerrick, 24 October 1980, Timber Sales Office Files, Coconino National Forest.

64. Michael A. Barton for John R. McGuire to Hon. Bob Stump, House of Representatives, 15 August 1978; Stump to McGuire, 28 July 1978; both in Flagstaff File 2410. "Periodic Reanalysis, Flagstaff Federal Sustained Yield Unit 1979"; "Summary of the Flagstaff Federal Sustained Yield Unit," 1979; "Not for Public Distribution: Summary of Public Response Relating to the Periodic Reanalysis of the Flagstaff Fed. Sus. Yield Unit," n.d. [ca. 1980]; all in Timber Sales Office files, Coconino National Forest.

65. Record of public hearing, 9 January 1980, Timber Sales Office Files, Coconino National Forest.

66. Max Peterson to regional forester, Albuquerque, 20 May 1980; press releases 28 May 1980; Flagstaff File 2410.

67. "Policy Statement for Flagstaff Federal Sustained Yield Unit Policy," effective 1 October 1981, submitted 12 August 1980, Flagstaff File 2410. Order Granting Dismissal (Judge Valdemar A. Cordova), United States District Court for the District of Arizona, filed 20 March 1981, and related correspondence, File 1570, "Appeals," Southwest Forest Industries [vs.] Dissolution of the Flagstaff Federal Sustained-Yield Unit, Coconino National Forest, TMO, Southwest Region.

an attempt to determine the economic structure of the community. The foresters' initial assumption that an industrial monopoly was the secret to Flagstaff's stability in the end led the Forest Service to support a corporation instead of the community. The service's traditional fear of monopolies was for the moment forgotten.

Lessons Not Learned

The Flagstaff unit's peculiarities—along with those of all the sustained-yield units created under the 1944 law—reflected national as well as local considerations. Certainly the Arizona Forest Service staff hopped onto the sustained-yield bandwagon because they saw the new unit as equivalent to their own earlier proposal for a hundred-year sales contract with the two combined large companies (a contract that would have constituted a sustained-yield unit by another name). Nevertheless, the real creators of the unit were the Forest Service's leaders in Washington. Christopher Granger was a great booster of sustained-yield units, which were his special charge, but it was Lyle Watts, more than anyone else, who saw the Flagstaff unit—questionable origins, conceptual warts, and all—into existence.

Despite initial misgivings, Watts and the Forest Service eventually wagered much of their public credibility on the sustained-yield program. The chief at first greeted the sustained-yield program with caution, especially while the war continued. Once he had taken the measure of the law, however, he became an enthusiastic supporter. Sustained-yield units appeared to serve a number of cherished Forest Service objectives. Properly framed, they could promote community stability, justify the existence of the national forests, and force operators to harvest conservatively on private lands. Watts was able to achieve only one cooperative unit, however. The Shelton plan sparked outrage from other "communities" disadvantaged by the arrangement. More effective opposition from a cross-section of the public scuttled all other attempts at cooperative units.

In response to this unaccustomed defeat, Watts and the Forest Service turned their attention to federal units, which as it happened also faced opposition. Flagstaff seemed to have promise, however. Organized opposition there appeared minimal, and potential support was widespread. Its establishment would save face for Watts and vindicate his objectives. The chief told the region to launch the proposal only after it had greased the public-relations skids. Yet even this experiment ran into heavy opposition.

As a realist, Watts quit urging the establishment of more units. He could not bring himself to admit that the program was dead, however. He told a newspaper in 1950 that there was "some difficulty with sustained yield units but my

mind was not changed one iota. That was one of the finest pieces of legislation passed." He did admit that no new units were contemplated immediately. In 1953 after Watts had retired, the Department of Agriculture effectively buried the program by requiring communities, rather than the Forest Service, to initiate proposals, reserving the right of final approval for the secretary of agriculture. The secretary announced four years later that it was departmental policy to establish no new sustained-yield units of either type, although established units would be "continued for the present."[68]

The sustained-yield unit program was the Forest Service's grandest and most systematic attempt to promote community stability through management of national forest resources. It was doomed by a complex mixture of faulty conception, compromise with monopoly, human nature, and questionable intervention into local and private affairs. The program provoked unexpectedly strong and often highly emotional opposition—not just from the timber industry, but from conservation groups, organized labor, civic organizations, and other traditional supporters of the Forest Service. Coalitions of these groups rose up in outrage, and defeated the proposals one by one. There were doubtless some bruised feelings among those federal foresters leading the campaign for unit establishment, as they heard themselves castigated as enemies of small business, disrupters of communities, friends of monopoly, and bedfellows of certain industries. The Forest Service had never heard such things from its friends before. Its political enemies previously had been well-defined and rather easy to dismiss as self-serving—large industry, mostly, especially during the Progressive and New Deal eras when large industry was a national whipping boy.

Such opposition from unexpected sources should have given the agency pause, causing it to reexamine its objectives and redefine its vision of the public interest. The wreck of the sustained-yield unit program might have been good preparation for an approaching era of increasingly vocal but not necessarily consistent attacks on the Forest Service by groups that once had supported it. Instead of taking the lessons of the sustained-yield program to heart, however, the service more often failed to consider whether the objections were valid, or really even listen to what opponents had to say, and in the process did itself a disservice. ▲

68. "Forester Acts on War Peril," *Portland Oregonian*, 15 August 1950. Steen, *U.S. Forest Service*, p. 252. Barton for McGuire to Congressman Bob Stump, 15 August 1978; "Briefing for Chief Peterson Regarding Flagstaff Federal Sustained Yield Unit," n.d.; both in Flagstaff File 2410.

Acknowledgement This article has been adapted from the author's forthcoming book, *Timber and the Forest Service* (Lawrence: University Press of Kansas, 1986. $29.95).

Domestic Trunk Air Transportation: From Regulatory
  Control to Deregulation

Paul A. Cleveland
State University of New York
at Geneseo

ABSTRACT

A concise history of the development of the
airline transportation industry in domestic U.S.
markets is presented. The presentation focuses on
the nature of regulatory control and how the industry developed within these confines. Finally, an
examination of the reasons for the successful move
to deregulate the industry is presented.

In this paper I plan to examine the historical
development of the United States airline industry. The
aim is to provide an understanding of the controlled
environment within which the domestic airlines operated
until 1978, when the industry was deregulated. Insight
emerges about the reasons for deregulation and several
consequences of that policy.

Today's U.S. domestic air transportation industry
originated with the mail delivery service begun by the
Post Office Department in 1918. Initially airmail service was operated on a limited basis by the Army Air
Corps. Then, in 1925, Congress passed the Kelly Act,
giving the Postal Service authorization to contract
with private carriers for airmail delivery. As this
service grew, passenger air travel emerged. In 1930,
Congress passed comprehensive legislation, giving the
Postmaster General the right to award airmail contracts

176

without engaging in a competitive bidding procedure. Subsequently, the majority of the contracts were awarded to four large carriers, which were the predecessor firms of American, Eastern, United, and Trans World. Although the legislation did not legally restrict entry into passenger air travel markets, it de facto limited such entry, since airmail contracts, which carried large subsidies, were crucial to the success of any operation.

Due to conflicts and problems associated with the 1930 legislation and the growth of the industry, Congress passed the McCarren-Lea Act (Civil Aeronautics Acts) in 1938, creating an agency to regulate and direct the air transportation business. This act created the Civil Aeronautics Board (CAB). The CAB was established as a five member board with several assigned duties: encouraging the development of the air-transport industry, regulating the industry to assure safety, fostering sound economic conditions for growth, and promoting adequate and competitive service. With on exception, these duties remained intact for the 40 year period from 1938 to 1978. In 1958, Congress passed the Federal Aviation Act which established the Federal Aviation Administration (FAA) whose purpose was, and remains to regulate air safety in the United States. Therefore, this act relinquished some of the CAB's authority to the FAA. However, its other functions remained substantially unchanged until the Deregulation Act of 1978.[1]

Since the CAB had authority to control several major areas of air transportation, the board's actions had a substantial impact upon the growth of the industry. First, consider the board's control over entry into and exit out of city-pair markets. This authority stemmed from the board's ability to grant or deny an airline a certificate of public convenience for operating in a particular city-pair market. After certification was awarded and service begun, such service could only be discontinued with the approval of the CAB. Although the board had the right to award certification, as well as the authority over discontinuation of service if a carrier wished to drop a route, its authority over the self-initiated removal of route certification was limited. Thus, once a carrier received such licensing, it could be substantially viewed as a permanent feature of the domestic route system.[2]

In practice, airlines wishing to receive a route certification first filed with the CAB for approval to operate in a particular market. Upon receiving such an application, the board would initiate a series of public hearings in order to discern the necessity of route certification for the public interest. These hearings could extend for as long as two years before a decision was rendered. Once the hearings were completed, the board would either award or deny certification.

This licensing procedure affected the growth of the industry in several ways. First, "grandfather rights" implied that firms with airmail contracts prior to the 1938 legislation were automatically issued certificates of public convenience on those routes, which helped establish the dominance of firms that held postal service contracts. In particular, the Big Four (Eastern, American, United, and TWA) controlled 60 percent of the domestic revenue passenger miles of service flown as a result of "grandfather rights."

Second, after the passage of the act in 1938, the CAB expanded operating rights by granting hundreds of route certificates. This expansion helped the other carriers in the industry so that 16 trunks emerged.

Third, during the 1940's, the board began to authorize temporary certificates to local carriers for routes not serviced by the trunks. These temporary certificates were later made permanent by congressional legislation in 1955. This act made local carriers a prominent feature of the air transportation industry.

Finally, given the board's control over mergers as well as route certification, mergers and acquisitions reduced the number of domestic trunks to 11 by 1962. In most cases these mergers occurred when one carrier took control of a failing counterpart.[3] On one occasion the board voted to disapprove a proposed merger--one by American and Eastern. In this decision, handed down in June 1963, the board stated that such a combination would be inconsistent with the public interest.[4] This decision had a major impact on market structure, given the relative size of the airlines involved and the potential market share of the merged firm. But, in most instances, mergers and acquisitions were approved, unless the board felt that such action would impede competition.

These were the basic ground rules for market entry and exit as well as the guidelines for mergers and how they were utilized by the board in practice. As a result of these rules, a group of large carriers, known

178

44

as trunks, emerged. The trunks dominated domestic air travel, although smaller carriers, known as locals, operated in small markets not serviced by the trucklines. To gain a better understanding of the participants in the industry, consider Table 1, which shows the number of carriers in each classification. In the initial years of the industry, we observe substantial entry. After 1931 the number of airlines in operation began to fall, until the Civil Aeronautics Act passed in 1938. Then, until 1945, the total number of carriers remained fairly constant, with no change taking place in the number of trunks. In 1945, we observe the entrance of local service carriers into airline markets. The number of firms in this class grew rapidly, then began to decrease somewhat after 1950. The 1950s and early 1960s also saw a reduction in the number of trunk carriers, down to 11 by 1962. These 11 trunks remained intact up until deregulation and are, for the most part, the major airlines today.

The board's actions in expanding operating rights have been in accordance with the law, in the sense of proceeding on a case by case basis, except where Congressional intervention has occurred. As a result of this format, there has been no long range or preconceived plan for the development of the industry. However, since the board tended to take prevailing economic factors into consideration in the certification process, a pattern of rapid expansion of route certification in competitive service markets occurred during periods of substantial growth in traffic, meanwhile, limitations on such additional certification occurred in periods of low growth or low profitability.[6] To see how growth in traffic and capacity has occurred over time, consider the data in Table 2. This information indicates that the 1950s and 1960s were periods of substantial growth.

Next, before considering price regulation, consider the impact of technological advances upon airline route certification and how such advances affected key variables in air travel. In the first place, larger, faster, and more efficient aircraft made certain routes accessible, which previously could not be flown. According to one report, "a proliferation of service has resulted from rapidly growing traffic and improved aircraft technology combined with additional operating rights. Nonstop service was expanded to many markets as soon as technology permitted and demand warranted. The steady evolution of larger aircraft with greater range and speed made feasible longer and longer nonstop flights."[8] Therefore, expansion of

179

route certification in many markets came as a result of the capability to serve those markets in the early years of the industry. Another factor to consider with respect to advances in equipment is how improvements in aircraft redefined air travel vis-â-vis other modes of transportation. These questions are illuminated by tracing some of the major developments in aircraft design.

From 1948-1957 aircraft manufacturers were producing and improving upon piston engine aircraft. They developed a wide variety of models, ranging in seating capacity from 45 to 95 passengers and able to cruise at speeds ranging from 270 to 350 miles per hour over various distances. Two of the most impressive aircraft were the Lockheed L-1049C and the Douglas DC-7. With their introduction in 1953, it was finally possible to fly coast-to-coast routes nonstop. The DC-7 had a range of 2,600 miles, with first class seating capacity of 68 passengers or coach seating for 85, and it cruised at a speed of 350 miles per hour. The Lockheed L-1049C could carry between 71-95 passengers with similar cruising speed and range.

The next major advance came in 1958 with the introduction of the first turbo jet aircraft. The Boeing 707-120 sported 4 engines, cruised at a speed of 590 miles per hour, and seated between 96 and 160 passengers, depending upon the interior configuration. Douglas Corporation was not far behind Boeing with the introduction of the DC-8. With the development of the turbo-jet and the soon to follow turbo-fan aircraft, the early 1960s saw the trunks switching their fleets over to modern aircraft. The most popular model produced in this time period was the Boeing 727 turbo fan. It is smaller than the 707, yet it remains the mainstay of most airline fleets today.

The last major advance came with the introduction of the wide-body desgin in the early 1970s. Three aircraft models of this type are the McDonnell-Douglas DC-10, the Lockheed L-1011 Tristar, and the Boeing 747, the largest of the three. These aircraft greatly expanded seating capacity, since they are able to carry between 300 and 490 passengers and are, therefore, generally used in long range markets.[9]

These advances in equipment are the most important in the industry to date. However, in recent years, as a result of rising fuel costs, aircraft manufacturers have developed more fuel efficient models. The impact of these models cannot currently be assessed due to

180

their limited use, and they are, therefore, not considered here.

Given these advances in aircraft design, we can consider some of the effects of improved technology on the air transportation industry. With the introduction of larger, longer range, and faster aircraft, we would expect several occurrences. First, an increase in the average flight stage length should occur as longer range aircraft were introduced, because route certifications took place in markets where previous nonstop traffic was not possible. Thus, early advances should lead to longer distance nonstop travel, which would lengthen the overall average stage length, other things equal. However, this effect would be somewhat offset, given that longer range aircraft tend to be the larger equipment. If larger aircraft are employed primarily in long distance markets, flight frequency in those markets, relative to the shorter haul routes, would decrease, which would tend to limit the increase in the overall flight stage at length.

Another factor that might affect the overall stage length is the higher cruising speeds of newly developed aircraft. Reductions in flight time, resulting from faster equipment, would make air travel relatively more attractive vis-à-vis other modes of transportation, especially in short haul markets. This effect would also tend to offset the expansion of the average stage length since market densities would be expected to increase most sharply on the short-haul routes. Table 3 shows the average overall flight stage length for scheduled domestic service by trunk carriers, the percentage growth in this stage length between years, and the average available seats per aircraft flown for the years 1949 to 1972. The data provide an interesting insight into the effects noted above. The 1950s were characterized by a relatively rapid increase in the average flight stage length. This increase could have resulted from the introduction of longer range aircraft, which made many more long-haul nonstop routes possible. This growth pattern dropped rather dramatically, however, with the initial introduction of jet aircraft. The reduction could have resulted from a combination of two factors. As jet aircraft were employed, the number of long-distance flights may have decreased due to the expanded capacity of the new equipment. Furthermore, the increased speed of these aircraft may have increased market densities in short-haul markets sufficiently to cause this reduction in the growth rate of the overall average flight stage length. By the middle of the 1960s the growth rate in

181

47

stage length had increased as a result of expanded route certification in long-haul markets, as well as from increases in market densities on these routes.

Finally, it is interesting to note what happened in 1971 and 1972 when wide-body aircraft were introduced. During these years the overall average flight stage length actually fell. This change can be explained by a reduction in flight frequency due to expanded capacity on each flight. This effect was understandably strong, given that wide-body aircraft doubled seating capacity on a flight. The growth rate fluctuations described here are shown over time in Figure 1.

Before considering price regulation, two final points of interest with respect to the aircraft manufacuturing industry require attention. First, aircraft manufactureres have been very reluctant to undertake the risks associated with the development of a new model. They have typically been characterized as willing to undertake a new design only when they have firm commitments for the resulting product. This type of behavior has led to collaboration between manufacturers and airlines in the development of new models. In most instances a manufacturer would enter an agreement with the consulting airlines to exclude nonparticipating carriers from early delivery dates and, usually, to subject those firms to higher prices. The manufacturer's fear of low sales without prior commitments is not unfounded. One example is Lockheed's experience with the L-1011 Tristar, which was developed independently. This venture cost the company dearly.

A second point of interest is the considerable success Boeing has enjoyed in aircraft manufacturing. Boeing's market share grew from 7 percent in 1960 to 75 percent in 1981. On the other hand, McDonnell-Douglas, the major rival of Boeing experienced a reduction in its market share from 43 percent to 18 percent over the same period. While a consideration of how this change affected the air transportation industry is not included in this paper, such a shift is worth noting.[11]

Next, let us consider the CAB's authority in controlling air fares. A firm operating in any particular market was required to seek approval from the board when it wished to alter its price or restructure its pricing policy. Airlines petitioned for a change in much the same way that they filed for route certification. While many hearings concerning pricing policies

182

took place, two major investigations established the CAB's basic stance regarding fare structure. These two investigations are known as the General Passenger Fare Investigation (GPFI) initiated in 1956 and the Domestic Passenger Fare Investigation (DPFI) undertaken in 1970.

The GPFI was initiated to establish a set of well-defined criteria on which fares would be based. The investigation was conducted over a four year period with the board's final decision being issued in November 1960. The board outlined rate-of-return guidelines on which fare structures would be based. Specifically, the board established a 10.25 percent allowable rate of return for the Big Four domestic trunks, while allowing an 11.125 percent rate of return for the other trunk carriers.[12] This decision provided the framework upon which the board considered all future petitions for fare increases. It was hoped that fares would be reflective of the costs of service, if the board made decisions based on this criteria.

The DPFI, undertaken in January 1970 in response to a pending court case, was the second major fare investigation conducted by the CAB. This case arose as a result of a congressional inquiry into the board's perspicacious action in endorsing a new fare-mileage formula to aid the carrier's profits, which had fallen in 1969. The congressional group argued that the action taken by the board ignored several statutory requirements and was, therefore, unlawful. In order to affect the outcome of the case, as well as examine the issues at hand, the board initiated the DPFI.

The investigation was divided into nine phases: (1) aircraft depreciation, (2) leased aircraft, (3) deferred federal income taxes, (4 joing fares, (5) discount fares, (6) load factors and seating configurations, (7) fare level, (8) rate of return, and (9) overall fare structure. By July 1971, the board had completed its work on phases 1,2,3,7, and 8, and it had issued a decision concerning them. The board affirmed the use of straight-line method of depreciation, allowed for the inclusion of deferred federal taxes as an expense, and disallowed the inclusion of leased aircraft when calculating the base for rate-of-return on investment. Further, the board ruled against discount fares, such as youth fares and standby fares, arguing that they were price discriminating in nature. Finally, the board ruled that fares should be based upon the average cost of providing reasonable service, so that a rate-of-return of 12 percent on investment would be generated.[13] This reaffirmed much that was

183

stated in the GPFI decision, with some specific alterations. These decisions provided the framework upon
which the CAB operated in deciding pricing policy and
structure. This framework, along with entry regulation, provides an understanding of the environment
within which the airline industry developed until
deregulation.

In 1978 Congress passed the Airline Deregulation
Act, calling for termination of the CAB by the end of
1985. The legislation outlined a plan to phase out the
CAB's authority, beginning with eliminating entry
barriers and ending with the dissolution of board
itself. Any remaining regulatory authorities, such as
those connected with international travel, were transferred to the Department of Transportation.[14]

This legislation came about amid an intellectual
debate over the usefulness of regulation. For example,
George Douglas and James Miller published a paper in
1974 dealing with nonprice competition in airline
markets.[15] Within the context of a full price demand
model, they showed how regulated air fares determined
flight frequency in airline markets and, hence, the
average load factor that prevailed. Furthermore, they
claimed that air fares under regulation tended to be
set above fares which would almost certainly apply in
an unregulated environment. Therefore, the authors
suggested that the traveling public would benefit from
deregulation. This view became accepted by a large
number of influential people during the 1970s,
including Alfred Kahn.

Prior to passage of the Deregulation Act, President Jimmy Carter appointed Alfred Kahn as chairman of
the CAB. Kahn's support of deregulation was reflected
in the type of leadership he brought to the board.
Under his direction the board instituted several new
policies. Among the most significant were looser
guidelines associated with route certification and a
new domestic fare policy that superseded the structure
given by the DPFI. The new pricing rules allowed
carriers a great deal of flexibility in constructing
fares. Therefore, the airlines had a great deal more
freedom than under any previous board. The Kahn board
had, in essence, established a form of de facto
deregulation.[16]

However, these policies were not well received by
industry executives and officials. Airline Newsletter
called Kahn's approach to regulation conducive to chaos
in the industry. The article stated:

184

50

In what looks like a throwback to the
1930's, the Carter/Kahn CAB seems to have embarked on a policy of awarding domestic U.S. routes
to the airlines promising the lowest fares. That
appears, at least, to be the main thrust of the
most recent route cases to be set for hearings.

After President Roosevelt arbitrarily cancelled all the airmail contracts in 1934 and
ordered the Army Air Corps to fly the mail--with
tragic results--the mail routes were again given
to the airlines, the winners being the carriers
bidding the lowest rates (usually with the expectation of having the rates increased later). A
mad scramble for routes and chaos ensued,
prompting Congress to pass the Civil Aeronautics
Act of 1938...

Now, CAB evidently wants to turn back the
clock, so to speak, by adopting the very kind of
short-sighted policies that produced the chaos
which CAB was created to eradicate. In a way,
though, the Board's apparent new policy is not a
lot different from the philosophy of certain
present and former Board members to put on the
competition and drive down fares, never mind the
economic consequences. Whatever the case, such a
policy is only a short step from deregulation, or
'regulatory reform', as it's euphemistically
called.[17]

From this articled it is clear that the industry was
strongly opposed to the permissive competitive-bidding
regulation of the Kahn board. This opposition came to
a head when several airlines, along with Airline Newsletter, reluctantly endorsed deregulation in preference
to continuing to operate under the regulatory control
of the Kahn variety. United Airlines, although fundamentally against deregulation, was one firm that
preferred total decontrol rather than continuing to
operate under the Kahn regime. United argued that anything less than complete decontrol would distort the
industry more than necessary. Furthermore, the airline
felt that deregulation would result in a shrinkage in
the number of air carriers, and United hoped to
thrive.[18]

This same sentiment was echoed by Airline
Newsletter. In an editorial the publisher reaffirmed
his opposition deregulation from the start, arguing
that it would "bring economic anarchy; that service

185

51

quality will deteriorate rapidly as interline reservations, ticketing and baggage handling become chaotic or non-existent; that smaller cities will lose service or their service will be reduced to jitney operation when the local service airlines pull out after their subsidy is terminated, or a cross-subsidy earned on profitable trunk-type routes is eroded by the flood of cut-throat competition; and that the end result will be monopoly or oligopoly."[19] Nevertheless, the publisher came out in favor of deregulation given the policy changes instituted by the Kahn board. The newsletter was of the opinion that deregulation, with freedom to adjust fares and abandon routes, was preferable to the CAB's policy of awarding new certification to carriers who promised to cut fares. Furthermore, the publisher predicted that the final result of deregulation would be a shakedown of the industry to a small number of large carriers, which would eventually be reregulated.[20]

Given this stance by industry executives and officials, coupled with the push for deregulation by others, little opposition to the passage of the Airline Deregulation Act resulted. As stated above, the act called for phasing out CAB control over the industry. Specifically, the board's control over route regulation was terminated at the end of 1981, its authority over air fares was relinquished at the beginning of 1983, and its final dissolution came at the end of 1985. It is important to note that de facto deregulation, however, had been instituted as a result of the leadership of the CAB prior to the Airline Deregulation Act.

Since the Deregulation Act, the airline industry has been marked by a great deal of variability and financial turbulence, including the bankruptcy of some air carriers. These carriers were either purchased or reorganized and are in current operation. Other problems include fare wars, employee unrest, rising fuel prices, and low economic activity. Recently fuel prices have stabilized, and there has been an upturn in the U.S. economy, although fare variability and employee unrest remain. This volatility might be expected given the alteration from control to decontrol and could be the result of the transition to a new operating environment. It will, however, take some time to assess all the ramifications of deregulation, a subject beyond the scope of this presentation.

In summary, this historical perspective provides us with a basic understanding of the development of the airline industry. Specifically, the paper identified

the origin of the industry, the reasons and context of
legislated regulatory control, the nature and practical
applications of that control, and finally, the move to
a deregulated environment. Understanding this background information can aid us in evaluating the future
industry's performance.

NOTES

1. P. Biederman, The U.S. Airline Industry: End of an
   Era (New York, 1982).

2. U.S. Civil Aeronautics Board (hereafter cited as
   U.S. CAB), The Domestic Route System: Analysis and
   Policy Recommendations (Washington, D.C., 1974).

3. Ibid.

4. U.S. CAB, Annual Congressional Report (Washington,
   D.C., annual).

5. U.S. CAB, Handbook of Airline Statistics (Washington, D.C., annual).

6. U.S. CAB, The Domestic Route System: Analysis and
   Policy Recommendations (Washington, D.C., 1974).

7. U.S. CAB, Handbook of Airline Statistics (Washington, D.C., annual).

8. U.S. CAB, The Domestic Route System: Analysis and
   Policy Recommendations (Washington, D.C., 1974).

9. U.S. CAB, Handbook of Airline Statistics (Washington, D.C., annual).

10. Ibid.

11. P. Biederman, The U.S. Airline Industry: End of an
    Era (New York, 1982).

12. U.S. CAB, Annual Congressional Report (Washington,
    D.C., annual).

13. G.W. Douglas, and J.C. Miller, "Quality Competi-
    tion, Industry Equilibrium, and Efficiency in the
    Price-Constrained Airline Market," American Eco-
    nomic Review, 64 (1974), pp. 657-669.

187

14. P. Biederman, The U.S. Airline Industry: End of an Era (New York, 1982).

15. G.W. Douglas, and J.C. Miller, "Quality Competition, Industry Equilibrium, and Efficiency in the Price-Constrained Airline Market," American Economic Review, 64 (1974), pp. 657-669.

16. U.S. CAB, Annual Congressional Report (Washington, D.C., annual).

17. "Routes to go to Lowest Bidder--or De Facto Deregulation by CAB?," Airline Newsletter, Vol. 5 (1 February 1978), p. 37.

18. "Deregulation and Reregulation," Airline Newsletter, Vol. 5 (15 March 1977), p. 253.

19. "A Reluctant Conclusion About Deregulation," Airline Newsletter, Vol. 5 (1 March 1978), p. 15.

20. Ibid.

REFERENCES

Airline Newsletter: "Deregulation and Reregulation," Vol. 5, March 15, 1977, 253.

Airline Newsletter: "Routes to go to Lowest Bidder--or De Facto Deregulation by CAB?" Vol. 5, February 1, 1978, 37.

Airline Newsletter: "A Reluctant Conclusion About Deregulation," Vol. 5, March 1, 1978, 15.

Biederman, Paul: The U.S. Airline Industry: End of an Era. New York: Praeger Publishers, 1982.

Douglas, George W. and Miller, James C.: "Quality Competition, Industry Equilibrium, and Efficiency in the Price-Constrained Airline Market," American Economic Review, 64 (1974), 657-669.

Douglas, George W. and Miller, James C.: "The CAB's Domestic Passenger Fare Investigation," The Bell Journal of Economics and Management Science, 5 (1974), 205-223.

188

U.S. Civil Aeronautics Board: <u>Handbook   of   Airline Statistics</u>. Washington, D.C.: U.S. Government Printing Office, annual.

U.S. Civil Aeronautics Board: <u>Annual Congressional Report</u>. Washington, D.C.: U.S. Government Printing Office, annual.

U.S. Civil Aeronautics Board: <u>The Domestic Route System: Analysis and Policy Recommendations</u>. Washington, D.C.: U.S. Government Printing Office, 1974.

Table 1

Number of Certificated Route
Carriers by Classification [19]

Year	Total domestic Operations	Trunks	Locals	Other
1926	13	13	NA	NA
1927	16	16	NA	NA
1928	31	31	NA	NA
1929	34	34	NA	NA
1930	38	38	NA	NA
1931	35	35	NA	NA
1932	29	29	NA	NA
1933	24	24	NA	NA
1934	22	22	NA	NA
1935	23	23	NA	NA
1936	21	21	NA	NA
1937	17	17	NA	NA
1938	19	16	NA	3
1939	19	16	NA	3
1940	19	16	NA	3
1941	18	16	NA	2
1942	18	16	NA	2
1943	17	16	NA	1
1944	17	16	NA	1
1945	18	16	1	1
1946	22	16	5	1
1947	26	16	8	2
1948	38	16	12	10
1949	47	16	19	12
1950	48	16	19	13
1951	46	16	17	13
1952	44	16	16	12
1953	41	14	15	12
1954	39	13	14	12
1955	39	13	14	12
1956	38	13	13	12
1957	36	12	13	11
1958	36	12	13	11
1959	36	12	13	11
1960	39	12	13	14
1961	39	12	13	14
1962	39	11	13	15
1963	38	11	13	14
1964	37	11	13	13
1965	37	11	13	13
1966	37	11	13	13
1967	38	11	13	14
1968	37	11	12	14
1969	32	11	9	12
1970	33	11	9	13
1971	33	11	9	13
1972	33	11	9	13

Table 2

Capacity and Traffic (000) [18]
Domestic Operations

	Available Seat Miles			Revenue Passenger Miles		
Year	Total	Trunk	Local	Total	Trunk	Local
1932	303,582	300,038		127,433	127,433	
1933	373,762	370,126		174,429	173,492	
1934	367,777	362,547		189,207	187,859	
1935	577,651	572,547		281,177	279,376	
1936	686,225	680,708		390,782	388,242	
1937	836,151	828,188		410,257	407,296	
1938	951,458	944,729		479,844	475,600	
1939	1,215,158	1,209,611		682,903	679,755	
1940	1,817,085	1,809,373		1,052,156	1,047,131	
1941	2,341,878	2,330,555		1,384,733	1,377,152	
1942	1,962,967	1,949,679		1,417,526	1,405,834	
1943	1,857,837	1,838,469		1,632,452	1,617,129	
1944	2,434,970	2,418,117		2,176,854	2,161,030	
1945	3,811,307	3,784,532	2,486	3,350,346	3,336,278	1,312
1946	7,549,644	7,490,387	17,964	5,944,926	5,903,111	6,812
1947	9,364,210	9,152,389	155,507	6,105,310	6,016,257	46,418
1948	10,417,043	9,980,163	323,942	5,996,644	5,840,211	87,928
1949	11,711,576	11,117,703	477,991	6,767,595	6,570,726	134,742
1950	13,124,889	12,385,635	599,159	8,029,131	7,766,008	188,782
1951	15,614,681	14,671,982	774,713	10,589,668	10,210,726	289,644
1952	19,170,377	18,068,123	905,796	12,559,332	12,120,789	339,644
1953	23,337,498	22,114,772	1,013,729	14,793,875	14,297,581	390,854
1954	26,921,925	25,623,314	1,092,906	16,802,424	16,234,638	461,175
1955	31,371,182	29,978,597	1,184,100	19,852,118	19,205,675	534,788
1956	35,366,158	33,752,551	1,382,543	22,398,589	21,643,140	633,228
1957	41,746,275	39,838,165	1,652,132	25,378,769	24,499,510	747,288
1958	42,723,508	40,695,035	1,793,463	25,375,489	24,435,657	820,192
1959	48,404,952	45,793,218	2,309,162	29,307,600	28,127,216	1,024,336
1960	52,220,182	49,153,265	2,724,666	30,536,616	29,233,199	1,141,593
1961	56,087,214	52,525,014	3,228,491	31,062,345	29,534,792	1,343,761
1962	63,887,578	59,736,760	3,797,465	33,622,636	31,827,840	1,607,673
1963	72,254,533	67,601.302	4,266,886	38,456,612	36,383,756	1,868,988
1964	80,524,404	75,242,408	4,836,305	44,141,261	41,658,368	2,244,488
1965	94,787,113	88,731,152	5,545,691	51,887,415	48,986,972	2,621,201
1966	104,668,839	97,174,719	6,908,077	60,590,826	56,802,788	3,467,510
1967	133,699,795	124,141,624	8,862,400	75,487,327	70,990,141	4,114,304
1968	166,870,750	153,864,640	12,153,586	87,507,677	81,611,832	5,489,224
1969	194,447,654	179,646,708	14,722,390	95,945,897	89,184,622	6,310,630
1970	213,159,879	194,461,931	17,024,403	104,146,807	95,899,744	7,430,666
1971	221,503,165	202,509,471	17,335,816	106,438,408	97,756,113	7,851,515
1972	226,621,029	206,617,921	18,074,128	118,137,978	108,189,968	8,899,388

Table 3

Average Market Distance Growth
and Plane Capacity [18]

Year	Average overall flight stage length	% Δ in average stage length	Average available seats per aircraft
1949	194.9	1.99 %	34.7
1950	198.6	2	37.1
1951	208.8	5.13	39.1
1952	224.1	7.33	42.2
1953	237.7	5.76	45.6
1954	248.6	4.58	49.6
1955	257.2	3.46	51.5
1956	270.8	5.29	52.1
1957	289.9	7.05	53.7
1958	304.6	5.07	55.5
1959	306.5	.62	58.7
1960	310.1	1.17	65.4
1961	321.5	3.68	72.9
1962	351.4	9.30	79.4
1963	362.7	3.21	83.4
1964	383.9	5.84	86.1
1965	411.3	7.14	89.2
1966	434.6	5.66	91.2
1967	454.4	4.56	94.4
1968	494.6	8.85	100.8
*1969	548.6	10.92	109.8
1970	587.0	7	110.4
1971	591.3	.73	115.3
1972	579.2	(-2.05)	118.1

Handbook of Airline Statistics; CAB; 1973 edition.

58

Figure 1

Percentage Change in Average Stage Length

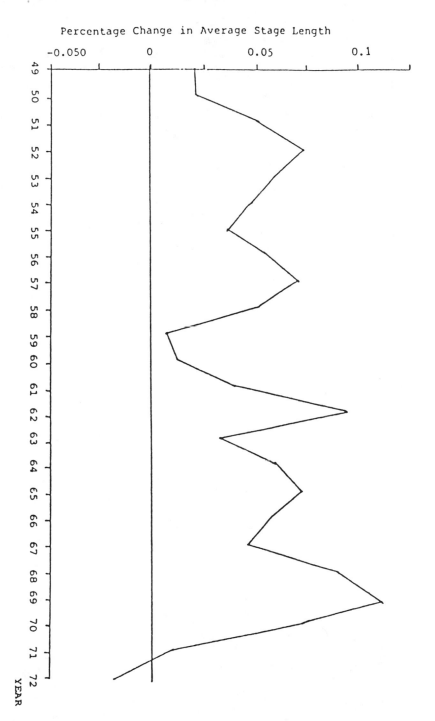

Eighty years of US petroleum pipeline regulation

LEONARD L. COBURN   US Department of Energy

Introduction

On 29 June 1906, petroleum pipelines came under the regulatory jurisdiction of the *Interstate Commerce Act*. For eighty years, petroleum pipelines have been regulated first by the Interstate Commerce Commission (ICC) and presently by the Federal Energy Regulatory Commission (FERC). It is the intention of this article to examine the history of petroleum pipeline regulation and to indicate the status of regulation today.

Industry characteristics

The regulated US petroleum pipeline industry is a substantial component of the US petroleum industry. In 1986, the last year for which statistics are available, the US pipeline industry had operating revenues of $7·3 billion and net income of $2·1 billion. Assets in place totalled $22·4 billion. The pipeline system within the USA is quite extensive, with about 170,000 miles in place. This system is made of three types of pipelines — gathering, crude, and products. In 1986, gathering lines comprised about 34,200 miles, crude lines about 54,100 miles, and product lines about 81,700 miles. The extent of the system can be measured in two other ways: the amount of deliveries from the pipeline network; and trunkline traffic measured in barrel-miles.[1] Deliveries from the pipeline network totalled 11·0 thousand million barrels in 1986, with crude lines contributing 6·3 thousand million barrels and product lines contributing 4·7 thousand million barrels to the total. Trunkline barrel-miles totalled 3·5 million million, with crude pipelines taking 55 per cent and product pipelines a 45 per cent share.

In 1986 there were 142 petroleum pipeline companies regulated by the FERC. Overwhelmingly these pipelines are owned by petroleum companies. A very small number are owned by companies that do not have other petroleum operations or are not considered integrated petroleum companies. In a study done

61

for the US Department of Energy, 147 pipelines were identified, of which 88 were owned by major integrated petroleum companies, 36 were owned by non-major integrated petroleum companies, and 23 were owned by independents (i.e. companies not otherwise affiliated with the petroleum industry).[2] The Department of Energy study also considered pipeline ownership based upon barrel-miles. For 114 pipeline systems, the majors accounted for about 91 per cent of total barrel-miles, non-majors for about 2·5 per cent, and independents for about 6·1 per cent. The major integrated petroleum companies own the largest pipelines, while the non-majors and independents tends to own the smaller systems. Another significant characteristic of the US petroleum pipeline industry is its joint ownership. Of the twenty largest pipeline systems, eleven are jointly owned and operated. These eleven systems account for about 63 per cent of total barrel-miles. All jointly owned pipelines account for about 75 per cent of total barrel-miles.[3]

Thus the US petroleum pipeline industry is primarily owned by integrated petroleum companies, usually operating as a wholly owned subsidiary of the petroleum company. The systems are also usually jointly owned with other petroleum pipelines. The largest of the individual pipeline systems are almost always jointly owned. The system is extensive, carrying large amounts of crude oil and petroleum products throughout the country. In fact the petroleum pipeline system carries about 25 per cent of all inter-city freight in the USA, based on ton-miles.

Oil pipeline operations

The petroleum industry can be viewed as discrete segments linked together into an integrated whole. Crude oil production, crude oil refining, and product sales to end users are linked together by an extensive transport system. The transport system provides the links to integrate the discrete segments into a workable, uni-fied chain. Transport can be ocean tankers, barges, railroads, tank trucks, and pipelines. In the USA, the pipeline is the most important overland link in the integrated system.

The pipeline is no more than lengths of pipes welded together and is usually buried in the ground. At various intervals a pump station is located to build up pressure on the liquid in order to move it along the pipeline. At the origin, ter-minus, and various in-between offtake points, tank farms are located to store the liquid until it is put into the pipeline, or when it is taken out of the pipeline. The entire pipeline operation is controlled by a central computer station.

Pipelines usually are thought of as gathering lines, crude lines, and product lines. Gathering lines are small-diameter pipelines, usually no more than six inches in diameter. They gather crude oil from the small wellhead lease tanks and bring the crude to a central tank farm within a field. At that point the crude is collected until sufficiently large batches are available to inject into crude trunk-lines. The crude lines operate from the field to the refinery. They are normally larger than 6 inches in diameter and can range up to 48 inches as in the Trans-Alaska Pipeline System. Most of the domestically produced crude oil in the USA arrives at the refinery by pipeline. By contrast, most of the imported crude oil arrives by tanker. In some situations the tanker offloads its crude into a pipeline for transporting to an inland refinery. At the refinery, the crude is offloaded into tanks until it is ready to be refined.

At the other end of the refining process, products waiting for distribution are loaded into tanks. Most products that can be moved by pipeline usually arrive at their retail area by pipeline. The products are then loaded into tanks to await their ultimate tank truck trip to the distributor or end user.

The beauty of the pipeline system is its ability to maintain a continuous flow of crude and products to keep the discrete segments of the petroleum industry operating smoothly. Most importantly, the pipeline is the least costly method of transporting crude and products across long overland distances. It has continuous economies of scale since as its diameter increases its unit operating costs decrease. These economies of scale lead many to consider that petroleum pipelines have natural monopoly characteristics and it is these natural monopoly characteristics that lead to the economic case for regulation. While modern economic theory relies upon the natural monopoly characteristics of petroleum pipelines to justify regulation, historically, pipelines were subjected to regulation because of the abuses of the Standard Oil Trust. To understand why pipelines were subjected to regulation in 1906, it is necessary to look at the situation before that date.

Historical sketch

Colonel Edwin Drake brought in the first oil well in the USA on 27 August 1859, near Titusville, Pennsylvania. Transporting the crude from the wellhead to refineries quickly became an important part of the industry. The first attempt at transporting the oil was in wooden barrels carried by horse and wagon teams, or put on flatbeds and floated down rivers. In 1862, a small-diameter pipeline was laid by James L. Hutchings from a well to a refinery 1,000 feet away. It operated on the gravity principle and used no pumps. In 1863–4 a 2-inch line was laid that traversed 3 miles to a railroad terminal, but had to be abandoned because it had too many leaks to be useful. Finally, on 7 October 1865, Samuel Van Syckel completed the first successful pipeline. It ran for 6 miles from the Pit Hole Field in western Pennsylvania to the Oil Creek Railroad railhead at Miller's Farm. It consisted of 2-inch, lap-welded, wrought iron pipes in 15-foot sections with three pumps giving it a capacity of 81 barrels per hour, or 1,900 barrels per day.[4]

It presented such a threat to the teamsters carrying oil in barrels on horse and wagons that Pinkerton guards were required to prevent the line from being ripped up. These early pipelines were not connected directly to the wells, but were connected to large dump tanks. In 1866 A. W. Smiley and G. E. Countnant constructed a 2 in. line across four miles of the Pit Hole Field to connect the tanks at the wells with the dump tank. Thus the first gathering line was developed and its use quickly spread throughout the industry. The high rate policy of the railroads and the adoption of the pipeline as the prime transport mode by Standard Oil caused the spread of the use of pipelines and within ten years of the Van Syckel pipeline, railroad domination of transporting crude oil was being challenged.

The railroads dominated both rail and early pipeline transportation. By using the pipeline to feed their rail systems, the railroads were able to capture both short-haul and long-haul movements. By the early 1870s the railroads had combined, either through their direct ownership of pipelines or through the formation of transportation pools with pipelines owned by others, to establish a transportation monopoly. Prices were dictated by the railroads to the producers and the shippers. To ensure the continuation of this transportation monopoly, the railroads refused any privately owned pipeline permission to cross the railroad right-of-way. After much debate and public outcry, the Pennsylvania and Ohio legislatures passed laws in 1872 granting common carrier pipelines the right of eminent domain in their acquisition of rights-of-way.[5]

In 1874, Dr David Hostetter organised the Columbia Conduit System in order to build a pipeline some 60 miles to Pittsburgh. The line was complete except for a railroad crossing near Pittsburgh. Despite the existence of the Pennsylvania eminent domain statute, the railroad refused permission to cross the track. While the legal controversy proceeded through the courts, two others bought the Columbia Conduit System and temporarily solved the delivery problem by building tanks on either side of the track and using wagons to transport the crude across the track. When the courts ruled in favour of the pipeline in 1875, the 100-foot gap in the line was completed.

The early development of pipelines was a struggle between the Standard Oil forces and those independents with the courage to fight the power of John D. Rockefeller and his Standard Oil Trust. Rockefeller started his business in Cleveland, Ohio, in the 1860s and through shrewd business acumen and heavy-handed tactics began his rise to the top of the oil industry. His major weapon was the control of transport, first railroads and then pipelines. The race for control of the industry in the late 1800s and early 1900s centred principally on the control of crude oil pipelines — both gathering lines and trunklines. By the late 1870s Rockefeller's tactics enabled him, through his Standard Oil Trust, to control both railroad and pipeline transport.[6] Standard Oil located its refineries in the centres of product consumption and was able to offer the railroads large volume shipments of crude oil in return for favourable rates. Railroads were played off against each other and the system of favourable rates was maintained as a result. As pipeline transport proved itself, the Standard Oil Trust utilised gathering lines to transport the oil cheaply to the railheads and later was able to build or acquire pipelines that ran parallel to the railroads as a further method of maintaining its competitive advantage.

In 1879 the Tide Water Pipe Line, a company independent of the Standard Oil Trust, opened and became the first overland long-distance trunk pipeline, running 109 miles from the Bradford, Pennsylvania, oilfields to Williamsport, Pennsylvania. This 6 in. line was extended five years later to Bayonne, New Jersey, and provided a direct link from the oilfields to the coastal refineries and the lucrative export trade. Standard Oil, at first unable to gain control of Tide Water, emulated this achievement and by the 1880s Standard Oil had lines serving Pittsburgh, Cleveland, Buffalo, and New York City. Discoveries of crude oil spread west to Ohio, Indiana, and Illinois and the use of pipelines spread as well. With the development of the Lima–Indiana Field, Standard Oil organised the Buckeye Pipe Line Company and used its pipeline to extend its control over that field. Refineries were built in the Chicago area and pipelines fed those refineries from the Ohio, Indiana, and Illinois fields.

Before 1926 mainly crude oil was shipped through the pipelines; products — mostly kerosene — were shipped by rail. Thus, refineries tended to locate near large consuming centres, since it was cheaper to ship crude oil via pipeline than to ship products by higher priced rail transport. The industry started to change with the discoveries of oil in the mid-continent and in Texas. The 1890s witnessed the development of the oilfields in Kansas and Oklahoma (the Mid-Continent field). Standard Oil was active in these fields through the Prairie Oil and Gas Company, which was formed in 1901. In the same year was the massive discovery at Spindletop, Texas — the start of the large flush production from the east Texas field. This discovery brought new companies to prominence due to the accessibility to water transport. With Spindletop came the rise of the Texas Company (now Texaco), Sun, and Guffey Oil Company (later acquired by the Mellons and developed into Gulf Oil).

Standard Oil's interest, besides its control of the Appalachian and Lima–Indiana Fields, centred on the Mid-Continent field. Standard's company, Prairie Pipe Line, extended its system from the Kansas and Oklahoma fields through St Louis and to the existing Buckeye system. Thus, by 1905, crude from the Mid-Continent field could be processed in the Atlantic coast refineries via Standard Oil's pipeline system. In the other direction, from the Mid-Continent field to the Gulf Coast, other companies, principally Texas and Gulf, built systems to connect with Gulf Coast refineries, or for shipment elsewhere by water.

Although pipelines were a significant development in the oil industry, more generally the early 1900s were a time of agitation for increased regulation of railroads. The abuses of the railroad monopoly were creating economic and political chaos. While railroads were regulated at the federal level in 1887, effective regulation did not occur until the early 1900s.

During the latter part of the nineteenth century, the explosion in railroad construction created the environment for railroad abuses and eventually for government regulation. Railroad control over transport was extremely abusive and especially so regarding the carriage of agricultural commodities. Rates in many instances were set at extortionate levels. Rate discrimination among shippers and among similar origins and destinations was rampant. Facilities were often inadequate or non-existent. Financial practices were scandalous.[7]

The first response was at the state level. Various states passed laws, known as the 'Granger Laws' since they were sponsored by the farmers' organisation known as the Grange. These laws attempted to control the most abusive aspects of the railroads. While the US Supreme Court upheld these laws as they related to local practices,[8] ultimately the Supreme Court undermined the efforts of the states. In 1886 the Supreme Court ruled that the states could not regulate the interstate segments of the railroads, regardless of the kind of regulation engaged in by the federal government.[9] Since the federal government was not regulating railroads, the railroads were left essentially unregulated.

Congress was aware of the railroad abuses and studied the issue for a number of years.[10] The Supreme Court's decision in 1886 brought action, however. In 1887, the *Act to Regulate Commerce*, more commonly known as the *Interstate Commerce Act*, was enacted.[11] The Act established the Interstate Commerce Commission (ICC) as the federal regulatory body to regulate the activities of the railroads. The *Interstate Commerce Act* gave the ICC the power to: receive complaints; obtain reports and other information; compel testimony; set up a uniform system of accounts; and make effective the Act's main provisions, such as just and reasonable rates, prohibition of discrimination, rebates and pooling, and the filing of all rate schedules.

Although these powers appeared extensive, the US Supreme Court soon emasculated the ICC through a series of court decisions. First, the court indicated that the ICC could not compel testimony relating to rebates and rate discrimination, since the compulsion could be self-incriminating and therefore a violation of the Fifth Amendment of the US Constitution.[12] This undermined the ICC's ability to obtain evidence on rebates and rate discrimination. Then the court held that the *Interstate Commerce Act* did not specifically give the ICC the power to set rates.[13] Without this power the ICC was powerless to establish just and reasonable rates. All it could do was set aside rates, but it could not prescribe them. Finally, the court held that all ICC orders could be re-examined entirely by the courts.[14] As a result, the ICC proceedings were not taken seriously, since all decisions were appealed to the courts for resolution.

This was the regulatory situation at the turn of the century. It was clear that the ICC's power had to be strengthened if it was to be an effective regulatory agency. The situation was so critical that it became a significant part of the presidential campaign and was one of the major activities of the presidential tenure of Theodore Roosevelt. The president took advantage of railroad abusive behaviour and strongly urged that their rate abuses be controlled by the federal government. On 5 December 1905, he delivered his annual message to Congress and declared that the most pressing need was for legislation eliminating unjust rates, specifically indicating his desire to empower the ICC to fix maximum rates only after shipper complaints, to eliminate the last vestiges of rebating, and to extend the ICC's powers to other matters.[15] In response to this call for action, Representative William P. Hepburn introduced his bill on 4 January 1906, to extend the ICC's powers according to the president's desires.

Congress was also concerned about Standard Oil's control of the oil industry and in 1905 ordered the recently formed Bureau of Corporations to study the transport of petroleum. The ICC was authorised to conduct a similar study, but the ICC's investigation was delayed by the president to avoid any conflict with the Bureau of Corporations' effort. During consideration of the Hepburn Bill in the Senate[16] Senator Henry Cabot Lodge offered an amendment to bring petroleum pipelines under the jurisdiction of the ICC. The original Lodge amendment subjected not only oil pipelines to the common carrier provisions of the *Interstate Commerce Act* but also natural gas pipelines and water pipelines. Other senators objected to the inclusion of the latter; Senator Lodge indicated that he only wanted to bring under control the oil pipelines and when the amendment was reintroduced on 4 May 1906, it applied only to oil pipelines. On the same day, President Roosevelt transmitted a summary of the Bureau of Corporations' Report to the Senate; however, the focus of the president's message was on the railroads' and Standard Oil's practices. The modified Lodge amendment was submitted moments after the receipt of the president's message and passed the same day 75 votes to 0, despite Standard Oil's effort to convince Senator Lodge of the folly of his amendment.

One month after passage of the Lodge amendment, Senator Stephen B. Elkins introduced a commodities clause amendment to the Hepburn Bill. The amendment applied to all *Interstate Commerce Act* common carriers. The commodities clause originally sought to prohibit a railroad owning a coal production facility from carrying on its railroad, so as to prevent undue preference *vis-à-vis* independent coal producers. The Senate, sensing the public distrust of big business and the railroads, in particular, forged ahead with consideration of Senator Elkins's amendment and passed it with its application to pipelines.

At about this time, the Bureau of Corporations' full report was sent to Congress (on 17 May 1906) and it hit hard at Standard Oil's practices. It concluded:[17]

The Standard Oil Company has all but a monopoly of the pipelines in the United

States. Its control of them is one of the chief sources of its power. While in the older oil fields pipelines are by the State laws common carriers, there has been little attempt by the States to regulate their charges. The Federal Government has not as yet exercised any control over pipelines engaged in interstate commerce. The result is that the charges made by the Standard for transporting oil through its pipelines for outside concerns are altogether excessive, and in practice are largely prohibitive. Since the charges far exceed the cost of the service, the Standard has a great advantage over such of its competitors as are forced to use its pipelines to secure their crude oil.

With varying Hepburn Bills, a House–Senate conference committee met to iron out differences. There was little concern in this first conference regarding pipelines, except that, as the Elkins amendment applied to pipelines, Senator Shelby Cullom said, the Elkins amendment 'was not discussed except to agree generally that whatever would curb the Standard Oil Company we ought to be for'. The results of this committee brought the oil industry into action. The debate in the Senate centred on the issue of whether pipelines should have their rates controlled and be available to all who wanted to use them. Senator Lodge argued that pipelines are like railroads (also monopolies) and should be restricted to transporting goods, not own them as well. Senators Foraker and Long argued from the opposing position, that pipelines were plant facilities and unlike railroads there should be no separation between the operation and ownership of the goods transported.[18]

The oil industry was overwhelmingly opposed to the commodities clause. In dependent producers feared that imposing common carrier status, and consequently the Elkins amendment on integrated pipelines, would hamper their competitive strength. If a pipeline were barred from carrying its own oil, independents could no longer sell to pipelines at the wellhead and might have to undertake the costs and risks of shipments and sale directly to refineries. Moreover, the independents were fearful that the impact would fall most heavily upon them, while the Standard Oil Companies would find a way around the commodities clause restriction. Senator Elkins was pressured by the many oil interests in his home state of West Virginia. Other senators, unhappy with the legislation, forced a reconsideration in a second conference committee.

In the second conference committee, the bill was changed so that the Elkins amendment would apply only to railroads and not to common carriers. Senator 'Pitchfork Ben' Tillman of South Carolina, the manager of the Hepburn Bill, refused to sign the report of the second conference committee. Senator Tillman commented, 'It simply means in plain English that the Standard Oil Company has got in its work . . . We released the Standard Oil people entirely from the control of the provision which divorces the producers of commodities from the transportation of commodities.' Other 'senators alleged that the Standard Oil Company used devious political devices in order to get pipelines exempted from the commodities clause.'[19] A third conference was held in order to reach agreement on all portions of the bill. The final bill dropped the commodities clause's application to petroleum pipelines while imposing common carrier and maximum rate regulation on them. The president signed the bill on 29 June 1906. Thus, President Roosevelt won a substantial victory and, with the *Hepburn Act*, the rates of both railroads and pipelines became subject to the maximum rate regulation of the ICC, but only after complaint.

The theory behind making pipelines common carriers in the *Hepburn Act* was that if pipelines could be used by all on payment of reasonable charges (cost plus a fair profit for risk) no monopolistic advantage would accrue to the owner. Thus, the benefits of pipeline transport would be available to all shippers.[20]

Statutory authority over petroleum pipelines

The *Hepburn Act* amended the *Interstate Commerce Act*. Section 1(*1*) of the *Interstate Commerce Act* provides:

> The provisions of this chapter shall apply to common carriers engaged in . . .
>
> (*b*) The transportation of oil or other commodity, except water and except natural or artificial gas by pipelines, or partly by pipeline and partly by railroads or water.

The most important regulatory provisions of the *Interstate Commerce Act* require that all pipelines: charge just and reasonable rates for their service; provide and furnish transport upon reasonable request; establish reasonable through routes with other carriers; and establish just and reasonable rates for through transport. Authority is granted under the Act to establish just and reasonable rates either for single carrier transport or for through transport. Pipelines cannot receive rebates, cannot make or give unreasonable preferences or advantages to shippers, and cannot charge more for a short haul than for a long haul. Tariffs for rates and service must be filed with the commission. The commission can conduct investigations and hearings upon complaint or on its own initiative. It can suspend newly filed rates for up to seven months pending investigation.

The commission has no power to require certificates of public convenience and necessity as a basis for starting operation. Pipelines do not need commission permission to abandon or terminate service. The commodities clause of *Interstate Commerce Act* does not apply to common carrier pipelines; neither do provisions regarding the extension of credit, nor those concerning merger, consolidation, common control, or interlocking directorates. The commission cannot order extension of lines nor can it order pipelines to offer facilities needed to provide adequate service such as storage or tankage for terminal operations.[21]

Regulation yesterday

Testing the ICC's jurisdiction

The ICC obtained jurisdiction over interstate petroleum pipelines in 1906. Its first order of business was to assert its jurisdiction. In 1911, the ICC ordered pipeline companies to file with the ICC schedules of their rates and charges for the transporting of oil. The pipeline companies resisted this assertion of jurisdiction, arguing that they were not common carriers. Oil pipelines, they argued, were really plant facilities purchasing oil in the field and carrying only the oil that they owned. The companies argued that they did not offer to carry oil for all who wanted to ship — the heart of the common carrier concept. Moreover they argued that applying the common carrier provisions of the *Interstate Commerce Act* to them would be a taking of property in violation of the due process clause of the Constitution.

In the *Pipe Line Cases*, the Supreme Court ruled that the *Hepburn Act* provided the ICC with the authority to regulate pipelines as common carriers. The Supreme Court found that there was no unconstitutional taking of property in violation of the due process clause. It was the intention of Congress to remedy the situation that gave control over pipelines to a select few companies. The Supreme Court made one very limited exception: a pipeline that moved oil from its own wells across a state line to its own refinery for its own use was not subject to the *Interstate Commerce Act*.[22] All other pipelines were swept under the regulatory umbrella of the ICC. With this decision, the pipelines filed their schedules of rates and charges. Besides issuing some routine administrative regulations, the ICC took no other action to enforce its jurisdiction for over twenty years, with only one exception.

The ICC, in two cases, dealt with the persistent complaints of the Brundred Brothers, who wanted to ship crude oil from the mid-continent producing fields to Pennsylvania over the Standard Oil controlled Prairie Pipe Line. The ICC heard the complaints and left the rates of the pipeline in place, stating that it had no basis upon which to determine the reasonableness of the rates. The ICC did deal with the pipeline's establishment of minimum tender requirements.[23] The ICC ruled that the 100,000 barrel tender requirement was unreasonable and ordered the pipeline to reduce the tender requirement to 10,000 barrels. No general reduction of tender requirements was ordered; only the tender requirement as it applied to the Brundred Brothers. With the disposal of this complaint, the ICC maintained its focus on railroad regulation and ignored petroleum pipelines for another decade.

New Deal activism

Rate cases
In 1934, bowing to the pressure of recent Congressional hearings and to complaints from shippers on crude oil pipelines, the ICC initiated a hearing into the rates and service practices of thirty-five pipelines serving the mid-continent oilfields. The hearing progressed slowly and finally in 1940 the ICC issued its

opinion in *Reduced Pipe Line Rates and Gathering Charges*. The ICC ruled on two important issues. It found that minimum tender requirements in excess of 10,000 barrels were excessive and unreasonable, and ordered the pipelines to institute 10,000-barrel minimum tender requirements. More importantly, the ICC, for the first time, dealt with the rates of crude oil pipelines. It adopted a generic approach to rate-making, ruling that oil pipeline companies could earn no more than 8 per cent of their valuation rate base. In the context of this proceeding, the ICC found that fourteen pipelines were not earning more than the 8 per cent standard, while twenty-one were earning more. The ICC entered an order to show cause why the twenty-one pipelines should not reduce their existing rates.[24] The importance of this proceeding is that it was the first time the ICC articulated how petroleum pipeline rates should be determined. The case applied the rate determination in a generic sense and not to specific rates of specific pipelines. The ICC left each pipeline to determine whether its overall rate structure complied with the general 8 per cent guideline.[25]

A year later the ICC dealt with rates on product pipelines. This time the ICC acted only after a group of shippers initiated the proceeding. The ICC applied the same methodology it used in the *Reduced Pipe Line Rates* case, but permitted a 10 per cent return on the pipeline's valuation rate base. The ICC indicated that it thought product pipelines were more risky than crude pipelines, and that increased risk justified the higher rate of return. In this proceeding, the ICC did establish specific rates for particular movements. Three years later the ICC again considered crude oil pipeline rates, again after the proceeding was initiated by shippers. It affirmed the methodology established in *Reduced Pipe Line Rates* and applied the 8 per cent return on valuation rate base to the crude oil pipelines under consideration. But unlike the *Reduced Pipe Line Rates* proceeding, the ICC made findings regarding specific movements rather than setting general guidelines.

The interesting aspect of these petroleum pipeline rate proceedings was that they came about because of the competition between the pipelines and railroads. Despite the inherent lower costs of pipelines, railroads were still able to compete with pipelines, primarily because pipelines kept their rates at, or near, railroad rates. In the *Reduced Pipe Line Rates* case the complaints poured in when the pipelines lowered their rates well below railroad rates. Since, in practice, only pipeline owners used the pipelines, oil shippers using the railroads were placed at a distinct competitive disadvantage. The attempt by the pipelines to capitalise on their efficiencies was challenged by those excluded from availing themselves of those efficiencies.

In the *Petroleum Rail Shippers' Association* case, the competition between rail and pipeline again created the pressures for the proceeding. Companies attempting to compete in distant markets found that they were unable to because both railroad and pipeline rates were too high. Even though pipeline efficiencies should have yielded lower transport rates, the pipeline rates equalled the railroad rates. Thus, refiners located near the product markets had an advantage over those shipping from a distance. Also, the owners of the pipelines, shipping essentially at cost rather than the tariff rate, were able to compete in distant markets, while the non-owners, whose cost was the tariff, could not meet the competition. These competitive pressures forced the ICC to act to lower pipeline rates.

Valuation cases

While these rate cases were going forward, the ICC was engaged in a parallel effort to clarify its jurisdiction regarding the valuation of pipelines. Congress had passed the *Valuation Act* in 1913[26] as a way of determining the rate base or value of the assets of the regulated companies upon which the companies could earn a rate of return. Since railroads were considered more important than petroleum pipelines, the ICC began its efforts to determine the valuation of railroad assets. It was not until twenty years after the passage of the *Valuation Act* that the ICC turned its attention to petroleum pipeline valuations.

In 1936, the ICC ordered the Valvoline Oil Company to file valuation data. The Valvoline Oil Company objected, claiming that it fell within the exception made by the Supreme Court in the *Pipe Line Cases* of 1914. Valvoline argued that it carried its own oil through its own pipeline to its own refinery — the very situation exempted by the Supreme Court. The ICC found, however, that Valvoline was buying the oil from others at the wellhead, rather than transporting oil from its own wells. This was enough of a distinction to apply the *Hepburn Act* and the common carrier provisions of the *Interstate Commerce Act* as well as the *Valuation Act*. The Supreme Court upheld the ICC on the same grounds.

The ICC's jurisdiction over crude lines was quite clearly spelled out in the *Pipe Line Cases* and the *Valvoline* decision. It was assumed that the ICC's jurisdiction over product pipelines was commensurate with its jurisdiction over crude pipelines. But in two cases, decided in 1946 and 1951, the Supreme Court indicated a somewhat anomalous and different result.

In 1941 the ICC ordered the Champlin Refining Company to file information with the ICC for its valuation work. The company refused. Again using the 1914 exception as its basis, Champlin argued that it carried only its own petrol from its own refinery across state lines to its own petrol terminals. It did not seek to carry any other shipper's petrol. The ICC rejected the Champlin argument and ordered the company to file the valuation information. The Supreme Court affirmed the ICC on the grounds that the petrol was part of interstate commerce, that is, the *Hepburn Act* applied to the transporting of commodities from state to state by pipeline. It was irrelevant that the commodity was for the use of Champlin only. With regard to the ICC's request for information, 'the commerce power is adequate to support this requirement whether the applicant be considered a private carrier or a common carrier'.

In 1948 the ICC ordered the same Champlin pipeline to file annual reports, to institute a uniform system of accounting, and to publish and file rates for the transporting of petroleum products. Again, Champlin refused, asserting the 'Uncle Sam' exception announced in 1914. Again, the ICC rejected the argument and ordered Champlin to comply. The Supreme Court agreed with the ICC over jurisdiction to compel the filing of annual reports and the institution of uniform accounts. But the Supreme Court rejected the ICC's jurisdiction with respect to the filing of tariffs. The court found in this instance that no other shipper sought to use Champlin's pipeline and that only Champlin's petrol was shipped in it. The court concluded that Congress did not intend to 'make common carriers for hire out of private pipe lines whose services were unused, unsought after, and unneeded by independent producers and whose presence fosters competition in markets heavily blanketed by large majors. Such a step would be pointless; it might well subvert the chief purpose of the Act.' As a result of this decision, Champlin did not have to file its tariffs with the ICC.

The ICC did not deal any further with its jurisdiction over petroleum pipelines. The cases that it did bring support the following propositions: (*1*) an interstate petroleum pipeline that offers to transport petroleum belonging to others for shipment in its own lines is a common carrier for all purposes; (*2*) an interstate petroleum pipeline that connects producing and refining facilities that are under common ownership with the pipeline is not a common carrier for any purpose; and (*3*) an interstate petroleum pipeline that ships its own refined products and no others between its own refinery and its own terminals, interconnecting with no other pipelines, is a common carrier for reporting or informational purposes, but is not for tariff or rate purposes, at least where there is no demand by others to use the pipeline.

Anti-trust cases
While most of the regulatory activity occurred at the ICC, it is impossible to leave the New Deal era without discussing the activities of the Department of Justice, Antitrust Division. These activities led to a form of regulation over petroleum pipelines that lasted over forty years. In the late 1930s, President Franklin Roosevelt asked Congress to authorise an investigation into the problem of monopoly power in the US economy. This request led to the creation of the Temporary National Economic Committee (TNEC) to study the problem. Using this committee, the Department of Justice was able to gather detailed data of the petroleum industry.

On 30 September 1940, the Department of Justice filed a series of cases against the petroleum industry. One case was known as the 'Mother Hubbard' case for its sweeping scope and attempt to correct many of the problems of the industry in one lawsuit. This suit was filed against twenty-two petroleum companies and 379 of their affiliates. Part of the lawsuit involved petroleum pipelines and part of the theory of the case rested upon the belief that control over the petroleum pipelines by the major petroleum companies was a way to control the price or output of the petroleum industry. That is, petroleum pipeline control led to the anti-competitive behaviour of monopolisation, a violation of one of the anti-trust laws, the *Sherman Act*. On the same day, the Department of Justice also filed a series of cases alleging that petroleum pipelines were violating the *Elkins Act*, which prohibited common carriers from giving rebates to shippers using the pipeline. The Act also provided for a treble damage remedy that could cost the petroleum pipelines billions of dollars in penalties. The allegations in the three cases filed focused on the payment of dividends to the owners of the pipelines as illegal rebates. The purpose of the lawsuits was to force rates down to a point that would yield a reasonable return to the owners and ensure that rates paid by outside companies related more closely to costs incurred by the owners.

The lawsuits against the petroleum companies became intertwined with the co-operative effort required by the Second World War. On 23 December 1941, the *Elkins Act* cases were settled through a consent decree. The consent decree applied to seventy-eight petroleum companies whose common carrier pipelines engaged in crude oil or petroleum product interstate transport. The decree applied to the situation where the shipper was also the owner and obtained a share of the profits through dividends. The dividends, in effect, lowered the cost of shipping through the pipeline. The most important provision of the consent decree affected the distribution of dividends. From 1942 a pipeline had to limit its dividend distribution to no more than 7 per cent of the valuation of the pipeline's property. The valuation to be used was the latest one made by the ICC.

The anti-trust consent decree became another form of regulation of petroleum pipelines rather than a correcting tool for many of the allegations found in the 'Mother Hubbard' case. Many pipelines structured their rates on a consent decree basis, that is, earning only the amount permitted under the consent decree rather than using the 8 per cent and 10 per cent limits established by the ICC. While the original intention of the consent decree was to act as a limitation on the return on invested capital, ensuing developments virtually vitiated this limitation. The Department of Justice permitted pipelines to include the debt portion of the pipeline's financing in the valuation base. It also permitted the interest on the debt to be deducted as an expense, in addition to depreciation allowances. With these developments, many pipelines altered their capital structures to have more debt than equity. Many wholly owned pipelines switched to 100 per cent debt, while many joint stock companies used a 90 per cent debt–10 per cent equity structure. This development permitted the owners to earn vast sums on their invested capital — a development unforeseen at the time the decree was entered in 1941.[27]

The New Deal activism of the 1930s and 1940s regarding petroleum pipelines disappeared by the end of the war. The few cases that were still alive were usually settled in a manner beneficial to the industry. Petroleum pipelines were to recede into benign neglect for more than twenty years.

Regulation today

The transition to today's regulatory scheme began in 1971 with Williams Brothers Pipe Line Company (Williams) filing new increased tariffs with the ICC. A group of shippers operating in the mid-continent area of the USA who used the Williams system protested against the tariff increase. The protest eventually led to a final decision fourteen years later by the FERC. It also led to a complete reassessment of the way in which petroleum pipelines were regulated, eventuating in a change in the mode of regulation.

The history of the *Williams* proceeding is tortuous; while a complete procedural history is available,[28] a short sketch of the highlights will illustrate the complexity of the proceeding and the importance of the outcome to the petroleum pipeline industry. The protest against the initial rate increase was filed in 1971. The protesters put several arguments to the ICC. The rate base of Williams, and indeed all other pipelines, was based on a valuation formula or fair value methodology established in the early 1940s. All other regulated industries had abandoned the fair value methodology, because of the Supreme Court rulings on the subject.[29] The petroleum pipeline industry alone maintained this archaic, and allegedly illegal form of rate-making. The protesters also argued that Williams should use as its rate base the original cost of the assets and not the increased value of the assets resulting from Williams' purchase of the pipeline from others.

The ICC completely rejected the arguments and affirmed its rate-making methodology established some thirty years earlier. The protesters appealed and nearly carried the day. The Court of Appeals for the District of Columbia Circuit indicated its displeasure with the valuation approach, but since the jurisdiction over petroleum pipelines now rested with the FERC, the court deferred to the FERC's argument that it should be permitted to decide the case expeditiously. More than five years passed during which the FERC held evidentiary hearings and two oral arguments before it issued its first decision on 30 November 1982. The decision was the longest ever issued by the FERC and probably one of its most controversial. There were very few citations to the record; rather, the decision was more like a treatise on the history and economics of the petroleum pipeline industry.

The first *Williams* decision attempted to find a way to impose little or no rate regulation on the industry. While it left intact the valuation rate base, it indicated that the rate of return would be established by each pipeline based upon a series of alternatives. The opinion itself indicated that these alternatives would lead to 'creamy returns' on investment. This attempt by the FERC was rejected completely by the same judge of the Court of Appeals for the District of Columbia Circuit that wrote the first decision in this matter. Having been completely chastised, the FERC went back to its proverbial drawing board. On 28 June 1985, the FERC issued its second decision in *Williams*, dramatically changing its approach to regulation. Rather than rely to any extent upon the valuation methodology established forty years before, the FERC abandoned it completely and changed to a hybrid form of regulation, relying upon original cost for the debt component of the rate base and trended original cost for the equity component of the rate base. The rate of return would be determined on a case-by-case basis for each petroleum pipeline system. With this approach the last vestiges of fair value disappeared.[30]

Original cost is a method of measuring the value of the property to be included in the rate base. Original cost methodologies start with the original cost of the property (i.e. the amount actually paid for installing the original plant and equipment), plus additions, when first devoted to public service. Accrued depreciation must be deducted from the property's valuation. Other elements of value also are accounted for, including working capital allowances, property held for future use, land, and intangibles.[31]

Trended original cost is a variation of the original cost methodology. Trended original cost's primary feature is the placement of an inflation component in the rate base. Rather than accounting for inflation in the rate of return as in original cost, the rate of return in trended original cost is the real cost of capital. The inflation component, normally a part of the rate of return, is taken out of the rate of return and made a part of the rate base. As a result, the time line for rates for a trended original cost methodology would show rates increasing for several years before peaking and then decreasing. Original cost rate time lines would start higher than trended original cost and decline over the entire life of the project. The use of trended original cost is an innovation. The FERC regulates natural gas pipelines and interstate wholesale transactions of electric power. For both of these regulated industries, the FERC uses original cost rate-making principles. The innovation of trended original cost is a departure from this past practice. It is an attempt to rely upon new concepts in rate-making that mitigate some of the harsher effects of the original cost methodology.

Effort to deregulate petroleum pipelines

The maturation of regulation in the USA has led to a reconsideration of the role of economic regulation in general. New studies indicated that economic regulation in some industries imposed more costs than benefits. Competition appeared to be more prevalent in some regulated industries than was thought. Consumers were paying more for the services of regulated firms than was necessary. As a result, the 1970s brought about increased pressures for regulatory reform. In the past decade regulatory reform has swept the airline, railroad, trucking, financial, and telecommunications industries. The energy industries have not escaped the regulatory reform movement. Complete deregulation of crude oil and petroleum prices occurred in 1 January 1985. Petroleum pipelines seemed to be a natural target for regulatory reform. Both rates and service have been regulated since 1906; however, in the *Williams* proceeding petroleum pipeline rates underwent their most detailed examination ever.

In 1981 the petroleum pipeline industry, represented by the Association of Oil Pipe Lines (AOPL), suggested that it was appropriate to consider the deregulation of petroleum pipelines. At the instigation of the AOPL, a bill was introduced into the House of Representatives. The bill proposed to deregulate the rates of all petroleum pipelines, but it would leave untouched service regulation, the common carrier and anti-discrimination provisions.

The industry position was justified by several studies.[32] These studies asserted that petroleum pipelines were not natural monopolies. They focused on the level of competition encountered by petroleum pipelines from other petroleum pipelines, from water transport, and, in some instances, from truck transport. The economists supporting the industry argued that, on the one hand, with market forces working effectively in the industry, rates no longer needed to be regulated by the FERC. On the other hand, the industry argued that service regulation should remain because common carriage was necessary for pipelines to take advantage of the eminent domain provisions of state laws. The AOPL also argued that the anti-discrimination provisions were a protection against the exertion by the pipelines of any residual market power. Besides these arguments advanced by the industry, a more important reason existed at the time that the industry advanced its proposal. By 1981 the *Williams* proceeding at the FERC had been going on for ten years with no end in sight. The industry thought that rate deregulation was the quickest and easiest way to extricate itself and the FERC from the morass of *Williams*.

The industry arguments met with uniform opposition from the Reagan Administration. The opposition was voiced at hearings that took place in 1982 to examine the industry bill. The Administration witnesses argued that if there was sufficient competition in the petroleum pipeline industry to warrant rate deregulation, then there was sufficient reason to deregulate all aspects of petroleum pipeline operations. They saw no reason to bifurcate regulation over the industry. Importantly, these Administration witnesses would not state that all petroleum pipelines operated in competitive markets. While no proof of these competitive concerns was submitted to these hearings, it was generally the opinion of these Administration witnesses that some petroleum pipelines had sufficient market power to warrant continued regulation and they promised to examine the industry carefully to determine whether their opinions on market

power were borne out. They also promised to develop an approach to deregulation that was consistent with their theories.

Three agencies — the Department of Energy, the Department of Justice and
the Office of Management and Budget — worked together to develop an
approach to deregulating petroleum pipelines. The discussion initially centred
on the idea of deregulating all petroleum pipelines quickly. Afterwards, the
Department of Justice or some other government agency could bring administrative or judicial proceedings to reregulate those petroleum pipelines with
competitive problems. After spending considerable time on this approach, the
decision was made that it was not workable.

The working group encountered a significant problem: it did not have a reliable study to determine the extent of competition in the industry. It was generally thought that few pipelines presented problems. The Department of Justice took the lead to study competition in the petroleum pipeline industry. In
order to formulate the Administration approach, it was necessary to determine
as accurately as possible which pipelines had market power. If none did, then
deregulation could proceed quickly. If they all did, then deregulation efforts
would grind to a halt. If only part of the industry had market power, then an
approach based upon that notion was required. A preliminary effort led to the
belief that a small number of pipelines had market power and should remain
regulated. This belief was backed up by a preliminary report by the Department
of Justice, issued in 1984 which spelled out the methodology for determining
which pipelines had market power and published much of the data to be used in
making the determination. Two years later, the Department of Justice issued its
final report, indicating that five pipelines should remain regulated and that six
other pipelines raised sufficient questions to warrant additional investigation.[33]
The Administration's approach, based upon the work of the Department of
Justice and finally submitted to Congress in the form of legislation in 1987, is to
deregulate quickly those petroleum pipelines that operate in competitive markets. The few pipelines that the Department of Justice thinks have market power
would have to go through an administrative proceeding to be held at the Department of Energy with the decision concerning market power to be made by the
Secretary of Energy. While this approach meets the objectives of the Administration — total deregulation for competitive pipelines and total regulation for non-
competitive pipelines — the industry dislikes it. This approach may leave some
pipelines completely regulated, an idea the industry thinks is a mistake.
Moreover, it is likely that some of the largest pipelines may remain regulated, so
that the industry leaders will be affected adversely. This approach also means
that some pipelines have to undergo an anti-trust type hearing. Even though the
proposal would limit the hearing process to no more than two years, the prospect
of more hearings is not an appealing one to an industry that has been tied up for
fifteen years in litigation in *Williams*. The industry also argues that elimination of

common carrier requirements could adversely affect their ability to invoke the eminent domain authority of state laws. Finally, some independent pipeline operators argue that there may be instances where deregulated pipelines could discriminate in their rates with adverse effects upon these independent pipelines. The present positions of the industry and the Administration almost produced an impasse in the efforts to deregulate petroleum pipelines. In early 1988, significant progress has been made to reach a consensus on a unified approach.

Conclusion

In this paper petroleum pipelines regulation over the course of its eighty-year history has been sketched. Petroleum pipelines came into being in the 1860s and developed without any government supervision until 1906. Petroleum pipeline issues were caught up in the furor over the abuses of the Standard Oil Trust and became intertwined in presidential politics. Petroleum pipelines were first regulated on 29 June 1906. Regulation since that time has been very sporadic. The ICC tested its jurisdiction in the decade after it acquired its regulatory authority, but did little else. The New Deal activism of the 1930s spread to the petroleum pipeline industry. Congressional hearings and shipper complaints forced the ICC to act. The result was a series of cases defining the ICC's rate regulation of petroleum pipelines and a series of cases defining the ICC's regulatory jurisdiction. By the early 1940s, petroleum pipelines, for the first time, had rate of return limitations imposed upon their valuation rate bases. The Department of Justice also was active in its attempt to break up major oil company control over petroleum pipelines. This effort failed owing to the need for co-operation during the Second World War. The effort devolved into another form of regulation — limiting the dividends that could be paid to owner–shippers. Regulation fell into benign neglect for another thirty years until the *Williams* proceeding of the 1970s and 1980s, resulting in the change in the form of regulation from the valuation rate base–general rate of return guideline approach, to a cost-based specific rate of return approach.

Petroleum pipeline regulation has not been activated by well-defined policies. Regulation has been responsive to crises or shipper activism. For most of the regulatory era the ICC was preoccupied with other regulatory problems and left petroleum pipeline regulation to founder. Recent shipper activism brought petroleum pipelines under increased regulatory scrutiny. This renewed scrutiny created problems in regulation, as regulatory methodologies changed and became stricter, impinging upon the pipelines' past regulatory prerogatives and raising the question of whether regulation is necessary at all. But varying views on how to deregulate have developed into an impasse that m v be on the verge of resolution.

Historically this important transport industry preferred to remain buried —
out of sight and out of mind. The industry is chafing under its recent exposure.
Only time will tell whether it remains exposed or whether it can resume its existence out of the daylight.

Notes

1 Deliveries from the system provide a measure of
the gross number of barrels the system handles.
Barrel-miles, the number of barrels shipped multiplied by the length of a pipeline, provide an indication of capacity and distance, perhaps a truer
measure of the size of the system. See 'Pipeline
Economics', *Oil and Gas Journal*, 23 November 1987,
pp. 56–8.
2 L. L. Coburn, *United States Petroleum Pipelines: an
Empirical Analysis of Pipeline Sizing*, U.S. Department
of Energy, Washington D.C. (1980).
3 L. L. Coburn, 'The case for petroleum pipeline
deregulation', *Energy Law Journal*, 3 (1982).
4 Petroleum Extension Service, *Introduction to the
Oil Pipeline Industry*, University of Texas at Austin
(1978). Association of Oil Pipe Lines, *Pipeline Transportation: a Review of the Oil Pipeline Industry*, A.O.P.L.,
Washington D.C. (1976). G. Wolbert Jr, *American
Pipelines*, University of Oklahoma Press, Norman,
Oklahoma (1952). G. Wolbert Jr, *U.S. Oil Pipe Lines*,
American Petroleum Institute, Washington D.C.
(1979). J. Loos, *Oil on Stream! A History of Interstate Oil
Pipeline Company 1909–1959*, Louisiana State University Press, Baton Rouge (1959).
5 Eminent domain is a law which permits the taking of private lands with compensation through a
court-enforced legal procedure in cases where a public interest is demonstrated.
6 A. M. Johnson, *Petroleum Pipelines and Public
Policy 1906–1959*, Harvard University Press, Cambridge, Mass. (1967). E. J. Mitchell (ed.), *Vertical
Integration in the Oil Industry*, American Enterprise
Institute, Washington D.C. (1976).
7 C. F. Phillips, Jr, *The Economics of Regulation*,
Richard D. Irwin Inc., Homewood, Illinois (1969),
pp. 441–7.
8 *Munn v. Illinois*, 94 U.S. 113 (1877).
9 *Wabash, St Louis and Pacific Railway Co. v. Illinois*,
118 U.S. 557 (1886).
10 G. Nash, *Origins of the Interstate Commerce Act of
1887*, 24 Pennsylvania History 183 (1957).
11 C. B. Aitchison, *The Evolution of the Interstate
Commerce Act: 1887–1937*, 5 George Washington
L. Rev. 289 (1937).
12 *Counselman v. Hitchcock*, 142 U.S. 547 (1892).
13 *Interstate Commerce Commission v. Cincinnati, New
Orleans and Texas Pacific Railway Co.*, 167 U.S. 479
(1897).
14 *Interstate Commerce Commission v. Alabama
Midland Railway Co.*, 168 U.S. 144 (1897).

15 A. Hoogenboom and O. Hoogenboom, *A
History of the ICC*, Norton, New York (1976).
16 The Hepburn Bill passed the House in February, 346 votes to 7.
17 Bureau of Corporations (1906), 'Transportation of petroleum', in Senate Committee on the
Judiciary, *Petroleum Industry Competition Act of 1976*,
S. Rep No. 94–1005, 1976.
18 It should be noted that Senator Foraker was a
former Standard Oil counsel.
19 R. Prewitt 'The operation and regulation of
crude oil and gasoline pipe lines', *Quarterly Journal of
Economics*, 56 (1942).
20 G. Harmon, 'Effective public policy to deal with
oil pipelines', *American Business Law Journal*, 4 (1966).
21 See W. Jones, *Authority of the Department of
Energy to Regulate Anticompetitive Aspects of Petroleum
Pipeline Operations*, U.S. Department of Energy,
Washington D.C. (1978).
22 This exception became known as the 'Uncle
Sam' exception to common carrier status because the
pipeline involved was owned by the Uncle Sam Oil
Company.
23 Minimum tender requirements concern the
amount of crude oil that must be offered to a pipeline
in order to ship through the pipeline.
24 A final order was not issued until 1948. By that
time the number of pipeline respondents was
reduced to twenty-six, mainly by consolidations, and
pipeline rates and earnings were reduced substantially. The ICC reaffirmed its adherence to the
8 per cent rate of return guideline.
25 It is important to note that the 8 per cent rate of
return applied to the pipeline company. If the company owned more than one pipeline, the rates of
return could be averaged to achieve the 8 per cent
overall rate of return. Thus, some pipelines could
earn more than the 8 per cent rate of return.
26 For a detailed analysis of the operation of ICC
valuation, see P. Navarro and T. Stauffer, 'The legal
history and economic implications of oil pipeline
regulation', *Energy Law Journal*, 2 (1981).
27 The Department of Justice made one attempt
to change the interpretations permitting the inclusion
of debt in the rate base upon which the 7 per cent was
applied. The Supreme Court, however, rejected this
attempt because of the long time between the entry of
the consent decree and the filing of the interpretive
suits in 1957. The consent decree was dissolved on
13 December 1982.

28 B. O'Neill and G. Knapp, 'Oil pipeline regulation after Williams: Does the end justify the means?', *Energy Law Journal*, 4 (1983). L. L. Coburn, 'Farmers' union II: Sisyphus starts up the hill again, *Energy Law Journal*, 5 (1984).
29 The fair value methodology emerged from a Supreme Court decision of 1898, in which the court ruled that 'The basis of all calculations as to the reasonableness of rates . . . must be the fair value of the property being used.' Fair value was determined by calculating original and present costs. The Supreme Court abandoned fair value in 1944. In 1944 the court indicated that the end result was the most important consideration, but it is clear that the court disliked the fair value approach and preferred an original cost approach.
30 For an explanation of the various petroleum pipeline methodologies, see L. L. Coburn, 'Oil pipeline regulation: has the FERC finally slain the Minotaur?', *Energy Law Journal*, 6 (1985).

31 C. F. Phillips, *The Regulation of Public Utilities*, Public Utilities Reports Inc., Arlington, Virginia (1984).
32 E. Mitchell, *A Study of Oil Pipeline Competition*, mimeo, (1982). R. Barber, *The Transportation of Alaskan North Slope Oil by Pipeline: an Assessment of the Competitive Issues Relevant to Rate Deregulation*, R. Barber and Associates, Washington D.C. (1982).
33 Department of Justice, *Competition in the Oil Pipeline Industry, A Preliminary Report* (1984). Department of Justice, *Oil Pipeline Deregulation* (1986). For other views, see J. Hansen, *U.S. Pipeline Markets — Structure, Pricing and Public Policy*, MIT Press, Cambridge, Mass. (1983). National Economic Research Associates, *Competition in Oil Pipeline Markets: a Structural Analysis*, NERA, Washington D.C. (1983). W. Adams and J. Brock, 'Deregulation or divestiture: the case of petroleum pipelines', *Wake Forest Law Review*, 19 (1983).

Oligarchic Tendencies
in
National Policy-Making:
the Role of the
Private Policy-Planning
Organizations

THOMAS R. DYE

T HE PURPOSE OF THIS ESSAY is to contribute to the development of a more specific and useful version of the "elitist" model of the policy-making process. We are not going to argue the theoretical merits of elitism, or re-open the seemingly endless debates regarding the concepts of power, elitism, or pluralism. We ask the indulgence of readers who find elitist theories and concepts unsatisfactory at the outset. We shall endeavor, first, to set forth a more detailed, working model of oligarchy in national policy-making; second, to identify the organizations which contribute to cohesion and consensus among top corporate, financial, and governmental leaders; third, to identify the individuals *by name* who direct these organizations and to note their linkages with the corporate and financial worlds; fourth, to observe their role in recruiting individuals for high government positions; and finally, to specify some

° Presidential Address delivered at the annual meeting of the Southern Political Science Association held in New Orleans, Louisiana, November 5, 1977.

I appreciate the assistance of G. William Dumhoff, University of California, Santa Cruz. I apologize to those eminent political scientists who told me that the activities of private policymakers was not "political science."

of the key decisions in which these private policy-planning organizations have been influential.

Elite Theory and Public Policy

The typical "elitist" model of public policy portrays policy as the preferences and values of a governing elite.[1] The governing elite is "structured"—that it, it is relatively stable over time. Issues and elections may come and go, but a fairly stable group of individuals continues over time to exercise a disproportionate influence over public policy. The model implies that the continuing influences of the elite is generally derived from its control over large corporate and financial institutions. Elected officials—the "proximate policy-makers" whose actions give official sanction to policy decisions—knowingly or unknowingly respond primarily to the values of the elite. While persons in the elite may disagree from time to time over the specifics of public policy, they generally share a consensus over the major goals and directions of society. The governing elite is fairly cohesive and exercises influence over a wide range of important domestic and foreign policies. The governing elite sets the major policy goals and directions, leaving to elected officials the task of deciding upon the details of public policy. Policy questions are not decided by "the people" acting through elections, or through political parties, or through the operation of the interest groups. Rather, the "elitist" model acknowledges only very *in*direct popular influence over the policy-making behavior of elites. Finally, elite theory suggests that the structure of society itself is designed in such a way as to suppress the emergence of issues which might result in policies adverse to the interest of the governing elite. We have come to label this process "non-decision-making".[2]

[1] Various contemporary descriptions of "elitism" in American society can be found in Thomas R. Dye and Harmon Zeigler, *The Irony of Democracy*, 4th ed. (Boston Duxbury Press, 1978); G. William Domhoff, *Who Rules America* (Englewood Cliffs: Prentice Hall, 1967); G. William Domhoff, *The Higher Circles,* (New York: Random House, 1970); Peter Bachrach, *The Theory of Democratic Election* (Boston: Little Brown, 1967); David M. Ricci, *Community Power and Democratic Theory* (New York: Random House, 1971); Thomas R. Dye, *Who's Running America? Institutional Leadership in the U.S.* (Englewood Cliffs: Prentice Hall, 1976); Geraint Parry, *Political Elites* (New York: Praeger, 1969).

[2] Peter Bachrach and Morton S. Baratz, "Decisions and Non-decisions," *American Political Science Review,* Vol. 57 (September, 1963) 632-642;

The problem with this elitist model to date has been its failure to tell us *how* the elite goes about making national policy. What are the institutions and organizations through which the elite function to make public policy? How is control over corporate and financial resources transformed into influence over public policy? What organizations or processes are employed to achieve elite consensus, and how are elite decisions communicated to government officials—the "proximate policy-makers"?

An Oligarchic Model of the Policy-Making Process

Let us suggest an "oligarchic model" of the policy-making process —a model derived from the literature on national elites. It will be an abstraction from reality—we will not expect every major policy decision to conform to our model. But we think the processes described by the model will strike many knowledgeable readers as familiar; that the model indeed actually describes the way in which a great many national policies are decided, and therefore at least deserves consideration by students of the policy-making process.

Our oligarchic model of national policy-making assumes that the initial resources for research, study, planning, and development of national policy-making *are* derived from corporate and personal wealth. This wealth is channeled into foundations and policy-planning organizations, in the form of endownments, grants, and contracts. Moreover, corporate presidents, directors, and top wealth-holders also sit on the governing boards of these foundations and policy-planning organizations to oversee the spending of their funds. In short, corporate and personal wealth provides both the financial resources and the overall direction of policy research and planning. Finally, the directors of these foundations and policy-planning organizations play a major role in the recruitment of personnel to high posts in the executive branch of government.

It is the policy-planning organizations which are central coordinating points in the policy-making process. Certain policy planning groups—notably the Council on Foreign Relations, the Committee on Economic Development, and the Brookings Institution— are influential in a wide range of key policy areas. Other policy

Geoffrey Debnam, "Nondecisions and Power," *American Political Science Review,* Vol. 69, (September, 1975) 889-907, with a response by Peter Bachrach and Morton S. Baratz.

planning groups—The Urban Institute, Resources for the Future, The Population Council, for example—specialize in a particular policy field.

These organizations bring together the leadership of corporate and financial institutions, the foundations, the mass media, the leading intellectuals, and influential figures in the government. They review the relevant university and foundation supported research on topics of interest, and, more important, they try to reach a consensus about what action should be taken on national problems under study. Their goal is to develop *action recommendations*—explicit policies or programs designed to resolve national problems. These policy recommendations of the key policy planning groups are distributed to the mass media, federal executive agencies, and the Congress. The White House staff, Congressional Committee staffs, and top executive administrators are contacted with increasing frequency by representatives of policy-planning organizations, when it is felt that the time has come for government action. The purpose is to lay the groundwork for making policy into law. Soon the results of elite decision-making and consensus-building will be reflected in the actions of elected officials—the "proximate policy-makers."

The Policy-Planning Organizations

Let us illustrate these propositions by examining three of the nation's leading policy-planning organizations—the Council on Foreign Relations, the Committee on Economic Development, and the Brookings Institution.

The Council on Foreign Relations. The most influential private policy-planning organization in foreign affairs is the Council on Foreign Relations. It was founded in 1921, and supported by grants from the Rockefeller and Carnegie Foundations and later the Ford Foundation. Its early directors were internationally-minded Wall Street corporation lawyers: Elihu Root, also Secretary of State; John W. Davis, also 1924 Democratic presidential nominee; Paul Cravath, founder of the prestigious New York law firm of Cravath, Swaine, and Moore.

The history of the CFR accomplishments are impressive: it developed the Kellogg Peace Pact in the 1920s, stiffened U.S. opposition to Japanese Pacific expansion in the 1930s, designed major portions of the United Nation's Charter, and devised the "containment" policy to halt Soviet expansion in Europe after World War II. It laid the ground work for the NATO agreement and devised the Marshall Plan for European recovery[3]. When top elites began to suspect that the U.S. was over-reliant upon nuclear weapons in the late 1950s, the CFR commissioned a young Harvard professor to look into the matter. The result was Henry Kissenger's influential book, *Nuclear Weapons and Foreign Policy*, which challenged the "massive retaliation" doctrine of John Foster Dulles and urged greater flexibility of response to aggression.[4]

The Council on Foreign Relations publishes the journal, *Foreign Affairs*, which is considered throughout the world as the unofficial spokesman of U.S. foreign policy. Few important initiatives in U.S. policy are not first outlined in articles in *Foreign Affairs*.

The Council on Foreign Relations limits itself to approximately 700 individual resident members (New York and Washington) and 700 non-resident members. There are few elites with an interest in foreign affairs who are not CFR members. Its list of former members includes every man of influence in foreign affairs from Elihu Root, Henry Stimson, John Foster Dulles, Dean Acheson, Robert Lovett, George F. Kennan, Averill Harriman, to Dean Rusk, Henry Kissinger, and Cyrus Vance.

Evidence of CFR interaction with corporate and financial world, as well as with universities, foundations, the mass media, and government, is found in extensive interlocking between the leadership of CFR and the leadership of these other sectors of society. In 1976, the CFR Board of Directors included the following:

David Rockefeller. Chairman of the Board of Directors of the Council on Foreign Relations. Chairman of Board and Chief Executive Officer, Chase Manhattan Bank. A director or trustee of the Rockefeller Foundation, Museum of Modern Art, Harvard University, the University of Chicago, and Rockefeller Center, Inc.

John J. McCloy. Former Chairman of the Board of Chase Manhattan Bank and Senior Partner of the New York law firm of Milbank, Tweed, Hadley & McCloy. Former Special Advisor to the President on Disarmament, 1961-63; Chairman of the Coordinating Committee on the Cuban Crisis, 1962; member of the Commission

---

[3] See Joseph Kraft, "School for Statesmen," *Harper's* (July, 1958), 64-68.

[4] Henry Kissinger, *Nuclear Weapons and Foreign Policy* (New York: Council on Foreign Relations, 1957).

on the Assassination of President Kennedy; U.S. High Commissioner for Germany, 1949-52; President of the World Bank, 1947-49; A director of Allied Chemical Corporation, American Telephone and Telegraph Company, Chase Manhattan Bank, Metropolitan Life Insurance Company, Westinghouse Electric Corporation, E. R. Squibb and Sons. A trustee of the Ford Foundation and Amherst College.

Gabriel Hauge. President Manufacturers Hanover Trust Co., Former Editor of *Business Week.* A director of New York Life Insurance, American Metal Climax, American Home Products. A trustee of the Committee for Economic Development, Juilliard School of Music, and the Carnegie Endowment for International Peace.

James A. Perkins. President of Cornell University. A trustee of Carnegie Corporation and the Rand Corporation; and a director of Chase Manhattan.

Hedley Donovan. Editor in Chief, *Time Magazine.* A trustee of New York University, and the Carnegie Foundation.

William P. Bundy. Editor of the Council on Foreign Relations' journal, "Foreign Affairs." Senior Partner, Covington and Burling (Washington law firm). Former Deputy Director of the C.I.A., Asst. Secretary of Defense (1961-64), Asst. Secretary of State for Far East (1964-68). A trustee of the Committee on Economic Development, the American Assembly, and Yale University.

Robert O. Anderson. Chairman of the Board, Atlantic Richfield Co., and a director of the American Petroleum Institute. A trustee of the California Institute of Technology, University of Chicago, and the University of Denver.

Nicholas DeB. Katzenbach. Former Attorney General of the United States, 1964-66, under President Johnson. Former University of Chicago Law School professor. A director and general counsel of the IBM Corporation.

Douglas Dillon. Chairman of Board of the New York investment firm of Dillon, Reed, and Co. A director of U.S. Foreign Securities Corp. and U.S. International Securities Corp., the Rockefeller Foundation, the Brookings Institution, New York Hospital, and the Metropolitan Museum of Art. Secretary of Treasury (1961-63) under President Kennedy.

Theodore M. Hesburgh. President of University of Notre Dame. Former Chairman, U.S. Civil Rights Commission. A director of

American Council on Education, the Rockefeller Foundation, Carnegie Foundation, Woodrow Wilson National Fellowship Foundation, United Negro College Fund, and the Freedoms Foundation.

Robert V. Roosa. Senior Partner in the New York investment firm of Brown Brothers, Harriman & Co. (which was founded by Averill Harriman). A director of American Express Co., Anaconda Copper Co., Owens-Corning Fiberglass, and Texaco. Former Under-Secretary of Treasury.

Peter G. Peterson. Chairman of the New York investment firm of Lehman Bros. Former Chairman of Board of Bell and Howell, Co. and former Assistant to President for International Economic Affairs (1971-72) under President Nixon. A director of Minnesota Mining and Manufacturing, General Foods, and Federated Dept. Stores. A trustee of Museum of Modern Art, and the University of Chicago.

Paul C. Warnke. Now U.S. Arms Control and Disarmament Advisor and SALT negotiator. Senior Partner, Washington law firm of Clifford, Warnke, Glass, McIlwain, & Finney. Former Assistant Secretary of Defense (1967-69).

Cyrus Vance. Now Secretary of State. Vice Chairman of the Board of Directors of the Council on Foreign Relations. Senior Partner in New York law firm of Simpson, Thacher and Bartlett. A director of Pan American World Airways, American Life Insurance Co., IBM, American Red Cross, University of Chicago, and the Rockefeller Foundation. Former Secretary of the Army and Under-Secretary of Defense and a U.S. negotiator at the Paris Peace Conference on Vietnam, during the Johnson Administration.

W. Michael Blumenthal. Now Secretary of the Treasury. President of the Bendix Corporation. Former director of Crown Cork Company and special representative on trade negotiation under President Kennedy. A trustee of Princeton University.

Zbigniew Brzezinski. Now Special Assistant to the President for National Security Affairs. Professor of Government at Columbia University, and Executive director of the Trilateral Commission.

Of the 25 current (1976) directors and 16 "directors emeriti," the Council now, according to fashion, boasts of one woman and one black. The woman is Elizabeth Drew, *Washington Post-Newsweek* journalist and commentator on Washington's WTOP-TV (which is also owned by *Washington Post-Newsweek*). The black is Franklin Hall Williams, former N.A.A.C.P. attorney and U.S.

Ambassador to Ghana (1965-68) under President Johnson. He is also a director of the Chemical Bank of New York and Consolidated Edison.

Political Scientist Lester Milbraith observes that the influence or CFR throughout the government is so pervasive that it is difficult to distinguish CFR from government programs: "The Council on Foreign Relations, while not financed by government, works so closely with it that it is difficult to distinguish Council actions stimulated by government from autonomous actions."[5]

In the Kennedy and Johnson Administrations the Council took the lead in the determination of U.S. policy in Southeast Asia—including both the initial decision to intervene militarily in Vietnam and the later decision to withdraw. Council members in the Kennedy-Johnson Administration included Secretary of State Dean Rusk, National Security Advisor McGeorge Bundy, Assistant Secretary of State for Far Eastern Affairs William P. Bundy, C.I.A. Director John McCone, and Under-Secretary of State George Ball. The Council consensus up to November, 1967, was clearly in support of the U.S. military commitment to South Vietnam.[6] (Of all top establishment leaders, only George Ball dissented from the War as early as 1965.) Following the Tonkin Gulf Resolution and the introduction of U.S. ground combat troops in February, 1965, President Lyndon Johnson created a private, informal group of CFR advisors, with the assistance of CFR chairman John J. McCloy, which later became known as the "Senior Advisory Group on Vietnam."[7] The group was not an official governmental body and it included more private elites than public office-holders. Twelve of the fourteen members of the Senior Advisory Group on Vietnam were CFR members; only Johnson's close personal friend Abe Fortas and General Omar Bradley were not CFR members. As the war continued unabated through 1967, the Council, at the urging of George Ball recruited Professor Hans Morganthau of the University of Chicago to conduct a new private study, "A Re-examina-

[5] Lester Milbraith, "Interest Groups in Foreign Policy," James R. Rosenau, ed., *Domestic Sources in Foreign Policy* (New York: Free Press, 1967), 247.

[6] Laurence Shoup, "The Council on Foreign Relations and American Policy in Southeast Asia," *The Insurgent Sociologist*, Vol. 7 (Winter, 1977), 19-30.

[7] Council on Foreign Relations, *Annual Report 1967-68*, (New York: CFR, 1968).

tion of American Foreign Policy."[8] Following the Tet offensive in February, 1968, President Johnson called a special meeting of this "Senior Advisory Group." The Group met for two days, March 25, and 26; key members Douglas Dillon, Cyrus Vance, Arthur Dean, Dean Acheson, McGeorge Bundy, switched from "hawks" to doves." They presented their new consensus to the President. Five days later, March 31, President Johnson announced a de-escalation of the war, the opening of peace talks in Paris with the Hanoi government, and his own retirement from public office.

At this point the CFR, doubtlessly relieved that Johnson and his immediate advisors were left as the scapegoats of the Vietnam disaster, immediately launched a new group—the "Vietnam Settlement Group"—headed by Robert V. Roosa and Cyrus Vance. The group devised a peace proposal allowing for return of prisoners and a standstill ceasefire, with the Viet Cong and Saigon dividing the territory under respective control.[9] Secretary of State Kissinger avoided direct attributions of U.S. policy to the CFR plan, but the plan itself eventually became the bases of the January, 1973, Paris Peace Agreement.

A discussion of the CFR would be incomplete without some reference to its multi-national arm—the Trilateral Commission. The Trilateral Commission was established by CFR Board Chairman David Rockefeller in 1972, with the backing of the Council and the Rockefeller Foundation. The Trilateral Commission is a small group of top officials of multi-national corporations and governmental leaders of industralized nations, who meet periodically to coordinate economic policy among the United States, Western Union, and Japan. At the request of J. Paul Austin, Chairman of Board of Coca Cola Co., with its headquarters in Atlanta, Rockefeller appointed the then little-known governor of Georgia, Jimmy Carter, to the Trilateral Commission. The Executive Director of the Commission was Columbia University Professor Zbigniew Brzezinski, now President's Carter's National Security Advisor. The Commission's membership was a compendium of power and prestige: it included Cal Tech President Harold Brown (now Secretary of Defense); Coca-Cola's J. Paul Austin; Time magazine Editor

[8] See Clark M. Clifford "A Viet-Nam Reappraisal," *Foreign Affairs*, Vol. 47 (July, 1969).

[9] Council on Foreign Relations, *Annual Report 1972-73*, (New York: CFR, 1973).

Hedley Donovan; Paul Warnke (now U.S. Arms Control and Disarmament Advisor); Alden Clausen, President, BankAmerica, the nation's largest bank; United Auto Worker's President Leonard Woodcock (now U.S. representative to the People's Republic of China); Bendix Corporation President W. Michael Blumenthal (now Secretary of the Treasury); Cyrus Vance (now Secretary of State); and U.S. Senator Walter Mondale (now Vice President of the United States). So while Carter nourished his image as an "outsider" to the general public in 1976, he had been in close contact with the nation's top elite through the CFR and Trilateral Commission as early as 1972.[10]

What is the CFR planning for us today? Currently the high priority item at CFR, under David Rockefeller's tenure as chairman, is something called "The 1980s Project."[11] This is an ambitious program even for so powerful a group as the CFR. The project began in 1975, and it includes (1) an international campaign in behalf of "human rights"; (2) a series of alternative approaches to nuclear stability, including a new strict policy toward nuclear proliferation; (3) an effort to restrict international arms sales; and (4) a study of "North-South global relations"—relations between richer and poorer countries. Each of these aspects of "The 1980s Project" has a separate study group. It should come as no surprise to CFR watchers that each of these concerns is currently reflected in the administration of President Jimmy Carter.

The Brookings Institution. Today the Brookings Institution may be the most influential policy-planning group in America in domestic policy. Since the 1960s, it has overshadowed the Committee on Economic Development, the American Assembly, Resources for the Future, The Urban Institute, the Twentieth Century Fund, and all other domestic policy groups. The Brookings Institution has clearly taken the lead in planning recent domestic policy—the war on poverty, welfare reform, revision of the nation's health care system, tax reform, and defense policy.

The Brookings Institution began as a modest component of the progressive movement of the early Twentieth Century. A wealthy St. Louis merchant, Robert Brookings, established an Institute of

[10] See Roger Morris, "Jimmy Carter's Ruling Class," *Harper's*, (October, 1977), 37-45.

[11] Council on Foreign Relations, *Annual Report 1975-76* (New York: CFR, 1976).

Government Research in 1916, to promote "good government," fight "bossism," assist in municipal reform, and press for economy and efficiency in government. It worked closely with the National Civic Federation and other reformist, progressive organizations of that era. Brookings himself was appointed to the War Production Board in World War I by President Woodrow Wilson. The original trustees of Brookings included Frederic H. Delano (wealthy banker and railroad executive, a member of the nation's first Federal Reserve Board, and an uncle of President Franklin Delano Roosevelt); James F. Curtis (banker and Assistant Secretary of the Treasury under President Taft); Arthur T. Hadley (President of Yale University); Herbert Hoover (then a self-made millionaire engineer); and Felix Frankfurter (then a Harvard Law Professor).

The first major policy proposal of the Brookings Institution was the establishment of an annual federal budget. The Brookings Institution proposed, and the Congress passed, the Budget and Accounting Act of 1921, which created for the first time an integrated federal budget prepared in the Executive Office of the President and presented to the Congress in a single budget message. This notable achievement was consistent with the early interests of the Brookings trustees in improving economy and efficiency in government.

The Brookings Institution directors today are as impressive a group of top elites as any assembled anywhere:

Robert V. Roosa. Chairman of Board of Trustees of the Brookings Institution; Senior Partner, Brown Brothers, Harriman & Co. a director of American Express Co., Anaconda Copper, Owens-Corning Fiberglass Co., and Texaco. A trustee of the Rockefeller Foundation and a director of the Council on Foreign Relations.

Louis W. Cabot. (Of the original Boston Cabots, whose ancestors discovered America.) Chairman of the Board of the Cabot Corporation. A director of Owens-Corning Fiberglass Co., New England Telephone and Chairman of the Federal Reserve Bank of Boston. A trustee of the Carnegie Corporation, M.I.T., and Northeastern University.

Robert S. McNamara. President of the World Bank. Former Secretary of Defense (1961-67), and former President of Ford Motor Company.

William McChesney Martin, Jr. Former Chairman of the Federal Reserve Board. Former chairman of the Export-Import Bank, governor of the New York Stock Exchange, and partner in the investment firm of A. G. Edwards & Sons. A director of IBM, Caterpillar Tractor, and General Foods. A trustee of the American Red Cross, Johns Hopkins University, and Yale University.

Douglas Dillon. Chairman of Board of the New York investment firm of Dillon, Reed, and Co. A director of U.S. Foreign Securities Corp. and U.S. International Securities Corp., the Rockefeller Foundation, New York Hospital, and The Metropolitan Museum of Art. He was Secretary of Treasury (1961-63).

Eugene R. Black. Former President, Chase Manhattan Bank. A director of Chase Manhattan, American Express Co., Equitable Life Assurance Society, I.T.&T., New York Times, Electric Bond & Share Co., Cummins Engine, F. W. Woolworth Co., Royal Dutch Petroleum, Trust Company of Georgia. A trustee of the J. P. Morgan Library, Harvard University, Johns Hopkins University, the Population Council, Planned Parenthood, Project Hope, and the Girls Club of America.

Luther G. Holbrook. Former President T. Mellon & Sons and trustee of the Mellon Foundation.

Arjay Miller. Former President Ford Motor Company; Dean of the Graduate School of Business of Stanford University.

Herbert P. Patterson. President, Chase Manhattan Bank. A director of American Machine & Foundry, and the Urban Coalition.

Edward W. Carter. President of Broadway Hale Stores, including Nieman Marcus and Bergdorf-Goodman. A director of A.T.&T., Southern California Edison, Del Monte Corporation, Western Ban-Corporation, Pacific Mutual Life Insurance Co.

Two women are listed among the 21 trustees and 10 honorary trustees of the Brookings Institution: Barbara W. Newell, President of Wellesley College; and Lucy Wilson Benson, former National President of the League of Women Voters; Secretary for Human Services, Commonwealth of Massachusetts; and a director of the Dreyfus Fund, Continental Can and Federated Department Stores.

Brookings boasts that in 1952, under the leadership of Robert Calkins, the Institution broke away from being "a sanctuary for conservatives" and recruited a stable of in-house liberal intellectuals. The funds for this effort came mainly from the Ford Foundation; later a Ford Foundation staff worker, Kermit Gordon, was named Brookings Institution director. (He served until his death in 1976.)

First, under Calkins and later under Gordon, Brookings fashioned itself into a policy-planning organization and rapidly gained prestige and prominence in elite circles. When Republicans captured the presidency in 1968, Brookings became a haven for unemployed liberal Democratic intellectuals and bureaucrats. Charles L. Schultz, now chairman of the Council of Economic Advisors, began the publication of an annual "counterbudget" as a critique of the Nixon budgets. Director Kermit Gordon, drawing on his experience as budget director under President Johnson, pressed forward with the notion of annual counterbudgets as an alternative to the presidential budget. Brookings "counterbudgets" continue to be published each year. Gordon also persuaded Charles Schultz and Alice Rivlin at Brookings to develop a proposal for a new congressional budget and Congressional Budget Office. Congress obligingly passed the Budget and Impoundment Act of 1974, establishing new budgetary procedures, creating new and powerful House and Senate Budget Committees, headed by Brock Adams (now Secretary of Transportation) and Edmund Muskie, and a new joint Congressional Budget Office, headed, of course, by a Brookings staffer, Alice Rivlin.

The Brookings Defense Analysis Project was begun in 1969. Perhaps the most important recommendation to emerge from the Defense Analysis Project was the recommendation to drop the B-1 bomber from the U.S. arsenal. Brookings made its B-1 report in February, 1976;[12] it was read by President Carter and announced as national policy in July, 1977, despite strong recommendations by military advisors to retain the bomber. But Brookings clearly overpowered the "military industrial complex." Brookings overpowered the military again in its recommendation that the U.S. withdraw ground combat forces from Korea. Brookings recommended the withdrawal in 1976,[13] and President Carter announced the withdrawal one year later in the face of overt military opposition to the move.

The Brookings section on Governmental Studies, led by political scientist Gilbert Y. Steiner, claims its major policy contribution of

---

[12] Alton H. Quanbeck and Archie L. Wood, *Modernizing the Strategic Bomber Force* (Washington: Brookings, 1976).

[13] Ralph N. Clough, *Deterrence and Defense in Korea* (Washington: Brookings, 1976).

recent years to be the Presidential Campaign Finance Law.[14] This is the law that allows us to check off one dollar of our income tax for presidential campaigns and establishes the Federal Elections Commission to oversee campaign spending. Finally, the Carter Administration tilt toward the Arab cause in the Middle East could have been predicted by a close reading of a 1975 Brookings report entitled, "Toward Peace in the Middle East," coauthored by Zbigniew Brzezinski.[15]

The Committee on Economic Development. The Committee on Economic Development (CED) is the most "business-oriented" of the major policy-planning organizations. It was created in 1942, as an outgrowth of the realization that large corporations would be required to work closely with government in World War II war production. The CED was initially composed of businessmen who viewed the New Deal as an essential reform to save the capitalist system. Early CED members were considered more progressive and far-sighted than the conservative businessmen in the National Association of Manufactures (NAM). As business gradually moved away from the "public be damned" attitudes of the 19th century robber-barons, and assumed a new liberal public-regarding, social consciousness, a new organization was required to reflect these views. The once powerful NAM became a discredited voice of conservatism and the CED became the chief spokesman of large corporate enterprise in America.

The CED's founder was Paul Hoffman (chairman of the Board of Studebaker-Packard Corporation; a U.S. Delegate to the United Nations; a trustee of the Ford Foundation, a trustee of the University of Chicago; a director of New York Life Insurance Co., Times, Inc., Encyclopedia Britannica, the Automotive Safety Foundation, and chairman of the Fund for the Republic). Another key figure in its formation was William Benton (former U.S. Senator from Connecticut; former Assistant Secretary of State; Chairman of the Board of Encyclopedia Brittanica; a trustee of the University of Chicago, University of Bridgeport, Brandeis University, the John F. Kennedy Library, and the American Assembly) who served as vice-chairman of CED under Hoffman.

The first important accomplishment of the CED was the Employ-

[14] See *The Brooking Bulletin*, Vol. 13 (Fall, 1976), 11.

[15] *Toward Peace in the Middle East*, Report of a Study Group (Washington: Brookings, 1975).

ment Act of 1946, creating the Council of Economic Advisors and officially committing the U.S. government to fiscal and monetary policies devised to avoid depression, maintain full employment and minimize inflation.[16] At this time the CED was heavily interlocked with an organization called the National Planning Association which did the actual lobbying for the Act. The NPA was then headed by Charles E. Wilson, President of General Electric Corporation. (Charles E. Wilson was then referred to as "Electric Charlie" to distinguish him from Charles E. Wilson, president of General Motors and later Secretary of Defense, who was called "Engine Charlie.")

The trustees of the CED today reflect extensive interaction with business, financial, foundation, and governmental institutions, and include such men as the following:

William H. Franklin. Chairman of the Board of Trustees of the Committee on Economic Development. He is chairman of the Board of Caterpillar Tractor Co. and a director of Exxon Corporation.

Robert O. Anderson. Chairman of the Board, Atlantic Richfield Oil.

William S. Anderson. Chairman of the Board, National Cash Register.

Roy L. Ash. Former Director Office of Management and Budget (1973-75) under President Nixon. Former Chief Financial Officer, Hughes Aircraft Co., and later co-founder and president of Litton Industries. A director of the Bank of America, Global Marine, Inc., and a trustee of the California Institute of Technology.

James F. Bere. Chairman of the Board, Borg-Warner Corporation. A director of Abbott Laboratories, Continental Illinois National Bank and Trust Co.

Edward W. Carter. President of Broadway Hale Stores. A director of A.T.&.T., Southern California Edison, Del Monte Corporation, Western Bankcorporation, Pacific Mutual Life Insurance Co.

Frank T. Cary. Chairman of the Board, IBM.

Clifton C. Garvin, Jr. Chairman of the Board, Exxon Corporation, and a director of Citycorp, and the American Petroleum Institute.

[16] See David W. Eakins, "The Development of Corporate Liberal Policy Research," Ph.D. dissertation, University of Wisconsin, 1966 (Ann Arbor: University Microfilms, 1966).

Gabriel Hauge. President Manufacturers Hanover Trust Co., former editor of Business Week. A director of New York Life Insurance, America Metal Climax, American Home Products. A trustee of the Committee for Economic Development, Julliard School of Music, and the Carnegie Endowment for International Peace.

H. J. Heinz, II. Chairman of the Board, H. J. Heinz Co. He is a director of Mellon National Bank and Trust and a trustee of Carnegie-Mellon University. His son, H. J. Heinz, III, is U.S. Senator from Pennsylvania.

Edward R. Kaye. President I. E. duPont de Nemours & Co. and a director of Morgan Guaranty Trust Co. An earned Ph.D. in chemistry from M.I.T.

C. Peter McColough. Chairman of the Board, Xerox Corporation and a director of Citicorp.

Richard D. Wood. Chairman of the Board, Eli Lilly & Co. A director of Chemical Bank of New York, Elizabeth Arden, Inc., Standard Oil of Indiana, Lilly Endowment.

Ralph Lazarus. President, Federated Department Stores, Inc. He is a director of Chase Manhattan Bank, Scott Paper Co., General Electric, and a trustee of Dartmouth College.

George C. McGhee. Sole owner, McGhee Oil Company. Former U.S. Ambassador to Turkey, former Chairman of Policy Planning Council of the Department of State, and former Under-Secretary of State, and U.S. Ambassador to West Germany.

Chauncey J. Medberry, III. Chairman of the Board, Bank-America, and a director of Getty Oil Co.

John B. M. Place. Chairman of the Board, Anaconda Copper Co. and a director of Celenese Corp., Chemical Bank of New York, Communications Satellite Corp., Lever Brothers, and the Union Pacific Railroad.

J. L. Scott. Chairman of the Board, Great Atlantic and Pacific Tea Co. (A & P).

George P. Shultz. Former Secretary of Labor (1969-70). Director of the Office of Management and Budget (1970-72), and Secretary of Treasury (1972-74). Currently President of Bechtel Corporation and a director of J. P. Morgan & Co. and the Morgan Guaranty Trust Co. Former Dean of Graduate School of Business, University of Chicago.

Joseph L. Black. Chairman and Chief Executive Officer, Inland

Steel Company. A director of Chicago Board of Trade, Commonwealth Edison Co., Chicago First National Bank.

Jevis J. Babb. Former President and Chairman of the Board of Lever Brothers. A director of Sucrest Corporation, Universal Foods, Gruen Industries, Guardian Life Insurance, American Can Co., Bank of New York.

The CED immodestly claims, "Recommendations made by CED have a penetrating impact on the development of the consensus from which national and international policies emerge."[17] The immodesty, however, may be an honest appraisal of its true influence. The CED program, "Achieving Energy Independence" (December, 1974) proposed many of the components of the energy package presented to Congress by President Carter, including energy conservation measures, standby fuel rationing authority, and improved efficiency in the use of energy. The only difference between the CED proposal and the Carter plan was the CED's call for deregulation of interstate natural gas and old oil. The CED proposed as early as 1970 a public-service jobs program with temporary public-service employment funds allocated to cities with especially high unemployment rates. The Act was passed in 1974, and expanded in 1977. It was the CED which recommended to both Presidents Ford and Carter a "go slow" approach on nuclear energy, a halt to commercial nuclear fuel reprocessing plants, and prevention of the sale of nuclear plants to non-nuclear countries by the U.S. and European nations. The CED recommended federal assumption of current federal-state-local welfare programs into a single reformed income maintenance program; the CED claims its views have been a "major ingredient" in Carter's welfare reform proposals.

The Policy Planning Directors

A collective portrait of the directors of CFR, CED, and Brookings confirms the impressions derived from our brief biographies. The biographies "flesh out" the statistics in Table 1, and "naming names" reminds us that the leaders of the policy-planning organizations are real people. But the aggregate figures on corporate, gov-

---

[17] Committee for Economic Development, *Report of Activities 1976* (Washington: CED, 1977). 3.

ernmental, university, and civic organizations interlocking, as well as education and social character, also deserve attention.

First of all, it is clear that the policy-planning organizations do in fact provide structured linkages with the corporate world. The directors of our three policy-planning organizations averaged nearly four corporate directorships each; only sixteen percent of the policy-planning directors were *not* members of corporate boards.

Second, the directors of the policy-planning organizations have extensive government experience. They averaged 3.5 government posts during their careers; only 22 percent failed to report any governmental experience. The CFR directors *all* held governmental posts at one time or another in their careers. In contrast, half of the CED directors had never served in government. This is an important comment on the two organizations: clearly the CED directors are much more experienced in business.

Third, the policy-planning directors maintain an active interest in education. The average director held 1.8 university trusteeships; only 22 percent of our directors had *not* held a university trusteeship.

Fourth, it is clear that the policy-planning directors also form a bridge between their organizations and a wide range of civic and cultural organizations. The average director held three reported posts (not merely memberships) in civic and cultural associations. These included, for example, the Metropolitan Museum of Art and Lincoln Center; the Rockefeller, Ford, and Carnegie Foundations; and other policy-planning groups such as the Urban Institute, American Assembly, the Resources for the Future. Only 19 percent did *not* report holding official posts in civic or cultural organizations.

The coordinating function of the policy-planning directors is made strikingly clear when we observe that the directors averaged over twelve interlocking positions each! Certainly the policy planning organizations provide extensive linkages with the corporate, governmental, university, and civic and cultural institutions.

Regarding educational background, the policy-planning directors are distinctively "Ivy League." Over three quarters of the directors of CFR, CED, and Brookings graduated from just twelve prestigious universities. (A significant number [11.9 percent] graduated from the 30 private prestigious prep schools.) Over one-third of the policy-planning directors are lawyers; lawyers are particularly

TABLE 1

THE POLICY-PLANNING DIRECTORS: A COLLECTIVE PORTRAIT[*]

	CFR $N = 25$	CED[3] $N = 22$	Brookings $N = 20$	Total $N = 67$
Interlocking				
Corporate directorships				
Average number	3.7	3.8	4.6	3.9
(% with none)	(28%)	(4%)	(10%)	(16%)
Government offices				
Average number	4.6	2.8	3.0	3.5
(% with none)	(0%)	(50%)	(20%)	(22%)
University trusteeships				
Average number	1.7	1.5	2.3	1.8
(% with none)	(16%)	(36%)	(20%)	(22%)
Civic Assn. offices				
Average number	2.2	3.8	3.0	3.0
(% with none)	(20%)	(14%)	(25%)	(19%)
Total institutional affiliation				
Average number	12.0	11.8	12.9	12.2
Education				
Percent private prep school[1]	16.0%	17.4%	5.0%	11.9%
Percent college education	100.0%	100.0%	100.0%	100.0%
Percent prestigious univ.[2]	86.4%	63.6%	80.0%	76.1%
Percent with law degree	52.0%	18.0%	30.0%	34.3%
Percent graduate degree,				
including law	92.0%	72.7%	90.0%	85.0%
Social Character				
Percent Female (number)	4%(1)	0	15%(3)	6.0(4)
Percent Black (number)	4%(1)	0	5%(1)	3.0(2)
Average Age	58.8	59.0	59.5	59.0
Private Clubs				
Average number	1.8	1.5	1.5	1.6
(% with none)	(36%)	(41%)	(30%)	(35%)

[*] All data are for 1976. Source: Marquis, *Who's Who in America 1976-77.* Data on six directors was not available.

[1] Andover, Buckley, Cate, Catlin, Choate, Cranbrook, Country Day, Deerfield, Exeter, Episcopal, Gilman, Groton, Hill, Hotchkiss, Kingswood, Kent, Lakeside, Lawrenceville, Lincoln, Loomis, Middlesex, Milton, St. Andrew's, St. Christopher's, St. George's, St. Mark's, St. Paul's, Shattuck, Taft, Thatcher, Webb, Westminister, Woodbury.

[2] Harvard, Yale, Chicago, Stanford, Columbia, M.I.T., Cornell, Northwestern, Princeton, Johns Hopkins, Pennsylvania, and Dartmouth.

[3] CED actually claims 200 trustees; 22 were randomly selected for analysis. Trustees for CFR and Brookings represent total number, less those whose biographies did not appear in *Who's Who in America 1976-77.*

prevalent in the CFR, which draws heavily from the large, well-known New York and Washington law firms.   More important, perhaps, is the prevalence of post graduate education among the policy-planning directors—including law school, business school, and an impressive number of Ph.D.'s.   Fully 85 percent of these directors held earned post baccaulureate degrees; this figure does *not* include the numerous honorary degrees that these directors regularly collect.   This finding supports specualtions by other writers of the growing importance of expertise in policy planning.

Finally, we might observe that only six percent of the policy-planning directors are women, and three percent are black.   This is a recent phenonema.   A check against earlier information on the directors of CFR, CED, and Brookings showed that as late as 1971, there were *no* women or blacks on the governing boards of these organizations.

In addition to their impressive educational credentials, and a great deal of experience in corporate, governmental, university, and civic affairs, the policy-planning directors bring considerable experience in life itself to their jobs—their average age is 59.   However youthful the *staffs* of the policy-planning organizations may be, overall direction of these organizations is secure in the hands of experienced men of public affairs.   Membership in private clubs (emphasized as a coordinating device by some writers) was common: the average director reported 1.6 club memberships.   However, one-third did not report any club memberships, casting some doubt on the centrality of club membership in developing policy consensus.

In brief, the policy-planners have a great deal of experience in directing affairs in the corporate, governmental, university, and civic worlds.   They are extraordinarily well-educated with the vast majority holding advanced degrees.   Over three-quarters of them obtained these degrees from prestigious "Ivy League" universities.   And, of course, the policy-planning directors are overwhelmingly white, male, and middle-aged.

The Role of the "Proximate Policy-Makers"

What is, then, the role of the proximate policy-makers?"[18]   The

[18] The phrase "proximate policy-maker" is derived from political scientist Charles E. Lindbloom who uses the term to distinguish between citizens and

activities of the "proximate policy-makers"—the President, the Congress, federal agencies, congressional committees, White House staff, and interest groups—in the policy-making process have traditionally been the central focus of political science. Political scientists usually portray the activities of the proximate policy-makers as the *whole* of the policy-making process. But our oligarchic model of public policy-making views the activities of the proximate policy-makers as only the *final phase* of a much more complex process. This final stage is the open, public facet of policy making, and it attracts the attention of the mass media and most political scientists. The activities of the "proximate policy-makers" are much easier to study than the private actions of corporations, foundations, the mass media, and the policy-planning organizations.

Many scholars concentrate their attention on this final phase of public policy-making and conclude that policy-making is a process of bargaining, competition, persuasion, and compromise among interest groups and governmental officials. Undoubtedly bargaining, competition, persuasion, and compromises over policy issues continue throughout this final "law-making" phase of the policy-making process. And admittedly many elite recommendations fail to win the approval of Congress or the President in the first year or two they are proposed. Conflict between the President and Congress, or between Democrats or Republicans, or liberals and conservatives, and so forth, may delay or alter somewhat the final actions of the "proximate policy makers."

But the agenda for policy consideration has been set by other elites *before* the "proximate policy-makers" become actively involved in the policy-making process—the major directions of policy change have been determined, and the mass media has prepared the public for new policies and programs. The formal law-making process concerns itself with details of implementation: who gets the "political" credit; what agencies get control of the program; and exactly how much money will be spent. These are not unimportant questions, but they are raised and decided within the con-

---

elected officials: "Except in small political systems that can be run by something like a New England town meeting, not all citizens can be the immediate, or *proximate*, makers of policy. They yield the immediate (or proximate) task of decision to a small minority." Charles E. Lindbloom, *The Policy-Making Process* (Englewood Cliffs: Prentice Hall, 1968), 30.

text of policy goals and directions which have already been determined. The decisions of the "proximate policy-makers" tend to center about the *means* rather than the *ends* of public policy.

Summary

Our "oligarchic model of the policy-making process" attempts to provide a more developed version of the elitist model of policy formation. It suggests *how* elites go about the task of deciding about national policy. It specifies the organizations—the Council on Foreign Relations, the Committee on Economic Development, and the Brookings Institution, for example—which research, initiate, and develop consensus on behalf of broad national policy objectives. It posits linkage between the corporate and financial worlds and government decision-making, through a complex pattern of interaction involving foundations, universities, the mass media, and especially policy-planning organizations. It suggests ways in which elite consensus is developed and then communicated to government decision-makers.

The data presented here on these three policy-planning organizations—the Council on Foreign Relations, Committee on Economic Development, and Brookings Institution—are meant to be illustrative. We do not pretend that this data provides an adequate test of our model. While data on interlocking directorates is not unimportant, it must be supplemented by further investigation into other means of interaction among policy organizations. We may want to ask "proximate policy-makers" about their interactions with, and perceptions of, the organizations and individuals who are posited by this model as influential in policy determination. We may want to trace carefully the origins of a number of other key policy decisions to ascertain what role, if any, was played by these organizations and individuals. In short, we hope to encourage research into the private, non-governmental phases of national policy-making.

Years ago, Harold Lasswell defined politics as "the study of influence and the influential."[19] But we have arbitrarily narrowed the discipline of political science to the study of government. Per-

[19] Harold Lasswell, *Politics: Who Gets What, When, How* (New York: McGraw Hill Co., 1936), 1.

haps we should reconsider Professor Lasswell's advice and rededi-
cate ourselves to the study of the origins of public policy, to the
uses of influence, and to the identification of the truly influential
organizations and individuals in American society.

The Prospects for Regulatory Reform: The Legacy of Reagan's First Term

Michael Fix†
George C. Eads††

Four years ago, when the Reagan Administration was about to embark on its first term in office, it announced that "regulatory relief" would be a cornerstone of its economic program.[1] The Administration spoke of eliminating hundreds of obsolete and inefficient regulations,[2] revising major regulatory statutes like the Clean Air Act,[3] and even abolishing several regulatory agencies.[4] As Reagan's second term begins, regulatory issues are no longer so prominent. The words "regulatory relief" are no longer heard. Indeed, the only politically realistic prospects for statutory change involve strengthening, not weakening, major social regulatory statutes. And the only regulatory agency abolished has been the Civil Aeronautics Board, a victim of legislation passed during the *Carter* presidency.[5]

It would be a mistake, however, to consider the Reagan Administration's regulatory activities during its first term a failure. The Administration has surely left its mark on regulation. And in some areas—like presidential control over the rulemaking process—its changes are likely to be permanent. Nevertheless, the Administration did not achieve many of its stated objectives. Perhaps more importantly, prospects for achieving some of these objectives are less favorable now than when the Administration first took office—due, in some part, to the way it has handled regulatory activities, particularly during its first two and a half years.

† Senior Research Associate, The Urban Institute.
†† Dean of the School of Public Affairs, University of Maryland, College Park. Between June 1979 and January 1981, member of President Carter's Council of Economic Advisors and chairman of the Regulatory Analysis Review Group. This article was written under the general auspices of The Urban Institute's Changing Domestic Priorities Project, which is examining changes in domestic policies advanced by the Reagan Administration. Support from the Ford and John D. & Catherine T. MacArthur Foundations is gratefully acknowledged. The opinions expressed are, however, those of the authors.

1. *See, e.g.,* D. Stockman, Avoiding a GOP Economic Dunkirk (1980) (arguing that regulatory relief is necessary to avoid a "quantum scale-up of the much discussed regulatory burden") (unpaginated memorandum on file with the *Yale Journal on Regulation*).
2. *See, e.g., id.*.
3. *See, e.g., id.*.
4. *See generally Deregulation HQ: An Interview on the New Executive Order with Murray L. Weidenbaum and James C. Miller III*, REGULATION, Mar.-Apr. 1981, at 14.
5. *See* Airline Deregulation Act of 1978, Pub. L. No. 95-504, § 40, 92 Stat. 1705, 1744 (1978) (codified at 49 U.S.C. § 1551 (1982)).

293

As the Administration begins its second term, it seems appropriate to examine the regulatory legacy of the first four Reagan years. Section I of this Article describes the proposals for regulatory reform that were competing for support at the end of the Carter presidency. Section II analyzes the Administration's regulatory efforts during its first term and draws on this analysis to speculate about what reforms are politically possible in the second term. Section III focuses on the second-term prospects for regulatory change in four major areas that tell us something about the legacy of regulatory relief: the expanded use of market mechanisms; the devolution of regulatory authority to the states; the White House regulatory oversight function; and the revision of major aspirational statutes. The Article concludes by noting that absent significant legislative change, the legacy of the Reagan regulatory program will be an expansion of administrative discretion and presidential control over social regulation. Ironically, this will leave future presidents better equipped to reconstruct the regulatory edifice Ronald Reagan once promised to dismantle.

I.   The Emerging Consensus in the Late 1970's for Regulatory Reform

By the end of the Carter Administration, a consensus had emerged among many economists and policymakers that economic and social regulation was overly expensive, inflexible, arbitrary, and ineffective. Although many disagreed over what should be done, recognition of the need for reform cut across party lines and traditional political affiliations. Many policymakers believed that the economic costs of regulation were excessive. This sentiment was bolstered by Murray Weidenbaum's estimate that the current regulatory policy was costing $100 billion a year.[6] Other estimates of the costs attributable to specific regulatory rules and of the costs incurred by specific sectors of the economy also supported this contention.[7] The EPA, for example, estimated the cumulative cost of achieving clean

---

6. Weidenbaum, *On Estimating Regulatory Costs*, REGULATION, May-June 1978, at 14 (costs of regulation in 1979 "may top $100 billion").

7. *See, e.g.,* Portney, *The Macroeconomic Impacts of Federal Environmental Regulation* in, THE MACROECONOMIC IMPACTS OF FEDERAL ENVIRONMENTAL REGULATION, 25, 30 (H. Peskin, P. Portney, A. Kneese eds. 1982).

Virtually all analysts offering cost estimates conceded that they had not attempted to measure the social benefits of regulation and offset those benefits against estimated regulatory costs. *See, e.g.,* M. WEIDENBAUM & R. DEFINA, THE COST OF FEDERAL REGULATION OF ECONOMIC ACTIVITY 3 (1978)(American Enterprise Institute Reprint No. 88). Indeed, studies failed to show that regulation was a significant factor affecting the conventional indicators of economic performance—inflation, production, economic growth and unemployment. *See, e.g.,* E. DENISON, ACCOUNTING FOR SLOWER ECONOMIC GROWTH 122-44 (1979). But these facts did not lessen the impact cost estimates had on regulatory policy.

air and water alone would total more than $360 billion between 1977 and 1986.[8]

Policymakers also noted that regulatory institutions tended to be highly inflexible and arbitrary, imposing costly inefficiencies on affected businesses.[9] Bardach and Kagan argued that regulators adopted strict, legalistic enforcement approaches to avoid the criticism and political pressure which accompany even the appearance of undue leniency.[10] They demonstrated that rigid adherence to rules left inspection routines insensitive to the unique characteristics of businesses and industries. Other critics observed that command and control regimes contributed to the system's arbitrariness and inflexibility. They argued that such regimes relied too heavily on highly prescriptive design standards and on detailed, inflexible rules that failed to account for diversity among regulated entities and created the impression of arbitrary patterns of enforcement.[11] The volume of information disclosure and paperwork required for regulatory compliance was also criticized.[12]

Perhaps the most damning criticism offered was that many regulatory schemes were simply not effective. This criticism focused on the lack of evidence of success by regulatory agencies. For example, although studies found that automobile accidents per mile traveled were decreasing, critics noted that the studies also showed that this trend predated the founding of the National Highway Traffic Safety Administration.[13] Similarly, Lave and Omenn attributed the major portion of improvements in air quality during the 1970's to the switch from coal to oil in electric power generation rather than to standards issued under the Clean Air Act.[14] Not surprisingly, such studies were controversial and were criticized for failing to consider what might have occurred in the absence of federal standards.

Some commentators went so far as to argue that regulation was *per se*

---

8. ADMINISTRATOR OF THE ENVIRONMENTAL PROTECTION AGENCY, THE COST OF CLEAN AIR AND WATER, S. DOC. NO. 38, 96th Cong., 1st Sess. 8 (1979) (figures presented in 1977 dollars).

9. E. BARDACH & R. KAGAN, GOING BY THE BOOK: THE PROBLEM OF REGULATORY UNREASONABLENESS 105 (1982).

10. *Id.* at 207-08.

11. *See, e.g.,* Kahn, *Regulation and the Imagination,* in INNOVATIVE TECHNIQUES IN THEORY AND PRACTICE 1, 5-7 (1980) (Proceedings of a Regulatory Council Conference).

12. As Charles Schultze stated in his Godkin lectures at Harvard University: "The more complicated and extensive the social intervention, the more difficult it becomes to accumulate the necessary information at a central level. It is relatively easy to set up a system for payroll records from which to determine social security benefits. . . ." In contrast, "an efficient regulatory scheme to control the discharge of pollution into the nation's waterways requires that regulatory authorities know the production function, the range of technologies for pollution control and the demand curve of every major polluter." C. SCHULTZE, THE PUBLIC USE OF PRIVATE INTEREST 20 (1977).

13. S. PELTZMAN, REGULATION OF AUTOMOBILE SAFETY 24 (1975). *But see* Graham & Garber, *Evaluating the Effects of Automobile Safety Regulation,* 3 J. PUB. ANAL. MGMT. 206 (1984).

14. L. LAVE & G. OMENN, CLEARING THE AIR: REFORMING THE CLEAN AIR ACT 1 (1981).

295

an unwise form of social control.[15] Others asserted that regulators lacked the ability to control more than a minute fraction of the billions of individual decisions made daily concerning health and safety.[16] These critics argued that market mechanisms, such as product liability laws and insurance, might be more effective means to influence social behavior.[17]

The above-mentioned critiques, taken together, represented a forceful indictment of regulatory excesses. Each of Ronald Reagan's three predecessors had tried to bring these excesses of regulation under control.[18] The legacy of those efforts—the broadest of which was advanced by the Carter Administration[19]—was the emergence of a rough consensus both inside government and among academic critics on the proper underlying principles for regulatory reform.

This consensus reflected a belief that individual reforms should be neutral in character and application, and should not be dictated by political expediency. It also included a recognition that, although reform did not require expanding the scale of regulatory institutions, it did require strengthening their capabilities. Moreover, most advocates of reform agreed deregulation was appropriate in traditional areas of economic regulation, but inappropriate in areas of social regulation. They believed that the inevitable market imperfections in areas into which regulation had been introduced in the 1960's and 1970's required that such regulation be made more efficient rather than eliminated.[20] Regulatory reform was also

---

15. *See, e.g.,* Reynolds, *A Free Market in Energy,* in INSTEAD OF REGULATION 67 (R. Poole, ed. 1982); Meiners, *What to do About Hazardous Products,* in *id.* at 285.

16. *See, e.g.,* L. LAVE, THE STRATEGY OF SOCIAL REGULATION 2-3 (1981).

17. *See, e.g.,* G. EADS & P. REUTER, DESIGNING SAFER PRODUCTS: CORPORATE RESPONSES TO PRODUCT LIABILITY AND PRODUCT SAFETY REGULATION 120-38 (1984).

18. *See, e.g.,* G. EADS & M. FIX, RELIEF OR REFORM? 45-68 (1984).

19. The Carter Administration attempted to reduce administrative expenses and compliance costs and to improve regulatory coherence by strengthening the power of the President to oversee regulatory activity. The Carter efforts included the creation of an explicit presidential oversight role through the Paperwork Reduction Act of 1980, Pub. L. No. 96-511, 94 Stat. 2812 (codified at 44 U.S.C. §§ 3501-3520) (1982), and the creation of the Regulatory Analysis Review Group as an expert regulatory "watchdog." The Administration also created the Regulatory Council to help develop and encourage the use of more cost-effective forms of regulation. The Council later prepared an agenda of regulatory reform proposals which stressed: (1) enhancement of presidential oversight; (2) institutionalization of cost-benefit regulatory assessment procedures; (3) adoption of flexible regulatory alternatives and market mechanisms in lieu of traditional command and control regulation; and (4) further examination of non-governmental solutions (such as greater insurance availability) to problems previously viewed as primarily regulatory in character. *See generally* U.S. REGULATORY COUNCIL, REGULATORY REFORM HIGHLIGHTS 1970-80: SUMMARY AND FINDINGS 1-5 (1980).

20. The term social regulation has over the past few years been applied to the set of federal programs that use regulatory techniques to achieve broad social goals—a cleaner environment, safer and more healthful workplaces, safer and more effective consumer products, and equal employment opportunities. (The term protective regulation is also used to refer to these programs.) *See, e.g.,* National Environmental Policy Act of 1969, 42 U.S.C. § 4321 (1970) (establishing EPA). Most programs of social regulation originated in the 1960's and 1970's, although some—the programs of the Food and Drug Administration and the Department of Agriculture—go back several decades. *See, e.g.,* Act of Oct. 31, 1949, ch. 792, § 401, 63 Stat. 1054 (current version at 7 U.S.C. § 1421-49

considered to be a slow, incremental process. Because regulators and regulated entities had substantial sunk costs in existing regulatory regimes, the constituency supporting reform was small and politically unstable. It was therefore seen as crucial that the reforms proceed in a careful manner, so that public support would not be undermined.

II. The Regulatory Relief Efforts of the Reagan Administration During Its First Term

The regulatory relief program implemented by the Reagan Administration was based upon an entirely different set of premises from those underlying the earlier consensus. These premises were grounded in the libertarian view that most economic and social regulation was an unwarranted intrusion of the federal government into private decision-making. The 1982 Economic Report of the President clearly articulated this position:

> Many government programs, such as detailed safety regulations or the provision of specific goods (rather than money) to the poor, are best described as paternalistic. Paternalism occurs when the government is reluctant to let individuals make decisions for themselves and seeks to protect them from the possible bad effects of their own decisions by outlawing certain actions. Paternalism has the effect of disallowing certain preferences or actions. . . . There is no reason to think that commands from government can do a better job of increasing an individual's economic welfare than the individual can by making choices himself. Moreover, the long-term costs of paternalism may be to destroy an individual's ability to make decisions for himself.[21]

Advocates of this perspective sought a wholesale repeal of economic *and* social regulatory regimes. The recent success of deregulatory efforts in areas of economic regulation was interpreted as indicating that deregulation in areas of social regulation was also feasible and desirable. Hence, the goal of regulatory relief was not to reform social regulation, but to elimi-

---

(1982)) (establishing price supports for agricultural commodities).

An important distinguishing feature of social regulation (especially to economists) is that one cannot expect even properly functioning markets to produce the goals that social regulation seeks. As far as economists are concerned, the problems of environmental pollution, excessive levels of workplace hazards, or unsafe consumer products exist largely because "commodities" like environmental quality, workplace safety, and product safety do not trade in markets. Economists work hard to devise ways to simulate markets for such "commodities," arguing that if this could be done, the goals of social regulation could be achieved at far less cost and with far less government interference in the details of business decision-making. But even the most optimistic of the economists' schemes contemplate some continued federal regulatory presence.

21. ECONOMIC REPORT OF THE PRESIDENT 42 (1982).

297

nate it, thereby removing impediments to economic growth and to the promotion of personal responsibility.

The new Administration originally accorded regulatory relief a place on its agenda equal to that given budget, tax, and monetary policy. The Reagan regulatory program was implemented much more quickly than the regulatory reform measures of previous administrations. It was based upon a theory of economic decisionmaking that places great weight on the value of "shocking" and was intended to "shock" regulatory expectations downward.[22] This objective is articulated in David Stockman's "Dunkirk" memo, which called for a "dramatic substantial rescission of the regulatory burden for the short-term cash flow relief it will provide to business firms and the long-term signal it will provide for corporate investment planners."[23]

The Reagan regulatory relief program consisted of three principal strategies. First, dozens of pending and existing administrative regulations would be delayed, rescinded, or revised. Second, agency enforcement policies and practices were to be altered to make the regulatory process more cooperative and less combative. Third, the federal regulatory bureaucracy was to be harnessed by strengthening presidential oversight of the regulatory process, by limiting the discretion of federal regulators, and by transferring their responsibilities to the states.

A. Strengthening Presidential Oversight

The centerpiece of regulatory relief was Executive Order 12,291,[24] which centralized regulatory oversight within the Office of Information and Regulatory Affairs (OIRA) of the Office of Management and Budget and called for the promulgation of a uniform cost-benefit standard that all regulations would be required to meet to ". . . the extent permitted by law."[25] In some respects the Order represented an extension of efforts

22. The Reagan Administration's economic game plan relied heavily on an immediate "expectations" shock — and on reaping its reward. Applying this approach to regulatory relief, it becomes immediately clear that the actual timing of any relief that might be forthcoming would have less impact on business decisions than the secure knowledge that relief would in fact occur. *See, e.g.,* G. EADS & M. FIX, *supra* note 18, at 42 (1984).

23. D. Stockman, *supra* note 1.

24. Exec. Order No. 12,291, 3 C.F.R. 127 (1982).

25. *Id.* at 128. In several respects, the Reagan program represented a departure from past policy. First, it effectively shifted the burden of demonstrating that proposed regulations were cost effective from the White House to the agencies. Second, although it preserved requirements for regulatory impact analyses for "major" regulations (i.e., those having an impact estimated at more than $100 million), it vested far greater discretion in the White House to designate as "major" regulations not meeting the dollar requirement and to exempt from analysis others that did. Third, for the first time cost-benefit analyses of regulations promulgated by executive branch agencies were made mandatory — except where prohibited by law. Fourth, where regulatory reviews had previously been distributed among several executive branch offices and departments (such as the Regulatory Analysis Review

taken during the Carter Administration to enhance the President's role in overseeing the regulatory process. Indeed, on its face the order did not constitute a major departure from Executive Order 12,044, promulgated during the Carter years.[26] The differences lay elsewhere—in practice and in the two administrations' underlying philosophies.

The Reagan order as implemented was criticized immediately for its lack of openness and questionable legitimacy.[27] By not requiring that OMB disclose comments made to agencies regarding changes in proposed or existing rules, the order converted OMB's role in the regulatory review process into an analogue of its behind-the-scenes efforts to prepare the federal budget. Critics pointed out, however, that while the President's budget is reviewed and revised by the Congress, federal regulations do not benefit from debate in a comparably democratic forum.[28]

Imprudent comments by OMB officials,[29] continuing criticism regarding OMB officials' vulnerability to *ex parte* and unrecorded contacts with regulated entities, and the small and diminishing resources of OIRA raised serious doubts about the possible neutrality of the new OMB review process.[30] These concerns eventually began to stimulate reform proposals. For example, a key provision of Congressman Sam Hall's generic regulatory reform bill would have expressly prohibited the director of

Group and the Council on Wage and Price Stability), Executive Order 12,291 concentrated those functions within OMB's Office of Information and Regulatory Affairs (OIRA). Fifth, the process established by the Executive Order provided officers at OIRA not one, but two occasions for reviewing proposed regulations: their adequacy was reviewed before their promulgation in both proposed and final forms and OIRA was given the power to order delay of publication of contested rules while differences with the relevant agency were ironed out. See STAFF OF HOUSE COMM. ON ENERGY AND COMMERCE, PRESIDENTIAL CONTROL OF AGENCY RULEMAKING: AN ANALYSIS OF CONSTITUTIONAL ISSUES WHICH MAY BE RAISED BY EXECUTIVE ORDER 12,291, at 12-13 (Comm. Print 1981) [hereinafter cited as PRESIDENTIAL CONTROL].

26. *See* Exec. Order No. 12,044, 3 C.F.R. 152 (1979).

27. PRESIDENTIAL CONTROL, *supra* note 25, at 60.

28. *Id.* at 54.

29. One of the most widely reported statements along these lines was made by Boyden Gray, Counsel to the Vice President, in a speech to the U.S. Chamber of Commerce. Gray told his audience to bring their problems with regulatory agencies to his attention. Gray reiterated his willingness to smooth out regulatory problems in an appearance before a House Subcommittee, declaring: "If you have a problem, if you think that they [the agency] are not recognizing and paying attention to the material that you give them, bring the material to me and or to us and we will see then what the problem is." *Role of OMB in Regulation, 1981: Hearing Before the Subcomm. on Oversight and Investigations of the House Comm. on Energy and Commerce*, 97th Cong., 1st Sess. 54 (1981).

30. *See* STAFF OF SUBCOMM. ON OVERSIGHT AND INVESTIGATION OF THE HOUSE ENERGY AND COMMERCE COMM., 98TH CONG., 2D SESS., REPORT ON THE PRESIDENT'S CLAIM OF EXECUTIVE PRIVILEGE OVER EPA DOCUMENTS, ABUSES IN THE SUPERFUND PROGRAM AND OTHER MATTERS 282-94 (Comm. Print 1984). The report observed that the OMB had at times "served as a conduit for affected industries by allowing the industries to comment directly to OMB on draft proposed rules and then passing the industry comments along to EPA as OMB's own." *Id.* at 292. Four Republicans on the 13 member committee dissented from the report. *Id.* at 295.

299

OMB from participating in "any way in deciding what regulatory action, if any, the agency will take in any rule-making proceeding."[31]

B. Constraining Agency Discretion

The Administration made three major managerial changes during the first term: steep budget cuts, agency reorganizations, and the appointment of ideologically uniform administrators. A number of regulatory agencies had their budgets reduced between fiscal year 1980 and fiscal year 1984.[32] Hardest hit were agencies regulating the environment, land use, and consumer affairs, and agencies administering traditional economic regulation.[33] A series of reorganizations also affected agency staffing and capacity. For example, proposed changes at the Federal Trade Commission[34] and at the Office of Surface Mining[35] led to an exodus of seasoned enforcement staff and to a concentration of agency authority and activities in Washington instead of at agency regional offices. Repeated reorganizations of the Environmental Protection Agency's Enforcement Division also left that critical agency office in disarray.[36] Finally, many of the Reagan Administration's early appointments, particularly those at the sub-Cabinet level, were characterized more by ideological uniformity than by relevant administrative or political experience.[37] Taken together, these strategies seemed designed to constrain agency discretion and were widely perceived as having reduced regulatory capabilities.

C. Transferring Regulatory Authority to the States

The third area in which the Administration attempted to leave an institutional imprint was the transfer of regulatory authority and responsibility to the states. The Administration expected the transfer to speed up the regulatory process, broaden it to involve parties with the most complete

31. H.R. No. 2327, 98th Cong., 1st Sess. § 624(a) (1983).

32. G. EADS & M. FIX, supra note 18, at 151.

33. ·Id.

34. See Proposed Closing of Four FTC Regional Offices: Hearing Before Subcomm. on Commerce, Consumer, and Monetary Affairs of the House Comm. on Government Operations, 97th Cong., 2nd Sess. 1 (1982).

35. See Office of Surface Mining, Denver, Colorado: Hearing Before the Subcomm. on Civil Service of the House Comm. on Post Office & Civil Service, 97th Cong., 1st Sess. 16 (1982). The Office of Surface Mining reorganization program led to a 49% attrition rate between January 1981 and June 1982 in the office's staffing in the GS-1 to GS-15 civil service grades, only about half of whom were replaced by the end of October 1982. Letter from Rep. Patricia Schroeder, Chairperson, Subcomm. on Civil Service, House Comm. on Post Office and Civil Service, to James Watt, Secretary of the Interior (Oct. 28, 1982) (letter on file with the Yale Journal on Regulation).

36. J. CLAYBROOK, RETREAT FROM SAFETY: REAGAN'S ATTACK ON AMERICAN HEALTH 128 (1984).

37. Anne Gorsuch's appointment as Administrator of the EPA is one example. See N. Y. Times, Feb. 20, 1981, at A23, col. 2.

knowledge of regulatory impact, and increase its efficiency by enhancing the flow of information between regulators and regulated entities. The 1982 Economic Report to the President demonstrates the Administration's whole-hearted endorsement of this transfer of authority:

> Regulation should take place at the appropriate level of government. The primary economic reason for most regulation is the existence of external effects. The costs or tolerance of these external effects may vary among locations. Economic efficiency, therefore, calls for the degree and type of regulation to vary also. National standards tend to be too severe in some regions, while being too lax in others. Federal regulations should be limited to situations where the actions in one State have substantial external effects in other States, constitutional rights are involved, or interstate commerce would be significantly disrupted by differences in local regulations.[38]

Consistent with these premises, the pace of formal delegation of federal regulatory responsibility to the states was quickened,[39] regulations governing the transfer of that authority were relaxed,[40] and both the formal and informal oversight of states activities by federal regulatory agencies was reduced.[41]

The Administration's *modus operandi* in effecting the transfer, however, undercut political support. At the same time states were being called on to assume a greater share of the national regulatory burden, the federal government sharply reduced its funding for state programs. For example, although new state obligations to control pollutants mounted between 1980 and 1984, EPA grants to support state environmental programs fell in real terms by one-third.[42] Moreover, budget restrictions hampered the

---

38. *See* ECONOMIC REPORT OF THE PRESIDENT, *supra* note 21, at 166.

39. For example, 27 state delegations of Phase I program authority under the Resources Conservation and Recovery Act, 42 U.S.C. § 6926 (1982), were completed during the first 24 months of the Reagan Administration. G. EADS & M. FIX, *supra* note 18, at 214-15. Although prior efforts of the Carter administration and program maturity are responsible for a significant proportion of these delegations, it is clear that the Reagan administration has accelerated the rate at which formal delegations such as these have proceeded. *Id.* at 220; *see also* COUNCIL ON ENVIRONMENTAL QUALITY, ENVIRONMENTAL QUALITY 1982, at 10 (1982).

40. For instance, in October 1981 the Office of Surface Mining revised by rulemaking what is termed the "State Window Rule" to relax requirements state programs would have to satisfy to be eligible for program delegation. 46 Fed. Reg. 53,376 (1981) (codified as amended at 30 C.F.R. §§ 730-732 (1984)).

41. An example is the Environmental Protection Agency's adoption of a revised review process, 47 Fed. Reg. 27,073 (1982) (to be codified at 40 C.F.R. pt. 52), which streamlined approvals of amendments to State Implementation Plans (SIP) under the Clean Air Act, 42 U.S.C. § 7410 (1982). From January 1981 through October 1982, the number of SIP revisions pending dropped 97%, from 643 to 20. G. EADS & M. FIX, *supra* note 18, at 226.

42. CONGRESSIONAL BUDGET OFFICE, THE BUDGET OF THE ENVIRONMENTAL PROTECTION AGENCY: AN OVERVIEW OF SELECTED PROPOSALS FOR 1985, at 7 (1984). State obligations to control pollutants are discussed at *supra* note 40.

301

implementation of innovative regulatory techniques, such as emissions trading, which relied heavily on state participation and required substantial front-end expenditures.

Furthermore, the Administration's selective enthusiasm for regulatory federalism called the neutrality of the strategy into question. The Administration's treatment of the regulation of hazardous workplaces provides a good example. Within weeks after Reagan took office, the Occupational Safety and Health Administration (OSHA) withdrew a proposed federal standard designed to provide information to employees about chemical hazards in the workplace.[43] After the withdrawal, a number of states and localities passed their own employee "right to know" statutes.[44] However, following complaints by affected companies over the stringent new state and local regulatory regimes[45] and assertions that a uniform federal standard was needed,[46] OSHA reentered the field promulgating new rules. OSHA prohibited states from adopting regulations more stringent than it had promulgated and from regulating industry categories not covered by federal regulations.[47] Federal preemption was complete.[48]

III.   The Impact of the Administration's Approach on Future Efforts for Regulatory Reform

At the end of its first term, the Reagan Administration was able to claim a measure of success for its regulatory relief program. It had reduced the number of new regulations promulgated by the federal government,[49] rescinded a number of regulations pending at the time of Reagan's election,[50] and strengthened and expanded presidential oversight of the regulatory process.[51] In some areas regulatory responsibility had been shifted to the states,[52] and some progress had been made in reducing regulatory costs.[53] Productivity gains for business had been stimulated, al-

---

43.   46 Fed. Reg. 12,214 (1981) (withdrawing notice of proposed rulemaking setting forth proposed standard requiring employers to identify hazardous chemicals in workplace).

44.   See Foote, *Beyond the Politics of Federalism: An Alternative Model*, 1 YALE J. ON REG. 217, 221-22 & n.18 (1984).

45.   See, e.g., *Office of Management and Budget Control of OSHA Rulemaking: Hearings Before the Subcomm. on Manpower and Housing of the House Comm. on Government Operations*, 97th Cong., 2d Sess. 21 (1982) (testimony of George H. R. Taylor, Director, Department of Occupational Safety and Health, AFL-CIO) [hereinafter cited as *Hearings*].

46.   See, e.g., *An OSHA Rule Industry Wants Despite the Cost*, BUS. WK., Nov. 7, 1983, at 47.

47.   48 Fed. Reg. 53,280 (1983) (codified at 29 C.F.R. § 1910 (1984)).

48.   See Foote, *supra* note 44, at 222-24.

49.   See, e.g., G. EADS & M. FIX, *supra* note 18, at 166-67.

50.   *Id.* at 168, 180.

51.   See generally *id.* at 108-12.

52.   See *id.* at 220.

53.   See *id.* at 236-37.

though not nearly to the extent claimed by the Administration.[54] The Reagan Administration, however, had not achieved its broader goal of rolling back social regulation permanently. Few enduring changes had been made, and, by 1984, institutional and political support for broad regulatory reform had eroded. The generally unpromising atmosphere for social reform resulted from two early strategic miscalculations.

The first miscalculation occurred close to the outset of Reagan's first term. The Administration imported into the arena of social regulation the deregulatory·strategies and rhetoric which had been previously employed in the realm of economic regulation.[55] The result was a set of strategies which led to a deterioration of institutional capacity in many regulatory agencies. Between 1980 and 1984, federal agencies responsible for regulating the environment, land use, and consumer protection were subjected to reductions in staff and budget on the same scale as a number of independent agencies which were being phased out of existence by statute.[56] This reduced strength made it virtually impossible for many agencies to carry out their unchanged statutory missions. Viewed as neglecting their legal obligations, the agencies became vulnerable to criticism from the press, the Congress, and the public. Reduced capacity also left rule changes vulnerable to legal challenge, since diminished resources made it difficult for agencies to provide the analytic support required to justify proposed shifts in agency rules.

The second miscalculation was the Administration's apparent indifference to the need for neutrality in regulatory procedures and outcomes. Critics condemned highly discretionary enforcement strategies, oversight procedures which remained shielded from public view, and delegation strategies that appeared indifferent to state and local capability.[57] These critics suspected that the lessened adversarial enforcement approaches, in-

54. *See* Christiansen & Haveman, *The Reagan Administration's Regulatory Relief Effort: A Mid-term Assessment,* in THE REAGAN REGULATORY STRATEGY: AN ASSESSMENT 49, 69-70, 78-79 (G. Eads & M. Fix eds. 1984) [hereinafter cited as REGULATORY STRATEGY].

55. Rhetorically, Administration spokesmen were reported to advocate the dramatic, wholesale revision of major social regulatory statutes. For example, in December 1983, Christopher DeMuth, then head of OIRA, reportedly called for the development of a second-term regulatory agenda which would "replace the Clean Air and Water Acts and related environmental laws with laws that emphasize economic incentives rather than mandatory federal standards." C. DeMuth, Regulatory Policy 8 (Dec. 9, 1983) (unpublished memorandum on file with the *Yale Journal on Regulation*).

56. After accounting for inflation, the percentage decreases in budget authority of the EPA, the Office of Surface Mining, and the Consumer Product Safety Commission between 1980 and 1984 were about as drastic as those experienced by the Civil Aeronautics Board. G. EADS & M. FIX, *supra* note 18, at 152-53.

57. *See, e.g., Hearings, supra* note 45, at 10 (1982) (statement of George H. R. Taylor, Director, Department of Occupational Safety and Health, AFL-CIO); *see also* PRESIDENTIAL CONTROL, *supra* note 25, at 7.

303

creased centralization, and accelerated delegation were simply attempts to bring about *de facto* deregulation.

Near the end of Reagan's first term, the Administration seemed to lose its interest in regulatory relief. The Administration had suffered a major public relations debacle at EPA. Moreover, the political divisions between proponents of regulatory restraint and regulatory activism deepened, with the debate over social regulation taking on a moral tone.[58] With an election approaching, Administration rhetoric became conciliatory,[59] abandoning the bellicose anti-regulation threats heard in the Republican Platform of August 1980.[60] Regulatory change moved very much off the center of the political stage.

The change was not merely one of style. A set of controversial appointees were replaced,[61] and, at least for the moment, agency budget cuts slowed. Indeed, at the most politically visible regulatory agency—EPA—previous budget cuts were reversed with the assent of the Office of Management and Budget.[62] Even the language of regulatory change was altered. The term "regulatory relief" was no longer operative, having been replaced by its more traditional forerunner, "regulatory reform."[63]

Did this mean that a chastened and wiser Reagan Administration was ready to return to the path charted by the Ford and Carter administrations? Certainly, by the end of its first term, the Administration appeared to be moving away from the political rhetoric of regulatory relief towards a more traditional if subdued policy of regulatory reform. At least in the short run, however, the charged political environment the Administration had created by the end of its first term was a serious impediment to such reform in the second term.

---

58. The tenor of regulatory debate that was taking place towards the end of the first Reagan term is reflected, in part, by the titles of the literature then emerging on the Reagan social regulatory effort. Among the most widely noted were: S. TOLCHIN & M. TOLCHIN, DISMANTLING AMERICA: THE RUSH TO DEREGULATE (1983); J. LASH, K. GILLMAN & D. SHERIDAN, A SEASON OF SPOILS: THE STORY OF THE REAGAN ADMINISTRATION'S ATTACK ON THE ENVIRONMENT (1984); J. CLAYBROOK, RETREAT FROM SAFETY: REAGAN'S ATTACK ON AMERICAN HEALTH (1984).

59. *See* Green, *Reagan: The Liberal Democrat,* N.Y. Times, Aug. 15, 1984, at A23, col. 5.

60. "The Republican Party declares war on government overregulation. We pledge to cut down on federal paperwork, cut out excessive regulation, and cut back on the bloated bureaucracy." 126 CONG. REC. 20,625 (1980).

61. *See* Stansfield, *Ruckelshaus and Clark Seek to Blunt Environmental Lobby's Political Swords,* NAT'L J., June 30, 1984, at 1256.

62. *See* Mosher, *Ruckelshaus's First Mark on EPA- Another $165.5 Million for Its Budget,* NAT'L J., June 25, 1983, at 1344.

63. *See, e.g.,* DeMuth, *A Strategy for Regulatory Reform,* REGULATION, Mar.-Apr. 1984, at 25.

304

IV.   The Prospects for Regulatory Reform in the Second Term: Four Crucial Areas

As the Reagan Administration begins its second term, prospects for sweeping regulatory change appear dim, though not universally bleak. This Section identifies three areas of reform in which the Reagan Administration has endorsed change and significant progress is possible: (1) the development and adoption of market-oriented regulatory innovations, (2) the transfer of regulatory authority to the states, and (3) increased presidential oversight of the regulatory process. The section also examines the possibility of obtaining statutory revision of "aspirational"[64] social legislation and makes clear that obtaining enduring regulatory reform requires a higher level of political commitment, skill, and patience than has been exhibited by the Administration's attempts at regulatory relief.

A.   *Market Oriented Regulatory Innovations*

By the late 1970's, substantial attention had focused on market-oriented regulatory techniques as a more flexible and efficient alternative to the traditional command and control regimes.[65] It was believed that by decentralizing decision-making and reducing the role of the federal government, market-based alternatives would better account for the diversity of regulated entities, reduce paperwork burdens, and conserve agency resources. Reformers hoped that the new strategies would provide regulated firms with a stronger incentive to comply with regulations, disclose information, and reduce litigation.[66]

Although market-based reforms were supposed to accomplish these sub-

---

64. *See infra* note 116.
65. The market-oriented alternatives to "command and control" regulatory techniques identified by the Regulatory Council during the Carter Administration included the following:
    1. MARKETABLE RIGHTS: the distribution of a limited number of rights to scarce resources that private parties can then buy, sell or trade as market needs dictate.
    2. ECONOMIC INCENTIVES: the use of fees or subsidies rather than government enforced standards to encourage private sector achievement of regulatory goals.
    3. PERFORMANCE STANDARDS: the replacement of regulations specifying the exact means of compliance (usually detailed design standards) with general targets that the regulated firms can decide how to meet.
    4. COMPLIANCE REFORM: the replacement or supplementing of governmental monitoring and enforcement with market oriented mechanisms including third party compliance monitoring, penalties that reflect the degree of non-compliance and supervised self certification.
    5. INFORMATION DISCLOSURE: providing users of a product with relevant information about the consequences of using it.
    6. VOLUNTARY ACTIONS: reliance on regulatory standards developed by third parties or the regulated firms themselves.
Supra note 11, at v.
66. *See generally* R. CRANDALL, CONTROLLING INDUSTRIAL POLLUTION (1983); Spence & Weitzman, *Regulatory Strategies for Pollution Control* in APPROACHES FOR CONTROLLING AIR POLLUTION 199 (A. Friedlaender ed. 1978).

305

stantial goals while illustrating the virtues of the marketplace, they received surprisingly little attention during the first term of the Reagan presidency. A review of the past year's activities, however, suggests that such reforms may be at the forefront of the Administration's regulatory agenda during the second term.

Since their inception, market-based regulatory mechanisms have enjoyed a modest political constituency among academics, and state and federal bureaucrats.[67] Although support from these constituencies is important, it only partially explains the favorable prospects for market-based reforms during Reagan's second term. Of at least equal importance is the prominence that such reforms have gained as a result of the Supreme Court's decision in *Chevron U.S.A. v. Natural Resources Defense Council*,[68] which made clear that some of these reforms could be achieved administratively, without the often elusive approval of Congress.

In *Chevron*, the Court upheld the authority of the EPA to implement without legislative approval its market-based "bubble policy"[69] in geographic areas which have not attained national air quality standards. The bubble policy allows pollution-emitting devices or facilities regulated under the Clean Air Act to set off less expensive pollution reductions at one source against more costly emissions requirements at other sources, as long as aggregate air quality is improved. Emissions trades, including the bubble policy upheld by the court, function as supplements to existing agency rules and are administered within the framework established in controlling legislation. *Chevron* did not disturb, and may indeed have reinforced, the agency's continuing practice of promulgating policies regard-

---

67. *See, e.g.*, Drayton, *Getting Smarter About Regulation*, HARV. BUS. REV., July-Aug. 1981, at 38.

68. Chevron U.S.A. Inc. v. Natural Resources Defense Council, Inc., 104 S. Ct. 2778 (1984). The narrow question posed by *Chevron* was whether the agency's construction of the term "stationary source" under the Clean Air Act was at variance with Congressional intent. Under the interpretation advanced by the agency, use of the netting element of the agency emissions trading policy could be extended to non-attainment areas and would no longer be limited to those areas of the country found to be in compliance with federal air quality standards. *Id.* at 2780.

69. EPA's emissions trading policy, issued in 1982 and supplemented in 1983, sets forth four related substantive reforms to comply with provisions of the Clean Air Act. The four consist of:

1. the *bubble*, which allows managers of one or more existing plants to trade additional control of cheaply controlled stacks or vents for less control of more expensive sources;

2. *offsets*, which allow new plants or modifications to emit pollutants in non-attainment areas if they secure sufficient reductions from others to improve air quality;

3. *netting*, which allows use of a bubble to avoid burdensome New Source requirements for inplant modifications, so long as plant-wide emissions do not increase significantly; and

4. *banking*, which allows sources to store surplus reductions in a legally protected manner for future use or sale.

M. Russell, *Incentives to Strengthen Regulation of Pesticides: The Uses of Regulatory Reform*, U. N. ENVIRON. PROG. IND. & ENVIRON. NEWSLETTER, July-Sept. 1984, at 8, 9.

306

ing the use of market mechanisms in the form of policy guidelines, rather than by statute, or by regulation.

In the wake of *Chevron*, EPA intensified its efforts to expand trading concepts to other programs. This effort was spurred by the appointment of the reform-minded William Ruckelshaus as administrator of the agency,[70] and encouraged by organizations and individuals often identified as supporters of the Reagan Administration.[71] The agency has extended trading principles to new areas within the purview of the Clean Air Act,[72] including mobile sources.[73] Moreover, trading principles have also been applied outside the air program,[74] and now cover areas such as the amount of leaded gasoline refiners are allowed to produce.[75]

A review of the evolution of market mechanisms reveals that despite the popularity trading principles now enjoy, adoption of market-based reforms remains a slow and complex process. Although the initial EPA experimentation has quieted much skepticism and solved some mechanical problems, many of the problems encountered by the EPA will doubtless resurface. Commentators have noted that when emissions trading was first developed no real constituency for the policy existed.[76] Even within the EPA, the air and water program staffs and the regional offices initially

70. William Ruckelshaus resigned as EPA administrator on November 30, 1984. Lee A. Thomas, former chief of the agency's hazardous waste control programs, was named to replace him. N. Y. Times, Nov. 30, 1984, at A1, col. 2.

71. *See, e.g.*, Clark, *The Environmental Protection Agency* in MANDATE FOR LEADERSHIP II 84 (1985). Clark writes:

> Excessive costs also result when regulators use "command and control" regulations . . . rather than using regulatory systems that permit the flexibility that results from market systems. Regulatory systems can introduce market flexibility by allowing manufacturers to exchange cleanup obligations, so that firms that face a high cost to reduce a given increment of a pollutant can contract with other firms to achieve the same level of cleanup at lower cost.

Id. at 84.

72. One example would be EPA's recent internal decision to allow new sources of air pollution to use emission credits, trading, banking, or a bubble under the Clean Air Act in non-attainment areas without a demonstrated attainment plan. *See Alm Approves New Source Bubble Proposals*, ENV'T REP. (BNA) 1468 (Jan. 11, 1985).

73. In October 1984, EPA proposed an averaging program for diesel particulate emissions from heavy duty trucks. The program would allow some engines with emissions that are more difficult to control to exceed the emission standard so long as the sales weighted total emissions level does not exceed federal designated minimum standards. 49 Fed. Reg. 40,248 (1984) (to be codified at 40 C.F.R. § 86).

74. The agency's Water Innovation Project is examining state experience with point source trades, trades between point and non-point sources, as well as the use of banking strategies to control water pollution. *See* EPA ANN. REG. REP. 7 (1983).

75. In November 1982, EPA introduced a policy of permitting lead trading among gasoline refiners and importers. The agency's lead trading policy was extended through 1987 under a policy which would encourage refiners and importers to take actions to reduce the lead content of the gasoline they produce or sell earlier rather than later. *See Extensions of Lead Trading Rights to 1987*, ENV'T REP. (BNA) 1469 (Jan. 11, 1985).

76. *See* Levin, *Getting There: Implementing the "Bubble" Policy*, in SOCIAL REGULATION: STRATEGIES FOR REFORM 59, 65 (E. Bardach & R. Kagan eds. 1982).

resisted the program. Agency officials feared that the trading would be unduly resource intensive and would distract from more pressing administrative functions.[77] Almost eight years of institutional commitment of political capital and resources were required to overcome political resistance to the policy. Led by the agency's regulatory reform staff, the process involved selling emissions trading to the agency's central and regional office bureaucracies, to national public interest groups, to industry, and to local and state officials.

Some of the pioneering work done at the EPA will make future attempts to implement market-based reforms easier. The agency's use of economic incentives to entice states to assume program responsibilities is one such innovation.[78] The agency's efforts to introduce regulatory negotiation[79] and to reexamine environmental auditing may also prove useful.[80]

Nevertheless, rapid and easy progress is improbable because trading principles tax the political, legal, and technical capacity of regulating entities in ways that are not susceptible to simple solutions. Indeed, a recent survey indicates that although most state and regional air officials believed that emissions trading is a good idea, the officials continue to experience many problems. Unresolved issues and procedural requirements continue to cause frustration in program implementation and significant delays. Finally, those surveyed often voiced dissatisfaction with the complexity of the trading policy and expressed a need for more detailed guidance.[81]

The prospect of severe budget cuts at federal regulatory agencies also poses a substantial threat to broader application of trading principles—at least in the near term. Budget cuts could disrupt research and development, and limit the scope of federal oversight and the amount of technical assistance provided to state regulators. Given the complexity of the review and enforcement process, and the incentives which polluters have to claim unjustified credits, steep cuts could be disastrous.

---

77. *Id.* at 69-71, 78-79.

78. *See, e.g.*, 47 Fed. Reg. 15,076 (1982); 48 Fed. Reg. 39,580 (1983).

79. The agency's regulatory negotiation project is exploring ways in which to develop regulations by negotiation. The proposed regulations governing diesel emissions from heavy trucks (*see* Levin, *supra* note 76) were worked out through an early experiment with the process. *See* N.Y. Times, Dec. 6, 1984, at A22, col. 1.

80. In the area of environmental auditing (the development of internal management systems for reviewing facility operations to determine compliance with environmental regulations), the agency has completed a large scale research effort on the use of auditing in agency enforcement activities. *See* ARTHUR D. LITTLE, INC., CURRENT PRACTICES IN ENVIRONMENTAL AUDITING (1984) (report prepared for EPA).

81. *See* JELLINEK, SCHWARTZ, CONNOLLY & FRESHMAN, INC., EMISSIONS TRADING IN SELECTED EPA REGIONS (1984) (report prepared for EPA).

308

B. *Regulatory Federalism: Continued Delegation of Regulatory Authority to the States*

Although market-based regulatory mechanisms received scant attention in the early years of the Administration's first term, the same cannot be said of regulatory federalism. Almost from the day Carter left office, the Reagan Administration vigorously pursued a policy of delegating regulatory authority to the states. Indeed, the Administration effected significant transfers of authority during its first term[82] and probably will continue to do so. Moreover, these delegations are likely to be among the most enduring of the Administration's regulatory actions.

It would be oversimplifying, however, to view regulatory federalism as an irresistible force. In fact, devolution seemed to slow toward the end of the first term as a somewhat more deliberate approach appeared to emerge, perhaps reflecting political resistance to regulatory federalism. During the past year, for example, EPA began a major review of state programs operating under the Clean Water Act.[83] Although second thoughts about state regulatory authority appear more the exception than the rule, it appears that regulatory federalism will be pursued with a more considered accounting of political costs.

1. *Factors Influencing Further Delegation*

The pace, scope, and endurance of regulatory decentralization in the second term are likely to be influenced by the availability of federal funds to support the regulatory activities assumed by the states, the receptivity of industry to strengthened state regulatory roles, and the opposition of state and public interest groups to delegations of authority that appear to be mere smokescreens for deregulation.

Rhetoric of the New Federalism campaign notwithstanding, when Administration budget priorities have clashed with state preferences, state interests have frequently been overridden. If this continues to be true, further budget cuts could impede delegation of regulatory responsibilities to the states. Severe cuts in federal funding of state environmental programs, combined with strong fiscal pressures on state government, would diminish the prospect for future delegation of EPA authority. Funding cuts will particularly chill delegation in spheres of expanding federal regulation, such as federal pre-treatment programs created by the Clean Water Act. In a recent letter to Senator Patrick Leahy, former EPA Administrator Ruckelshaus stated that a tenfold increase in federal staffing would be

---

82. *See supra* note 39.
83. *Ronald Reagan's Second-term Agenda*, FORTUNE, Oct. 1, 1984, at 26, 30.

required to implement the program.[84] Staff increases of similar scope are expected to be necessary in the twenty-five states that have assumed authority for administering the pre-treatment program.[85] In the absence of assured federal funding, it is unlikely that additional states will seek authorization to administer their own program.

Industry can also act as a formidable check on the delegation of regulatory authority to the states, especially when regulatory authority is fragmented in a manner which imposes substantial costs on powerful industries. In business spheres where uniform federal standards promote economies of scale, support for nationally administered regulatory programs, rather than state delegation, is dominant.[86] In instances where conflicts between state and business interests have arisen over delegation to date, the Administration has shown a strong predilection to sacrifice its oft-enunciated federalism principles and side with business.[87]

When the delegation of federal regulatory responsibility appears to cloak an effort by the Administration to abandon statutory responsibility, opposition by the states themselves, as well as public interest groups, is a further check on regulatory federalism. For example, attempts by the Army Corps of Engineers to abandon responsibility for policing headwaters and inland lakes[88] have met with united and forceful opposition from a group of state governments.[89] Similarly, the National Wildlife Federation recently led a successful legal challenge to regulations issued by the Office of Surface Mining that would have improperly delegated to states the power to approve surface mining plans on federal lands.[90]

---

84. *Significant Increase in Staff Level Needed to Carry Out Pre-treatment Program, EPA Says,* ENV'T REP. (BNA) 534 (August 8, 1984).

85. *Id.*

86. *See* G. EADS & M. FIX, *supra* note 18, at 230.

87. In Pacific Gas & Elec. Co. v. State Energy Resources Cons. & Dev. Comm., 457 U.S. 1132 (1983), the federal government joined the petitioners in arguing successfully that a California statute authorizing a moratorium on nuclear power plant construction was preempted by the Atomic Energy Act of 1954, 42 U.S.C. §§ 2011-2284 (1982). In Silkwood v. Kerr-McGee Corp., 104 S. Ct. 615 (1984), the Court rejected the government's argument and held that federal law did not preempt state laws allowing punitive damages awards against companies which allowed their employees to become contaminated with radiation.

Note also the Administration's preemption of state hazardous workplace rules. Hazard Communication, 48 Fed. Reg. 53,280 (1983) (codified at 29 C.F.R. § 1910.5); *see also* G. EADS & M. FIX, *supra* note 18, at 230-31 (describing willingness of federal government to preempt state law when desirable).

88. *See* 47 Fed. Reg. 31,794 (1982) (codified in scattered sections of 33 C.F.R.).

89. *See* G. EADS & M. FIX, *supra* note 18, at 223-24.

90. *In re* Permanent Surface Mining Regulation Litigation, 21 ENV'T REP. (BNA) 1724 (D.D.C. July 6, 1984).

310

2. *Why Delegation is Likely to Continue*

As the above discussion indicates, the Administration obviously cannot treat regulatory federalism as trouble-free. Additional delegation will require attention to political cost and expedience. Nonetheless, regulatory devolution will continue during the second term and those delegations that have already occurred will for the most part endure. These two facts can be attributed to three characteristics of the delegation of regulatory power: (1) it is supported by the delegatees; (2) it attracts little publicity; and (3) it is consistent with the policies of prior administrations.

Delegation enjoys considerable political support among the delegatees. State legislators and administrators consistently place a high value on program autonomy.[91] These officials recognize that heightened regulatory autonomy provides them with greater influence over the context within which trade-offs between regulatory protections and economic developments take place.[92] They are also aware that state regulatory autonomy gives them the opportunity to assume credit for successful regulatory programs. Although this makes it harder for them to shift blame for regulatory failures onto federal bureaucrats, state regulators generally prefer the enhanced power and autonomy promised by regulatory federalism.[93]

Delegation also has the advantage of achieving reform through relatively informal administrative channels that are removed from public attention and media focus. With few exceptions, delegations completed to date have generated little political controversy. Often, transfers of regulatory authority do not require agency rulemaking or even conformance with the modest dictates of the Administrative Procedure Act.[94] A comparatively small group of professionals structures the labyrinthine relations between local, state and federal regulatory agencies.[95] Such a concentrated locus of policy-making power, to which outsiders have limited access, enables allocative decisions to take place without significant public debate or media attention. As a result, external political pressures sufficient to produce policy reversals will probably not be brought to bear on the Admin-

---

91. Fix, *Transferring Federal Regulatory Authority to the States*, in REGULATORY STRATEGY, *supra* note 54, at 153, 163.

92. Mashaw & Rose-Ackerman, *Federalism and Regulation*, in REGULATORY STRATEGY, *supra* note 54, at 111.

93. *Id.* at 122-27.

94. For example, regulatory authority is de facto transferred when federal oversight of state regulatory activity is diminished. *See* G. EADS & M. FIX, *supra* note 18, at 211.

95. Obviously, this is a characteristic which delegation shares with emissions trading policy. *See generally* E. Meidinger, The Politics of Market Mechanisms in U.S. Air Pollution Policy: On the Emerging Culture of Regulation (March 1984) (paper presented at the Conference on Distributional Conflicts in Environmental-Resource Policy, Berlin, West Germany).

311

istration's movement toward regulatory decentralization with any ease or frequency.

A third reason delegation should endure is that Reagan's transfer of regulatory authority to lower levels of government represents an accelerated continuation of policies put in place by previous administrations. Regulatory federalism is not a radical break from past policy, or from the principles upon which such policy rests. The policy of regulatory delegation, like that of reliance on market mechanisms, is premised on political and economic theories of greater maturity and broader currency than those regulatory policies driven by the "supply-side" economics which the Reagan Administration embraced. This foundation in accepted theory and recent history should render regulatory federalism less vulnerable to attack by academic and political critics.

C.   Future Directions for White House Oversight

The beginning of Ronald Reagan's second term, like the beginning of his first, witnessed the issuance of an executive order concerning regulatory oversight.[96] The content of that second order, as well as the virtual absence of controversy surrounding it, reveals a great deal about the likely course of White House oversight of regulation during Reagan's second term. The most recent order establishes, in effect, a regulatory budget without numbers. It creates a process by which OMB, working with executive branch agencies, will develop and publish an administration regulatory program.[97] This program will reflect "the administration's regulatory goals and objectives,"[98] much as the President's annual financial budget reflects his administration's economic goals and objectives.

In its most extreme form, the concept of a regulatory budget is closely analogous to that of a financial budget. Costs and benefits would be estimated in dollar terms for all proposed regulations. Through a process akin to that employed in putting together a financial budget, agencies would be allotted ceilings representing the total regulatory costs they would be permitted to impose on the economy. Once these ceilings were set, the precise details of how regulations were written and imposed would be left to the agencies. OMB's work would be done.[99]

The idea of a regulatory budget—with or without numbers—is not new. While many economists viewed the increased use of cost-benefit

96. Exec. Order No. 12,498, 50 Fed. Reg. 1036 (1985).
97. Id.
98. Id.
99. See DeMuth, Constrain Regulatory Costs: Part II, The Regulatory Budget, REGULATION, Mar.-Apr. 1980, at 30-31.

312

analysis as the tool by which "excessive and inefficient" regulation might be controlled, others had long argued that executive oversight by itself would accomplish little of value.[100] They believed that increased oversight would be nothing but window dressing unless the incentives facing regulators were fundamentally changed. Their solution was to put the regulators on a "budget," making them balance the costs of regulatory programs against perceived benefits. Proposals for a regulatory budget, however, created only a brief stir. Economists debated whether the numbers necessary for such a budget could ever be developed, and the debates themselves resulted in widespread recognition that a full-blown regulatory budget was impractical.[101]

The 1985 Reagan executive order resurrects the regulatory budget concept in a radically altered form. Those who previously advocated establishing a regulatory budget had focused on its utility as a technique for program control.[102] But such a budget can also serve as an instrument for political control. Budgets are political statements which are manifestations of a government's priorities.[103] Reagan's new "regulatory budget without numbers" has the potential of fulfilling this political purpose.

Assembling a workable regulatory budget document will be a formidable undertaking. It remains to be seen whether OMB—and especially OIRA—is capable of the task. Certainly, institutionalization of regulatory budgets will require a significantly increased commitment of resources by OMB. It will also require that the OMB Director have the ability and desire to understand the scope and content of executive branch regulatory programs. The position of OMB director must thus evolve from that of a professional budgeteer to a political professional with a broader, more policy-oriented perspective.[104] Preparation of a regulatory budget without

100. Among the most vocal of these economists was Christopher DeMuth, who later became head of Reagan's Office of Information and Regulatory Affairs. In a 1980 two-part article in *Regulation*, DeMuth first reviewed the history of presidential efforts to control regulation and found them fatally flawed. He then proposed the idea of the regulatory budget—although he was not the first to do so. *See* DeMuth, *Constrain Regulatory Costs: Part I, The White House Review Programs*, REGULATION, Jan.-Feb. 1980, at 13; DeMuth, *supra* note 99, at 29.

101. For a summary of the arguments in these debates, see R. LITAN & W. NORDHAUS, RE-FORMING FEDERAL REGULATION 133-58 (1983).

102. G. EADS & M. FIX, *supra* note 18, at 99-100.

103. Presidents in the early part of this century moved to create a unified Executive Branch budget. Individual agencies had previously submitted their budgets directly to the Congress. The change has enabled presidents to develop a coherent set of priorities that reflect the aims of their administrations as well as to exert detailed control over various programs.

104. The current OMB director, David Stockman, fits the latter description. Prior to becoming head of OMB he had served for two terms as a Republican Congressman from Michigan. In that capacity he was heavily involved in observing and shaping federal regulatory activity. *See, e.g.,* Stockman, *Address*, in GOVERNMENT, TECHNOLOGY, AND THE FUTURE OF THE AUTOMOBILE 393 (D. Ginsberg & W. Abernathy eds. 1980).

313

numbers will shift the agency's focus further away from preparation of a financial budget and toward a broader executive branch managerial role.

It is unclear how Congress will greet such a change. In a real sense, the creation of a regulatory budget without numbers represents a greater shift in power from the Congress to the President than did the consolidation of oversight power within OMB in 1981. Reagan's 1981 executive order followed in the tradition of similar efforts by Reagan's three predecessors to exercise control over regulations issued by agencies of the executive branch.[105] Only in the order's implementation was there a break from tradition. In contrast, the 1985 executive order asserts that the President has the power to take various regulatory programs established by the Congress and combine them into an "administration regulatory program" that reflects his priorities.[106] Where Congressionally-mandated guidelines do not exist, OMB can set the level and scope of social regulation. Given the apparent immunity of oversight to legal challenges,[107] this program gives the President enormous power to shape the regulatory process—provided he is able to appoint regulators who can avoid the legal pitfalls and congressional problems that hampered the Reagan Administration during its first term.[108]

Congress might react to the introduction of a regulatory budget and the accompanying shift of power to the executive in many ways. Some committees have already indicated that they will require agencies over which they exercise oversight to submit their regulatory agendas to Congress *before* they submit them to OMB.[109] Presumably, this would enable the committees to gauge how much OMB alters these agendas in developing the Administration's annual regulatory program.[110] Congress could also respond by revising agency authorizing legislation to reduce executive discretion, as it did in the recent revision of the Resource Conservation and

105. G. EADS & M. FIX, *supra* note 18, at 45-67.

106. Exec. Order No. 12,498, *supra* note 96.

107. *See, e.g.*, Center for Science in the Pub. Interest v. Dep't of Treasury, 573 F. Supp. 1168, 1178 (D.D.C. 1983) (Administrative Procedure Act did not require agency to disclose contacts and information received in informal rulemaking); Center for Auto Safety v. Peck, 751 F.2d 1336 (D.C. Cir. 1985) (scope of arbitrary and capricious standard is narrow and court is not to substitute its judgment for that of agency).

108. *See supra* notes 27-32 and accompanying text.

109. Agencies under the purview of the House Energy and Commerce Committees will have to satisfy this requirement. *See Broadened Powers Give Budget Office Control Over Rules*, N.Y. Times, Dec. 20, 1983, at A1, col. 1.

110. Indeed some legislative movement along these lines may already be perceptible. S. 2433, 98th Cong., 2d Sess. § 8(g)(1)(A) (1984), proposing revisions to the Paperwork Reduction Act of 1980, 44 U.S.C. § 3501-3520 (1982), would have required that the administrators of federal regulatory agencies make publicly available a copy of any draft of a proposed or final rule submitted by an agency for review to the Office of Information and Regulatory Affairs.

Recovery Act.[111] Alternatively, it could achieve the same result by imposing tight deadlines and narrow requirements on the scope of permissible regulations. This would prevent the Administration from developing its own separate regulatory program by removing the leverage that regulators in the executive branch have to influence the timing and content of agency rules and regulations.

Congress itself could attempt to become involved in the regulatory budgeting process. The role that OMB has come to play in reviewing regulations is not substantially different from the role it plays in assembling the Administration's financial budget or in "clearing" Administration testimony and legislation. Secrecy and behind-the-scenes bargaining characterize all of these processes. Compared to the process of regulatory review, however, budget review and legislative clearance generate relatively little controversy. This is because the results of these reviews go to the Congress. If Senators or Representatives do not like the results, they are in a position to act directly to change them. This is not the case with regulation. To be sure, Congressional committees can hold oversight hearings or use budget riders to try to control how agencies regulate.[112] These avenues of control, however, are less satisfactory methods of expressing legislative intent than is actual legislation. It is thus not clear how successful Congress could be in exercising control through its own regulatory budgeting.

Congress' likely response to regulatory budgeting is as yet unclear. We believe, however, that the simultaneous referral of a draft regulatory agenda to OMB and to the Congress would probably be an ineffective technique for Congressional control, as simultaneous submission of independent regulatory commission budgets has been. We have no evidence that this dual review has given Congress any additional leverage in setting those agencies' budgets. We, however, also believe that it would be extremely undesirable for Congress itself to start drafting regulations. Congress originally delegated rulemaking authority to executive agencies because it recognized that it could not handle the job itself.[113] Much of the arbitrariness and inefficiency of regulation results from regulators being forced to implement highly detailed statutory standards which leave little room for administrative flexibility. If anything, regulators need more, not less, discretion. Congress should, therefore, focus on promoting the responsible use of discretion and not second-guess day-to-day decisions of

---

111. Hazardous and Solid Waste Amendments of 1984, Pub. L. No. 98-616, tit. 2, 98 Stat. 3221, 3226-66 (amending the Resource Conservation and Recovery Act, 42 U.S.C. § 6921 (1982)).

112. Until it was declared unconstitutional, see INS v. Chadha, 462 U.S. 919 (1983), Congress increasingly resorted to the use of the legislative veto as a means of controlling agency action.

113. See, e.g., R. CUSHMAN, THE INDEPENDENT REGULATORY COMMISSIONS 74, 425 (1941).

315

regulators who seek to fashion coherent regulatory programs. Congress does have an important role to play in setting the tone of regulatory activities by taking a comprehensive look at regulatory priorities. Unless such broad scale reviews are conducted, the Congress will surrender to the executive the power to set regulatory priorities.

D. *The Prospects for Legislative Reform*

In stark contrast to its attempts to encourage the adoption of market mechanisms, delegate regulatory authority, and expand executive oversight, the Administration's record in pressing for and obtaining legislative changes has been dismal.[114] For a number of reasons, the prospects for legislative change during the second term are no brighter.

First, the spillover effects of the political controversy which characterized the early years of Reagan's regulatory relief program have been most acutely felt in the legislative arena.[115] By 1980, bipartisan political support was beginning to center around revising what have been termed the "aspirational" provisions of a number of prominent pieces of social legislation.[116] The statutes' aspirational goals were seen as creating institutional tensions among the three branches of government, between agencies and firms, and between federal and state regulators. The regulatory misadventures of the Administration's early years, however, provided a textbook lesson on how to stimulate public support for strengthening the na-

114.   In a memorandum to the Cabinet Council on Economic Affairs, Christopher DeMuth, then head of OIRA, stated "[I]n the [first] three years [of the Reagan Administration] we have not advanced a single detailed proposal of our own for reform of any of the major health, safety, or environmental statutes." C. Demuth, Regulatory Policy 5 (Dec. 9, 1983) (unpublished memorandum on file with the *Yale Journal on Regulation*).

115.   Murray Weidenbaum's comments in a paper prepared for a June 1983 Urban Institute Conference provide a fitting assessment of the political climate: "We will be lucky if, by January 1985 we are back where we were in January 1981 in terms of the public's attitude toward statutory reform and social regulation." Weidenbaum, *Regulatory Reform Under the Reagan Administration*, in REGULATORY STRATEGY, *supra* note 54, at 15, 38.

116.   The term, coined by Yale Law School Professor Jerry Mashaw, refers to an absolute legislative approach. *See* J. Mashaw, Remarks at Urban Institute Conference (June 22-23, 1983). A short list of these provisions would probably start with the Delaney Clause to the Federal Food, Drug and Cosmetic Act which bans all food additives "found . . . to induce cancer in man or animal" even if some putatively safe level for human use could be established. 21 U.S.C. § 348(c)(3)(A) (1982). The clause is, thus, thought to set a no-risk goal for the carcinogenicity of food additives and to prohibit, in effect, a weighing of costs or an assessment of comparative health risks associated with the ban. *See generally* L. LAVE, THE STRATEGY OF SOCIAL REGULATION: DECISION FRAMEWORKS FOR POLICY 11-15 (1981).

Another likely candidate for the "short" list of aspirational enactments would be the provisions setting National Ambient Air Quality Standards under the 1970 Clean Air Amendments. 40 C.F.R. § 50.1-12 (1984). The 1970 Amendments have been criticized as costly, inefficient, indifferent to location, inhibiting modernization, and, paradoxically, increasing the total amount of pollution exposure. *See* Harrison & Portney, *Remedy for the Clean Air Act*, REGULATION, Mar.-Apr. 1981, at 27.

Moreover, the Act has been interpreted in a manner which does not permit the balancing of costs and benefits in designating exposure levels. *See id.* at 25.

316

tion's social legislation. When Ronald Reagan took office in 1981, the percentage of citizens believing that some relaxation of federal environmental laws would be appropriate was at an eight-year high.[117] Midway through the President's first term, the polls showed not only a sharp drop in the percentage of citizens believing that environmental laws and regulations had gone too far, but also a substantial rise in the percentage of respondents believing that they had not gone far enough.[118]

Second, legislative change is often politically expensive. If the Reagan Administration has provided future presidents with a valuable lesson on achieving their political objectives, it is that success comes from concentrating political capital on a narrow and achievable agenda.[119] Judging from the Administration's first term, it can be assumed that the President and his staff will deploy their political capital to control the shape of budget and tax measures, choosing not to expend such capital on reform measures for social regulations.

Finally, as we have documented,[120] substantial change in the day-to-day administration of the regulatory process, in the focus of regulatory authority, and even in the designation of selected regulatory standards can be accomplished without legislative change. These administrative opportunities may make the bruising, relatively public process of legislative change seem unnecessary, if not politically inadvisable.

In sum, the unfavorable political climate for legislative action, its high political cost, and the opportunities for regulatory change available elsewhere indicate that legislative stasis is likely. Indeed, it is clear that regulatory relief objectives did not underlie legislative activity in the 98th Congress. While the term ended with a host of major environmental laws (including the Clean Air Act, the Clean Water Act, and the Safe Drinking Water Act) remaining to be reauthorized, the one bill which did pass—the amendments to the Resource Conservation and Recovery Act[121]—provided evidence that proposals for regulatory relief have had little effect on current legislation. The bill not only expanded EPA's regulatory responsibilities,[122] but also eliminated agency discretion by setting very specific agency priorities in the processing of permits.[123]

---

117. The group, though, remained small, representing only 23% of those polled. See THE CONSERVATION FOUNDATION, STATE OF THE ENVIRONMENT 1982, at 425, fig. 9.11 (1982).

118. Id.

119. See Salamon & Lund, *Governance in the Reagan Era—An Overview* in THE REAGAN PRESIDENCY AND THE GOVERNING OF AMERICA 17-18 (1985).

120. G. EADS & M. FIX, *supra* note 18, at 179-89.

121. Hazardous and Solid Waste Amendments of 1984, Pub. L. No. 98-616, § 221, 98 Stat. 3221, 3248-51 (codified at 42 U.S.C. § 6921) (1984).

122. It required for the first time that generators disposing between 100 and 1000 kilograms of hazardous waste per month dispose of their waste at a RCRA-approved facility.

123. *See, e.g., id.* § 201(e) (prohibiting land disposal of solvents and wastes containing dioxin

317

Conclusion

After having failed to take advantage of a significant opportunity for change during its first term, the Reagan Administration has apparently reconciled itself to spending the next four years on the legislative sidelines as well. As James C. Miller III, Chairman of the Federal Trade Commission, recently said, "The President is just going to let the glue dry on deregulation."[124] If Miller's prognosis is correct, the Administration's regulatory legacy will be quite different from the one which the President might have hoped for and expected. In the absence of legislative change, the Reagan legacy will be broadened administrative discretion and a greater presidential control over the course of social regulation. While this might give deregulation-minded presidents like Ronald Reagan an opportunity to reduce perceived regulatory burdens, it also gives presidents with differing philosophies the power and the tools they need to turn regulation to quite different ends.

---

beginning 24 months after enactment); § 201(d) (banning hazardous wastes on the "California list"—cyanide, arsenic, lead, mercury, etc.—from land disposal beginning 32 months after enactment); § 103(a) (appointing an ombudsman to respond to citizen inquiries regarding RCRA programs); § 202(a) (requiring the promulgation of regulations within 30 months requiring that all new landfills, surface impoundments, waste piles, underground tanks, and land treatment units use approved leak detection systems); § 231 (ensuring that 12 months after enactment every hazardous waste treatment, storage, or disposal facility has a permit and shall be inspected at least every two years).

124. *Ronald Reagan's Second-term Agenda*, FORTUNE, Oct. 1, 1984, at 26, 30.

Deregulation: Looking Backward and Looking Forward

Alfred E. Kahn†

We have a surfeit of deregulatory anniversaries to celebrate or deplore: it is now more than thirty years since the Federal Communications Commission (FCC) authorized substantial competition in long-distance communications,[1] more than eleven since we deregulated the airlines, and almost ten years since we did substantially the same to the railroad and trucking industries.[2] Can we, by examining this long and varied experience with deregulation, draw any conclusions about the likelihood and desirability of its continuation in the decade ahead?

In this attempt to place deregulation in historical perspective, I feel compelled to emphasize, in contradiction of the widespread

† Robert Julius Thorne Professor of Political Economy, Emeritus, Cornell University; Special Consultant, National Economic Research Associates, Inc.; Chairman, New York Public Service Commission, 1974-77, and Civil Aeronautics Board, 1977-78. This is a revised and expanded version of a paper presented at the fiftieth anniversary session of the American Economic Association, Transportation and Public Utilities Group on December 28, 1989. I acknowledge with gratitude the criticisms of Richard Rapp, Douglas Jones, Irwin Stelzer, William Shepherd, Judith Greenman and Robert Crandall, and the assistance of Tina Fine.

1. Allocation of Frequencies in the Bands Above 890 Mc, 27 F.C.C. 359 (1959), *modified on reconsideration* 29 F.C.C. 825 (1960) (authorizing large users to provide their own communications services via microwave).

2. Other major milestones were the deregulation of stock exchange brokerage commissions in 1975-76, see Roberts, Phillips & Zecher, *Deregulation of Fixed Commission Rates in the Securities Industry*, in THE DEREGULATION OF THE BANKING AND SECURITIES INDUSTRIES 151 (1979); the progressive relaxation of FCC restrictions on cable television competition with over-the-air broadcasters during the 1970s, see S. BESEN, T. KRATTEN-MAKER, A. METZGER JR., & J. WOODBURY, MISREGULATING TELEVISION 4-20 (1984); see also Besen & Crandall, *The Deregulation of Cable Television*, 44 LAW & CONTEMP. PROBS. 77 (1981); the FCC's reluctant allowance of direct competition in the offer of interexchange telecommunications service on a common carrier basis. MCI Telecommunications Corp. v. FCC, 561 F.2d 365 (D.C. Cir 1977); In re Establishment of Policies and Procedures for Consideration of Application to Provide Specialized Common Carrier Services in the Domestic Point-to-Point Microwave Radio Service, 29 F.C.C. 2d 870 (1971); In re Applications of Microwave Communications, Inc., 18 F.C.C. 2d 979 (1967). *See generally* 2 A. KAHN, THE ECONOMICS OF REGULATION: PRINCIPLES AND INSTITUTIONS 129-52 (1988); G. FAULHABER, TELECOMMUNICATIONS IN TURMOIL: TECHNOLOGY AND PUBLIC POLICY (1987). *See also* text accompanying *infra* note 20.

popular impression that President Reagan deserves most of the credit—or blame—how much of it occurred between 1978 and 1980.[3]

While deregulation has dramatically transformed the transportation industries, its effect on the traditional public utilities, while substantial, can easily be exaggerated. Two years ago, in a symposium on "The Surprises of Deregulation," Robert Crandall shrewdly observed that the greatest surprise in the case of telecommunications was how little had actually occurred.[4]   Customer premises equipment aside, the overwhelming majority of transactions continue to be thoroughly regulated. And AT&T, which had agreed to divest its putatively naturally monopolistic services and confine itself to competitive operations, continues nonetheless to be heavily regulated.[5]

I have been guilty of some such exaggeration myself, in speculating several years ago that we might at last be witnessing the fulfillment of Horace Gray's ancient celebration of "the passing of the public utility concept:"[6]

> Gray intended his title to be historically descriptive, and not merely hortatory. The celebration was premature. . . .

> In contrast, the last decade has witnessed such dramatic modifications and abandonments of the traditional institution that I suggest it is now possible to talk realistically about the passing of the public utility concept. . . .

> The institution of closely regulated, confined, franchised monopoly, which produced reasonably satisfactory results for all parties, including the public, until around 1970, has proved progressively unsuited to the drastically altered condition of the American economy since that time. I think history is on the way to proving that Horace Gray was something of a

---

3.   Even so knowledgeable a student as Roger Noll has credited President Reagan with dismantling the Civil Aeronautics Board (CAB), merely because it happened during his term. Noll, *Regulation After Reagan*, REGULATION, Number 3, 1988, at 13. Also, most people credit Reagan with deregulating crude oil, even though it was President Carter who set the process on a definite two and a half year time schedule; his successor's contribution was to compress the remaining nine months into one immediately on taking office.

4.   Crandall, *Surprises from Telephone Deregulation and the AT&T Divestiture*, 78 AM. ECON. REV., PAPERS & PROCEEDINGS 323 (1988). The same is true of electric power and local distribution of gas.

5.   *See* G. FAULHABER, *supra* note 2, at 85-87.

6.   Gray, *The Passing of the Public Utility Concept*, 16 J. LAND & PUB. UTIL. ECON. 8 (1940).

prophet—a premature one (if it is not excessively redundant of me to say so), and a simplistic one, but something of a prophet nonetheless.[7]

More cautious than Gray, I hedged my predictions and prescriptions. Where deregulation had been incomplete, I observed, the reciprocal interpenetration of markets by regulated and unregulated companies required regulatory prevention of cross-subsidization and abuse of monopoly power. I also professed agnosticism about the feasibility of competition across the board in electric generation, dithered on the desirability of deregulating basic cable television service and petroleum pipelines, described my own efforts to ensure effective protection of shippers captive to the otherwise deregulated railroads, and recognized that similar exploitation was almost certainly happening in some thin airline markets. Still, considering the continuing pervasive regulation of the public utilities, I, like Gray, could justly be described as a "premature prophet" of their passing.

There is, however, also a great deal going on, almost all of it in the direction I predicted. Of especial significance, the major issues of regulatory policy these days in the public utility arena are not whether or how to return to the closed world of franchised, thoroughly regulated monopolies, but how to accommodate traditional regulation to the increasing intrusion of competition. Among the leading examples of that intrusion are:

the growth of electric generation by non-utility enterprises—both "qualifying facilities" under the Public Utility Regulatory Policies Act (PURPA)[8] and so-called independent power producers;[9]

7.   Kahn, *The Passing of the Public Utility Concept: A Reprise*, in Telecommunications Today and Tomorrow 3, 4, 5, 27 (E. Noam ed. 1983) (footnotes omitted) [hereinafter Kahn, *A Reprise*].

8.   Pub. L. No. 95-617, 92 Stat. 3117 (1978) (codified at 16 U.S.C. § 2601 (1988)). *See generally* Joskow, *Regulatory Failure, Regulatory Reform, and Structural Change in the Electric Power Industry*, 1989 Brookings Papers on Economic Activity: Microeconomics 124, 153-74, 184-85.

9.   Non-utility generation accounts for only about four percent of total national capacity. *See* Edison Electric Institute, 1989 Capacity and Generation of Non-Utility Sources of Energy (1989). But it accounts for one third or more of planned additions. J. Wile, The Demand for New Generating Capacity (Nat'l. Econ. Res. Assoc. 1989), provides an estimate of 30 percent of planned additions. Mason Willrich quotes a figure of 44 percent of "capacity under construction or advanced development." *The Competitive Wholesale Electric Generation Act, 1989: Hearings on Amend. 267 to S. 406 Before the*

327

- the deregulation of certain wholesale bulk power sales, where the Federal Energy Regulatory Commission (FERC) has satisfied itself that the transactions were at arms' length and untainted by monopoly or monopsony power;[10]

- the requirement by an increasing number of state utility commissions that local electric companies obtain their additional power requirements via competitive bids;[11]

- the decision by many states to permit electric companies to exercise discretion in pricing, within a stipulated range, in order to meet competition, forestall cogeneration, and retain or attract industry;[12]

- the proposal by FERC to permit local gas distribution companies to replace long-term commitments to buy gas from open access pipelines with arrangements to purchase transportation alone;[13]

- the total deregulation of telephone equipment, which is now highly competitive;[14] and

- the burgeoning of private communications networks, to such a point that more business phones are now linked in the

Senate Comm. on Energy and Natural Resources, 101st Cong., 2d Sess. 5-6 (1989) (statement of Mason Willrich, Pres. and CEO, PG&E Enterprises).

10. R. FITZGIBBONS, BEYOND THE FERC NOPRS: TRENDS IN ELECTRIC UTILITY REGULATION (Nat'l. Econ. Res. Assoc. 1989).

11. Fourteen commissions have done so, twelve others are considering it. Willrich, *supra* note 9, at 5.

12. R. FRAME, COMPETITIVE INDUSTRIAL RATES (Nat'l. Econ. Res. Assoc. 1987).

13. Batla, *Order 500 Joins Order 451 on the Critical List*, NATURAL GAS, Dec. 1989, at 1. In 1982, interstate pipelines owned 78 percent of the natural gas they carried; by 1987 that share had fallen to less than one-third. For the remainder, the pipelines provided the transportation as a separate service. ENERGY INFORMATION ADMIN., OFFICE OF OIL & GAS, U.S. DEP'T OF ENERGY, GROWTH IN UNBUNDLED NATURAL GAS TRANSPORTATION SERVICES: 1982-87, at ix-x (1988).

14. *See* Crandall, After the Breakup: U.S. Telecommunications in a More Competitive Era (Nov. 1989) (unpublished manuscript on file with author). *See also* Noll & Owen, *United States v. AT&T: An Interim Assessment*, in FUTURE COMPETITION IN TELECOMMUNICATIONS 172-86 (S. Bradley & J. Hausman ed. 1989).

first instance to their own switches than to those of the local telephone company.[15]

Among such quasi-public utilities as financial service institutions and transportation, the processes of market interpenetration and unregulated pricing are even further advanced.

Despite these developments, most transactions at the core of the traditional public utilities, such as the local provision of telephone, electric and gas service, continue to be tightly regulated, and there seems little prospect or desirability of that situation changing fundamentally in the next decade. In these circumstances, my predictions and prescriptions about the future course of deregulation in the structurally competitive industries, on the one side, and the structurally monopolistic markets, on the other, will necessarily differ from one another.

There will, however, be a common theme and a consistent set of conclusions:

The case for deregulation has been that direct regulation typically suppressed competition, or at least severely distorted it, and that competition, freed of such direct restraints, is a far preferable system of economic control. I read the recent experience as having essentially vindicated that proposition, making substantial reversal of the deregulatory trend unlikely.

Where competition is not feasible throughout an industry or market, as in the traditional public utilities, entry of unregulated competition can introduce distortions so severe as to make the mixed system the worst of both possible worlds. The preferable remedy is not to suppress the competition, but to make the residual regulation as consistent as possible with it. That seems to be the direction in which regulators are moving.

The abolition of direct economic regulation is by no means synonymous with *laissez faire*. On the contrary, it may call for government interventions no less vigorous than direct regulation itself, but fundamentally different in character and intent. The progressive realization of this fact in recent years makes

15. P. W. Huber, The Geodesic Network: 1987 Report on Competition in the Telephone Industry 2.5-2.7 (Antitrust Division, U.S. Dep't of Justice 1987).

329

for a bifurcated prognosis for the 1990s: the historic trend of direct economic deregulation is unlikely to be reversed, but government will play an increasingly active role in attempting to preserve competition and remedy its imperfections. And that is what it should do.

I. The Prospects for Reregulation

One way of trying to judge whether the recent deregulatory trends are likely to continue or be reversed is to consider the root causes of these remarkable historical changes[16] and appraise the likelihood of their persistence.

Perhaps the most fundamental of these has been the rediscovery all over the world of the virtues of the free market. It was obviously no accident that many of the comprehensive governmentally-administered cartelizations overturned during the late 1970s and early 1980s were established during the Great Depression, when confidence in the market economy was at its nadir. While the present enthusiasm for market capitalism will doubtless be subject to ebbs and flows in the years ahead, it is difficult to envision an early return to centralized governmental command and control systems, of which our regimes of economic regulation were an exemplar in microcosm.

There is no sign of let up, either, in the technological explosion that made inevitable the collapse of almost all the historic regulatory barriers against competitive interpenetrations in telecommunications, and bids fair to do the same among financial institutions. It was the development of microwave that presented large users with the irresistible opportunity to escape the regulatorily-dictated overcharging of interexchange services. Similarly, the geometrically declining cost and increased versatility of switching has made possible the proliferation of privately-owned networks and privately-provided sophisticated telecommunications services; and fiber optics will probably doom the present artificial separation of cable television and information services from telephony.

A. Vested Interests in Deregulation

The deregulations of the last fifteen years were powerfully motivated also by changes in the configuration of the private

---

16. *See generally* Kahn, *The Political Feasibility of Regulatory Reform: How Did We Do It?*, in REFORMING SOCIAL REGULATION: ALTERNATIVE PUBLIC POLICY STRATEGIES 247 (1982).

interests most directly affected. The Staggers Act[17] was passed in large measure because of the growing disenchantment of the railroads with their historic regulatory bargain with government that protected them from competition but also systematically impeded them from competing effectively, forced them to maintain thousands of miles of track on which they were losing money, and limited their ability to raise their charges to customers with relatively inelastic demands. Similarly, airline deregulation owed a great deal to the unhappiness of United Airlines with the CAB's systematic denial to it of the ability to enter new markets or desert old ones. The insistence of large customers that they be released from the burdens of cross-subsidization to which they had been subjected by the FCC and state commissions was an important part of the reason for the breakup of AT&T's monopoly; in the same way, the competitive encroachments on the formerly protected markets of the electric and gas utilities came about because of the desire of large industrial customers to take advantage of emerging opportunities to make bulk purchases at bargain rates in the field and from outside suppliers with excess capacity. And one reason for the receptivity of the electric industry to competitive generation was the reluctance of many of its members to undertake construction of new baseload generating stations, because of the stunning regulatory disallowances of previously incurred construction costs to which they had been subjected in the early and mid-1980s.[18]

It is the converse of the foregoing proposition that is the more relevant for the future. There are now vested interests in deregulation itself—politically or economically powerful entities that, having now achieved freedom from regulation, will not readily surrender it. That is part of what I intended when I said that my colleagues and I at the CAB were going to get the airline eggs so scrambled that no one was ever going to be able to unscramble them. Although many of the thousands of new truckers and small bus companies

---

17. Staggers Rail Act of 1980, Pub. L. No. 96-448, 94 Stat. 1895 (1980) (codified as amended in scattered sections of 11, 45, and 49 U.S.C.).

18. As the foregoing account already suggests, while the deregulation movement was powerfully motivated by historical factors affecting the economy at large and economic policy generally, its explanation must be sought also in circumstances peculiar to the individual industries affected. For example, it is highly unlikely that our regulatory policies affecting the electric utilities would have been so substantially changed had that industry continued to perform as it had during the decades of the 1950s and 1960s. In contrast with telecommunications, where the most powerful motivating force was technological progress, in the energy sector the motivating force was, in important measure, technological and institutional failure. See, e.g., Joskow, supra note 8, at 149-63; R. F. HIRSH, TECHNOLOGY AND TRANSFORMATION IN THE AMERICAN ELECTRIC UTILITY INDUSTRY (1989).

331

and many of the hundreds of railroad ventures that have taken over the trackage and thin routes that larger companies were unable to operate profitably, and many of the cogenerators and small-scale generators of hydro- and wind power that have eagerly entered the doors opened by deregulation have already gone bankrupt, and many more will, the survivors are not going to permit the government to retract the invitation to compete. Moreover, the previous incumbents now have a freedom to manage their own operations, configure their own service offerings and set their own prices that will be very hard to take away. Where the deregulatory process has been only partial, the companies that remain thoroughly regulated devote most of their energies to demanding "symmetry," by which they mean not a restoration of restraints on their newer competitors, but corresponding freedom for themselves. The principle applies symmetrically to deregulation and regulation: once instituted, they tend to be progressive and cumulative.[19]

These forces explain why the process can be essentially inadvertent, as it was in the case of telecommunications. No planner laid out in advance the path of decisions from Hush-a-Phone and Above 890 through Carterphone, MCI, Specialized Common Carriers, Execunet, AT&T's stonewalling response, the Modified Final Judgment concluding the ensuing antitrust litigation, and the FCC's MTS/WATS Market Structure and three Computer Inquiries. Yet each step led logically to the next, and they were all in the same direction.[20]

The same process is underway in the financial services field. Once we permitted brokerage houses to offer the equivalent of demand deposits and retail chains to provide home mortgages and credit card services, once we removed ceilings on interest rates payable by savings institutions, it was inevitable that we would loosen the previous restraints on the permissible lending and investment activities of the savings institutions and permit commercial banks to underwrite commercial paper.

---

19. On the tendency of regulation to spread, see, e.g., A. KAHN, *supra* note 2, at 28-32. For a study of the effects of deregulation, see Kahn, *Applications of Economics to an Imperfect World*, 69 AM. ECON. REV., PAPERS & PROCEEDINGS 1 (1979).

20. *See* text accompanying *supra* notes 1-2. *See also* Kahn, *The Future of Local Telephone Service: Technology and Public Policy*, in TOWARD THE YEAR 2000 88-90 (1987); Crandall, *supra* note 14.

B. *Distortions and Tensions of Partial Deregulation*

In the electric and gas utilities, similarly, partial deregulation has introduced a host of asymmetries and distortions, which have been and are still being resolved primarily by further liberalizations. The basic problem is that the rates charged by the utility companies, which inevitably play a central role in deciding which competitive transactions take place and which do not, contain a very large component of capital carrying charges on investments valued at embedded (i.e., at depreciated original) cost, not marginal cost. Under partial deregulation, therefore, many competitive purchase and production decisions are made on the basis of comparisons between those economically meaningless, traditionally regulated rates, on the one side, and competitive costs or prices on the other. Businesses will decide whether to generate their own electric power or construct their own communications systems by comparing the current, true economic cost to them of doing so with the regulated rates they would otherwise have to pay. Where those rates are higher than the marginal or avoided costs of the electric or tele- phone company itself—as they have been by wide margins in recent years, because of the presence in rate base of high-cost, excess generating capacity, or inadequately depreciated telephone plant[21]—the decisions by customers to provide the service themselves can produce inefficient results.

For the same reason, when differences in regulated rates cause large-volume buyers to shift their patronage from one electric company to another, or from a gas pipeline or distribution company to producers in the field, it need not be that the marginal costs of the new supplier are lower than the avoided costs of the former one. Often, in fact, their short-run marginal costs are identical—for example, when both suppliers are part of the same power pool. The most powerful inducement for high-volume gas customers to desert their historic pipeline and distribution company suppliers has been the billions of dollars of sunk costs embodied in the rates of their former suppliers because of commitments they had made to take or pay for very high-cost gas at a time when supplies were critically short. As a result, a large number of transactions have been entered into because of decisions distorted by regulation itself, and there is

---

21. *See* Rohlfs, *'Miles to Go': The Need for Additional Reforms in Capital Recovery Methods,* TELECOMMUNICATIONS IN A COMPETITIVE ENVIRONMENT 63 (Nat'l Econ. Res. Assoc. 1989). *See also* A. KAHN, *supra* note 2, at 146-50; Kahn, *The Uneasy Marriage of Regulation and Competition,* TELEMATICS, Sept. 1984, at 1, 2, 8-17.

333

no assurance that the supply function is distributed among competitors on the basis of their comparative efficiency.

The legal obligation of utility companies to serve on demand, which requires them to incur the costs of installing the capacity necessary to fulfill that obligation, creates a similar distortion. So long as they were monopolies, their customers had, in effect, a corresponding obligation to pay rates reflecting those sunk costs if prudently incurred. In contrast, the customers who are now free to shop around or to supply their own needs can escape that obligation. If their shift is feasible only because, while evading the costs of keeping the option available to them, they nevertheless retain the right to return to their local utilities and demand service without penalty when their economical supplies elsewhere dry up, or their own generators fail, or their own telephone circuits are busy, the shift may involve not an improvement, but a loss in economic efficiency.[22]

C. *Regulatory Adaptations*

The still emerging resolution of these distortions has had several components.

Legislatures and regulatory commissions have been giving the utility companies increased freedom to reduce prices as low as their incremental costs to meet competition. Occasionally, this freedom has extended to the point of total deregulation of some services or transactions, such as Centrex, telephone equipment on the customer's premises, and some electric bulk power sales.

Also, both regulators and the passage of time have presided over a partial writing off, settling out, accelerated recovery, and disallowance of the heavy sunk costs—the multi-billion dollar take-or-pay obligations of the gas pipelines, the long-term contractual purchase obligations of the local gas distribution companies, the

---

22. On the separate problem of option demand and the possibility of market failure in satisfying it, see Weisbrod, *Collective-Consumption Services of Individual-Consumption Goods*, 78 Q. J. OF ECON. 471 (1964); Kahn, *The Tyranny of Small Decisions: Market Failures, Imperfections, and the Limits of Economics*, 19 KYKLOS 23 (1966). On the possible distortion of competition consequent on the failure to impose such a charge in the telephone industry, see A. KAHN, *supra* note 2, at 238-39. For the most thorough exposition of the case for such charges, see Weisman, *Default Capacity Tariffs: Smoothing the Transitional Regulatory Asymmetries in the Telecommunications Market*, 5 YALE J. ON REG. 149 (1988). *See also* Weisman, *Competitive Markets and Carriers of Last Resort*, PUB. UTIL. FORT., July 6, 1989, at 17; Weisman, *Optimal Re-contracting, Market Risk and the Regulated Firm in Competitive Transition*, 12 RES. IN L. & ECON. 153 (1989).

334

inflated costs of recently constructed or abandoned electric generating plants, and inadequately depreciated telephone company plant—that have constituted the major source of discrepancy between the companies' average revenue requirements for regulatory purposes and their own incremental costs.[23]

In a few cases, regulators have partially relaxed the utility's obligation to serve customers who choose to escape their *de facto* obligation to help carry fixed costs. Regulators have also considered permitting the utility companies to impose a capacity reservation charge—the leading example of which is the gas inventory holding charge contemplated by FERC—on customers who wish to retain the option of service on demand.[24] In a few recent cases, where buyers have had access to alternative suppliers, FERC has permitted the utility's obligation to be limited explicitly to the volumes and circumstances stipulated in long-term contracts.[25]

The importance and promise of individually negotiated long-term contracts can hardly be exaggerated, both as a newly permissible form of competition and as a device for reestablishing and redefining the relationship between utility companies and individual customers in a manner compatible with competition. In the electric power industry, for example, the increasing tendency of the utility companies to acquire their supplies by long-term contract has helped to introduce competition into generation. Before the Staggers Act, such contracts for rail transport were legally unenforceable: all rail and truck carriage had to be at openly posted, uniform spot rates. As a result, electric companies that had built generating plants in the Southwest designed to burn coal from Wyoming and Montana found themselves subjected to very sharp increases in the rail rates charged them by the single railroad or pair of end-to-end carriers to which they were captive. Since 1980, in contrast, most of the coal shipped by rail has been covered by long-term contracts.

The ability, newly available under deregulation, to enter into such arrangements, adapted to the particular needs of the individual shipper and providing for rewards and penalties based on performance of the transportation function, is said to have been an essential

23. In the case of the electric companies, the discrepancy has been reduced in many areas by marginal costs moving up toward average charges as growth in demand has outpaced additions to capacity.

24. *See* Kahn, *A Reprise*, *supra* note 7, at 18-21 (tracing dissolution of this obligation in the case of the airlines and motor carriers, and even incipient efforts in the electric utilities).

25. R. FITZGIBBONS, *supra* note 10, at 11.

335

factor in the rapid spread of just-in-time inventory and logistical control systems, which have produced cost savings estimated in the scores of billions of dollars a year.[26]

There has been no abatement in the zeal of regulatory commissions to protect residential and small commercial customers, almost all of whom remain captive to the local utility companies, from being forced to assume the sunk costs that the competitive markets can no longer be forced to bear. To some extent, they have continued to do so by discouraging "cream-skimming" competition—for example, by competitive providers of long-distance telephone service intrastate, or by proprietors of "smart buildings," providing telecommunications services for their tenants.[27] Increasingly, however, regulators have been developing methods consistent with, rather than obstructive of, the new competition—a tendency most fully developed in the field of telecommunications.

The simplest of these new methods has been a rate freeze for basic telephone service, accompanied by stipulations that service quality not deteriorate. The freeze may consist in a simple directive or undertaking to maintain existing rates for a number of years. Alternatively, it may provide for automatic adjustment to reflect inflation or changes in taxes or interstate separations. The indexations typically incorporate an automatic downward adjustment predicated on a targeted improvement in productivity, thereby ensuring a continuation of the long-term decline of these rates in real terms.

Such freezes or "social compacts" have some obvious virtues, both political and economic. They provide direct, straightforward protection for consumers of the services that are the subject of most

---

26. R. DELANEY, FREIGHT TRANSPORTATION DEREGULATION, SEMINAR T9 ON ROAD TRANSPORT DEREGULATION: EXPERIENCE, EVALUATION, AND RESEARCH 6 (Arthur D. Little, Inc.).

27. At times regulatory commissions have simply prohibited the utility companies under their jurisdiction from offering special competitive rates to attract customers, particularly where (1) the competitor's marginal or avoidable costs were no lower than those of the customer's traditional supplier, and (2) the consequence of the transaction would have been merely to shift the sunk costs inflating the rates of the latter from the departing customer to the remaining ones. See, e.g., In re Lukens Steel Co., No. P-810310 (Pa. Pub. Util. Comm'n, Jan. 13, 1984) (petition denied). In this case, the Pennsylvania Power and Light Co. sought to attract a large industrial customer from the Philadelphia Electric Co. with a favorable rate, even though both companies were generating their electricity from a common pool dispatching power from the lowest marginal-cost supply source. Similarly, the New York Public Service Commission dismissed the petition by some towns in Westchester County to be served by New York State Electric and Gas rather than Consolidated Edison. Interoffice Memorandum from Jean Cleary, Staff Counsel, to State of New York Public Service Commission (July 12, 1974).

336

intense regulatory concern. More important in the present context, they sever the link between those rates and the revenues from the more competitive services, and in this way, in principle, prevent cross-subsidization of the latter offerings by the former. By so doing, once again in principle, they make it possible to give the utility companies greater freedom to compete for the business on which they are challenged. Finally, by focusing regulation on prices rather than rates of return, and fixing the course of those prices over a period of time, these freezes or indexations mitigate the cost-plus character of traditional regulation, and therefore enhance the incentives of the companies to improve their efficiency.

These beneficent tendencies are sometimes reinforced by an explicit or implicit acceptance of a wider than usual range within which achieved rates of return are permitted to vary. Sometimes there is an accompanying provision for companies and ratepayers to share surplus profits, up to limits (before sharing) that would have seemed unacceptably high by historical standards. The consequently wider range of possible earnings, for longer periods of time, presumably provides carriers with enhanced incentives not only to minimize costs, but also to undertake risky investments and innovations that would be discouraged if the returns from successful ventures were limited to levels traditionally regarded as reasonable.[28]

Finally, the FCC now subjects AT&T's basic and non-basic interstate services to separate rate caps—ceilings on average prices (rather than on each individual one) indexed to inflation minus a productivity target. It has decided to do the same with the services

---

28. The accompanying divorce of basic service rates from the companies' overall costs and revenues relieves regulators to some extent of responsibility for scrutinizing the heavy expenditures the companies are making in fiberoptic transmission and digital switching, with a view to their possible disallowance. Since these outlays are typically justified only partly in terms of minimizing the costs of basic service, and in part in order to be able to offer new services the market for which is highly uncertain, regulators have naturally been concerned that subscribers interested only in the former not be burdened by the costs and greater risks properly attributable to the latter. Threatened with disallowance of some portion of these outlays from rate base, while lacking the prospect of being permitted to retain supernormal profits if the ventures prove successful, the companies may refrain from undertaking relatively risky innovations that may nevertheless be socially desirable. Freezes and indexations of basic service rates and variable rates of return tend to remove those obstacles. See Kahn & Shew, *Current Issues in Telecommunications Regulation: Pricing*, 4 YALE J. ON REG. 191 (1987).

337

of the local companies under its jurisdiction, and some states as well are now actively considering rate caps for intrastate services.[29]

These various regulatory devices tend to permit the utility companies to compete effectively for business by offering rates as low as their incremental costs, if necessary. In this way, they correct the worst competitive distortion introduced by partial deregulation, while limiting the ability of a company to recoup net revenue losses from basic service customers. They also limit the extent to which the company may compensate for reductions in competitive rates by raising rates for non-basic services.

Of course, such arrangements openly invite the companies—and, insofar as the adoption of rate caps is coupled with the opportunity for a wider range of achieved rates of return, encourage them—to introduce a finer discrimination in the prices they charge for their several services. This is only a more polite way of saying that deregulation permits a fuller exploitation of monopoly power.[30]

The counter-considerations—in my judgment compelling—are the necessity of giving the utility companies freedom to meet the

---

29. In re Policy and Rules Concerning Rates for Dominant Carriers, No. 87-313 (F.C.C. Supplemental Notice of Proposed Rulemaking, adopted March 8, 1990); In re Policy and Rules Concerning Rates for Dominant Carriers, No. 87-313 (F.C.C. Report and Order and Second Further Notice of Proposed Rulemaking, adopted March 16, 1989). For a description of the FCC's plan and of a similar one adopted by the California Public Utilities Commission, see Norris, *Price Caps: An Alternative Regulatory Framework for Telecommunications Carriers*, PUB. UTIL. FORT., Jan. 18, 1990, at 44. On the pioneering British "RPI minus 3" scheme, see Stelzer, *Regulating Telecommunications in Britain: A New Alternative to the U.S. Approach*, TELEMATICS, Sept., 1986, at 7.

The Florida Commission has in effect grafted a kind of rate cap on the formal scheme of variable rates of return that it accepted for Bell South, by explicitly excluding the Company from the right to share in any surplus earnings that are the consequence of increases in its average rates: "Southern Bell will not be permitted to enhance its profits through rate increases. . . . We will allow any rate increases to be netted against rate decreases." In re Petitions of Southern Bell Telephone and Telegraph Company for Rate Stabilization etc., No. 880069-TL and 870832-TL, Order No. 20162, slip. op., at 7-8 (Fla. Pub. Serv. Comm'n, Oct. 13, 1988).

These direct restraints on prices—whether in the form of freezes, indexation provisions, "social compacts," or rate caps—do not represent an abandonment of traditional rate of return regulation. They typically contemplate periodic reexamination of the results and readjustment of the formulas when and as rates of return range outside of acceptable limits. In the last analysis, therefore, they are all forms of rate of return regulation. See, e.g., Noll, *Telecommunications Regulation in the 1990s*, in 1 NEW DIRECTIONS IN TELECOMMUNICATIONS POLICY 11 (P. Newburg ed. 1989). The potentially significant difference, in principle, is that these various formulas may contemplate substantially longer regulatory lags, and therefore imply a willingness on the part of both the commission and the company to accept returns fluctuating and persisting within some range wider than would be permitted under traditional regulation.

30. This is Joseph P. Gillan's objection to rate caps. Gillan, *Reforming State Regulation of Exchange Carriers*, TELEMATICS, May, 1989, at 17.

increasing competition they encounter in the provision of "non-basic" services, and their entitlement to recover prudently incurred costs. The former is grounded in considerations of both economic efficiency and of retaining whatever contribution the competitive markets may continue to make to holding down the rates for basic service. The latter requires that the companies be allowed an opportunity to recover the consequent net revenue losses elsewhere, as the market will allow. The resulting discriminations are therefore in the interest of subscribers to basic service, and they tend also to minimize the aggregate distortions in customer choices created by the need to price above marginal cost in order to recover total costs.[31]

D. *Possible Reversions to Regulation*

Each of these adaptations of regulatory policy to competition represents a further loosening of restraints, rather than a reversal of the deregulation process. Each therefore seems to support the general expectation that the trend of the last ten to fifteen years will persist. There are, however, two opposing possibilities.

The first is the far-from-negligible danger of a misguided intensification of protectionism, in the event that we either fail to cure the fundamental macroeconomic causes of our national balance of trade deficit or we "solve" the problem by falling into a recession. The public's enthusiasm for free competition varies inversely with the unemployment rate.

The second possibility lies in the microeconomy of the electric utility industry. Major sections of the country are likely to need substantial additions to generating capacity within the next several years. At present, a large portion of the increase is expected to be supplied by non-utility generators using natural gas as their fuel. It seems likely, however, that the present large natural gas supply bubble will be exhausted during the 1990s, resulting in a sharp increase in the field price. In that event, a large portion of those expected additions to non-utility generating capacity may well not materialize, and we may see the commissions and the public alike turning back toward total reliance on their local utility companies. In these circumstances, the recent vogue of regulatorily-required

---

31. *See* Baumol & Bradford, *Optimal Departures From Marginal Cost Pricing*, 60 AM. ECON. REV. 265 (1970).

least-cost planning[32] could well result in restoration of the traditional "regulatory compact"—the mutual commitment on the part of the companies to ensure the required expansions of capacity and of the commissions, having lent their approval, to provide reasonable assurances to the companies of recovering prudently incurred costs.[33]

II. The Merits of Continued Non-Regulation

The future course of regulation and deregulation will be determined not only by the changing configurations of private interests, prevailing political and economic philosophies and macroeconomic conditions, but also by how we collectively appraise the record so far. The difficulty is that the performance of even a single industry is multi-faceted and never susceptible to a definitive evaluation; even less is it possible to reach a simple, unequivocal verdict about the effects of deregulation on the diverse collection of industries that have been affected by it in varying ways and degrees over the last fifteen years.

Nevertheless, I believe most economists would agree on the following two broad propositions:

> *First*, wherever even quite imperfect competition is feasible, it is superior to command-and-control regulation. This proposition has a corollary: where such regulation continues to be necessary, as in major sectors of the traditional public utilities, it should, to the greatest extent possible, be designed in such a way as to be compatible with competition rather than obstructive of it; and

> *Second*, if competition is to work well, it requires a great variety of governmental interventions to remedy imperfections and market failures—interventions that, however validly they may be characterized as regulatory, differ fundamentally from the kind of direct economic regulation previously administered by such agencies as the CAB and ICC, and still practiced by most of the state public utility commissions.

---

32. Burkhart, *Least-Cost Planning: A State Survey*, PUB. UTIL. FORT., May 14, 1987, at 38.

33. On the previous dissolution of this implied "regulatory compact," see Kahn, *Competition: Past, Present, and Future—Perception versus Reality*, in UTILITIES STRATEGIC ISSUES FORUM 2, 3, 9-10 (Elec. Power Res. Inst. 1988), and Kahn, *Who Should Pay for Power Plant Duds?* Wall St. J. Aug. 15, 1985, at 26, col. 3.

340

To these propositions I would attach a third, somewhat less obvious one. A central part of the case for deregulation is the severe deficiencies of regulation—deficiencies of information, wisdom, and incentives, along with a strong inherent tendency to suppress competition.[34] If, however—as I will argue presently—the response to the imperfections we have observed in the performance of the deregulated industries is that a large share of the fault lies in the failure of government to perform its essential competition-supplementing functions, such as antitrust enforcement, then the case for deregulation may rest upon assumptions about the ability of the government to fulfill those supplementary responsibilities just as unrealistic as the assumptions behind the case for direct economic regulation. This last consideration could, in some situations, take us full circle, back to an acceptance of full-scale regulation as the less imperfect of the two alternatives. In most instances, I believe, it does not.

A. *Reading the Record: The Superiority of Competition*[35]

The deregulated industries are unquestionably more competitive today than they were previously. This is not to deny the significance of the increased concentration at the national level in less-than-truckload (LTL) carriage or, marginally, in airlines,[36] or to claim that the competition is sufficiently effective in all markets to have fully taken over the role previously played by governmentally-enforced price ceilings. It is to say that market concentration route-by-route has definitely declined, on average, in markets of all sizes and dimensions,[37] and that the several indicia of competitive behavior

---

34. *See* A. KAHN, *supra* note 2, at 1-46.

35. Not surprisingly, the record of the effects of deregulation on performance is much fuller and more susceptible to the drawing of conclusions—favorable or unfavorable—in the case of industries and markets that have been thoroughly deregulated than for the core public utilities; for this reason, the following account has relatively little to say about the latter.

36. For a discussion of the anticompetitive consequences of the same air carriers meeting one another in market after market, see Shepherd, *The Airline Industry*, in THE STRUCTURE OF AMERICAN INDUSTRY 217, 225 (W. Adams ed. 1990), echoing my own almost identical observation with respect to the chemical industry many years earlier. Kahn, *The Chemicals Industry*, in THE STRUCTURE OF AMERICAN INDUSTRY 197, 208-09 (W. Adams, ed. 1950).

37. For the changes in airlines between 1983 and 1987, see CONGRESSIONAL BUDGET OFFICE, POLICIES FOR THE DEREGULATED AIRLINE INDUSTRY 17 (1988) [hereinafter CBO REPORT] and, for 1978-83, see CIVIL AERONAUTICS BOARD, IMPLEMENTATION OF THE PROVISIONS OF THE AIRLINE DEREGULATION ACT OF 1978 14 (1984). *See also* SECRETARY'S

341

support the same conclusion.[38] The same is true of telecommunications, particularly in customer and central office equipment, long-distance telephony, and the provision of high-speed, high-volume transmission of data. Because of the competition unleashed by deregulation, average prices of air travel, trucking, and long-distance telephoning are down substantially, producing not only

TASK FORCE ON COMPETITION IN THE U.S. DOMESTIC AIRLINE INDUSTRY, U.S. DEP'T OF TRANSP., 1 INDUSTRY AND ROUTE STRUCTURE 3, 11-12 (1990) [hereinafter SECRETARY'S TASK FORCE REPORT]. The mutual interpenetration by the dominant carriers of their respective regional markets, which that result, has occurred also in LTL trucking. *See* U.S. GENERAL ACCOUNTING OFFICE, TRUCKING REGULATION: PRICE COMPETITION AND MARKET STRUCTURE IN THE TRUCKING INDUSTRY 18 (1987).

38.   On the case of the railroads, see MacDonald, *Railroad Deregulation, Innovation, and Competition: Effects of the Staggers Act on Grain Transportation*, 32 J. L. & ECON. 63, 64-65 (1989); *Hearings Before the Joint Economic Committee*, 101st Cong., 2d Sess. (Oct. 19, 1989) (testimony of Darius W. Gaskins, Jr., former chairman of the Interstate Commerce Commission) [hereinafter Gaskins Statement]. With respect to the increased inter-railroad competition in the Powder River Basin, see BUREAU OF LAND MANAGEMENT, CASE STUDY: IMPACT OF COAL TRANSPORTATION ON WESTERN COAL DEVELOPMENT AND THE FEDERAL COAL PROGRAM (1987).

Critics have laid heavy emphasis on the substantial air fare increases in late 1988 and early 1989, which have reflected the industry's increased facility in playing oligopolistic follow-the-leader. But those criticisms have clearly minimized the underlying competitive tensions—which showed up, for example, in a sharp decline in average yields in the ensuing months, practically all the way back to 1988 levels. This experience elicited universal moaning in the investment community about the consequent erosion of yields and profits. For example:

> [t]he airline industry remains a very competitive business. If Congress thinks this is not a competitive business, perhaps a brief review of some of the promotional fare activity spreading—as competitive battles heat up—in a number of regions will convince them. American, Pan Am and Eastern are battling it out in Miami; America West is entering the Hawaii free-for-all; Eastern will take on Delta in the Northeast-Florida markets and Atlanta in hopes of regaining lost market share. USAir is attempting to slow Midway's expansion plans in Philadelphia. And, it seems everyone wants a bigger piece of the West Coast Corridor market, from American (San Jose) to United (San Francisco-SFO) to Delta (Los Angeles-LAX) to USAir (LAX & SFO) to Southwest (Oakland) to Alaska Airlines (Seattle).

Derchin & Tortora, *The Airline Industry: What Happen [sic] to the Oligopoly?*, in DREXEL BURNHAM LAMBERT, Research 4 (Dec. 8, 1989).

Shortly thereafter, First Boston estimated the industry's operating profits in 1989 at $1.95 billion, or 33 percent below the $2.95 billion reported in 1988—with the entire decline occurring in the second half of the year. PAUL P. KAROS, FIRST BOSTON, EQUITY RESEARCH, INDUSTRY: AIRLINES, FLIGHTLINES: EXPECT BRUTAL FOURTH QUARTER COMPARISONS 1 (Nov. 30, 1989).

342

consumer savings but net welfare improvements in the billions of dollars each year.[39]

The effect of deregulation on the relationship between the structure of prices and costs has been more complicated. In general, regulators tend to equalize rates to different customers despite differences in the costs of serving them; correspondingly, competition since deregulation has apparently—despite some increases in price discrimination, to which I will return—forced prices for the several categories of service into closer conformity with their respective costs.[40] Prominent examples of this economically beneficial change have been the increased sensitivity of air fares to the effects on cost of length of trip and traffic density, and of transportation rates generally to the differences between peak and off-peak and front- and back-haul. In telephony, the prices of long-distance calling and basic residential service have likewise come into closer conformity with their respective costs.[41]

---

39. S. MORRISON & C. WINSTON, THE ECONOMIC EFFECTS OF AIRLINE DEREGULATION (1986); Rose, *The Incidence of Regulatory Rents in the Motor Carrier Industry*, 16 RAND J. ECON. 299 (1985). In the telephone case, see reference to the L. Perl study in Kahn & Shew, *supra* note 28, at 209. It is of course impossible to say with certainty how much of the observed decline in price can be attributed to deregulation—a consideration especially pertinent in the case of the airlines, whose average fares declined secularly under regulation as well. *See* Brenner, *Airline Deregulation—A Case Study in Public Policy Failure*, 16 TRANSP. L.J., 179, 198-99 (1988); Kahn, *Airline Deregulation—A Mixed Bag, But a Clear Success Nevertheless*, 16 TRANSP. L.J., 229, 235-36 (1988). Morrison and Winston have come closest to resolving the question by reconstructing for the post-deregulation period the Standard Industry Fare Level (SIFL) index, according to which the CAB used to set fares, and demonstrating in this way that actual fares have indeed been consistently lower, by many billions of dollars a year, than they would have been had those CAB policies continued in effect. Morrison & Winston, *The Dynamics of Airline Pricing and Competition*, 80 AM. ECON. REV., PAPERS & PROC. 189 (1990).

40. MacDonald observes that the widespread use of long-term contracts for rail carriage has been especially beneficial to large shippers; it could therefore have made possible price discriminations that were previously impermissible. His major finding, however, is that the Staggers Act deserves substantial credit for the accelerated replacement of single-car with much lower-cost multiple-car and unit-train shipments, which have required the predictability and larger volumes that large shippers have been best able to provide. The resulting breakdown of the ICC's historic policy of equalizing rates to large and small shippers and the abandonment of unprofitable routes—the previous mandatory service of which had likewise been beneficial mainly to small shippers—have therefore evidently involved a closer alignment of rates with costs and so resulted, on balance, in a diminution of discrimination. *See* MacDonald, *supra* note 38.

41. Between December 1983 and December 1989, the local telephone charges component of the Consumer Price Index increased 19.3 percent in real terms, while the average price of long-distance calling declined 44.5 percent interstate and 24.1 percent intrastate. FEDERAL-STATE JOINT BOARD, U.S. BUREAU OF LABOR STATISTICS, MONITORING REPORT CC DOCKET NO. 87-339, at 246 (1990). This has been more the indirect than the direct consequence of intensified competition: the FCC initially required local exchange companies to charge long-distance companies rates far above marginal costs for access to

343

Purchasers are being offered a greatly expanded range of price/service options, most strikingly in financial services, telecommunications and transportation.[42]

The removal of regulatory restrictions and the pressures of competition have yielded marked increases in productivity.[43] The failure of the airline industry to realize the huge potential economies of hub and spoke operations under regulation testifies eloquently to the inefficiency of centralized government planning and the superiority of unconstrained profit-seeking in free markets. Similarly, the freedom of both airlines and truckers to vary their effective charges from one moment and one route to another, depending on the relationship between demand and capacity, has contributed powerfully to improved use of equipment and consequent reductions in cost.

All of this has occurred with no evident sacrifice of safety.[44] And, with the glaring exception of the general decline in the quality of the air travel experience, it has on the whole resulted in improved quality as well as variety of service, just as any student of competition would have predicted.[45]

B. *Imperfections of Competition and Derelictions of Government*

There remain three glaring apparent exceptions to the beneficent consequences of deregulation—the deterioration in the quality of air travel, a sharp increase in certain kinds of price discrimination,

interstate callers. When institutional customers and interexchange carriers began to bypass the local phone companies in order to evade these inflated charges, the FCC gradually reduced them and substituted a direct charge on ultimate subscribers. *See* Kahn & Shew, *supra* note 28, at 196-97.

42. Prominent among the expanded range of service offerings in transportation have been long-term contract as well as spot rates, sharply increased intermodal carriage, and—thanks to the spread of airline hub and spoke operations—an increased variety of available destinations. SECRETARY'S TASK FORCE REPORT, *supra* note 37, at 3, 149-289 (especially the discussion at 160).

43. For the case of the railroads, see Gaskins Statement, *supra* note 38.

44. *See generally* Rose, Profitability and Product Quality: Economic Determinants of Airline Safety Performance (1989) (unpublished manuscript on file with author, publication forthcoming in J. POL. ECON.); TRANSPORTATION SAFETY IN AN AGE OF DEREGULATION (L. Moses & I. Savage ed. 1989). Statistics compiled by the Federal Highway Administration show a decline in fatal trucking accidents of about 20 percent in 1981-85, as compared with 1976-79, on a per mile basis. Letter from Edward H. Rastatter of the Regulatory Review and Planning Division to Alfred E. Kahn (Sept. 16, 1987). *See also* CAL. PUB. UTIL. COMM'N & HIGHWAY PATROL, REPORT ON TRUCK SAFETY, JOINT LEGISLATIVE REPORT AB 2678 (1987).

45. The one qualification of that prediction would have been a recognition of the strong tendency of the previous regulatory regimes to encourage an inefficient inflation of service quality. *See* text accompanying *infra* note 46.

344

and—reflecting a loss of the safety or stability that the previous pervasive restrictions on competition were supposed to preserve—the savings and loan fiasco.

1. *Discomfort and Congestion in Air Travel*

The first thing to observe about the increase in congestion, crowding and delay in aviation is that they reflect success, not failure. A major criticism of regulation had been that, by discouraging price competition, it had on the one side encouraged inefficient competition of a cost-inflating, quality-enhancing character,[46] and, on the other, failed to probe the price elasticity of potential demand. Deregulation has eliminated the distortion and made good the failure. The result has been deeply discounted fares—necessarily for service in fuller planes, with tighter seating and a lower ratio of ticket agents and flight attendants to passengers. It has been the enthusiastic response of travelers to this new option that has taxed the capacity of our airports and air traffic control systems, and the patience of travelers.

Neither an economist nor a government official is competent to decide whether the lower-quality service provided at a lower price is superior to the higher price/quality option exclusively available before. It is the task of an efficiently-functioning market to offer customers the choice, to the extent it is feasible to do so. The inefficiency of regulatory cartelization, corrected by deregulation, was that it suppressed the former option.

To some extent, unregulated competition has had the equally deplorable opposite effect: travelers who pay full fare suffer along with the ones who buy the discount tickets from long lines, uncomfortable seating and delays. This spillover effect might suggest there is no basis for concluding that there has been a net welfare improvement.

There are several reasons for rejecting that implication. First, the superior service option has not disappeared: the airlines compete strenuously for the patronage of the regular full-fare-paying customers, with frequent flyer credits, upgrades, separate lines, and, where feasible, separate business class service.

Second, to the extent that it is not feasible to provide full-fare-paying passengers a fully differentiated service—wider seating than

---

46. For a broad exposition of this proposition across various industries, see A. KAHN, *supra* note 2, at 10, 189 (trucking), 206-20 (securities brokerage and airlines).

their discount-fare-paying fellow travelers, for example—it is a general principle, and on balance a beneficent one, that in a market economy the majority of dollar votes rules, at the necessary expense of minority preferences, when the two cannot be reconciled.[47]

Finally, the general increase in congestion and the failure of the market to offer delay-free travel to customers willing to pay for it are, above all, a consequence of severe derelictions on the part of government. During my tenure as Chairman of the Civil Aeronautics Board, I pointed out that it was the responsibility of government to respond to the increased demands generated by the competitive forces we were unleashing, by expanding airport and air traffic control capacity, and by pricing access to those scarce facilities rationally.[48]

2. *Intensification of Price Discrimination*

Most of the history of economic regulation can be written around the phenomenon of price discrimination. Discriminations by the railroads inspired our first major venture in regulation. Regulators, hostile to even cost-justified price differentiations, have frequently required discrimination, in the interest of "equity." On the other hand, regulators have long recognized the possible economic benefits of discrimination in the presence of economies of scale and scope, and of overall revenue constraints defined in terms of historic or embedded costs.[49]

---

47. *See* Kahn & Shew, *supra* note 28, at 229-32 (discussing "collective consumption decisions").

48. *See, e.g.*, Address by Alfred E. Kahn, Federal Aviation Administration Consultative Planning Conference (Mar. 22, 1978). *See also* Levine, *Landing Fees and the Airport Congestion Problem*, 12 J. L. & Econ. 63, 79-108 (1969).

The Massachusetts Port Authority (Massport) in 1988 shifted the basis for landing fees at Boston's Logan Airport from weight of aircraft to the number of operations. The Department of Transportation (DOT) ordered Massport to withdraw those altered charges on the ground that they were discriminatory, because, among other reasons, they entailed higher charges per passenger on smaller than on larger planes. What DOT failed abysmally to understand was that it was the previous charges that were discriminatory: the change to which it objected was fully justified by differences in the respective marginal costs of serving the two classes of customers. On the other hand, the new fee schedules' failure to differentiate peak and off-peak landings was admittedly an imperfection, which Massport had promised to remedy.

49. Observe, for example, the unrestricted pricing freedom conferred on the railroads by the Staggers Act, within the limits of 180 percent of average variable costs and overall revenue adequacy. 49 U.S.C. § 1701a (d)(2). *See also* T. KEELER, RAILROADS, FREIGHT AND PUBLIC POLICY 98-101 (1983).

346

Even ardent deregulators have understood that unregulated price competition in the public utility industries would probably be highly selective and localized, with its benefits available only to some well-situated customers, because of the ubiquity of the monopoly power that counselled regulation in the first place. Many of us have been surprised, however, to find discrimination increasing also with the deregulation of industries that we thought were potentially structurally competitive. Borenstein and Rose have demonstrated unequivocally that price discrimination in the airline industry has in some respects increased, substantially and significantly, as markets have become less concentrated.[50]

Manifestly, the instances of sharply increased price discrimination that deregulation has made possible in airlines and railroads are both a competitive and a monopolistic phenomenon. They reflect intense competition for the traffic most likely to be attracted by price differences among competitors. They have also promoted economic efficiency in very important ways. The ability of the railroads to price down toward incremental cost has improved the distribution of the transportation function among the competing modes; their ability to charge rates for demand-inelastic traffic incorporating wider margins above variable costs has contributed to an improvement in their financial condition, which has helped them to finance major improvements in trackage, equipment and service, without yielding excessive returns in the aggregate. The deeply discounted fares to discretionary air travelers fill seats that would otherwise remain empty and help make possible more frequent scheduling, which is particularly valuable to the full-fare travelers.

Manifestly, however, the discriminations also reflect the exercise of monopoly power no longer curbed by direct price regulation. The reasons for the return of monopoly power to the airline industry, following upon the intensified competition of the early 1980s, and the way in which it has been exercised to produce sharp increases in the unrestricted fares paid by about 10 percent of the

---

50. Borenstein & Rose, Competitive Price Discrimination in the U.S. Airline Industry (1989) (unpublished manuscript available at University of Michigan Institute of Public Policy Studies). Their results do not necessarily conflict with my previous observation that in other respects price discrimination has been reduced significantly. Borenstein and Rose's findings relate to an increased dispersion of the fares charged different passengers on individual routes; my observation related to the structure of fares for different routes, times of day and modes of travel. On the other hand, a marked increase has occurred in discrimination in the fares carriers charge on different routes depending on the extent to which they encounter competition on them. See text accompanying infra note 51.

347

travelers, is by now a familiar story.[51] The increasing sophistication with which the leading carriers—particularly the ones with the most fully developed computerized reservations systems—have learned to practice what the industry euphemistically calls "yield management" has enabled them to take full advantage of that monopoly power, while also erecting possibly insurmountable barriers to entry by truly new competitors.[52]

There are three possible ways in which government might respond to this equivocal situation.

It could do nothing. We put up with a great deal of competitive imperfection in industries that we would not think of regulating. It is by no means clear that unrestricted fares exceed the stand-alone costs of serving the minority of passengers who pay them, or that the discrimination to which those travelers are subject is not compensated for by frequent flyer credits[53] and the improved convenience of scheduling that the high fares help make possible. The airline industry is far more competitive than it was; the benefits of that competition have been widely distributed; and the industry is evidently not earning monopoly profits. In these circumstances, it would not be ridiculous to conclude that no remedy was required.

Second, however, the government clearly has neglected responsibilities of which it was never the intention of deregulation to relieve it. These include vigilant policing of safety practices, the provision of the requisite airport and air traffic control capacity[54] and pricing access to them rationally, and vigorous enforcement of the antitrust laws, along with other policies designed to remove

51.   See, e.g., Hearings Before the Subcommittee on Aviation of the Senate Committee on Commerce, Science, and Transportation, 101st Cong., 1st Sess. 6-61, 131-41 (1989) (statement of Kenneth M. Mead, Director, Transportation Issues, Resources, Community and Economic Development Division, U.S. General Accounting Office) [hereinafter Mead Statement]; CBO REPORT, supra note 37, at 23-36; SECRETARY'S TASK FORCE ON COMPETITION IN THE U.S. DOMESTIC AIRLINE INDUSTRY, U.S. DEP'T OF TRANSP., 1 PRICING 3-4 (1990); Borenstein, Hubs and High Fares: Airport Dominance and Market Power in the U.S. Airline Industry, 20 RAND J. ECON. 344 (1989); Levine, Airline Competition in Deregulated Markets: Theory, Firm Strategy, and Public Policy, 4 YALE J. ON REG. 393 (1987).

52.   For these complicated reasons, Shepherd is both correct and at best telling only part of the story when, under the heading of "price discrimination," he concludes that "airline pricing behavior has virtually ceased to be a competitive weapon and has become instead a complex process by which an airline tries to maximize the revenue it extracts from its customers." Shepherd, supra note 36, at 232.

53.   On the especial attractiveness of these credits as a device for retaining the patronage of the full-fare-paying passenger, see Levine, supra note 51, at 452-54.

54.   An alternative clearly worth considering would be to permit private entrepreneurs to fulfill this function in whole or in part. A leading proponent of privatization is Robert W. Poole, Jr., of the Reason Foundation. See Poole, Toward Safer Skies, in INSTEAD OF REGULATION (R. Poole ed. 1982).

348

barriers to competition. Prominent among such supplementary policies would be expansion of airport capacity sufficient to keep open opportunities for competitive challenges to hub-dominating carriers and dissolution of preferential arrangements between those carriers and their hub airports.[55] The bill recently introduced by Senators Danforth and McCain is a long overdue initiative along the latter lines.[56]

Finally, however, it is not possible in principle to reject the reimposition of price ceilings to protect travelers subject to monopolistic exploitation, where restoration of more effective competition proves to be infeasible.

My own endorsement of the second approach and reluctance to embark upon the third—a position with which most economists would probably agree—is heavily influenced by the lesson of history that, once introduced, direct (as contrasted with competition-supplementing) regulation has both a logical and almost irresistible tendency to spread. Price ceilings would be of little value if they were not accompanied by the introduction of floors under quality of service. It takes little imagination to see where that logic might lead—to prohibitions of reductions in the frequency of scheduling and in the frequency with which full-fare paying customers are upgraded to first class; stipulations about the minimum quality of meals; maximum charges for head sets; and maximum length of lines at the ticket counter. These examples are not fanciful: all but one of them were adopted under regulation, in mirror image, to prevent competitive evasions of governmentally-set price floors.

3. *The Savings and Loan Fiasco*

The flood of savings and loan bank failures and the consequent multi-hundred-billion-dollar cost to the Federal Government dramatically underscores the second of the three propositions with which I introduced this appraisal of the record—namely, that economic deregulation cannot mean firing the police force. It also, however, inescapably raises the question implicit in the third one: may not

---

55. *See* Mead Statement, *supra* note 51, at 4-5; SECRETARY'S TASK FORCE ON COMPETITION IN THE U.S. DOMESTIC AIRLINE INDUSTRY, U.S. DEP'T OF TRANSP., AIRPORTS, AIR TRAFFIC CONTROL AND RELATED CONCERNS (IMPACT ON ENTRY), ch. 3 (1990).

56. S. 1741, 101st Cong., 1st Sess. (1989). The bill, entitled "A Bill to Amend the Federal Aviation Act of 1958 to Increase Competition Among Commercial Air Carriers at the Nation's Major Airports and for Other Purposes," was introduced by Senators McCain, Danforth and Bradley on October 6, 1989.

349

deregulation in some circumstances put on police forces burdens heavier than they can realistically be expected to bear?

In retrospect, the causes of the massive failures are clear. They were the consequence of our having removed the regulatory ceilings on interest rates payable to depositors, which in turn necessitated a relaxation of the restrictions on the kinds of lending and investment activities in which those institutions were permitted to engage. What we evidently failed to recognize was that removal of these restrictions, while retaining Federal deposit insurance, openly invited the more speculative if not reckless lending and outright fraud that, along with a good deal of bad luck, produced the present debacle. So long as the government guaranteed their deposits, institutions whose assets may have been worth far less than their liabilities could nevertheless continue to attract deposits by offering higher interest rates, and could engage in additional risky investments—as well as continued peculation. If those ventures proved successful, the owners could not only remain in business but could make large profits; if they failed, it would be the Federal Savings and Loan Deposit Insurance Corporation that would be left holding the bag—as indeed it was.[57]

In short, deregulation, particularly in the presence of Federal deposit insurance, enormously increased the necessity for vigilant bank examination, enforcement of capital requirements sufficient to provide a cushion against losses, varying deposit insurance premiums with the riskiness of the lending and investing activities of the insured institutions, and a readiness to close down S&Ls that were effectively insolvent.

C. The Future Direction: Coming Full Circle?

This kind of defense of the deregulation record—"It wasn't my fault, the trouble is you other people didn't do your job"—is a trifle glib. It contains more than a trace of justifying the abandonment of direct regulation, because of its severe imperfections, in terms that implicitly demand perfection of performance by such agencies as the Department of Transportation, the Savings and Loan Bank Board

---

57. See Andrews, Is There Any Way Out of the Deposit Insurance Crisis?, INSTITUTIONAL INVESTOR, Sept. 1988, at 86; Bush, Former FHLBB Regulators Offer Solutions to the Current FSLIC Crisis, SAVINGS INSTITUTIONS, Oct. 1988, at 81; O'Driscoll, Bank Failures: The Deposit Insurance Connection, CONTEMP. POL'Y ISSUES, Apr. 1988, at 1. O'Driscoll would disagree with this diagnosis only to the extent it assigns blame to the removal of restrictions on the asset side; he contends that diversification alone would have reduced risk.

350

and Congress—higher levels of prescience, conscientiousness, information, incorruptibility or simple effectiveness than can reasonably be expected.

To some extent, similarly, thrusting upon the antitrust authorities both blame for some of the monopolistic consequences of airline deregulation and responsibility for their future remedy implicitly expects more of competition-preserving policies than they can deliver. It is possible to identify fewer than a handful of mergers and code-sharing (i.e., traffic-interchange) agreements that probably should not have been permitted on antitrust grounds; most of the mergers that have reconcentrated the industry were more a reflection of the economies of networking and the inability of smaller competitors to survive in open competition than they were an independent cause of its attenuation. Again, the greatest disadvantage borne today by airlines dependent on the computerized reservations systems of their major rivals is apparently the high booking fees they have to pay; but these raise the inescapable consideration that the high profits of the system owners may be a reasonable reward for an important innovation; and the possible divestiture cure has never, to my knowledge, confronted the possible sacrifice of economies of integration. Yet again, frequent flyer credits augment the monopoly power of the larger carriers, and particularly the ones dominating the hubs used by business travelers; but it would be difficult to attack them directly, because they are a form of price competition. Moreover, the logical remedy of subjecting them to income tax when the purchases that generated them were treated as deductible business expenses would apparently be an administrative nightmare. Finally, an attack on predatory pricing would involve all-too-familiar difficulties of distinguishing unacceptable price discriminations from legitimate competitive responses and welfare-enhancing exploitations of the economies of scale and scope.[58]

58. These reservations about the likely efficacy of antitrust should not be construed as in any way diluting my firm advocacy of vigorous competition-preserving and enhancing policies, in preference to reregulation.

On the desirability of a forthright attack on practices that might be regarded as predatory, for example, I am among the minority of American economists who feel that our profession and the courts have gone much too far in the direction of minimizing the likelihood of predation and the threat to competition it may pose. See, for example, the decision by the CAB, under my Chairmanship, to limit the permissible competitive response of the International Air Transport Association carriers to the intensified competition on trans-Atlantic routes of the charters and Freddie Laker—an effort ultimately overturned by President Carter; my warning of the dangers (which have in fact materialized) of a successful price response of the incumbent carriers to the prospective entry of World and Capitol into the transcontinental market, in Kahn, *Deregulatory Schizophrenia*, 75 CALIF. L.

351

Competition can in some circumstances make unrealistic demands on consumers as well—assuming a greater ability on their part to make complex choices, on pain of suffering penalties to which they had not previously been subjected, than they either have or are willing to take the trouble to acquire. A poignant illustration of the resulting dilemma has been provided in recent years by providers of alternate telephone operator services, which have entered into arrangements with non-telephone-company owners of public telephones, hotels, and other such institutions serving transient customers, under which, in exchange for commissions to the owners, they receive the right to provide operator services and charge what they please. The problems arise because the transient caller is an often unwitting captive to such arrangements between the other two parties. The competitive solution would be to permit this kind of free entry, while requiring comprehensive disclosure of the system of charges and, probably also, that callers be offered the opportunity to be transferred without charge to the long distance carrier of their own choice. Conceivably, however, the burden on consumers of digesting such information and choosing may outweigh the benefits of competition; one is reminded of Oscar Wilde's analogous observation: "The trouble with Socialism is that it uses up too many evenings."

Conclusion

I can take solace from the equivocal nature of these observations in the fact that I have been consistent in my equivocation. The beginning of wisdom in the devising of regulatory and deregulatory policies must be, as I put it in celebrating the "passing of the public utility concept,"

> a skepticism of the universal efficiency of both the unregulated market, on the one side, and of government enterprise on the other, sufficient to make it impossible for me simply to abandon the regulatory tool. Competition and regulation are both highly imperfect institutions. So is antitrust. It should not

REV., 1059, 1060-68 (1987); *see also* Kahn, The Macroeconomic Consequences of Sensible Microeconomic Policies, The First Distinguished Lecture on Economics in Government, Annual Meeting of the American Economic Association and Society of Government Economists 11-15 (Nat. Econ. Res. Assoc. 1985).

352

be surprising, therefore, that there is no single choice between them equally valid for all times and places. . . .[59]

The experience of the last decade or so justifies a somewhat less fatuous conclusion. I believe it has confirmed our historic presumption in favor of competitive markets: against the deregulatory fiasco of the S&Ls must be weighed the regulatory fiascos of nuclear power plant construction and the shortages and extreme distortions of natural gas markets during this same decade. Our recent experience demonstrates also that free markets may demand governmental interventions just as pervasive and quite possibly more imaginative than direct regulation; but its lesson is that those interventions should to the greatest extent possible preserve, supplement, and enhance competition, rather than suppress it. Finally, to the extent direct economic regulation continues to be required, it is preferable that it be of a kind compatible with competition, rather than obstructive of it.

In short, the lesson I take from recent history is that the evolution of regulatory policy will never come to an end. The path it takes—and we should make every effort to see that it takes—however, is the path not of a full circle or pendulum, which would take us back to where we started, but of a spiral, which has

---

59. Kahn, *A Reprise*, *supra* note 7, at 26. For a recent, persuasive exposition of the ubiquity of market failure—as well as regulatory failure—in transportation, see Kay & Thompson, Regulatory Reform in Transport in the UK: Principles and Application (Oct. 1989) (unpublished manuscript on file with Center for Business Strategy, London Business School).

It is important for me to make clear what it is that I have been consistently equivocal about. It has to do with selecting the set of institutional arrangements best suited to achieving economically optimal results, not with the propriety of economic efficiency as the primary goal of regulatory (or deregulatory) policy.

In contrast, the debate between advocates of regulation and deregulation is in very large measure about the latter, not the former issue. Opponents of deregulation will often protest—sometimes truculently, I can attest—that efficiency is not and should not be the sole or even the primary end of economic regulation. While I endorse the proposition that fairness and a more equitable distribution of income should be central goals of public policy, I also insist that proponents of such goals have every obligation to be just as rigorous in thinking about how they may best be served as the advocates of pure economic efficiency. And "best," in a world of scarcity, must mean "at minimum social cost." Restrictions on entry and price competition and distortions of the relationship between prices and marginal cost are usually irrational ways of achieving those ends, and to the extent regulation has served them in these ways, it has typically done so at excessive social cost. From this standpoint, one of the major accomplishments of deregulation has been to force us to seek more rational ways of achieving those goals. Neither privately nor governmentally-administered syndicalism or cartelization is a sensible way either to remedy the failures of unregulated market capitalism or to achieve a more humane distribution of income.

353

a direction. This is in a sense only an expression of a preference for seeking consistently to move in the direction of the first-best functioning of a market economy, rather than the second- or third-best world of centralized command and control.

TO WHICH FIDDLE
DOES THE REGULATOR DANCE?
SOME EMPIRICAL EVIDENCE

DAVID L. KASERMAN*
L. ROY KAVANAUGH**
RICHARD C. TEPEL***

ABSTRACT

This paper presents an empirical test of the economic theory of regulation which holds that regulators behave as optimizers facing pressures from opposing interest groups. The data employed pertain to the decisions made in the early 1970's by state public service commissions to award or reject automatic fuel adjustment clauses for 34 electric utilities located in the northeast. A probit model of this binary decision outcome is specified, incorporating those variables suggested by the economic theory of regulation. The results obtained provide empirical support for that theory. Moreover, the results strongly reject what has come to be known as the simple capture theory of regulation which holds that regulators unerringly dance to the industry's fiddle.

I. Introduction

At least three views of the regulatory process may be discerned in the extant literature, and one's choice among these views is largely dependent upon one's perception of the underlying motives or, more formally, the objective functions of regulators.(1) First, what Posner (1972, 1974) terms the "public interest" concept of economic regulation sees the governmental control of industry prices, entry, quality, capacity, etc. as a manifestation of the consumers' desire to avoid exploitation by naturally monopolistic or otherwise non-competitive industries. Here, regulators are viewed as social welfare maximizers or as career civil-servant automatons that have been programmed by welfare economists to selflessly serve the interests of society at large.(2) Second, what may be called the "simple capture theory" of regulation views observed regulatory behavior as a perversion of originally pristine legislative intents where such perversion is brought about by the regulated industries gaining control over the agencies created to regulate them. Here, regulators are viewed as pure wealth maximizers who are willing to compromise their mandated objectives for monetary gain (either in the present as graft or in the future as industry-related employment).(3) And third, the "effective political group" theory portrays the regulator as an elected official who holds a monopoly over legal coercive powers. The regulatory process is seen as a system for marketing the benefits of such powers to the highest bidder (or coalition of bidders) of votes where the regulator's costs are also expressed in terms of votes. Here, the regulator is seen as a vote or majority maximizer that produces regulatory favors in exchange for political support.(4)

Since both consumers and producers possess an economic interest in the outcome of regulatory proceedings, the "effective political group" theory of regulation may be viewed practically as a generalization of the other two views.(5) If consumers are able to muster sufficient votes, we will obtain results that are consistent with the "public interest" view; and if producers wield the power necessary to elect or defeat candidates at the polls, we have the "simple capture theory."(6) Consequently, we do not have three separate theories of the regulatory process that one can hope to distinguish empirically. Instead, we have only one economic theory of regulation with two special-case situations in which a given group is thought to dominate consistently.

In this setting, empirical investigations of the regulatory decision-making process can add credence to that theory by: (1) observing outcomes to see whether a single interest group consistently dominates all decisions; and (2) analyzing regulatory decisions to see whether those factors implied by the "effective political group" theory appear to operate in directions consistent with that theory.(7) In this paper, we carry out this sort of empirical investigation.

The regulatory decision process that we attempt to model is the awarding of automatic fuel adjustment clauses by public service commissions in the northeast in the early 1970's. The awarding of these clauses represents a major shift in the process through which utility company prices are set and, in an inflationary environment, effectively provides a significant transfer of wealth from consumers to producers (or, more accurately, prevents a transfer of wealth from producers to consumers).(8) In the long run, such a transfer may be entirely consistent with the "public interest" view of regulation since a failure to obtain compensatory returns could result in an increase in the regulated firm's cost of capital. Also, if the output of the firm is underpriced (without an adjustment clause), misallocations occur. Thus, regulators and consumers may be better off by eliminating the deadweight loss (using improved rate design) to achieve revenue requirements. Also, there may be conflicts between today's consumers and tomorrow's consumers that regulators must mediate. In the short run, however, the regulatory commissions facing these issues were, in fact, subjected to diametrically opposing pressures from these two interested groups.

II. The Automatic Fuel Adjustment Clause

The automatic fuel adjustment clause is a formula that is incorporated in utility tariff schedules which permits allowed rates (on both electricity and gas) to respond to changes in fossil fuel prices without a formal hearing process. While the specific formulas adopted by the various regulatory commissions differ somewhat in detail, the basic effect is to hold the difference between output price and fossil fuel cost per unit of output constant at some base year difference. The purpose of the adjustment clause is to maintain

Kaserman et. al.   247

the financial position of the regulated firm during periods of rapidly rising fuel prices while, at the same time, conserving the resources that would be required for otherwise more frequent rate hearings.

Although the use of fuel adjustment clauses may be traced as far back as 1917, their widespread application to the residential sector did not occur until the inflationary and environmental pressures of the 1970's placed many utility companies in severe financial trouble.(9) In the early 1970's, many public service commissions (particularly those in the northeast whose constituent companies had an historically heavy reliance on oil and relatively high pollution levels) found themselves faced with continuous rate hearings as the regulated firms found it necessary to apply for additional rate increases prior to the conclusion of hearings on previous requests.(10) In response to this kind of pressure, the application of the automatic fuel adjustment clause to residential sales was expanded from 35% of all utility companies in 1970 to 65% in 1973. As fuel prices have continued to rise, the adjustment clause component of the customer's bill has grown in importance and, at times, has dominated the non-clause portion of the bill. In 1976, total rate changes increased electric utility companies' revenues by $8.5 billion — $6 billion of which was due to application of automatic fuel adjustment clauses and $2.5 billion of which was the result of formal rate cases.(11)

With regulatory lag and the use of historical cost data in traditional rate setting cases, the granting of an automatic fuel adjustment clause to an electric utility during inflationary periods, although necessary to maintain the financial integrity of the regulated firm, represents an indirect but clear short-run transfer of wealth from consumers to producers. Such transfer occurs because, in the absence of the clause, the rate of increase in electricity prices would be slowed by the formal hearing process. Since it involves a relatively clear transfer of wealth, the process through which these clauses are awarded provides fertile ground for an empirical investigation of the regulatory decision-making process. Variation in the experiences of individual utility companies requesting these clauses in the early 1970's provides useful data for an analysis of the economic theory of regulation.(12)

III. A Model Of Adjustment Clause Awards

In this section, we specify a simple single equation model of the process through which individual utilities are awarded or denied automatic fuel adjustment clauses. Assuming that regulators attempt to maximize utility, the probability of a firm obtaining an adjustment clause will be dependent on the level of utility of the regulatory body with and without this regulatory instrument. If regulator utility is higher with the clause than without it, then the clause will be awarded. The level of utility that the regulator derives from the act of granting the adjustment clause is, then, hypothesized to be dependent on the level of demand for this regulation and the perceived costs of supplying it, both of which may be viewed as functions of utility company and public service

Kaserman et. al.   248

commission characteristics.

Thus, we hypothesize that

$$<1> \quad p(GFAC) = p\left[U(GFAC) > U(RFAC)\right],$$

where GFAC represents the act of granting an automatic fuel adjustment clause, RFAC represents the act of refusing an adjustment clause (i.e., maintaining the existing regulatory environment), U is the level of utility of the regulatory authority, and p denotes probability. Let CO be a vector of utility company characteristics, and let PSC be a vector of public service commission characteristics. Then, the economic theory of regulation implies that the utility that the regulator derives from granting an adjustment clause will be dependent upon these vectors, i.e.,

$$<2> \quad U(GFAC) = f(CO, PSC)$$

The following sections describe the specific variables that enter the CO and PSC vectors in this study and indicate the various hypotheses implied by the economic theory of regulation.

<u>Company Characteristics.</u> Regulator utility that results from awarding the company an automatic fuel adjustment clause should be dependent upon the financial need that the company exhibits as well as the political support that the company can muster in favor of the award. Financial need, in turn, is primarily dependent upon the rate of increase in the fuel prices that the firm faces. Thus, the CO vector contains the variables PL(-1) and PC(-1), which are the percentage increases in the company's oil and coal prices, respectively, each lagged one year. Increases in either of these variables are expected to shift the firm's demand curve for this regulatory instrument to the right and thereby increase the utility that the regulator derives from granting an automatic adjustment mechanism.

Financial need might also be reflected in the company's observed return on equity, which we also lag one year, ROE(-1). This variable, however, is subject to a certain amount of ambiguity in interpretation. The observed return on equity may, in fact, more closely represent the behavior of the public services commission in setting rates and, consequently, may belong on the supply side in the PSC vector. The sign of the coefficient attached to ROE(-1) should reveal which effect this variable is capturing. If ROE(-1) proxies the company's financial need, it will bear inverse relation to the demand curve and carry a negative sign (lower returns increasing the company's demand for this regulation and the regulator's utility from granting an adjustment clause). But if ROE(-1) proxies the regulator's empathy with the regulated firm, it will bear a positive relation to the supply curve and carry a positive sign (more generous regulators deriving more utility from granting the adjustment clause).(13)

Finally, the political strength that the utility company exerts is quite difficult to measure objectively. At first blush, one might assume that the larger the company the more clout it will carry in the political arena. Bigger firms have more resources at their

Kaserman et. al.   249

disposal, and these resources can be devoted to campaign and/or lobbying efforts. They also provide more remunerative employment possibilities to cooperative ex-regulators. The problem with this view, however, is that larger companies also serve more customers. Since the awarding of an adjustment clause involves a transfer of wealth away from consumers, we should expect the public service commissions to be more reluctant to grant clauses to the larger companies if the "effective political group" theory of regulation is accurate since each customer has a vote. This expectation of a negative sign on the company size variable is strengthened by the fact that the adjustment clause portion of the affected group's (customers') bill is large in magnitude (even on a per capita basis) and discovery of its effect requires very little investment in information acquisition since it is generally stated explicitly on the monthly bill. Thus, unlike many regulatory actions that impact consumers' wealth in subtle, difficult-to-detect ways, the effect of the automatic fuel adjustment clause is readily apparent to the consumer/voter. Due to these considerations, we should expect the consumers to represent a relatively effective political group in these decisions. Therefore, we anticipate a negative sign on the coefficient of the company size variable, which we measure by the firm's total kilowatt hour sales, KWH.

Public Service Commission Characteristics.(14)   Keeping in mind that ROE(-1) may, in fact, represent the public service commission's generosity in setting rates or empathy with relatively efficient firms, we incorporate two additional variables in the model that are expected to influence the commission's willingness to grant an automatic adjustment clause. First, we include SC, which is the size of (number of people serving on) the public service commission. Since the approval of an adjustment mechanism represents a departure from the status quo, we expect a larger commission to be more reluctant to grant such approval. From the "effective political group" theory of regulation, a larger commission should be expected to raise the costs to the company of influencing the regulators' decisions since lobbying efforts must be spread over a larger number of participants in order to influence the decision. In effect, the costs of group decision making are assumed to increase as the size of the group increases. Consequently, this theory implies that the coefficient of SC should carry a negative sign.

Finally, we incorporate in the PSC vector the number of utility companies that the public service commission has jurisdiction over, JD. Since traditional rate cases must be conducted for each company individually, we expect increases in the number of companies to increase the commission's willingness to grant an automatic fuel adjustment clause. This, in effect, shifts the supply curve for this regulatory instrument to the right. Consequently, we expect the coefficient of JD to be positive. This expectation is also in line with the "effective political group" theory of regulation. The more companies the commission has jurisdiction over, the less severe the political consequences of granting a given company an adjustment clause is likely to be, ceteris paribus.

Assuming linearity of the functional relationship in equation <2>, the level of utility that the regulator derives from the act of

Kaserman et. al.   250

granting the automatic adjustment clause may now be written out as:

$$\langle 3 \rangle \quad U(GFAC) = \beta_0 + \beta_1 \cdot PL(-1) + \beta_2 \cdot PC(-1) + \beta_3 \cdot SC$$
$$+ \beta_4 \cdot JD + \beta_5 \cdot KWH + \beta_6 \cdot ROE \ (-1) + \mu$$

If we now assume that the level of utility that the regulator derives from maintaining the status quo (i.e., from rejecting the automatic adjustment clause) is a normally distributed random variable with zero mean and unit variance (i.e., $U(RFAC) \sim N(0, 1)$), then equations $\langle 1 \rangle$ and $\langle 3 \rangle$ yield the probit regression model.(15)

IV. Empirical Results

Definitions of the independent variables contained in equation $\langle 3 \rangle$, along with the data sources, are reported in Table 1. These data apply to 34 privately owned electric utilities in the northeast in 1972. This point in time was selected so that sufficient observations could be obtained for firms both with and without adjustment mechanisms. The results of estimating the model with the probit maximum likelihood estimation technique are reported in Table 2. Overall, these results lend fairly strong support to the "effective political group" theory of regulation. All coefficients for which an hypothesis was expressed attain the anticipated sign and are significant at the .10 level or above. In addition, the equation as a whole is significant as we are able to reject the null hypothesis that $\beta_1 = \ldots = \beta_6 = 0$.

Individual coefficient estimates indicate the following five results. First, increases in the rate of fuel price escalation improves the utility company's chances of being awarded an automatic adjustment clause. Second, the more members on the public service commission the less likely it is to grant an adjustment clause. Third, the more firms the commission regulates the more likely it is to grant such a clause. Fourth, our expectation that the consumer group would dominate this particular decision process is supported by the negative coefficient attained by the company size variable. And fifth, the evidence indicates that ROE(-1) is serving as a proxy for the regulatory commission's overall disposition in favor of the regulated firm (perhaps reflecting a reward for outstanding efficiency by the firm - footnote 13).

V.   Conclusion

We have attempted to model the regulatory decision-making process whereby automatic fuel adjustment clauses were awarded to individual utility companies in the early 1970's, and the results of that effort were found to be broadly consistent with the economic theory of regulation. Variables which this theory implies as important determinants of the regulatory decision outcome were found to be significant in the expected directions. Such empirical verification, while far from conclusive, does add some credence to the view that regulators behave as optimizers facing constraints from the opposing interests of both consumers and producers.

Kaserman et. al.   251

In addition, the results we obtained for the company size variable clearly rejects the "simple capture theory" of regulation which holds that regulators unerringly dance to the industry's fiddle. As Peltzman (1976) states: ". . . regulatory agencies will not exclusively serve a single economic interest." (p. 211) Under the economic theory of regulation, it is likely that no single group can ever completely capture the regulator but that several groups will temporarily and alternately hold him hostage. Indeed, at times the regulator appears to be attempting to dance not to a single fiddle but to an entire orchestra, the individual members of which are all playing different tunes.

TABLE 1

Variable Names, Definitions, and Data Sources

Variable	Definition	Source
PL (-1)	Percentage annual change in the price of oil (¢/10^{6}Btu), lagged one year.	1
PC (-1)	Percentage annual change in the price of coal (¢/10^{6}Btu), lagged one year.	1
ROE (-1)	Percentage return on equity, lagged one year.	2
KWH	Total annual kilowatt hour sales of electricity.	2
SC	Size of commission board.	3
JD	Number of companies under PSC's jurisdiction.	3

Sources: 1. Steam Electric Plant Construction Cost and Annual Production Expenses, 1970-71.

2. Statistics of Privately Owned Electric Utilities in the United States, 1972.

3. Telephone conversations with the public service commissions in each state.

Kaserman et. al.   253

171

TABLE 2

Regression Results

Variable	Hypothesized Sign	Parameter Estimate	Likelihood Ratio Test Statistic[*]
Intercept	(?)	-19.631	-
PL(-1)	(+)	15.545	12.217
PC(-1)	(+)	14.701	11.352
SC	(-)	-1.398	4.283
JD	(+)	2.420	17.755
KWH	(-)	-3.521 E-07	5.233
ROE(-1)	(?)	1.249	8.089

n = 34

Likelihood ratio test statistic for H_0: $\beta_1 = \ldots = \beta_6 = 0$ is 25.883 with the X^2 critical value (10%) of 10.645.

[*]X^2 critical value (10%) = 2.7055.
X^2 critical value (5%) = 3.8415
X^2 critical value (1%) = 6.6349

Kaserman et. al.   254

*   The University of Tennessee
**   Tennessee Gas Transmission
***   Oak Ridge National Laboratory

(1) See Posner (1974) for a more complete discussion of these three alternative views of regulation. Brock (1981) identifies a total of six alternative views of regulation, but several of these may be seen as special cases of the three discussed here. For a discussion of regulator objectives, see Hilton (1972), Eckert (1973), Hirshleifer (1976), and Michaels and Kalish (1981).

(2) Posner (1974) cites Bonbright (1961) as representing the "public interest" view.

(3) Posner (1974) cites Bernstein (1955) as being representative of this view of the regulatory process. Eckert (1981) provides some empirical evidence on the frequency of ex-commissioner employment in industry-related jobs. Notice that in referring to this view we place the quotation marks so as to include the word "theory".

(4) This theory is attributed to Stigler's (1972) pathbreaking paper. Important extensions are provided in Posner (1972, 1974) and Peltzman (1976).

(5) See Posner (1974), and Peltzman (1976).

(6) The "effective political group" theory also allows for coalitions to be formed among subsets of these two groups. This provides a potential explanation for cross-subsidization schemes. See Posner (1972, 1974) and Peltzman (1976).

(7) These factors include such items as the size of the affected groups, the magnitude of the per capita benefits and costs, and the difficulty of acquiring information. See Peltzman (1976). Joskow's (1972) study could easily be interpreted to provide this sort of empirical support. For instance, the presence of intervenors in a formal rate hearing (which is an obvious indication of fairly cohesive political opposition) is found to influence the commission's decision.

(8) The shift toward adoption of the partial cost pass-through form of price regulation is by no means limited to electric utility regulation. See Harvey and Roush (1981) and Kendrick (1975).

(9) See Baron and DeBondt (1979) and Trigg (1958) for discussions of the history of this regulatory instrument. Our discussion here draws heavily on the former reference.

(10) See Joskow and MacAvoy (1975).

(11) Automatic fuel adjustment clauses have been the subject of much criticism in recent years. See Gollop and Karlson (1978), Baron and DeBondt (1979), Atkinson and Halvorsen (1980), and Kaserman and Tepel (1982).

(12) The failure of a firm to obtain an automatic fuel adjustment clause at a given point in time does not, of course, preclude that firm from obtaining such a clause at a later time. In the interim, however, the firm without the clause will lose revenues if fuel prices continue to rise.

(13) The observed return on equity may also reflect the regulated

Kaserman et. al.   255

firm's operating efficiency. Regulators may wish to reward the relatively efficient firms and may do so by awarding adjustment clauses to them. Joskow's (1972) results indicate that regulators will tend to be more lenient with relatively efficient firms.

(14) One potentially relevant public service commission characteristic that is excluded from our PSC vector is a dummy variable to distinguish between elected and appointed commissions. Exclusion of this variable was necessitated by lack of variation in the sample. With the sole exception of New York, all public service commissions in our sample are elected.

(15) Judge, et al (1980, p. 591) provide an argument for assuming normality of the critical value of the index in the probit model. If there are many independent factors determining U(RFAC) for each public service commission, the central limit theorem may be called upon to justify this assumption.

(16) In part, the difficulty of testing the economic theory of regulation can be traced to the absence of sufficient data to specify and estimate a structural simultaneous model of the demand for and supply of a given regulation. For example, B_6 in equation <3> cannot be signed a priori because it is, in effect, a reduced form coefficient. As interpreted, ROE(-1) simultaneously shifts the demand curve to the left and the supply curve to the right, leaving its net effect on p(GFAC) indeterminate on theoretical grounds.

REFERENCES

1. Atkinson, S. E. and R. Halvorsen, "A Test of Relative and Absolute Price Efficiency in Regulated Utilities," REVIEW OF ECONOMICS AND STATISTICS, Vol. 62 (February 1980), pp. 81-88.
2. Baron, D. P. and R. R. DeBondt, "Fuel Adjustment Mechanisms and Economic Efficiency," JOURNAL OF INDUSTRIAL ECONOMICS, Vol. 27 (March 1979), pp. 243-261.
3. Bernstein, M., REGULATING BUSINESS BY INDEPENDENT COMMISSION, Princeton: Princeton University Press, 1955.
4. Bonbright, J. C., PRINCIPLES OF PUBLIC UTILITY RATES, New York: Columbia University Press, 1961.
5. Brock, G. W., THE TELECOMMUNICATIONS INDUSTRY: THE DYNAMICS OF MARKET STRUCTURE, Cambridge, Massachusetts: Harvard University Press, 1981.
6. Eckert, R. D., "On the Incentives of Regulators: The case of Taxicabs," PUBLIC CHOICE, Vol. 14 (1973), pp. 83-99.
7. Eckert, R. D., "The Life Cycle of Regulatory Commissioners," JOURNAL OF LAW AND ECONOMICS, Vol. 24 (April 1981), pp. 113-120.
8. Gollop, F. M. and S. H. Karlson, "The Impact of the Fuel Adjustment Mechanism on Economic Efficiency," REVIEW OF ECONOMICS AND STATISTICS, Vol. 60 (November 1978), pp. 574-584.
9. Harvey, S. and C. T. Roush, Jr., PETROLEUM PRODUCT PRICE REGULATIONS: OUTPUT, EFFICIENCY, AND COMPETITIVE EFFECTS, Washington, D. C.: Staff Report of the Bureau of Economics to the Federal Trade Commissions, 1981.
10. Hilton, G. W., "The Basic Behavior of Regulatory Commissions," AMERICAN ECONOMIC REVIEW, Vol. 62 (May 1972), pp. 47-54.
11. Hirshleifer, J., "Comment," JOURNAL OF LAW AND ECONOMICS, Vol. 19 (August 1976), pp. 241-244.
12. Joskow, P. L., "The Determination of the Allowed Rate of Return in a Formal Regulatory Hearing," BELL JOURNAL OF ECONOMICS AND MANAGEMENT SCIENCE, Vol. 3 (Autumn 1972), pp. 632-644.
13. Joskow, P. L. and P. W. MacAvoy, "Regulation and the Financial Condition of the Electric Power Companies in the 1970's," AMERICAN ECONOMIC REVIEW, Vol. 65 (May 1975), pp. 295-301.
14. Judge, G. G., et al., THE THEORY AND PRACTICE OF ECONOMETRICS, New York: John Wiley and Sons, 1980.
15. Kaserman, D. L. and R. C. Tepel, "The Impact of the Automatic Adjustment Clause on Fuel Purchase and Utilization Practices in the U. S. Electric Utility Industry," SOUTHERN ECONOMIC JOURNAL, Vol. 49 (January 1982), pp. 687-700.
16. Kendrick, J. W., "Efficiency Incentives and Cost Factors in Public Utility Automatic Revenue Adjustment Clauses," BELL JOURNAL OF ECONOMICS, Vol. 6 (Spring 1975), pp. 299-313.
17. Michaels, R. and L. Kalish, "The Incentives of Regulators: Evidence from Banking," PUBLIC CHOICE, Vol. 36 (1981), pp. 187-192.
18. Peltzman, S., "Toward a More General Theory of Regulation," JOURNAL OF LAW AND ECONOMICS, Vol. 19 (August 1976), pp. 211-240.
19. Posner, R. A., "Taxation by Regulation," BELL JOURNAL OF ECONOMICS AND MANAGEMENT SCIENCE, Vol. 2 (Spring 1971), pp.

Kaserman et. al.   257

22-50.

20. Posner, R. A., "Theories of Economic Regulation," BELL JOURNAL OF ECONOMICS AND MANAGEMENT SCIENCE, VOL. 5 (AUTUMN 1974), pp. 335-358.

21. Stigler, G. J., "The Theory or Economic Regulation," BELL JOURNAL OF ECONOMICS AND MANAGEMENT SCIENCE. Vol. 2 (Spring 1971), pp. 3-21.

22. Trigg, R. S., "Escalator Clauses in Public Utility Rate Schedules." UNIVERSITY OF PENNSYLVANIA LAW REVIEW, Vol. 106 (1958), pp. 964-997.

176

Quarterly Review of Economics and Business
Vol. 20, No. 2 (Summer 1980)
© 1980 Board of Trustees of the University of Illinois

Big Business and Public Policy in Contemporary United States

Kim McQuaid

CHALLENGE AND RESPONSE

American corporations faced important threats to their stature and legitimacy during the 1970s. Problems abroad, symbolized by the OPEC oil embargo and resulting petroleum price increases, ended an era of cheap energy and shocked a nation accustomed to relative self-reliance in strategic resources. Popular backlash against policies aiming at economic restraint was often directed at big business, particularly the multinational energy conglomerates which were perceived as having helped engineer an outrage.

On the domestic scene, an avalanche of scientific findings regarding the environmental and health impacts of industrial operations produced increased skepticism about corporate claims to social responsibility and responsiveness. Reforms of congressional accountability, oversight, and access regulations spawned by the reaction against the Vietnam and Watergate crises testified to widespread concerns about the activities of special interests inside and outside of government. Large corporations were not exempt from their share of the resulting censure. Washington, presumably, had to do something to forward the general welfare in more effective ways.

Businessmen were among those calling for government assistance in the 1970s, for American corporation managers are in the market for government just as are the members of other interest groups. In good times businessmen, like labor leaders and others, tend to advocate laissez-faire. In bad times, however, these same groups seek to make use of government nonmarket controls to ameliorate economic and industrial problems.[1]

Businessmen, however, found themselves speaking in a babble of tongues as they went into the market for government assistance in the early 1970s. Frictions between industries, and particularly between smaller and larger firms, severely limited the ability of large corporations to perfect their interests — oligopolistic and otherwise — and a good deal of regulatory legislation was passed which big businessmen did not particularly like.

These laws were of a functional variety which posed uncustomary problems to businessmen, especially those responsible for administering the nation's most powerful companies. Functional regulation, exemplified by the energy, environmental, and "affirmative action" initiatives of the 1970s, evidenced a clear break with past federal activities and traditions.

Until the 1970s, almost all federal regulation was industry-specific in nature. Laws were passed for particular industries rather than for "business" generally. Firms and trade associations within given industries possessed their own peculiar regulatory problems, and had relatively few occasions to form ongoing political alliances across industrial lines. Under the terms of industry-specific regulation, it was also comparatively easy for individual industries, or for powerful trade associations or firms within those industries, to dominate regulatory activities over the long term. The Interstate Commerce Commission, Civil Aeronautics Board, and the Federal Communications Commission provide classic examples of this phenomenon.[2]

As Murray Weidenbaum and others have pointed out, however, functionally oriented regulatory agencies are not amendable to domination by any one industry, trade association, or firm, however large. OSHA, EPA, and EEOC — to name but three of the score of new alphabetical agencies created in Washington in the 1970s — were not established to regulate a particular industry, but rather, to oversee a segment of the operations of all industries. The panindustrial scope of these new functional agencies' concerns "makes its impractical for any single industry to dominate these regulatory activities in the manner of the traditional [industry-specific] model." Functional regulation affecting almost all businesses also made chief executive officers in widely separated industries more aware of business's common regulatory problems and more willing to evolve collective means to resolve them [28, pp. 13–16; and 26, p. 16].

Until the 1970s, however, the most important and influential business lobbying and advisory groups active on the national level were either industry-specific in nature (for example, the American Iron and Steel Institute) or were so panindustrial as to defy any quick or effective mobilization of corporate resources (for example, the US Chamber of Commerce and the National Association of Manufacturers). Larger American corporations could not use either type of organization to lobby effectively against environmental, energy, safety, health, and minority-hiring standards which simultaneously offended managerial instincts and imposed significant compliance costs. The broad and heterogeneous membership of the US Chamber and the NAM, for example, was composed of bevies of small- and medium-sized firms which neither supported big business efforts to influence public policy councils in specific ways nor paid their share of the bills for such efforts. Larger corporations, in short, were often placed in the position of being generals in command of nonexistent armies. "Business" was split in almost as many directions as the heroine of an existential romance, and its political clout was accordingly fragmented.

As big businessmen became increasingly aware of the fact that they needed new avenues of collective and individual access into government to influence the formulation and implementation of regulatory legislation, they began evolving new types of lobbying and advisory groups to accomplish their goals.

THE BIRTH OF THE BUSINESS ROUNDTABLE

Cohesion and credibility were key items on the corporate agenda. The nation's largest firms had somehow to organize relationships among themselves so that big business could speak with a common voice on broad questions of national importance and influence policymakers in new ways by arriving early, proposing consistently, and formulating long-term political strategies. To accomplish such goals, chief executive officers of massive companies including General Electric, General Motors, duPont, US Steel, American Telephone and Telegraph, and Exxon — joined by the chief executive officers (CEOs) of scores of other *Fortune* 100 and *Fortune* 500 companies — created a new breed of business organization whose corporate membership was restricted to the active managers of the largest firms in the country. The Business Roundtable is an embodiment of this newest stage of corporate organizational dynamics.

The Business Roundtable is, in effect, a sort of super holding company for big business political influence. The Roundtable's origins and early development, however, were not the simple unfolding of some grand entrepreneurial design. For several years, in fact, the organization underwent complicated changes in derivation and emphasis.

Initially, the Business Roundtable was a loose alliance of groups interested in lessening organized labor's powers — particularly in the strategic construction industry. These groups, notably the Construction Users Anti-Inflation Roundtable (CUAR) and the Labor Law Study Committee (LLSC) were formed in the wake of a surge in construction industry labor costs late in the 1960s that helped topple the voluntary wage/price guidelines program of the Johnson Administration. Shortly after the beginning of the Nixon presidency, the CUAR and its allies cooperated with Republican leaders in efforts to force construction unions to moderate their wage demands, chiefly by threatening presidential suspension of the Davis-Bacon Act. Having firmed Nixon's political resolve to get the AFL unions to the bargaining tables, the CUAR broadened its efforts to solve growing inflationary problems by rolling back union power. In the fall of 1972, the like-minded CUAR and LLSC joined forces and re-named themselves the Business Roundtable as a matter of organizational convenience.[3]

At this point in its development, the Business Roundtable was an alliance of construction contractors, large firms, and corporate lawyers interested in weakening well-entrenched trade unions. In the following year, however, the focus and tactics of the organization changed substantially.

The agents of the change were the members of an informal gathering of corporate CEOs known as the "March Group." Created in the spring of 1972 by John Harper, the chairman of Alcoa, and Fred Borch, chairman of GE, the March Group existed to try and improve big business's standing in the eyes of citizen, congressman, and federal bureaucrat alike. The group's concerns were considerably broader than those of the nascent Business Roundtable. Alcoa's Harper and GE's Borch had reason for their concern. They had, among other things, been told by highly placed Nixon appointees including Secretary of the Treasury John Connally and Federal Reserve Board Chairman Arthur Burns that (in the words of one participant) "business had to shape up in sophistication and techniques in Washington or else go down the political tube."[4] To follow through upon Connally and Burns's rather alarming suggestions, Harper and Borch sought to energize the members of the Business Council, an organization of which both men were members.

Since its founding in 1933, the Business Council has occupied a shadowy but almost unique place in Washington. Created to provide a confidential forum for contact, cooperation, and recruitment for federal administrators and interested business leaders during the New Deal, the council was, and has remained, an exclusive organization composed of the CEOs of the largest corporations in the country.[5]

The history of the Business Council has been told in detail elsewhere [12 and 13]. What is important to understand here is that the council was not explicitly created as a lobbying agency, and that the organization's bylaws specifically prohibited the activity. Lobby its members did — but carefully, and deep within the executive branch. As an organization, the Business Council had no great interest in going public. The very existence of the Business Council, however, allowed it to be used as a recruitment center for corporate expertise. The March Group of the Business Roundtable was, in essence, a short-lived bridge over which interested council members like Borch and Harper moved to affiliate themselves with the Business Roundtable while simultaneously broadening the latter organization's purposes and strategies.[6]

March Group organizers had one overarching objective: to increase business stature and influence in Washington by bringing corporate CEOs into direct and continuing contact with government in general and governmental leaders in particular. From 1972 on, March Group insisted that CEOs of member corporations attend meetings regularly. Few underlings were allowed, and staff was kept to a minimum. CEOs were further required to take personal responsibility for implementing policies arrived at in meetings, in particular by face-to-face lobbying within the executive branch and in an increasingly powerful post-Watergate Congress.

Here was an important new corporate political approach. Until the 1970s, corporate CEOs only rarely lobbied government officials directly. When they did so, moreover, their efforts were usually connected with the affairs of their particular firms or industries, rather than with those of big business generally.

The day-to-day work of looking after company or industry interests was, for the most part, left in the hands of lobbyists. As reforms such as the Legislative Reorganization Act of 1970 democratized congressional operations, however, power centers proliferated. Fragmentation of the executive branch in the wake of the Watergate debacle produced the same effect. It became harder and harder for comparatively low-status corporate representatives to discover where power or influence regarding particular policy issues resided, or to obtain easy access to such influence brokers as existed.[7]

March Group members intended to solve the resulting access problems by putting CEOs directly on the front lines in Washington, and, moreover, by targeting CEOs from specific corporations on congressmen whose districts contained plants or other subsidiaries of their firms. The group, however, needed an organizational base. Informal meetings were not enough. Faced with a choice between refining its own infrastructure, broadening that of a reticent and secretive Business Council, or affiliating itself with a third party, the members of the March Group opted for the latter, and merged with the recently established Business Roundtable by the middle of 1973.[8]

THE ROUNDTABLE IN ACTION

The organization that resulted from this affiliation was, as one perceptive student of Roundtable dynamics remarks, a patchwork of interests.

From the Labor Law Study Group and the Construction Users League [sic], the Business Roundtable inherited a commitment to fight organized labor through legislation and regulation. But the March Group and the Business Council moderated the stridency in the antilabor mission, diluting it with the Council's history of compromise and the March Group's preoccupation with image. The Business Roundtable is the product of clear but competing visions. [2, p. 34]

Organizationally, however, the Business Roundtable possessed attributes which restrained corporate divisiveness on important policy matters: specifically, a "Policy Committee" composed of an average of 45 members.

The Business Roundtable's Policy Committee is, in effect, a council of elders within the larger organization. Its members — and its members alone — are publicly affiliated with the Roundtable. All other memberships (currently totaling about 160) are kept secret to the greatest possible extent. The Policy Committee is a cross-section of the largest firms in the nation. It is also the membership of the Business Council under another name. In 1977, for example, 37 of the 45 CEOs on the Roundtable's Policy Committee were also members of the council; in 1978, 31 of 47; and, in the first six months of 1979, 35 of 47. Given such figures, it is not surprising that leadership positions in both organizations are often held by the same people, and that these people are the presidents or board chairmen of firms such as GM, GE, duPont, and AT&T.[9]

The Business Roundtable's Policy Committee performs many important functions. First, it sets the annual legislative and lobbying priorities of the organization, selecting only a small handful of matters for attention each year to ensure that organizational influence is not diffused over a too-wide spectrum of issues. Second, it appoints all members of Roundtable committees and "task forces" given long-term responsibility for developing common programs in specific policy areas including taxation policy, government regulation, labor legislation, national planning and employment, energy use, energy supply, antitrust, environment, consumer interests, national health, and wage and price controls. Lastly, it ratifies all reports, recommendations, and other policy statements made in the Roundtable's name [8, pp. 1965–66; 17, p. 7; and 7, pp. 53–54].

Important tensions continue to exist within the Roundtable's blue ribbon corporate membership, particularly in the areas of energy, foreign trade, and defense policy. The existence of the Policy Committee, however, allows the leaders of the nation's largest corporations to exercise effective control over the Roundtable's activities and emphases. All Roundtable member corporations can — and do — involve themselves in the organization's short-term lobbying, but effective control over longer-term strategies and tactics remains in Policy Committee hands. The committee, in short, can restrict the growth of subgroups within the membership that could dissent effectively on controversial issues that the Roundtable may wish to take stands upon. Industrial interest groups cannot "load" specific Roundtable committees with representatives of a particular point of view, nor can they obtain organizational backing for their positions without the agreement of the Policy Committee. The organization's secretiveness about its membership and internal procedures also serves to ensure that such disagreements or resignations as do take place will not be widely reported — if they are reported at all. The Roundtable, then, is an umbrella organization engaged in issuing political "hunting licenses" to segments of its membership through its Policy Committee [3, p. 625; 4, p. 17ff; and 14, pp. 92ff].

As presently structured, the Business Roundtable is relatively well qualified to serve big businessmen's political interests in Washington. The top-drawer character of the organization's membership commands respect in Congress, in the executive branch, and on the baronial levels of the civil service. The strategy of face-to-face lobbying by corporate chief executive officers pays off in terms of access in a comparatively atomized Congress where committee chairmen, whips, and other party leaders can no longer effectively deliver large blocs of votes or guarantee legislative results.

Another major reason for Roundtable effectiveness is that the organization does not make the mistake, so common among older, panindustrial business associations including the NAM and the US Chamber, of seeming to "oppose everything." Instead of merely arguing against particular legislation, Roundtable spokesmen more often support alternative legislation, legislation aimed at doing something about problems in a manner congenial to businessmen. Though not always successful, the Roundtable's efforts do give it a reputation as a positive, as opposed to negative, force. A strategy of "yes, but . . ." provides long-term dividends.[10]

But the Roundtable's greatest strength lies in its members' awareness — varying though it is — that they do not want less government but, rather, "more efficient" government — as defined by themselves. Since the Great Depression, American big businessmen have gradually come to the realization that they can exist and prosper in an era of big government. The uncluttered marketplace world beloved of neoclassical economists has progressively less relevance to a world in which big business and government are tied together in complicated webs of mutual dependence.

The very existence of an organization such as the Business Roundtable, then, serves to increase big businessmen's collective returns on their political investments. By arriving early, proposing consistently, and coordinating lobbying and other advisory activities early enough in the political game so that its members do not get behind the power curve on particular issues, the Roundtable hopes to institute a new era of "partnership" between large corporations and the state.

An illustration of what this partnership consists of is provided by Roundtable support for the voluntary wage/price guidelines program of the Carter Administration. Such Roundtable (and also Business Council) positions irk the *Wall Street Journal* no end. For the *Journal*'s editorial writers rightly recall that partnership of this sort — first begun during the Nixon Era controls of 1971–74 — has precious little to do with free enterprise as discussed in economics textbooks. This fact, however, bothers the Business Roundtable relatively little. Rhetorically, Roundtable leaders maintain a clear preference for the staples of conservative economic thinking. Privately, however, many are not loath to admit that the doctrines of Adam Smith are dead and that businessmen can no longer afford even to attempt to ignore the fact that Washington, DC exists.[11]

For all its influence, real and apparent, in contemporary Washington, the Business Roundtable is not a perfected institution. Some prominent Roundtable leaders, Irving Shapiro among them, have privately voiced discontent with the fact that the organization has become too much of a "super-lobby," and too little of a long-term policy forum in which corporate understandings of and relationships with prominent federal bureaucrats can be broadened and refined.

The Roundtable remains important, however, as an indicator of a clear watershed in corporate political affairs in the United States. Using the Business Roundtable as an organizational base, businessmen are becoming increasingly innovative, and increasingly savvy to the ways in which various segments of the federal establishment operate. Problems still exist. Comparatively few member-companies, for example, are administratively structured to allow their in-house planning or public affairs departments to follow through upon decisions or goals that corporate CEOs have enunciated within Roundtable policy forums, and this problem is only gradually being addressed on an ad hoc, firm-by-firm basis.[12]

For all the problems, Roundtable CEOs are learning how to make use of new tools at their collective disposal in agencies such as the Business Roundtable. They are not merely using techniques such as mass demonstrations and petition campaigns perfected by the left in the 1960s and used with increasing frequency by the right in the 1970s and 1980s. They are, instead, formulating a new generation of strategies, strategies exemplified by the face-to-face lobbying of congressmen and their staffers and by political campaign contributions aimed at supporting incumbents, often liberals, who might be persuaded to swing their way on crucial votes.

In recent years, indeed, the Business Roundtable has begun flexing its muscles. In 1978, for example, the Roundtable grabbed national headlines when it helped orchestrate the defeat of a Labor Law Reform Bill which enjoyed wide backing among the leadership of AFL-CIO unions. Organized labor's defeat was as symbolic as it was real, for congressmen and senators hitherto reluctant to oppose a united AFL-CIO, sensing a change in the political weather, began talking about the labor law battle as (in Senator Orrin Hatch's words) "a starting point for a new era of assertiveness by big business in Washington." In a city where symbol is as important as substance, the Business Roundtable's political stock has risen accordingly [22, p. 138; and 2, pp. 144–59].

Next to feel the weight of Roundtable influence were federal regulators, particularly those in functionally oriented agencies such as EPA, EEOC, OSHA, and the FTC. The FTC, in particular, began to enjoy the status of a symbolic enemy. Attacks upon the agency and its chairman, Michael Pertschuk, appeared to be designed to send a message to regulators generally either to cool their ardor or face increasing big business opposition emanating through amenable congressmen. The messages being sent are not being lost on any regulator or politician directly concerned.[13]

Roundtable efforts, of course, have not been uniformly successful. All the deals being cut are not equally to the liking of individual corporations, or of the membership generally. The Roundtable, for example, was heavily criticized for first opposing, and then belatedly supporting, the passage of a small-business-backed "Steiger Amendment" to a 1978 tax bill that drastically lowered capital gains tax rates. Roundtable attempts to horse-trade with the Carter Administration on tax issues infuriated segments of the organization's membership. Continuing efforts to muzzle the AFL construction unions by repealing the Davis-Bacon Act have, similarly, gone nowhere fast.[14]

The Roundtable, then, does not exercise any formalized domination, and is not equally effective in the resolution of all types of policy issues. What the organization does do is to give officers of the nation's largest corporations new forms of political leverage in Washington. This, in turn, increases Roundtable visibility and power. For, as Roundtable repute among Washington cognoscenti and "insiders" has grown, congressmen and White House officials have been quicker to try to obtain Roundtable assistance in solving pressing political problems. The petitioners have included President Jimmy Carter who in 1977 cosponsored and helped pass into law a Roundtable-engineered compromise on the vexing question of legislation to restrict US corporations from complying with Arab boycotts aimed at the State of Israel [1, pp. 17–19; and 20, pp. 1 and 5].

THE FUTURE

The new quasi-public role that American big business leaders are working out for themselves in forums such as the Business Roundtable, then, illustrates a wider process of change at work throughout the commanding heights of US corporate economy. The American CEO is, gradually and often reluctantly, coming of political age. In the process, the managers of the nation's largest corporations are learning the simple (but in a US context, slightly stupefying) truth that government and business are engaged in an increasingly symbiotic relation. Whether the actors on either side like it or not, big business and big government are moving into an era in their relations that cannot be explained by the staples of neoclassical economic theory. The painful corporate and governmental adjustments required to deal with threatening issues such as the moving target of rising energy costs and proliferating environmentalist concerns will spur consultation at the highest levels. The prospects of a period of slower economic growth and continued inflationary uncertainty throughout the 1980s will almost certainly increase desires for the enunciation of comprehensive industrial, taxation, and trade policies among businessmen and bureaucrats alike.

During the forthcoming decade, it even appears possible that the largest corporations will evidence greater and greater degrees of tolerance for what in Western European terms is known as "indicative planning." The process involved here is not likely to be a simple one; it will, more probably, be of a distinctly ad hoc and non-Cartesian variety. Businessmen, for example, are certainly not going to turn into enthusiastic public advocates of tax-based incomes policies, and "planning" of an overtly nonmarket variety is not calculated to become a popular item in the Rotary Club, or Business Roundtable, lexicon.

Corners, however, are being turned. The earlier mentioned Business Roundtable and Business Council support for voluntary peacetime wage/price controls during the Nixon and Carter presidencies illustrates a marked departure from American big business custom. Peacetime America has not seen the like since the long-departed days of Franklin Delano Roosevelt's NRA, and defenders of the neoclassical faith such as the *Wall Street Journal* and *Barron's* know it very well. Marxists of varying persuasions are also interested observers of such developments, not least because they are waiting for big businessmen to step out in front of the political curtains and institute a "corporate state," in cooperation with their supposed political, academic, labor, and agrarian allies.

The realities of change, however, will be less cataclysmic than neoclassicists and neo-Marxists suppose. Barring catastrophic escalations of political frictions in the underdeveloped nations, it seems safe to conclude that the United States will continue a fairly steady drift towards a more fully planned society. Such additional planning as takes place will continue to be a complex mix of federal, state, private, and even international, responsibility. But those concerned to understand the evolving structure of America's corporate economy must pay more heed to the fact that managers of the nation's largest firms are no longer operating on the assumption that the public sector is an aberration, or a factor in their economic life that can, or will, be materially reduced. Understanding this fact, scholars can, perhaps, become less anxious or antiquarian, and more relevant and predictive.

NOTES

1. This paper could not have been written without the assistance of present and former Washington hands. Among the people who talked with me, I especially wish to thank Carlton Spitzer, Edward Merlis, Michael Pertschuk, Dan Fenn, Mark Green, Gerald Rosen, Andrew Buchsbaum, Evelyn Dubrow, Bryce Harlow, and Leonard Silk. None are responsible for my conclusions, but all informed whatever intelligence I could muster. For well-written overviews of the paradoxes of business-government relations in the US, see [11 and 9].

2. The academic literature regarding regulatory problems is voluminous and unusually dull. For better written journalistic treatments, see [10 and 6].

3. By the time this essay appears, Andrew Buchsbaum and Mark Green of Ralph Nader's "Congress Watch" will have produced a useful study on the Business Roundtable and the US Chamber of Commerce which will be of interest to all students of business-government relationships. See also [5, pp. 256–62 and 310–40; 27, pp. 6–7 and 99; and 2, pp. 29–30].

4. Bryce N. Harlow to author, 18 January 1979.

5. For the evolution of the Business Council, see [12 and 13].

6. Among the most cogent summaries of internal Business Council procedures is a mimeographed memorandum entitled "Observations of a BAC Wife" and another titled "Advantages and Disadvantages of BAC — With Suggestions for Improvement." Both memos, circa 1961, are available in Box 126 of the John W. Snyder Papers in the Truman Presidential Library, Independence, Missouri. For journalistic treatments of the council, see [18 and 19].

7. For easy-to-read summaries of the relevant congressional changes, see [15 and 16].

8. A great many journalistic articles regarding Roundtable strategies have appeared in recent years. Thus far, academicians seem generally to have ignored them. Why they have done so is unclear. For cogent examples, see [7, 8, 23, 24, 25, and 2].

9. Examples of the interlocking noted here are many. In 1979, for example, Reginald Jones of GE was a cochairman of the Business Roundtable and the chairman of the Business Council. Irving Shapiro (duPont), Clifton M. Garvin (Exxon), and Thomas Murphy (GM) are also numbered among those corporate leaders who have been especially prominent in the affairs of both the council and the Roundtable for most of the past five years.

10. Buchsbaum described Roundtable political strategies thus: "Fight until acceptable terms are offered, then negotiate and assume a moderate position" [2, p. 62].

11. For *Wall Street Journal* editorials attacking the cooperative stances of the Business Roundtable, see the issues of 12 January 1979, 26 April 1979, and 3 October 1979.

12. One indication of the process of change outlined here is that about 25 percent of Washington representatives for larger corporations are (according to a recent poll) former congressional or White House staffers. See *Wall Street Journal* 15 January 1980, p. 1, and 11 January 1980, p. 34, for specifics regarding this ongoing phenomenon.

13. Reference 21 provides an important example of the results of this regulatory offensive.

14. The infighting between small and large business interests regarding the Steiger Amendment is reflected in *Wall Street Journal* editorials such as those of 8 May 1978 and 11 May 1978. The Roundtable, it appears, was (initially) anxious to avoid angering Carter by trying to pass the capital gains tax reduction bill over administration opposition. The Roundtable leadership apparently wanted time to broker a compromise. But disgruntlement within its own membership, and heightened small business opposition, led Roundtable spokesmen finally to reverse their position.

REFERENCES

1. Edgar M. Bronfman, "How to Succeed in Business and Public Policy by Really Trying," *New Republic,* 4 June 1977, pp. 17–19.

2. Andrew Buchsbaum, "Lords of the Chamber, Knights of the Roundtable: A Study of Big Business Lobbying Associations" (Senior thesis, Harvard University, 1979).

3. Thomas Ferguson and Joel Rogers, "Knights of the Roundtable," *Nation,* 15 December 1979, pp. 620ff.

4. ———, "Labor Law Reform and Its Enemies," *Nation,* 6–13 January 1979, pp. 17ff.

5. Craufurd D. Goodwin, ed., *Exhortation and Controls: The Search for a Wage-Price Policy, 1945–1971* (Washington: Brookings, 1975).

6. Mark J. Green and others, *The Closed Enterprise System* (New York: Grossman, 1972).

7. Walter Guzzardi, Jr., "Business Is Learning How to Win in Washington," *Fortune,* 27 March 1978, pp. 53ff.

8. Barry M. Hager, "Business Roundtable: New Lobbying Force," *Congressional Quarterly,* 17 September 1977, pp. 1964ff.

9. Jonathan R. T. Hughes, *The Governmental Habit: Economic Controls from Colonial Times to the Present* (New York: Basic Books, 1977).

10. Louis M. Kohlmeier, Jr., *The Regulators: Watchdog Agencies in the Public Interest* (New York: Harper, 1969).

11. Grant McConnell, *Private Power and American Democracy* (New York: Knopf, 1966).

12. Kim McQuaid, "Big Business and Government Policy in Post-New Deal America, From Depression to Détente," *Economics and Political Science Review,* Vol. 4 (February 1979), pp. 41–72.

13. ———, "The Business Advisory Council of the Department of Commerce, 1933–1961: A Study in Corporate-Government Relations," in Paul Uselding, ed., *Research in Economic History . . . Volume 1 — 1976* (Greenwich, CT: JAI Press, 1976), pp. 171–97.

14. D. Quinn Mills, "Flawed Victory in Labor Law Reform," *Harvard Business Review,* Vol. 57 (May-June 1979), pp. 92–102.

15. Walter J. Oleszek, *Congressional Procedures and the Policy Process* (Washington: Congressional Quarterly, 1978).

16. Norman J. Ornstein and Shirley Elder, *Interest Groups, Lobbying, and Policymaking* (Washington: Congressional Quarterly, 1978).

17. Steven Rattner, "Big Industry Gun Aims at Hill," *New York Times*, 7 March 1976, Section 3, p. 7.

18. Hobart Rowen, *The Free Enterprisers: Kennedy, Johnson, and the Business Establishment* (New York: Putnam, 1964).

19. ———, "America's Most Powerful Private Club," *Harper's*, Vol. 221 (September 1960), pp. 79–84.

20. Agis Salpukas, "How Big Business Grappled with the Arab Boycott," *New York Times*, 21 August 1977, Section 3, pp. 1 and 5.

21. George Schwartz, "The Successful Fight Against a Federal Consumer Protection Agency," *Michigan State University Business Topics* (Summer 1979), pp. 45–57.

22. Philip Shabecoff, "Big Business on the Offensive," *New York Times Magazine*, 6 December 1979, pp. 134ff.

23. Irving Shapiro, "The Process," *Harvard Business Review*, Vol. 57 (November-December 1979), pp. 98ff.

24. James W. Singer, "Business and Government: A New 'Quasi-Public' Role," *National Journal*, 15 April 1978, pp. 596ff.

25. Peter Slavin, "The Business Roundtable: New Lobbying Arm of Big Business," *Business and Society Review* (Winter 1975–76), pp. 28ff.

26. David Vogel, "Businessmen Unite," *Wall Street Journal*, 14 January 1980, p. 16.

27. Arnold Weber, *In Pursuit of Price Stability: The Wage-Price Freeze of 1971* (Washington: Brookings, 1973).

28. Murray Weidenbaum, *Business, Government, and the Public* (Englewood Cliffs: Prentice-Hall, 1977).

EMERGING STRUCTURAL CHANGES
IN TRANSPORT AND PUBLIC UTILITIES

Northeast Railroads: Restructured or Nationalized?

By ALEXANDER LYALL MORTON*

The intractability of the current Northeast rail problem owes to the fact that the demands of shippers, the demands of rail employees, the claims of creditors, and the demands of public transport policy cannot all be met by the Northeast rail system— they add up to more than the rail system, operating in the competitive environment it does, can produce. Even if the claims of the creditors on the bankrupt estates were to be extinguished, the present demands of the other three claimants could not be met by a self-supporting rail system. Briefly stated, the situation is thus: various labor practices on the railroads (by no means the fault solely of rail labor unions) raise rail costs to the point that most freight traffic (and virtually all passenger traffic) has been lost to other modes of transport and to the point that railways are only marginal competitors for most remaining freight traffic. Large rail shippers use their muscle, playing railroads off one against another and against competing modes to hold down rail freight rates and to extract services from the carriers at prices below cost. Government policy imposes a host of common carrier obligations on the railroads, requiring "essential public services" to be performed and cross-subsidized by profits on other services. Intense competition from other modes and the power of large shippers have eroded such profits

* Harvard Business School.

(which once derived from markets in which railroads enjoyed monopoly powers). The owners of the Northeast railroads have for some decades been the victim of this squeeze play, but now their resources have been largely exhausted, and the Northeast rail plant is in shambles. To whom do employees, shippers, and the beneficiaries of public policies turn next to fill the gap created by their excessive demands upon the rail system?

The political process has intervened in the search for a solution. Declaring the bankrupt railroads to be of concern to the national interest, Congress passed the Regional Rail Reorganization Act of 1973, thereby removing the solution from the exclusive jurisdiction of the bankruptcy courts. In fact, the political process did not have to intervene; conventional thinking has for many years exaggerated the importance of the railroads to the Northeast economy (as we will suggest below). There is, of course, a risk to the government's taking on this responsibility: Will the political process be able to force compromise and sacrifice upon the competing interest groups, or will it ultimately resort to the public purse to squeeze past the crisis?

The proper remedy is to force the claimants to moderate their demands so as to create a viable, self-supporting rail system, for there is no good reason why freight transport should be a subsidized factor of production. Happily, the medicine need not be too bitter, but it does require some rather radical departure from past practice.

First, let us look at the changes labor must accept. Restrictive labor practices raise the labor cost of rail freight transportation to roughly equal the labor input of private and exempt motor carriage, thereby contributing to the loss of rail traffic to trucks. Work rules, craft lines, seniority agreements, and a host of related restrictions severely limit and constrain the specific tasks that may be assigned to any individual rail employee. The purpose of these rules is to share the "available work" more widely, thereby protecting jobs and income. But these understandable goals of labor can be served in a much better way. Slow, unreliable train service and the run-down condition of track and equipment reveal that there are plenty of opportunities for using extra useful service from every present employee to improve service and upgrade plant. To guarantee that greater labor productivity is not turned against labor, employment and income guarantees should be issued. In fact, improved rail service would generate rail freight traffic, actually improving employment prospects in the future. Greatly improved rail labor productivity is one essential remedy for the Northeast rail problem.

Let us turn now to the reform required of shippers and public transport policy. Shippers, local communities, and passengers exploit the common carrier obligations and regulation of the railroads to obtain and preserve rail services at prices below their true cost. The bankruptcies of Northeast railroads were caused to a large degree by forcing the carriers to provide many services at unremunerative rates, and the restoration of these carriers to profitable operation requires an end to this practice.

The proper way to do this is to release railroads from common carrier obligations altogether. Free railroads to negotiate de-

tailed service contracts with individual shippers that specify what services will be provided and what price will be charged, and let the railroads abandon all services whose cost the market refuses to bear, just as most other private industry is permitted to do.

To understand why such a radical cure is necessary and, at the same time, feasible or safe, one must look at the intense competition Northeast railroads now face. American industry has a variety of transport modes to choose among to move its freight; the railroads receive only about one out of every eight dollars spent on intercity freight movement. Equally important, industry has a rich variety of alternatives to the purchase of transportation; among the most important of these are decentralization of production and substitution of locally available materials for those which must be moved longer distances. Thus rails are but one alternative in an array of logistical options that industry has. Let us focus more intently on the truck as a competitor of and alternative to rail. The cost functions of rail and private and exempt truck operations are today nearly identical. This is perhaps astonishing because of the apparent broad differences between the two technologies, but it is nonetheless true. Any commodity can move by truck and move at a cost that is, at best, only slightly higher than the current cost (to the railroad) of rail movement. Trucks can and do carry large amounts of virtually every commodity there is to be moved. (Coal is the commodity whose movement railroads most dominate; yet trucks move about one-sixth as much coal as rail and their share is growing.) Virtually every shipper and every community has unhindered access to trucking for its freight needs. Modern highways serve virtually every location; there is no legal restriction on entry into private trucking; and the near total absence of economies of scale associated with truckload operations means that even the comparatively small shipper whose freight needs will fully utilize only a truck or two has access to virtually all the benefits of truck transport. Because of its broad availability, cost competitiveness with rail, and generally better service and greater convenience, trucking has grown to be the dominant mode. Trucks presently receive five times the revenues of railroads for intercity freight movements.

Trucks, then, can and do compete on a cost basis for virtually every type of traffic the railroads carry, and the cost of private and exempt trucking places a very firm and reasonable ceiling on the price an unregulated railroad industry could possibly demand for its service. The one area where railroads can, one may argue, develop distinct cost advantages over trucks is in high-volume, long-distance movements of bulk commodities such as coal, ore, petroleum products, chemicals, construction aggregates, lumber, and grain. Industries that rely on these raw materials have come increasingly to locate along the expanding network of navigable waterways, however, and water carriers, either alone or in conjunction with truck, now offer cost-competitive and surprisingly widespread competition to the railroads for that one type of traffic that may be somewhat insulated from truck competition. Also, production and distribution of these bulk commodities have become highly concentrated in the hands of a few, very large firms. The size and market power of these firms more than protect them from abusive treatment by railroads.

Shippers no longer require common carrier obligations and regulation to protect them from the railroads. Rather, freedom from these obligations may even be necessary to the survival of railroads in the Northeast. Competing modes are closing in on rail freight transport. They have already diverted vast amounts of rail traffic in the Northeast and they are becoming ever more cost and service competitive for the rest. The point is being approached where the volume of rail traffic remaining in the Northeast fails to achieve the economies of scale and density necessary to support the Northeast rail system in anywhere near the form we know. The grip of the Northeast railroads on the freight market is so tenuous and uncertain that, far from being restrained, they must be given the freedom and encouraged to compete aggressively for all the traffic they can get.

Given this freedom, the railroads may once again carve out for themselves a defensible position in the Northeast. The opportunity is there. The dedicated, or unit, train—a train composed of cars designed specially for their load that shuttles back and forth between specified origin(s) and destination(s)—permits substantial savings in labor, fuel, and capital costs over conventional train operations. It should be used more widely for the movement of bulk commodities and those manufactures that generate repetitive, high-volume movements. Piggybacking—the movement of truck trailers on railway flatcars—enables the railroads to recapture other traffic that has been lost to trucks. The railroad's cost advantage over trucking lies primarily in line-haul efficiency. Piggybacking permits railroads to capture the line-haul portion of intercity freight movements while leaving to trucks the local pickup and delivery functions that trucks clearly do best. Northeast railroads have been moving toward greater use of unit trains and piggybacking, but the common carrier obligations imposed on railroads severely retard what should amount to a technological revolution, a massive restructuring of the industry.

Having intervened in the Northeast rail problem, is the political process facing up to the hard decisions outlined above? The signs are not encouraging. The Regional Rail Reorganization Act itself virtually foreclosed the possibility of substantial reform of restrictive labor practices. The one lever the authors of the Act possessed to goad management and labor into work-rule revision was the offer of protection for any employees that might be affected in rationalizing the Northeast rail system. The Act, however, grants this protection, on extraordinarily generous terms, without requiring any meaningful change of labor practices.

It is still too early to say what success the Act and the instrumentalities it creates—the United States Railway Association (*USRA*) and the Consolidated Railway Corporation—will have in ending the exploitation of the common carrier obligations imposed by the Interstate Commerce Act. While some pruning of rail operations in the Northeast has been spoken of, hearings held throughout the region have revealed strong political opposition to service cutbacks of any kind. The representation of shippers, states, cities, rail labor, and the Interstate Commerce Commission on the Board of Directors of *USRA* suggests that meaningful reform on this front can be little more than a hope.

There are, on the contrary, disturbing signs that we are being prepared for an assault on the public purse to get us past this crisis. Any employee whose job is eliminated will be generously protected by public funds, according to the Act, though there are few if any precedents for public protection of workers who have lost jobs when the fortunes of an industry have turned. Branch line subsidies will preserve "essential rail service" along rail lines that might otherwise be abandoned, though the decline of traffic on these lines is itself evidence that rail service is no longer essential to more than a few shippers. Fixed rail plant is to be rebuilt with federal grants and loan guarantees.

One can even hear the rhetoric that is to prepare us for continuing subsidy of Northeast rail operating deficits after these initial excuses—labor protection, branch-line subsidies, etc.—begin to pall. The railways, we are told, are a "valuable natural resource," the "low-cost carrier," a "fuel-conserving mode of transport." Is it cynical to ask why, if railroads are so inherently efficient, have they sunk to their present state and why must they be subsidized and protected from higher-cost competitors? Judging from present deficits, the drain of the Northeast rail system on public funds will run on the order of $500 million to $1 billion annually even at the onset.

But the present drift of events will almost certainly carry us further than nationalization of Northeast railroads. Clever, solvent rail carriers may find it profitable to encourage federal involvement and public subsidy for the bankrupt railroads. Freight cars today absorb over half of all rail capital expenditures. The Penn Central, western and southern carriers claim, has long beggared other railroads for freight cars because of its own inadequate ownership. What an opportunity to reverse the score now that the public treasury will be buying cars. The argument for branch-line subsidies does not lose validity at the Potomac, Ohio, and Mississippi Rivers; once the principle is accepted for the Northeast, solvent carriers should be able to tap easily into a branch-line subsidy program.

Then look further to the future. The entire American railroad industry has earned a subnormal return on invested capital for decades. Net railway operating income in 1973, a good year, was one-third lower than in 1929, without adjustment for the greatly reduced purchasing power of those dollars. The railroads' rate of return on transportation investment has not exceeded 5 percent since 1929 and has not exceeded 4 percent since 1955. Railroad executives constantly face a difficult decision in committing and recommitting capital to an enterprise whose return has been so marginal for decades, particularly now that interest rates have risen to the 10 percent level. With the low returns and the vast appetite for capital that railroads have, the owners may welcome a chance to unload the business, if only some sucker may be found to buy it. The settlement with the creditors of the Northeast bankrupts may set the terms at which the owners of solvent railroads can expect to sell out. While the Regional Rail Reorganization Act may not have intended it, it appears that the courts may award the estate reasonable value for any properties taken over. Once management of solvent carriers decides that liquidation of rail assets and

ultimate sale of the remains to the government are more attractive than perpetual reinvestment for inadequate returns, the properties of these carriers will begin the long slide into disrepair, down the same track as the Northeast bankrupts.

Other industries may some day find it attractive to play the same game. Once the government commits itself to solving industrial crises like the Northeast rail situation and doing so from the public purse, an important restraint upon the demands of other interest groups in the economy will have been sacrificed. Already several large airlines have applied, though unsuccessfully to date, for Federal subsidies. Distant early warnings of trouble in the electric utility industry have also appeared. Is it time to ask what precedents we wish to set?

The CAB's Struggle to Establish Price and Route Rivalry in World Air Transport

By R. D. PETERSON*

ABSTRACT. Almost from the beginning of *international air transport,* this industry, while *regulated* by the U.S. Government, has enjoyed exemption from
prosecution under the *antitrust laws.* In 1946 leading airlines of Western Europe,
Canada and the United States organized the *International Air Transportation
Association,* which the *Civil Aeronautics Board* later charged was a *cartel* regulating prices, schedules and routes in the interest of the profits of the carriers.
In 1978 the board began trying to establish price and route competition in the
industry's foreign operations, as well as in the domestic services. The board's
efforts to *deregulate* the industry to make it responsive to *market* forces continued through the *Ford, Carter* and *Reagan presidencies* and the evidence so
far available suggests that they have achieved a substantial degree of success.

I

Overview

AFTER MORE THAN THREE DECADES of protectionism, the Civil Aeronautics Board
(CAB) publicly began to question the need for antitrust immunity enjoyed by
the International Air Transport Association (IATA). Under the leadership of Dr.
Alfred E. Kahn, the now defunct CAB was successful in sterilizing the potency
of the international air cartel over the North Atlantic. This paper traces the controversy between the CAB and IATA during the deregulation era.

Regulation of selected industry groups in the American economy has persisted
for more than a century.[1] In 1938, the Civil Aeronautics Act[2] established the
Civil Aeronautics Authority (CAA),[3] later replaced by the Civil Aeronautics Board
(CAB).[4] Congress granted that agency the power to exempt airlines from the
antitrust laws.[5] In 1946, the International Air Transportation Association (IATA)[6]
was created by leading airlines of Western Europe, Canada, and the United
States to coordinate the otherwise disorganized air traffic over the North Atlantic.

In that same year, the CAB granted immunity from prosecution under the
antitrust law to U.S. and foreign flag airlines that participated in rate-making
conferences held by IATA.[7] This exemption continued for more than 30 years.
In 1978 the CAB threatened to withdraw this privilege from American air carriers

* [R. D. Peterson, Ph.D., J.D., is professor of economics, Colorado State University, Fort Collins,
CO 80523.]

American Journal of Economics and Sociology, Vol. 49, No. 1 (January, 1990).
© 1990 American Journal of Economics and Sociology, Inc.

and thereby discontinue the long period of stable regulated competition which had characterized international air transport. The CAB alleged that IATA was a cartel which engaged in anti-competitive collusive activities. It sought to replace *regulated* with *open* competition in domestic (and *significant* competition in international) air transport markets to benefit shippers, carriers and the economic status of the airlines in order to substitute the discipline of natural market forces for public regulation. IATA argued that it was *not* a cartel but operated in the public interest because of the "unique features" of foreign air transportation.

II

Cartelization

THE WORD "CARTEL" is derived from the Italian, *cartello,* a diminutive of *carta,* or "paper."[9] In the extreme, a cartel is a formal agreement (recorded on paper) among otherwise independent firms to coordinate combined business activities for their mutual benefit.[10] "Cartel" is an emotionally charged word which involves degrees of collusive business conduct.[11]

The Perfect Cartel

In a full, or perfect cartel, firms reach a monopoly solution of profit maximization rather than a competitive equilibrium of price and output from independent efforts of individual firms.[12] A perfect cartel is created when all producers of a substitutable product agree, in a written and legally binding contract, to empower a designated representative to determine aggregate output and assign market territories among members as well as to allocate investment in plant and equipment, establish a price for each market area and to share profits.[13] These conditions result in a monopoly price and output when the cartel manager operates member firms as if they were one giant company (and hence the sole producer of the output sold in the market).[14]

In a perfect cartel, member firms report information to the cartel headquarters on costs, productivity, output, capacity, and other accounting, production and marketing activities.[15] The cartel manager thereby achieves joint profit maximization.[16] The tighter the control by the cartel manager, and the more rigidly cartel members follow the assigned allocations, the greater the expected success of the cartel in achieving the monopoly outcome. As control and followership are weakened, results deviate from monopoly price and output.

Degrees of Collusion

The perfect cartel is an idealistic extreme because control and followership may be *incomplete* rather than *complete.*[17] Toward the monopoly end of the spectrum of market organizations, which includes oligopoly, Bain describes collusion as being complete, incompletely observed, indefinite in its terms and participation, and interdependent without agreement.[18]

A perfect cartel involves *complete collusion* whenever an agreement was signed by all sellers in the industry to be enforceable on all signers by definite terms, and which specifies and unambiguously fixes outputs, prices, production capacities, and market shares. This agreement also includes a formula for sharing profits (not necessarily in proportion to market shares or output) and is followed rigorously if all parties adhere to its terms.[19] Price and output closely approach a monopoly situation.

In an *incompletely observed collusion,* a collusive express or tacit agreement exists among firms in the industry to establish a common price and output but is not rigorously observed by *all* the sellers. Actual prices do not necessarily follow agreed prices because of some price cutting.[20] Price (output) is slightly less (more) than in monopoly.

Collusion with indefinite terms and incomplete participation requires that an express or tacit agreement exists on prices and output among most, but not all, sellers in the industry, with terms being neither rigid nor clear. Price and output policies are at variance among those sellers who are members to the agreement; but there may be some collusion and some independent action among the parties to an agreement.[21] The result deviates from price and output in a monopoly position.

For *interdependent action without agreement,* no express or implied agreement exists among firms over time, but sellers condition their price and output decisions in light of anticipated actions by each other. Depending on the number of firms in the industry, the degree of product differentiation, and the extent of interdependency recognized, some price leadership and price cutting exist.[22] Price and output occur somewhere between the monopoly and competitive levels.

Cartel Criteria

There is no absolute either/or dichotomy between the independent-competitive and the joint-monopolistic activities of oligopolistic firms. Instead, there is a *continuum* between oligopoly and monopoly embracing various degrees of collusion by which firms in an industry coordinate their price and production policies. Bain's classification of collusion helps to distinguish between perfect and imperfect (or full and partial) cartels.[23] His scheme depends on numbers of activities, proportion of output, completeness of agreement, and enforcement of provisions. Four factors affect whether collusive behavior by an organization is cartel-like. The tendency for monopoly price and output is greater: the larger the number of production and marketing activities covered in the arrangement; the larger the proportion of industry output produced by firms that are party to an arrangement; the greater the clarity and completeness of an arrangement; and the greater the enforcement of the arrangement.

III

International Air Transport Association

INDUSTRIAL FIRMS can often reduce certain hazards leading to the risk of loss by creating a voluntary organization which influences their business environment.[24] IATA is such an arrangement.

History

On August 25, 1919, the International Air Traffic Association was created to monitor international air navigation and to set up a permanent structure for its administration.[25] A short agreement was signed then to establish a central office and to pledge mutual cooperation.[26] This first IATA was an organization of airline carriers, not of individual governments; membership was voluntary but new members could be approved by a majority of existing members.[27]

During its first 20 years, regular meetings were held and a committee structure was developed and expanded. During that time, IATA made contributions about safety and standardization for aircraft design and construction, weather navigation, and flight communications.[28] Membership had expanded by the mid-1930s. It conducted studies and encouraged the sharing of information for topics such as icing, weight, balance, aircraft size, landing field requirements, and high altitude flights.[29]

The last meeting of the original IATA was held in 1938 when World War Two was erupting.[30] In late 1944, a convention of international aviation authorities was held in Chicago to create the International Civil Aviation Organization (ICAO).[31] In 1945, a successor to the first IATA emerged[32] with officers, committees, and organizational ties to ICAO-represented governments.[33] A mechanism for various "conferences" was developed so that IATA members could meet to discuss mutual marketing and other economic problems.[34] IATA grew in size and responsibility during the post-World War Two period.[35]

Organization[36]

As a nongovernmental organization, IATA derives legal stature from an act of Canada's Parliament which granted it a corporate charter of existence and operation. More than 125 internationally scheduled air carriers representing nearly 100 countries belong to IATA, an organization providing technical, medical, legal, research, finance, and tariff information to its members. IATA is voluntary, non-exclusive, non-political and democratic. Any airline can become a member if it has been licensed to provide scheduled air service by a government eligible for membership in ICAO. Day-to-day administration of IATA is carried out by a nine-member Executive Management Board, headed by a Director General. Its budget is financed from dues paid by members, generally in proportion to the international air traffic carried by each airline.

Activities

International air transportation is a highly complex activity. Passengers and cargo moving from one nation to another become involved with different airlines, currencies, national aviation policies, and customs laws. IATA coordinates these differences to create an integrated, global air transport system which links users, airlines, and governments.[37] It operates a clearing house for handling interline accounts among carriers (nearly $10 billion annually). It lobbies for lower taxes, provides data-processing equipment and programs, and monitors fuel prices. It also urges international security standards; compiles information from members for their sharing; assists the development of landing procedures; studies airmail conveyance rates of various governments; and disseminates public relations materials to governments, civic groups, and the general public.[38]

Conferences

One of the primary functions of IATA is to provide a forum for members to participate in "conferences" at which airline representatives meet to discuss, negotiate, and agree on rights to carry traffic on routes flown, prices charged, and standards adopted for various kinds of service. Recommendations are forwarded to respective governments of home nations of the delegates.[39] Conference results eventually become embodied in a *bilateral agreement*[40] by which fares, routes, and conditions of transport between two nations are established, published, and followed. These agreements carry the force of law in international air travel when specific governments "ratify" the agreements and the filed tariffs are accepted.

IATA conducts several types of conferences.[41] First, several Procedures Conferences establish a common system of air transport operations among member airlines and their nations: Passenger Services Conferences for matters of travellers' baggage, reservations, ticketing, and scheduling; Passenger Agency Conferences for relationships between airlines and sales agents; Cargo Services Conferences for handling, documenting and loading freight; and Cargo Agency Conferences for monitoring the sale and shipment of international air cargo.

Second, the heart of IATA operations lies in a dual mechanism of Traffic Conferences and Tariff Coordination. Traffic Conferences meet on a regular basis to coordinate international fares and to establish conditions and procedures relating to fares. Tariff Coordination meetings enable IATA members to discuss matters of fares and commissions on sales openly and collectively. Observers from ICAO—government representatives from the nations of IATA member airlines—attend Traffic Conferences along with air carrier representatives.[42]

Third, World-wide Tariff Coordination Conferences are held so members can review matters of *overall* passenger fares and air cargo rates. For this purpose, IATA established three broad geographic regions: the Western Hemisphere;

Europe, Africa, and the Middle East; and Asia, Australia and the South Pacific. These conferences help IATA and its members understand developments in the volume of freight and travel on a global basis and create schedules, fares, and routes vis-a-vis world-wide demand conditions.[43]

IATA administrators sought to create multilateral forward agreements among the national governments of its members as a means of building cohesiveness, solidarity, and cooperation in promulgating and enforcing IATA policy. Bilateral agreements continue to exist among IATA members and their governments but multilateralism has not yet been achieved.[44]

IV

U.S. Air Transport Policy

BEFORE THE MID-1920s, aviation was in its infancy and essentially competitive. Regulation of U.S. civil air transport began with the passage of the Kelly Act (1925), the Air Commerce Act (1926), the McNary-Watres Act (1930), and the Air Mail Act (1934). Primary air transport policy is found in the Civil Aeronautics Act (1938)—now the Federal Aviation Act of 1958—which features a dual policy: to remedy past abuses of safety and competition, by promoting the former, and controlling the latter. The CAA, and its successor, the CAB, largely monitored entry and fares. Safety was assigned to several agencies but now resides in the Federal Aviation Administration (FAA) in the Department of Transportation (DOT). U.S. domestic air transport policy emphasized regulated competition after 1938, but its international policy since 1946 allowed for self-determination and cooperation among carriers and their nations. In the late 1970s these policies underwent a rapid change. By 1985, the CAB ceased to exist and its functions were transferred to the DOT.

Policy from 1946 to 1975

In November, 1944, ICAO was created to promote free air traffic among nations.[45] Five "freedoms of the air"[46] were advocated, but only two were adopted because European nations wanted a tightly regulated structure. As a result, a *multi*lateral approach was avoided and a policy of *bi*lateral agreements was adopted.[47]

In April, 1945, IATA was resurrected and reformulated in Havana, Cuba. Cooperation among IATA air carriers and their governments (through ICAO) was affirmed.[48] At successive meetings, an international rate-making structure was created and placed into operation under the aegis of IATA.[49] Pan American Airways then announced a plan to reduce fares 30 percent on its transatlantic flights.[50] Concern by Great Britain over such destructive price cutting of air transport rates by the U.S. prompted the Bermuda Conference in January 1946.

200

This meeting gave birth to a bilateral agreement by which the U.S. agreed to participate in IATA's route and rate conferences, and Britain agreed to allow freedom of U.S. air carriers to fly trans-Atlantic routes.[51] In February, 1946, the CAB granted to U.S. carriers flying international routes an antitrust exemption from their participation in IATA conferences.[52] This immunity was reviewed in 1955 and continued into the 1970s.[53]

Policy During Ford's Presidency

In September, 1976, President Gerald Ford began the drive for deregulation of domestic air travel when he released a report of the Economic Policy Board Task Force on International Transportation Policy.[54] A new economic philosophy of competition was initiated with multilateral discussions and bilateral agreements. Five principal objectives were stated for international air transport policy: (1) to rely on competitive market forces; (2) to provide low-price air transportation; (3) to generate sufficient profits for U.S. air carriers; (4) to foster national defense and foreign relations; and (5) to encourage safety and efficiency for the airways and environment.[55] The possibility of excess capacity and predatory pricing was acknowledged, resulting in a call for restrained competition.[56] Although the Task Force sought route competition among carriers, it was admitted that multiple U.S. carriers might not be needed for all foreign routes. The report foresaw a continued role for IATA to negotiate tariffs for U.S. international air flights. IATA members were warned to allow market forces to set innovative and flexible fares, routes and schedules for *individual* carriers.

Policy During Carter's Presidency

President Jimmy Carter appointed an economist, Dr. Alfred E. Kahn, to be CAB Chairman in 1977. Kahn believed that air transport possesses basic competitive features: a price elastic demand (so that a modest reduction in fares will increase air carriage significantly); few economies of scale exist (so that cost per ton or passenger mile is similar for fully loaded small and large aircrafts); and mobile resources (so that an aircraft can be moved quickly into and out of different market areas as demand changes).[57] Kahn suggested deregulating the airlines and eliminating the CAB.

Kahn and his staff supported four official policy changes embraced by: (1) the Air Cargo Deregulation Act of 1977;[58] (2) the Airline Deregulation Act of 1978;[59] (3) the June 9, 1978, Order to Show Cause on IATA Conference Agreements;[60] and (4) the International Air Transportation Competition Act (IATCA) of 1979.[61] The purpose of the "Show Cause" order was to put IATA and the airlines on notice of CAB's intent to withdraw antitrust immunity from rate conferences and to invite interested parties to a hearing to provide reasons (*i.e.,* to show cause) why the immunity should not be withdrawn.

The purpose of IATCA was to foster low-price international air carriage by relying on competitive market forces. The Act specifically encouraged entry of new carriers, promoted the introduction of innovative fares, and urged pricing freedom for individual air carriers. Moreover, CAB entry criteria for certificates of operating authority were expanded under the Act to a "fit, willing and able" standard which is "consistent with the public convenience and necessity" for regular, temporary, and charter international air carriage.[62]

Policy During Reagan's Presidency

Marvin Cohen, appointed by President Carter in 1979, continued to be CAB Chairman under President Ronald Reagan, and followed a policy of deregulating domestic and international air transportation. The international goal was to create a "broad based free trade zone in air transportation" based on price competition, open entry, low and innovative fares, unique services, and new markets.[63] Cohen asserted that deregulation and competition would result in efficiency, variety, profit opportunities, and wise energy allocation.[64]

Although world airlines were losing money,[65] Cohen believed that the new competitive policy was not a threat to international carriers. He suggested that it is healthy in competition for carriers to "fall by the wayside" if they are not as efficient as airlines able to compete and survive.[66] Cohen attributed recent declines then in airline profits to strikes, the recession and higher fuel costs because of the OPEC oil cartel, not to the results of open competition.[67] Despite these words of support for the free market, international competitive policy continued to be questioned. The CAB supported a proposed Show Cause Order on IATA Conference Agreements but postponed twice the promulgation of that order at the request of the Reagan administration. The House of Representatives legislated that no funds could be spent by the CAB to enforce the 1978 Show Cause Order.[68] It was finally ordered in 1985. Smaller U.S. airlines who have lost money in recent years, and subsidized European airlines and their govern-ments who decry the open competition policy tried to dissuade the CAB. The CAB continued to pursue its deregulation policies even after its functions had been absorbed by DOT.

V

The Cartel Debate: CAB Versus IATA

THE ROLE OF IATA was at the center of a debate over an alleged international air cartel. The two sides to this controversy involved charges by the CAB and responses of IATA.

Allegations by CAB

Kahn argued that IATA performs a cartel role because of its Traffic and Tariff Conferences. He labeled IATA a "smoothly oiled price-fixing cartel" and called participants in IATA multi-lateral negotiations "protectionists and cartelizers."[69] Kahn claimed that multilateralism among air carriers of leading Western nations, through the leadership of IATA, fixed binding floors under prices, restricted entry and capacity, and restrained competition. IATA's cartel activities were manifest in its meetings for coordinating otherwise competitive air fares which increased prices and reduced services.

Kahn believed that the CAB should repeal the antitrust immunity enjoyed by U.S. airlines participating in IATA rate conferences. Instead, he suggested replacing these conferences with *uni*lateral price determination (wherein representatives of nations negotiate and agree, *separately* but *in pairs,* as to what the overall air transport policy between them shall be).[70] Multilateralism, for Kahn, was appropriate for conflict resolution rather than for price and route negotiation.

The CAB charged that IATA was a cartel organization because its members include most of the world's scheduled airlines who meet regularly to discuss international air fares, routes, and schedules for various sectors of the globe. In its Show Cause Order aimed at IATA in June, 1978, the CAB explained how the organization had served for more than 30 years as an approval agency for IATA's basic fare structure agreements.[71] CAB officials thereby observed the influence of IATA Traffic Conferences and concluded that multilateral rate-making through IATA obviates price competition.

The CAB believed that if IATA conferences did not exist, international air fares would be lower than they were during the 1946-to-1978 period. In its 1978 statement, the CAB suggested that price-fixing agreements of IATA members are *per se* violations of the antitrust laws and that IATA Traffic Conference Resolutions and related agreements are not in the public interest.[72]

In a May, 1979, statement, CAB reiterated its belief that IATA was stifling competition in international air transportation: the multilateral conference mechanism for *discussing* rates (which are subsequently *established* and *approved*) destroys price rivalry.[73] In November, 1979, CAB found that a proportional fare structure proposal of IATA amounted to manipulation for the purpose of reducing competition among its members. The CAB subsequently held that such agreements were adverse to the public interest.

In April, 1980, the CAB responded to an IATA proposal to establish a two-tier structure for its organization: a Trade Association for activities other than rate-making, and a Traffic Conference for rate-making activities.[74] All IATA members were required to belong to the former, whereas membership in the latter would be optional. The purpose of such restructuring was to isolate the subject of the cartel allegations from IATA's total operations.

In their assessment of market impact, CAB believed that this new arrangement was inimical to competition as a probable violation of Section 1 of the Sherman Act, but that IATA may not be a *complete* cartel. CAB noted that IATA's meetings involved discussions which are more aimed at "adjusting" and "harmonizing" air fares than at sharing information.[75] In this regard, even the proponents of joint and through fares admitted that IATA provided a forum in which members could be certain that price competition by one carrier would not hurt other carriers.[76]

In May, 1981, the CAB concluded that IATA was a voluntary organization of carriers (but not of governments) whose conferences deliberately obtain uniform price agreements between direct competitors; that IATA's rate-making conferences and U.S. air carrier antitrust immunity from them reduces competition; that IATA multilateral fare setting may reduce rather than increase interlining services; and that in markets where all carriers are not IATA members, fares and services had not been disrupted.[77] The CAB did not claim that IATA was a complete cartel, but that the forum provided by IATA allowed its members to behave collusively.[78]

Response by IATA

Knut Hammarskjold, Director General at that time, contended that IATA was not a cartel engaged in anti-competitive practices. He claimed that IATA fostered world cooperation among airlines to solve the many complex problems inherent in international air transportation, and that it was a *trade association* serving airlines, passengers, shippers, travel agents, and governments.[79] IATA controlled neither entry into air transport nor loading capacities on individual flights; and its pricing agreements were merely *recommendations* to governments, not binding orders to airlines. Furthermore, he argued that IATA neither required a carrier to participate in Traffic Conferences nor excluded it from them, that observers from various governments were allowed to attend IATA conferences, and that IATA opposed discrimination and unfair business practices.[80]

Hammarskjold believed that international air carriage does not possess key elements of a competition market. The commodity—the supply of air carriage—is perishable (because space cannot be stockpiled); although an aircraft is mobile and can move in and out of markets, markets themselves are immobile. Moreover, international aspects of air transportation—scheduling flights through countries with diverse laws—are not akin to competitive distribution of output in unfettered markets. As a result, international air transportation is more conducive to self-regulation through mutual cooperation and communication such as with IATA, than to open or government-sponsored competition.[81]

In its first response to CAB's Show Cause Order, IATA described how its activities were in the public interest and called for the CAB to withdraw its tentative findings.[82] Specifically, IATA claimed that an open market for international aviation was unrealistic because foreign air transport requires a carefully integrated coordination among airlines and governments.[83] In a second response, IATA rebutted CAB's legal analysis by arguing that Section 42 of the revised FAA rules required tariff and traffic coordination of through-rate and interline problems.[84] Moreover, IATA criticized the CAB's unilateral approach to making international air transport policy and called for an intergovernmental approach among nations to deal with the CAB's allegations.[85]

In its official publications, IATA tried to counter the cartel accusation: "Cartel" is an extreme concept not applicable to IATA—it is not a monster but faces monstrous problems. The organization is a mechanism for reconciling the marketing problems in world air travel. It does not allocate markets because individual governments perform this function for their own flag air carriers. IATA neither establishes nor controls airline schedules and routes, nor sets prices, nor discriminates among the rights of its members in favor of one over another. Indeed, there is healthy rivalry in international air transport for market shares among IATA members, non-scheduled operators, and surface carriers. In fact, IATA limits neither membership nor their outputs of air services, but is open to any air carrier meeting its admission criteria.

VI

Assessment

GIVEN THE ADMITTED STRUCTURE and activities of IATA, to what extent is it a cartel? Considering the allegations of the CAB, at which cartel element(s) were its efforts directed? By its threat and ultimate issuing of a Show Cause Order against IATA, did the CAB introduce competitiveness into the market for international air transport?

IATA a Cartel?

A cartel is a collusive organization of otherwise competing producers in a line of commerce which encourages joint harmonization of combined business interests. A cartel is not absolute, but exists by degrees of collusion. One cartel may be full, or perfect, whereas another may be partial, or imperfect. Tendency toward fullness of perfection can be judged by the nature of collusive activities facilitated by a suspected cartel organization.

IATA was not a *full* cartel for several reasons. It did not control total industry output, dictate prices and directly allocate markets, investment, or profits among its members. Moreover, no formal written agreement binds IATA and its members for their combined business decisions.

205

The existence of IATA provided a forum for its members to discuss, negotiate and agree on production and marketing practices which lead to collusive behavior. Collusion among international airlines is facilitated by the administrative structure of IATA which helped to coordinate members' interests through ICAO to foreign governments. IATA's entire conference structure allowed cross coordination by its members of policies for prices, inputs, output and terms of trade. That Traffic and Tariff Conferences fostered cartel-like collusive behavior is difficult to deny. It is difficult to argue that competitiveness results from those conferences which establish parallel procedures for reservations, ticketing, baggage, sales-agent relations, cargo handling, and other aspects of air travel.

Based on the collusive continuum of Bain, IATA fostered a partial, or imperfect, cartel described by "incompletely observed collusion" as measured by numbers, proportion, completeness, and enforcement. IATA members produced 75 percent of industry output. A large number of production and marketing decisions was coordinated at IATA meetings. In conjunction with ICAO, national airlines and foreign governments, an enforcement mechanism was operative. Recommendations, resulting from IATA discussions, were largely followed even though no formal written agreement was signed by members. Governments were bound through bilateral agreements.

CAB's Target

Control over prices, and prevention of price cutting, are crucial to collusive cartel behavior. CAB efforts to reduce the effectiveness of IATA's alleged cartel activities was a several-pronged policy to promote competition in international air transport. The primary CAB policy weapon was the withdrawal of antitrust immunity from airlines participating in IATA Traffic and Tariff Conferences. This eliminated the central feature of cartel goals: common prices in individual market subgroups and therefore, no price rivalry among cartel members. Without antitrust immunity, U.S. airlines participating in rate meetings are exposed to legal action for price fixing.[86]

The withdrawing of antitrust immunity fosters price rivalry among international air carriers. When this goal is combined with the already existing policy of relaxed entry requirements into the industry (*i.e.,* new carriers), and into individual markets (*i.e.,* multiple routes), the number of air carriers increase and pressures develop for price cutting. When several airlines fly a route, it is difficult to enforce a stabilized price at a high level than when only a few fly the route.

The CAB Show Cause Order and amendments allowing U.S. air carriers to participate in IATA's trade association activities constituted a procompetitive policy. One of the primary features of competition is adequate knowledge of market prices, costs, productivities and capacities. These conferences allowed air carriers, especially U.S. companies, to share data with one another. This information helps all airlines make rapid adjustments to changing demand and supply conditions of fares, routes, and schedules.

A Restructured Market

Prior to the drafting of the 1978 Show Cause Order, competitive forces were already beginning to undermine the effects of IATA's cartel activities. The stable pricing structure began to collapse for several reasons because both public and private policies changed. The British government ordered BOAC to avoid IATA. Sir Freddie Laker entered the overseas air travel market with jumbo jets and cut-rate fares. Other airlines instituted low stand-by and 40-day advance fares, along with a penalty clause. Although these cracks appeared in the cartel foundation built by IATA, the CAB apparently wanted to make sure that IATA did not regain control of the cartel price structure in air travel over the North Atlantic.

The CAB Show Cause Order on Traffic Conferences was served on IATA in May, 1985,[87] but some of its intended effects had already been achieved. IATA's maneuver to separate trade-association from rate-making activities was tacit recognition that price coordination took place. This result, coupled with the CAB policy of relaxed entry requirements, both into the industry and on specific routes, introduced price, schedule, and route rivalry into international air transport. Moreover, domestic deregulation fostered a competitive climate which had spilled over into the international sector. Competitive-like forces ostensibly exist in the international air transport market.

In a competitive market, economists expect firms to operate at capacity and prices to be bid down near average cost of production so that profit rates are low. For international passenger carriage by U.S. airlines after deregulation, fares and profit rates decreased, but revenues and capacity increased, despite skyrocketing fuel costs. To illustrate, the average passenger-mile rate, in constant 1967 dollars, rose from .040 in 1973 to .045 by 1977, but then fell to .042 in 1979 and to .034 by 1983.[88] Likewise, average profit rates on equity which were 3.8% in 1977, dropped to 0.8% in 1981 and to −0.5% by 1983.[89] With respect to output and capacity, 44 billion revenue passenger miles were flown in 1977, but increased to 55 billion by 1983, while the revenue passenger load factor grew from 56% to 61% during that same period.[90] These performance measures occurred as fuel costs increased 42% from 1977 to 1979, and then 82% from 1979 to 1981.[91] Whether the breakup of the IATA cartel was responsible for these conditions requires additional investigation and analysis but these revealing statistics support the competitive hypothesis.

Notes

1. Banking was regulated in the early 1800s, and states regulated safe and sanitary employment conditions in 1877. See Clair Wilcox, *Public Policies Toward Business* (Homewood: Irwin, 1966), p. 5.

2. Public Law No. 75-706, 52 Stat. 973 (1938).

3. *Ibid.,* Section 1102.

4. Paul S. Dempsey, "The Rise and Fall of the Civil Aeronautics Board: Opening Wide the Floodgates of Entry," *Transportation Law Journal,* Vol. 11, 1979, p. 11.

5. 49 U.S. Code 1384, Section 414.

6. IATA, *50 Years of World Airline Cooperation,* 1969, p. 6.

7. CAB Agreement No. 493, "IATA Traffic Conference Resolution," 6 CAB 639 (1946).

8. The U.S. has had a long-standing commitment to fostering the free, competitive market in its economy. This is especially notable in its antitrust policy. See Willard F. Mueller, *A Primer on Competition and Monopoly* (New York: Random House, 1970), pp. 127-72. But the Webb-Pomerene Act of 1918 allowed participation in foreign cartels by export traders.

9. *The American Heritage Dictionary,* Second College Edition (Boston: Houghton Mifflin, 1982), p. 243.

10. William G. Shepherd, *The Economics of Industrial Organization* (Englewood Cliffs: Prentice-Hall, 1985), pp. 242-44.

11. Frederick M. Scherer, *Industrial Market Structure and Economic Performance* (Chicago: Rand McNally, 1970), pp. 158-61.

12. Edwin Mansfield, *Microeconomics* (New York: Norton, 1970), pp. 318-20.

13. James V. Koch, *Industrial Organization and Prices* (Englewood Cliffs: Prentice-Hall, 1980), pp. 419-28.

14. Campbell R. McConnell, *Economics* (New York: McGraw-Hill, 1981), p. 576.

15. Scherer, *op. cit.,* pp. 208-10.

16. In theory, industry marginal revenue is equated with the aggregate marginal costs of cartel firms to determine industry output. The next step is to assign each member a part of that output based on its own marginal costs.

17. Robert Lanzillotti, "Pricing Objectives in Large Companies," *American Economic Review,* Vol. 62, 1958, pp. 921-40.

18. Joe S. Bain, *Industrial Organization* (New York: Wiley, 1968), pp. 306-10.

19. *Ibid.,* pp. 311-12.

20. *Ibid.,* pp. 312-13.

21. *Ibid.,* pp. 313-14.

22. *Ibid.,* pp. 314-15.

23. According to Bain's forms of collusion, a perfect cartel is an extreme form of collusion tending toward the monopoly price and output but that several degrees of imperfect collusion are associated with forms of oligopoly which are suggestive of imperfect cartels.

24. Mancur Olson, *The Logic of Collective Action* (Cambridge: Harvard Univ. Press, 1965), p. 144.

25. 50 Years, *op. cit.,* p. 2.

26. *Ibid.,* p. 3.

27. *Ibid.*

28. IATA, *World Airline Cooperation,* 1981, p. 3.

29. IATA, *Trends in International Aviation and Governmental Policies,* 1979, pp. 6-7.

30. 50 Years, *op. cit.,* p. 6.

31. World Airline, *op. cit.,* pp. 3-4.

32. *Ibid.*

33. 50 Years, *op. cit.,* p. 6.

34. World Airline, *op. cit.,* pp. 6-8.

35. Statement of Knut Hammarskjold, *Hearings Before the House Committee on Public Works and Transportation on International Aviation Policy,* 97th Congress, 1st Session, 1981, p. 10.

36. This section is derived from information in Trends, *op. cit.,* and 50 Years, *op. cit.*

37. World Airline, *op. cit.,* p. 2.

38. *Ibid.,* pp. 5–14.

39. Many western developed nations either regulate their airlines or have nationalized them. This tendency makes it easy to promulgate fares, rates, routes, and schedules, especially in international aviation because such arrangements carry the force of law.

40. A "bilateral agreement" is one between two nations regarding the rights, privileges, duties, and legal relations concerning foreign aviation. In international aviation, dozens of "bilaterals" exist among most western developed nations whereby each country agrees individually with every other country.

41. World Airline, *op. cit.,* pp. 6–10.

42. Trends, *op. cit.,* p. 10.

43. IATA, *Backgrounder,* 1980, p. 3.

44. IATA, *The International Multilateral Interline System: Its Benefits and Requirements,* 1980, pp. 1–7.

45. 50 Years, *op. cit.,* pp. 6–7.

46. The "five freedoms" involve the privilege: (1) to fly across a territory without landing; (2) to land for non-traffic purposes; (3) to put down passengers/cargo from a carrier's flag country in another; (4) to take on passengers/cargo destined for any state and put passengers/cargo down in any other state. See Benjamin A. Sims, "International Air Transportation: The Effect of the Airline Deregulation Act of 1978 and the Bermuda II Agreement," *Transportation Law Journal,* Vol. 10, 1978, p. 240.

47. 50 Years, *op. cit.,* pp. 6–7.

48. Trends, *op. cit.,* p. 10.

49. *Ibid.,* p. 11.

50. *Ibid.,* p. 12.

51. *Ibid.,* p. 13.

52. *Ibid.,* p. 14.

53. CAB Order E-9305, June 15, 1955.

54. President Gerald Ford, *Statement of International Air Transportation Policy of the United States,* 1976, p. 9.

55. *Ibid.,* pp. 3–4.

56. *Ibid.,* p. 17.

57. Alfred E. Kahn, *The Economics of Regulation* (New York: Wiley, 1971), pp. 209–20.

58. 91 Statutes 1278, 1977.

59. Public Law 95-504, October 24, 1978.

60. CAB Order to Show Cause 78-6-78 (1978). This is a tentative finding order, Docket 32851, Agreement CAB 1175, as amended.

61. Public Law 96-192 (1980).

62. 94 Statutes 37.

63. Marvin Cohen, *Competition in Air Transportation on the North Atlantic,* Third International Aviation Conference, Paris, 1981, p. 14.

64. *Ibid.,* pp. 2–3.

65. *Ibid.*

66. *Ibid.,* p. 9.

67. *Ibid.,* pp. 4–6.

68. Private correspondence, Office of Aviation Operations, U.S. Department of Transportation, Washington, D.C.

69. Alfred Kahn, "Protecting Airlines From Freedom," *Washington Post,* November 5, 1981, p. A29.

70. *Hearings Before House Committee on Public Works and Transportation on International Aviation Policy,* 97th Congress, 1st Session, 1981, p. 12 (from "Statement of Alfred E. Kahn").

71. CAB Order to Show Cause 78-6-78 (Docket 32851), Agreement CAB 1175, As Amended.

72. *Ibid.,* pp. 1–7.

73. CAB Order 79-5-113.

74. CAB Order and Statement of Tentative Conclusions 80-4-113.

75. *Ibid.,* pp. 7–8.

76. *Ibid.,* p. 9.

77. CAB Final Order Terminating Proceeding 81-5-27.

78. CAB Order 8-4-113, p. 9.

79. Hammarskjold, *op. cit.,* pp. 1–4.

80. *Ibid.,* p. 1.

81. IATA, "This 'Cartel' Nonsense," 1980, pp. 1–2.

82. IATA, Response to the Board's "Order to Show Cause," Docket 32851, Agreement CAB 1175, 1978. pp. 1–5.

83. *Ibid.,* p. 82.

84. IATA, Comments on the Board's "Statement of Tentative Conclusions" in Order 80-4-113, 1980, pp. 1–16.

85. *Ibid.,* pp. 116–117.

86. Public Law No. 190, 26 Stat. L. 209, 1890.

87. Feldman, "IATA Could Finalize Restructuring At Geneva AGM," *Transportation World,* 1978, pp. 25–28.

88. *Statistical Abstract of the United States* (Washington, DC: U.S. Department of Commerce, Government Printing Office), selected issues, 1975 to 1984-5.

89. *Air Transport 1986* (Washington, DC: American Air Transport Association, 1986).

90. IATA, *Annual Report,* Geneva, 1985.

91. Statistical Abstract, *op. cit.,* p. 88.

Federal Advisory Committees, Interest Groups, and the Administrative State

MARK P. PETRACCA

University of California, Irvine

Abstract

The current system of federal advisory committees in the United States is both extensive and expanding. While there are significant differences between specific advisory bodies regarding their constitution, construction, and role in the process of public policy-making, the system itself facilitates the permanent institutionalization of linkages and dependencies between interest associations and federal administrative agencies. Indeed, it moves the role of pressure group influence on the policy-making process from that of a suspect input to that of a welcome withinput. Utilizing data derived from advisory committee compliance with the 1972 Federal Advisory Committee Act and selected case study material this article begins the process of exploring how the system functions, who participates in it, what impact it has on the development and formation of public policy, and who are its ultimate beneficiaries. It concludes by developing a framework for the assessment of potential advisory committee power and influence on the process of administrative policy-making and advances a preliminary assessment of the domination of industry interests on departmental advisory committees.

Federal advisory committees constitute one of the most significant vehicles for interest group representation and influence on the policymaking processes of the national government. Unlike many other pathways of interest group influence, federal advisory committees facilitate the permanent *institutionalization* of linkages between interests and the national executive.[1]

Utilized in many forms and for a wide variety of purposes, advisory committees have been with us since the presidency of George Washington. Often extolled and praised, more recently condemned and "regulated," this particular form of "government by committee" has been aptly termed the "fifth arm of the Federal establishment" (U.S. Congress, House, 1970:5).[2] Despite their apparent importance, David Brown's (1972:336) claim that "we have not, despite extensive usage, adequately understood or appreciated" the advisory committee system is largely accurate today. Indeed, it is only since the passage of the 1972 Federal Advisory Committee Act [P.L. 92-463] that we have been in a position to undertake any systematic research about them.[3]

This article seeks to remedy that oversight by examining: (1) a variety of trends in the development of advisory committees from 1972-1984 including their expansion, frequency and openness of meetings, changes in the construction of representational forms, and the distribution and concentration of interest group membership; (2) the potential advisory committees have for influencing the process of policy making; and (3) the possibility that industry interests have a disproportionate influence on advisory committee decisions.

While there is no consensus about what constitutes a federal advisory committee (compare MacMahon, 1930 and 1965; Mansfield, 1968; Brown, 1955), for empirical research purposes we have accepted the definition provided by the 1972 Federal Advisory Committee Act which has, for the first time, produced reliable advisory committee data.[4] That act defines an advisory committee based on how it is established (i.e., those established by law; directed by law; authorized by law; and by presidential directive); where its authority is located (i.e., presidential or administrative agency); its length of tenure (i.e., *ad hoc* or continuing); and who serves on it (i.e., excluded is any committee composed wholly of full-time offices or employees of the federal government). In addition, the term "advisory committee" means any committee, board, commission, council, panel, task force, or similar group established in the interest of obtaining advice or recommendations for the President or one or more agencies or offices of the federal government.

The proliferation and increased utilization of advisory committees, which began with the New Deal and in the years following World War II, is a product of the American state's response to the needs of the citizenry (Brown, 1955; Reagan, 1983), the needs of government officials (Gill, 1940), and the demands of interest groups (Wiedenbaum, 1977; Aug, 1975; and Schlozman and Tierney, 1983).

Advisory committees perform important functions for both the federal government and private interest groups. They are presumptively valuable to government in primarily three ways: (1) improving the quality of government by fostering closer ties between the public and the government (see Reagan, 1983; Reynolds, 1939; Ruin, 1974); (2) making for better decisionmaking inputs, such as good advice, technical expertise, idea generation, and demand articulation and translation (see Brown, 1955; Gill, 1940; Kvavik, 1974/75; Useem, 1979; Yarmolinsky, 1966); and (3) facilitating important strategic political values, such as the cooptation of interest groups, information dissemination, development of legitimacy and consensus, and assistance with policy implementation (see Brown, 1955; Derthick, 1979; Hart, 1937; Leiserson, 1942; Rodgers, 1974; Spector, 1971).

The benefits which advisory committee relations provide for organized interests are also compelling: (1) insider's information on what the government is doing and intends to do (Aug, 1975; W. Miller, 1976); (2) incentives and resources which groups so desperately need to maintain their organizations (see DeParle, 1983; Offe, 1981; Olson, 1965; Wilson, 1973); (3) influential access and direct involvement in government policymaking (Boyce, 1964; Bottin, 1973; Leiserson, 1942; Perritt and Wilkinson, 1975; Price, 1954; Rodgers, 1974; Roose, 1975; Spector, 1971); and (4) the creation and maintenance of important inter- and intra-interest group policy networks (Herman, 1981; Mokken and Stokman, 1978; Useem, 1979, 1984).

The advisory committee system not only fundamentally alters the style of pressure group politics, but also changes the structure of the relationships which define the processes of policy formation. When it comes to the relationship between administrative agencies and interest groups, the advisory committee system moves

TABLE 1

Federal Advisory Committees: An Overview, 1972-1984

Year	Number of Committees[a]	Members	Cost
1972	1439	b	$25,215,882
1973	1250	b	31,110,810
1974	1242	22,702[c]	42,380,636
1975	1267	22,256[d]	51,769,400
1976	1159	23,375	59,726,365
1977	875	17,400	54,428,015
1978	816	18,040	62,638,772
1979	820	18,742	80,026,293
1980	865	19,724	79,363,229
1981	853	20,412	70,668,757
1982	878	18,605	71,228,753
1983[e]	884	21,941	75,896,547
1984	930	25,162	71,078,408

[a] As of December 31 of that respective year.

[b] Data unavailable from *Report of the President to the Congress.*

[c] The total number of members that served during 1974.

[d] The total number of members on committees in existence at the end of each year—1975-1984.

[e] Denotes change to fiscal year (as opposed to calendar year) reporting.

Sources: *Federal Advisory Committees: Annual Report of the President to the Congress* (Washington, D.C.: GPO, 1972-1984). *Congressional Record,* Senate, September 28, 1976: S-3294-3295. *Congressional Record,* Senate, October 20, 1977: S-34625-34627.

Note: All data in subsequent tables and figures are from *Federal Advisory Committees: Annual Report of the President to the Congress* (Washington, D.C.: GPO, various years), unless otherwise indicated.

the role and position of pressure group influence from that of an input to that of a withinput (Kvavik, 1974/75:110-103; Peters, 1977:196). During the Reagan administration we have seen an unprecedented proliferation in the number of advisory committees in response to the demands of modern governance. This expansion is justified by the administration's policy of promoting public/private sector partnerships in the decisionmaking and problem solving activities of government (Reagan, 1983:4). The public/private partnership facilitated by the advisory committee system may well be the "buckle that fastens the administrative process to the dominant institutions, elites, and values in society" (Cottin, 1973:1140; Steck, 1975). It is to the task of exploring how tightly the buckle is fastened that we now turn.

TRENDS IN THE DEVELOPMENT OF ADVISORY COMMITTEES

Committee and Membership Expansion

One indicator of the impact of advisory committees on the governmental process is their sheer number [see Table 1]. Despite the initial success of the Carter administration in reducing the number of advisory committees—dropping from

1159 when Carter entered the White House to a low of 816 in 1978—the number of committees has been increasing ever since [see Figure 1] (see *U.S. News and World Report*, 1978). By 1984, there was a net growth of 114 committees, bringing the total number up to its highest level since 1976 at 930 committees.

The Reagan administration has been pleased with this trend in that it coincides with their efforts to establish public and private sector "social partnerships." In a 1985 message to Congress, Reagan (May 23, 1985) extolled the value of advisory committees: "Federal advisory committees have been referred to variously as the fourth arm of government or as a public-private partnership. Known by many names and descriptions, these committees play an important role in determining

FIGURE 1
Federal Advisory Committees: An Overview, 1972-1984

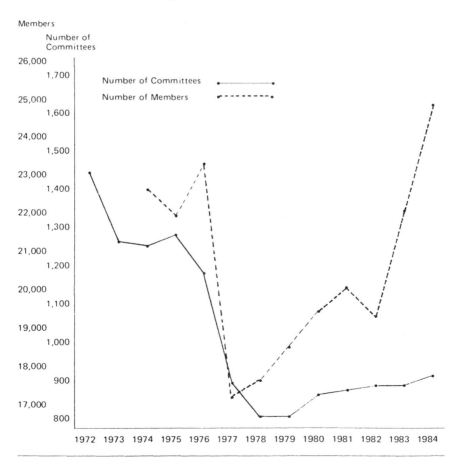

214

TABLE 2
The Establishment of Federal Advisory Committees, 1974-1984

Year	Directed by Law	Authorized by Law	Established by Agency	Presidential Directive
1974	262 (17%)	504 (33%)	747 (48%)	28 (2%)
1975	295 (20%)	440 (29%)	742 (50%)	23 (2%)
1976	288 (20%)	424 (29%)	714 (49%)	20 (1%)
1977	253 (32%)	469 (35%)	598 (45%)	23 (2%)
1978	348 (37%)	383 (36%)	322 (30%)	26 (2%)
1979	348 (37%)	279 (30%)	285 (30%)	29 (3%)
1980	437 (45%)	252 (26%)	254 (26%)	31 (3%)
1981	427 (44%)	251 (26%)	258 (27%)	31 (3%)
1982	434 (46%)	241 (25%)	249 (26%)	24 (3%)
1983	430 (44%)	242 (24%)	265 (27%)	31 (3%)
1984	409 (41%)	242 (24%)	331 (33%)	28 (3%)

This table shows the number and percentage of advisory committees for each year by the means of establishment.

public policy and contribute to our Nation's security, economic vitality, scientific achievements, and quality of life."

As information in Table 2 suggests, the major impetus for the increase in the number of committees has come primarily from the congressional formation of committees by statutory directive. Between 1974 and 1984, the number of committees created by statutory directive has increased by 64%, while the number created by agency discretion and those authorized by law have declined by 66% and 62% respectively. The number established by presidential directive has remained relatively stable. While the precise causes behind this change remain unclear, such a shift does reflect a general trend toward the institutionalization of the advisory committee system. It is likely that a change in the arena establishing an advisory committee will have important implications for the type of representational structure created.

The number of individuals appointed to advisory committees has also increased dramatically [see Table 1 and Figure 1]. The 25,162 advisory committee members in 1984 constitute the largest number of members since systematic data on membership were first made available in 1974. Between 1977 and 1984 the number of advisory committee members increased by 31%. Just during Reagan's first term membership rose by a sizable 19%. This increase can probably be attributed to (a) the Reagan administration's general position on the value of private citizen participation in the policy making process and (b) rising demands on the part of newly mobilized and inspired interest associations to be included in the advisory committee system. Thus, while the number of committees has been reduced since 1972, the opportunity for "citizen participation" and for the representation of organized interests has increased. Of course, whether or not the expansion of membership has really increased the input of the "public" remains to be seen.

A significantly different picture of advisory committee expansion emerges, however, when we examine separate departmental constellations of advisory committees.

Table 3 presents data on the growth and decline of advisory committees for the executive departments of Agriculture, Commerce, Defense, HEW, Labor and Treasury. HEW and Agriculture have some of the largest number of committees, while Labor and Treasury have some of the smallest number during this period. Commerce and Defense have been in the middle to higher range. These committees were selected for detailed study for two reasons. First, as Table 3 indicates, these six departments have over 50% of the total number of advisory committees throughout the twelve-year period. They also contain over 40% of all advisory committee members. Second, these departments are the likely focus of attention for the main organized interests from various sectors of American society (such as business/industry, labor unions, trade associations, farmers, etc.).

Important differences have occurred in committee development among these six departments. First, between 1972 and 1984, every department except for Commerce experienced a general decline in the number of advisory committees. In fact, with the exception of the past two years, Commerce was the only department of the six to actually increase its advisory committees during the period when general committee reduction was most severe—1972-1978.[5]

During the post-1978 period, there was a steady increase in Agriculture and Defense and a decline in Labor committees. Commerce (with the '83/'84 exception), HEW (HHS), and Treasury all remained relatively stable. Not surprisingly, the general decline of the labor movement in America is reflected in the diminished status of Department of Labor advisory committees, while at the same time the increasing importance of the defense establishment (or "military-industrial complex") has led to a rise in the prominence of Defense Department advisory committees.

Second, consider the over-all and post-1978 data on committee membership. For the eleven-year period, 1974-1984, only Commerce increased the size of committee membership during the period when widespread cutbacks were occurring. For example, from 1974-1978 the total number of all advisory committee members fell by 21% (see Table 1). During the same period Commerce *increased* committee membership by 44%. In the post-1978 period, Agriculture, Defense, and most recently Treasury and HHS have all increased their membership rolls. On the other hand, during the same period when general membership has been on the rise, the number of Labor committee members has generally been declining.[6]

Finally, we can comment on the stability of these departmental advisory committees by identifying those departments that have witnessed large numbers of newly created or terminated committees. A rank ordering of the administrative units having the largest number of newly created or terminated committees between 1972 and 1984 was calculated. Committees ranked 1st in any given year were assigned 3 points, a 2nd rank gained 2 points, and 3rd received 1 point. While this is no doubt a very crude measure for calculating the degree to which there is a change in an administrative unit's advisory committee system, it should minimally provide a sense of comparative stability between administrative units.[7]

HEW received the highest cumulative scores: 59. This was followed by Agriculture and Interior, both with 27, and then Commerce with 17. The Small Business

TABLE 3

Federal Advisory Committees: Number and Membership—Selected Executive Departments, 1972-1984[a]

	1972	1973	1974	1975	1976	1977	1978	1979	1980	1981	1982	1983	1984
AGRICULTURE													
Number of Committees	172	136	163	168	108	26	50	61	57	71	80	89	85
Members			2013	1734	1879	1289	655	873	868	825	1156	1398	1514
COMMERCE													
Number of Committees	76	41	72	74	88	102	96	93	84	75	83	57	56
Members			1337	1387	1713	1868	2396	2306	2561	2330	2092	2327	1644
DEFENSE													
Number of Committees	95	81	97	66	59	41	36	37	34	37	40	44	50
Members			1306	1186	1071	900	790	777	814	897	848	1100	1238
LABOR													
Number of Committees	46	44	19	23	23	20	20	22	15	13	13	15	13
Members			3603	4005	4341	4427	4119	3978	3644	4347	3362	3797	4780
HEW/HHS													
Number of Committees	367	286	299	322	349	298	257	258	237	233	221	240	237
Members			677	740	695	693	846	749	779	558	373	579	523
TREASURY													
Number of Committees	29	25	10	16	26	9	8	9	10	8	8	9	9
Members			336	291	456	414	151	172	161	129	114	147	227
Percent of Total[b]	55	49	53	53	56	57	57	59	51	51	50	51	48

[a] Includes only those committees that were in existence at the end of the calendar year.

[b] Percentage of total number of departmental committees relative to total number of committees for all administrative agencies.

Administration had a score of 9, the National Science Foundation a score of 5, and Defense a score of 3. The Departments of Labor and Treasury did not make the top three ranking at all in any given year. While most of the change in Commerce is attributable to increases in committees between 1973 and 1980, HEW seems truly to be in a constant state of flux. Given the vitality of the defense establishment alluded to earlier, it comes as no surprise that change would come slowly to that advisory system.

Why did Commerce advisory committees (and to a lesser extent Defense committees) display a different pattern of development during this period? First, when it comes to committee and membership reductions, there may simply have been less initial "fat" (or nonproductivity) to trim from the Commerce advisory committee machinery. Second, the interests which dominate the Commerce advisory committees may have been more persuasive than their counterparts in making a strong functional case for their continued survival. This persuasive capacity could be attributable to the significant increase in business lobbying resources dedicated to influencing the federal government occurring at the same time (see Schlozman, 1984; Vogel, 1983; McGrath, 1979; and Weidenbaum, 1977).

Third, this persuasive capacity may have little to do with the sizable increases in traditional lobbying resources on the part of business and far more to do with the inherently "privileged position" of business in American politics (Lindblom, 1977). This privileged position is due not to large campaign contributions (although business does make them), advertising campaigns (although business does engage in them), or to traditional pressure group politicking (although business does pressure), but rather to the fact that American prosperity and the politicians' electoral well-being requires that government anticipate the needs of business and act accordingly. In addition to economic health, government needs big business because "the technology of modern warfare is provided by giant industrial firms" (Fusfeld, 1972:172). The military-industrial complex is the offspring of the dependence of national power upon the economic base provided by big business (A. Miller, 1972 and 1976). This business-defense-government nexus also helps to explain the surge in Defense Department advisory committees and members, as well as the general stability of that committee system.

Committee Activity: Opening up the Meetings

Two of the main criticisms of the advisory committee system leading to the passage of the 1972 FACA were that: (1) committees were stacked in favor of special interests—primarily big business; and (2) committees met in secret, keeping their proceedings confidential.[8] Businessmen frequently attempt to have "most or all of their dealing with the state handled administratively out of view" (Elkin, 1985:193). As a response to this problem, Section 10 (a) (1) of the 1972 Act stipulated that "Each advisory Committee meeting shall be open to the public." Making the government-industry complex visible was one possible way of breaking down the connection and opening it up to the "fresh air" of the public interest.

Appendix 1 presents the percentage of open, closed, and partially closed meetings for all committees between 1974 and 1984. When all committees are considered, the percentages have not changed drastically over the eleven-year period. On average, 57.4 percent of the meetings are fully open, 21.4 percent are fully closed, and 21.3 percent are partially closed (i.e., some portion of the meeting is closed to the public). However, during the last four years the percentage of closed meetings has increased by roughly 20 percent. Indeed, the total percentage of closed meetings for 1983 and 1984 are at a post-1973 high at 25 and 24 percent respectively.

If we examine departmental committee data, however, some important distinctions between departmental advisory systems once again become apparent (see Appendix 2).

Agriculture (at 83% open) and Labor (at 65% open) have, on average, far more open meetings than Defense, which averages only 19% open. While one would justifiably expect Defense advisory committee meetings, which deal with sensitive national security issues, to be closed more often, that rationale is not persuasive for Commerce (at 56% open) or Treasury (at 36% open). [A totally unexpected finding is that HEW (HHS) closes part of its meetings to the public 66 percent of the time. This finding requires further analysis.] Indeed, during the last four years over 38% of all Commerce meetings have been closed to the public compared with Labor and Agriculture at 20% and 18% respectively.

As discouraging as these statistics appear for some departments, they may hide an even bleaker reality. Available statistics are based on known meetings. Some groups do not even bother to publish a meeting announcement in the Federal Register, oftentimes because they consider themselves merely subcommittees or groups not subject to the Act (Turkheimer, 1975: 67-68; Rodgers, 1974:724). The process of advisory committee decisionmaking is secret if no one is let in the door, if no one is in the room, or if no one knows about the meeting. There are a variety of techniques employed by advisory committees to prevent or at least forestall widespread public participation. These techniques include: (1) proclamations that space is limited; (2) locations for meetings that are held in restricted access areas such as the Executive Office Building, State Department, or the Exxon Building in New York City; and (3) manipulation of the meeting's agenda to partially close the meeting (Turkheimer, 1975). Through these devices advisory committees can effectively exclude the public from decisionmaking.

The American tradition of public access to the process of governmental decisionmaking is an important underpinning of American democratic theory (Perritt and Wilkinson, 1975; Schattschneider, 1960). Regrettably this principle has more often than not remained only an ideal and not a matter of political practice. Openness in the advisory committee process is not much better off today—indeed it is significantly worse—than it was over a decade ago. If the relationship between the potential for interest group influence and closed committee meetings is accurate, then there is little evidence to suggest that the government-industry complex is any less secure today than it was in 1971. In fact there is good reason to believe that the connection has been strengthened.

The Construction of Representation

Section 5(b)(2) of the 1972 Act requires "the membership of the advisory committee to be fairly balanced in terms of the points of view represented and the functions to be performed by the advisory committee." However, this "fair balance"

FIGURE 2
The Construction of Representation

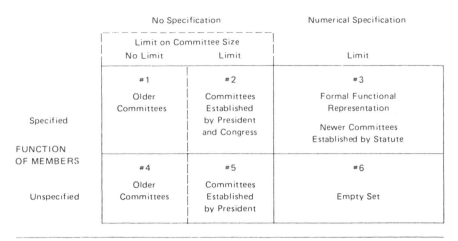

remains, for the most part, an unfulfilled statutory goal. Federal agencies have generally avoided the issue of representation of opposing viewpoints, concentrating instead on the less controversial factors (in this context) of geography, race, and sex as the overriding indicators of balance (Gage and Epstein, 1977:50004).[9]

There are, however, some fairly discernible patterns in the formal construction of interest representation which merit consideration. Figure 2 represents one possible method for distinguishing between the different constructions of interest representation. This method focuses on two descriptive dimensions: first, the extent to which the function or role of a member is specified (i.e., is the member there to ostensibly "represent" a particular interest—labor, consumers, farmers, etc.—or not); and second, the extent to which there is an actual numerical distribution specified or not in the enabling authority. There is also a distinction worth making between those authorizations which do not specify a particular distribution of members but do place a limit on committee size AND those authorizations which neither specify a particular distribution of members nor limit the size of the committee. This creates a six-cell matrix. Cell #6 is empty because when there is no specification of function then the only issue of classification is one of a specified limit on committee size. Logically then, there will be no cases to classify in this cell because the two-fold dimension of size limitation is captured already in cells #4 and #5. Eventually, as data gathering continues we will be able to classify all committees under investigation between 1972 and 1984 in a systematic fashion. However, for now we have to be content to provide examples of each cell and to identify some possible patterns in the classificatory scheme.

Cell #1 contains committees whose members are supposed to represent specific functional categories, but without any specific distribution between the categories or limit on the size of the committee.[10] For the most part such committees were established by the Congress and came into existence prior to 1973.

Cell #2 differs from #1 only because the size of the committee is limited.[11] For the most part, these committees seem to be newer ones established mainly by executive order and occasionally by Congress. Cell #3 contains those committees that most resemble "corporatist" forms of functional representation. The construction is corporatist in the limited sense that in these committees there is often an attempt to balance the distribution of interests between functional areas (see Anderson, 1979; Brenner, 1969; Lawson, 1978; Lehmbruch, 1979; Panitch, 1980; and Schmitter, 1979). Not only are the interests to be represented specified by function, but the distribution of particular members by interest affiliation is also specified. An increasingly large number of advisory committees, primarily established by acts of Congress, specify functional representation. As the number of committees established by Congress has increased, so too has the extent of functional representation.[12]

Despite the proliferation of these committees coming out of Congress, only a very few advisory committees established by presidential directive provide for functional representation. For example, Jimmy Carter's Pay Advisory Committee [E.O. 12161 of September 28, 1979] required five members each from labor, management and the public. As part of the President's anti-inflation program, this committee was directed to advise the Council on Wage and Price Stability on developing policies that encourage anti-inflationary pay behavior by employers and labor. Why are there so few advisory committees established by presidential directive that require formal functional representation? We will return to answer this question momentarily.

Cell #4 contains committees that have neither functional specification nor a limit on committee size. Based on our previous analysis of cell #1 we might infer that this group would contain older committees, established before the 1972 Act. While there are some established by acts of Congress, there are also quite a number of recently established by presidential directive which fit these conditions.[13] Cell #5 differs from #4 only because these authorizations limit the size of the advisory committees. Like Cell #2 this classification contains mostly advisory committees established by presidential directive.[14]

Why do so few advisory committees established by presidential directive require formal functional representation, while those that do seem to be emerging from the Congress? What does this tell us about the relationship between interests, these two institutions and the distribution of political power? To answer such questions we have to take seriously the explicit goals of functional representation in the first place. Functional representation makes it possible: (1) For interests affected by an issue to be present during the deliberation over it; and (2) To attempt to equalize the balance between such interests in the particular deliberative forum. Presumably, such a construction provides advantages to those interests which would ordinarily be excluded from consideration were it not for their required presence. Functional representation then, may serve to benefit those with less political clout. (Of course, it can also be used as a ploy to incorporate less powerful interests into the policy-making process in order to coopt them and enhance the legitimacy of the deliberations.) Powerful interests, on the other hand, have no incentive to lobby for such a construction because it could be used to compromise their potential for over-representation where the appointment of members is discretionary rather than required.

One possible implication of this is that the modern presidency is more responsive to powerful organized interests in this society than is the Congress. This argument stands in direct contradiction to the position expressed best by Grant McConnell (1966:351-52) that the presidency was uniquely situated to serve the public interest—"all the people." If our earlier analysis is accurate, the more powerful organized interests are likely to be those of industrial capitalism.

Why might this be the case? First and most obvious, the individuals who advise the president on these matters are likely to be interconnected with the business establishment. For example, Peter Freitag (1975: 141; also Sklar and Lawrence, 1981) has found that between 1897 and 1973 over 76% of all cabinet members were interlocked with big business. Second, because there is a convergence of the president's role as economic planner and politician *and* the interests of the corporate sector, "the president stands to gain when corporate capitalism gains" (Katznelson and Kesselman, 1975:216). The President and his party will be better off electorally when economic times are good (Tufte, 1978).

Third, there is a logic to the economic system which requires presidents to respond as the economy dictates. As James Livingston (1983:52) explains, "it was no accident that the rise of the modern presidency went hand in hand with the corporate reconstruction of the American economy." The expansion of capitalism, the argument suggests, cannot continue without the enforcement by the state of its worldwide claims. Since the presidency has become the embodiment of the American sovereign state, capitalism requires presidential action on its behalf—not to mention a powerful "sovereign," i.e., a powerful president. Indeed, the structure of national and international economics demands that the President become the leader and guardian of the economic system (Wolfe, 1981:25).

To the extent that the state (in this case represented by the President) or the interests of capitalism see a need to create an advisory apparatus, then it is more likely to be accomplished through a presidential directive than an act of Congress (see Elkin, 1985). In either case (even if the advisory committee is established by statute) that directive is unlikely to create a "balance" among potential interests by requiring formal functional representation.

How then do we explain Jimmy Carter's Pay Advisory Committee? In fact, this may be an exception which validates the proposition. The Pay Board was authorized to make recommendations on how to administer pay policy or wage policy. The final judgment would be made by the Chairman of the Council on Wage and Price stability, but the presumption was that the advice of the board would be weighed quite heavily. *Business Week* (Oct. 15, 1979:33) claimed that the board would "set whatever wage guideline is used in the second year and (would) consider individual pay cases for exceptions to the guidelines."

Business leaders were outraged, opposing the whole set up as favoring labor. In fact, the Business Roundtable refused to submit a list of candidates to the administration for inclusion on the panel. However, as specified in the executive order six members of the general public, six members of labor, and six from business were eventually selected for the board. After selections were made *Business Week* (Oct. 29, 1979) journalists commented that "The business makeup of the committee partly reflects opposition to the pay board concept by such groups as the Business Round-table." One way to interpret that statement is that with the Roundtable's support a different group of business representatives would be serving on the board—arguably a group of business "heavy-weights." As it turned out, despite its authority and potential, the Pay Advisory Committee accomplished little during its brief tenure. Without the support of the Roundtable this anti-inflationary effort may have been doomed to failure anyway.

Congress, on the other hand, may be a more open and diffuse arena for pres-sure politics. As Benjamin Page and Mark Petracca (1983:334) observe, "Presidents are uniquely situated to pursue the national interest of economic growth and stabil-ity, perhaps with a tilt toward labor or (more often) business, but standing above the clamor of particular local and occupational groups, that often animate Con-gress." We are likely to see, therefore, statutes establishing advisory committees which seek to empower those interests (e.g., occupational and local) by creating forums for functional representation. The classic pattern of congressional interest-group liberalism (Lowi, 1979; McConnell, 1966) will also result in demands for func-tional representation on advisory committees created by statute. In addition, Con-gress may specify the distribution of interest representatives on advisory committees because a failure to do so would allocate the additional discretion of appointment to administrative agencies already possessing an excessive delegation of authority (see Lowi, 1979).

The Distribution and Concentration of Interests

Unlike Carter's Pay Advisory Committee, the majority of authorizations creat-ing advisory committees do not provide for an equal distribution of members among represented interests. Considerable discretion remains in the selection of members for most advisory committees—by an administrative agency, cabinet official, or president. To begin analyzing the distribution and concentration of interests repre-sented on federal advisory committees a membership analysis of the 1972 and 1977 advisory committees in the Departments of Agriculture, Commerce, Defense, Labor, Treasury, and Energy (for 1977 only) was undertaken.[15] Table 4 presents the percentages of each identified "interest" that was represented on the respective executive department's advisory committees for 1972 and 1977.[16]

The data reveal a striking imbalance in the representation of diverse interests on most committees. First, in 1977 industry representation on *all* committees never fell below 20 percent of the total number of members. In only one instance—Agriculture —was industry representation below 24 percent in 1972. Indeed, for 1972 industry representation in Commerce and Treasury constituted a majority-plus of the com-mittees' members.

Second, industry representation has gone down. In some committees, it declined by a little less than 50% from its 1972 total. However, at the same time, at both Commerce and Treasury large increases occurred in the number of special interest organizations represented. These special interests included such industrial trade associations as: Motor and Equipment Manufacturers Assn., Assn. of Home Appliance Manufacturers, Man-Made Fiber Producers Assn., National Canners Assn., Ferroalloys Assn., U.S. Brewers Assn., U.S. Chamber of Commerce,

TABLE 4

Interest Representation on Federal Advisory Committees: Selected Executive Departments, 1972 and 1977 (in percent)[a]

	Industry	Labor	Special Interests	University	Government	Law, Accounting, Consulting	Farmers	Consumer	Other
AGRICULTURE									
1972 (n = 168)	13.14	.28	4.66	5.24	15.42	.57	44.10	—	15.12
1977 (n = 24)	22.00	1.09	34.00	17.75	13.37	.70	1.04	—	10.50
COMMERCE									
1972 (N = 76)	79.13	.68	3.68	8.51	1.00	2.58	—	.11	3.22
1977 (N = 93)	42.76	1.50	18.77	10.37	12.99	3.87	—	.56	10.61
DEFENSE									
1972 (N = 95)	28.37	.20	4.24	29.26	23.43	5.26	—	—	8.61
1977 (N = 41)	20.90	1.06	9.46	32.32	23.42	6.32	—	—	6.17
LABOR									
1972 (N = 44)	26.85	25.30	18.84	13.91	6.68	2.82	—	—	3.33
1977 (N = 31)	24.79	51.46	10.59	5.60	5.90	2.30	—	—	1.89
TREASURY									
1972 (N = 27)	89.16	—	1.21	.56	.74	1.05	—	—	7.23
1977 (N = 9)	46.90	4.06	11.19	5.79	19.06	7.35	—	.44	6.95
ENERGY									
1977 (N = 21)	44.91	.60	20.11	13.63	10.92	5.43	—	.33	4.28

[a]The percentage of each interest (industry, labor, etc.) represented on each executive department's particular advisory committees. N = the number of committees in each department surveyed. This corresponds to the total number of advisory committees submitting reports for inclusion in the Annual Report of the President. Columns do not add up to 100% due to rounding.

National Assn. of Manufacturers, Tanners Council of America, National Handbag Assn., and the National Sporting Goods Assn. As Murray Weidenbaum (1977:252) explains, as part of growing business lobbying efforts, "Companies are more frequently drawing upon trade associations to assist them in participating in the process of government decision-making." If only half of all special interest groups represented in Table 4 were pro-industry trade associations (the figure is actually closer to 89%) the interests of industry once again had over 50% of the representatives in Agriculture, Commerce and Treasury for 1977.

Third, during this period labor has increased the extent of its representation in all departments. However, its gains have been small. Labor made the largest stride in Department of Labor committees where its representation jumped from 25.3% in 1972 to 51.5% in 1977. Fourth, despite concern for balanced representation, there is almost no explicit consumer group representation worth mentioning. Some of the members classified as "others" are private citizens without affiliation. However, even those percentages are not high.

These data, however, give us only the general distribution of interest representation. Table 5 provides more precise information on the concentration of interests in individual committees. We assume that where there are larger concentrations of interests, those interests are more likely to exercise greater influence on the committee's decisionmaking processes. This is not an assumption that advisory committees make decisions on the basis of majority rule. Rather we assume that given the functions that committees serve for government, larger concentrations of interests will be in a better position to render information, advice, legitimacy, support, and so forth. As a result of this particular currency of exchange between agency officials and organized interests, concentrated interests are more likely to be in a position to be influential (see Alford and Freidland, 1975; and Useem, 1979).

Table 5 shows the percentage of committees in which a particular interest had either majority (M) or plurality (P) representation. Once again, the concentration of industry representation is significant in Commerce, Labor, Treasury, and Energy. In Defense, industry, university, and government representation share in the concentration of interests for 1972 and 1977. In Agriculture, the predominance of individual farmers in 1972 seems to have been replaced by a larger representation of special interests. Once again these organizations are primarily associations of high economic status farmers (see Wilson, 1977).[18] If we take industry representation and special interest representation as a distinctly business-oriented group, then a pro-business concentration is evident in Agriculture as well.

Labor unions, associations, and federations increased their concentration of interest, but unlike the representation figures in Table 4, only in Department of Labor committees. There were no instances where consumers had a majority or a plurality concentration.

A survey of recently established committees supports the general finding on the concentration of business interests. During the Carter and Reagan administrations a number of important new advisory committees were established. Of the fifteen committees analyzed, eight have a majority of industry representatives, while three of them have plurality industry representation. Only four of the committees are not dominated by industry representatives.[18]

225

TABLE 5

Interest Concentration: Majority and Plurality Interest Representation on Advisory Committees in Selected Executive Departments: 1972 and 1977

	Industry		Labor		Special Interests		University		Government		Law. Accounting Consulting		Farmers		Other		Membership Split
	M	P	M	P	M	P	M	P	M	P	M	P	M	P	M	P	
AGRICULTURE																	
1972 (N = 168)	5%	6	—	—	2	1	1	2	4	5	—	—	48	4	5	10	8
1977 (N = 25)	4%	12	—	—	24	16	12	—	8	—	—	—	8	—	4	—	12
COMMERCE																	
1972 (N = 76)	84%	3	—	—	1	—	5	1	—	—	1	1	—	—	1	—	1
1977 (N = 93)	38%	10	—	—	3	13	4	4	5	5	1	—	—	—	3	5	7
DEFENSE																	
1972 (N = 95)	17%	15	—	—	2	1	21	8	15	9	—	1	—	—	2	1	7
1977 (N = 41)	15%	10	—	—	5	—	22	10	22	5	2	—	—	—	—	5	5
LABOR																	
1972 (N = 44)	23%	11	16	7	2	9	—	9	—	4	—	—	—	—	—	—	18
1977 (N = 31)	25%	3	45	3	—	—	3	3	6	—	—	—	—	—	—	—	10
TREASURY																	
1972 (N = 27)	89%	—	—	—	—	—	—	—	—	4	—	—	—	—	7	—	—
1977 (N = 9)	33%	11	—	—	—	—	—	—	22	—	—	22	—	—	11	—	—
ENERGY																	
1977 (N = 21)	52%	14	—	—	10	5	5	5	—	5	—	—	—	—	—	—	5

This table shows the percentage of committees in which a particular interest has either majority (M) or plurality (P) representation. Cases where representation was evenly divided among two or more sets of interests are listed in the last column. Columns do not add up to 100% due to rounding.

THE IMPACT OF ADVISORY COMMITTEES ON PUBLIC POLICY

At this juncture in the research it is difficult to draw any firm conclusions about: (a) the extent to which the pattern of interest representation directly serves to shape the process of advisory committee decisionmaking; or (b) the extent to which the process of advisory committee decisionmaking has an impact on the process of administrative policymaking. The first issue is discussed in the concluding section. As for the second issue, immediately below we consider the different sources of advisory committee authority and set forth a framework for the development of propositions about advisory committee influence and power on the process of administrative policymaking.

The Formal Sources of Authority

By analyzing a large number of advisory committee authorizations—presidential directives, statutes, and administrative orders—we can identify three major sources of formal authority given to the committees. These sources can be placed on a continuum of varying degrees of public coercive capacity.

The first and most coercive source of authority is a *direct delegation of public authority to private interests*. While the number of instances are few, we have had occasional experience in this area.[19] The NRA was probably the "highpoint" of the "institutionalization of quasi-public agencies in policymaking and policy implementation in the U.S." Under the NRA "trade associations were permitted to draft and supervise codes of fair trade competition, each code becoming 'law merchant' for all members of the relevant industry" (Brand, 1983:100). This effort at a "cooperative recovery movement" (Fainsod et al., 1959:531) was eventually overturned by the Supreme Court on the grounds that Congress had delegated excessive authority to the executive branch. According to Theodore Lowi (1969:126, 298), this was the last time that the court invalidated a major statute for excessive delegation of power.

Not only have there been numerous examples of delegations of power from Congress to the executive—Lowi's "policy without law"—but there have also been occasional examples of the delegation of public authority to private interests since the NRA was disbanded. The most notable recent instance of this was Nixon's Pay Board. In October 1971, as part of the Nixon Economic Stabilization Program (Phase II), a Pay Board, "composed of 5 representatives of organized labor, 5 representatives of business, and 5 representatives of the general public" was created to "take such steps as may be necessary, . . . to stabilize prices, rents, wages, and salaries" [E.O. 11627]. Similar to Carter's Advisory Pay Committee, the Nixon Board was given final authority to: establish standards, criteria and procedures for their implementation; render final decisions on individual cases; and recommend legal action to assure compliance to the Justice Department. While both the Carter and Nixon Boards served at the President's discretion the respective boards were assured of their independence and full presidential support. While very few advisory committees ever receive this sort of "binding" delegation of authority it does remain an option for those seeking to utilize and empower a particular advisory committee. For analytic purposes, of course, such committees constitute some of the most interesting case study possibilities, even if few in number.

The second source of formal authority is *policy creation*. While instances of the delegation of public authority enable an advisory committee to make decisions which are directly enforceable on the private sector, policy creation authority may "bind" only the administrative agency attached to the advisory committee. Examples of this kind of authority would include the authority to: develop rules and standards for administrative decisionmaking processes; develop rules and standards for the private sector which are binding at the discretion of the administrative agency; make grant or other funding allocations; review standards and decisions of an administrative agency; and resolve and render judgments on appeals from agency decisions.[20]

The third and final source of authority we call *specified prior consultation*. This constitutes the requirement that the administrative agency consult with the advisory committee prior to the promulgation of rules, standards, or decisions as outlined in that particular area of administrative discretion.[21]

Informal Sources of Authority

Except in the case of the direct delegation of public authority, an advisory committee's ability to successfully utilize these formal allocations of authority will also be a function of the informal sources of authority which they are able to bring to bear on the decisionmaking process. These informal sources can also be used on their own to influence the decisionmaking process. By considering the differential resources that interest associations can bring to the advisory committee system we can identify four different informal sources of authority.

The enabling capacity of knowledge or information is the first such source. We live in a world where information is a key power base. The ability of an advisory committee to provide (or alternatively withhold) information will influence the capacity of an agency to render decisions and will serve to shape the form that the decision will take.[22]

The persuasive capacity of individual committee members as well as the persuasive position of the committee as a whole is a second source of informal authority. Beyond individual abilities at rhetorical success, a committee's persuasive capacity will be a function of its level of recognized expertise. In a study of F.D.A. advisory committees, Robert S. Friedman (1978:210) discovered that while F.D.A. officials "constantly hammer at the idea that panels are advisory, not decision making . . . when experts speak, however, they speak with authority and their views cannot be neglected." Due to the inherent persuasive power of expertise, advisory committees are often able to render advice to official agencies "that can be rejected only at considerable risk" (McConnell, 1966:164). An advisory committee's ability to provide absolute expertise, which will be especially prominent in military, scientific, and technical areas, will greatly enhance their capacity to influence an administrative agency (Nadel and Rourke, 1975:379).

Advice is potentially one of the most powerful weapons in an administrative arsenal (Seidman, 1975:23). The nature of that advice may also constitute an additional informal source of authority. The potential influence of committee advice will be a function of the "fit" of such advice with: (a) the direction of administrative decisions; (b) presidential or congressional proclamations, goals, or commitments; or (c) the trend of public opinion. Advice which is acceptable and/or expedient is more likely to be heeded than advice which offers a major challenge to any of the previously specified conditions.

A final source of informal authority is expectation. Advisory committee recommendations, reviews, and general advice will be influential in the policymaking process as a function of the extent to which administrative (and other political) officials believe that such advice either should or will in fact matter.

There are at least five ways in which such expectations can be created. First, governmental philosophy which extolls the value and legitimacy of such advice will create an inherent susceptibility to it. The closer defenders of such a philosophy are to the advisory committees, the greater the probability that the advice will be followed. Second, the extent to which there is a need for such advice will shape administrative susceptibility to it. Need will be strongest in cases where advisory committees are established to perform investigatory tasks for agencies which are supposed to lead to rule-making proceedings. Third, expectations privileging advisory committee advice will result when a symbiotic relationship has developed between agency officials and committee members. The development of mutual norms of accommodation between advisory committees and administrative agencies will strongly influence the impact of committee advice. Promises given by agency officials, presidents, or the Congress that advisory committee advice will be followed is the fourth means for creating an expectation.[23] Finally, expectations will also be a function of past behavioral precedents. Where their advice has been followed in the past, a presumption favoring future advice will be likely.[24]

An Impact Typology

The previous two sections have established a set of conditions which vary along a continuum of coercive authority. This authority/coercion dimension is either formally allocated to an advisory committee or stems from the inherent nature of the advisory committee-administrative agency relationship. But there are two other dimensions worth detailing for the purposes of classifying and analyzing different types of advisory committees.

The second dimension is committee penetration or discretion. This is a measure of the extent to which the advisory committee has been given a broad (high) or a narrow (low) operational mandate in their particular arena of concern. Greater penetration increases the probability of committee impact. Unlike the authority/coercion dimension, which is concerned with a committee's capacity to fulfill its mandate, this dimension attempts to specify the key variables which differentiate and qualify the mandate itself. The potential impact then, of an advisory committee on the policymaking process will also be a function of the number of specific mandate variables.

A comparison of advisory committee authorizations results in the identification of three variables. [While clearly not mutually exclusive, these variables attempt to focus on different mandate qualities.] First, there is the *sphere of committee involvement* in the operational affairs and procedures of the administrative agency. Some committees will be required to play an active role in the process of administrative decisionmaking, while others will have only tertiary interaction. Committees

FIGURE 3
An Advisory Committee Policy Impact Typology

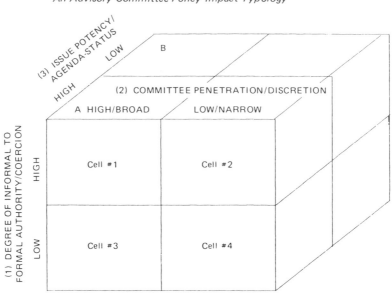

authorized to review administrative standards, play a role in information gathering, and meet frequently with the agency will penetrate much further into the routines of an agency.

The second variable is the *expanse of turf* or the jurisdictional boundaries established for the advisory committee. Some committees are established to render advice on a very narrow topic, while others are delegated jurisdiction over considerable policy ground.[25] Of course, turf may be granted by statute but not fulfilled in practice. Conversely, an expansion of turf may occur during the tenure of a committee which is not specified in its initial authorization.

The third variable is the *logistics of inquiry*—the resources, devices, and mechanisms that the advisory committee can utilize to fulfill its mandate. The stronger the logistical support the greater the probability of impact. Some of these logistics would include: (a) the ability to hold hearings; (b) the ability to hire outside consultants; (c) the ability to appropriate funds for special investigatory projects; (d) budgets; (e) the ability to obtain needed information from other government agencies; and (f) to enter into contracts.

Because these variables are not mutually exclusive we find many instances of patterned variability among them. In addition, the ability of an advisory committee to pursue its mandate will not necessarily be based on cumulative resources. Not only must we take into account the variation along the authority/coercion dimension, but we must also be sensitive to the orientation of an administrative agency to the efforts of an advisory committee.

230

These two dimensions are juxtaposed graphically in Figure 3 to create a four-cell matrix. Figure 3 also illustrates the third dimension—the potency or salience of a particular issue or issue area. (We are using issue in the Eastonian (1979:140) sense of a demand that is the subject of great controversy.) The potency of an issue is the relative status of that issue on the public governmental or decision agendas. The public agenda is the point at which issues have achieved a high level of public interest and visibility. The governmental agenda is the list of subjects that have the attention of government officials and people outside of government closely associated with them, while the decision agenda is the list of subjects within the governmental agenda that are actually up for an active decision (Kingdon, 1984:3).

The process by which such agendas are established is complex and multifaceted (see Cobb and Elder, 1983; Berger and Luckmann, 1967; Dery, 1984; Gusfield, 1981; Nelson, 1984; and Petracca, 1985). While not a sufficient condition, agenda status (or issue potency) is most often a necessary one for political action. Some issues will be highly placed, while others will receive very little attention. The potential for an advisory committee to have a significant impact on the policymaking process will, therefore, vary with the relative agenda status of the issue or area which defines the committee's jurisdictional mandate. Since agenda status varies across time we should expect to see considerable movement of advisory committees along this dimension. Of course, the ultimate in movement is when the committee is terminated because it simply no longer fulfills a useful function.

Figure 3 represents a three-dimensional typology from which we can deduce a number of descriptive and propositional insights about the potential impact of advisory committees. Some will have the potential to exercise power, others only influence, and probably the greatest number will have only minor effects. First, the smallest number of actual committees are likely to be found in cells 1B or 1A where there is both high authority and high penetration, but variable potency. However, these may also be the committees that have the most potential for impact on the policy process—especially those in 1A. Following the distinction made by R. J. Mokken and F. N. Stokman (1976:37) between power and influence, committees in cell 1A are likely to have the greatest capacity "to fix or to change (completely or partly) a set of action alternatives or choice alternatives" due to their broad definitional penetration and to the coercive authority to "enforce" them. This is power.

Second, the largest number of committees are probably to be found in cells 3B, 4A, and 4B. Since the agenda status of an issue changes over time, it is likely that committees once mandated to advise the government on a very salient issue will have diminished policymaking effects as that issue moves down or off the agenda. Committees in cells 3B and 4B are likely to be the least influential committees, while committees in 4A, because of the potency variable should have some impact opportunities.

A medium number of committees are likely to be found in cells 3A, 2A, and 2B. Committees in 3A will have the opportunity to define important alternatives, but will have to rely extensively on informal sources of authority and whatever mileage is forthcoming from high agenda status in order to achieve a policy impact. To the extent that committees in 2A and 2B are able to "determine the actions or choices of other actors [in this case agency officials] within the set of action or choice alternatives available to those actors" they will have what Mokken and Stokman

(1976:37) call influence. Committees in 2A and 2B are most likely to have narrowly prescribed mandates (i.e., alternatives have already been established), but have the authority to make varying degrees of binding choices within that mandate.

CONCLUSION: THE CASE OF INDUSTRY INFLUENCE

Some advisory committees—especially those in cell 1A—are likely to play a major role in the process of policy formation and decisionmaking. We have ample preliminary evidence to suspect that such an effect is likely to be strongly biased in favor of business interests. Industry dominates the current membership of many advisory committees and is especially prominent in those government departments most concerned with important economic matters, e.g., Commerce, Defense, Labor, and Treasury. Industry interests are in a better position to stave off demands for functional representation. Instead, they serve on committees without balanced representation and with broad jurisdictional mandates. Industry interests are also likely to possess a very compelling arsenal of informal authority resources. Given the importance of industrial growth as a policy issue, it should not be a surprise to find that industry representatives dominate those advisory committees with the greatest potential for policy impact—cell 1A committees. A membership survey of all advisory committees might reveal a very modest percentage of over-all industry representatives. However, if we analyze the concentration and distribution of membership on those committees with the greatest potential for policy impact (see Figure 3), according to the reasoning presented above, we are likely to discover overwhelming industry and trade association domination.

We fully recognize that power cannot be equated with participation, although there is usually a strong relationship between these analytically separable dimensions. It is not necessarily the case that inequalities of representation are translated into proportional inequalities of power or influence (Schlozman, 1984:1028). We cannot automatically conclude that the overrepresentation of industry members on key advisory committees implies that they are decisively shaping the policies of those committees. Additional investigation on the actual operation, output, and impact of advisory committees is clearly required.[26]

However, the preliminary conclusion that industry interests do dominate key advisory committees is validated, in part, by the few case studies we have on the impact of advisory committees on public policy. Murray Weidenbaum (1977: 252-53) documents the impact of the Industrial Advisory Committee [I.A.C.] (of the Department of Defense) on Pentagon procurement policy and the influence of Treasury Department advisory committees (dominated by industry interests) on Treasury's quarterly financing of the public debt. Diane Roose (1975) documents the very close relationship between the defense establishment and representation of some of the nation's largest military contractors in the I.A.C. Like many others, according to Roose (1975:62), "this Council represents a previously unexamined institution which actually concretized the military-industrial complex."

In a study of F.D.A. advisory committees, Robert S. Friedman (1978:210-11) discovered that committee advice was accepted and adopted 76-99% of the time and that industry was most influential (compared to consumers) in shaping recommendations. Regarding trade advisory committees, Deputy Assistant Secretary of Commerce Stephen Strauss (1982) explained that 695 businessmen and women are members of the advisory committees established by the 1974 Trade Act and the 1979 Trade Agreements Act. "All meetings [of these committees] are closed to the public. . . . These advisory committees exist to maintain a constant dialogue between government and private business on international trade issues and concerns. And they are the linchpin for the effort to improve America's competitiveness in international markets. . . . A review of the work of the industry advisory committees shows they have been a dependable and effective force, frequently relied upon by the government in forging international trade policy." Strauss goes on to commend the efforts of the chemical industry for assisting the U.S. negotiating team during the Multinational Trade Negotiations process.

Finally, consider the case of the National Industrial Pollution Control Council (NIPCC), established by Richard Nixon in 1970 to "encourage the business and industrial community to improve the quality of the environment" [E.O. 11523]. Only corporate board chairmen and presidents from the largest corporations were eligible to serve, 53 members in all. By the time Congress refused to renew its appropriation in 1973, the NIPCC had become one of the most discredited advisory committees of all time, especially for the illegal campaign contributions from its members in 1972. Yet in terms of its functions and concentration of industry representation it is like many other advisory committees currently in existence. Richard Vietor's (1979) study of the NIPCC reveals two particularly blatant examples of the impact that an advisory committee can have on policy making processes.

In 1972 the Forest Industries Council (a subcommittee of the NIPCC), which had become an umbrella organization for the National Forest Products Association, became the industry's key link to the White House in averting a ban on clear-cutting. This policy continued throughout the remainder of the Nixon Administration until the courts intervened in 1975. Another example concerns the EPA. When the EPA began promulgating the rules necessary to implement the Clean Air Act in 1971, the NIPCC was instrumental in getting many of the rules revised and diminished— including the elimination of the "no significant deterioration" policy. Commenting on the NIPCC, William Rodgers charges that industry was being "supervised only by the sympathetic" (Cottin, 1973:1143).

During the 1960's Grant McConnell and Theodore J. Lowi were among the first to warn us about the dangers of interest group liberalism. The "conquest of segments of formal state power by private groups and associations" had become a major characteristic of American government (McConnell, 1966:162). The broad delegation of authority to administrative agencies enabled these interest groups to "shut out the public . . . at the most creative phase of policymaking, the phase where the problem is first defined" (Lowi, 1969:86). The public interest was not and could not be served under these conditions.

The potential for industry domination of the key elements in the federal advisory committee system should renew our concern about whether or not government is operating to serve the public interest. The concentration of industry representatives on those advisory committees with the greatest potential to influence the policymaking processes of administrative agencies may not, however, simply be another case of interest groups capturing those agencies most relevant to their concerns. As Stephen Elkin (1985) reminds us, the state is neither inert nor neutral.

Rather it is active and independent. Industry is able to dominate key advisory committees because of the structure of the American regime—not simply because, in a classic battle of pressure group politics, industry has emerged as the victor.[28]

The construction of interest representation in the advisory committee system raises serious questions about: (1) the balance of viewpoints in our policymaking process; (2) the extent to which that process contributes to fair and equitable forms of representation; and (3) the forces which are responsible for the direction of policy development. Regarding these questions, the nature of this effort has been by necessity exploratory and speculative. Future research in this area must address these issues far more systematically. During a time when we hear many calls for the creation of even more "public-private partnerships" and "social contracts" (see: Thurow, 1981, 1984; Rohatyn, 1982, 1983; Reich, 1984; Business Week, 1980; Johnson, 1984), presumably to solve the problems of industrialization, we should be hesitant about answering those calls in haste.

APPENDIX 1
Advisory Committee Meetings: All Committees, 1974-1984

Year	Total Number of Meetings	Percent Open	Percent Closed	Percent Partially Closed
1974	3626	55 (N=1994)	20 (N=919)	25 (N=913)
1975	4179	52 (2164)	20 (836)	28 (1179)
1976	4694	59 (2779)	18 (845)	23 (1070)
1977	4495	59 (2677)	21 (941)	20 (877)
1978	4146	60 (2479)	22 (900)	18 (767)
1979	4204	59 (2500)	22 (936)	19 (768)
1980	4074	62 (2539)	19 (768)	19 (767)
1981	3459	58 (2022)	22 (746)	20 (691)
1982	3352	57 (1898)	22 (749)	21 (705)
1983	3733	55 (2047)	25 (936)	20 (750)
1984	3865	55 (2111)	24 (941)	21 (813)
Average		57.4	21.4	21.3

APPENDIX 2

The Meetings of Federal Advisory Committees: Open, Closed, or Partially Closed, 1974-1984

		1974	1975	1976	1977	1978	1979	1980	1981	1982	1983	1984
AGRICULTURE	N	191	206	205	111	119	193	110	98	145	161	158
	%O	98	87	86	86	53	68	100	99	75	77	79
	%C	2	12	14	14	47	32	0	1	25	23	21
	%PC	0	1	0	0	0	0	0	0	0	0	0
COMMERCE	N	177	269	409	580	564	474	397	392	357	280	243
	%O	72	57	47	44	53	67	72	64	59	41	39
	%C	0	19	36	46	34	23	14	26	32	48	47
	%PC	28	23	18	10	9	11	15	11	10	10	16
DEFENSE	N	362	376	348	349	328	344	322	311	238	427	489
	%O	24	18	23	26	19	19	19	17	12	13	19
	%C	73	79	71	71	78	74	72	75	82	80	72
	%PC	3	3	6	3	3	6	8	8	6	7	9
HHS/HEW	N	951	1133	1237	1194	1046	912	765	655	657	898	800
	%O	24	28	39	49	46	46	34	25	22	24	23
	%C	2	1	1	1	1	0	0	1	0	0	5
	%PC	75	71	60	50	53	54	66	74	78	76	72
LABOR	N	91	129	162	129	186	185	142	117	59	60	54
	%O	100	88	74	85	77	71	91	84	76	82	78
	%C	0	12	26	15	23	27	7	16	24	18	22
	%PC	0	0	0	0	0	3	2	0	0	0	0
TREASURY	N	53	39	49	24	27	20	23	14	17	15	27
	%O	6	8	74	38	26	25	30	0	41	60	59
	%C	94	62	27	63	74	75	70	100	59	40	41
	%PC	0	0	0	0	0	0	0	0	0	0	0

Notes

[1] This is a much reduced version of a paper originally delivered at the 1985 Meetings of the American Political Science Association. It is part of a larger research project on advisory committees currently receiving funding from the Academic Senate at the University of California, Irvine. Assistance with the collection of information for this paper was variously provided by Heather O'Loughlin, Charles Edelman, Mark Lerner, and Courtney A. Wiercioch. Comments by Irvine colleagues Kristi Monroe, Bernie Grofman, and Barbara Mikalson as well as by Burdett Loomis, Norman Thomas, Robert Salisbury and the editors of this journal have been greatly appreciated.

[2] Consult the following sources for historical overviews of advisory committees and presidential advisory commissions: Popper, 1970; Marcy, 1945; Galloway, 1931; and Wolanin, 1975.

[3] For information on the legislative history of the 1972 Act, see: U.S. Congress, Senate, Committee on Governmental Affairs, 1978; Levine, 1973; Markham, 1974; and Cardoza, 1981. It is interesting to note that there are apparently a large number of commissions, boards, councils, etc., which are not "advisory" by the standards set forth in the 1972 Act. Some of these organizations are actually formally part of the executive branch, for example, many government boards of directors. Others are purely private organizations which consult regularly with administrative agencies, for example, the Government Borrowing Committee of the American Bankers Association and the Government Fiscal Policy Committee of the Securities Industry Association. According to Murray Weidenbaum (1977:253), these two groups meet regularly with Department of the Treasury officials. Many of these groups, to the extent that they are comprised of private citizens, raise many of the same questions about the concentration and distribution of influence as well as potential impact on the policymaking process that are addressed in this paper.

[4] Systematic and reliable data on advisory committees is not available prior to 1972.

[5] The recent 1983 and 1984 decline in the number of Commerce committees is wholly attributable to the elimination of a large number of regional fishery management councils which were deemed unnecessary because of a lack of productivity (e.g., the Caribbean, Gulf of Mexico, Mid-Atlantic, New England, and Pacific Fishery Management Councils and their various subcommittees).

[6] The 1984 decline in Commerce membership, which is quite significant, is due to the elimination of the committees mentioned above (see fn. 5).

[7] Data are not presented in this paper but are available from the author. This is a limited measure because: (a) we are considering only the creation and termination of committees—not the attrition of members; and (b) we have only identified the top three committees undergoing committee changes during each year.

[8] As Robert W. Dietsch (1971:19 and 21) put it: "This government by committee is really a giant lobby for business and industry. . . . Thirty-two hundred advisory bodies have helped breed an invisible government-industry complex." While there was no way to know precisely how many advisory bodies there were at the time, it was alleged with considerable analytic and empirical validity that industry would be more effective at wielding "inappropriate" and "unbalanced" influence if the doors to the committee meetings were closed.

[9] Efforts even in these areas have not been particularly successful. Of the number of membership positions in 1976, for example, only 12.6% were held by women; 4.77% by blacks, and less than a total of 4% by Hispanics, Asians, or American Indians or Alaskan Natives (Metcalf, 1977, pp. S-13751-13753).

[10] Examples include: the Plant Variety Protection Board, established on December 24, 1970 [P.L. 91-577], which provides that: "Membership of the Board shall include farmer representation and shall be drawn from the sector of government or the public" (Sec. 7(a)). Another example is the Labor Market Advisory Council, established on December 28, 1971 [P.L. 92-223] which provides that: "Any such Council shall include representatives of industry, labor, and public service employers from the area to be served by the Council" (Sec. 432(C)(f)(2)).

[11] For example, the National Advisory Commission on Resource Conservation and Recovery, established on October 21, 1980 [P.L. 96-482] provides that: "The Commission shall be composed of nine members to be appointed by the President. Such members shall be qualified by reason of their education, training, or experience to represent the view of consumer groups, industry associations, and environmental and other groups concerned with resource conservation and recovery" (Sec. 33(a)(2)). Other recent examples include: (1) the President's National Security Telecommunications Advisory Committee [E.O. 12382 of September 13, 1982]; (2) the President's Commission on Strategic Forces [E.O. 12400 of

January 3, 1983]; (3) the National Industrial Technology Board [P.L. 96-480, October 21, 1980, Sec. 10]; and (4) the President's Commission on Industrial Competitiveness [E.O. 12428 of January 28, 1983].

[12]For example, the Towing Safety Advisory Committee, established on October 6, 1980 by P.L. 96-380, which provides that: "The Committee shall consist of sixteen members with particular expertise, knowledge, and experience regarding shallow-draft inland and coastal waterway navigation and towing safety as follows: (1) seven members from the barge and towing industry, reflecting a regional geographic balance; (2) one member from the offshore mineral and oil supply vessel industry; and (3) two members from each of the following—(A) port districts, authorities, or terminal operators; (B) maritime labor; (C) shippers (of whom at least one shall be engaged in the shipment of oil or hazardous materials by barge) and (D) the general public." Other recent examples include: (1) The Toxicology Advisory Board [P.L. 95-631, November 10, 1978]; (2) The Travel and Tourism Advisory Board [P.L. 97-63, October 16, 1981]; (3) The National Driver Register Advisory Committee [P.L. 97-364, October 25, 1982]; (4) The Dispute Resolution Advisory Board [P.L. 96-190, February 12, 1980]; (5) The Motor Carrier Ratemaking Study Commission [P.L. 96-296, July 1, 1980]; and (6) The National Council on Health Care Technology [P.L. 95-623, November 9, 1978].

[13]For example, the President's Economic Policy Advisory Board [E.O. 12296] established by President Reagan on March 2, 1981, provides that: "The Board shall be composed of members from private life who shall be appointed by the President" (Sec. 1). Similarly, Reagan's National Productivity Advisory Committee [E.O. 12332], established on November 10, 1981 requires that: "The Committee shall be composed of distinguished citizens appointed by the President, only one of whom may be a full-time officer or employee of the Federal Government" (Sec. 1). It would be difficult to imagine any less precision in the determination of committee membership.

[14]Jimmy Carter's White House Coal Advisory Council [E.O. 12229] established on July 29, 1980 stipulates only that "The Council shall be composed of nine members appointed by the President, none of whom shall be an officer or a full-time employee of the United States Government" (Sec. 1-102). Ronald Reagan's Advisory Committee on Mediation and Conciliation [E.O. 12462], established on February 17, 1984, states that: "The Committee shall be composed of not more than twelve members who shall be appointed or designated by the President from among persons with special knowledge and familiarity with labor relations problems" (Sec. 1). In both of these cases—Coal Advisory and Mediation and Conciliation—one might expect that given the importance of the issues at hand to members of business and labor (not to mention consumers) that a "balanced representation" would have been specified.

[15]These two years were selected out of necessity because they are the only two years for which a membership index for all advisory committees was released as a congressional document. The membership information, for all other years, which is required by the 1972 Act, exists only in the Federal Advisory Committee Depository in the Library of Congress. That data will be coded and analyzed during the summer of 1986.

[16]This is not a sample of the committees, but rather a complete analysis of every committee listed for these departments in the 1972 and 1977 membership indexes.

[17]These associations include: the American Soybean Assn., National Farmers Assn., American National Cattlemen's Assn., State Granges, National Pork Producers Council, Poultry and Egg Institute of America, and Burley Leaf Tobacco Dealers Assn.

[18]Data are available from the author. Examples of the committees under examination included: (1) White House Coal Advisory Committee [E.O. 12229, 1980]; (2) Auto Industry Committee [D.O.T. Secretarial Directive, 10-17-80]; (3) President's Economic Policy Advisory Board [E.O. 12296, 1981]; (4) Advisory Committee on Small Business and Minority Business Ownership [E.O. 12190, 1982]; and President's Advisory Council on Private Sector Initiative [E.O. 12427, 1983].

[20]The Editors of the Columbia Law Review (1937:447; see Comer, 1927), for example, observed in 1937: "In recent years American legislatures as part of a general tendency towards increased delegation of powers, have granted government powers to non-official groups on an unprecedented scale." This delegation of power took a variety of forms: (1) the requirement that in appointing administrative officials, the appointing officer shall act upon the recommendation of a private group; (2) placing the power of appointment in the hands of nonofficial parties; (3) entrusting to a private body the power of administering law; and (4) statutes which declare violations of rules formulated by lay groups to constitute a crime (Jaffe, 1937:231-32).

The major national examples of these forms of delegation included: Marketing agreements under the Agricultural Adjustment Act of 1933 which authorized agreements between the Secretary of Agriculture and processors, producers, and associations of producers'; Stockmen's Associations composed of local stockmen under the Taylor Grazing Act of 19344; District Boards composed primarily of coal producers under the Bituminous Coal Act of 1937; interest group participation in rule-making by the Securities and Exchange Commission during the late 1930's (Leiserson, 1942, pp. 189-220), and the National Recovery Administration Act of 1933.

[20]Examples of each include: the Winegrape Varietal Names Advisory Committee, established on March 30, 1982 by the Director of the Bureau of Alcohol, Tobacco, and Firearms; the Product Safety Advisory Council, established on October 27, 1972 [P.L. 92-573]; the Dispute Resolution Advisory Board, established on February 12, 1980 [P.L. 96-190]; the Advisory Committee for Trade Negoations [P.L. 93-618—Jan. 3, 1975]; and the Plant Variety Protection Board [P.L. 91-577 of Dec. 24, 1970].

[21]For example, the Secretary of Health and Human Services is required to consult the Technical Electronic Product Radiation Safety Standards Committee [P.L. 90-602—Oct. 18, 1968] before prescribing any standards under the rubric of this act. Similarly, the Secretary of Transportation is required to consult with the Towing Safety Advisory Committee [P.L. 96-380—Oct. 6, 1980] "before taking any significant action affecting shallow-draft inland and coastal waterway navigation and towing safety" (Sec. C).

[22]Herbert Simon (1957) has emphasized the utility of being able to shape the value or factual control over decisions. According to Mark Nadel and Francis Rourke (1975:376), "it is precisely in this way that bureaucratic information and advice often function in the policy process." In a book advising business how to respond to increases in government regulation, Murray Weidenbaum (1979:109-110) explains that "the most effective type of lobbying is neither stereotyped arm-twisting nor providing financial contributions to politicians. Rather it is the timely provision of accurate and pertinent information on the issues of public policy being . . . considered in government agencies." Of course, not all of the interests represented on advisory committees will have an equal ability to offer up "accurate and pertinent information." Differential capacities to provide needed information will be a function of information-gathering resources, skill in presentation, and presence on the particular advisory committee. Interests, like business, will be in a better position to influence agency decisions if they are able to maximize their information-providing capacities.

[23]What bothered the Business Roundtable most about Jimmy Carter's Pay Advisory Committee was the President's public declaration that the "advice of this pay board will have a heavy weight, both with me and with (the) Council on Wage and Price Stability" (Carter, 1979: p. 1859).

[24]F.D.A. staff respondents in Robert S. Friedman's study (1978:210), for example, claimed that advisory committee recommendations were accepted and adopted from 76% to 99% of the time. That must certainly create a compelling norm for future staff behavior. Similarly, Martha Derthick (1979:89) discovered in her comprehensive study of social security that "The student of social security policy-making soon learns that he is *expected* by program executives and close observers of social security affairs *to take citizen advisory councils seriously,* as places where important decisions will be made" [emphasis added]. Derthick's study gives ample testimony to the repeated influence of social security advisory committees throughout the policy's entire history.

[25]For example, the President's Advisory Committee on Mediation and Conciliation [E.O. 12462 of Feb. 17, 1984] is charged with undertaking a review of regulations promulgated by the Federal Mediation and Conciliation Service that affect established arbitrarion and mediation procedures and offering a single report on that topic to the President. That is a fairly narrow expanse. On the other hand, the National Commission for Employment Policy [P.L. 97-300 of Oct. 13, 1982] is authorized to identify the employment goals and needs of the nation, determine the quality of the programs of this law (i.e., the Job Training Partnership Act), develop further recommendations on this field, investigate the effectiveness of federally assisted programs in this field, evaluate the role of tax policies on employment and job opportunities, and to advise the Secretary of Labor on the development of national standards of performance for these programs. That advisory committee covers alot of ground.

[26]The preceding interpretation evokes the long-standing debate among elitists (Mills, 1956; Hunter, 1953), pluralists (Dahl, 1961; Polsby, 1980); and neo-elitists (Bachrach and Baratz, 1970; Crenson, 1971; Schattschneider, 1960) regarding the relationship between political participation and political power. Pluralists would argue that the overrepresentation of certain interests does not necessarily translate into the capacity to exercise political power at the exclusion of other relevant interests. In addition, groups not represented on particular advisory committees may still have their views taken into account indirectly by the anticipation of advisory and administrative officials. Pluralists would rightly challenge us to examine

the outcome of particular issues that advisory committees are involved with before rendering a conclusion about industry influence. Attention to actual cases of advisory committee decision-making constitutes a major part of the next stage in this research project.

[27]For other examples of the influence of organized interests, see Steck (1975); Turner (1972); and Cronin and Thomas (1971).

[28]This is contrary to a pluralist explanation which would view the regime (i.e., state apparatus) as a neutral arbiter between disputing interest groups. The outcomes of such disputes would largely be a function of the various resources that respective groups can bring to bear on the political conflict. Given the assumptions that pluralists make about the widespread distribution of political resources it is unlikely that industry would have an institutionalized advantage in the advisory committee system.

References

Alford, R. R. and R. Friedland. 1975. "Political Participation and Public Policy." *Annual Review of Sociology* 1: 429-479.

Anderson, C. 1979. "Political Design and the Representation of Interests." In P. Schmitter and G. Lehmbruch, eds. *Trends Toward Corporatist Intermediation.* Beverly Hills: Sage.

Aug, S. M. 1975. "Why Advise?—To Get Ears of High Officials." *Washington Star* 23 November.

Bachrach, P. and M. Baratz. 1970. *Power and Poverty: Theory and Practice.* New York: Oxford University Press.

Berger, P. L. and T. Luckman. 1967. *The Social Construction of Reality.* New York: Anchor Books.

Boyer, W. 1964. *Bureaucracy on Trial.* Indianapolis: Bobbs-Merrill Co.

Brand, D. 1983. "Corporatism, the NRA, and the Oil Industry." *Political Science Quarterly* 98: 99-118.

Brenner, M. J. 1969. "Functional Representation and Interest Group Theory." *Comparative Politics* 2: 111-134.

Brown, D. S. 1972. "The Management of Advisory Committees: An Assignment for the 1970's." *Public Administration Review* 32:334-342.

———. 1955. "The Public Advisory Board as an Instrument of Government." *Public Administration Review* 15: 196-203.

Business Week. 1979. "What Carter's Payboard Cost." 15 October: 33-34.

———. 1979. "Raw Business Recruits Dig in at the Pay Board." 29 October: 46-47.

———. 1980. "Revitalizing the U.S. Economy." 30 June, 56-57.

Cardoza, M. H. 1981. "The Federal Advisory Committee Act in Operation." *Administrative Law Review* 33: 1-62.

Carter, J. 1979. *Public Papers of the Presidents of the United States, Jimmy Carter 1979.* Washington, D.C.: GPO. Book II. October 11.

Cawson, A. 1978. "Pluralism, Corporatism, and the Role of the State." *Government and Opposition* 13: 178-198.

Cobb, R. and C. Elder. 1983. *Participation in American Politics: The Dynamics of Agenda Setting.* 2nd Edition. Baltimore: Johns Hopkins University Press.

Columbia Law Review. 1937. "Delegation of Power to Private Parties." March: 447-461.

Comer, J. P. 1927. *Legislative Functions of National Administrative Authorities.* New York: Columbia University Press.

Congressional Quarterly. 1976. "Ban Sought on Closed Advisory Sessions." *Congressional Quarterly Weekly Report* 20 March: 588.

Cottin, J. 1973. "Private Access to Government Policymakers Brings Hint of Tighter Legislative Controls." *National Journal* 5: 1138-1145.

Crenson, M. 1971. *The Un-Politics of Air Pollution.* Baltimore: Johns Hopkins University Press.

Cronin, T. E. and N. C. Thomas. 1971. "Federal Advisory Processes: Advice and Discontent." *Science* 26: 771-779.

Dahl, R. A. 1961. *Who Governs?* New Haven: Yale University Press.

DeParle, J. 1983. "Advise and Forget." *The Washington Monthly* 15 May: 41-46.

Derthick, M. 1979. *Policymaking for Social Security.* Washington, D.C.: Brookings.

Dery, D. 1984. *Problem Definition in Policy Analysis.* Lawrence, Kansas: University of Kansas Press.

Dietsch, R. W. 1971. "The Invisible Bureaucracy." *The New Republic* 20 February: 19-21.

Easton, D. 1965, 1979. *A Systems Analysis of Political Life.* Chicago: University of Chicago Press.

Elkin, S. L. 1985. "Pluralism in Its Place: State and Regime in Liberal Democracy." In Roger Benjamin and Stephen L. Elkin, eds. *The Democratic State*. Lawrence, Kansas: University of Kansas Press.

Fainsod, M., L. Gordon, and J. C. Palamountain, Jr. 1959. *Government and the American Economy*. 3rd Edition. New York: W.W. Norton.

Freitag, P. J. 1975. "The Cabinet and Big Business: A Study of Interlocks." *Insurgent Sociologist* 23: 137-152.

Friedman, R. S. 1979. "Representation in Regulatory Decision Making: Scientific, Technical, and Consumer Inputs to the F.D.A." *Public Administration Review* 39: 205-214.

Fusfeld, D. R. 1972. "The Rise of the Corporate State in America." *Journal of Economic Issues* 6: 1-20.

Gage, K. and S. S. Epstein. 1977. "The Federal Advisory Committee System: An Assessment." *Environmental Law Reporter* 7: 50000-50012.

Galloway, G. 1931. "Presidential Commissions." *Editorial Research Reports* Vol. 1; 28 May: 356-364.

Gill, N. 1940. "Permanent Advisory Committees in the Federal Government." *Journal of Politics* 2: 411-439.

Gusfield, J. 1981. *The Culture of Public Problems*. Chicago: University of Chicago Press.

Hart, J. 1937. "The Exercise of Rule-Making Power." In *The President's Committee on Administrative Management*. Washington, D.C.: GPO.

Herman, E. 1981. *Corporate Control, Corporate Power*. Cambridge: Harvard University Press.

Hunter, F. 1953. *Community Power Structure*. Chapel Hill: University of North Carolina Press.

Jaffe, L. L. 1937. "Law-Making by Private Groups." *Harvard Law Review* 51: 201-253.

Johnson, D., ed. 1984. *The Industrial Policy Debate*. San Francisco: Institute for Contemporary Studies.

Katznelson, I. and M. Kesselman. 1975. *The Politics of Power*. New York: Harcourt, Brace, Jovanovich.

Kingdon, J. W. 1984. *Agendas, Alteratives, and Public Policies*. Boston: Little, Brown.

Kvavik, R. B. 1974/75. "Interest Groups in a 'Cooptive' Political System: The Case of Norway." In Martin O. Heisler, ed. *Politics in Europe; Structures and Processes in Some Postindustrial Democracies*. New York: David McKay.

Lehmbruch, G. 1977. "Liberal Corporatism and Party Government." *Comparative Political Studies* 10: 91-126.

Leiserson, A. 1942. *Administrative Regulation; A Study in Representation of Interests*. Chicago: University of Chicago Press.

Levine, R. O. 1973. "The Federal Advisory Committee Act." *Harvard Journal on Legislation* 10: 217-235.

Lindblom, C. 1977. *Politics and Markets*. New York: Basic Books.

Livingston, J. 1983. "The Presidency and the People." *democracy* 3: 50-57.

Lowi, T. J. 1969, 1979. *The End of Liberalism*. New York: W.W. Norton.

McConnell, G. 1966. *Private Power and American Democracy*. New York: Random House.

McGrath, P. S. 1979. *Redefining Corporate-Federal Relations*. New York: The Conference Board, Inc.

MacMahon, A. W. 1930. "Board, Advisory." *Encyclopedia of the Social Sciences*. Vol. 2. New York: Macmillan Co.

_____. 1965. "Responsibility and Representation in Advisory Relations." In R. Martin, ed. *Public Administration and Democracy*. Syracuse: Syracuse University Press.

Mansfield, H. C. 1968. "Commission, Government." *International Encyclopedia of Social Science*. Vol. 3. New York: Crowell, Collier and Macmillan.

Marcy, C. 1945. *Presidential Commissions*. New York: King's Crown Press.

Markham, J. W. 1974. "The Federal Advisory Committee Act." *University of Pittsburgh Law Review* 35: 577-608.

Metcalf, L. 1976. "New Index Shows Personal Corporate Influence on Federal Advisory Committees." *Congressional Record*, 28 September: S. 32954-32956.

_____. 1977. "New Index Shows Personal and Corporate Influence on Federal Advisory Committees." *Congressional Record*, 20 Oct.: S. 34625-34627.

Miller, A. S. 1972. "The Legal Foundations of the Corporate State." *Journal of Economic Issues* 6: 59-79.

_____. 1976. *The Modern Corporate State*. Westport, Conn.: Greenwood Press.

Miller, W. 1976. "Advisory Committees: The Invisible Branch of Government." *Industry Week* 23 February: 38-48.

Mills, C. W. 1956. *The Power Elite*. New York: Oxford University Press.

Mokken, R. J. and F. N. Stokman. 1976. "Power and Influence as Political Phenomena." In Brian Barry, ed. *Power and Political Theory: Some European Perspectives*. London: Wiley.

_____. 1978. "Traces of Power III: Corporate-Governmental Networks in the Netherlands." In Hans J. Hummell, ed. *Mathematische Ansatze zur Analyse Sozialer Macht*. Duisburg, Germany: Sozialwissenschaftliche Kooperative.

Nadel, M. V. and F. E. Rourke. 1975. "Bureaucracies." In Fred I. Greenstein and Nelson W. Polsby, eds. *Handbook of Political Science* 5: 373-440.

Nelson, B. 1984. *Making an Issue of Child Abuse*. Chicago: University of Chicago Press.

Offe, C. 1981. "The Attribution of Public Status to Interest Groups: Observations on the West German Case." In Suzanne D. Berger, ed. *Organizing Interests in Western Europe*. Cambridge: Harvard University Press.

Olson, M. 1965. *The Logic of Collective Action*. Cambridge: Harvard University Press.

Page, B. I. and M. P. Petracca. 1983. *The American Presidency*. New York: McGraw-Hill.

Panitch, L. 1980. "Recent Theorizations on Corporatism: Reflections on a Growth Industry." *British Journal of Sociology* 31: 161-187.

Perritt, H. H. Jr. and J. A. Wilkinson. 1975. "Open Advisory Committees and the Political Process: The Federal Advisory Committee Act After Two Years." *Georgetown Law Review* 63: 725-747.

Peters, B. G. 1977. "Insiders and Outsiders: The Politics of Pressure Group Influence on Bureaucracy." *Administration and Society* 9: 191-218.

Petracca, M. P. 1985. "The Agenda-Building Process: A Critique and Analysis of the Field." Unpublished Manuscript. University of California, Irvine.

Polsby, N. 1980. *Community Power and Political Theory*. 2nd edition. New Haven: Yale University Press.

Popper, F. 1970. *The President's Commissions*. New York: Twentieth Century Fund.

Price, D. K. 1954. *Government and Science*. New York: New York University Press.

Reagan, R. 1983. "Message to the Congress Transmitting the Annual Report." U.S. President. *Federal Advisory Committees: Eleventh Annual Report of the President*. Washington, D.C.: GPO. 16 June.

_____. 1985. "Message to the Congress Transmitting the Annual Report." U.S. President. *Federal Advisory Committees: Thirteenth Annual Report of the President—Fiscal Year 1984*. Washington, D.C.: GPO. 23 May.

Reich, R. B. 1983. "Industrial Evolution." *democracy* 3: 10-20.

_____. 1984. *The Next American Frontier*. New York: Penguin.

Reynolds, M. T. 1939. *Interdepartmental Committees in the National Administration*. New York: Columbia University Press.

Rodgers, W. 1974. "Advisory Committees: The Back-Room Arm Twisters." *Nation* 8 June: 722-724.

Rohatyn, F. G. 1982. "Reaganomics." *New York Times Magazine* 5 December: 72 ff.

_____. 1983. "Time for a Change." *New York Review of Books* 18 August: 46-48.

Roose, D. 1975. "Top Dogs and Brass Hats: An Inside Look at a Government Advisory Committee." *Insurgent Sociologist* 5: 53-63.

Rourke, F. 1984. *Bureaucracy, Politics and Public Policy*. Boston: Little, Brown.

Ruin, O. 1974. "Participatory Democracy and Corporatism: The Case of Sweden." *Scandinavian Political Studies* 9: 171-186.

Schattschneider, E. E. 1960. *The Semisovereign People*. New York: Holt, Rinehart, and Winston.

Schlozman, K. L. 1984. "What Accent the Heavenly Chorus? Political Equality and the American Pressure System." *Journal of Politics* 46: 1006-1032.

Schlozman, K. L. and J. T. Tierney. 1983. "More of the Same: Washington Pressure Group Activity in a Decade of Change." *Journal of Politics* 45: 351-377.

Schmitter, P. and G. Lehmbruch, eds. 1979. *Trends Toward Corporatist Intermediation*. Beverly Hills: Sage.

Seidman, H. 1975. *Politics, Position and Power*. 2nd Edition. New York: Oxford University Press.

Simon, H. 1957. *Administrative Behavior*. 2nd Edition. New York: Macmillan.

Sklar, H. and R. Lawrence. 1981. *Who's Who in the Reagan Administration?* Boston: South End Press.

Spector, M. 1971. "Involving Clients and the Public in Federal Administration Through Advisory Committees." In David S. Brown, ed. *Federal Contributions to Management*. New York: Praeger.

Steck, H. J. 1975. "Private Influence in Environmental Policy: The Case of the National Industrial Pollution Control Council." *Environmental Law* 5: 241-281.

Strauss, S. B. 1982. "The Industry Consultations Program: A Major Tool for Formulating Trade Policy." *Business America* 31 May: 1.

Thurow, L. 1981. *The Zero-Sum Society*. New York: Penguin.

_____. 1984. "Building a World-Class Economy." *Society* 22: 16-36.

Tufte, E. R. 1978. *Political Control of the Economy*. Princeton: Princeton University Press.

Turkheimer, B. W. 1975. "Veto By Neglect: The Federal Advisory Committee Act." *American University Law Review* 25: 53-83.

Turner, W. W. 1972. "Advisory Committees: The Fifth Branch of Government." *Bureaucrat* 1: 142-149.

U.S. Congress. House. 1972. *Federal Advisory Committee Standards Act*. Report No. 92-1017. 92nd Congress, 2nd sess. Washington, D.C.

_____. 1970. *The Role and Effectiveness of Federal Advisory Committees*. Report No. 91-1731. 91st Congress, 2nd sess. Washington, D.C.

U.S. Congress. Senate. Committee on Government Operations. 1972. *The Federal Advisory Committee Act*. Report No. 92-1098. 92nd Congress, 2nd sess. Washington, D.C.

_____. Committee on Governmental Affairs. Subcommittee on Energy, Nuclear Proliferation, and Federal Services. 1978. *Federal Advisory Committee Act* (P.L. 92-463); *Sourcebook: Legislative History Text, and Other Documents*. 95th Congress, 2nd sess. Washington, D.C.

_____. Subcommittee on Reports, Accounting, and Management. 1977. *The President's Advisory Committee Reduction Program*. 95th Congress, 2nd sess. Washington, D.C.

U.S. President. 1980. *Federal Advisory Committee. Eighth Annual Report of the President to the Congress*. Washington, D.C.: GPO.

U.S. News and World Report. 1976. " 'Cheap' Brainpower in Washington—Boon or Boondoggle." 1 March: 63-64.

_____. 1978. "Carter's Uphill War on Those Outside Advisors." 17 July: 61-62.

Useem, M. 1979. "The Social Organization of the American Business Elite and Participation of Corporate Directors in the Governance of American Institutions." *American Sociological Review* 44: 552-572.

_____. 1984. *The Inner Circles*. New York: Oxford University Press.

Vietor, R. H. K. 1979. "NIPCC: The Advisory Council Approach: Advisory Councils Often Served the Interests of the Politically Powerful. . ." *Journal of Contemporary Business* 8: 57-70.

Vogel, D. 1983. "The Power of Business in America: A Reappraisal." *British Journal of Political Science* 13: 19-43.

Weidenbaum, M. L. 1977. *Business, Government and the Public*. Englewood Cliffs: Prentice-Hall, Inc.

_____. 1979. *The Future of Business Regulation*. New York: AMACON.

Wilson, G. 1977. *Special Interests and Policymaking*. London: Wiley.

Wilson, J. Q. 1973. *Political Organizations*. New York: Basic Books.

Wolfe, A. 1981. "The Presidency and the People." *democracy* 1: 19-32.

Wolanin, T. R. 1975. *Presidential Advisory Commissions*. Madison: University of Wisconsin Press.

Yarmolinsky, A. A. 1966. "Ideas Into Programs." *Public Interest* 2: 70-79.

Corporate Power & Political Resistance: The Case of the Energy Mobilization Board*

Sidney Plotkin
Vassar College

Professor Plotkin examines here the controversy over President Jimmy Carter's Energy Mobilization Board proposal to bring out the limits on corporate control of public policy. Focusing on the role of land use and environmental controls as elements of procedural democracy that can frustrate business objectives, he assesses the relevant pluralist, neo-pluralist, and structural theories for their ability to explain corporate power-public policy relationships in the United States.

Sidney Plotkin is Assistant Professor of Political Science at Vassar College. His work in the areas of policy studies and political economy has been included in Politics and Society *(1980) and* The Politics of San Antonio *(1983).*

In 1979, after a series of aggravating defeats in their efforts to build large-scale energy projects, American fuel corporations won Presidential backing for a new bureaucratic ally—an Energy Mobilization Board (EMB)—designed to "cut red tape" and expedite construction. Local opposition to power plants would be channelled into a more efficient and disciplined decision-process, one that would furnish national overrides of local vetoes. Congressional defeat of EMB and its implications for the study of corporate power in the United States are examined below. We begin with a discussion of recent trends in the analysis of business power, and then sketch out the opposition to energy expansion, drawing on the notion of an exclusionary bias in contemporary land-use and environmental policy that is closely connected to fundamental property rights. The case study centers on the defense of this bias, locating it not only in

*I want to thank Professors Robert Engler, William E. Scheuerman, and Peter Stillman for their comments on an earlier draft of this paper.

active pressure group resistance, but the electoral interest and tactics of the Republican Party. Theoretical implications for the study of corporate power are re-examined in the conclusion.

Corporate power is once again an important issue in American political science. Though many scholars have identified corporations as a special power factor in the society,[1] advocates of the dominant pluralist model of power in the United States rarely elevated corporations into prominent positions. Large businesses were seen as merely one among many different forms of organized power contending for political control. With the recent publication of Lindblom's *Politics and Markets* and several newer works by Dahl, however, it is clear that leading figures in mainstream political science have begun seriously to re-examine pluralist ideas on business power. As Dahl and Lindblom wrote in 1976, the part played by businessmen in "polyarchal politics [is] much more powerful than an interest-group role." Industrial corporations, Lindblom now concedes, "are taller and richer than the rest of us and have rights that we do not have."[2]

But, in fact, just how much of an advantage does corporate height afford when large companies are challenged by political and economic groups positioned outside the strongholds of the larger industrial firms? Are there circumstances under which corporations can be defeated on key issues? And what is the theoretical significance of such events for the revisionist approach to corporate power? Given the strong emphasis in pluralist theory on the need to study power empirically, in the heat of conflict, it is notable that the neo-pluralist revisionism has not been accompanied by much concrete investigation of political battles against the use of corporate power. This absence weakens the neo-pluralist case. For without solid foundations in empirical work, the neo-pluralist revision tends to be an observation rather than a reconstructed theory of power in the United States.

---

1. Thorstein Veblen, *Absentee Ownership,* intro. by Robert Lekachman (Boston: Beacon Press, 1967); Robert A. Brady, *Business as a System of Power,* intro. by Robert S. Lynd (New York: Columbia University Press, 1943); C. Wright Mills, *The Power Elite* (New York: Oxford University Press, 1956); Robert Engler, *The Politics of Oil* (New York: Macmillan, 1960).

2. Charles E. Lindblom, *Politics and Markets* (New York: Basic Books, 1977), p. 5, and "The Market as Prison," *Journal of Politics* 44, 2 (May 1982): 324–336; Robert A. Dahl, *Dilemmas of Pluralist Democracy* (New Haven: Yale University Press, 1982), and *After the Revolution* (New Haven: Yale University Press, 1970). For comments on the leftward shift of these writers see John F. Manley, "Neo-Pluralism: A Class Analysis of Pluralism I and Pluralism II," *American Political Science Review* 77, 2 (June 1983): 368–383, and the replies that follow by Lindblom and Dahl, pp. 384–389; Lawrence Joseph, "Corporate Power and Liberal Democratic Theory," *Polity* 15, 2 (Winter 1982): 246–267.

The research vacuum is especially impressive in light of recent work in Marxist state theory which stresses that democratic political institutions complicate and often restrict the ready transfer of corporate demand into public policy. In what has come to be known as the structural theory of power, "relative autonomy" is attributed to the state in its relations with business. Indeed, this is regarded by Marxists as both a logical and empirical pre-condition of government's need to represent multiple and contradictory social interests and to perform both accumulation and legitimation functions for the political economy as a whole. Here the state is no longer viewed as a tool or instrument of a cohesive business class. As a capitalist political structure, its coercions and policies are certainly oriented to the interests of monopolistic capital—the most technologically and economically advanced sectors of business. But in the face of numerous rival social interests, including divisions within monopolistic capital itself, state policies and actions are seen to assume a highly mediated political form, not reducible to the economic power advantages of a particular class or class fraction.[3] That is, much of the recent work in Marxist state theory actually seems to have resurrected one of the basic questions of pluralism—the problematic nature of the translation of economic into political power.[4] As David Truman put it over thirty years ago:

> Relationships in the economic and political spheres differ, even when the holders of power in the two may to some extent be identical. These relationships differ both in the techniques that leaders must employ and in the expectations and demands of those who participate in the institutions. . . . It is likely, therefore, that economic power can be converted into political power only at a discount, variable in size which accounts for some of the heat and frustration generated in corporate directors' meetings . . . over the past twenty years.[5]

Truman's approach is especially valuable because it places the accent where it belongs: on the dynamic but ambiguous aspect of corporate power in the democratic capitalist state. Like Franz Neumann, Truman

3. Ralph Miliband, *Marxism and Politics* (New York: Oxford University Press, 1977); Nicos Poulantzas, *Political Power and Social Classes,* trans. and ed. Timothy O'Hagan (London: New Left Books, 1975); Bob Jessop, *The Capitalist State* (New York: New York University Press, 1982).

4. Claus Offe, "Political Authority and Class Structures," in *Critical Sociology,* ed. Paul Connerton (New York: Penguin Books, 1976), pp. 388–421; Jurgen Habermas, *Legitimation Crisis,* trans. Thomas McCarthy (Boston: Beacon Press, 1973).

5. David B. Truman, *The Governmental Process* (New York: Alfred A. Knopf, 1962), p. 258.

would insist that "the translation of economic power into social power and thence into political power becomes the crucial concern of the political scientist."[6] Each would ask the student of corporate power to assess both the processes by which "discounts" are established and the prevailing social power relationships which govern the context for discounting. They compel us to recognize that unless one is prepared to assume at the outset that corporate-state relations are permanently centered within a pre-established range of policies, that is, to deny the material importance of historical change, the issue of corporate power and the limits to it must be studied on the level of concrete political conflicts.

The defeat of EMB is a promising vehicle for such an inquiry. It isolates a direct collision of the interests and policy preferences of the President and a major industry (one with a fabulous reputation for political influence) with those of regional and environmental interests lodged well below the command posts of "the power elite." It illustrates how democratic norms, procedures and institutions require corporations to respond to political criteria in the deployment of capital, and not always successfully. Indeed, it suggests the importance of an exclusionary bias in the political economy that is powerful enough to turn corporations into opponents of the status quo. Looked at from this perspective, the proposal to establish an Energy Mobilization Board represents an opportunity to study the mobilization of rules of the game against corporate power. And as an example of industrial challenge to widely held values, it is, in Bachrach and Baratz' sense, an "important" issue. For it illuminates conflict over "values and biases that are built into the political system and that, for the student of power, give real meaning to those issues which do enter the political arena."[7] The starting point for an analysis of EMB must, therefore, be the mobilization of bias favoring exclusion of corporate capital from economically necessary sites.

I. The Expansion-Exclusion Dialectic

Although expanding profit is the main goal of capitalist economies, it should not be overlooked that accumulation is channelled through social relationships of exclusion, called private property. For owners of an immobile commodity such as land, however, exclusion is inordinately difficult to preserve. Externalities abound in industrial economies and the spill-over effects of noise, fumes, traffic, and explosion, easily pour

6. Franz Neumann, "Approaches to the Study of Political Power," in *The Democratic and the Authoritarian State,* ed. with a preface by Herbert Marcuse (New York: The Free Press, 1957), p. 12.

7. Peter Bachrach and Morton Baratz, *Power and Poverty* (New York: Oxford University Press, 1970), p. 43.

over backyard fences and well-trimmed hedges. As a result, the law of landed property has maintained for centuries that owners must use their property so as not to injure that of another. In practice, writes one legal scholar, proprietors have long enjoyed rights to extend their fences across neighboring property lines and exercise "an implied easement restricting nearby uses" when they endanger one's own. Exclusion is thus a traditional social power of landed property.[8]

Today's land-use and environmental policies are modern extensions of this ancient heritage. They establish appropriate conditions of industrial action within specified geographic jurisdictions. As Robert Nelson has noted, state and local environmental policies represent the exercise of "collective property rights" on behalf of local landowners. Typically implemented in a manner reminiscent of feudal towns, they exclude development that threatens to undermine local economic stability and environmental quality, independent of the growth needs of the larger society.[9] Nelson sees an anti-progressive, anti-developmental bias in exclusionary policy, a view widely reflected in the land-use literature. Many large corporations, corporate-sponsored research institutions, and the federal government have generated studies of the economic penalties associated with local and regional growth management, and have issued calls for more centralized expansion-oriented land-use programs.[10] Leading intellectuals, meanwhile, urge the public to tolerate more willingly the social costs of rapid economic change while officials in the Reagan administration are studying proposals aimed at "educating the public on economic change."[11]

8. Charles M. Harr, *Land-Use Planning* (Boston: Little, Brown and Co., 1976), pp. 124–125; Robert R. Wright, "Constitutional Rights and Land Use Planning: The New Era and the Old Reality," *Duke Law Journal,* 1977, no. 4: 843.

9. Robert H. Nelson, *Zoning and Property Rights* (Cambridge, Mass.: The MIT Press, 1977).

10. The literature of complaint is huge, but notable examples include: Fred Bosselman and David Callies, *The Quiet Revolution in Land Use Control,* prepared for the U.S. Council on Environmental Quality (Washington, D.C.: U.S. Government Printing Office, 1971); Richard Babcock, *The Zoning Game* (Madison: University of Wisconsin Press, 1966); National Commission on Urban Problems, *Building the American City* (Washington, D.C.: U.S. Government Printing Office, 1968). For critical perspectives on this movement see James O'Connor, *The Fiscal Crisis of the State* (New York: St. Martin's Press, 1974); Sidney Plotkin, "Policy Fragmentation and Capitalist Reform: The Defeat of National Land-Use Policy," *Politics and Society* 9, 4 (1980): 409–445; Richard A. Walker and Michael K. Heiman, "Quiet Revolution for Whom?" *Annals of the Association of American Geographers* 71, 1 (March 1981): 67–83.

11. Robert Reich, *The Next American Frontier* (New York: New York Times Books, 1983); "Some in Administration See Industrial Policy Alternatives," *National Journal,* January 28, 1984, pp. 182–184.

Critics of the dominant view, such as K. William Kapp, argue that the debate over environmental policy really reflects "a shift in the balance of power from those groups responsible for initiating economic change (that is, private entrepreneurs) to those who bore the brunt of the social losses in the past." The latter use their "growing political and economic power . . . to protect themselves against the undesirable consequences of progress." The unfolding battles are thus "an integral part of the general expansion of democracy" in the twentieth century.[12]

However one may choose to evaluate them, land-use and environmental policies complicate the translation of corporate power into expansionistic public policy. Corporations have had to learn hard lessons of political accommodation with local land interests, though for the most part, patterns of mutual acceptance have been forged. The energy industry has not been so fortunate, however. Its huge, pollution-prone projects and highly explosive product occasion anxiety and resistance in many areas.[13] Thus, even as the United States encountered major energy shortages in the 1970's, the nation also found itself in the anomalous position of deterring the energy giants from extending the country's fuel supply network.

II. Not Here!

In the 1970's, the proposed siting of oil refineries, utilities, pipelines, port facilities and electric transmission lines seemed everywhere to provoke fierce and effective resistance. "Keep out" became an all-too-familiar cry in the politics of power. Coastal residents fought off-shore drilling in the Atlantic and Pacific. Conservationists used the National Environmental Policy Act to delay oil pumping in Alaska, and the Clean Air Act to block the giant Kaiparowitz coal plant in Utah and the PACTEX oil pipeline, slated to connect Long Beach, California, and Midland, Texas. In the Mid-west, farmers, ranchers, and the railroads kept up their nearly twenty-year battle opposing delegation of eminent domain powers to coal slurry pipeline companies, while nearby in Minnesota, farmers used guerilla tactics to knock down 765KV power lines. According to industry figures, no fewer than twenty major projects were

12. Kapp, *Social Costs of Private Enterprise,* p. 16. For similar perspectives see Karl Polanyi, *The Great Transformation,* intro. by Robert MacIver (Boston: Beacon Press, 1957).
13. *Energy and Human Welfare—A Critical Analysis, Vol. 1: The Social Costs of Power Production,* eds. Barry Commoner, Howard Bousenbaum, Michael Corr (New York: Macmillan, 1975). "Harris Poll: A Call for Tougher—Not Weaker—Anti-Pollution Laws," *Business Week,* January 24, 1983, p. 87; William Schneider, "The Environment: The Public Wants More Protection, not Less," *National Journal,* March 26, 1983, pp. 676–677.

cancelled as a result of political opposition, and dozens of others suspended due to regulatory miasma and seemingly endless conflict. Corporations lost millions on investment, interest costs, and legal fees as they struggled vainly to justify the expansion of energy capital. As one sympathetic Senator explained, "Our problem is that you cannot get anything built in the United States today." Or as Secretary of Energy James Schlesinger put it, "We have reached the stage of participatory democracy where almost everyone in the society can say 'no,' but none can say 'yes.' "[14]

To answer their needs energy firms sought Federal control of facility siting decisions. Along with other branches of business, most notably construction, the large oil and utility companies appealed for a National Land Use Planning Act formalizing the States' responsibility to furnish space for essential projects. But the corporations were frustrated. Although it passed the Senate twice, national land-use policy legislation was rejected by the House of Representatives in 1974 and 1975.[15]

In the absence of centralized administrative power, the industry's revised strategy centered on gaining Congressional exemptions from the nation's environmental policies. Four Alaskan oil and natural gas pipelines were granted "procedural" waivers from judicial review under the National Environmental Policy Act. In 1978, Congress amended the Endangered Species Act to create a special inter-agency cabinet body empowered to set aside regulations protecting the nation's wildlife. Indeed, as early as 1975, when it became obvious that national land-use policy was dead, the Edison Electric Institute (EEI), trade association of the nation's private utilities, proposed the rationalization of waiver authority as an alternative to a national industrial locations policy. It urged Congress to create a formal process through which energy construction

14. Statement of James R. Schlesinger, United States Secretary of Energy, cited in "Controversy Abounds Over Authority of the Proposed Energy Mobilization Board," *Congressional Quarterly Weekly Report,* September 29, 1979, p. 2134; U.S. Congress, Senate, Statement of Senator J. Bennett Johnston on S. 1308, 96th Cong., 1st sess., 2 October 1979, *Congressional Record* 125: 13863 (hereafter cited as *Senate, Debate*). For background on the various energy resistance battles see U.S., Senate, *Energy Development Project Delays: Six Case Studies,* a report prepared by the Congressional Research Service of the Library of Congress for the Committee on Environment and Public Works, 96th Cong., 1st sess., October 1979 (hereafter cited as *Project Delays*); Barry M. Casper and Paul Wellstone, *Powerline* (Amherst: University of Massachusetts Press, 1981); Louise B. Young, *Power Over People* (New York: Oxford University Press, 1973); K. Ross Toole, *The Rape of the Great Plains: Northwest America, Cattle and Coal* (Boston: Atlantic Monthly Press, 1976).

15. Noreen Lyday, *The Law of the Land: Debating National Land Use Legislation, 1970-1975* (Washington: Urban Institute, 1976); Plotkin, "Policy Fragmentation and Capitalist Reform" (see note 10 supra).

variances could be obtained when essential sites were blocked by opposition under federal, state, or local law. The Institute asked that the President of the United States be given authority to expedite the building of critical facilities by "granting waivers of particular federal, state or local laws and regulations if found necessary in the public interest."[16] Under these rules the "discount rate" on the industry's power would be generously reduced.

Although Congress failed to act on the EEI's initiative, it was clear that the zoning variance model, so useful to expansionist interests at the local level, was fast becoming the corporations' preferred way of dealing with local and regional resistance. Despite its implications for procedural democracy, the corporate drive for centralization of siting authority failed to capture public attention. Predictably, media coverage focused on the individual siting battles, not the broader institutional drift. It took shrinking fuel supplies in the spring of 1979 to illuminate the threat to procedural democracy.

III. Energy Crisis and Emergency Action

The early months of 1979, dominated by revolutionary changes in Iran, brought the United States its second major fuel crunch in five years. Since little had been done to rationalize American energy policy following the 1973 crisis, the relatively minor supply problems created by Iranian stability were quickly magnified. Once more, gasoline lines spread and fuel prices crept upward.[17]

Industry and government blamed the newest shortages on revolutionaries and panicky consumers. Indeed, President Jimmy Carter actually welcomed the situation for confirming the need for comprehensive action, especially the creation of fuel rationing authority. In early May 1979, he told reporters, "We may have to have a few demonstrable shortages . . . to show that it is necessary."[18]

By late June, however, matters were out of hand. The President was informed by chief domestic advisor Stuart Eisenstat that public opinion identified Mr. Carter himself as the principal culprit behind the nation's

16. Testimony of F. W. Mielke, Jr., Chairman, Power Plant Siting and Land Use Committee, Edison Electric Institute, U.S., Congress, Senate, Committee on Interior and Insular Affairs, *Land Resource Planning Assistance Act and the Energy Facilities Planning and Development Act,* Hearings Before the Subcommittee on Environment and Land Resources on S.984 and S.619, 94th Cong., 1st sess., 1975, p. 911f.

17. For general discussions of energy policy in the 1970's, see Robert Engler, *The Brotherhood of Oil* (Chicago: University of Chicago Press, 1977); David Howard Davis, *Energy Politics,* 3rd ed. (New York: St. Martin's Press, 1983).

18. "Carter Would Sign Oil Control Extension," *Washington Post,* May 5, 1979, p. 1.

newest energy mess: "Nothing else has so frustrated, confused, or angered the American people—or so targeted their distress at you personally." Eisenstat recommended a "new approach to energy"—the blaming of domestic ills on OPEC price manipulators. National policy disarray was best projected as the intrigue of "wiley" Arabs. Given the alien threat to national security, public opinion could be marshalled behind "new" programs, permitting the administration to rise above the political confusion and bureaucratic tangling. Among the initiatives Eisenstat gathered from the Department of Energy files were a massive synthetic fuels program already under consideration by Congress, and "a National Energy Mobilization Board" to bypass "the normal regulatory tangle that slows such projects down."[19] Industrial proposals for a national variance agency were now to be resurrected as bold executive action.

Carter turned the memo's essentials into a major nationally televised address, the now-famous "malaise" speech. He urged establishment of the Energy Mobilization Board "to make absolutely certain that nothing stands in the way of achieving" our energy goals. "The red-tape, the delays, and endless roadblocks" must be eliminated. "We will protect our environment," said Carter. "But when this nation critically needs a refinery or a pipeline, we will build it."[20] Although Carter was not especially popular in oil circles—industry leaders resented his charges that they had failed to cooperate during the June crisis—his speech firmly expressed the corporate view that exclusion must yield to expansion. An entity like EMB would insure this.

The Board's task, said Carter, was "to eliminate or modify procedural impediments to the construction of non-nuclear energy facilities." It would be authorized to designate projects for "fast-tracking," to devise binding Project Decision Schedules (PDS) of not longer than one year, and to issue waivers of "procedural requirements imposed . . . by Federal, State or local law." These would include, but not be limited to, "timetables and requirements for hearing and notice." The failure of agencies at any level of government to comply with a PDS would be penalized by yielding decision-making authority to EMB. This so-called "bump-up" or "in lieu" power would have to be exercised in line with relevant statutes. However, the Board could suppress substantive and procedural rules enacted by any level of government following the commencement of construction on a "critical energy facility." This grand-

19. "Memorandum for the President from Stu Eisenstat, Subject: Energy," *The Washington Post*, July 7, 1979, p. A10.

20. "Carter Television Address Text," *Congressional Quarterly Weekly Report*, July 21, 1979, p. 1472.

father waiver was intended to limit the ability of local and state governments to harass project sponsors with ex post facto laws. But it also meant that unforeseen dangers might not be corrected through legal remedy if EMB officials thought rapid construction of the plant to be essential. Finally, judicial review of agency actions was to be curtailed. The designation of priority projects would be exempt from review altogether and other agency decisions would not be reviewable until after EMB certified that the permitting processes were complete. Suits could be entered no later than 60 days following such certification.[21]

Carter's plan exuded confidence, even daring, traits rarely visible in his earlier energy moves. Widely criticized for indecisiveness, he was finally showing his nerve. Democracy's deadlock would no longer cripple the "power elite." Yet, characteristically, for all the tough talk, Carter failed to show Congress how procedural cutbacks could be made without undermining environmental values, for the central mechanism of environmental protection was precisely the detailed process of project review.

Sacrifice was certainly inherent in the Carter administration's plan. Public rights to exclude were to be checked by federal power in the interest of national security. But the public did not believe that a real energy crisis existed, or that large private corporations could be entrusted to lead the country out of it, except at ever-higher economic and ecological costs.[22] Given the widespread disillusionment with the nation's private energy elites, and his own sympathies for environmental protection, Carter was inclined to minimize the implications of EMB for a change in the prevailing exclusionary bias. He also wanted to avoid a direct confrontation with environmentalists, a constituency crucial to the Democratic party, and one of its few solid connections to the suburban middle class. Caught between commitments to energy capitalism and consensus politics, the administration's proposal embodied the contradiction between expansion and exclusion without resolving it. But the problem was inescapable. Procedural waivers must have substantive implications; otherwise they would be irrelevant to the President's goal of rapidly

21. "Specifications for Establishment of Operation of an Energy Mobilization Board" in U.S., Congress, House, *Priority Energy Project Act of 1979. Hearings Before the Subcommittee on Energy and Power of the Committee on Interstate and Foreign Commerce on H.R. 4499, H.R. 4573, and H.R. 4862,* 96th Cong., 1st sess., pp. 144–146 (hereafter cited as House, Commerce, Hearings).

22. A May 1979 survey by NBC News and the Associated Press, for example, found that 71 percent of those questioned believed "the oil companies have created the shortage of gasoline so they could raise prices and increase their profits." Cited in Richard Corrigan, "The Gasoline Shortage—It's Real, But Is It Necessary?" *National Journal,* June 23, 1979, p. 1028.

increasing energy supplies. But if they did carry substantive implications, then they would not be merely procedural. In fact, procedural change and policy change were inseparable, for as one Senate aide put it, "In our laws, the procedure is the substance." Energy mobilization really implied a re-mobilization of bias in favor of expansion.[23]

The administration's reluctance to admit the need for environmental sacrifice led inexorably to its loss of control of the EMB debate. For interest group and Congressional reactions focused precisely on the implications of the substance-process distinction, not on energy policy at all. At least three reasonably distinct political groupings formed around this issue: defenders of the exclusionary status quo, conservative Republican advocates of a new, more explicit commitment to economic expansion, and mainstream corporate liberals, mostly Democrats, who struggled to defend and refine the President's policy against the assaults of the left and right.

IV. Excluders and Conservatives

Environmental groups and organizations of state and local officials publicly conceded the President's central contention: the regulatory system needed streamlining. But more than this they would not accept. Conservationists strongly criticized centralized schedule-making and procedural short-cuts that would likely inhibit serious analysis of a project's effects. They warned of a "full-fledged panic in progress," of "normally prudent people . . . stampeding to endorse solutions which have the apparent short-term advantage of being quick and the probable long-term drawback of being wrong."[24] They recommended two alternatives to EMB. First, the President was urged to continue previously established mechanisms of informal inter-agency coordination, such as the Critical Energy Facility Program under the Office of Management and Budget, which fostered integrated scheduling and review, but not at the cost of existing statutory requirements.[25] More important, they insisted that the

23. Charlene Sturbitts, Senate Environment and Public Works Subcommittee on Environmental Pollution, cited in "Controversy Abounds Over Authority of the Proposed Energy Mobilization Board," *Congressional Quarterly Weekly Report,* September 29, 1979, p. 2137.

24. Testimony of Louise C. Dunlap, Executive Vice-President, Environmental Policy Center, U.S., Congress, House, Committee on Interior and Insular Affairs, *Priority Energy Project Act, Hearing before the Subcommittee on Energy and the Environment,* 96th Cong., 1st sess., on H.R. 4573, July 11, 1979, p. 62; Testimony of Jonathan Gibson, Sierra Club, in ibid., p. 65.

25. Dunlop testimony in House, Interior, *Hearings,* p. 63; and Statement of Roy N. Gamse, Deputy Assistant Administrator for Planning and Evaluation, U.S. Environmental Protection Agency, in ibid., pp. 101–104.

energy debate should concentrate not on techniques for bypassing rules, but on alternative technology to render large-scale fossil-fuel investment socially unnecessary.[26] Environmentalists, in short, challenged Carter's primary policy assumption: that the forms of future energy production should be determined by private corporations with vast sunk capital in the established means of fuel production.

Local officials also paid lip-service to rationalization. They welcomed improved coordination of Federal decision making, but groups such as the National Governors Association demanded extensive inter-level consultation concerning project designations and scheduling. Governors maintained that state and local decisions should "be strictly voluntary and consistent with State statutes and regulations."[27]

Like the protectionists, conservatives rejected the terms of the EMB debate. For them, administrative delay was only the symptom of a more basic problem: the existence of public policies that systematically opposed economic activity. Rep. Phil Gramm (D-Texas) put it this way: EMB "is a copout on going back and looking at all this [environmental] legislation [sic] and seeing where we really made mistakes . . . and here we need to repeal legislation."[28] Conservatives saw the path to energy abundance marked "de-regulation." Letting market forces determine resource allocation would not only increase output, it would also avoid federal intrusion into states' rights. Most conservatives argued as if land-use and other protectionist controls were unconnected to exclusionary property rights and interests in economic stability, as if environmental policy was a kind of socially disembodied bureaucratic interest. In short, they assumed an automatic harmony between capitalism, federalism, and landed property. But not all conservatives were so sure of the benign relations between capitalism and local political-economic rights. Representatives such as Manuel Lujan (R-New Mexico), James Santini (D-Nevada), and Senator Malcolm Wallop (R-Wyoming), all from areas targeted as major energy production sites, were extremely sensitive to exclusionary inclinations back home.[29]

American business was, of course, delighted with the conservative emphasis on expansion, but wisely refrained from an all-out attack on environmental regulation.[30] Most corporate lobbyists believed variances

26. Gibson testimony in House, Interior, *Hearings,* p. 65.

27. Testimony of Edward A. Helme, Associate Director of the National Governors Association Energy Resources Program, House, Commerce, *Hearings,* p. 188.

28. House, Commerce, *Hearings,* pp. 204, 113, 209.

29. For the exclusionary views of westerners see: Neal R. Pierce and Jerry Hagstrom, "Western Governors Seek Stronger Voice Over Energy Policy for Their Region," *National Journal,* October 13, 1979, pp. 1692–1693.

30. For the business press's generally dismal reviews of the Carter proposals see John M. Berry, "Carter's Energy Policy: The Vital Ingredient is Still Missing," *Fortune,* August 13,

were the most that could be won from a government controlled by the Democratic party. For waivers to make a difference, however, energy men insisted the agency must explicitly control substantive as well as procedural rights. They believed, quite reasonably, that the courts would closely scrutinize the Board's constitutionality. Unless Congress clearly mandated EMB's national prc-eminence, a pre-eminence that included Congress' will to by-pass environmental commitments when necessary, the Courts would almost surely force EMB to respect the exclusionary bias of existing law. Ramming the big projects through the fences of local and state government would remain as difficult as ever. Hence the American Petroleum Institute, Interstate Natural Gas Association, the National Coal Association, and similar groups pushed for a measure that included authority to waive substantive law when required by "national security." This was seen as the only sure basis for gaining what one executive called "a favorable regulatory attitude."[31] After all, as a coal industry lobbyist added, there is, practically speaking, "very little difference between procedural and substantive issues," though legally and constitutionally, judges have always insisted upon the distinction. He advised Congress "to find a way around that . . . constitutional problem and certainly to provide language withdrawing those requirements imposed pursuant to Federal law."[32]

This position was far more unequivocal than the President's. It was not clear how far his administration would go in following the substantive implications of procedural waivers. In testimony before the House Commerce Committee, the Chairman of the Federal Energy Regulatory Commission, Charles B. Curtis, suggested an executive branch perspective directly parallel to the corporate view. Insisting that it would be impossible both to protect the environment and expedite decisions, he concluded that EMB must be "equipped with substantive powers to cut through the generic substantive requirements."[33] Still, the President con-

---

1979, p. 106; *Business Week,* "Start at Square One," editorial, July 23, 1979; "Business Wary on Carter Plan," *New York Times,* July 17, 1979, p. D1.

31. Testimony of Carlton B. Scott, Director, Environmental Sciences Department, Union Oil Co. of California, on behalf of the American Petroleum Institute, House, Commerce, *Hearings,* p. 79; Testimony of John G. McMillian, Chairman and Chief Executive Officer, Northwest Energy Co., Salt Lake City, Utah, U.S., Congress, Senate, *Energy Supply Act (Title II), Synthetic Fuels Production Act (Title VI), Hearings Before the Committee on Energy and Natural Resources,* 96th Cong., 1st sess. on S.1308 and S.1377, June 20, July 9, 13, 1979, p. 9.

32. Testimony of Chris Farrand, Director, Corporate Planning, Peabody Coal Co., on Behalf of the National Coal Association, House, Commerce, *Hearings,* p. 86.

33. Testimony of Hon. Charles B. Curtis, Chairman, Federal Energy Regulatory Commission, House, Commerce, *Hearings,* p. 150.

tinued to stress that the "Board could not waive substantive environmental standards."[34]

V. The Corporate Liberals

Most Congressional Democrats backed the President's initiative, but even within his party, important differences surfaced over the meaning and implications of the procedure-substance distinction. Liberal Democrats, especially those with ties to the environmental lobby, wanted a strict separation of form and substance. Led by Rep. Morris Udall of Arizona, Chairman of the House Interior Committee, Rep. Timothy Wirth of Colorado, and Senators Edmund Muskie of Maine and Abraham D. Ribicoff of Connecticut, the liberals hoped to establish a waiver system that would not undermine the exclusionary power of Federal, state or local agencies. Many of these legislators represented areas of the nation already experiencing serious energy expansion pressures.[35] By contrast, more conservative Democrats, led by Rep. John Dingell of Michigan, Chairman of the Commerce Subcommittee on Energy and Power, House Democratic Majority Leader, Jim Wright of Texas, and Senators Henry Jackson of Washington, Chairman of the Energy and Natural Resources Committee, and his lieutenant for EMB legislation, J. Bennett Johnson of Louisiana, wanted a clear commitment to rapid development. More inclined to concede industry arguments that substantive exemptions were sometimes essential, these legislators worked to place the waiver power on a firmer legal footing.

Democrats of all persuasions agreed with the President that administrative rationalization was necessary for national energy policy and national security. For example, opening hearings on the EMB bill, Udall complained that "paralysis all too often overtakes the Government when evaluating major energy projects." It is perfectly reasonable, he urged, to press for a more predictable decision system that will "minimize business uncertainty, expedite . . . applications, and still protect the rights of affected citizens and their communities." The EMB had an appropriate role as "schedule expediter."[36]

Conservative Democrats described the situation more graphically.

34. "Carter Environmental Message Text," *Congressional Quarterly Weekly Report,* August 11, 1979, p. 1670. Conservation groups were unimpressed. "It was kind of underwhelming," said one in response to the messages, ibid., p. 1667.

35. Western and New England legislators, such as Udall, Muskie, Ribicoff, and Jackson also controlled key committee chairmanships on energy and environmental policy, a fact which accentuated exclusionary views throughout consideration of EMB.

36. Statement of Rep. Morris Udall, House, Interior, *Hearings,* p. 18; also see Statement of Senator Abraham D. Ribicoff, *Senate, Debate,* p. 13863.

Jackson spoke of an "institutional crisis" in which "you can't get anything done in this country." Majority Leader Wright lamented that the "Government [was] tied down like Gulliver by the Lilliputians."[37] Furthermore, these Democrats charged, paralysis was stimulating a right-wing reaction against environmental policy. Excluders were warned that unless they joined in accepting some form of substantive variance, "the steamroller is going to go over you,"[38] as Ohio's Senator Howard Metzenbaum put it.

Protectionist-minded Democrats responded that strictly limited procedural waivers were enough. Udall thought we only needed to "knock heads together" to obtain a fast-track schedule. "Our energy problems must not be used as an excuse to make an end run around all the existing laws."[39] Consistent with this logic, Udall's Committee produced a bill that was faithful to the President's wish not to alter legal standards "established prior to the commencement of construction" on priority projects. According to the Interior Committee's report, EMB would be authorized to modify "the time taken to reach decisions, not the basis upon which decisions are made."[40]

Senate Democrats went further. Johnston failed to win support for a full substantive waiver, but did manage to add language to his Committee's Report which established the panel's intention to authorize administrative "changes . . . whether or not they can be categorized as procedural or substantive and whether or not they have substantive or procedural implications."[41] It was in the House Commerce Committee, however, that the waiver power was most clearly set forth.

Dingell was persuaded—in part, by corporate arguments, and in part by a growing personal skepticism about the place of environmental regulation in a stagnant economy—that substantive variances must be made a permanent feature of policy if expansion and exclusion interests were to be harmonized.[42] The Commerce Committee, naturally, was quite sympathetic to this view. Committee support quickly galvanized behind the power to waive all legal obstructions, at any level of government,

37. Statement of Senator Henry Jackson, Senate, Energy, *Hearings,* p. 187. Statement of Rep. Jim Wright, House, Interior, *Hearings,* p. 25. A moment later Wright used a different image: "we are nibbled to death by the minnows and the piranha fish."

38. For this argument see Senate, Energy, *Hearings,* pp. 189–191.

39. U.S., Congress, House, Statement of Rep. Morris Udall on H.R. 5660, 96th Cong., 1st sess., 30 October 1979, *Congressional Record* 150: 9940 (hereafter cited as House, Debates); House, Interior, *Hearings,* p. 18.

40. U.S. Congress, House, Committee on Interior and Insular Affairs, *Priority Energy Project Act of 1979,* H. Rpt. 96–410, 96th Cong., 1st sess., Part 1, p. 4.

41. Senate, Energy, *Report,* p. 39.

42. For background on Dingell's changing regulatory views see Irwin B. Arieff,

whether passed before or after commencement of construction on a priority project.

To justify this step, the Committee argued that, historically, Congress had not been reluctant to issue waivers when faced with roadblocks to the completion of key facilities, such as the Alaska pipelines. But these actions were often in the nature of "last minute decisions" to attach "a barely germane amendment to an unrelated piece of legislation." If particularism was inevitable in regulating the affairs of a modern industrial society, it was all the more important to base exceptions on a predictable, general process. The substantive meaning of due process, protection against arbitrary state action, would be preserved by requiring that waivers be treated as a form of legislation. "Problems are more likely to be resolved in a rational and desirable fashion if a generic process is adopted which will permit orderly review of waiver proposals . . . pursuant to a clearly defined process."[43] This could be achieved by adding a legislative veto provision to the waiver authority. Without it, excluders would sue, on the ground that executive actions to change the law were an unconstitutional violation of Congress' right to make the law. In Dingell's words, "the only way [to] avoid the most appalling case of litigation would be to permit action subject to Congressional veto."[44]

When Rep. Wirth announced that he would offer an amendment to strike the waiver, President Carter was invited to confirm, once and for all, his commitment to the exclusionary bias. After all, Carter himself had declared it to be "vitally important" that the administration "speak and act with a single voice" on every policy. But White House lobbyists joined industry representatives in opposing Wirth. After the amendment was twice rejected by Commerce, protectionists became incensed at what they regarded as Carter's duplicity.[45] Instead of mediating corporate

---

"Dingell: Stubborn, Abrasive and at Center of Energy Issue," *Congressional Quarterly Weekly Report,* November 10, 1979, pp. 2517-2520; also Richard E. Cohen, "House May Get an Energy Committee, and Dingell May be Left Out in the Cold," *National Journal,* February 2, 1970, pp. 188-191. Dingell's increased sympathies for industry complaints about over-zealous environmental control were strongly influenced by his representation of northwest Detroit, an area with obvious ties to auto-industrial interests.

43. U.S. Congress, House, Committee on Interstate and Foreign Commerce, *Priority Energy Project Act of 1979,* H. Rpt. 96–410, 96th Cong., 1st sess., Part 2, p. 24.

44. House, Commerce, *Hearings,* p. 242.

45. The Commerce Committee voted 16–26 against deletion of the full waiver. After the decision, three top environmental officials—Gus Speth, Chairman of the White House Council on Environmental Quality, Cecil Andrus, Secretary of the Department of Interior, and Douglas Costle, administrator of the Environmental Protection Agency—sent a letter of protest to the President—which was soon leaked to the press—complaining that opposition to Wirth's amendment "undermines our credibility." "Curb Panel in Energy Aides Ask," *New York Times,* September 13, 1979, p. 27.

power with a concern for the environment, the administration merely joined hands with energy capital. But Carter's aides demurred. They replied that the White House opposed Wirth not because Carter favored substantive waivers, but because he feared that a waiver-less House bill would increase pressure on the Senate to delete its procedural waiver, leaving the administration with an impotent EMB. Excluders found little to cheer in this explanation.

VI. Congressional Action: The First Round

By autumn, then, three versions of the Energy Mobilization Board legislation were ready for consideration by Congress. Each offered a new executive agency authorized to designate priority energy projects, set binding decision schedules for regulatory agencies, and enforce fast-track schedules by restricting the scope of environmental analysis, including judicial review. They differed primarily with respect to their means of enforcement. On the one hand, the House Commerce and Senate Energy bills either directly or indirectly permitted waivers of substantive law, while the Udall proposal would only abbreviate schedules.

In each chamber, excluders challenged the stronger bills. Senators Muskie and Ribicoff introduced a counter-proposal that favored court orders as the Energy Mobilization Board's main enforcement tool. A similar alternative was offered in the House. In late summer, Morris Udall read the Commerce Committee vote for full waivers as a warning that his colleagues desired a stronger EMB than the one the Interior Committee promised. Joining forces with Wirth and conservative Republican Don Clausen of California, Udall prepared a substitute modeled on the Muskie-Ribicoff bill, with the exception that his plan included authority for EMB to act "in lieu" of other Federal agencies and to issue grandfather waivers.

Pro-EMB forces then toned town somewhat their earlier conception of the agency. On the Senate floor a compromise was hastily arranged following the Ribicoff-Muskie amendment's narrow defeat,[46] that would

---

46. An assorted ideological grouping of 18 Republicans joined 21 mostly liberal Democrats in supporting the substitute. Among the Republican backers were Senators as ideologically diverse as Jacob Javits (N.Y.), Lowell Weicker (Ct.), Orin Hatch (Utah) and Jesse Helms (North Carolina). Interestingly, Senators representing coastal states, where oil drilling was a proximate danger to local fishing and tourism, voted 12-5 in favor of the substitute, while those representing the four Mountain states (Montana, Wyoming, Colorado, Utah) slated for large-scale coal and synfuel development, split their votes 4-4. The Colorado, Montana and Alaska delegations all split their votes, reflecting uncertainty about the implications of EMB more than party loyalty (e.g., Democratic votes from Montana and Alaska went against the President's bill). Senate, *Debate,* p. 13940.

authorize the administrator of the Environmental Protection Agency and Secretary of the Interior to reject proposed waivers of laws enacted after commencement of construction on a priority project. Having successfully added one more veto to the energy decision system as the price of gaining a "fast-track" agency, the Senate proceeded to reject a last effort to include substantive waiver authority. Finally, the Senate passed the Energy Mobilization Board bill by a vote of 68–25, on October 4, 1979—less than three months after President Carter's television address.[47]

John Dingell also tempered his legislation. Seeing many members inclined to accept the Udall-Wirth-Clausen substitute, the Commerce Committee Chairman let it be known that he was disposed to accept an amendment revoking EMB waiver authority over state and local laws. This amendment, proposed by the conservative westerners, James Santini (D-Nevada) and Manuel Lujan (R-New Mexico), also added the grandfather waiver and bump-up authority to Dingell's measure.

In the House, this turned out to be a popular reply to the bill's critics. But local and state officials continued strongly to oppose Dingell, despite his acceptance of the Santini-Lujan amendment. Following its nearly unanimous adoption, the National League of Cities issued a statement predicting that the amendment would return "to haunt members who voted for it in good faith, not realizing the impact of such sweeping power on local communities and states."[48] Their concern stemmed from a fundamental fact about post-New Deal federalism: Much of state and local administrative power is interlocked with organic federal law. For a vast range of policies—including education, transportation, health, welfare, housing, and environmental protection—state action depends on congressionally mandated national requirements, not to mention national funding.[49] Under the Santini-Lujan amendment, Congress' decision to waive national environmental standards could effectively nullify state and local enforcement powers.[50] Thus Udall and Wirth

47. Of the 25 votes against EMB, conservative Republicans were prominent. They included Helms (North Carolina), Garn and Hatch (Utah), Lugar (Indiana), Roth (Delaware), Schmitt (New Mexico) and Armstrong (Colorado). Western Democrats also tended to dissent. They included Baucus (Montana), Burdick (North Dakota), Gravel (Alaska), and McGovern (South Dakota), Senate, *Debate*, p. 14054.

48. Cited in "House Endorses 'Fast Track' Energy Board," *Congressional Quarterly, Weekly Report,* Nov. 3, 1979, p. 2448.

49. For a review of this criss-crossing maze of responsibilities see David B. Walker, *Toward a Functional Federalism* (Cambridge, Mass.: Winthrop Publishers, 1981).

50. For a list of many of the State laws indirectly subject to waiver under Santini-Lujan, see U.S., Congress, House, Statement of Rep. Henry Waxman, 96th Cong., 2nd sess., 27 June 1980, *Congressional Record,* pp. H 5726–5727 (hereafter cited as House, Conference, *Debate*).

insisted that unless the federal mandates were secure, states and local communities would be vulnerable to suppression of their exclusionary powers—precisely because those powers were already, to a considerable degree, national in character.[51] What Washington gave, it could deny.

Dingell responded by shifting the debate onto his preferred terrain of red tape. Labeling the Udall substitute "the Slow-Track, Sidetrack, Massive Litigation and Lawyer's Full Employment and Enjoyment Act of 1979," he cited administration charges that the measure would cause up to seven years delay in energy project decision making. Protectionists fought back by attacking what Udall called a "phony letter" by "some junior lawyer down at the Justice Department" who "assumes that every judge is stupid."[52] But enough doubt had been planted about the efficiency implications of judicial enforcement. By a narrow majority, 192–215, the House rejected Udall's substitute. Almost immediately, Congressman Bob Eckhardt of Texas moved to rally support for deletion of the Federal waiver provisions, but his amendment failed by a wider 100-vote margin. The House of Representatives now decisively moved toward the Commerce Committee bill, accepting it by a vote of 299–197 on November 1, 1979.[53]

VII. Shutting Down the Fast Track

After four weeks of wrangling over appointments to the EMB conference Committee, thirty-six members were given the responsibility to engineer a compromise. Predictably, the conferees deadlocked over the variance issue. Senate members struggled to preserve whatever semblance remained of the procedure-substance distinction, while their House counterparts, a majority representing the Commerce Committee, demanded full waivers. The stalemate lasted until late April 1980. At last, the necessary bargains were struck. The Committee recommended that the agency be authorized to propose for Presidential consideration the suspension of any Federal statute or rule presenting a "substantial impediment" to a critical project. With Presidential concurrence, the

51. House, *Debate,* p. H 10005. It should be added that Walker's views derive from a perspective as Assistant Director of the Advisory Commission on Intergovernmental Relations.

52. House, *Debate,* pp. H 10014, 9948–9949.

53. The voting pattern on these decisions—the Udall substitute, Eckhardt Amendment, and the final vote—was dominated by the traditional Southern Democrat-Republican coalition prevailing against a fragmented Democratic Party. This was a kind of "business-as-usual" vote reflecting conservative corporate power in American politics. By contrast, delegations from States most exposed to new energy pressures overwhelmingly favored the substitute.

recommendation would be forwarded to Congress where it would be referred "immediately . . . to the committee having jurisdiction over the relevant statute or requirements."[54] The proposed variance could now be killed without ever reaching the floor of Congress. As one utility executive lamented, "There's no jumping for joy" about climbing onto this fast-track.[55]

When the House of Representatives finally took up the Conference Report in late June, the energy worries of the previous spring were displaced by higher prices, increased supplies, and a new national focus on American hostages in Iran. The Ayotallah Khomeini now provided just the kind of unifying symbol Stuart Eisenstat had envisioned a year earlier. But it conveyed an image of Presidential impotence as much as that of foreign intrigue. Meanwhile, as the Presidential election campaign sped toward the summer conventions, the Republicans' top candidate, Ronald Reagan, missed few opportunities to attack the President's record. Reagan's Republican Congressional allies, whose votes proved crucial to passage of the original House bill, now had little interest in giving Jimmy Carter a legislative victory. Energy mobilization had better be left to a Reagan administration, where it could be accomplished without "Even More Bureaucracy."[56]

Despite the months of debate, doubts about EMB were more pervasive than ever. Early opponents of the variance power, such as Udall and Clausen, were joined by former Dingell allies such as Manuel Lujan. Corporate lobbyists criticized the waiver process as overly politicized. Adding vetoes to waivers of other vetoes only deepened the problem of regulatory miasma and legal deadlock. It attracted few adherents. Nonetheless, Congressman Dingell pleaded for votes, once more warning liberals and environmentalists that only EMB could hold back the impending conservative assault on the environmental laws.[57] The House rejected this appeal, voting 232–131 to recommit the bill to Conference.

As *Congressional Quarterly* summarized the outcome, "Republicans clearly played the key role" in EMB's defeat. Only 9 of the 134 Republicans voting sided with the President. And, 123 Republicans joined 109

54. U.S. Congress, House of Representatives, Conference Report on S. 1308, H. Rpt. No. 96-1119, *Priority Energy Project Act of 1980,* Title II, Sec. 317, 96th Cong., 2nd sess., 21 June 1980, *Congressional Record* 12: 5486–5487.

55. Douglas C. Bauer, Senior Vice-President, Edison Electric Institute, cited in Christopher Madison, "New Board to Cut Red Tape May Cause Some Problems of its Own," *National Journal,* May 10, 1980, p. 763.

56. Opponents of the Board appeared on the House floor sporting lapel buttons emblazoned with the words "*Even More Bureaucracy,*" the first letter of each word given special emphasis.

57. House, Conference, *Debate,* p. 5790.

mostly liberal Democrats in defeating the establishment of an Energy Mobilization Board.[58]

VIII. A Reagan-era Postscript

The election of Ronald Reagan in November 1980 did little to raise energy industry hopes for early establishment of a national land clearance agency. Reagan promised oil men not another bureaucratic outpost, but a return to freedom for their private government of energy. In fact, he presided over the worst recession of the post-war era, leading to sharp cuts in demand for current, as well as future, supplies. The land hunger of the oil giants had temporarily abated. As one former Energy Department official put it, "At the moment, the economics have changed. . . . [The] hysteria to get these projects on line" has been supplanted by "a deep sense of complacency."[59] This was clearly reflected in the Reagan administration's 1984 budget proposals for the Department of Energy, where conservation and renewable fuels programs were slashed by 400 percent and 100 percent respectively.[60] It is also reflected in corporate hesitancy to undertake the massive production of syn-fuels envisioned by President Carter in 1979. At least six projects were cancelled between January 1982 and May 1983, leaving only two that were actually under construction. And, as of the latter date, the U.S. Synthetic Fuels Corporation, created by Congress in 1980 to spur construction of forty new plants capable of producing the equivalent of two million barrels of oil per day, had not committed funds in loan or price guarantees to a single project.[61] Still, the Edison Electric Institute continues to remind us that "the licensing and regulatory process must be streamlined so that new generating plants can be brought into service more quickly."[62]

58. "House Shelves Energy Mobilization Board," *Congressional Quarterly Weekly Report,* June 28, 1980, pp. 1790–1792. A good deal of heat was generated during the debate over the Conference Committee's intent that the waiver of Federal law also applied to state policies derived from national law. Since this point was made quite clear during the earlier discussions, many conservatives were now feigning innocence to justify a partisan vote.

59. John M. Deutch, cited in "Synthetic Fuels Appeal Fades," *New York Times,* May 6, 1983, p. D14.

60. "Summary of Proposed DOE Budget," *The Power Line,* February 8, 1963, p. 2; U.S., Congress, Congressional Budget Office, *An Analysis of the President's Budgetary Proposals for Fiscal Year 1984* (Washington, D.C.: U.S. Government Printing Office, 1983), pp. 124–127.

61. Lawrence Mosher, "Synfuels Subsidies—What Some Call 'Insurance,' Others Call a Giveaway," *National Journal,* May 7, 1983, pp. 965–968; "Synthetic Fuels' Appeal Fades," *New York Times,* May 6, 1983, pp. D1, 14.

62. Their advertisement appeared in newspapers and magazines around the nation.

IX. Conclusion

We have reviewed above the defeat of the proposed Energy Mobilization Board. Originally sought by energy companies to undercut their environmental opponents, the Board was advocated by a debilitated Carter administration to rally the country behind a drive for energy security and to renew the public faith in its leadership. Though ties between Jimmy Carter and the energy industry were not especially close, the major energy trade associations and firms backed the administration's bill, while lobbying hard for an even stronger agency, one capable of waiving substantive environmental regulations at any level of government.

The White House backed away from proposals to waive substantive law. Its lobbyists opposed attempts to weaken the House Commerce Committee bill, which included the full waiver, but the President himself insisted on maintaining the sanctity of existing law. He only wanted to "cut red-tape." But the administation never explained how procedural reform could be separated from substantive implications. Why were procedures to be cut if not to change the mobilization of bias from exclusion to expansion? Organizations of state and local officials joined with environmental interest groups to pose these questions. Though they were frequently warned by Democratic Congressional leaders to accept EMB as a way of forestalling a more radical pro-expansion shift led by Republicans, opponents of EMB saw the agency itself as an ominous threat to their exclusionary rights.

Republicans were inconsistent. In the fall of 1979, when energy was still a prominent issue, they voted heavily in the agency's favor. In the summer of 1980, as the Presidential campaign moved into high gear, they defected, opposing "Even More Bureaucracy" with a revival of trust in market forces and the promise of strong leadership from Ronald Reagan. Looking out for their party's interest, and less for the interest of business as a whole, Republicans were not reluctant to trade EMB for an improved chance to control the White House and the larger drift of public policy in the 1980's.

What are the broader theoretical implications of EMB for an understanding of corporate power in the democratic capitalist state? The EMB was proposed because citizens believe they have a right to place controls on economic change in their communities, and because those controls can be wielded to frustrate corporate plans that have strategic significance for the national economy. This right is now a widely held expectation of procedural democracy in the United States. Rooted deep in the assumptions and traditions of landed property rights, the modern land-use and environmental policy apparatus make it difficult for corporate power to control public policy, not to mention land. As K. William Kapp observes, there has been "a gradual shift of the balance of power away from those producers and innovators who were formally able to transfer part of the costs of production to the community." The EMB represented an awkward attempt to acknowledge the legitimacy of this democratic shift while at the same time opening new administrative space for centralized control of economic change. The contradiction became all too obvious in the debate that followed its introduction.

The case of EMB shows that the impact of corporate power on the political process cannot be explained by sheer industrial might alone. Both neo-pluralist observations about the special role of business in polyarchal systems and instrumental theories of the capitalist state fail to explain adequately the complex discounting involved in the translation of corporate into political power. As the Marxian theory of relative autonomy suggests, even the most strategically located firms encounter the state as a perplexing structure of opposing interests and programs. Winning policy battles is rarely a simple task even for the biggest companies. It is especially difficult when non-corporate interests use their bridgeheads at all levels of the policy process to fight corporate aspirations.

David Truman's "discount" metaphor is useful shorthand for this complex idea. It neatly conveys the image of the mediating role of government as regulator of the class and interest group relationships of capitalist society. But it should not be overlooked that Truman introduces this concept in the course of a discussion which very persuasively argues the thesis that business' long-term success in political propaganda campaigns has depended directly on its structural position and cultural preeminence in the society. Given the sizable prestige gap between business and government in the American tradition, one which the Reagan administration has tried hard to expand, it may be expected that Truman's discount rate, "variable in size," will continue to be applied to the more obtrusive demands of individual firms and industries, though not to the integrity and legitimacy of corporate capitalism as a system of centralized, private economic power. That framework endures.

Bailout: A Comparative Study in Law and Industrial Structure

Robert B. Reich†

Economies are like bicycles: the faster they move, the better they maintain their balance. Changes in consumer preferences, technologies, international competition, and the availability of natural resources all require economies to reallocate capital and labor to newer and more profitable uses. Societies that redeploy their capital and labor more quickly and efficiently than others are apt to experience faster growth and greater improvements in productivity.

Redeployment is particularly difficult in regions that are dependent on a few large manufacturing firms. In such regions, a substantial portion of the plant, equipment, and labor force has been dedicated to making certain products. When markets for these products change radically, capital and labor are not always able to keep up. The investment required to redeploy these resources may involve too many workers and too much plant and equipment, entail too serious risks, and affect too large a portion of the regional economy to be undertaken without substantial sacrifice and dislocation. Failure to adapt, however, raises the specter of sudden liquidation, massive loss of jobs, erosion of the local tax base, and area-wide economic decline.

In some instances, the process that might normally be applied to effect the necessary redeployment—a bankruptcy under the protection of a court receiver or even an informal "workout" among creditors—is perceived to be inadequate. Although such a proceeding might entail concessions from employees, suppliers, and others with a direct stake in the company, it does not involve the participation of other "constituents"—manufacturers in the area, service businesses, communities dependent upon a healthy tax base—who have an indirect stake in a major firm's continued operations. Inevitably, politics has interceded. Governments have been called upon to save jobs by "bailing out" the companies.

In recent years the U.S. government has responded with increasing fre-

† Mr. Reich teaches business, law, and public management at the John F. Kennedy School of Government, Harvard University. I am indebted to many friends and colleagues for their helpful insights: in particular, Mark Moore, William Hogan, Raymond Vernon, Steven Kelman, Ezra Vogel, George Lodge, Richard Nelson, Owen Fiss, and the members of the Legal Theory Workshop at Yale Law School.

163

quency to calls for aid to certain large, distressed businesses. Conrail,[1] Lockheed,[2] Chrysler,[3] and Continental-Illinois Bank[4] are only the most visible "bailouts." Tariffs, quotas, and tax and regulatory relief are examples of additional efforts also directed at failing enterprises. These responses have released a storm of criticism and debate. Some people, recoiling from the ad hoc nature of these government actions, have called for a new government institution to aid troubled industries and companies.[5] They typically point to Japan's Ministry of International Trade and Industry (MITI) as a model.[6] Opponents of this approach typically point to the failures of Britain's National Enterprise Board or similar institutions.[7]

The debate to date has had a strange, disembodied quality, as if its participants were arguing over the best way to start up an old machine. There has been too little discussion of the social context in which economic change occurs—the vast network of rules, informal codes, shared understandings, and values which help determine how economies adapt. Broad policies cannot be borrowed wholesale from Japan or anywhere else. But smaller-scale rules and social understandings *can* be altered, if only incrementally. By understanding the detailed context of economic change, we can perhaps begin to face these more subtle possibilities.

The underlying question, then, is not that which many economists and policy analysts want to ask: "Are bailouts *good?*" It is a fact of social and political life that governments inevitably will respond to such calls for help. This essay, therefore, is not a search for normative judgments, so much as it is a quest for explanations and hypotheses. What accounts for the differences in how societies have responded to roughly similar problems? What are the underlying social realities? Perhaps most impor-

---

1. The U.S. Government's response to the problems of several failing northeastern and midwestern railroads is embodied in the Regional Rail Reorganization Act, 45 U.S.C. §§ 701-797 (1982). For a discussion of Conrail's return to profitability, see *Making More Hauling Less*, FORTUNE, Aug. 23, 1982, at 7.

2. The bailout of Lockheed Aircraft Corp. was effectuated through the Emergency Loan Guarantee Act, 15 U.S.C. §§ 1841-1852 (1982).

3. For a discussion of the bailout of the Chrysler Corp., see *infra* at 180-87.

4. For a discussion of the problems at the Continental Illinois Bank, see, e.g., Wall St. J., July 19, 1984, at 1, col. 6.

5. *See, e.g.*, Eizenstat, *Reindustrialization Through Coordination or Chaos?*, 2 YALE J. ON REG. 39, 49 (1984); Weil, *U.S. Industrial Policy: A Process in Need of a Federal Industrial Coordination Board*, 14 LAW & POL'Y INT'L BUS. 981 (1983).

6. *See* C. JOHNSON, MITI AND THE JAPANESE MIRACLE: THE GROWTH OF INDUSTRIAL POLICY, 1925-1975, at 30-32, 305-24 (1982); Weil, *supra* note 5, at 994-97.

7. Many commentators have warned against the United States following the lead of Great Britain or other Western European countries in the industrial policy area. *See, e.g.*, Krauss, *"Europeanizing" the U.S Economy: The Enduring Appeal of the Corporatist State*, in THE INDUSTRIAL POLICY DEBATE 71-90 (C. Johnson ed. 1984) ("European experience shows that the real myth is the notion of an efficient industrial policy in the first place."); Miller, Walton, Kovacic & Rabkin, *Industrial Policy: Reindustrialization Through Competition or Coordinated Action?*, 2 YALE J. ON REG. 1, 23-27 (1984).

164

tantly, what can we learn through these comparisons about our own system of economic adaptation, and about its limitations and possibilities?

The article is organized into three parts. Part I examines in detail four large manufacturing companies—AEG-Telefunken, A.G., in West Germany; British Leyland in Great Britain; Toyo Kogyo in Japan; and Chrysler in the United States—and the "rescues" that were arranged to bail them out. Each of these major regional employers began to experience substantial losses at some time during the last decade, but for one reason or another did not make the investments required to shift their resources to potentially more profitable uses. Part II analyzes the responses to these four crises and identifies various underlying patterns in their politics, economics, and administration. In each case, the company dismissed employees, reduced capacity, and shifted some employees and assets to new, more productive uses after the bailout was initiated. However, the extent and pace of such shrinkage and shifting varied. Part III discusses possible explanations for these differences.

I.   Cases

The four cases described in this section are not intended to be representations of how these political-economic systems typically redeploy people and capital within normal business reorganizations. To the contrary, the four cases are atypical; they depict systems under stress. These major business failures threatened, or were perceived to threaten, entire regions of the country and, to some extent, the entire national economy. Each case occurred during a particularly turbulent economic period. Each was perceived as exceptional and generated controversy, debate, complex negotiations, and a search for new solutions. Each case tested the system of normal political and economic arrangements among finance, labor, management, and government, and thereby illuminated the detailed rules and understandings that shape the relationships among these groups.

Typically, we see only the gross movements—the large deals, lawsuits, statutes, and economic aggregates—and mistake these for the social organization lying beneath them. It is only when the system is under stress, when the normal institutional relationships are stretched and tested, that we can see these underlying patterns more clearly, and understand what is unique about them and why their uniqueness matters.

The comparisons which are drawn in the following pages are not intended as a controlled experiment, in the sense that differences in how each of these large-firm crises was handled clearly indicate systemic differences among these four political-economic systems and their capacities to adapt to economic change. No such experiment is possible, because

165

there is an almost infinite number of variables which might have affected public and private approaches to these four cases and their eventual outcomes. Instead, the comparisons are intended merely to suggest systemic differences in the approaches and outcomes, and in social organization.

A. AEG-Telefunken, A.G.[8]

AEG-Telefunken, A.G., was founded in Berlin in 1883. After the Second World War, the company was dismembered because ninety percent of its production facilities were in East Germany. But the company capitalized on the consumer boom of the 1950's and 1960's, becoming a giant conglomerate. It bought up small companies that made washing machines, ranges, and household appliances. By 1970, it was the second-largest electronics manufacturing company in West Germany, after Siemens, and the fifth-largest in Western Europe. It also was responsible for approximately one percent of the nation's GNP.

In the mid-1970's, AEG's successes began to wane. Japanese manufacturers of consumer products started to invade the West German market, cutting into AEG's sales. The *deutschmark* rose relative to foreign currencies, making imports even more attractive and AEG's exports even less so. Moreover, having never fully digested its various acquisitions or imposed any coherent management structure upon them, the firm seemed incapable of cutting costs. The many acquisitions also had left the company deeply in debt. As costs rose, the company dipped into pension reserves, creating a large deficit in the pension fund.

The crisis came in 1979. Losses for that year mushroomed to $580 million. In October, management presented to the company supervisory board a plan to reduce costs. The plan included elimination of 20,000 jobs, 13,000 to occur in 1980 alone. Labor representatives on the board strongly opposed the plan.

AEG's labor leaders met in Bonn with Count Lambsdorff, Minister of Economics in Helmut Schmidt's coalition government, and Hans Matthöfer, Minister of Finance. They argued that the government should invest in the firm, possibly taking over the company, and thereby saving jobs. Matthöfer, a union member and also a leading member of the Social Democratic party, was sympathetic, but concerned about the government's

8. This case study is based on data obtained from a wide variety of sources, including company reports of AEG-Telefunken, interviews, news accounts, and other materials. For the reader interested in learning more about this case one very useful source is D. Anderson, AEG-Telefunken, A.G. (July 1981) (Harvard Business School Case No. 1-381-187). For the purposes of this case and the cases which follow (*see infra* notes 16, 23, and 32), all foreign currencies have been converted into equivalent dollar values at the exchange rate applicable when the transaction discussed occurred.

mounting deficits. Lambsdorff, a Free Democrat and economic conservative, opposed the plan. There was no agreement on a remedy for AEG's problems.

The Dresdner Bank, AEG's lead bank and the second largest bank in West Germany, then took the initiative. In December, Dr. Hans Friderichs, chief executive of Dresdner and a director of AEG's supervisory board, hosted a meeting of sixty-six of West Germany's most powerful business and financial leaders at the bank's headquarters in Frankfurt. Friderichs' message was clear: AEG needed financial help. If the help did not come from the banks, insurance companies, and other industrial giants there assembled, it would have to come from the government. If help came from the government, it would come with strings, and the strings would be tied to organized labor, giving it more power within management. One managing director of the Dresdner Bank put the matter bluntly: "Let's face it, either we are going to provide the subsidy or the State will, and if the State does then the State will want control . . . and there are certain voices in our political system that will be happy to ease the way."[9]

The assembled financiers and industrialists also were aware of mounting public concern about the powerful role banks played in the West German economy.[10] The government was then considering legislation to limit the amount of equity any bank could hold in a given company. The bankers feared that an admission that they could not handle the crisis without state intervention would raise serious questions about why they should enjoy such sweeping power in corporate boardrooms.[11]

The meeting produced a plan to aid AEG. Under the plan, a consortium of twenty-four banks would provide the company with the equivalent of $376.2 million in new equity, bringing the banks' combined holdings to around sixty-five percent of the firm's outstanding shares. The banks also would reschedule about $1.16 billion of the company's long-term debt and some $700 million in short and medium-term debt. Insurance companies would subscribe to $90 million in unsecured bonds at a rate one percent below that on long-term government bonds; other large industrial firms would subscribe to about $125 million in similar bonds. In addition, shareholders would be asked to approve a two-thirds reduction in the nominal value of the company's stock. The company, in turn, would reduce its West German work force by ten percent in 1980, and would replace its chief executive with Heinz Dürr.

9. D. Anderson, *supra* note 8, at 15.

10. *See id.*, at 12-15. For a discussion of the role German banks traditionally play in the economy, see *infra* at 207-09.

11. Wall St. J., Nov. 26, 1979, at 16, col. 3.

167

The plan proved to be inadequate and losses continued to mount. In 1981, the firm lost $260 million on sales of $6.2 billion. Nearly the same results befell the firm in 1982. Accumulated debt rose to $3.2 billion. Equity shrunk to ten percent of indebtedness. The 1981 recession, coupled with high interest rates, was partly to blame; the firm was still struggling to repay loans for its 1960's expansion.

Once again, the Dresdner Bank took the initiative. It sought to get the group of lenders to reschedule the existing debt and provide new loans. This time, however, the government's help would be needed. The company's debt was now too large, and its future too precarious, to rely any longer on a private-sector solution.

In the spring of 1982, Hans Friderichs and Heinz Dürr met with Count Lambsdorff and the new finance minister, Manfred Lahnstein. The recession had pushed unemployment up to more than seven percent from an average rate of 3.5% between 1977 and 1980. Prospective job losses were on everyone's mind. Friderichs and Dürr proposed that the government become involved in the company's plight. The banks would write off the firm's 1982 debt repayments of $105 million, and would provide new loans up to $800 million. But the government would have to guarantee to repay the loans if the firm went into bankruptcy. Labor leaders met separately with the government officials to ask for government assistance, but argued, as they had three years before, that in return the government should obtain an ownership interest in the company.

A few months later the government announced its decision. It would immediately provide AEG with loan guarantees equivalent to $239 million for the purpose of financing export sales, on condition that the banks provide $100 million in new loans. Additional loan guarantees would be made available to the company on the condition that an independent audit showed that the firm was still viable and could survive without aid in two or three years' time. Lambsdorff made it clear, however, that any solution to the company's problems was primarily the responsibility of the company and of West German industry, not of the state.[12]

AEG then dropped the other shoe. On August 9, 1982, after an emergency meeting of AEG's supervisory board, the firm announced that it had run out of cash, that its losses for the year could be as much as $200 million, and that it would therefore seek reorganization under a court proceeding known as *Vergleich*, a type of partial bankruptcy under which sixty to sixty-five percent of a company's debt can be written off so long as the company's reorganization plan is approved by a majority of creditors

12. Wall St. J., July 15, 1982, at 34, col.1.

168

holding among them at least seventy-five percent of the debt.[13] If successful, the reorganization would wipe the company's slate clean of more than $2 billion of debt. Reorganization would have the added advantage of eliminating $520 million of unfunded pension liabilities, which would be taken over by the Pension Security Association, a semi-public corporation established in the early 1970's to insure the pensions of employees of insolvent companies. In addition to seeking reorganization, the company announced that 20,000 employees would be laid off.

The announcements shocked the West German financial community and labor unions. Labor leaders again called upon the government to buy the company in order to stop job losses. The government held firm, although Chancellor Helmut Schmidt's Social Democrats were about to face an important contest with the Christian Democrats in the State of Hesse, in which labor support was crucial. The conservative Free Democrats, on whom Schmidt depended to maintain his increasingly fragile coalition-government, opposed state intervention. The unions were philosophical. "The times have changed," stated Eugen Loderer, a chief of the labor union, IG Metall. "A cave-in has occurred that cannot be handled in the usual bombastic way. Union policy must accept the realities."[14]

Several weeks later the government formally agreed to guarantee up to $440 million of new loans to the firm. The independent audit commissioned by the government had concluded that the firm had a good chance of survival so long as the court-supervised settlement of AEG's current debts was approved, the new loans were provided, and the company continued to slim down. Half of the loan guarantees would come from individual state governments, in proportion to their share of AEG's work force. In addition, certain states agreed to provide low-interest loans. For example, the State of Hesse would grant loans of up to $400,000 at subsidized rates to any AEG supplier headquartered within the state.

AEG's creditors approved the reorganization plan. The banks then came up with more than $800 million of new loans, half of which were guaranteed by the government. The crisis seemed to be over. Indeed, in 1983, AEG appeared to be back on a relatively even keel. Its stock price had rebounded to around $47 a share, up from a low of around $12 in 1979. Its worldwide payroll was down to 76,500 people—60,000 of them in West Germany. Although the company "celebrated" its hundredth birthday with losses of just under $333 million for 1982, it cut its losses to

---

13. Vergleichsordnung §§ 7, 20, 73, 74, 1935 Reichsgesetzblatt [RGBl] I 321 (W. Ger.).
14. *Labor is Bracing for AEG's Collapse*, BUS. WK., Sept. 6, 1982, at 42, 43.

169

less than $13 million in 1983, and it was expected to approach the break-even point in 1984.[15]

B.   *British Leyland*[16]

British Leyland (BL) was created in 1968 when Harold Wilson's Labour government decided that the only way to preserve a strong British automobile industry that could compete worldwide was to merge the two remaining British-owned automobile companies, British Motor Company and Leyland Motor Company, into a larger-scale enterprise. The government, therefore, offered funds to induce the change.

The merger occurred on paper only. The two companies, which themselves resulted from more than thirty mergers over the years, remained fragmented. There were more than seventy plants scattered around England, many too small to achieve economies of scale. More than 200,000 employees were divided among eight divisions, seventeen different unions, and 246 bargaining units. In 1970, five million work-hours were lost to strikes and work stoppages; by 1972, the loss had reached ten million work-hours. Fierce inter-union rivalries also existed because many of the companies that had been merged into BL had been rivals for decades. According to one industry executive, "[t]he people at Longbridge [where Austins were made] wouldn't talk to the people at Cowley [the Morris plant], and the snobs at Jaguar wouldn't speak to any of them."[17]

Despite these problems, BL managed during the early 1970's to coast along on rising automobile sales generated largely by the government's decision to lift restrictive credit and tax measures. BL sold all the cars and commercial vehicles it could produce, though profit margins were extraordinarily low: in 1973, it sold 1.2 million cars, but earned the equivalent of $66 million on $3.8 billion of sales (a paltry 1.7%).

Then came the oil crisis and soaring inflation of the mid-1970's. BL's costs were so high relative to other auto companies and its quality so poor, that it could not compete. It began to lose money. The Austin 1300 sedan became one of the few cars ever to be awarded a "silver lemon" by the West German Automobile Club, a dubious honor bestowed for "horrible" mechanical faults. BL's share of the British market tumbled from forty-

---

15.   German Trib., Jan. 8, 1984, at 7, col. 1.

16.   The sources for this case study, as for the study of AEG, are too numerous to list comprehensively. *See generally* G. Lodge, British Leyland: The Ryder Report (Feb. 1982) (Harvard Business School Case No. 9-376-052); D. RYDER, R. CLARK, S. GILLEN, F. MCWHIRTER & C. URWIN, BRITISH LEYLAND: THE NEXT DECADE (1975) (abridged version of a report presented to the Secretary of State for Industry by a Team of Inquiry led by Sir Don Ryder) [hereinafter cited as RYDER REPORT]; BRITISH LEYLAND, 1974 REPORT AND ACCOUNTS (1975).

17.   Wall St. J., Apr. 11, 1975, at 1, col. 6.

170

five percent, just prior to the 1968 merger, to thirty-three percent in 1974; its share of the continental European market declined from ten to seven percent.

In July 1974, BL executives met with the firm's principal bankers—Barclays, Lloyds, Midland, and National Westminster—to ask them to lend the company the equivalent of $1.2 billion for new investment over the next six years. The company already had borrowed $315 million. The banks, however, were unwilling to extend any more loans. By September, BL's cash position was deteriorating quickly. Losses for the fiscal year amounted to $46.2 million. With its share capital valued at only $360 million, the company had a worrisome debt-to-equity ratio of approximately one-to-one.

The crisis was deepening. In a few months, BL would not be able to pay its bills. BL executives and their bankers met in late November with Tony Benn, Secretary of State for Industry in the Wilson government. On December 6, 1974, Benn announced that the government would seek Parliament's approval for public aid to the company, perhaps including some degree of public ownership. He immediately appointed a team of business and labor leaders, under the direction of Sir Don Ryder, a noted industrialist, to assess both BL's present situation and its future prospects, and report back to Parliament.

The *Ryder Report*,[18] issued on March 26, 1975, blamed BL's troubles on inadequate capital investment, poor labor-management relations, and inefficiently organized production. According to the report, however, the situation was not hopeless: the company could become profitable again with an infusion over the next seven years of the equivalent of $6.2 billion for new investment. Half of this money would come from the government; the other half would be generated internally. Through its purchase of old and new shares, the government would own a majority of the company. In addition, the report proposed the establishment of a new structure of "industrial democracy" within the company, in order to take advantage of the ideas and enthusiasm of the work force and overcome hostilities. It also suggested reorganizing the company into four separate profit centers with responsibility, respectively, for cars, trucks and buses, international sales, and other special products.

On April 24, 1975, Prime Minister Harold Wilson, the leader of the Labour Party, described the government's plan to rescue BL to a packed and somber House of Commons. Wilson explained that the company's importance to the national economy necessitated such a vast investment.[19]

18. RYDER REPORT, *supra* note 16.
19. N.Y. Times, Apr. 25, 1975, at 45, col. 1. *See also* RYDER REPORT, *supra* note 16, at 3

171

After a bitter and acrimonious debate, Parliament agreed.[20] BL announced in a letter to its shareholders that it had accepted the plan. The company's managing director resigned and was replaced with a new chief executive. BL's aged chairman, Lord Stokes, was given the figurehead position of president, and a new chairman was installed.

The government immediately provided BL with the equivalent of $426 million of new equity capital; the rest would come in stages, as BL met certain performance benchmarks. The National Enterprise Board (NEB), a semi-independent government agency, then headed by Sir Don Ryder, would provide these funds. The Board soon began working with BL's new management, restructuring the company along the lines that had been suggested in the *Ryder Report*.

Labor disputes increased as a result of these efforts. Ryder's plan for industrial democracy involved a complex hierarchy of plant committees, divisional committees, and senior councils. Shop stewards, who had the greatest power under the old arrangement, feared that the new system would create a rival channel of communication. A compromise was reached which gave the shop stewards responsibility for putting forth a slate of worker delegates to the committees and councils.

There were other problems. Middle managers felt excluded from the process, while senior managers had all they could do to attend the 760 weekly meetings of the various groups. Confidential company information leaked out to the press. Rank-and-file workers continued to engage in wildcat strikes. There were stoppages at the Triumph works over track speed, at Bathgate over pay, at Coventry's Jaguar plant over a management decision to install a new paint shop at Castle Bromwich—which the workers feared would jeopardize the independence of Jaguar. Moreover, workers continued to complain about salaries and responsibilities, as well as about other company policies.

Productivity in 1977 was lower than in the crisis year of 1974. The company estimated that strikes and work stoppages reduced production by 225,000 vehicles. Losses amounted to the equivalent of $110.5 million. The company sold 785,000 vehicles (down from 1.2 million in 1973), and BL's share of the British automobile market slipped to twenty-three percent (from thirty-three percent at the time of the *Ryder Report*). The National Enterprise Board continued to hand out money, but the government threatened to review and revise the entire Ryder plan.

("[V]ehicle production is the kind of industry which ought to remain an essential part of the UK's economic base. We believe, therefore, that BL should remain a major vehicle producer, although this means that urgent action must be taken to remedy the weaknesses which at present prevent it from competing effectively in world markets.").

20.   892 PARL. DEB., H.C. (5th ser.) 1542 (1975). *See also infra* note 64.

172

A turning point of sorts came in the fall of 1977, when Leslie Murphy took over from Don Ryder at the NEB. Among Murphy's first acts was to dismiss BL's chief executive and its chairman. The NEB appointed Michael Edwardes to both positions. As chief executive of Chloride Group, Britain's largest battery maker, Edwardes had earned something of a "whiz kid" reputation; he had also been one of the first members of the NEB.

Edwardes immediately set out to reduce BL to profitable size. He revised the firm's production targets downward to 800,000 vehicles and twenty-five percent of the British market, and announced the need for a corresponding cut in employment. He offered workers bonuses of up to $3000 if they would leave the company voluntarily. Simultaneously, Edwardes took a tough line with the unions. He closed the Speke plant in Liverpool, which had been plagued by work stoppages and poor workmanship, thereby laying off 3000 workers. When the machinists at Scotland's Bathgate truck and tractor factory went out on strike, Edwardes announced a $70 million cut in planned investment at the plant.

By late 1979, as Margaret Thatcher moved into Downing Street and the Conservatives took over the reigns of government, BL's share of the British auto market had fallen for the first time to under twenty percent. Only 625,000 vehicles were manufactured, down from 785,000 in 1977, and 1.2 million in 1973. The company had slimmed: it now employed 165,000 people (down from 211,000 in 1975). With under two percent of the world's automobile market, BL was the smallest full-range automobile manufacturer on the globe. Losses for the fiscal year ending in September were the equivalent of $242 million, double the losses for 1977 and almost four times the losses for the crisis year of 1974. All told, the Labour government had invested more than $1 billion and lent the company more than $500 million.[21]

It was now the Tories' turn to deal with BL's problems. Union leaders met with Keith Joseph, the new Secretary of State for Industry, and argued for more government assistance. Joseph opposed generous concessions to BL. Edwardes announced that substantial new public investment was needed both to launch new models and to encourage voluntary layoffs. He warned that, without the funds, BL would be forced into bankruptcy and he would resign. He also unveiled a plan to scale back BL still further by closing thirteen more plants and cutting an additional 25,000

21. The poor performance could no longer be blamed entirely on the company. Sales of North Sea oil had strengthened the pound, thereby making all British exports less attractive. At the same time, higher oil prices dampened demand for larger cars, on which BL made its highest profits.

173

workers from the payroll. Joseph relented. The Conservatives agreed to provide the equivalent of an additional $660 million in cash.

However, this new infusion of capital did not help. Although 1979 had been a bad year for BL, 1980 was even worse. Losses were $1.2 billion on sales of $6.5 billion. The world auto industry was generally in a slump. BL had invested a substantial portion of the government's money in developing new models, but they were still months away from appearing in showrooms. In the meantime, new cash was needed desperately. After a stormy meeting of the Cabinet in February 1981, Joseph announced that the government would provide BL with another cash infusion—this one the equivalent of $1.2 billion. One ministerial colleague commented dryly: "There's a job waiting for Sir Keith Joseph in Oxford Street. He's been practicing the role of Father Christmas."[22]

The rest of the story is more upbeat. Losses for 1981 were slightly less than the year before. By 1982, losses had been reduced to $275 million and in 1983 the company nearly broke even. Certain divisions, like Land Rover and Jaguar, actually turned a profit. The new models were enormously successful. The Metro became Britain's most popular compact. The Maestro, a 5-door hatchback, was introduced to much acclaim in early 1983. News reports featured Mrs. Thatcher at the wheel, proudly motoring up and down Downing Street for the cameras. BL's share of the British market bounced back almost to twenty percent. Productivity was up and the company was now considerably leaner. Capacity had been reduced to roughly a half-million vehicles; employment was down to 100,000. Industry observers predicted a rosy future.

C. Toyo Kogyo[23]

Toyo Kogyo, founded in 1920 in Hiroshima, began as a manufacturer of cork products. The company's first automobile, introduced in 1931, was little more than a wagon attached to a motorcycle. During the Second World War the company produced rifles, rock drills, and gauges to measure the accuracy of precision-engineering instruments. When the United States dropped the atomic bomb on Hiroshima on August 6, 1945, Toyo Koygo's factory and its 10,000 workers were shielded by a small hill separating them from the rest of the city.

Tsunjei Matsuda, son of the company's founder, took over as president

---

22. *BL: It's the Thought that Counts*, ECONOMIST, Jan. 31, 1981, at 48.

23. This case study is based on data obtained from a wide variety of sources including company reports of Toyo Kogyo, interviews, news accounts, and other materials. *See, e.g., The Turnaround at Mazda—Is there a lesson for Chrysler?*, L.A. Times, Oct. 25, 1981, § 5, at 1, col. 5; TOYO KOGYO, SUMMARY OF TOYO KOGYO (1983).

174

in 1951. The company became one of Japan's leading truck makers under the brand name "Mazda," a contraction of Matsuda. Matsuda was intent on using Toyo Kogyo's expertise in engineering to compete with the much-larger Toyota and Nissan automobile companies. In 1960, the firm produced its first "real" car, a tiny sixteen horsepower two-seater.

Soon thereafter Toyo Kogyo turned for help to the Sumitomo Bank, one of Japan's largest banks. Until that time Toyo Kogyo's lead bank had been the Hiroshima Bank, but the firm was now sufficiently large that it needed the backing of a larger financial institution. The new relationship proved auspicious. Shozo Hotta, the chairman of Sumitomo Bank, introduced Matsuda to West Germany's Konrad Adenauer, and Adenauer in turn arranged for Toyo Kogyo to obtain from Audi-Wankel a license to produce a rotary engine which Audi engineers had just designed.

By 1967, Toyo Kogyo was the world's only commercial manufacturer of cars equipped with rotary engines. The cars were wildly successful: rotary engines produced relatively little pollution (an important advantage, as the Japanese government progressively tightened pollution-control standards in the 1970's), were snappy and responsive, and were novel.

Before introducing rotary engine models, Toyo Kogyo produced about 150,000 cars and trucks a year; after it began to concentrate on rotary engines, production increased dramatically. By 1973, Toyo Kogyo was building 740,000 vehicles annually and had become Japan's third largest automaker. Its export sales, mostly to the United States, were booming. It was expanding its facilities to accommodate annual production of one million vehicles. Its workforce also expanded rapidly, reaching 37,000 by 1973—4.5% of the working population of Hiroshima prefecture. If component suppliers are included in the calculation, 7.4% of total jobs in the prefecture derived from Toyo Kogyo, one-quarter of the total manufacturing employment. Hiroshima's other major industry, shipbuilding, was in steep decline, so that the regional economy was growing even more dependent on Toyo Kogyo.

Toyo Kogyo's success was abruptly shattered by the oil crisis of the mid-1970's. With all their advantages, rotary engines had one telling disadvantage: they were inefficient. According to a 1974 report of the U.S. Environmental Protection Agency, Mazdas with rotary engines got only ten miles per gallon in city driving.[24] Rapidly rising oil prices therefore meant rapidly falling sales. In 1974, U.S. sales of Mazdas declined by more than 43,000 cars, and Japanese sales also plummeted. Inventories bulged.

24. U.S. ENVIRONMENTAL PROTECTION AGENCY, 1974 GAS MILEAGE GUIDE FOR CAR BUYERS: FUEL ECONOMY TEST RESULTS FOR AUTOMOBILES AND LIGHT-DUTY TRUCKS 4-5 (1974).

175

Nevertheless, throughout 1974 Kohei Matsuda, the president of the firm and grandson of the founder, continued to make rosy projections. Late in the year he called a press conference to announce that a new rotary engine with forty percent better fuel efficiency would be in production before the end of 1975. (In fact, it took Toyo Kogyo engineers six more years to achieve this feat.) Despite declining sales, Matsuda refused to cut production, with the result that by the end of 1974 the company was left with 126,000 unsold cars. Not surprisingly, the company's performance in 1974 was a disaster; it lost the equivalent of more than $75 million on $2 billion of sales. The firm had sunk even more deeply into debt than normal for debt-laden Japanese firms. By the end of 1974, the firm's bank indebtedness had grown to $1.5 billion, and its debt-equity ratio had mushroomed to four-to-one.

Sumitomo Bank officials were not standing idly by. They suggested to Kohei Matsuda that the firm cut production and stop its expansion program, but Matsuda would not listen. Meanwhile, Toyo Kogyo dealers from around Japan expressed their concerns about the company to bank officials. The dealers' lack of confidence, coupled with Matsuda's intransigence and the rapidly deteriorating position of the firm, forced the bank's hand.

In October 1974, the bank sent two of its senior officers to Toyo Kogyo to join the firm's management temporarily. This action was intended to "strengthen the company's financing operations [and] prepare for a possible deterioration in the company's business."[25] The Sumitomo officers took charge of the biggest trouble spots: financing the ballooning inventories of unsold Mazdas in the United States, and projecting the firm's performance over the next year or two. These emissaries were followed by others. In all, over the next two years, Sumitomo Bank and Sumitomo Trust Company placed eleven of their top-level executives in key positions within Toyo Kogyo. These included Tsutomu Murai, managing director of the bank, who took over as executive vice president of the automaker. Murai described the changeover bluntly: "For now, we're an army of occupation. Active intervention is unavoidable."[26]

The Sumitomo rescue team acted quickly. Kohei Matsuda, Toyo Kogyo's president, was made chairman of the company without any operating duties. Two-thirds of the company's section chiefs were shifted to new positions. Costs were slashed in all areas. Production was cut back, expansion plans were dropped, $54 million in stock and real estate was sold off, dividends were reduced by twenty percent for three years, hiring

25. Wall St. J., Oct. 3, 1974, at 11, col. 1.
26. *Where is Toyo Kogyo Going?*, Toyo Keizai [Oriental Economist], Feb. 14, 1976.

176

of new assembly workers was halted for four years, pay levels were frozen for all managers at the rank of section chief or above (about four percent of the total payroll), directors' salaries were cut and bonuses ended for three years, and the union accepted pay raises lower than those received by auto workers at other automobile companies.

One major cost remained. With production cut, the company no longer needed one-quarter of its workforce. Ten thousand employees were now redundant. Rather than lay off the workers, the new Toyo Kogyo managers devised a scheme for training them as auto salesmen and sending them to Mazda dealers around Japan to sell the excess cars door-to-door. About 5000 employees, mostly from the shop floor, took part in the plan between 1975 and 1980. The other 5000 employees gradually retired from the firm over the five years. Each participating employee spent two years in sales work before returning to his factory job. Most were assigned to Tokyo and Osaka, hundreds of miles north of Hiroshima. The company paid each participant his incidental expenses, provided a supplemental wage in order to match his factory salary, and housed him in company-owned dormitories.

Mazda dealers were delighted to have the extra help. It is common in Japan to sell automobiles door-to-door, and a larger sales force means more sales. The displaced workers, however, were less enthusiastic. The two-year shift often meant absence from family and friends. Many found the transition from production to sales to be difficult. Hayato Ichihara, who later became president of the company's union, explained why workers went along: "[W]e feared that if we didn't accept the proposal the company would demand we accept dismissals of workers in exchange for wage increases. And union members did understand that there were too many workers for the work that existed."[27]

Simultaneously with their cost-cutting efforts, Toyo Kogyo's new managers shifted the firm's competitive strategy. Rather than compete solely on the basis of engineering, the company henceforth would compete on the strength of its sales organization and its low costs. But the new managers also knew that Toyo Kogyo's future would depend on new models. The company continued to hire engineers and pour money into developing cars both with conventional piston engines and with rotaries. Between 1977 and 1980 Toyo Kogyo introduced five new models, including a fuel-efficient rotary.

Sumitomo Bank financed much of this transition and arranged financing for the rest. By 1976, when Toyo Kogyo's accumulated debt reached the equivalent of $1.6 billion, the bank's share reached $256 million, six-

27. *Hard Times Make Tenjin a Top Auto Salesman*, L.A. Times, Oct. 25, 1981, § 5, at 1. col. 3.

177

teen percent of the total. The following year it boosted its lending by $70.9 million, to a peak of $327 million. When the other sixty banks and insurance companies which had lent money to Toyo Kogyo threatened to cut off future credit, Ichiro Isoda (later president of Sumitomo Bank and then an executive in charge of the Toyo Kogyo account) called the other lenders to a meeting at Sumitomo's headquarters in Osaka and assured them that regardless of what happened to Toyo Kogyo in the future, the Sumitomo Bank would "stand by the company to the end" and would be making additional loans in the near future.[28] Isoda then asked the other lenders not to desert Toyo Kogyo either, and promised them that all creditors would share equally in repayment of any new loans. In the end, only a few of the lenders came forth with additional loans, but none called in the loans then outstanding.

Sumitomo Bank also twisted arms. Members of the Sumitomo keiretsu[29] provided additional loans. They bought most of the $54 million in stocks and real estate which Toyo Kogyo was forced to sell. They also purchased large numbers of Mazdas from Toyo Kogyo's bloated inventories. Sumitomo Bank branch offices around Japan steered bank customers to Mazda dealers. The bank also provided a large loan to C. Itoh, a major trading company which was not a member of the keiretsu, on condition that Itoh take over Toyo Kogyo's sales organization in the eastern United States and purchase its inventory of 10,000 unsold cars. Finally, in 1979 the bank arranged for Ford Motor Company to purchase twenty-five percent of the outstanding shares of Toyo Kogyo, a move which dramatically improved Toyo Kogyo's cash position.

Additional help came from the city of Hiroshima. Business leaders formed an association called a Kyoshinkai ("Home Heart Group") to promote Toyo Kogyo sales in the region. The prefectural government cooperated by enacting a new and far stricter pollution-control law. Because rotary engines produced less pollution than conventional engines, this

---

28. Interview with Satoshi Yamada, General Manager of Sumitomo Bank, in Osaka, Japan (Sept. 16, 1983) [hereinafter cited as Yamada Interview].

29. Keiretsu, groups of companies united by stock ownership and financial support, are the postwar descendants of the great zaibatsu, whose hand in the Japanese war effort led to their dissolution during the American occupation after World War II. The four most famous pre-war zaibatsu—Mitsubishi, Mitsui, Sumitomo, and Yasuda—included firms in every sector of the economy from heavy industry to banks, each bearing the zaibatsu's name and all centered around a single holding company exercising strict control. Unlike the zaibatsu, the keiretsu is centered around a large bank which exercises considerable influence over the keiretsu's members. The power of this lead bank is assured not only by its debt and equity arrangements with the firms in the keiretsu, but also by the interlocking financial and operating linkages among the firms and by the efforts of the group's trading company. See R. CAVES & M. UEKUSA, INDUSTRIAL ORGANIZATION IN JAPAN 62-68 (1976); see also K. HAITANI, THE JAPANESE ECONOMIC SYSTEM 120-25 (1976). The main role of the lead bank within a keiretsu is to guarantee a member's debt and thereby permit heavy leveraging of investment. C. JOHNSON, supra note 6, at 206.

178

change had the effect of reducing the pollution tax on rotary-engine vehicles relative to the tax on conventional engine models. These efforts served to raise Toyo Kogyo's share of the regional market from twenty to thirty-five percent, and further reduced inventories.

The national government did not intervene directly, but its presence was felt. From the beginning Sumitomo Bank officials understood that the Ministry of Finance was vitally concerned about the future of the company and that the central bank would make every effort to cooperate. The Ministry of International Trade and Industry (MITI) at first considered merging Toyo Kogyo with Mitsubishi or Honda. However, in a widely circulated speech Tomatsu Yoguro, vice-minister of MITI, announced that MITI would not look favorably upon a merger. MITI also encouraged Toyo Kogyo's large suppliers, such as Mitsubishi Steel, to continue their dealings on normal terms. The Ministry of Finance encouraged major banking institutions, like the Industrial Bank of Japan and the Long-term Credit Bank, to provide Toyo Kogyo with additional credit. In 1979, MITI obligingly cleared away legal hurdles for Ford's purchase of one-quarter of Toyo Kogyo.

Toyo Kogyo's new models were successful and, because they could all be produced on the same production line at the same time, the company had the flexibility to vary its output while fully utilizing its plant and equipment. This new organization of production fueled productivity improvements, from nineteen cars a year per worker in 1973 to forty-three cars in 1980.

By 1980 the company was profitable once again. Its debt had been reduced to the equivalent of $943.5 million, and the infusion of new equity from Ford had reduced its debt-to-equity ratio to under two-to-one. It sold more than one million vehicles, slipping past Chrysler to become the world's ninth-largest auto maker.

Successes continued. Export sales ballooned. Ford began to rely on Toyo Kogyo's supply of subcompacts and components. In 1983, its most popular export model, the Mazda 626, was named United States "Import Car of the Year" by *Motor Trend* magazine.[30] That year the company sold 1.2 million vehicles, earning the equivalent of $91.4 million on $4.3 billion of sales. In the fall of 1983, looking back on nine years of rebuilding the company, Satoshi Yamada, general manager of Sumitomo Bank's credit department and one of the bank executives who had spent time at Toyo Kogyo, said: "[I]t was a difficult period. Many people sacrificed. We didn't know how it would come out in the end. We are very pleased."[31]

30. MOTOR TREND, Apr. 1983, at 9.
31. Yamada Interview, *supra* note 28.

179

D.   *Chrysler*[32]

The Chrysler story began in 1922 when several bankers, worried about their outstanding loans to the faltering Maxwell Motor Company, persuaded Walter P. Chrysler to take over management of the auto company. The company had expanded too rapidly and haphazardly during the First World War and the short boom following it. It had been unprepared for intense competition from other upstart automakers and a decline in demand when the market returned to normal. Chrysler persuaded the bankers to extend new loans to Maxwell and forgive much of the old debt in exchange for stock and stock options. He also raised more funds by hurriedly redesigning Maxwell's old line of cars and slashing the price. In 1924, he unveiled a new car with a high-compression engine capable of extraordinarily quick starts. More than 32,000 Chryslers were sold that year at a profit of over $4 million, and the name of the company was changed to the Chrysler Corporation. The company continued to flourish, purchasing Dodge in 1928. It weathered the Depression better than most businesses.

Chrysler's performance after the Second World War was less impressive. Walter Chrysler was gone. The company was slow to ready new models to meet the postwar boom; its historic strength lay in engineering rather than in marketing and styling, which were now the keys to capturing Americans' growing demand for autos. It gained twenty-two percent of the U.S. automobile market in 1951, but then entered a long downward trend that would take its share below ten percent in 1962. It bounced back a bit in the mid-1960's under the direction of Lynn Townsend, who emphasized design and sales. Townsend also launched the firm on an ambitious expansion program which drained the firm of cash and made it vulnerable to sudden changes in demand.

Chrysler's first brush with bankruptcy came in 1970, when it lost $27 million in the first quarter and plunged deeply into debt. The Penn Central bankruptcy that year made investors wary of any company with heavy debt and current losses. A rescue mission was mounted by John McGillicuddy, then a vice-chairman of Manufacturers Hanover Trust Co., Chrysler's lead bank. He organized a syndicate of banks to pump $180 million into Chrysler's critical financial subsidiary, which in turn continued to provide loans to car buyers. The firm got a second wind.

However, the oil shock and the 1974 recession caused auto sales to plummet. Chrysler went into a tailspin. Lynn Townsend was replaced by

---

32.   The data on which this case is based were obtained from company reports, interviews and news accounts. A much more detailed version of this study appears in R. REICH & J. DONAHUE, NEW DEALS: THE CHRYSLER REVIVAL AND THE AMERICAN SYSTEM (1985).

John Riccardo, whose strategy was basically to keep the company solvent by selling off the foreign subsidiaries that Townsend had created and closing marginal factories around the United States. Eventually, even these cuts proved to be insufficient. In 1978, the firm lost $204.6 million on under $13 billion in sales.

By the summer of 1979, Chrysler's lenders had become extremely worried. The firm by now owed more than $1 billion to almost 400 separate financial institutions spread around the globe. Chrysler needed more loans, but its creditors were in no mood to accommodate. McGillicuddy, now chairman of Manufacturers Hanover, persuaded Chrysler to host a meeting of its major creditors to allay their fears. The meeting was held at Chrysler's headquarters; one participant described it as little more than a pep rally, in which no new information was forthcoming but Chrysler executives expressed determination and confidence.[33] The bankers agreed to keep available to Chrysler $750 million in short term credit, but warned that they could not arrange additional funding. Their fears and warnings mounted in July after Riccardo announced Chrysler's performance for the second quarter: the company had suffered a loss of $207 million on sales of $3 billion. This loss was worse than the total losses for 1978.

Politicians also were becoming worried. Chrysler had closed a number of plants in 1978 and more closings seemed imminent. The firm directly employed 140,000 people, and hundreds of thousands more worked for suppliers. Most of the workers were concentrated around the Great Lakes. Riccardo hoped that the new Democratic administration would be sympathetic to Chrysler's problems and the hardships that would result from massive layoffs. Since President Carter's election, Riccardo had made repeated trips to Washington, seeking financial assistance to modernize certain plants and relief from fuel efficiency and environmental regulations. At first, his requests fell on deaf ears. As the company's position deteriorated, however, senators and representatives from affected states became increasingly active. In June 1979, Riccardo met with administration officials to seek legislation that would permit the company to convert its mounting tax losses into a $1 billion cash advance, but the Carter Administration still was not receptive. The Treasury Department feared that any such plan would pervert the tax code and open the floodgates to other companies in dire straits. Nevertheless, Treasury officials organized a task force to gather information on Chrysler and devise alternatives.

By August, the Carter Administration had decided to help Chrysler. It

---

33. Interview with officials of Manufacturers Hanover Trust Co. (names withheld by request), in New York City (Jan. 10, 1984) [hereinafter cited as Manufacturers Hanover Interview].

181

was likely that Congress would act even if the Administration did not. In addition, Douglas Fraser, president of the United Auto Workers Union, and Coleman Young, Mayor of Detroit, had impressed upon the President and his immediate staff the importance of maintaining Chrysler jobs. With an election little more than one year away, their advice struck a responsive chord. On August 9, 1979, G. William Miller, the newly-appointed Secretary of the Treasury, met with Chrysler's board of directors. He told them that the administration would support neither the tax plan nor regulatory relief, but might be persuaded to introduce legislation guaranteeing up to $750 million in new loans if the company came up with an acceptable restructuring plan, including financial concessions from lenders, employees, dealers, and state governments.[34] Another requirement—well understood, although unstated—was that John Riccardo would step down as chairman of the company.[35]

Riccardo resigned and Lee Iacocca, who had come to Chrysler from Ford in 1978, took over. The firm hired an investment banking firm and a management consultant to help devise its restructuring plan. It also shifted its public-relations strategy: the firm no longer argued that relief was warranted by the burdens of the government's tax and regulatory policies; instead, it blamed itself for past failures, but warned that a bankruptcy would force 600,000 people out of work. It also shifted its lobbying efforts from Congress's tax committees to the banking committees.

Chrysler and the Treasury negotiated throughout October 1979. Secretary Miller continued to demand that the plan include larger financial concessions from the banks and employees, and that the earnings projections on which the plan was based be better substantiated. The Treasury commissioned several independent studies of Chrysler, the automobile industry, and the possible effects of a Chrysler bankruptcy. Meanwhile, Chrysler's cash situation continued to deteriorate. Its losses for the third quarter reached more than $450 million. No company in history had lost so much money in so short a time. Chrysler was approaching default on its loans. Its share of the U.S. automobile market was now down to less than nine percent.

Chrysler's congressional allies were growing impatient. Senator Don Riegle and Representative James Blanchard, both from Michigan and both members of their respective chambers' banking committees, introduced loan guarantee legislation. Both committees held hearings at which Lee Iacocca, Douglas Fraser, and Coleman Young argued for loan guar-

34. Interview with G. William Miller, former Secretary of the Treasury, in Washington, D.C. (Jan. 17, 1984) [hereinafter cited as Miller Interview].

35. Id.

182

antees. John McGillicuddy of Manufacturers Hanover explained that Chrysler executives have "substantially exhausted their remedies in the private sector, from a lending point of view, and are now in a position where they need Federal assistance if they are to implement their plan and bring their organization back on its feet."[36]

On November 1, 1979, Secretary Miller announced the administration's support for a $1.5 billion loan guarantee. He explained that the administration's original estimate of $750 million was far short of what was needed to put Chrysler back on a sound footing.[37] Immediately, Chrysler swung into action, seeking congressional relief before the end of the year. Chrysler dealers, members of the United Auto Workers (UAW), and key suppliers all visited congressional offices, armed with printouts showing Chrysler and Chrysler-related jobs in each district. There was no organized opposition, save for relatively weak lobbying by the National Association of Manufacturers, the National Taxpayers Union, and Ralph Nader's Congress Watch.

Nevertheless, certain members of Congress did press for specific provisions in the loan guarantee legislation. At the behest of Senator Russell Long, the proposal was amended to include an employee stock ownership plan.[38] Senators Richard Lugar and Paul Tsongas held out for greater concessions from the employees.[39] Other members simply opposed the whole idea on the basis that the "free market" should be allowed to work its will.[40]

The final bill was enacted on December 20 in the House and on the following day in the Senate.[41] A few weeks later, in a subdued White House ceremony, President Carter signed the Chrysler Loan Guarantee Act while Douglas Fraser and Lee Iacocca watched. The law provided guidelines for approximately $2 billion of financial concessions required of the banks, employees, dealers, suppliers, and states, to be matched by $1.5 billion of federal loan guarantees.[42] It also established a loan guarantee

---

36. *Chrysler Corp. Loan Guarantee Act of 1979: Hearings on H.R. 5805 Before the Subcomm. on Economic Stabilization of the House Comm. on Banking, Finance and Urban Affairs*, 96th Cong., 1st Sess. 824 (1979) (statement of John McGillicuddy, Chairman, Manufacturers Hanover Trust Co.) [hereinafter cited as *House Hearings*].

37. N.Y. Times, Nov. 2, 1979, at 1, col. 6.

38. 125 CONG. REC. 27,180-81 (1979).

39. 125 CONG. REC. 36,638-44 (1979).

40. *See, e.g.*, 125 CONG. REC. 37,059 (1979) (statement of Sen. Goldwater) ("I think this [bailout of Chrysler] is probably the biggest mistake that Congress has ever made in its history."); 125 CONG. REC. 36,220-22 (1979) (extension of remarks of Rep. D. Crane) ("Clearly, such largesse [to the Chrysler Corp.] would be the end of the free enterprise system.").

41. Chrysler Corporation Loan Guarantee Act of 1979, Pub. L. No. 96-185, 93 Stat. 1324 (1979) (codified at 15 U.S.C. §§ 1861-1875). The authority of the Loan Guarantee Board to issue new guarantees for loans to Chrysler expired on December 31, 1983. 15 U.S.C. § 1875 (1982).

42. 15 U.S.C. § 1863(c) (1982) (requiring $1,430,000,000 in concessions from creditors); §

183

board comprised of the Secretary of the Treasury, the Chairman of the Federal Reserve Board, and the Comptroller General to monitor the company's compliance with the legislation and to authorize issuance of guarantees upon finding that the company continued to be "viable."[43]

Chrysler's losses for the year totaled $1.1 billion. Iacocca said, "The hard part starts now"[44]—getting the various groups to agree to come up with $2 billion worth of concessions. Chrysler's workers were the first to cooperate. Annual pay increases specified in the industry-wide "pattern" contract (which Chrysler workers already had agreed to delay in their October contract talks) would be postponed further, putting Chrysler workers six months behind Ford and General Motors employees that year and another five-and-one-half months behind the next year. The 250-member Chrysler Council approved the new contract on January 9, 1980; three weeks later it was approved by more than seventy-five percent of the workers voting in seventy-five Chrysler locals. One UAW official explained the large margin of victory: "The debate in Congress over federal aid and all the publicity convinced them. They voted to save their jobs."[45] In addition, the UAW leaders agreed to allow Chrysler to postpone its periodic payment to the union pension fund. Chrysler viewed this as a "contribution" worth $413 million, even though the government, as insurer of pensions through the Pension Benefit Guarantee Corporation,[46] ultimately would pick up the tab should Chrysler fall into bankruptcy.

Creditors were more recalcitrant. The Act required that creditors contribute $650 million in loan concessions.[47] But by January Chrysler had stopped paying both principal and interest on its outstanding debt. It was now technically in default, and some lenders argued that their forebearance from seeking bankruptcy was a form of contribution. Many of the 400 lenders were convinced that Chrysler eventually was going to fail. They feared that the government loan guarantee, which had priority over their claims, would only drain away assets that might otherwise go to the banks at liquidation. The banks also fought among themselves: European banks, and some small U.S. banks, demanded payment in full from the larger U.S. lenders. Some banks seized funds Chrysler had deposited with them and applied the funds against Chrysler's debts. The larger U.S.

1865(a)(1) (requiring $462,500,000 in concessions from Chrysler employees); § 1867 (limiting Board authority to extend loan guarantees to $1,500,000,000).

43.   15 U.S.C. § 1862 (1982).
44.   N.Y. Times, Jan. 8, 1980, at D1, col. 5.
45.   Detroit Free Press, Feb. 2, 1980.
46.   29 U.S.C. §§ 1301-1309 (1982).
47.   15 U.S.C. § 1863(c)(1) (1982) (requiring at least $500,000,000 from U.S. banks, financial institutions, and other creditors in the form of new loans or credits); § 1863(c)(2) (requiring at least $150,000,000 from foreign banks, and other creditors).

lenders insisted that every lender must sacrifice directly in proportion to its outstanding loans. Negotiations dragged on through March and April, with Chrysler and Manufacturers Hanover executives trying to strike a deal with the others. Eventually the lenders agreed to defer certain debt payments until after 1983, in exchange for $200 million in Chrysler preferred stock.

The new plan which Chrysler submitted to the Loan Board at the end of April did not meet the legal requirements set out in the Loan Guarantee Act. State and local governments had not yet committed funds; suppliers and dealers only had agreed to "softer" terms on purchases; the lenders' agreement to defer payments did not represent "new" money for Chrysler. Nevertheless, the Loan Board conditionally approved the plan.[48] Chrysler would receive $500 million in loan guarantees so long as the various parties actually came up with the sacrifices to which they had agreed.

Despite the Loan Board's leniency, the deal almost fell through. A few small banks and several foreign banks still held out. By June, Chrysler was without cash. It stopped paying its suppliers. Had they then stopped supplying Chrysler, the company would have shut down. Secretary Miller and his staff, now firmly committed to Chrysler's plan, applied pressure. They met with the bank officials, explained that with anything less than one-hundred-percent participation the entire deal would unravel, and subtly threatened retaliation.[49]

Final agreement was reached on June 24. Chrysler received its $500 million loan guarantee. The Loan Board approved a second draw-down of up to $300 million on July 15, 1980.[50] The transaction, said Lee Iacocca, represented "the most complex financial restructuring program in history . . . for one purpose—to protect the jobs of 600,000 American workers who build American cars for American buyers."[51]

Throughout this period, Iacocca and other Chrysler executives reported monthly to Secretary Miller, and daily to the Loan Board staff. "We were like a board of directors," Miller said. "I tried to convince them that they could no longer be a big car company, offering a full range of models.

48. The conditions are set forth in STAFF OF SUBCOMM. ON ECONOMIC STABILIZATION OF THE HOUSE COMM. ON BANKING, FINANCE AND URBAN AFFAIRS, 96TH CONG., 2ND SESS., FINDINGS OF THE CHRYSLER CORPORATION LOAN GUARANTEE BOARD 39-45 (Comm. Print 1980).

49. Interview with Wendell Larsen, former Chrysler Vice-President for Public Affairs, in Chicago, Ill. (Feb. 14, 1984). Legislation affecting bank regulation was pending in Congress; in addition, one member of the Loan Board was Chairman Paul Volcker of the Federal Reserve Board, the government agency which directly regulated many of the banks.

50. STAFF OF SUBCOMM. ON ECONOMIC STABILIZATION OF THE HOUSE COMM. ON BANKING, FINANCE AND URBAN AFFAIRS, 96TH CONG., 2ND SESS., REPORT OF THE CHRYSLER CORPORATION LOAN GUARANTEE BOARD 10-14 (Comm. Print 1980).

51. L. Iacocca, Statement at Press Ceremony (June 25, 1980).

185

They had to downsize the firm. They resisted the notion at first."[52] This resistance, however, soon disappeared. Chrysler abandoned the full-size car business, cut its production, and concentrated on compacts and sub-compacts, including the much-vaunted K-car. Plants were closed, with corresponding cuts in employment. When a UAW official charged in October 1980 that the Loan Board was putting "undue pressure on Chrysler Corporation to strip down its operations," Secretary Miller insisted that the Board's "sole objective" was to put Chrysler back on a "sound financial and operative plan."[53]

Despite the new money, Chrysler's plight did not improve. The K-car did not sell, in part because the Federal Reserve Board was drastically restricting the money supply, forcing interest rates to more than twenty percent and thereby discouraging automobile sales. By the end of 1980, Chrysler was back to the Loan Board for a third installment. This time Secretary Miller and the Board demanded even greater sacrifices from the constituent groups. The Board held all the cards: if the Board did not approve additional loan guarantees soon, responsibility for resolving the situation would shift to the Reagan Administration, which was not likely to be sympathetic.

Miller summoned Chrysler executives, bankers, and union officials to an eleventh-hour meeting at the Treasury Department in early January 1981. There he met separately with representatives of each group, squeezing them for more concessions. In the end, the union agreed to cut wages by $1.15 an hour and freeze them at that level until September 1982; the banks agreed to convert $1 billion of Chrysler's $2 billion debt into preferred stock, and accept repayment on the other half at a rate of thirty cents on the dollar. No one was happy with the deal. William Langley, an executive from Manufacturers Hanover, claimed that the banks had been forced to the wall and had borne the brunt of the sacrifice.[54] Douglas Fraser called it "the worst economic settlement we ever made. The only thing worse is the alternative—which is no jobs."[55] The Board approved a final installment of $400 million in loan guarantees.

Chrysler came back from the dead, earning a small profit in 1982. Helped by the strong upturn in the U.S. car market in 1983, the company earned more than $700 million, a swing of more than $1 billion from the same period two years before. Chrysler had cut its long-term debt from $2.15 billion in 1983 to $1.07 billion, paid $116.9 million in back divi-

---

52. Miller Interview, *supra* note 34.

53. N.Y. Times, Oct. 21, 1980, at D5, col. 4.

54. Interview with William Langley, Executive Vice-President of Manufacturers Hanover Trust Co., in New York City (Jan. 10, 1984).

55. N.Y. Times, Jan. 25, 1981, § 3, at 15, col. 2.

186

dends on preferred stock, strengthened its capital structure by exchanging $1.1 billion in preferred stock and warrants for common shares, and retired 14.4 million warrants held by the Treasury for $311 million. Its share price rose to $35 during the summer of 1983—more than seven times higher than its low in 1982.

The company was now "lean and mean," in the words of Lee Iacocca.[56] Its production capacity had been slashed to approximately 750,000 cars, down from a peak of almost 1.6 million in 1968. Its total employment was down to approximately 70,000, from 160,000 just five years before (U.S. employment shrank from 110,000 to 60,000). It produced far fewer models, had no foreign subsidiaries (except for a plant in Mexico), had a far smaller budget for developing new models and technological innovations (though it was now producing several new models, including a highly successful mini-van), and was relying heavily on Japanese producers to fill out its product line and supply it with technology. Nevertheless, the company had survived and had, according to Iacocca, "won its long battle for independence."[57]

II.   Patterns

These four cases appear to have a great deal in common. Each manufacturing company was highly successful in the past. Each expanded rapidly during the boom years of the 1960's, becoming extremely large by the start of the 1970's. Each had difficulty consolidating and "digesting" its expansion. Each became deeply in debt. In each case, the combination of past successes and the rapid build-up made the company unable or unwilling to change direction, even in light of signs that the market for its products was leveling off or declining. Each company therefore was highly vulnerable to the oil shocks, deep recessions, and sharp changes in international competition which characterized the middle and late 1970's.

In addition, each of these companies was a major regional employer. By the early 1970's, each accounted for five to ten percent of the manufacturing jobs in areas like the State of Niedersachsen in West Germany, the British Midlands around Coventry and Liverpool, the Hiroshima Prefecture in Japan, and the Great Lakes region around Detroit and northern Ohio. Each also purchased a significant percentage of materials and components produced within the region or in regions nearby. Although estimates of indirect employment vary, each of these companies clearly had a pivotal position within at least one regional economy, producing the larg-

---

56.   Interview with Lee Iacocca, President of Chrysler Corp., in New York City (Nov. 9, 1983).
57.   N.Y. Times, Feb. 24, 1984, at 3, col. 1.

187

est item of trade between the region and the national and world economies, and thereby supporting countless smaller businesses producing both goods and services.[58]

In each instance, the first clear sign of crisis was a shortage of cash which compelled company executives to seek additional short-term credit from the company's lead bank. Within months, the shortage of operating capital grew significantly. Losses ballooned. Company executives denied the extent of the crisis. They continued to view it as a temporary cash-flow problem which would sort itself out as soon as the economy improved, when the company developed a technical "fix" for its declining competitiveness, or when its new product line was unveiled. In each case the lead bank forced the company's hand by refusing to make additional loans.

As the crises deepened, control of each company shifted out of the hands of the incumbent executives to a third party which oversaw the transition to a new management team. This third party also negotiated with the various interests who had a continuing stake in the company, seeking financial sacrifices from them in order to keep the company going. In return, the third party agreed to bear a considerable share of the cost itself, including the investment of new money. Although government was involved in every case, the third party was the lead bank for AEG-Telefunken and Toyo Kogyo; for British Leyland and Chrysler the third party was a government agency.

There is, however, a deeper set of comparisons to be drawn. In none of these four cases was the company formally liquidated. Although AEG-Telefunken resorted to a limited type of formal reorganization under court protection, in none of the cases did a receiver or trustee oversee a full, formal reorganization under the bankruptcy laws. Nevertheless, a reorganization of sorts did take place. The companies were refinanced and reorganized, assets were redeployed, new products were developed, and various parties had to sacrifice in the short term for the sake of longer-term rewards. Parts of the companies were "liquidated" in the sense that certain assets were sold off and employees let go. In each case the bailout was effected by a mix of shrinking the company and shifting some workers and assets.

---

58. *AEG: Weltfirma am Abgrund*, DER SPIEGEL, Nov. 19, 1979, at 75 (discussing the role of AEG in the West German economy); RYDER REPORT, *supra* note 16, app. B, at 74 (discussing regional employment by BL); Interview with Ichiro Maeda, Assistant General Manager of Toyo Kogyo for Corporate Planning, in Hiroshima, Japan (Sept. 16, 1983) [hereinafter cited as Maeda Interview] (discussing effects on Japan); *The Chrysler Corp. Financial Situation: Hearings before the House Subcomm. on Economic Stabilization of the House Comm. on Banking, Finance and Urban Affairs*, 96th Cong., 1st Sess. 187-227 (1979) (report on the employment and economic effects of a shutdown or major reduction of business by Chrysler).

A. *Shrinking the Company*

Given the size and importance of these companies, the groups requesting government aid argued that the free market and the profit motive on which market transactions are based could not be relied upon to ensure the well-being of citizens dependent on the enterprise. And yet, paradoxically, each of the companies ended up substantially smaller than it was originally.[59] This paradox appeared repeatedly in public discussions and debates over what to do about these companies: the company had to be saved because so many people were dependent on it, but the only way to save it was to reduce drastically its size and thereby harm the very people who depended on it. Market processes, including bankruptcy, would result in a significant portion of the company being sold off or liquidated for scrap, so it was necessary to subsidize the company while it sold off or liquidated a significant portion of itself.

The bailout of AEG-Telefunken is a case in point. Count Lambsdorff justified the West German government's decision to provide AEG-Telefunken with loan guarantees by reference to how important the firm was to the West German economy.[60] His secretary, Otto Schlecht pointed to the hundreds of thousands of workers who depended on the company and the 30,000 separate companies which provided it with materials and supplies, and noted that a "[bailout] in this instance is less costly for Germany than bankruptcy."[61] But Lambsdorff had approved the loan guarantees only after an independent audit concluded that the company could survive as long as it continued to cut drastically its size and payroll.

We see a similar apparent inconsistency in the case of Toyo Kogyo. Tsutomi Murai, managing director of the Sumitomo Bank, who took over as vice president of Toyo Kogyo, made the rounds of business leaders in Hiroshima to assure them that the bank's intention in taking over the troubled company was to save jobs. The bank also requested assistance from the prefecture on the same grounds. The new Toyo Kogyo managers then proceeded to cut employment. "Obviously, we had to reduce costs," one bank official later explained, "and labor costs are among the most important to reduce."[62]

The same tension was present in the British Leyland case. The initial

---

59. AEG-Telefunken shrank from 105,000 West German employees at the start of the crisis to 60,000 by the time it was over (a 43% drop in employment); British Leyland, from 211,00 to slightly more than 100,000 (52%); Toyo Kogyo, from 37,000 to 27,000 (27%); and Chrysler, from 110,000 U.S. employees to around 60,000 (45%).

60. Fin. Times, July 15, 1982, at 1, col. 1.

61. Schlecht, *Darf der Staat sanierungsreifen Unternehmen helfen? [Should the Federal Government Support Enterprises That Have Economic Problems?]*, WIRTSCHAFTSDIENST, Sept. 1982, at 423, 425.

62. Yamada Interview, *supra* note 28.

189

debate in Parliament[63] clearly pitted Conservative against Labour, free-market ideology against the socialization of costs. The conservatives argued that the free market should be allowed to function, that letting BL go bankrupt would facilitate the redeployment of labor and capital to more efficient uses. Labour countered by focusing on the hardships such a bankruptcy would impose on the many people dependent on the automaker.[64] Not surprisingly, the initial Labour plan for British Leyland relied on a combination of new investment and more participation by the workers in company management to restore the company to profitability.[65] There was no mention of reducing the size of the company and cutting its work force. Indeed, Lord Stokes, British Leyland's chairman, publicly criticized this lack as the "worst aspect" of the plan."[66] Just two years and more than $500 million later, the Labour government's National En-

---

63. 892 PARL. DEB., H.C. (5th ser.) 1419-1538 (1975).

64. Mr. Enoch Powell summed up the Conservative view:

[W]hat bankruptcy brings about, and it does so harshly, is to make it possible for the resources which have been devoted to making a loss to be reapplied in ways which are more likely to make a profit.

We use the terms "loss" and "profit", but they disguise a much cruder reality—and that cruder reality is destruction and creation. When men are employed in an undertaking which, year after year, is making a loss, those men—who are the last people to blame—are actually destroying that which their fellow workers are creating. Less is going out than comes in; they are involuntary parasites upon the economy. The benefit which bankruptcy confers, the benefit which makes it indispensable, is that it enables resources which would otherwise be locked in the work of destruction to be released for different applications, different combinations, different circumstances, in which they can again be creative.

Immediately, however, public money comes upon the scene, immediately public money is to be injected into an undertaking, all the criteria which would otherwise be brought to bear fly out of the window and are replaced by a very different outlook. The private, cautious, calculated, experienced, almost cynical estimation of the likely prospects for the future is replaced by the public commitments, by the political pressures and by the freedom from responsibility which comes out of spending public money, money which is there to hand. . . .

[B]ankruptcy is indispensable and . . . there is no substitute for the judgment of bankruptcy and for the liberating power of bankruptcy.

Id. at 1481-84.

Tony Benn, Secretary of State of Industry in the Labour government, responded to Powell and several other Tories:

I am listening intently to the hon. Gentleman, who speaks with great clarity and seriousness on these matters, but the more I listen to him the more I am utterly convinced that his argument leaves out of account that there is not only the balance sheets but the ballot box. He speaks of people as if they can be moved at the behest of the owners of industry without regard to the political and social factors which are the basis of our standing in the House . . . [T]he people represented through the ballot box intend to exercise, and do exercise, a countervailing power to the use he would wish to make of them as pawns in a financial game.

Id. at 1493.

Soon after the Parliamentary debate, Keith Joseph, a member of the Conservative Shadow Cabinet who was to be Secretary of State for Industry in the Thatcher government, condemned Benn's position: "In order to preserve jobs in over-manned, inefficient British Leyland, Mr. Benn will take astronomic money from the rest of the country and thus cause many other firms to fail. . . . Mr. Benn is the real manufacturer of poverty." Fin. Times, May 3, 1975, at 1, col. 3.

65. *Our Very Own British Leyland*, ECONOMIST, Apr. 26, 1975, at 88.

66. Fin. Times, May 8, 1975, at 1, col. 3.

190

terprise Board hired a new chief executive for the company who, with the full approval of the government, set about slashing its work force.[67] By then it was clear that such cuts were the only way to save the company.

When the Conservatives regained power in 1979, the reduction in employment at BL was well underway. Job cuts accelerated over the next two years. At the start of 1981, however, Margaret Thatcher's government decided to give British Leyland more than $2.4 billion, a far larger infusion of new equity than had ever been contemplated by the Labour Party, because Sir Geoffrey Howe, the Chancellor of the Exchequer, had determined that liquidation of the firm would increase unemployment in Britain by 150,000 people (including the employees of suppliers), and thereby boost public welfare spending by approximately $7 billion a year.[68] Keith Joseph, the Industrial Secretary who approved the payment, told the press: "We tried to find a middle way but there was no middle way. Whether we accepted or rejected [British Leyland's request for more aid] the taxpayers would have been clobbered."[69]

The debate in the United States over Chrysler followed a similar path. In the congressional hearings on the loan guarantee, Detroit's Mayor Coleman Young cited estimates that a Chrysler bankruptcy would double the number of unemployed in Detroit to about twenty percent of the city's population.[70] Other cities would be hit hard as well: the Wilmington-Newark, Delaware area would lose 14,000 jobs; St. Louis would lose more than 25,000; Syracuse, N.Y., and Huntsville, Alabama would have their unemployment rates doubled; Newcastle, Indiana, would lose one-third of its jobs; Kokomo, Indiana, faced a forty percent cut in its jobs.[71] The individual suffering caused by such losses would be considerable:

[A]lthough economic theoreticians may be comforted by the fact that over the long term our economy would adjust, this is no comfort to those in so many of our cities who face the loss of a job. Because of age, some of those, as a matter of reality, will never be able to find a job again, or at least will never be able to find a job at anything close to comparable wage rates or in the places where they now live.[72]

Congressman Jim Wright, the House Majority Leader, urged his col-

---

67. Ball, *Saving Leyland is a Job for Hercules*, FORTUNE, July 3, 1978, at 58, 61.

68. *BL: It's the Thought that Counts, supra* note 22, at 48; *Brighter Future for British Cars?*, NEWSWEEK, Feb. 9, 1981, at 77.

69. *Brighter Future for British Cars?, supra* note 68, at 77.

70. *Chrysler Corporation Loan Guarantee Act of 1979: Hearings on S. 1965 and S. 1937 Before the Senate Comm. on Banking, Housing and Urban Affairs*, 96th Cong., 1st Sess. 1033 (1979) (statement of Coleman Young, Mayor of Detroit) [hereinafter cited as *Senate Hearings*].

71. *Id.* at 1032.

72. *House Hearings, supra* note 36, at 343 (statement of Coleman Young, Mayor of Detroit).

191

leagues to support the aid bill, arguing that a Chrysler bankruptcy would cost the federal government $14 billion to $15 billion and plunge the nation into a full-scale recession.[73] The $15 billion figure included $11 billion in lower taxes and higher welfare and unemployment payments, a $1.1 billion drain on the Pension Benefit Guarantee Corporation, and a $3 billion rise in the trade deficit as foreign cars picked up much of Chrysler's market share. Wright warned that the failure of Chrysler would trigger an economic calamity. A loan guarantee would be in keeping with the tradition that says if "your neighbor's barn caught fire and burned down, then all of the rest of those who lived in the community would provide a little bit of their substance to help and that that was part and parcel of the American spirit."[74]

These sentiments were opposed by those who urged that the market be allowed to work its will. Walter Wriston, the chairman of Citicorp, testified against the loan guarantees:

> There is no avoiding the fact that it is an attempt by the Government to move economic resources to places where they would not otherwise go. Such distortions inevitably lead to less, not more, productivity—and therefore to fewer jobs, less return on investment, and fewer bona fide lending opportunities for banks and everyone else.[75]

Peter G. Peterson, chairman of the investment banking firm of Lehman Brothers Kuhn Loeb, Inc., and a former Secretary of Commerce under the Nixon Administration, warned that a loan guarantee would make Chrysler a permanent ward of the state: "There is clearly a grave danger here that the ultimate costs of government assistance may escalate far beyond the initial projections and that even then, the problem will not have been resolved."[76] Peterson implied that he would let Chrysler fail rather than set a precedent for other federal bailouts.[77] His sentiments were echoed by the Business Roundtable, a group of chief executives of very large companies, which issued a statement in opposition to the loan guarantees: "Whatever the hardships of failure may be for the particular companies and individuals, the broad social and economic interest of the nation are best served by allowing this system to operate as freely and as fully as possible."[78]

The proponents of the loan guarantee, many hoping to save jobs, won

---

73. *Id.* at 684 (statement of Rep. Wright).
74. *Id.*
75. *Senate Hearings, supra* note 70, at 1286 (statement of Walter Wriston, Chairman, Citicorp).
76. *Id.* at 777 (statement of Peter G. Peterson, Chairman, Lehman Brothers Kuhn Loeb, Inc.).
77. *Id.* at 778.
78. 37 CONG. Q. 2752 (Dec. 1, 1979).

the legislative battle. Once administration of the loan guarantee program was firmly in place within the Treasury Department, however, a different viewpoint seemed to predominate. Treasury officials were bent on restoring Chrysler to competitive health as soon as possible, thereby protecting the government's investment. "My job was to make sure that the government was protected," said Brian Freeman, who served as executive director of the Loan Guarantee Board. "That meant making sure that Chrysler was viable."[79] The objective of restoring Chrysler to quick health required that the firm cut costs and lay off workers. Treasury officials pushed Chrysler to drastically reduce its size. G. William Miller, who was Secretary of the Treasury at the time, talked about the difficulties involved:

> The truth is Lee [Iacocca] didn't want a downsized company when we started this; we had to fight for it. We weren't on the same wavelength. The first proposal he gave me I just slid . . . back across the table and said, "you haven't thrown any ballast off yet. When the ship starts to sink, the first thing you do is get rid of ballast."[80]

In the end, the Treasury view prevailed, and Chrysler shrank to almost half its size.

One way to explain the apparent shift in objective, from saving jobs at the expense of efficiency to saving the company at the expense of jobs, is to view the reorganization process as moving from a political to an administrative frame of reference. At the political stage, the company's plight is described as a public problem requiring a public response. Bankruptcy would result in huge social costs, falling disproportionately on certain groups of people. Such a result would be unfair, and in any event would require vast public assistance. Therefore, it is far more equitable, and less costly to the public, for the company to be given special aid.

With the political battle won, the problem then becomes one of administering aid to the troubled company. Financial specialists now take charge. Their professional training is in helping companies to improve their cash flow and balance sheets, not in keeping people employed. They are judged by how quickly they restore companies to financial health, not by how well they maintain the income streams of employees and subcontractors. They work within ministries of finance, treasury departments, and commercial loan departments of large banks—institutions whose traditional roles involve ensuring fiscal responsibility and prudence, rather

79. Interview with Brian Freeman, former Executive Director of the Chrysler Loan Guarantee Board, in Cambridge, Mass. (Feb. 2, 1984).
80. Miller Interview, *supra* note 34.

193

than promoting social welfare or distributional justice. These administrators naturally come to see their task as making a financial "deal" similar to other deals with which they have been associated. Former Secretary of Treasury G. William Miller described the Chrysler loan guarantee from the vantage point of the Treasury Department:

> It was just a professional reorganization outside of bankruptcy. One of the problems of doing it as public policy is that you can't count on every administration to have people in place who can do that sort of thing. We happened to have a set of industrialists and lawyers who were not strange to deals like this.[81]

Because the political mandate to save jobs inevitably is short-lived, and because political agendas are crowded and public attention can be focused on such a problem for only a short time before other issues predominate, administrators have considerable leeway in shifting to the objective of saving the company and minimizing the financial exposure of their own institution, even at the expense of jobs. Moreover, a goal like "saving jobs" is difficult to define and measure with certainty; by the time the crisis is apparent, many jobs already will have been lost, and additional job losses are to be expected. The administrators, however, face at least two constraints on their discretion.

The first is the limited ability of democratic politics to withstand the pressures generated by extremely rapid change: political and administrative goals are precariously balanced. If administrators move too quickly to restore the company through cuts in employment, the issue may move back into the political realm. We see elements of this constraint in all four cases. In the AEG-Telefunken rescue, Dresdner Bank officials justified an industry-led bailout to other banks and insurance companies on the ground that continued rapid job losses otherwise would force a political solution. When this "private" bailout itself began to result in rapid job losses, labor leaders pushed for nationalization of the company.[82] In the British Leyland case, after the National Enterprise Board finally acceded to substantial job cuts, the Labour Party grew deeply divided over the proper course of the rescue, with back-benchers calling for a change in management.[83] As Sumitomo Bank executives began to shrink Toyo Kogyo, leaders of Hiroshima expressed growing concern, with the implicit

---

81. *Id.*

82. *See, e.g., Labor is Bracing for AEG's Collapse*, BUS. WK., Sept. 6, 1982, at 42, 43; Fin. Times, Aug. 12, 1982, at 16, col. 2.

83. *Can British Leyland Survive?*, NEW STATESMAN, Jan. 27, 1978, at 108-09.

194

threat of political recourse if the situation grew markedly worse.[84] When the Loan Guarantee Board began to press Chrysler to reduce its size, labor leaders pressed Congress and the Carter Administration to intercede.[85] Under this view, the threat of political intervention caused these administrators to temper their enthusiasm and slow down their efforts to save the company by cutting labor costs.

This shift from a political to an administrative frame of reference, however, cannot explain the administrators' apparent willingness to pour additional funds into the company, and their corresponding reluctance to allow the company to fall into bankruptcy, even when it showed no signs of revival. This tenacity is particularly interesting in the two cases in which governments ostensibly committed to the free market significantly increased public assistance, at a time when both companies seemed destined for eventual bankruptcy: AEG-Telefunken under a fragile coalition between the Social Democrats and the conservative Free Democrats and British Leyland under the Conservatives. When asked to explain their sharp departures from party ideology and rhetoric, both West Germany's Count Lambsdorff and Britain's Keith Joseph pointed out that providing government assistance to the company was far cheaper than providing it to all the people who would be unemployed in the event of a bankruptcy.[86] Each government had every incentive to do its calculation carefully, taking full account of any segments of the company that probably would find another use in short order. Nevertheless, each determined that company assistance would be cheaper than social assistance.

At first blush this conclusion seems especially curious, coming as it does from conservative leaders, none of whom was particularly dependent on labor support. To be sure, the rather generous programs of unemployment assistance for which unemployed workers are eligible in these countries are themselves the results of earlier political compromises. But even with these social programs firmly in place, it seems strange that these governments would have preferred subsidies for the ailing companies. Though costly, unemployment insurance at least would permit workers to find alternative employment eventually. Bankruptcy at least would allow assets of the ailing company to be released into the economy, eventually to be put to better use. The bailout alternative might be a permanent drain on public resources, and a permanent misallocation of resources in the economy. One would expect free marketeers to argue that though in the

84. Yamada Interview, *supra* note 28.
85. Interview with Douglas Fraser, former President of the United Auto Workers, in Washington, D.C. (Oct. 19, 1983).
86. *See, e.g., supra* text accompanying notes 61 and 69.

195

short term it may be more expensive to allow the company to go under, in the long term this route is far cheaper than any other.

The surest explanation for the support of free market advocates for corporate bailouts is that company assistance was not seen as a permanent subsidy. It was, rather, a means of *slowing down* the inevitable shrinkage of the enterprise. Bankruptcy would work too quickly; the resulting market disruption would be too great. If the company suddenly dissolved its least competitive parts, large numbers of workers in particular regions of the country would simultaneously lose their jobs. This sudden burst of unemployment would have devastating effects on the economy, with multiplier effects as suppliers and services lost customers and could not collect on accounts. By extending the decline over a longer period of time, however, policymakers could ease the adjustment. Fewer people would be out of work at any given time, and growing businesses might be able to absorb many of them. Suppliers might lose the failing company as a customer, but would have time to develop alternative customers. Fewer workers and small businesses would face a credit crunch, and this would reduce the pressure on other small businesses, services, and lending institutions. Seeing the coming decline, creditors and shareholders also could make gradual adjustments, writing down their loans and altering their portfolios with minimal disruption. In short, given the size and importance of these companies to their economies, bankruptcy would release vast resources far more quickly than the market could absorb them. What was needed, therefore, was *slow* bankruptcy. This need is the source of the second constraint on administrative discretion: the reduction in the size of the company must be sufficiently gradual so as not to cause severe economic problems.

As we have seen, the shift from a political to an administrative frame of reference—with the ever-present possibility that the issue would regain public attention—also meant a slow shrinkage of the company. Under this view, the administrators' willingness to provide additional assistance to the company and thereby slow down the decline was a response to political reality. If the shrinkage were too rapid and the resulting unemployment too great within a particular time period, there would be political demands to preserve the status quo. These demands in turn would make it difficult, if not impossible, to restore the company to financial health. The administrators' goal, therefore, was to shrink the company as fast as politics would permit in order to regain solvency and protect their institutional investment. Under the slow bankruptcy view, on the other hand, a very different constraint governed administrators' decisionmaking. This second constraint was imposed by the economy's limited ability to adjust to extremely rapid change. Operating under this limitation, the administrators'

196

goal was to shrink the company only as fast as the economy would permit in order to ease the process of economy-wide adjustment.

The British Leyland bailout seems to have moved from concern with the first constraint to concern with the second over its seven-year course. Between 1975 and 1977, when the issue of saving British Leyland jobs was highly politicized, there were almost no layoffs. Between 1977 and 1979, still under the Labour government, the National Enterprise Board and BL's new executives cut employment by about 30,000, a pace that was as fast as these administrators could manage without politicizing the issue once again. Between 1979 and 1981 the Conservatives, unconcerned about union support, cut employment by almost 50,000. However, in 1981, faced with the possibility of an even more rapid dissolution, the Tories held back. The social costs of unemployment were rising, not just for former BL employees and subcontractors, but for the nation as a whole, and it seemed that a quicker decline would imperil the entire economy. The Thatcher government decided to give BL a major infusion of new capital. Job cuts thereafter slowed down to the earlier pace of around 15,000 per year.

The Chrysler pattern is slightly different. In this case, the greatest number of layoffs—30,000 of them—came in 1979, the very year that Chrysler was ostensibly seeking government assistance to save jobs. The magnitude of the layoffs served to put Chrysler on the political agenda. In 1980 and 1981, after the issue had moved from Congress to the Treasury Department, the pace of layoffs slowed. About 17,000 workers were laid off during those two years. As we have seen, once the loan guarantee legislation was passed, the Treasury Secretary and the staff of the Loan Board urged Chrysler to slim down. It is interesting to note, however, that by then Chrysler had already done most of its slimming. Had Chrysler maintained the same pace of layoffs in 1980 and 1981 that it had in 1979, the company would have ended 1981 with a mere 10,000 employees—fewer than were expected to be employed after a formal bankruptcy. Presumably the company would have cut back its suppliers to a similar degree. However, given the problem of high, and rising, unemployment, particularly in the Midwest and the industrial belt of the Northeast, the social costs of such a sudden demise would have been prohibitive.

B. *Shifting Workers and Assets*

So far we have assumed that the only reason for subsidizing these companies was, paradoxically, to shrink them, but to do so more slowly than would have been possible had they been left to the market and bankruptcy. The evidence suggests this pattern, although it is unclear whether

197

it was attributable to financial administrators who were engaged in a kind of tug-of-war with politicians, or to economic ministers who were keeping a watchful eye on how quickly the economy could adjust to the company's gradual demise, or to some combination of both. To round out our discussion, however, we need to recognize another pattern in these cases. It concerns the shift which occurred within each company during its crisis toward more competitive products and processes, and better use of employees.

If the market for the company's products had irrevocably declined, or if the company had simply grown too large and ungainly to serve its market profitably, then we could understand the crisis simply as a failure of the company to shrink in a timely manner. Resources were kept too long, as if the company had erected a dam to block the natural outward flow of such resources in pursuit of more profitable uses. By the time the crisis appeared, the company was huge, and the dam extraordinarily high. If the dam broke, the pent-up resources would have inundated the economy, or else politics would have interceded to shore up the dam at all costs. The challenge was to reduce the reservoir of misallocated resources gradually, so that they could be absorbed elsewhere without igniting more political demands.

But this metaphor is too tidy. Markets change; new markets develop. Each company might have shifted its research, plant, equipment, cash, and employee resources in the direction in which the markets seemed to be moving or in the direction of new, emerging markets. In other words, to avert crisis the company whose old market was declining need not have watched passively as its productive resources flowed out to more profitable uses. It could have put its resources to better uses internally by shifting them to new products and more efficient processes. Even after the crisis occurred, the company still had the option of shifting instead of shrinking. The reservoir of misallocated resources lying behind the dam could have been rechanneled in other directions rather than simply allowed to flow out.

In each of our cases, some such shift occurred after the crisis broke. AEG-Telefunken invested anew in telecommunications and defense related technologies. British Leyland developed new automobile models, and improved the quality of its Land Rover and Jaguar. Toyo Kogyo invested in new models and the development of a fuel-efficient rotary engine. Chrysler developed several new compacts and a new mini-van. All these shifts appear to have been successful. All adapted to new markets. All entailed a redeployment within the company of certain resources, including people, that otherwise might have flowed out. All the shifts were en-

198

couraged by the financial administrators who presided over the reorganization.

Shifting resources, however, requires money. New products must be designed and tested, plant and equipment converted, employees retrained, the production system reorganized, dealers prepared, and consumers reoriented. The well-managed company, highly sensitive to potential changes and new opportunities in the market, is constantly investing in such shifts. On the other hand, the company that has disregarded such changes and new opportunities, or is caught unaware by a sudden shock to the market (such as that brought about by the introduction of a pathbreaking technology or a substantial increase in the price of a raw material), may need to make a dramatic shift all at once, but lack the large sums necessary to do so. This was the problem faced by all four of the described companies. Once the crisis became apparent each of them shifted, but the shifts were only partial. The companies could not redeploy all of their resources internally because they did not have enough money to make a complete transition. In addition, because their market shares were declining and almost all their divisions were losing money, there was no likelihood of finding another company to purchase all or a substantial part of the ailing company.[87]

To some extent, shrinking and shifting are complementary strategies for companies in distress. By liquidating the most costly and least profitable operations, cash flow is enhanced. The new cash can then be invested in shifting the remaining resources to more profitable uses. This shrink-and-shift strategy was used by all four companies to some degree. All cut their payrolls and, as we have seen, some of the revenues resulting from these changes were invested in new products and improved manufacturing processes.

The irony, of course, is that shrinking and shifting ultimately are inconsistent. Human and capital assets that flow out of the company no longer are available to be shifted. Even if the shrink-and-shift strategy is enormously successful—so much so that the shrunken company finds itself growing rapidly once again—the company may have difficulty summoning back old suppliers, employees, dealers, customers, and certain specialized assets. Time has elapsed. The discarded employees and suppliers are

---

87. Occasionally, parts of large failing firms may be sold off to other companies or groups of investors, who expect that—due to their superior managerial acumen or "synergistic" aspects of their other businesses—the newly spun-off divisions will offer a better return to them than they did as part of the failing firm. This occurred to a limited extent in Chrysler, which sold off its tank division; it occurred to a substantial extent in AEG-Telefunken, which sold off its consumer-products divisions. In these transactions, title to plant, equipment, and employees are transfered to the new owners. From a social standpoint, there has been no change, particularly no net loss of jobs. Wholesale transfers like these, therefore, may represent a socially preferable alternative to shrinkage.

199

likely to have linked up with other companies in the interim. Having once been jettisoned by the old company, they may be unwilling to resume what seems to be a precarious relationship. Under these circumstances it may be more costly for the company to bid them back and shift them to new uses than simply to find new suppliers, employees, dealers, customers, and specialized assets.

If markets adjusted to such changes with ease, and transactions such as these were relatively costless, then it would not matter what combination of shrinking and shifting were chosen. The company could be as profitable after a great deal of shrinking and a small bit of shifting as the other way around. The economy as a whole could adapt as easily to a dramatic shrinkage in one of its largest companies as to a major shift.

The selection of a balance between shifting and shrinking does matter, however. Markets do not always adjust with ease. Market transactions are costly because parties often have difficulty getting adequate information. Individual suppliers, employees, and other participants may find it difficult to attempt a shift for themselves—locating new uses for their services, determining precisely what retraining they need, and ferreting out reliable buyers and sellers. On the other hand, networks of suppliers, managers, employees, dealers, and customers who have dealt with one another over a long period of time may have a sufficiently subtle understanding of one another's needs and performance that transactions among them are highly efficient. Under these circumstances, it is likely to be less costly for the company to shift them as a group than for individual actors to engage in a large number of "retail" transactions among strangers.

Besides potential efficiency advantages of internal redeployment, there may be social advantages as well. Companies like these exist at the center of intricate social networks. They anchor communities and define relationships and obligations over time. They shape community values as they order social life. Their sudden demise may rend the community irreparably.

This is not to suggest that shifting is always preferable to shrinking, either for the company or for society as a whole. Even if workers, financial intermediaries, and other constituents were perfectly willing to invest in a wholesale shift, there simply may be no profitable alternative for the specialized networks of people that would justify the investment. The point is that shifting is *sometimes* preferable.

Such shifts nevertheless are unlikely to take place if each of the company's constituencies remains unwilling to sacrifice, either waiting for other constituents to make the first move, or appropriating assistance for its own outside uses. Under this logic, the outside assistance provided in the cases described above should have been used for shifting, rather than

200

for compensating employees, suppliers, creditors, or other parties for sacrifices they were making in light of the cash crisis then affecting the companies. Otherwise, the assistance would simply amount to a transfer of wealth from one group (taxpayers or shareholders of the lead bank) to those being compensated. No real shift would occur.

The tension between wealth transfer and investment exists to a degree in all of our cases. For example, Alfred Kahn, then chairman of the Council on Wage and Price Stability, caused a stir when he pointed out that the initial deal struck between the United Auto Workers and Chrysler, while saving the firm between $203 million and $206 million in wages and benefits relative to the old contract, nevertheless would cost the company $1.3 billion over current wages during the three years of the contract.[88] This amount was just shy of the $1.5 billion loan guarantee that the company was seeking. Without more sacrifice from the union, therefore, it appeared that the government assistance would merely go into the pockets of Chrysler workers, leaving the company unchanged. As we might expect, more sacrifices were demanded as a condition of the loan guarantee. British Leyland, by contrast, did not have to cope with an Alfred Kahn. The bulk of government assistance to the troubled company in that case went to the workers for salary increases and severance payments, rather than toward new products and processes.

To the extent that the tacit goal of the assistance was simply to slow the pace of shrinkage, it did not matter that funds were diverted from investment into such payoffs. After all, the payoffs accomplished approximately the same underlying objective—they helped ease the pain of adjusting to a much smaller company by compensating those who otherwise would be hurt. But to the extent that new investment and internal redeployment was considered socially preferable to an "orderly" shrinkage and external redeployment, then the diversion was perverse. It prevented internal shifts.

Of all our cases, Toyo Kogyo shifted the most and shrunk the least. Its employment declined by only twenty-seven percent during the crisis. At the same time it completely transformed its manufacturing process and produced a wide array of new models. Most of the assistance provided to the company by the Sumitomo Group and, indirectly, by the regional and national governments, was invested in the shift. There were no payoffs, aside from continued interest payments to the banks on the company's accumulated debt. Suppliers and dealers continued to absorb losses; managers and employees took major cuts in wages and benefits; five thousand

88. *Senate Hearings, supra* note 70, at 701 (statement of Alfred Kahn, Chairman, Council on Wage and Price Stability).

201

production employees were temporarily transferred to dealers. Even when Toyo Kogyo sold its stock and real estate holdings to raise additional cash, it maintained the ability to summon these resources back to the fold, the purchasers being other members of the Sumitomo Group which, in effect, merely held these assets until Toyo Kogyo was able to reclaim them.[89] Thus, Toyo Kogyo managed better than the other companies in our sample to preserve its network of people and assets during the crisis, and simultaneously to shift them to new production.

At the other end of the spectrum lies British Leyland, which shrunk more than it shifted. It cut the size of its workforce by fifty-two percent during its crisis, but did not fundamentally alter its products, manufacturing processes, or organization. As we have seen, most of the assistance was diverted into payoffs. Neither the employees, suppliers, dealers, nor banks bore any special sacrifice. Most of the bailout amounted to a simple transfer by which British taxpayers compensated those who otherwise might have been burdened by the company's contraction.

III.   Explanations

The discussion above has identified two related phenomena in the four crisis-ridden companies—shrinking and shifting. Once the company received extraordinary assistance, the pace of its shrinkage was linked both to the likelihood of continued political interference in financial administrators' efforts to return the company to solvency, and to the economy's overall ability to absorb idled resources. The extent to which the company shifted its resources to more profitable pursuits rather than simply let them flow out, however, seems to have been related to how tightly the extraordinary assistance was tied to company investments instead of payoffs to its constituents.

Interestingly, the two relationships appear to have moved in the opposite direction: the slower the pace of shrinkage, the smaller the proportion of resources ultimately shifted. British Leyland's overall pace of shrinkage while it received assistance was the slowest of our four examples, and it also shifted the least. Toyo Kogyo's pace of shrinkage during its crisis was faster than that of British Leyland, but it shifted the most. AEG-Telefunken and Chrysler were in the middle on both scales.

Explanations are not difficult to find. The Japanese economy was performing relatively well during this period. Its unemployment averaged under 2.5% of the labor force, and overall productivity was improving

89. Yamada Interview, *supra* note 28.

202

3.8% a year.[90] So we might expect that such adjustments—substantial internal shifts of resources coupled with the rapid release of whatever marginal resources could not be used even if the shift were highly successful—would characterize many large companies. On the other hand, during British Leyland's crisis, the British economy was performing poorly, with unemployment averaging six percent of the labor force and creeping upward. Yearly productivity improvements averaged only about 0.1%.[91] Under these circumstances rapid shrinkage was politically problematic, and shifts were far more difficult to negotiate because every major transaction was a zero-sum game.

It seems equally plausible, however, that cause and effect ran in the opposite direction. Perhaps one explanation for Japan's relatively low unemployment and high rates of productivity improvement during these tumultuous years of oil shocks, world recessions, and rapid technological changes was the capacity of its large manufacturing enterprises to respond very rapidly—in our parlance, to shrink quickly and shift substantially. And perhaps one explanation for Britain's relatively poor performance lay in the comparative inability of its large manufacturers to do the same. The United States and West Germany, whose economic performance during these years fell between the two poles, also occupied intermediate points in the relative responsiveness of their larger manufacturers to rapid economic change.

Viewed in this light, the important distinction among our examples concerns not so much the intensity of political demands to save jobs—the pressures were intense and the governments highly responsive in all four cases. Rather, the important distinction is how the companies, and the set of institutions of which they were a part, responded to these demands. Toyo Kogyo's response was to jettison quickly a relatively small number of jobs and to shift the rest. British Leyland's response was to jettison slowly many of its jobs. AEG and Chrysler each attempted some of both.

How can we account for these differences in the patterns of response? A rescue was organized in all four cases, but the rescues were substantially different. Key institutions—labor, finance, and government—assumed different sets of responsibilities and undertook them in different ways. These variations resulted from the formal laws and informal understandings which governed the relationships among key institutions. The following sections explore some of these differences and the effects they had on the nature of the bailout in each instance.

90. For an analysis of all four countries' economic performances over the past five years, see U.S. Dep't of Commerce, 10 INT'L ECON. INDICATORS (1984).
91. *Id.*

203

A. *Information and Control*

One important difference is found in the timeliness and accuracy of information received about the company's difficulties by those with sufficient resources or influence to effectuate a rescue. Presumably, the earlier, more reliable, and more detailed that information, the easier it was to set a new course by shifting resources. Information coming much later, or of poorer quality, impaired the ability of the rescuers to do very much other than preside over a gradual shrinkage.

In the Toyo Kogyo case, the Sumitomo Bank knew of the firm's problems almost at once. Toyo Kogyo had done well in 1973, but the rapid rise in oil prices during the year made 1974 a disaster, causing the company to post a loss of $75 million. By October 1974, the bank had sent two of its senior officials over to Toyo Kogyo to take on financial management of the firm temporarily. These officials thereafter supplied the bank with highly detailed information about all aspects of the firm's problems, and paved the way for a larger rescue team which took over day-to-day management entirely.[92]

It was somewhat more difficult for the Dresdner Bank to get timely and accurate information about AEG's problems. Although the bank's chief executive also served as director of AEG's supervisory board, the board was slow to obtain detailed information, largely because of the tensions between labor and management representatives on the board.[93] Losses mounted steadily for six years before they reached the crisis level of $580 million in 1979, finally forcing Dresdner Bank's hand.

Chrysler's problems were even better hidden. Manufacturers Hanover Trust Co. received the same quarterly reports that investment analysts and shareholders received, but these merely summarized Chrysler's gradually worsening position, without explanation. Sometimes the figures masked reality. In 1978, for example, when slumping car sales began to push the company into the red and forced it to halt production at many plants and slash dividends by sixty percent, the company still managed to project a fourth-quarter profit. Thanks to a little-noticed actuarial adjustment, Chrysler merely changed the assumed rate of return on its employee pension portfolio to seven percent from six percent, reducing pension costs and adding about $50 million to its profits.[94] Manufacturers Hanover did not receive even moderately accurate projections of the firm's earnings or explanations of its problems until the Treasury Department's auditors

---

92. Yamada Interview, *supra* note 28.
93. *See infra* text accompanying notes 106 and 107.
94. Wall St. J., June 20, 1980, at 1, col. 6.

and research began to obtain better information as a condition for the loan guarantee.[95] By then, the crisis was well underway.

British Leyland is the extreme case. Although news that British Leyland had problems came relatively early, there was very little information about the problems themselves, or the prospects for solving them. When the firm went to the government at the end of 1974, its losses for the year were only $46 million—small by comparison with AEG-Telefunken or Chrysler. BL's banks, which had just refused to provide the company with any more loans, knew only that the firm's cash position was deteriorating rapidly. The government thereupon appointed a special commission to investigate, but the resulting *Ryder Report* contained no detailed assessments or projections. Its authors had done little more than ask BL management what new strategies the firm would pursue if money were no object, and report the results back to the House of Commons.[96] Nor was the National Enterprise Board equipped to diagnose BL's disease and prescribe a remedy, since it dealt with BL's managers at arm's length. Moreover, although BL officials filed reports with the NEB, the NEB—in sharp contrast to Sumitomo Bank—had no staff with particular expertise in the automobile industry.

The four sets of rescuers also differed considerably in their ability to affect a change in management or impose a new direction on the firm. Both the Sumitomo Bank and Dresdner Bank took the initiative in removing top managers who had presided over the firms' deepening problems and found new managers to replace them. The Sumitomo Bank continued to maintain tight control over Toyo Kogyo's rescue; the Dresdner Bank had a less direct role. At British Leyland, the National Enterprise Board selected the company's chief executives, but had no direct role in managing the company; the banks played no part. In the Chrysler case, the government also initiated the change by making it clear to Chrysler's board of directors that a management change was a precondition for a loan guarantee. The government, however, had no direct role in selecting a successor or in managing the company. As with BL, the banks to which Chrysler was indebted played no part.

These differences are attributable largely to differences in the relationships between banks, companies, and governments in the four nations, a subject to which we now turn.

---

95. Manufacturers Hanover Interview, *supra* note 33.
96. *See generally* RYDER REPORT, *supra* note 16.

1.   *Financial Linkages: Japan*

In Japan, the lead bank for a company plays a key role in that company's long-term development, as well as in the long-term development of other companies in the same industrial group. Banks are permitted to lend substantial portions of their capital to individual companies, and may also hold up to five percent of the outstanding shares of any company. Other companies within the industrial group also hold shares in the bank and in one another.[97] In 1975, at the start of Toyo Kogyo's crisis, the Sumitomo Bank was responsible for more than sixteen percent of Toyo Kogyo's accumulated debt and it held five percent of Toyo Kogyo's shares. Toyo Kogyo held three percent of the shares of the bank. Given these relationships, it is not surprising that Toyo Kogyo routinely shared confidential information with the bank, and that when the crisis occurred Kohei Matsuda, the company's president, put up only minor resistance to the bank's rapid takeover.

In addition to close relations to companies, Japanese banks are linked tightly to government agencies—the Ministry of Finance, the Ministry of International Trade and Industry, and the central bank. Banks are the primary intermediaries between savers and borrowers, but the banks must rely on the central bank for some of their capital. Because government officials set interest rates at the central bank lower than the demand for funds otherwise would dictate, the banks must depend on the discretion of the central bankers and government authorities for the amount of funds they receive. This "window guidance" makes bank officials particularly sensitive to the inclinations of policymakers and politicians.[98] In the Toyo Kogyo case it was clear that government officials were concerned about the firm's future and wanted to restore its competitiveness, but they also wanted to preserve jobs.

These two binding relationships—between the lead bank and its client companies on the one hand, and the lead bank and the government on the other—make the lead bank one of the major channels between government and individual companies in Japan. Rescues of companies in distress are timely and effective largely because of this deeply-entrenched public role of the lead bank. Commenting on the Sumitomo Bank's rescue of Toyo Kogyo, one of the bank executives who had temporarily managed the troubled firm explained:

---

97.   *See* Anti-monopoly and Fair Trade Maintenance Act, art. 11 (Japan), *reproduced in* Z. KITA-GAWA, DOING BUSINESS IN JAPAN, app. 7a-16 (1984).

98.   *See* J. ZYSMAN, GOVERNMENTS, MARKETS, AND GROWTH: FINANCIAL SYSTEMS AND THE POLITICS OF INDUSTRIAL CHANGE 248-50 (1983).

[I]n Japan, banks are private profit-making operations. But at the same time, banks have a social obligation to make sure that their clients are healthy. Had Sumitomo Bank merely tried to get its loan to Toyo Kogyo repaid, it might have succeeded by forcing the company into bankruptcy. But the bank would have been criticized by society. It would have gotten a reputation for being unreliable. One of the bank's goals is to avoid that kind of criticism.[99]

2. Financial Linkages: West Germany

The relationship between banks and companies in West Germany is similar to that in Japan. West German banks exercise extraordinary control over company access to capital; there are few other institutions which channel savings to borrowers.[100] By law, the banks can represent shareholders who deposit their shares with the banks.[101] Because only the banks are allowed to trade on the floor of the West German stock exchanges, and therefore have the best knowledge of stock performance, most shareholders take advantage of this service. In 1974, the latest date for which such data are available, West German banks held proxies for sixty-three percent of the shares of the nation's seventy-four largest publicly-held companies.[102] Banks are also permitted to purchase directly up to 100% of the shares of a company,[103] although it is considered imprudent for them to invest substantial portions of their capital in any single company.

As a result of these linkages, the banks in West Germany control a majority of the shares of companies to which they lend money. In 1974, for example, banks were represented on practically all of the supervisory boards of the seventy-four largest companies in the nation, and bank representatives chaired half of them.[104] Control is further centralized in West Germany's three largest banks—the Deutsche, Commerz, and Dresdner —which in 1974 supplied two-thirds of the bankers chairing such supervisory boards and voted thirty-five percent of the outstanding shares of the largest companies.[105]

The banks' control of AEG-Telefunken fits this pattern. At the height of the firm's crisis, the Dresdner Bank was its chief creditor; the bank also

---

99. Yamada Interview, *supra* note 28.
100. *See* J. CARRINGTON & G. EDWARDS, FINANCING INDUSTRIAL INVESTMENT 117, 120 (1979).
101. Aktiengesetz § 135, 1965 Bundesgesetzblatt [BGBl] I 1089 (W. Ger.).
102. SCHRIFTENREIHE DES BUNDESMINISTERIUMS DER FINANZEN, BERICHT DER STUDIENKOMMISSION, GRUNDSATZFRAGEN DER KREDIDWIRTSCHAFT, heft 28 (1979).
103. Aktiengesetz § 135, 1965 BGBl I 1089 (W. Ger.).
104. SCHRIFTENREIHE DES BUNDESMINISTERIUMS DER FINANZEN, *supra* note 102, heft 28.
105. *Id.*

207

directly held more than eighteen percent of the company's outstanding shares. With the proxies of AEG shares deposited with the bank or lent to it by other banks, the Dresdner Bank effectively controlled a majority of the company's shares. This explains why Hans Friderichs, the bank's chief executive, also came to be the chairman of AEG's supervisory board. It also helps explain why the bank assumed responsibility for arranging first the "private" bailout of the firm, and then the public one: the bank simply had too much at stake in AEG to let the firm go under all at once.

In these respects, the relationship between the Dresdner Bank and AEG paralleled that between the Sumitomo Bank and Toyo Kogyo. There were important differences, however. The Dresdner Bank did not have access to the same quality of information about AEG that Sumitomo had about Toyo Kogyo, nor at quite such an early stage of the crisis. The Dresdner Bank could neither place bank officers in key positions within AEG, as Sumitomo had done with Toyo Kogyo, nor accomplish the dramatic changes that the Sumitomo Bank managed at Toyo Kogyo in a relatively short time.

The ability of Dresdner Bank to control outcomes at AEG was also compromised by divisions on AEG's supervisory board. As AEG's financial position deteriorated in the middle and late 1970's, its board was unable to agree on a diagnosis or a plan of action. Not trusting the bank representatives to act in the best interest of labor, the representatives of labor on the board withheld certain information in their possession.[106] Not trusting labor to maintain confidentiality, management and the bank representatives also withheld information.[107] As the crisis deepened in 1979, the board was deadlocked. The Dresdner Bank refused to seek assistance from the government because it feared that such a move would give labor a greater voice in the management of the company, and ultimately in the management of the economy. It therefore turned for help to other banks, industrial companies, and insurance companies, while labor simultaneously sought help from the government. Even by 1982, when the bank was forced to go to the government, it negotiated separately from labor. In short, the ongoing power struggle in which the Dresdner Bank found itself impaired its ability to manage AEG's rescue.

In addition, it is important to note that West German banks are not politically accountable for their major decisions[108] despite all their power over the economy. The Dresdner Bank thus never assumed the same pub-

---

106. Interview with an official of the Dresdner Bank (name withheld by request), in Cambridge, Mass. (Jan. 12, 1984) [hereinafter cited as Dresdner Interview].

107. *Id.*

108. *See, e.g.,* J. ZYSMAN, *supra* note 98, at 260.

208

lic responsibilities for West German economic development that the Sumitomo Bank assumed for Japanese development. Unlike the Sumitomo Bank, the Dresdner Bank was not an agent of government policy.

3. *Financial Fragmentation: United States*

Banks in the United States maintain arm's-length relationships both with companies and with the government. This helps to explain why Chrysler's lead bank, Manufacturers Hanover, had neither early warning of Chrysler's problems, nor the ability to solve the problems even if it had received warning. The arm's length relationship between banks and companies is required by law. In general, financial institutions in the United States may not hold shares in separate business enterprises.[109] National banks, bank holding companies and insurance companies are typically permitted to engage (either directly or through a subsidiary) only in businesses bearing a close relationship to traditional banking or insurance functions.[110] In addition, the Glass-Steagall Act limits the role of commercial banks in underwriting and purchasing securities and specifically prohibits them from making investments in corporate securities for their own account.[111] Further restrictions on bank investments were embodied in the Bank Holding Company Act, which was designed to extend the principle of separation of banking from commerce to entities that own or control banks.[112] Similar restrictions on investments by state chartered banks exist

109. The Bank Holding Company Act, 12 U.S.C. § 1843 (1982), generally prohibits bank holding companies from engaging in nonbank activities.

110. *See, e.g.,* Bank Holding Company Act, 12 U.S.C. § 1843(c)(8) (1982) (a bank holding company may invest in a company which the Board of Governors of the Federal Reserve determines "to be so closely related to banking or managing or controlling banks as to be a proper incident thereto"); N.Y. BANKING LAW § 96.1 (McKinney 1971 & Supp. 1984) (banks may "exercise all such incidental powers as shall be necessary to carry on the business of banking"); N.Y. INS. LAW § 46-a1(a) (McKinney 1971 & Supp. 1984) (insurance companies may invest in subsidiaries engaged in insurance or investment related business); CONN. GEN. STAT. § 38-146a (1983) (Connecticut mutual life insurance companies can invest in subsidiaries engaged in insurance or investment-related business).

111. 12 U.S.C. § 24 (1982). Under 12 U.S.C. § 335, the provisions of 12 U.S.C. § 24 also apply to restrict the investment of state member banks of the Federal Reserve System.

112. Section 4(c)(5) of the Bank Holding Company Act (BHCA), 12 U.S.C. § 1843(c)(5) (1982), permits a bank holding company to invest in "shares which are of the kinds and amounts eligible for investment" by a national bank under 12 U.S.C. § 24 (thus embodying the limited exceptions to the Glass-Steagall Act). Section 4(c)(6) of the BHCA, 12 U.S.C. § 1843(c)(6) (1982), permits a holding company to own no more than five percent of the outstanding voting shares of any company. Although an equity investment of up to five percent might be insignificant, investments of five percent each by a number of bank holding companies could be substantial in the aggregate. However, there is a substantial risk that such joint investments of less than five percent each could be unprotected by § 4(c)(6). *See* 12 C.F.R. 225.137 (1984) ("the exemption was not intended to allow a group of holding companies, through concerted action, to engage in an activity as entrepreneurs"). Section 4(c)(2) of the BHCA provides an exemption to bank holding companies or any of their subsidiaries for shares acquired in satisfaction of "a debt previously contracted." 12 U.S.C. § 1843(c)(2) (1982). Unless such shares represent less than five percent of the total outstanding shares, they may only be held for a period of two years (which may be extended at the discretion of the Federal Reserve Board).

209

under various state laws.[113] Although insurance companies are generally permitted to make equity investments under state laws, such laws frequently require the investments to be made in corporations with a specified level of financial performance and strength.[114]

In addition to these limitations on equity ownership, banks in the United States may not extend loans which exceed ten percent of the bank's capital to an individual company.[115] Moreover, banks generally may not do business in more than one state.[116] On the other hand, specialized investment banks are permitted to hold shares,[117] but, because they are not allowed to accept deposits, they have comparatively few resources to invest. Such banks function primarily to maintain secondary markets for commercial paper and corporate bonds.

Most of these restrictions originated in the 1930's to help ensure bank solvency and credibility, and some are gradually succumbing to the forces of deregulation and competition.[118] These restrictions have had the effect of fragmenting and decentralizing financial intermediaries in the United States, so that no large company is particularly dependent upon any single financial institution, or vice versa. Chrysler was indebted to more than 400 separate banks; it also had substantial amounts of commercial paper and corporate bonds outstanding. By the same token, even Manufacturers Hanover, Chrysler's chief lender, regarded Chrysler as but one of a large number of clients about whom the bank knew relatively little.[119] The loan officer in charge of the Chrysler account had no particular knowledge about Chrysler or the automobile industry; indeed, his portfolio of ac-

---

113. For example, New York banks generally may not purchase the stock of other corporations. Although Section 97.5 of the New York Banking Law provides that a New York bank may acquire "[s]o much of the capital stock of any other corporation as may be specifically authorized by the laws of this state or by resolution of the banking board upon a three-fifths vote of all its members," the investments which are "specifically authorized" are not numerous. A provision similar to the exemption in 12 U.S.C. § 1843(c)(2) is also present in the New York statute, N.Y. BANKING LAW § 97.5 (McKinney 1971 & Supp. 1984).

114. McCarran-Ferguson Act, 15 U.S.C. § 1011 (1982) (states given authority to regulate the business of insurance). Under New York law, an insurance company may not invest in common stock unless the issuing institution earned enough in the aggregate to pay a dividend of four percent on all stocks and shares outstanding for each of the seven years preceding the acquisition by an insurer. N.Y. INS. LAW § 81(13)(a) (McKinney Supp. 1984). Various limitations are also placed on such equity investments in terms of a percentage of the insurer's total assets. See N.Y. INS. LAW § 81(13)(b) (McKinney Supp. 1984).

115. This restriction applies only to national banks. See 12 U.S.C. § 84(a)(2) (1982).

116. 12 U.S.C. § 36(c) (1982).

117. Banking Act of 1933, §§ 20-21, 12 U.S.C. §§ 78, 377, 378 (1982); see also 4 F. SOLOMON, W. SCHLICHTING, T. RICE & J. COOPER, BANKING LAW § 80.22(3) (1984) [hereinafter cited as F. SOLOMON]; Clark & Summers, Judicial Interpretation of Glass Steagall: The Need for Legislative Action, 97 BANKING L.J. 721 (1980).

118. See, e.g., Nationwide Banking: Barriers Fall, N.Y. Times, June 4, 1983, at 29, col. 3; America's Debut in Offshore Banking, N.Y. Times, Nov. 22, 1981, at F1, col. 2.

119. Interview with Manufacturers Hanover Trust Co. loan officer (name withheld by request), in New York City (Jan. 10, 1984).

counts was arranged geographically, rather than by industrial sector.[120] He periodically reviewed Chrysler's balance sheets and income statements to assure that they technically conformed to bank credit requirements. He was not trained to analyze financial projections or strategic plans, even had Chrysler been willing to give them to him.[121]

Even if bank managers possessed the skills, knowledge, and authority needed to deal with problems such as those experienced by Chrysler, it was not clear that they would have wanted to become deeply involved in developing a solution. Financial institutions in the U.S. which wish to participate in the debtor's management risk creating a relationship that will cause them to be deemed "in control" of the debtor. This may subject them to substantial liability under United States bankruptcy, securities and tax laws.[122] Even if a lender is not actually in control of a debtor, allegations that such control exists can result in expensive litigation.

In addition, corporate laws of various states draw a relatively sharp distinction between the fiduciary duties owed creditors and those owed shareholders.[123] Chrysler managers had a legal responsibility to act in the best interest of Chrysler shareholders, not in the best interest of the bank's shareholders.[124] Had the bank required as a condition of a loan that

---

120. *Id.*

121. *Id.*

122. Under the Bankruptcy Code, "insiders" are subject to possible recovery preferences during the one year period preceding the commencement of a bankruptcy case, while other persons are subject to such recoveries only during the ninety-day period preceding the commencement of a case. 11 U.S.C. § 547(b)(4) (1982). An "insider" is defined to include a director, officer, or person in control of the debtor. 11 U.S.C. § 101(25) (1982). Moreover, the bankruptcy court has the power to subordinate one claim to another on considerations of equity and fairness. 11 U.S.C. § 510(c) (1982). A creditor in control of a debtor can expect that it will be met with allegations that its claim should be equitably subordinated if not disallowed.

Although there is no specific statutory definition of "control" in either the Securities Act of 1933, 15 U.S.C. § 77b (1982), or the Securities Exchange Act of 1934, 15 U.S.C. § 78c (1982), the Securities and Exchange Commission broadly defines control as "the possession, direct or indirect, of the power to direct or cause the direction of the management and policies of a person, whether through the ownership of voting securities, by contract, or otherwise." 17 C.F.R. 230.405 (1984). Therefore, a creditor which directly participates in or selects management runs the risk of being considered to be in control of the debtor. *See, e.g., In re* Falstaff Brewing Corp. Antitrust Litig., 441 F. Supp. 62 (E.D. Mo. 1977) (lender that controls the daily affairs of borrower corporation can be held liable for corporation's Securities Exchange Act of 1934 violations).

123. The fiduciary duty of corporate directors and officers to stockholders includes a duty to act loyally, in good faith, and without assuming any position in conflict with the interest of the corporation. 19 C.J.S. *Corporations* § 761 (1940). No such fiduciary duty automatically exists with respect to creditors; directors and officers are merely agents of the corporation. 19 C.J.S. *Corporations* § 837 (1940).

124. *See, e.g.,* Newman v. Forward Lands, Inc., 418 F.Supp. 135, 136 (E.D. Pa. 1976) (the directors "had a duty to exercise in managing [the company's] affairs, but the duty was owed only to the corporation itself and not to" those outside the corporation); Rosebud Corp. v. Boggio, 39 Colo. App. 95, 561 P.2d 367 (1977) (managers of solvent corporation are primarily responsible to the corporation, though managers of insolvent corporation may be trustees for the entity and for its creditors).

211

Chrysler change its management or take some other action that might harm Chrysler shareholders—for example, selling off a valuable property to pay off corporate debts—Chrysler's shareholders could have a right of action against the bank.[125]

These fiduciary obligations obviously constrain the banks from asserting control over distressed companies. It is interesting to note that during the years immediately preceding Chrysler's crisis, the chairman of the board of Manufacturers Hanover, Gabriel Hauge, also was a member of Chrysler's board of directors—an interlocking relationship of the sort which flourished between Sumitomo Bank and Toyo Kogyo, and Dresdner Bank and AEG-Telefunken. Unlike the situations in Japan and West Germany, however, this relationship was purely cosmetic. It may have impressed a few shareholders or smaller creditors, but as a practical matter Hauge had to be careful not to pass information he learned at the Chrysler board meetings to the commercial loan department of the bank, lest he place himself in a conflict of interest and thereby invite a suit by Chrysler shareholders.[126]

The U.S. government, like the West German government, has no particular substantive authority over the banks, although it closely regulates them to ensure solvency and prudence. The government collects a large amount of information about individual companies in tax filings, securities filings, reviews of regulatory compliance, and reviews of proposed mergers and acquisitions. Most of these data, however, are in the wrong form to provide adequate warning that a major company is in trouble, or are dispersed among so many agencies that they often cannot be reconstructed without contravening laws which protect confidentiality.[127] This inadequacy explains why, when Chrysler came to the White House seeking help, the Carter Administration had to commission a variety of studies by

125. *See, e.g.*, State Nat'l Bank of El Paso v. Farah Mfg. Co., Inc., 678 S.W.2d 661 (Tex. App. 1984) (creditor held liable to debtor for damages resulting from creditor's efforts to prevent one individual from becoming chief executive officer and to retain in his place management more sympathetic to the creditor's concerns); Connor v. Great Western Sav. and Loan Ass'n, 68 Cal.2d 850, 864-66, 447 P. 2d 609, 616-17, 73 Cal. Rptr. 369, 376-77 (1968) (lender became participant in home construction enterprise by entering business relationships with the developer as well as lending capital, and thus was liable to the home buyers for structural defects).

126. Interview with Paul Hunn, Vice-President, Manufacturers Hanover Trust Co., in Cambridge, Mass. (March 7, 1984) [hereinafter cited as Hunn Interview].

127. Most agencies forbid inter-agency and inter-governmental flow of information. For example, in the Tax Reform Act of 1976, Congress provided that all tax returns and information were confidential and, thus, not routinely subject to disclosure to federal or state agencies. 26 U.S.C. § 6103 (1982). Similarly, information gathered by the Federal Trade Commission is confidential and may be shared with other federal agencies only in disaggregated form, with limitations on the use of such data. 15 U.S.C. § 57b-2 (1982). The Bureau of the Census may not disseminate census data in any form whereby an individual establishment might be identified, nor use the data for other than statistical purposes. 13 U.S.C. § 9(a) (1982).

212

private accountants, investment bankers, and management consultants in order to elicit useful information about the company's plight and future prospects, rather than rely on data already in the government's possession.

4. Financial Fragmentation: Great Britain

If anything, British banks are even further removed from the companies to which they lend money than are U.S. banks. The City of London, Britain's "Wall Street," is oriented to an international financial market in which capital is highly mobile. As a result, financial relationships are fragmented. Loans tend to be short-term (more than eighty percent are due to be paid within a year),[128] and British companies typically finance their expansion through retained earnings and new issues of stock.[129] In addition, the fiduciary obligations governing banks and company managers are at least as strict as those in the United States.[130] For these reasons, the banks play no significant role in monitoring or rescuing large firms in distress. British Leyland's major creditors had no inside information about the company's mounting problems, and no particular capacity to do anything about them.[131]

---

128. J. CARRINGTON & G. EDWARDS, supra note 100, at 129.

129. J. ZYSMAN, supra note 98, at 193.

130. For a comprehensive analysis of fiduciary duties in England, see H. SHELDON & P. FIDLER, SHELDON & FIDLER'S PRACTICE AND LAW OF BANKING 35-65 (11th ed. 1982).

131. Although the relationships between a troubled company and its bank, and the bank and the government, are more attenuated in Great Britain than in our other examples, the relationship between distressed companies and the goverment is closer. Britain is the only nation of the four to have embraced public ownership as a general solution to the problem of large companies in distress, or to have permanently created a special institution of government to oversee such rescues. Perhaps the two phenomena are related: with the banks unwilling to back up such companies or help oversee their revival, the burden has fallen entirely upon government to meet resulting political demands for special assistance.

The National Enterprise Board, which oversaw most of the rescue of British Leyland, was conceived as a kind of state "holding company" whose purpose, according to its guidelines, was to "combine the advantages of public sector financial resources and the private sector's entrepreneurial approach to decisionmaking." NATIONAL ENTERPRISE BOARD, ANNUAL REPORT AND ACCOUNTS 1977, at 56-59 (1978). Board members were appointed by the Secretary of State for Industry; the director and deputy of the board during this period were drawn from industry, and four of the nine part-time members were trade unionists. The board was authorized to make loans to troubled companies only at "commercial" rates of interest, and only to companies that eventually could become viable on their own. Lord Don Ryder, its first director, who presided over the initial stages of the British Leyland rescue, stated that "it is not part of NEB's policy to prop up non-viable companies simply to maintain jobs." NATIONAL ENTERPRISE BOARD, ANNUAL REPORT 3 (1976), cited in W. GRANT, THE POLITICAL ECONOMY OF INDUSTRIAL POLICY 106 n.13 (1982).

In addition, the NEB was not equipped to anticipate problem companies or to monitor and supervise the restructuring of the sort that a large company such as BL required. The Board had no particular knowledge of individual companies or industries; its relationship with BL, for example, was entirely by way of the chief executives whom the Board selected. The government could only approve or disapprove company decisions on the basis of limited financial data. Every request for funds or for additional funds, therefore, became a choice between acceding to the company or allowing it to fail. W. GRANT, supra, at 104-110.

213

B.   *Sacrifice*

Even if a rescuer has early and reliable information about a company's growing problems and asserts managerial control over the company, the "rescue" still is more likely to be an orderly shrink than a substantial shift, unless the other participants cooperate. In particular, workers must be willing to accept lower pay at least for a time, and to shift to new jobs within the company. Lenders must maintain their outstanding loans even in the face of higher risks, and perhaps advance additional credit. Without these sacrifices, new funds from the rescuer merely preserve the status quo for a time—maintaining existing wages and commercial credit while the company gradually shrinks.

The four cases represent a spectrum of sacrifice, with Toyo Kogyo and British Leyland once again occupying the extremes. Toyo Kogyo workers accepted major pay cuts, and many of them agreed to transfer temporarily to automobile dealers hundreds of miles away from Hiroshima. Similarly, Toyo Kogyo's banks, insurance companies, and suppliers agreed to maintain loans or advance credit. On the other hand, British Leyland workers resisted pay cuts and changes in work rules and job classifications, while private lenders called in their loans and refused to make new ones. AEG and Chrysler lie in between: AEG's lenders sacrificed, but its workers balked at major reductions in wages and benefits; Chrysler's lenders and workers both sacrificed, but only to a limited extent. This section attempts to account for these differences in the degree of sacrifice parties were willing to undertake.

1.   *Financial Interdependency*

One explanation is found in the structures of national financial markets. For the same reasons that lead banks in Japan and West Germany receive more timely and detailed information about their clients than "arm's-length" banks in the United States and Britain, they also are more committed to maintaining their clients. In these countries, even a gradual liquidation would be likely to impair the value of the bank's equity and jeopardize its major loans, both with the distressed company and also with a larger network of suppliers and industrial purchasers which depend on the company. These lead banks therefore are more likely to finance resource shifts than banks in the United States or Great Britain.

In addition, these lead banks are linked financially and strategically to other banks, insurance companies, and trade creditors. The lead banks, therefore, can facilitate the agreement of these other lenders to maintain their own outstanding loans to the troubled company, and even on occasion to provide new financing. These interdependent networks function as

214

systems of mutual aid. Lenders, in effect, insure one another against relatively sudden market changes which might threaten their survival.

In 1975, at the start of Toyo Kogyo's crisis, the Sumitomo *keiretsu* as a whole held almost eleven percent of Toyo Kogyo's shares and Toyo Kogyo had considerable holdings in other group members. The Sumitomo Bank also held nine percent of the shares of C. Itoh, the trading company outside the group on which the bank later called to help Toyo Kogyo. In addition to this financial tie, several members of the Sumitomo *keiretsu* supplied parts to Toyo Kogyo, or had common technological needs and therefore were engaged in joint ventures or joint purchasing arrangements. These financial and strategic ties enabled the bank to spread the cost and risk of the Toyo Kogyo rescue among many cooperating institutions. They also enabled the bank to make credible guarantees about the company's survival and thereby reduce the perceived riskiness on new loans. Given all these interdependencies, the Sumitomo Bank's announcement that it would stand by Toyo Kogyo made other lenders more willing to maintain their outstanding loans and commercial credits with the company.[132]

Like Sumitomo in the Toyo Kogyo case, the Dresdner Bank was able to call on other banks and insurance companies to help AEG. For some of these participants the stake was more direct: twenty four of these banks held almost fifty percent of the AEG's outstanding shares; the Deutsche Bank alone held nine percent. The Dresdner Bank could also count on the support of a small group of industrial companies. Although this group was not as formally organized and integrated as the Sumitomo Group, its ties were similarly strategic and financial. Through its close relationship with AEG, the Dresdner Bank gradually had developed expertise in the electronics and capital goods industries in which AEG competed; the bank therefore organized its industrial loan department along these sectors.[133] In this way, over time, many AEG suppliers and industrial purchasers became clients of the bank. These interdependencies were reinforced as the bank took equity positions in these companies.

There was no similar, mutually dependent network on which Chrysler or British Leyland could rely. As we have seen, British Leyland's banks backed out early in the crisis.[134] Chrysler's banks agreed to extend the maturity of some notes in 1980, and in 1981 they agreed to convert approximately one-third of the company's outstanding debt to equity and to write down another one-third. The banks, however, demanded full pay-

---

132. Yamada Interview, *supra* note 28; Maeda Interview, *supra* note 58.
133. Dresdner Interview, *supra* note 106.
134. *See supra* at 171.

215

ment on the final one-third, and throughout the crisis, they adamantly refused to extend new loans to the company. The few concessions they did make came largely as a result of pressure from the Treasury Department and the Federal Reserve Board.

To some extent, the comparative reticence of U.S. and British banks can be explained by differing auditing practices and financial regulations. Auditors and bank examiners in Japan and West Germany take a far more lenient view of non-performing loans than do their colleagues in the United States and Britain. In Japan and West Germany, debtors may violate loan covenants or miss interest payments without necessarily forcing the bank to write down the asset on its books. Because the debtor may well shift into a more profitable line of business, the loan is not necessarily considered to be riskier, or of lesser value, than it was before.[135] For the same reason, the bank also may advance new loans to such a company and carry the new loan as an asset.

In the United States and Britain, on the other hand, bank auditors and regulators are more concerned about the risk of inadequate capitalization. A bank typically is required to write down its non-performing loans;[136] it also may have to expand its loan-loss reserves in coming years. These items are charged off against earnings. If the distressed company subsequently repays the loan and any lost interest, these payments can be applied against whatever provisions have been made for the losses.[137] In the interim, however, the damage has already been done to the bank's reported profits, thereby impairing its ability to raise more capital. By the same token, new loans to a distressed company are scrutinized carefully; the bank probably would not be able to carry them as assets.

This cautious approach obviously makes banks more reluctant to accept temporary sacrifices. A Manufacturers Hanover vice president in charge of problem loans explained that the bank would never extend a new loan to a distressed company except as part of a plan to reduce the bank's overall embedded debt. Indeed, the bank followed this rule with respect to Chrysler and other banks took the same position.[138] Such a rule ultimately favors shrinkage over shifts.

Financial structures are only part of the story, of course. To understand why sacrifices were more widespread in Toyo Kogyo than in British Leyland—with AEG and Chrysler in between—we also need to examine the organization of labor.

---

135. Yamada Interview, *supra* note 28; Hunn Interview, *supra* note 126; *see also* Commercial Code, art. 281 (Japan), *reproduced in* Z. KITAGAWA, *supra* note 97, app. 5a-104.

136. *See* F. SOLOMON, *supra* note 117, at § 44.08(2).

137. Hunn Interview, *supra* note 126.

138. *Id.*

216

2. *Labor Interdependency*

By a variety of formal and informal rules, Japanese workers are tightly linked to their companies. The links are somewhat more attenuated in large West German companies. In the United States and Great Britain, such links are almost non-existent. These patterns are evident in the ways unions are organized, in the relations between unionized workers and managers, and in ways of providing job security and regulating wage differentials among workers.

In each of the four countries, workers are organized at several levels. At the bottom are local shop-floor organizations, which are aggregated into company unions or affiliates, then into industry unions, and finally into multi-industry labor federations. The locus of control differs in each country, however. In Japan, company unions predominate; most of the important decisions about wages and working-conditions are made at this level.[139] Company unions also are important in West Germany.[140] Unlike their Japanese counterparts, West German workers also participate through their unions in national negotiations over wages and macroeconomic policies.[141] Company unions are less important in the United States and Great Britain. In the United States, most bargaining occurs at the level of the industry union.[142] In Britain, bargaining occurs both at the shop floor and at the industry level.[143]

Formal relations between managers and unionized workers within the company are structured quite differently in the four countries. In most large Japanese companies there is no sharp distinction between supervisors and blue-collar workers. Japanese companies typically employ elaborate systems of joint consultation through which confidential management information is shared with lower-level employees. Japanese company unions include many white-collar supervisors, and the links between management and labor are reinforced by the fact that many company directors were once union leaders.[144] In West Germany, distinctions between production workers and supervisors are more clearly drawn, yet there exist a variety of consultative mechanisms. By law, union representatives occupy

---

139. *See, e.g.*, W. GOULD, JAPAN'S RESHAPING OF AMERICAN LABOR LAW 2 (1984); R. CLARK, THE JAPANESE COMPANY 50-55, 98-139 (1979).

140. E. CULLINGFORD, TRADE UNIONS IN WEST GERMANY 22 (1976); C. HANSON, S. JACKSON & D. MILLER, THE CLOSED SHOP: A COMPARATIVE STUDY IN PUBLIC POLICY AND TRADE UNION SECURITY IN BRITAIN, THE USA AND WEST GERMANY 191 (1982).

141. E. CULLINGFORD, *supra* note 140, at 17, 21.

142. *See* E. SMITH, TRADE UNIONS IN THE DEVELOPED ECONOMIES 169-70, 172-73 (1981).

143. *See* K. COATES & T. TOPHAM, TRADE UNIONS IN BRITAIN 166-67 (1980).

144. W. GOULD, *supra* note 139, at 4 ("of 313 major Japanese companies . . . 74.1 percent had at least one executive director who once had served as a labor union leader"). *See also* R. CLARK, *supra* note 139, at 109.

217

one-third to one-half of the seats on company supervisory boards, which have responsibility for major decisions affecting the company.[145] In the United States and Great Britain, on the other hand, managers and workers are sharply separated.

The National Labor Relations Act (NLRA), for example, presumes a fundamental conflict between managers and employees. Section 8(a)(2) makes it an unfair labor practice for employers to "dominate or interfere with the formation or administration of any labor organization or contribute financial or other support to it."[146] This provision has been construed broadly to bar management from supporting certain formal mechanisms of worker participation.[147] By the same token, supervisory employees are excluded from the provisions of the NLRA on the theory that the supervisor-employee relationship is necessarily adversarial and supervisors represent management; union membership, it is assumed, would involve them in a conflict of interest.[148] An American employer is under no obligation to open its financial records to its unions unless the company specifically pleads an inability to pay during collective bargaining.[149] Nor do employers have a duty to bargain about management decisions to close part of an operation.[150] The cumulative effect of these rules is to maintain an arm's length, adversarial relationship between management and employees.

Like American labor law, British labor law seems to presume a fundamental tension and separation between management and labor. For example, although British employers are obligated to disclose to the trade unions information without which the union representatives' collective bargaining efforts would be severely hampered,[151] this obligation is subject

145. Betriebsverfassungsgesetz, 1952 BGBl I 681 (W. Ger.); Mitbestimmungsgesetz, 1976 BGBl I 1153 (W. Ger.).

146. See 29 U.S.C. § 158(a)(2) (1982).

147. See, e.g., Homemaker Shops, Inc., 261 N.L.R.B. 441 (1982); Kaiser Foundation Hospitals, Inc., 223 N.L.R.B. 322 (1976); Midwest Piping and Supply Co., 63 N.L.R.B. 1060 (1945). When the United Auto Workers' president, Douglas Fraser, took a place on Chrysler's board of directors as a condition of union cooperation with the troubled company, the general counsel of the National Labor Relations Board declined to issue a complaint. The general counsel did so largely because the appointment created no financial ties between the company and the union. See N.L.R.B. Advice Memorandum, Case 7-CB-4815 (Oct. 22, 1980).

148. Justice Douglas' dissenting opinion in Packard Motor Co. v. NLRB, 330 U.S. 485 (1947), appears to have formed the rationale for the exclusion of supervisors under the 1947 Taft-Hartley amendments to the NLRA. In that case, Douglas argued that foremen should not be included as "employees" because a foreman's act—if attributable to management—might be an unfair labor practice, although—if the foreman were characterized as an "employee"—management would not be similarly liable. See id. at 496-497 (Douglas, J., dissenting).

149. NLRB v. Truitt Mfg. Co., 351 U.S. 149 (1956).

150. First Nat'l Maintenance Corp. v. NLRB, 452 U.S. 666 (1981).

151. Employment Protection Act, 1975, ch. 71, §§ 17-21.

218

to numerous qualifications and exceptions.[152] The ability of workers to obtain data from management is further compromised—and, thus, the separation between workers and management is preserved—by the uncertainty of the procedures for enforcing whatever obligations do exist.[153] British employers are required to give trade unions advance notice of and the reasons for plant closings; however, they, like their American counterparts, are under no affirmative duty to bargain over such managerial decisions.[154]

Finally, important differences also exist among these four countries in ways of providing job security and regulating wage differentials among workers. In Japan, employees of most large companies are hired directly from high school and expect to remain with the company until retirement; their wages and benefits depend largely on their age.[155] In West Germany job security is built into most labor contracts within large firms, as are generous severance payments in the event of necessary layoffs. Wage and benefit levels rise with the number of years the employee has served. In both West Germany and Japan, employers are required to provide employees with at least one month's advance notice of a plant shutdown.[156] In addition, employees have substantial rights in the event of an employer's insolvency: In West Germany, employees have a priority in bankruptcy, entitling them to sixty-eight percent average pay for one year; in Japan, they receive full wages for two years and eighty percent of the first three months' salary is provided by the state.[157]

In the United States and Great Britain, job security and relative wages have been more closely linked to job classifications, work rules, and seniority; rights and benefits vary with the category in which a worker is classified. Particularly in the United States, income-security provisions have substituted for job security. The government administers unemploy-

---

152. Employment Protection Act, 1975, ch. 71, § 18. One of these exceptions excuses the employer from disclosure "where the compilation or assembly [of the requested information] would involve an amount of work or expenditure out of useful proporation to the value of the information in the conduct of collective bargaining." Employment Protection Act, 1975, ch. 71, § 18(2)(b).

153. See P. DAVIES & M. FREEDLAND, LABOUR LAW: TEXT AND MATERIALS 154 (1979); see also Civil Service Union v. Central Arbitration Committee, [1980] INDUS. REL. L. REP. 274 (giving a broad reading to the exceptions to the disclosure requirement).

154. The elimination of jobs through plant closings in England is governed by the Redundancy Payments Act of 1965, codified in the Employment Protection Consolidation Act, 1978, ch. 44, §§ 81-92. The Redundancy Payments Act was designed to increase managerial freedom in the elimination of jobs, by providing lump sum payments to workers to make the dismissals more palatable. P. DAVIES & M. FREEDLAND, supra note 153, at 166. Although constraints on managerial discretion were imposed in 1975, see Employment Protection Act, 1975, ch. 71, §§ 99-107, British managers remain free of the duty to bargain over plant closings.

155. W. GOULD, supra note 139, at 1-11.

156. See generally I. MAGAZINER & R. REICH, MINDING AMERICA'S BUSINESS 143-54 (1983).

157. Id.

219

ment insurance, which pays approximately sixty percent of previous wages.[158] In many industries these benefits have been supplemented by unemployment benefits built into wage contracts.[159] If the company cannot then offer "suitable employment," workers who are at least forty-five years old can collect regular pensions, plus $400 monthly supplements until they become eligible for Social Security.

These different patterns of organization presumably influence workers' willingness to sacrifice in order to help a distressed company shift. Such shifts require flexibility in wages, benefits, and work responsibilities as alternatives to layoffs. Shifts also require external *inflexibility*—meaning that employees tend not to move between firms, but to remain with the same firm during the course of their career. This combination results in a great deal of mutual dependence between the company and the employee; both sides can draw upon a reservoir of trust and simultaneously rely on the discipline of future dealings. In consequence, unionized workers will be more willing to reduce wages and shift jobs during bad times than they would be otherwise.[160]

Japan's system of company negotiations, combined with lifetime job security (in the largest firms) and age-based wages, is the most internally flexible of the four. When a Japanese company suddenly begins to lose money, it can quickly reduce its workers' wages and benefits, and shift job responsibilities. The Japanese system is also externally rigid: with lifetime employment as the norm, it is difficult for a worker to leave one large company and find employment with another. Like those of the lead banks, workers' fates are linked to that of the company. Toyo Kogyo's company union accepted pay raises lower than those received by workers

---

158. Unemployment insurance is administered jointly by the federal and state governments. Because the states administer the programs—setting eligibility requirements and compensation rates—the benefits paid may vary from state to state. Most states pay unemployment benefits at a rate equal to about sixty percent of a worker's salary prior to loss of employment, subject to certain limits. *See, e.g.*, CONN. GEN. STAT. § 31-231a (1983); MICH. COMP. LAWS § 421.27(b)(1) (West Supp. 1984). The states collect taxes to pay unemployment benefits; these taxes are then paid into the federal government's Unemployment Trust Fund, from which the states are reimbursed for their expenditures. 42 U.S.C. § 1104 (1982). The federal government also disburses funds to the states to help pay the costs of administering unemployment benefit programs. 42 U.S.C. §§ 501-503 (1982).

159. In steel, aluminum, and canmaking, for example, workers with twenty years of service are guaranteed supplemental unemployment benefit (SUB) payments for two years, even if the union's own SUB funds are exhausted.

160. A moment's reflection will suggest how this relationship works. Suppose that a firm's managers contend that demand has declined and that workers therefore should reduce their wages. If the workers agree, the firm can have the same work as before but at a lower cost. But why should the workers believe the managers? They might believe them if they had built up a long-term relationship of trust and confidence, and the managers had shared company data with the union. But if the workers did not believe the claim, they could reduce the rewards to misrepresentation by refusing to cut their wages and forcing the firm to reduce its wage bill by cutting employment instead. For a general treatment of this subject, see Goldberg, *Relational Exchange: Economics and Complex Contracts*, 23 AM. BEHAV. SCI. 347 (1980).

at other automobile companies and agreed to the transfer of 5000 workers to Toyo Kogyo dealers.

AEG's workers were less inclined to accept wage and benefit reductions. In West Germany, national labor negotiations may have reduced the flexibility of the company union. Officials at IG Metall, the national union that represented many of AEG's workers, were concerned that any concession at the company level might strengthen the hand of management nationally, not only with regard to wages and benefits of workers in other companies but also with regard to larger questions about the role of financial institutions in shaping economic development. AEG's workers had not participated in planning either the initial private rescue or the subsequent federal loan guarantee; the unions viewed both actions as disturbing precedents.

Chrysler's workers resisted wage cuts even more adamantly. The United Auto Workers did not want to depart from "pattern bargaining" in which wages and benefits are established for the entire industry. Nor was the union willing to give up work rules and job classifications, a move which would have permitted Chrysler management to shift workers to other responsibilities. Under the pressure of the Loan Guarantee Board, the union ultimately acceded to wage cuts in 1981, but only after tens of thousands of Chrysler workers already had been laid off.

Indeed, at no point in Chrylser's crisis did the union express a willingness to exchange wage concessions for job guarantees. The union seniority system may have been partly to blame for this, since the axe would fall on younger workers with less influence in the union. The majority of union members who voted on wage concessions knew that they were less likely to be laid off. This dynamic was most apparent in the fall of 1982, when Chrysler's workers were offered a no-raise, no-layoff contract. Fifty thousand Chrysler workers, including 45,000 still on the job and 5000 most recently laid off, were entitled to vote; a majority of them wanted pay raises. But 42,000 Chrysler workers were not allowed to make this choice between pay raises and job security. This group had been laid off for so long that they had lost their union voting rights. Had they voted, the results might have gone the other way, and many of these laid-off workers might have gotten their jobs back.

Workers at British Leyland were the least cooperative of all. Many of their disputes were not with BL management, but with other workers. With seventeen different unions arranged into 246 bargaining units, and an elaborate system of work rules and job classifications, every negotiation over wages and benefits for one group potentially altered the relative positions of every other group. The firm was wracked by disputes over union jurisdictions and pay differentials. Shop stewards vied for control. With so

221

many groups and individuals competing for leadership and influence, none could risk appearing to concede too much. In the end, most of the rescue money went to maintaining wages and providing lump-sum severance payments. Shrinking was far easier to accomplish than shifting.

Conclusion

The broader lessons that emerge from this study must be stated with the tentativeness they deserve. We have, after all, investigated only four cases, and explored only some of the plausible explanations for their patterns and outcomes. Nevertheless certain conclusions seem warranted.

First, the cases suggest that these sorts of large manufacturing enterprises are *more* than mere productive enterprises. They are also the centers of vast social and economic networks of suppliers, dealers, financial institutions, employees, and service industries. They anchor communities, define relationships, and structure social obligations. How these companies respond to crisis is therefore intimately conditioned by, and profoundly affects, the way these social systems respond. When large companies that employ substantial portions of a region's workforce begin to falter, political pressures invariably mount to "save jobs." Even if politics did not intercede initially, rapid dissolution of such companies might so disrupt social and economic life that governments and other institutions would be compelled to respond. The fact that they did respond in the four cases thus is less interesting than is the fact that they responded in very different ways.

Second, the responses can be arranged along a continuum. Some responses merely slow down the company's inevitable shrinkage. Other responses help the company to shift its resources internally to more profitable pursuits. We have looked at four examples. At the extremes, Toyo Kogyo quickly jettisoned a relatively small number of its jobs and shifted the rest; British Leyland slowly jettisoned most of its jobs and shifted comparatively few. Yet the British government intervened far more directly to save British Leyland jobs—effectively nationalizing the company—than did the Japanese government to save Toyo Kogyo jobs. Chrysler and AEG both lie midway on this continuum; both companies shrunk considerably after they were "rescued," although the Chrysler and the AEG loan guarantees also were premised on "saving jobs."

Third, the pattern of response seems related to the laws and detailed understandings which shape relationships between management, finance, and labor. There are other possible explanations, of course. Some have to do with the overall pace of economic activity surrounding these companies. Presumably shifts are easier to negotiate when the economy is expanding

222

and all participants can anticipate a larger income in the future. Culture also obviously plays a part; shifts are probably easier to arrange if people think of themselves more as group members—as in Japan—than as isolated individuals—as in the United States.

Between economics and culture, however, lies a detailed set of laws, regulations, and social norms which frame institutional relationships. These formal and informal rules both establish and represent responsibilities. They define institutional loyalties and shape patterns of negotiation among different groups of people. They thereby give rise to different types of transactions—some between parties that perceive their dealings to be only temporary and convenient; others, between parties whose ties to one another arise from perceived mutual dependencies stretching over long periods of time.

At one extreme we find companies which are tied to lead banks, and through the lead banks to other financial and industrial units, and regional and national governments. This network functions as a system of early warning and mutual aid. It insures against unexpected changes in the market, helping companies restructure themselves by shifting their resources internally at the first sign of trouble. The corresponding organization of labor is internally flexible, but externally inflexible. Although wages, benefits, and responsibilities can vary significantly within the company from one period to the next, employees find it relatively difficult to leave one company and obtain a new job at another. Employees' fates are as inextricably linked to the fate of the company as is the fate of the lead bank. This overall organization of finance and labor, typified by the case of Toyo Kogyo, strongly favors shifts over shrinkage, internal over external redeployment.

At the other extreme, we find companies which have no special ties to any particular financial institution, and financial institutions which are similarly fragmented and distanced from one another, from other companies, and from governments. Most of the financial transactions in this system are at arm's length; parties deal with one another on the basis of information available to them at the time and do not necessarily assume repeated dealings in the future. Each separate company or institution takes responsibility only for its own profitability. The corresponding organization of labor is internally inflexible, but externally flexible. Wages, benefits, and responsibilities do not vary significantly within the company from one period to the next, but employees find it relatively easy to leave the company. Management and labor deal at arm's length, because they are presumed to have conflicting agendas. As a result, neither employees nor financial institutions are especially dependent on the fate of a particular firm. Furthermore, neither can draw upon a reservoir of trust or rely

223

on the discipline of future dealings. This overall organization of finance and labor, typified by the case of British Leyland, favors shrinkage over shifts, external over internal redeployment.

Fourth, the government's role in rescuing large failing companies is likely to be far more visible and targeted when management, finance, and labor deal with each other at arm's length than when these groups are more tightly linked. When tightly linked to the firm, both financial and labor organizations are likely to be actively involved in responding to the crisis. Government therefore can do its work indirectly through these mediating groups. It can act on behalf of affected communities merely by supporting the financial institutions or the labor organizations which already have a stake. In contrast, when they are at arm's length from the firm, neither financial nor labor organizations are necessarily involved in the crisis. Much of the real burden of redeployment therefore falls on individuals, some of whom have no direct contractual relationship with the firm, and on local governments and relief organizations. These individuals and institutions in turn make political demands for direct government intervention to save jobs and communities. The irony, as the BL case reveals, is that government is able to do little more than slow the pace of shrinkage without the active cooperation of finance and labor.

Finally, the analysis suggests that the practical question in these circumstances is not whether the government should intervene to "save jobs," but how it might intervene to preserve social networks. The answer to *that* question has a great deal to do with how finance and labor are organized. There are some reasons why internal redeployment might be preferable to external for very large companies whose activities and employment is concentrated in certain regions. If internal redeployment is preferred, then centralized planning boards or national development banks, as have been suggested by some proponents of "industrial policy,"[161] may be less useful than changes in the detailed rules and understandings by which financial institutions and labor organizations undertake their day-to-day responsibilities—changes which strengthen the bonds between the company's workers, managers, and financial institutions.

---

161. *See, e.g.,* Eizenstat, *supra* note 5, at 49; Weil, *supra* note 5, at 981.

224

Policy Studies Review, Summer 1990
Vol. 9, No. 4, pp. 649-663

ARTICLES

COMPETITION AND PERFORMANCE IN THE AIRLINE INDUSTRY
Fred Siegmund

Between 1938 and 1978 the airline industry operated under the Civil Aeronautics Act. Entry, exit, fares, mergers, subsidies and trade practices were controlled by a five member Civil Aeronautics Board. The Airline Deregulation Act of 1978 (ADA) allowed for a gradual phasing out of C.A.B. regulation. Carriers were first allowed to set fares in a zone of reasonableness without prior approval. By 1983, all C.A.B. fare authority expired. Market entry restrictions were eliminated in January 1982. Anti-trust immunity was replaced with more traditional Sherman Act and Clayton Act guidelines.

For those who have learned to squeeze into a deregulated airline seat, the contrast could hardly be more striking. Before ADA, the C.A.B. did not approve the entry of any new trunk carriers. New routes were parcelled out very slowly because the notice and hearing requirements often took over a year. Applicants were required to show that new routes were in the public interest and would not harm an existing airline. Fare changes required a hearing. Competitors were allowed to challenge changes or to propose their own changes so that changes were usually made in unison.

I. POLITICS AND DEREGULATION

The impetus for change came as the introduction of jets lowered costs much faster than fares. The result gave the carriers the incentive to compete over service rather than price. Briefly, the problem was that competitive conduct centered on non-price competition when entry and prices were controlled. Airline managers realized that an increase in flight frequency in city pair markets would begin to cause travelers to identify their airline as the one to use when they needed flights, especially on short notice. Thus, increased flights would tend to cause a disproportionally large market share increase over a broad range of flight frequencies. Unfortunately, all the airlines realized this quality effect. Once competition centered on quality, a cycle of poor market performance resulted. As flight frequencies increased, the percentage of seats filled per airline flight decreased so that coasts per passenger went up; profits disappeared and the airlines went back to the C.A.B. requesting fare increases. Fare increases would inject new profits into the airlines but a new round of increased flight frequencies as well as seat width, leg room, meals, drinks, movies and stewardess skirt length, would set off another round of debilitating cost increases leading to more fare increases.

Further pressure developed when comparisons were made between the C.A.B. regulated interstate carriers and the unregulated California and Texas intra state carriers (Keeler, 1977). The intra state carriers were stable, profitable carriers but maintained much lower fares than regulated carriers. The comparison helped build support for the changes that economists had been suggesting since the 1950s (Caves, 1962).

To economists, the changes made by the ADA would be superior to the regulatory framework because experience with other markets had demonstrated that freedom of entry and exit and the freedom to set prices had proved to be an effective mechanism for holding down prices and costs. Ten years of experience with ADA accompanied by a large amount of research seems to vindicate this view (Meyer & Oster, 1984; Bailey et al., 1985). The focus of attention in these studies has been on comparing the performance experience under deregulation with the performance under the period of regulation. While few dispute that airline performance has improved, I would like to suggest comparing today's airline performance with the standards of performance economists typically associate with competition rather than just the previous regulatory period. Since ADA is merely one among many possible institutional frameworks in which to operate the airline industry, maybe some modifications in ADA might improve performance even further.

II. COSTS AND COMPETITION

Competition, in the textbook sense of the word, implies a market where price falls and output expands until price equals marginal cost equals average cost where marginal cost is the additional costs of resources used to produce one more unit of output and average cost is the unit cost determined by dividing total cost by the units produced. $P = mc$ assures that the value in the current use of the marginal unit produced and sold is equal to the value of resources in their next best use. $P = ac$ assures that the profit return on all the units produced and sold will be no more or no less than the return in their next best use. Without belaboring the intricacies of Marshallian economics, it is important to remember such a condition requires a cost structure that limits a firm's output expansion, at least in the short run. Rising marginal and average costs limit a firm's ability to increase market share with lower prices because they encounter rising costs that prevent expansion.

A. Costs

For a deregulated airline industry, the self regulating nature of competition with price $= mc = ac$ performance is complicated somewhat by the peculiarities of decreasing average and marginal cost. To examine how cost per passenger might vary with passenger loads consider a single city pair market. The costs of operating service have both a fixed and variable component. The fixed costs include the capital costs of owning aircraft and equipment as well as the costs of administration and management. The variable costs depend on the number of flights and the number of passengers. Flight costs include fuel, crew salaries, maintenance, service and any landing fees. Passenger costs include schedule-reservations, information, ticket processing, baggage handling and on board food and amenities.

Starting from one passenger and then adding passengers until the plane is full determines marginal and average costs. The first passenger requires the full flight costs plus a small component of passenger costs. Marginal cost for the first passenger is very high. The second passenger generates a smaller marginal cost. Except for a small amount of extra fuel from added weight of passenger and baggage, there are virtually no extra flight costs. Extra passenger costs would include on board amenities, ticket reservations and sales. Since the costs of having airline employees needed to service traffic, collect tickets, serve meals and handle baggage will not increase in proportion to traffic, marginal and average costs will continue to decline as passenger loads increase to the plane's capacity. However, average costs do not decline as rapidly as marginal costs and therefore remain above marginal costs after the first passenger. Figure 1 gives an example of cost profile for a single flight per hour. One hundred and fifteen passengers is a normal capacity for the 737-200.

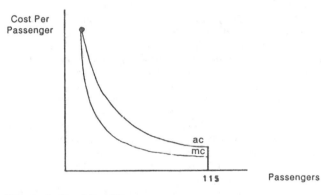

Figure 1. Cost Profile

The marginal and average costs of having two or more flights per hour is a continuation of the costs for one flight as shown in Figure 2.

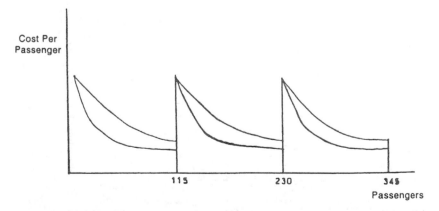

Figure 2. Cost Profile for Multiple Flights

Larger airlines with a full schedule of flights in a city pair market may have some cost savings from economies of scale because cost for airplane maintenance and the costs of reservations, sales and general traffic servicing may not increase in proportion to the number of flights and traffic. Most researchers have concluded economies of scale are small in the airline industry (Gordon, 1965; Strazheim, 1969; Eads et al., 1969; Jordan, 1970; Reid et al., 1973; White, 1979). Unfortunately, the data for such studies comes from system wide costs rather than city pair markets. Results also may be influenced by data that came partially from regulation periods. Thus, these results should be regarded with caution, but at least so far, evidence does not exist to indicate anything more than modest economies of scale.

B. Competition

When costs decrease through the relevant range of demand, marginal cost pricing implies p = mcac. The dual performance conditions are not feasible, at least not for private enterprise. Price must equal average cost for airlines to be viable but also to bring the airline industry to one of the standards of competitive performance. Improved performance implies higher output and lower pricing than before ADA but the achievable competitive performance implies a price and quantity where resources used earn a return no more and no less than the next highest valued use.

To apply the p = ac standard to airlines, it is necessary to ask what percent of an airplane's seats should be filled for price to equal average cost? Suppose we have a hypothetical city pair market that has day to day demand curve D_0 in Figure 3. Ordinarily day to day demand fluctuates somewhat but for this market assume for simplicity that demand is stable. At \$30.00, 115 passengers per hour are willing and able to fly in this market. Suppose further that we are the managers of the only airline serving this market and that average cost is cost per passenger for our 737-200 equipment. Average cost ac, represents the lowest cost equipment for this market.

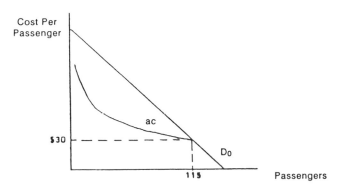

Figure 3. City Pair Market

In our hypothetical market p = ac at 115 passengers that is 100% load in the 737-200. It tells us that the competitive performance is achievable in this market and because we have assumed for simplicity that demand is stable, it is achievable everyday. Notice, however, there is a monopoly and given the usual profit maximizing assumptions for managers there is no reason to think the price will be set at average cost. It is likely to be much higher. The monopoly price, set to equalize marginal revenue and marginal cost, is a possibility. However, managers might find a long term limit price would be more profitable. A limit price is a price set low enough to prevent entry by new firms or expansion by established firms. It is often difficult for entrants to achieve costs as low as established firms, even with resources readily available. For example, capital financing may be more expensive since the costs of market research and advertising cannot be recovered by lenders if assets are sold. A price set below the monopoly price but high enough to exploit any cost differences and limit entry may be the most profitable in the long run. Whatever the price, the main point here is that the single carrier in this example could achieve, but almost certainly will not achieve, a city pair market performance, where p = ac at 100% load factor. Since our interests is in achieving a competitive performance, the question becomes, "What are the possibilities that entry will force the price down to average cost in our example?"

Suppose as managers we decide to set price at the limit price, $90 in Figure 4. Assume the same demand and cost conditions from Figure 3. Entry is likely to set off a price war. The demand remaining for entrants, D_{ent}, is everywhere less than average cost for the established carrier. Entrants cannot be profitable with the demand that remains and therefore must take over part of the traffic from the established carrier. Entry must be gained through price cutting, assuming the established sellers are operating the lowest cost equipment at the lowest cost. If the entrant prices at $30 and begins flights, the two airlines will have capacity of 230 seats on two flights with only 115 passengers to divide up between them. Competition is viable if the carriers can cover cost per passenger at 50% load factor. In the hypothetical example above, they cannot, but the possibility exists that they could if the monopoly carrier had been charging a price above the limit price.

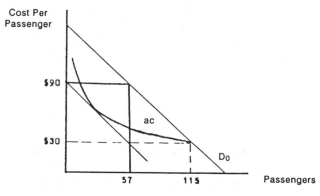

Figure 4. Limit Pricing

Entry in the example above lowered price and increased flights for consumers but left the load factor remaining in the 50% range. In practice, of course, demand is not stable, nor perfectly known and firms may not have equal costs. Following ADA, market entry did take place. The number of carriers increased from 36 in 1978 to 63 in 1980 and 106 by 1985 (Air Carrier Traffic Statistics, 1978, 1980, 1985). The number of single carrier markets fell from 3,978 or 77.1% of markets in the 1978 to 3,592 or 66.1% of total markets in 1984 (U.S. GAO, 1985). All of the markets with two or more carriers had a larger share of total markets in 1984 than in 1978. The index of air fares as reported by the Air Transport Association indicates average fares did rise substantially from 1978 to 1980 but the index of air fares in 1987 was 133.12 compared to 132.43 in 1980 (Annual Reports, ATA, various years). Thus, airfares after 1980 have remained stable despite 3 to 5% inflation in the general price level.

It is possible that some of this entry and improved performance resulted because the old firms had developed a cost structure and marketing practices that were not ready for deregulation. For one, established airlines had costly labor contracts with pilots, machinists and flight attendants. Entry may have been gained from the price cutting allowed by lower costs.

Second, pricing practices in our hypothetical market are assumed to be determined from perfect knowledge of demand where product differentiation is neutral or at least unimportant. After ADA, new carriers were free to try a range of discounting and product differentiation strategies in order to serve previously unserved or unknown demand or attract traffic from other carriers. While established carriers were accustomed to setting fares by formula, entrants began experimenting by scheduling flights at new times or peak times and at a range of discount fares.

Bailey, Graham, and Kaplan (1985, p. 106) provide some data of an excellent example of deregulatory entry in the Buffalo-Newark, N.Y. market. In July 1981 USAir operated 325 flights per month at 90.36 load factor for a market total of 25,699 passengers. Their fare was $97. In August, People's Express entered the market with 285 flights and a $35 fare. Just as predicted earlier, entry set off a price war. USAir matched the $35 fare and increased its flights from 325 to 412 per month. In August, the first month following entry, USAir had 31,847 passengers while People's Express flew 29,321. The market total of 61,168 represents an increase of 35,469 passengers. While the increase is very large, it is smaller than the percentage decrease in price so that the total change is actually an inelastic response and total revenues in the market declined. The results indicate the favorable effects of entry under deregulation--prices fall. Flights and passengers increase. It appears also that USAir's preentry price was so high that the unserved share of the market was able to support an additional carrier profitably. However, USAir's share of the market remained above 50% and their load factor over the new year was above those of People's Express. While the move toward competition is impressive, there was only one month over the next year when load factors equalled their preentry level. Otherwise they declined. Even though loads were still frequently above industry averages and competition shows impressive results like it did in the hypothetical market, there is still room for improvements.

ADA brought on a level of marketing experimentation by low cost entrants that was previously unknown. It is quite possible that established firms in monopoly or near monopoly markets, pricing above a limit price, combined with the uncertainties of cost and demand during the change over from regulation to deregulation have served to bring about most of the improvements in competitive performance observed so far. But whatever the cause of improvements the most important question after 10 years of ADA is--"What standards of performance is the industry capable of achieving?"

In practice, there is nothing about airline markets that assures demand will equal average cost at 100% load factor as it did in our hypothetical market. Price could equal average cost at 75% or some other load factor just as well. But the 100% load factor is not as implausible as it might seem because for markets with lower demand than D_0 in Figure 4, there are smaller airplanes with cost profiles that have lower cost per passenger. In the hypothetical 737-200 example above, planes for say 40 to 50 passengers are available such as the Fairchild F27. Likewise for larger markets, there is larger equipment or multiple flights that will allow cost profiles to be matched to demand.

For a market with 140 passengers per hour, the 727-200 with normal seating of 145 will likely have the lowest cost per passenger. A larger airplane like the 747-200 would be less than half full with 145 passengers while a smaller plane like the 737-200 would need two flights to accommodate 140 passengers. Both would have higher cost per passenger because of the lower load factor. Notice that higher load factors are consistent with adjustable service quality. Suppose in a lightly traveled market an airline offers one round trip per day in 737-200 equipment. Even at 100% load factor, a potential entrant might regard service quality as too low and enter with four round trips, using the smaller Fairchild F27. If better service increases demand to two or three hundred per day with four round trips, empty seats still imply a potential for further improvement in load factors. Either prices could be lower or service and equipment could be changed.

While demand cannot be controlled by airlines, it can be identified through experimentation. As different schedules and services are tried to identify demand, cost minimizing and profit maximizing under deregulation should be pushing the carriers to have the right equipment available for flights. The right equipment will be the type that results in a higher load factor. A theoretical competitive standard of performance for the airline industry is to have price equal average cost with load factors approaching 100%.

III. PUBLIC POLICY

After ten years of deregulation, the airline industry shows signs of competition that are closer to competitive performance. Yet continued deregulation leading to a p = ac performance at a load factor consistent with a competitive utilization of resources cannot be assumed under existing practices and policies. In 1975, the revenue passenger load factor was 53.7% (Air Carrier Traffic Statistics, 1975). By 1978, the first full year of ADA, it jumped to 61.5% (Air Carrier Traffic Statistics, 1978). In 1987, it reached its highest rate of 62.4% (Air Carrier Traffic Statistics, 1987). If the airlines of 1987 had been operating at 1975 load factors, 62,365 fewer people a day would have had service. It is impressive but 37.6% of the seats were still empty in the industry's best year. It is a figure that is high enough to warrant a more active role for public policy.

A. Antitrust Policy

For devotees of competitive performance the run of mergers is a sobering spectacle. The 15 mergers since 1986 have not always involved small airlines. Northwest-Republic, Texas Air-Eastern and TWA-Ozark are among this group (Air Carrier Traffic Statistics, 1987). As well, the largest strongest carriers prior to deregulation are emerging as the largest strongest carriers after deregulation while the newer carriers have had a tendency to disappear, either by merger or bankruptcy. The top carriers of the late seventies, measured by revenue passenger miles, were United Airlines, American Airlines, TWA, Eastern, Delta, Pan American, Northwest, Braniff, Continental and Western (Annual Reports, ATA, various years). By the late eighties only Braniff dropped out of this group; replaced by USAir. Continental was relatively larger while TWA was relatively smaller and Western has merged with Delta. Eastern's future remains somewhat uncertain but in general the big carriers of the seventies have maintained their market position by merger or internal growth. United Airlines ranked first in 1978 with 17.37% of revenue passenger miles. By 1987 they still ranked first with 16.3% (Annual Reports, ATA, 1978, 1987). American Airlines ranked second in 1978 with 12.78% of revenue passenger miles. By 1987 they still ranked second with 14.04% of revenue passenger miles (Annual Reports, ATA, 1978, 1987).

The four firm industry concentration ratio, representing the percentage of the industry revenue passenger miles served by the four largest carriers was 53.14% in 1978 at the beginning of deregulation and 60.58% in 1987 (Air Carrier Traffic Statistics, 1988). But while the higher rate indicates a less competitive market following deregulation, it tells nothing about concentration for individual city pair markets. Because the relevant market for the airline industry is the individual city pair market, any proposed merger will very likely involve concentration in many markets.

Suppose two carriers propose a merger. Say the first carrier flies to 30 cities and the second carrier flies to 20. The first carrier serves a combination of 435 city pair markets. The second carrier serves 190 city pair markets.[1] Suppose further that only 10 of the cities overlap for the two carriers. This means of the total of 625 city combinations served only 45 are actually in direct competition and the remaining city pairs would be unaffected. If the merger results in a monopoly in the 45 markets, should the merger be disallowed? Should it be allowed only if gates are available to new entrants? Or if no gates are available should the carriers be required to sell some percentage of their gates in the affected cities?

The problem of assessing mergers is further complicated because of the changes in route systems that have developed since deregulation. Increasingly, airlines have adopted a hub and spoke system where passengers at a single airport, a hub, are collected by routing flights from a large number of spoke cities into and out of the hub. Passengers boarding at spoke cities can make connections at the hub for flights from the hub back to spoke cities. The hub-spoke system makes the comparison of city pair markets somewhat harder because of the necessity of comparing circuitous, one stop routs with direct non-stop routes.

For example, someone who wants to travel from Chicago to Pittsburgh would probably find direct service on either United Airlines or USAir because United has a hub in Chicago and USAir has a hub in Pittsburgh. TWA with a hub in St. Louis can offer service from Chicago to Pittsburgh but if they use their St. Louis hub, it means the trip would be Chicago to St. Louis and then a change of planes to Pittsburgh. While the example is hypothetical, the growing use of hub-spoke systems requires evaluating the effects of a merger where overlapping city pair markets are offering different quality service.

In addition, the hub cities take on a special significance. In order for the hub-spoke system to work, incoming flights must land at about the same time so that passengers can make connections and depart as quickly as possible. Thus, a hub requires an airline to have a large number of gates, close enough together, to handle peak travel schedules. The use of hub-spoke systems has the advantage of helping to increase load factors because passengers boarding at spoke locations can be going to many different locations. While a higher load factor will unquestionably lower costs per passenger, the issue for public policy is whether competition after a merger will be strong enough to keep prices falling as load factors are rising.

Mergers for airlines operating at the same airport appear destined to reduce competition. First, two airlines developing a route system around the same hub are almost certain to have similar routes. Second, the need for gates at peak times almost assures the two carriers will be dominating the available gates. The merger of TWA and Ozark airlines offers an example (U.S. GAO, 1988). At the end of 1985, TWA handled 56% of enplanements at Lambert Field, St. Louis; Ozark had 26%. After the merger TWA's share was 82%. No other carrier had even 3%. Before the merger TWA/Ozark operated 85 routes with direct service; after the merger they operated 91. All other carriers had 83 direct routes before the merger but only 66 after it. The number of routes served by one carrier increased 42% after the merger. Four carrier, three carrier and two carrier routes decreased by 7%, 16% and 36% respectively. Similarly, the TWA/Ozark combination increased their dominance of non-stop routes. In 1986, they had a monopoly on 39% of non-stop routes; by June 1987, after the merger, they held a monopoly in 76% on non-stop St. Louis routes. Only 3% of the non-stop St. Louis routes were served by other carriers. While airline fares increased an average 2% nationally from 1986 to 1987, fare increases for St. Louis routes increased 18% in the first quarter of 1987 over 1986 and 13% in the second quarter and third quarter of 1987 over 1986. Of the 75 gates at Lambert Field, TWA has a long term lease for three fourths of them. No other carrier has greater than three gates.

While it is not certain a merger of airlines operating from the same hub will increase route dominance, fares, and airport gate control, the result has to be strongly suspected. Unless a third airline has a hub or enough gate capacity exists for potential entry of another hub carrier, hub mergers seem destined to repeat the St. Louis experience.

Evaluating mergers for airlines operating from different hubs is a somewhat harder process. Service between the same city pairs is still the most important issue in evaluating mergers but where different hubs are used, service quality will be different because one airline will offer direct service while another will have one-stop service, possibly with more circuitous routing.

To illustrate these issues consider a proposed merger of two hypothetical airlines. Assume one has a hub at Denver with 9 spokes to San Francisco, Los Angeles, Phoenix, Houston, Dallas, Kansas City, St. Louis, Chicago and Detroit. Assume the second has a hub at St. Louis with 9 spokes to Kansas City, Denver, Los Angeles, Dallas, Houston, Atlanta, pittsburgh, Detroit and Chicago. Figure 5 below shows the Denver carrier with solid lines and the St. Louis carrier with dotted lines. Both airlines operate service to 45 city pairs. Assume for simplicity that both operate only hub-spoke flights. Then both carriers operate non-stop service from the spokes to the hub and one stop service from the spoke city pairs.

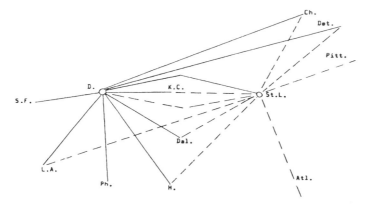

Figure 5. Hypothetical Hub-Spoke Routes

Should a merger take place, competition for non-stop service is affected for only one city pair, Denver-St. Louis. Only 28 city pairs are affected at all. Because Pittsburgh and Atlanta are not in the Denver system and San Francisco and Phoenix are not in the St. Louis system, 17 city pairs do not overlap. On the remaining 28 city pairs, however, the quality of service may differ between the two carriers. Suppose a passenger in Denver would like to go to Los Angeles. The Denver carrier offers a direct non-stop. The St. Louis carrier using the hub and spoke system offers a service into the St. Louis hub to make connections for a flight back to Los Angeles. How much do these flights compete? Of course, the St. Louis carrier might add a leg to Los Angeles on its Denver spoke, if it has or can get gate space. But even then the Denver carrier has an advantage here because they can cumulate passengers from other cities for the Denver-Los Angeles connection. The St. Louis carrier would be siphoning off some of its passengers for the St. Louis-Los Angeles spoke as well.

Service quality does not differ this much for all the other overlapping routes. Detroit to Los Angeles, for example, is almost the same quality. For some markets quality will be the same; for others different. But in evaluating the whole merger, there is no substitute for evaluating the individual markets. The complexity of its rules out easy formulas.

Even if the hypothetical market merger raises the concentration of enplanements 20 points, competition might not be affected significantly if there is at least one other carrier, or gate space is available for entry or expansion. As well, a merger agreement might include the sale of gate space to other carriers in affected markets. Without formulae or the ability to easily apply guidelines, Antitrust enforcement must weigh the potential a merger might improve service and raise load factors against the possibility competition will not be strong enough to keep price close to cost.

B. Non Antitrust Policy

While vigorous Antitrust enforcement is probably sound policy, the foregoing discussion suggests it may not be sufficiently adaptable for the airline industry to rely on it as a primary policy. Other policy within the existing regulatory framework can be tried. Any policy that raises load factors should improve performance as long as fares remain deregulated and entry is at least possible.

Airports are an important part of competition in the airline industry. If there is no gate or terminal space, competition is blunted. However, the crowding at airports is with flights rather than passengers. Since the planes are on average 37.6% empty, hidden capacity exists if the planes can be filled up a little more. One way to improve the allocation of resources would be to charge a graduated landing fee to encourage higher load factors. Such a program would work by lowering the landing fees for airlines operating with higher load factors. With thousands of flights and limited ability to avoid having some flights with low load factors, a graduated fee would probably lead to inequities if it were levied on a flight by flight basis. The average load factor for a time period with a small percentage of flights dropped from the measure could be used instead. Once the fee schedule was worked out, the fee times the average load factor for a given period of time at each airport times the number of flights would determine a landing payment per time period. With payments graduated for load factors poor performance is discouraged. Since one way to raise load factors and improve performance is to lower fares, airline efforts to reduce fee payments directly benefit consumers.

A slightly different policy would put a cap on daily flights for an individual carrier for specific city pair markets. Entry of other carriers and pricing would remain deregulated. Existing carriers would be prevented from raising prices without the threat of entry, yet available seats or rising demand would force them to develop strategies to improve their load factor instead of merely adding flights. If established carriers cut price under the threat of entry, consumers would be better off, load factors would rise and thereby improve the utilization of resources. The worst effects of price wars would at least be reduced because cost per passenger would fall as the load factor rises. System wide, a city pair flight frequency cap would force the larger carriers to operate in a larger number of markets, ensuring service to more cities and channeling competitive efforts in a direction that improves the performance in the industry.

Using the load factor to reallocate gate space might also be used to encourage a better utilization of resources. To pressure the airlines to fill up the seats, airport authorities could begin writing a separate lease agreement for each gate. The lease might include an automatic yearly renewal except a cancellation clause could allow airport authorities to cancel the gate lease for the gate with the lowest average daily load factor for the year. The gate lease would then be put up for auction with any certified carrier, including the previous leaseholder, eligible for bidding. A minimum bid price would be designated. Currently airports are usually owned by local governments and managed by local airport authorities. Gate space carries a long term lease with the airlines having paid for capital improvements such as ticket counters and gate facilities. These investments would have to be purchased or paid for by airport authorities before an auction plan started. While this complicates implementation, such a plan would still pressure airline managers to fill up their seats or face having to bid up the lease price to retain their gates from expansion minded carriers.

Load factors might also be improved by more flexible pricing. Pricing in the airlines is complicated because the consumers willing and able to pay the highest price are business travelers who expect to reserve flights on short notice. Discount seats are sold first and have restrictions the business traveler cannot or will not meet. Despite the difficulties airlines have begun adjusting thousands of fares on a daily basis. When the ratio of business travelers to discount travelers is lower than normal a few days before departure, more discount seats are opened up. While it is not quite an auction, it is getting close and such practices should certainly be encouraged.

Accurate information about all flights is needed by consumers to encourage competitive pricing. The current computer reservation system used to book flights by travel agents has been suspected of doing the opposite by limiting information. The computer reservation systems were developed by the major airlines in the mid 1970s. Because they made booking much easier, many travel agents began using them. Often they chose to use the system of the carrier that already had the largest share of the market in that region. Agreements between the agents and the airlines often had exclusive arrangements and practices that biased the displays in favor of the airline owning the computer reservation system. Complaints multiplied until the Civil Aeronautics Board investigated and issued a "Final Rule on Carrier-owned Computer Reservations Systems" in 1984.

The rules continued to allow the airlines to operate computer reservations systems but attempted to regulate the abuses by preventing exclusive agency contracts, requiring equal booking fees to carriers, and requiring any service improvements be made available equally to all. The complaints have not stopped however. Travel agents for computer reservations system owners can provide boarding passes and last seat availability, suggesting travel agents may not be entirely unbiased in recommending flights. Entry has not occurred and there is some sign, although no proof, that computer reservations systems earn their owners excellent profits (U.S. GAO, 1986).

An alternative policy would require all computer reservations systems to put their flight information on a centralized F.A.A. computer. Information on all flights would be available at airports or by phone. Comprehensive information about flights would be separated from those who owned the computer reservations systems and have a vested interest in one carrier over another. If consumers know the flight that best suit their needs before they call a travel agent to book the flight, they stand a better chance of getting the lowest fare.

A final suggestion for price flexibility is to use a bid board for a walk on fare beginning an hour or two before departure. Any unsold seats would go up for auction with some low minimum bid required. The remaining seats would go to the highest bidder. This system allows the harried business man or woman to get a seat at the last minute since presumably they would outbid the bargain hunters. It also raises the load factor.

IV. CONCLUSIONS AND POLICY ISSUES

Regulation and deregulation are not all or nothing terms. After ten years of deregulation, almost no one is suggesting a return to C.A.B. type regulation and it is not recommended here. But regulation dos not have to mean that a regulatory agency becomes directly involved in management decisions to adjust service or to meet market conditions. Changes in the institutional frame work in which airlines compete are still consistent with a deregulated environment. Notice that the policy suggestions outline above do not require a large bureaucracy. Existing airport authorities, the Federal Aviation Administration and congressional committees reviewing the airline industry are capable of making institutional policy changes. The committees could act to set policy goals and guidelines by establishing a schedule of landing fees, gate auction rules or city pair caps with local airport authorities and F.A.A. actually implementing policy. Congress could then conduct a yearly evaluation of policy effects. The lengthy hearings conducted before the C.A.B. would be unnecessary because the standard of evaluation would be a competitive performance, with prices, profits and passenger loads as the principal basis for determining improvement or lack of it.

The policy suggestions outline above concentrate on improving the utilization of existing resources, especially filling up the airplanes. Other important policy issues surround product performance and expansion of the existing system. It is implied in competition that consumers have perfect knowledge of economic and technical information about the product or services purchased. While that is rarely true in practice, effective competitive performance should improve product quality over time. Effective performance in the airline industry should mean airlines with good safety, on time and baggage handling records expand relative to others, leading to a rise in industry averages over time.

Unfortunately data to measure the quality of airline service is sparse and hard to measure. Safety, as measured by fatal accidents per 100,000 departures, was .1 in 1978 but lower than that every ear since then (Annual Reports, ATA, 1988). Is it safer now than before deregulation? Virtually all of jet aircraft in commercial service in 1978 are still in service. Perhaps an aging airline fleet makes the industry less safe in spite of the data? It seems doubtful but not certain. Most fatal accidents occur in bad weather. Perhaps safety could be improved if more flights were delayed or cancelled in bad weather? But this conflicts with the desire to improve service quality since delays and cancellations are not going to improve on time performance.

Product quality is not as amenable to public policy as price competition. The air traffic control system, the weather and airport congestion cannot be controlled by airline managers but they do lower on time performance and cause accidents. Policy that improves on time performance may jeopardize safety. Public policy can improve consumer information. For example, the publication of flight delays could be listed by cause to help pressure better performance from the airlines. But the conflict between safety and on time performance makes more aggressive policy action questionable.

Making better use of existing airport space as discussed earlier is an important issue to competition but airports do reach capacity so that without new construction or expansion entry is limited and competition more uncertain. Currently airport leases tend to be long term with established carriers having a direct voice in expansion decisions (U.S. GAO, 1988). Where hub carriers have the majority of gate space and flights as they do, say at Lambert Field, they are not likely to support expanded facilities for their competitors. Direct investment in a second airport would allow entrants to challenge dominant carriers. A new airport offers a better substitute for expanding an existing airport than before deregulation because fewer and fewer passengers are connecting to flights of other carriers (Annual Reports, ATA, 1989). Trips between airports are less problematic when passengers stay on the same airline. However, land acquisition has become such a problem in major cities that new airports away from city pair markets offers another less expensive option. Since no one would be going to such a hub except to change planes, this plan would improve competition for one stop service but non-stop service would be unaffected. For example, TWA already has to compete with other airlines when a passenger is considering a trip from say Chicago to Los Angeles. They could go through St. Louis on TWA or through Denver or Kansas City on another carrier. While a new hub away from a market improves the entry of one stop competition, travelers are likely to have more choices for one stop flights than non-stops already. As long as hub carriers dominance of non-stop service is unchallenged, an isolated hub is not a perfect substitute for a second airport in a major market.

The problem inherent in building new airports make the policy toward expanding existing ones all the more important. Since the established carriers are not likely to be eager to support new airport construction intended for new entry, expansion policy should be determined independently of established carriers.

The policy suggestions outlined above are not meant to be exhaustive. ADA has had ten years to improve performance. Happily things have improved at least in the way in which economists like to evaluate them. Enough time has passed, however, to realize that further improvements are unlikely without some policy changes to help them along.

NOTES

[1] $_nC_r$ where n = cities and r = 2 at a time.

REFERENCES

Annual Report of the U.S. Schedule Airline Industry. (1980, 1988). Air Transport Association. Washington, D.C.

Air Carrier Traffic Statistics. (1975, 1978, 1980). Civil Aeronautics Board. Washington, D.C.

Air Carrier Traffic Statistics. (1985, 1987). U.S. Department of Transportation. Washington, D.C.

Bailey, E., Graham, D., & Kaplan, D. (1985). *Deregulating the airlines.* Cambridge, MA: Harvard University Press.

Caves, R. (1962). *Air transportation and its regulators: An industry study.* Cambridge, MA: Harvard University Press.

Eads, G., Nerlove, M., & Raduchel, W. (1969). A long run cost function for the local service airline industry: A long run cost function for the local service airline industry. *Review of Economics and Statistics, 51.*

Gordon, R. (1965). Airline costs and managerial efficiency. *Transportation Journal, 61.*

Jordan, W. (1970). *Airline regulation in America: Effects and imperfections.* Baltimore, MD: John Hopkins University Press.

Keeler, T. (1977). Lower airline costs per passenger are possible in the United States and could result in lower fares. Washington, D.C.: U.S. Comptroller General, CED-77-34.

Meyer, J., & Oster, C. (1984). *Deregulation and the new airline entrepreneurs.* Cambridge, MA: M.I.T. Press.

Morrison, S., & Winston, C. (1986). *The economic effects of airline deregulation.* Washington, D.C.: Brookings Institution.

Reid, S., & Mohrfeld, J. (1973). Airline size, profitability, mergers and regulation. *Journal of Air Law and Commerce, 39.*

Strazheim, M. (1969). *The international airline industry.* Washington, D.C.: Brookings Institution.

U.S. General Accounting Office. (1985). Deregulation: Increased competition is making airlines more efficient and responsive to consumers. Washington, D.C.

U.S. General Accounting Office. (1986). Impact of computerized reservation systems. Washington, D.C.

U.S. General Accounting Office. (1988). Fare and service changes at St. Louis since the TWA-Ozark merger. Washington, D.C.

White, L. (1979). Economies of scale and the question of natural monopoly in the airline industry. *Journal of Air Law and Commerce, 44.*

Richard H. K. Vietor

Contrived Competition: Airline Regulation and Deregulation, 1925–1988

Although many have studied regulatory policy in the United
States, few have viewed it as a process, shaping markets and
industries and, in turn, being affected by the structures it
helped to create. By looking at the forty-year history of airline
regulation and then focusing on one company's adaptations
to deregulation, this article demonstrates that monocausal
explanations fail to capture the complex and dynamic nature
of the interaction between regulation and competition in
America.

Airline regulation and deregulation, taken together, provide a
uniquely interesting laboratory for testing basic concepts of
political economy. During the forty years of federal regulation (from
1938 to 1978), a number of economists studied airlines to understand how federal intervention affected key aspects of market
structure—especially entry, price, and supply and demand.[1] Political
scientists and historians also cited this experience to illustrate theories
of regulatory origin or capture.[2] Students of business administration

RICHARD H. K. VIETOR is professor of business administration at the Harvard Business School.

[1] Among the best studies by economists are Richard E. Caves, *Air Transport and its Regulators: An Industry Study* (Cambridge, Mass., 1962); Samuel B. Richmond, *Regulation and
Competition in Air Transportation* (New York, 1961); and William A. Jordan, *Airline Regulation in America: Effects and Imperfections* (Baltimore, Md., 1970); Alfred E. Kahn, *The Economics of Regulation* (New York, 1971), 2: 209–20.

[2] Samuel P. Huntington, "Clientalism: A Study in Administrative Politics" (Ph.D. diss.,
Harvard University, 1951); Marver H. Bernstein, *Regulating Business by Independent Commission* (Princeton, N. J., 1955); Emmette S. Redford, *The Regulatory Process: With Illustra-
tions from Commercial Aviation* (Austin, Texas, 1969); Robert C. Fraser, Alan D. Donheiser,
and Thomas G. Miller, Jr., *Civil Aviation Development: A Policy and Operations Analysis* (New
York, 1972); David D. Lee, "Herbert Hoover and the Development of Commercial Aviation, 1921–1926," *Business History Review* 58 (Spring 1984): 78–84; Ellis Hawley, "Three
Facets of Hooverian Associationalism: Lumber, Aviation, and Movies, 1921–1930," in *Regulation in Perspective: Historical Essays*, ed. Thomas K. McCraw (Boston, Mass., 1981), 95–123.

Business History Review 64 (Spring 1990): 61–108. © 1990 by The President and Fellows
of Harvard College.

focused on the regulated airlines' marketing, logistics, and competitive strategy.[3]

More recently, scholars have been fascinated by the unanticipated consequences of deregulation. The business conduct and market performance of deregulated airlines have challenged even the most sophisticated ideas about contestability, information and transaction costs, economies of scale, and the public and private interest theories of government.[4] For the theorists of regulation, deregulation has proven hard to explain.

Despite the richness of this scholarly output, economic and political explanations remain relatively unintegrated: the economic studies tend to be cross-sectional, seldom focusing on the dynamic process of an evolving market structure; the policy explanations strive unsuccessfully for monocausality. With some exceptions (for example, the work of John Meyer and Michael Levine), neither the economic nor the policy explanations take into account the strategic conduct of the firm or its effects on market structure. By examining the history of regulation and deregulation, this article suggests an interpretation of regulation that is grounded in a dynamic view of market structure, political interests, and the strategic behavior of firms.

The article is organized in five parts: 1) an analysis of the origins of airline regulation, 1925–38; 2) its effects on market structure, 1938–69; 3) a discussion of the causes of deregulation, 1969–78; 4) a description of American Airlines' strategic adjustment to deregula-

---

[3] Paul W. Cherington, *Airline Price Policy: A Study of Domestic Airline Passenger Fares* (Boston, Mass., 1958); Stanley C. Hollander, *Passenger Transportation, Readings Selected from a Marketing Viewpoint* (East Lansing, Mich., 1968); William Fruhan, *The Fight for Competitive Advantage* (Boston, Mass., 1972).

[4] Among the economic studies of deregulation are John Meyer, et al., *Airline Deregulation: The Early Experience* (Boston, Mass., 1981); John Meyer and Clinton Oster, *Deregulation and the New Airline Entrepreneurs* (Cambridge, Mass., 1984), and *Deregulation and the Future of Intercity Passenger Travel* (Cambridge, Mass., 1987); Elizabeth E. Bailey, David R. Graham, and Daniel P. Kaplan, *Deregulating the Airlines* (Cambridge, Mass., 1985); Elizabeth E. Bailey and Jeffrey R. Williams, "Sources of Rent in the Deregulated Airline Industry," *Journal of Law and Economics* 31 (April 1988): 173–202; Steve Morrison and Clifford Winston, *The Economic Effects of Airline Deregulation* (Washington, D.C., 1986); Robert J. Andriuliatis, et al., *Deregulation and Airline Employment: Myth Versus Fact* (Vancouver, B.C., 1987); and Michael E. Levine, "Airline Competition in Deregulated Markets: Theory, Firm Strategy, and Public Policy," *Yale Journal of Regulation* 4 (Spring 1987): 393–494. On the politics of deregulation, see Bradley Behrman, "Civil Aeronautics Board," in *The Politics of Regulation*, ed. James Q. Wilson (New York, 1980), 75–120; Stephen Breyer, *Regulation and Its Reform* (Cambridge, Mass., 1982); Thomas K. McCraw, *Prophets of Regulation* (Cambridge, Mass., 1984); Martha Derthick and Paul J. Quirk, *The Politics of Deregulation* (Washington, D.C., 1985); and Anthony E. Brown, *The Politics of Airline Deregulation* (Knoxville, Tenn., 1987).

U.S. Aerial Mail Service, 1918 · The earliest airline routes were inaugurated by the Post Office, with army men trained during the First World War serving as pilots. The airplane pictured is a Curtiss JN–4H. (Photograph reproduced from the records of the U.S. War Department.)

tion; and 5) an overview of deregulation's impact on market structure and performance, 1978–88.

Origins of Airline Regulation, 1925–1938

The airline business in America started out as a dangerous, heavily subsidized, mail delivery service. Government virtually created the market, long before the technology could sustain nationwide passenger service. During the First World War, Congress funded the development and large-scale production of military aircraft. As the war ended, the Post Office inaugurated scheduled airmail service, with operations provided by army pilots. For several years, the industry limped along with a short supply of skilled pilots, few control systems, rudimentary airports, and an uncoordinated route structure. Recognizing these weaknesses, the industry itself sought government help, asking for regulation of the airways and subsidies for commercial airmail.[5] Congress tried to meet these needs with the Kelly Airmail Act of 1925, which provided for competitive bidding and subsidies for contract airmail service, and the Air Commerce Act of 1926, which authorized the Department of Commerce to regulate air navigation and safety.[6]

The subsidies, amounting to $7 million a year by 1930, stimulated demand for airmail service and intense competition among sup-

[5] Lee, "Herbert Hoover and the Development of Commercial Aviation," 78–84.
[6] Paul T. David, *The Economics of Air Mail Transportation* (Washington, D.C., 1934); Francis A. Spencer, *Air Mail Payment and the Government* (Washington, D.C., 1941), 29–39; and Charles C. Rohlfing, *National Regulation of Aeronautics* (Philadelphia, Pa., 1931).

Passengers in a Ford Tri-Motor, c. 1930 · Early airline development was inhibited by a lack of infrastructure and by an airplane technology not yet ready for large-scale passenger travel, although Ford's advertising billed the plane pictured as "more stable than a yacht, swifter than the wind." (Photograph reproduced from R. E. G. Davies, *Airlines of the United States since 1914* [Washington, D.C., 1972], p. 87.)

pliers. Route mileage increased tenfold, with more than a dozen carriers organized to provide regular service. But competitive bidding for subsidies severely limited profits and prevented the development of any significant passenger service. Frustrated by the industry's slow development, Walter F. Brown, Herbert Hoover's postmaster general, proposed legislation to give himself wide-ranging authority over routes, mail rates, and discretionary contract awards. Congress granted Brown his request, save for the waiver of competitive bidding, in the McNary-Watres Act of 1930.[7]

Brown immediately called a meeting of the principal airmail carriers, none of whom were breaking even on passenger service at the time, and asked them to "agree among themselves as to the territory in which they shall have the paramount interest."[8] After several days of discussions and some arm-twisting by Brown, three transcontinental routes were designated and awarded: a southern route to American Airways, a central route to Trans Continental and Western Air (TWA; after 1950, Trans World Airlines), and a northern route to United

[7] J. Howard Hamstra, "Two Decades—Federal Regulation in Perspective," *Journal of Air Law and Commerce* 12 (April 1941): 108–14.

[8] Irving Glover, Second Assistant Postmaster, "Memorandum to the Postmaster General," 20 May 1930, reprinted in U.S. Congress, House, Committee on Post Office and Post Roads, *Air Mail Hearings*, 73d Cong., 2d sess., Feb.-March 1934, 227.

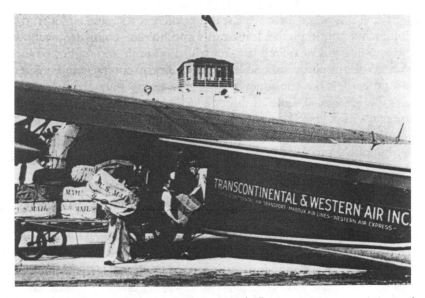

Inaugural Flight on TWA's New York–Los Angeles Route • TWA was awarded one of three airmail-passenger routes under the revised McNary-Watres Act of 1930. By 1932, the coast-to-coast flight for passengers required just under twenty-seven hours. (Photograph reproduced from TWA, Inc., Flight Operations Department, *Legacy of Leadership: A Pictorial History of Trans World Airlines* [n.p., 1971], p. 53.)

Airways. Six other carriers received the remaining contracts. "There was no sense," as Brown later explained, "in taking the government's money and dishing it out to every little fellow that was flying around. . . . " Administrative integration and consolidation, he believed, would "make the industry self-sustaining."[9]

With this government-sponsored cartel in place, the airline business made some rapid advances. Improvements in aircraft technology, together with noncompetitive mail contracts, stimulated the growth of passenger service. The principal carriers grew by merger as well as by extension. TWA was acquired by General Motors (along with Eastern, Western, and Douglas Aviation); United formed a holding company with National Air Transport, Pratt & Whitney, Boeing, and Sikorsky; and American was acquired by Aviation Corporation (along with Texas Air, Continental Air, Robertson Aircraft ["the Lindbergh Line"], and several others).[10]

[9] Quoted in Robert J. Serling, *Eagle: The Story of American Airlines* (New York, 1985), 65.
[10] U.S. Congress, Senate, Committee on Post Office and Post Roads, *Revisions of Air Mail Laws*, 73d Cong., 2d sess., March 1934, 76–86.

In 1934, when Brown's "spoils conference" came to light in a full-blown political scandal, the cartel and holding-company pyramids came crashing down. President Franklin Roosevelt, responding to allegations of conspiracy, canceled all existing airmail contracts and ordered the army to deliver the airmail.[11] Congress hastily revised the Air Mail Act (with the Black-McKellar Act of 1934), curtailing the postmaster general's authority, reimposing strict competitive bidding, and giving the Interstate Commerce Commission control of entry through a certification process. The act's most distinctive feature was its punitive thrust: it prohibited existing carriers from bidding on contracts, banned interlocking directorates, and restricted airlines with mail contracts from "engag[ing] in any other phase of the aviation industry." These measures destroyed the aviation trusts.[12]

The 1934 act restructured the airline industry, creating the horizontal oligopoly that would last until 1978. With new executive officers, new names, and new incorporation papers, eleven carriers emerged from the conglomerates. The "Big Four"—American Airlines, United Airlines, TWA, and Eastern Airlines—held about 80 percent of market share (in revenue-passenger miles). Seven others—Northwest, Pennsylvania Central, Braniff, Western Air Express, Chicago & Western, Mid-Continent, and National—shared the remaining 20 percent. The act also imposed a competitive bidding system, which, as the only feasible means of entry, resulted in absurdly low bids.

The industry as a whole operated at a loss for the next few years, giving the impression that "excess competition" was a sort of market failure. A blue-ribbon panel, appointed by Congress to evaluate long-term aviation policy, concluded that air transport was "not a natural monopoly," but that it did suffer from the wrong sort of competition. The panel recommended that Congress appoint an independent commission to regulate entry and to set minimum standards of service: "There must be enough competition to serve as a spur to the eager search for progress, but there must not be so much as to raise costs materially through the duplication of facilities. There must be no arbitrary denial of the right of entry of newcomers. . . . "[13]

---

[11] Franklin D. Roosevelt, Executive Order No. 6591, 9 Feb. 1934; also, U.S. Congress, Senate, Special Committee, *Investigation of Air Mail and Ocean Mail Contracts*, 73d Cong., 2d sess., parts 1–9, 1934.

[12] *Public Law 308*, 48 Stat. 933, 39 U.S.C. 463 (1934); Charles Rhyne, *The Civil Aeronautics Act Annotated* (Washington, D.C., 1939), 29–31.

[13] Federal Aviation Commission, "Report of the Federal Aviation Commission," *Senate Document No. 15*, 74th Cong., 1st sess., Jan. 1935, 52–53.

Douglas DC–3 · From its inauguration in 1936 until the Second World War, the DC–3 dominated the aircraft fleet. It had a seating capacity of twenty-one, seven more than the older DC–2s. (Photograph reproduced from the records of United Air Lines.)

The airline industry lobbied hard for regulation. Half the total investment in aviation had allegedly been lost, complained Edgar Gorrell, president of the Air Transport Association. Without regulation, "there is nothing to prevent the entire air carrier system from crashing to earth under the impact of cut-throat and destructive practices."[14] Congress (and eventually the Roosevelt administration) agreed, and, in 1938, passed the Civil Aeronautics Act.[15] The act created a Civil Aeronautics Authority (later renamed Board) with broad authority to control entry and exit by certification, approve or amend tariffs, set mail rates, control mergers, authorize interfirm agreements, and control methods of competition.[16] These extraordinary powers were

[14] U.S. Congress, House, Committee on Interstate and Foreign Commerce, *To Create a Civil Aeronautics Authority*, 75th Cong., 3d sess., March 1938, 38; and Edgar S. Gorrell, "Rationalization of Air Transport," An Address Presented at the Seventh Annual Convention of the National Association of Aviation Officials, 1–3 Dec. 1937, reprinted in *Journal of Air Law* 9 (1938): 43.

[15] The Roosevelt administration preferred that all regulatory responsibilities for transportation be consolidated in a single agency—either the ICC or a new cabinet department. See Franklin D. Roosevelt, "Message of Transmittal," 31 Jan. 1935, in Federal Aviation Commission, *Report*, iii–iv; and, U.S. Congress, Senate, Subcommittee on S. 3659, Committee on Interstate Commerce, *Civil Aviation and Air Transport*, 75th Cong., 3d sess., April 1938, 1–2.

[16] The original (1938) act actually combined regulatory and developmental (air traffic control and safety) functions under the same administrative roof. But after just two years, Congress amended the act, restoring air traffic control and safety to the Commerce Department (and changing the name of the Civil Aeronautics Authority to the Civil Aeronautics Board); see *Reorganization Act of 1940*, 54 Stat. 735; also, U.S. Congress, House, *House Report No. 2505*, 76th Cong., 3d sess., 1940.

based on two criteria: "the promotion of adequate, economical, and efficient service . . . at reasonable charges," and the promotion of "competition to the extent necessary to assure the sound development of an air-transportation system. . . . "[17]

The act represented neither the "public interest" concept that had evolved from *Munn v. Illinois* nor the simple "capture" of policy by industry.[18] Rather, the Civil Aeronautics Act was a muddled attempt to guide competition toward a socially optimal mix of service, innovation, and economic growth. This approach, of course, was perfectly consistent with the prevailing economic wisdom in the context of the Great Depression. Congress had already responded in a similar manner to depressed conditions in other industries, with the Emergency Railroad Transportation Act of 1933, the Banking Act of 1933, and the Motor Carrier Act (for trucking) of 1935. In 1938, interstate pipelines were placed under similarly tight federal controls in the Natural Gas Act.

Regulation-Defined Airline Markets, 1938–1968

During its first thirty years, the Civil Aeronautics Board (CAB) tried several tactics, depending on its makeup (particularly its chairman) and on airline market conditions. Prior to 1955, the board fostered rapid growth through route extensions, tight control over mergers and new entrants, and "route strengthening" for the smaller trunk carriers. Since the act had grandfathered the routes of the major carriers, the Big Four started out from a dominant position. As the CAB added 56,000 miles of new routes in the late 1940s (doubling the prewar network), it favored the growth of the smaller trunk carriers (for example, Northeastern, Northwestern, Braniff, Continental, Delta, National, Western, Mid-Continent, and Southern) (see Table 1).[19] The board also promoted growth by certifying and nurturing noncompeting "feeder lines," which by 1954 had grown into thirteen relatively stable local carriers with 22,000 miles of routes and $54 million in revenues (see Table 2).

Control of entry was a difficult issue for the Civil Aeronautics Board. Because airmail subsidies artificially stimulated entry, and because low natural entry barriers encouraged cream-skimming, entry

[17] *Civil Aeronautics Act of 1938*, 52 Stat. 973; also, Rhyne, *Civil Aeronautics Act Annotated*.
[18] The board itself drew this distinction in Civil Aeronautics Board, "Acquisition of Marquette by TWA—Supplemental Opinion," 2 CAB 409 (1940), 411–13.
[19] Civil Aeronautics Board, *Annual Reports*, 1946–1949 (Washington, D.C.).

Table 1
Market Share of Certified Carriers, 1939–1954
(percent of revenue-passenger miles)

	1939	1949	1954
Big Four	82%	70%	71%
Other Trunks	18	28	25
Local Carriers	—	2	4

Source: Civil Aeronautics Board, *Handbook of Airline Statistics, 1973* (Washington, D.C., 1973), 23.

Table 2
Certified Local Carriers in 1954

Allegheny	Ozark
Bonanza	Piedmont
Central	Southern
Frontier	Southwest
Lake Central	Trans-Texas
Mohawk	West Coast
North Central	

restrictions appeared warranted, even necessary. But with the glut of aircraft and pilots after the Second World War, hundreds of "irregular" carriers commenced service, exempt from certification. For a time, these irregulars showed extraordinary imagination and flexibility in skirting each new CAB rule. At its peak in 1951, market share of the irregular carriers reached 7.5 percent of revenue-passenger miles and 21 percent of cargo. It took the board nearly a decade to close every loophole, alienating quite a few members of congress in the process.[20]

On the major trunk routes, the board had no real decision-rule for dealing with requests for competitive entry or with service rivalries. Case-by-case decision making reflected a balancing act, slightly tilted toward a "presumption in favor of competition on any route which offered sufficient traffic to support competing services without

[20] *Investigation of Nonscheduled Air Service*, 6 CAB (1946), 1049; *Large Irregular Carriers, Exemption*, 11 CAB (1950), 609; U.S. Congress, Select Committee on Small Business, *Future of Irregular Airlines in United States Air Transportation Industry*, 83d Cong., 1st sess., 1953, and U.S. Congress, House Judiciary Committee, *Report Pursuant to H. Res. 107 on Airlines*, 85th Cong., 1st sess., 5 April 1957.

Douglas DC–4 · An unpressurized, forty-four–seat aircraft, the four-engine DC–4s came into widespread use immediately following the Second World War. Transcontinental DC–4 service began in March 1946, with flying time at thirteen to fourteen hours. (Photograph reproduced from Davies, *Airlines of the United States*, p. 327.)

unreasonable increase of total operating costs."[21] Too much service rivalry, without pricing flexibility, clearly threatened to raise costs, add excess capacity, and dilute traffic.[22] The board's case-by-case development of service authority produced a linear, point-to-point route structure that merely extended the early mail routes. Discussions of more comprehensive plans never surmounted the apparent limits to the board's authority—or to its vision.[23] Regulation was bounded on one end by a lack of faith in real competition, and on the other end by a fear of centralized administration. This was perhaps the essential dilemma of American-style regulation and a critical element in subsequent regulatory failures.

While the CAB fumbled to regulate competition, technological change and the business cycle periodically rocked airline markets. In

[21] *Transcontinental and Western Air North-South California*, 4 CAB 373 (1943), and *Colonial Air et al., Atlantic Seaboard Op.*, 4 CAB 552, 555 (1943).

[22] In a 1947 case, for example, this ambivalence toward city-pair competition (among trunk carriers) was clear, as the examiner sought to distinguish "between the cut-throat, disruptive type of competition where the existing carrier is fighting for financial survival and the constructive kind of competitive service imposed to stimulate traffic, reduce costs, encourage better service, and otherwise promote the development of the industry"; see Civil Aeronautics Board, Docket No. 679, *Detroit Washington Service Case*, "Report of Examiner," 17 March 1947, 84.

[23] See for example, the President's Air Policy Commission, *Survival in the Air Age* (Washington, D.C., 1948); U.S. Congress, Congressional Aviation Policy Board, *National Aviation Policy*, 80th Cong., 2d sess.; and, James M. Landis, "Air Routes under the Civil Aeronautics Act," *Journal of Air Law and Commerce* 15 (Summer 1948): 299.

1947, the industry plunged into a second re-equipment cycle (the first had been the prewar shift to DC-3s), converting to larger, faster four-engine aircraft capable of seating forty to sixty people. As the carriers incurred new debt to expand capacity, recession struck (in 1948), load factor (the proportion of available seats filled—that is, capacity utilization) plummeted, and operating margins turned sharply negative.[24]

The CAB responded to this crisis by urging all major carriers to raise rates by 10 percent and to offer promotional fares to fill empty seats.[25] Accused by the incumbent airlines of encouraging "competition for competition's sake," the board substantially curtailed its encouragement of city-pair rivalry—competition among carriers for the same city-pair market—and shut the door to new entry.[26] Eventually, it approved most of the mergers precipitated by recession; by 1954, the sixteen trunk carriers were reduced to thirteen, and the twenty-three locals to thirteen.

Shortly after the Korean War, this policy of structural stability was completely reversed. In April 1955, President Dwight Eisenhower appointed Ross Rizley, previously a congressman from Oklahoma, to chair the Civil Aeronautics Board. With prosperity helping to fill seats and to sustain record high airline earnings, Rizley concluded that more competition would best serve the public interest.[27] In a series of fourteen decisions over the next eighteen months, the CAB reduced the number of noncompetitive city pairs—cities served by only one carrier—in the top 100 markets from forty to sixteen. In all, competition was introduced or strengthened in 559 city-pair markets.[28]

At this moment of intensified rivalry, the jet age commenced. First turbo-props, developed in England, and then jets were introduced into commercial aviation. Pan American ordered the first Boeing 707s and McDonnell-Douglas DC–8s in October 1955. The other carriers followed suit, and within a year, the industry had committed $1.4 billion to new equipment—about $200 million more than its total previous net investment.[29]

---

[24] Load factor dropped from 79 to 60 percent in two years; Civil Aeronautics Board, *Annual Report, 1948*, 3.

[25] Cherington, *Airline Price Policy*, 186–289.

[26] Civil Aeronautics Board, Docket No. 1102, *Southern Service to the West*, "Report of the Hearing Examiner," 21 June 1959, 99, and 12 CAB 518 (1951), 534.

[27] Ross Rizley, "Some Personal Reflections after Eight Months as Chairman of the Civil Aeronautics Board," An Address to the Enid Chamber of Commerce, Enid, Okla., 13 Nov. 1955, in *Journal of Air Law and Commerce* 22 (Autumn 1955): 445–52.

[28] Richmond, *Regulation and Competition*, 112–90.

[29] Caves, *Air Transport*, 307–13. Net investment, as of 1955, was reported as $1,239,305,000, in U.S. Congress, Antitrust Subcommittee, *Report on Airlines*, 18.

Lockheed Constellation · Favored by TWA, the Constellation had a cruising speed 70 mph faster than the Douglas DC–4, and the pressurized cabin enhanced passenger comfort; the Constellation also had sixteen more seats than the DC–4. (Photograph reproduced from Davies, *Airlines of the United States*, p. 327.)

Once again, this re-equipment cycle added capacity and debt and undermined return on investment. An investigation of passenger fares opened in 1956 evolved into a collective rate case that brought fare increases of 10 percent in 1958 and 5 percent in 1960. The board justified these increases by an array of utility-like rate-making standards, with a rate of return pegged at 10.25 percent.[30]

The crux of this rule-making was a target load factor of 63 percent. Airline passengers, the board proclaimed, should not be burdened with the cost of excess capacity. Rather, "airline management [was] both responsible and capable of exercising control of load factors over reasonably extended periods by tailoring capacity to the requirements of traffic."[31]

Nowhere was the hubris of regulated competition more evident. The CAB's view that capacity utilization was a managerial prerogative, independent of price and entry regulation, was myopic. It separated the economic links between the firm and the market—between price, capacity investment, market share, and earnings.

Excess capacity was just the most perverse consequence of a hybrid regulation that prevented price competition, but not service rivalry (see Figure 1). Carriers could maintain market share only by adding capacity (more frequent departures) and service. These costs drove

[30] Jordan, *Airline Regulation in America*, 62–65.
[31] Emmette S. Redford, *The General Passenger Fare Investigation*, Inter-University Case Program No. 56 (University, Ala., 1960), 43–44.

Douglas DC–8 · With the Boeing 707, the Douglas DC–8 inaugurated the jet age in American commercial aviation. All of the airlines at this time continued to concentrate on fleet improvements designed to enhance long-haul flights. Shown here is a Pan American DC–8–33 at Kennedy International Airport in New York. (Photograph reproduced courtesy of the New York Port Authority.)

up prices, which in turn weakened demand and resulted in lower capacity utilization. The utility-type rate making that tied fares to the weaker performers among diverse corporations also discouraged cost effectiveness. Pricing under regulation tended to bundle a variety of services into one or two simple packages that hid the real costs and left travelers with little choice about the number and level of services they could purchase.

The effects of regulation on route structure and aircraft fleet were among the most important. By allocating routes piecemeal through individual certification proceedings, CAB regulation produced fragmented, politically stylized, point-to-point route systems. Although they provided convenient nonstop service, often to locations where maintaining that level of service made no economic sense, such route structures afforded air carriers none of the economies of scale or scope that would have been possible with a more integrated, centralized structure.

Rivalry restricted to service had a positive effect on the technological development of the aircraft fleet. Modernity, speed, and comfort were critical aspects of service rivalry. No major carrier could afford to fall behind in new aircraft acquisition—hence, the repetition of frantic re-equipment cycles. Development of the DC–3, for example, and later of the DC–10, were the direct results of American Airlines' efforts

Figure 1
Load Factors and Rates of Return
Domestic Trunk Airlines, 1948–1972

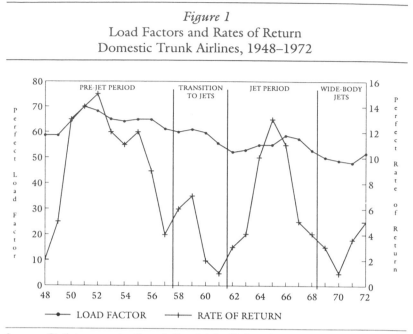

Source: Civil Aeronautics Board, Special Staff, *Regulatory Reform: Report of the Special Staff* (Washington, D.C., 1975), 130

to be more competitive. Similarly, Pan American played a major role in Boeing's development of the 747. The immense investment in re-equipping, moreover, was made possible by the economic security (and protection from competitive entry) that regulation afforded.[32]

Regulatory Failure and Reform, 1969–1978

Prior to 1969, healthy economic growth (with low inflation) and productivity gains from technological innovation had more than com-pensated for the inefficiencies caused by regulation. But the macro-economy began to change at the end of the decade. Slower economic

[32] This rapid turnover of aircraft, however, may not have been an unmixed benefit. Richard Caves pointed long ago to the fact that excessive equipment competition may have precluded some desirable utilization of older aircraft for lower fare service; see Caves, *Air Transport and its Regulators*, 241, and Kahn, *Economics of Regulation*, 2: 213–14. On the re-equipment cycle, see Louis J. Hector, "Problems in Economic Regulation of Civil Aviation in the United States," an Address before the New York Society of Security Analysts, 28 Nov. 1958, in *Journal of Air Law and Commerce* 25 (1958): 101–7.

Douglas DC–10 · The first of the wide-bodied jets, the DC–10 was introduced by American Airlines on its Los Angeles–Chicago route in August 1971. Even as the airlines struggled with excess capacity, they continued to promote the growth in plane size; the DC–10s carried 250 seats. (Photograph reproduced from Davies, *Airlines of the United States*, p. 574.)

growth, rising inflation, and higher interest rates staggered airline markets. Demand, which had been growing at an annual rate of 18 percent from 1965 through 1969, slowed to 4 percent between 1969 and 1975. Fuel supply shocks in the early 1970s, combined with the ratcheting upward of wage costs, sparked an explosion of airline operating costs. Between 1969 and 1978, the price of jet fuel increased 222 percent, amounting to nearly one-fifth of operating costs; and labor costs, which accounted for 45 percent of airline expenses, increased 135 percent (to $22,422 per employee).[33]

New technology and a fourth re-equipment cycle coincided with a downturn in the business cycle. Pan American, as before, acted first, buying twenty-five wide-bodied Boeing 747s (with 350 to 450 seats). Domestic carriers followed suit, ordering McDonnell-Douglas DC–10s and Lockheed L–1011s as well as 747s. By 1975, trunk carriers were operating 282 wide-bodied aircraft. At $22 to $25 million a plane, this capacity cost more than $6 billion—nearly four times cumulative operating profits.[34]

Together, these dramatic changes in demand for service—downward—and in supply of available seats—upward—amounted to a reversal of the airline industry's economic structure. Since the conversion to jet aircraft began in the late 1950s, the industry had enjoyed declining unit costs of capacity (with productivity growth outstripping inflation).[35] In effect, technological gains had been masking the

[33] Civil Aeronautics Board, *Handbook of Airline Statistics*, 1972, 464; 1978, 136.
[34] Civil Aeronautics Board, *Handbook of Airline Statistics*, 1974, 134–35.
[35] Fruhan, *The Fight for Competitive Advantage*, 24.

Lockheed L. 1011 Tristar · Lockheed's response to the Douglas DC–10, the L.1011, went into service in April 1972. Once again, a re-equipment expansion in capacity occurred during a downturn in the business cycle. (Photograph reproduced from Davies, *Airlines of the United States*, p. 575.)

inefficiencies of airline regulation. But in 1969, real capacity costs stopped declining, and they remained at their 1970 levels for the next seven years. Meanwhile, nominal unit costs, driven by wage gains and fuel prices, shot up 77 percent over the next seven years (see Figure 2). And since capacity utilization was so low, nominal costs per revenue-passenger mile rose even more sharply. Dramatic price increases were necessary, forcing the CAB to open an industry-wide rate case that threw the political spotlight on its own regulatory failings.

It was excess capacity that actually triggered the regulatory crisis. Customers, especially business travelers, desired convenience and choice in frequency of departure and nonstop service. In the absence of pricing flexibility, the addition of capacity by one competitor in a city-pair market was likely to take market share from the others. In fact, market share appeared historically to vary disproportionately to capacity share—an empirical relationship called the "S Curve." A city-pair rival with a minority share of capacity was likely to have a lower load factor than competitors—that is, airlines that had fewer seats were likely to fill a lower percentage of them than were competitors with greater capacity. And since overall load factors were often near the break-even point, it was difficult for a minority-share competitor to make a profit. This condition created a perverse incentive to increase capacity, even though capacity utilization would fall if a company's rival(s) followed suit. For carriers serving the same city-pair, this phenomenon posed a kind of prisoners' dilemma.[36]

[36] Ibid., 126–39.

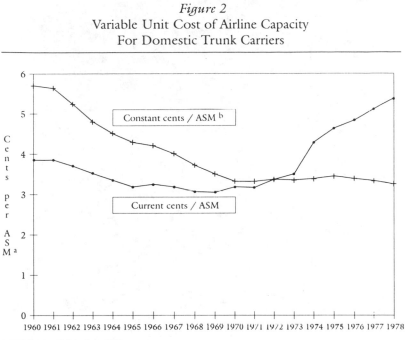

Figure 2
Variable Unit Cost of Airline Capacity
For Domestic Trunk Carriers

a ASM - Available Seat Mile
b1972 base year

Load factor, falling since 1965, hit a record low of 48 percent in 1971. Rapid growth in the number of flights, meanwhile, had already caused severe air traffic congestion, especially in the largest urban markets—Chicago, Los Angeles, New York, and Washington. On those routes, where price-insensitive business customers sought maximum convenience, excess capacity was rampant. Load factor on domestic 747 flights fell to 33 percent in 1971–72.

Between 1971 and 1974, the CAB approved a series of capacity agreements among the major carriers that reduced the number of weekly round-trip flights by 10 percent (on the Washington–Los Angeles route) to 38 percent (on the New York–San Francisco route).[37]

---

[37] In these markets, load factor improved considerably, to the point where travelers actually complained of difficulties getting tickets. William A. Jordan, "Airline Capacity Agreements Correcting a Regulatory Imperfection," *Journal of Air Law and Commerce* 39 (1973): 184–86; U.S. Congress, Senate, Judiciary Committee, Subcommittee on Administrative Practices and Procedure, *Civil Aeronautics Board Practices and Procedures—A Report*, 94th Cong., 1st sess., Committee Print (Washington, D.C., 1975), 145–46. These capacity agreements were ruled unlawful in Civil Aeronautics Board, Docket No. 22908, *Capacity Reduction Agreements Case*, "Report of the Examiner," 18 Nov. 1974.

American Airlines' 747 Piano Bar · With route and rate structures regulated, airlines were left to compete on the basis of service, and "lounge wars" ensued. (Photograph reproduced courtesy of American Airlines.)

Secor Browne, the CAB chairman from 1969 to 1973, also imposed a near-moratorium on new route authorizations. In the five years beginning in July 1969, only two applications were granted.[38]

With capacity and route expansion foreclosed as outlets for product differentiation, the trunk carriers devised new means of service competition. "Capacity wars" gave way to "lounge wars." On wide-bodied aircraft, lounges were introduced in first class, then in coach. When American installed piano bars, TWA countered with electronic draw-

[38] Commissioner G. Joseph Minetti, quoted in U.S. Senate, *CAB Practices and Procedure*, 84–86.

poker machines. Live entertainment proliferated, with musicians, magicians, wine-tasters, and Playboy bunnies.[39] This heightened service rivalry, meanwhile, spilled over into other city-pair markets, where some of the grounded aircraft were put to use. When smaller carriers complained, the industry's consensus on behalf of regulation began to waiver.

The Domestic Passenger Fare Investigation was the CAB's most constructive response to this crisis in capacity utilization. This proceeding, begun in January 1970 and concluded five years later, yielded fare increases totaling 38 percent. Although the fare investigation produced several regulatory innovations, its impact on economic efficiency was debatable.[40] Mileage-based pricing prevented fare flexibility and marginal-cost pricing, and the industry-averaging of costs protected the least efficient carrier. By 1975, the CAB's efforts had done little to improve airline performance; gross overcapacity, high prices, and weak earnings prevailed.

The policy debate on airline regulation came unraveled with great speed. The political process, especially in view of its active support by regulators, confounded the conventional wisdom of the policy literature. What could have broken the symmetry of the "iron triangle"— the regulated industry, congressional interests, and regulators—to which theory had attributed such immutable power? How, indeed, could a "captured" agency cross its captors to advocate its own demise?[41] No single explanation can suffice. Changes in basic economic factors, technological innovation, and regulatory failure were necessary, but not sufficient, preconditions. New ideas about government regulation and a degree of "policy entrepreneurship" also contributed.

Academic professionals, especially economists, played an unusual role in the process of airline deregulation. The work of John Meyer,

[39] Jordan, "Airline Capacity Agreements," 203.

[40] The CAB's procedure and methodology had been subject to criticism since the late 1950s, when commissioner Louis Hector resigned and sent an open letter to President Eisenhower, criticizing the board's lack of rational criteria, policy flip-flopping through case-by-case, oral decisions, justified after the fact by written opinions; Louis J. Hector, "Problems of the CAB and the Independent Regulatory Agencies," A Memorandum to the President, 10 Sept. 1959. In the DPFI, the board adopted an elaborate new set of standards, including 1) determination of an industry-wide average cost; 2) a target load factor of 55 percent; 3) a 12 percent rate of return; 4) a rate structure based on mileage; 5) an assumed price elasticity of demand of -0.7 percent; and 6) an automatic quarterly process for reporting costs and calculating fare adjustments. See U.S. Congress, Senate, *CAB Practices and Procedure*, 109–13.

[41] For a detailed analysis of the theoretical literature that pertains to airline deregulation, see Jonathan L. Katz, "The Politics of Deregulation: The Case of the Civil Aeronautics Board" (Ph.D. Diss., Columbia University, 1985), chaps. 2 and 3.

The Arrival of the In-Flight Movie · As part of service-based competition, TWA introduced in-flight movies on its longer routes in 1961; other airlines quickly followed suit—American and United in 1964. (Photograph reproduced from *Legacy of Leadership*, p. 191.)

Richard Caves, and Michael Levine had earlier established a scholarly thread of criticism. Now, as the industry's performance worsened, other critical voices joined in.[42] In the early 1970s, their critique of regulation was disseminated widely through the economic policy literature familiar to Washington insiders.[43] And the criticism was mag-

---

[42] In addition to those previously cited, see John R. Meyer, et al., *The Economics of Competition in the Transportation Industries* (Cambridge, Mass., 1959); Michael E. Levine, "Is Regulation Necessary? California Air Transportation and National Regulatory Policy," in *Yale Law Journal* 74 (1965): 1416–47; Theodore E. Keeler, "Airline Regulation and Market Performance," *Bell Journal of Economics and Management Science* 3 (Autumn 1972): 399, George W. Douglas and James C. Miller III, *Economic Regulation of Domestic Air Transport: Theory and Policy* (Washington, D.C., 1974), and Paul MacAvoy and John W. Snow, *Regulation of Passenger Fares and Competition among the Airlines* (Washington, D.C., 1977).

[43] Derthick and Quirk, *The Politics of Deregulation*, 29–39.

nified by the broader loss of faith in the federal government that stemmed from problems in the macroeconomy and, especially, from the political disasters of the Vietnam War and Watergate. This regulatory critique, which extended to trucking, railroads, natural gas, and electric power, began to diffuse through a dozen agencies and executive departments in Washington. In the second half of 1974, with the presidency weakened and the polity very much confused by the first oil crisis, the time for reform, and for political entrepreneurship, was ripe.

Stephen Breyer and Senator Edward Kennedy were the first to seize this political opportunity. Kennedy hired Breyer, from the Harvard Law School faculty, to revitalize the Subcommittee on Administrative Practice, which Kennedy chaired. Together, they chose regulatory reform as a strategic issue.[44] Breyer shrewdly suggested that they start with the airline industry, for several reasons: 1) its visibility and glamour; 2) the weak theoretical reed (excess competition) by which airline regulation was justified; 3) the industry's failing performance; 4) its relatively simple political-interest structure (only firms and unions, neither of which had much political clout); and 5) the existence of unregulated intrastate airlines whose performance compared favorably with that of CAB-regulated trunk carriers.

Senator Kennedy's subcommittee held hearings on airline regulation in the spring of 1975. Orchestrated by Breyer to present a "story" and to maximize attention in the press, these hearings were immensely successful. The central theme was that CAB regulation had caused airline fares to be higher than necessary. Witnesses from the airlines and from the CAB found it impossible to rebut the critical logic of Senator Kennedy and his well-prepared staff.[45]

What had been an academic debate now became a political issue, into which a wider array of interest groups were drawn. Gerald Ford's administration proposed legislation to reform airline regulation in 1975, and a coalition of consumer activists, together with a number of airport authorities and municipalities, lent support to the administration's initiative.[46] CAB chairman Richard O'Melia appointed a special staff to review the board's performance, and in July 1975, the special staff issued a lengthy critique that recommended deregulation.[47]

---

[44] K. Harrigan and D. Kasper, *Senator Kennedy and the CAB* (Boston: Harvard Business School, Case No. 9–378–055, 1977).

[45] Breyer, *Regulation and Its Reform*, 321–22.

[46] *Economic Report of the President, February 1975* (Washington, D.C., 1975), chap. 3.

[47] CAB Special Staff, *Regulatory Reform: Report of the CAB Special Staff* (Washington, D.C., 1975); also, 284–91.

During the next two years, congressional committees held hearings on various legislative proposals to liberalize restrictions on entry and fares. The idea of complete deregulation and shutdown of the CAB was not seriously advocated by anyone, including Alfred Kahn, until the final stages of legislative debate.

Organized labor was uniformly and adamantly opposed to deregulation. Pilots, machinists, clerks, flight attendants, engineers, teamsters, and transport workers realized the implications of increased competition for wages, work rules, and job security.[48] The airlines themselves started out in unanimous opposition to any significant reform, let alone general deregulation. Eventually, a few of the carriers broke ranks and supported regulatory reform. Some of the regionals saw an opportunity for growth; Pan American hoped for domestic routes; and United realized that its market dominance might be a competitive advantage.

Still, most carriers remained vehemently opposed. Although a self-styled "great believer in market forces," Frank Lorenzo, the chairman of Texas International, anticipated some structural problems from unfettered competition:

> [If] the Aviation Act of 1975 goes into effect, we will, over a period of years, end up with a couple of very large airlines. There will be many small airlines that will start up here and there, but they will never amount to a very significant amount of the transportation market. . . . The operating and financial advantages will go to the large carriers with substantial resources, and to very small carriers that temporarily have lower labor costs, primarily because they are non-unionized.

When asked by Senator Howard Cannon if regulatory liberalization "would be an attack on the labor movement," Lorenzo answered, flatly, "yes."[49]

Executives at American Airlines opposed deregulation as adamantly as anyone. Albert Casey, American's chairman, was so intransigent that Senator Cannon (once he had come around to the idea himself) facetiously nominated him for "dinosaur-of-the-month." Likewise, Robert Crandall, who eventually became president of American, warned that deregulation needlessly risked degradation of service, safety, and the integrated air-transport network.[50]

---

[48] See U.S. Congress, Senate, Commerce Committee, Subcommittee on Aviation, *Regulatory Reform in Air Transport*, 94th Cong., 2d sess., April-June 1976, 827; and, U.S. Congress, Senate, Committee on Commerce, Science, and Transport, Subcommittee on Aviation, *Regulatory Reform in Air Transportation*, 95th Cong., 1st sess., March-April 1977.

[49] *Regulatory Reform in Air Transportation*, March-April 1977, 510.

[50] Rush Loving, Jr., "The Pros and Cons of Airline Deregulation," *Fortune*, Aug. 1977,

While Congress deliberated, the CAB experimented. John Robson, whom Ford appointed chairman in 1975, liberalized charters, expanded competitive route authority, and experimented with fare competition—the off-peak "peanuts fare" by Texas International and American's broad rejoinder, the "Super Saver." In 1977, President Jimmy Carter appointed Alfred Kahn to chair the CAB. This quintessential policy entrepreneur took charge at the perfect time. With a powerful intellect, a dedication to microeconomic efficiency, and a quick and infectious humor, Kahn set about reorganizing the CAB.[51] Under Kahn, the Board decided several landmark cases, testing open entry and unrestricted price competition.[52]

Early in 1978, both houses of Congress passed bills to liberalize regulation (not to eliminate it). But as the policy options narrowed, airline executives, such as American's Crandall, faced with the prospect of a policy "that would leave the airlines half free and half fettered," now shifted gears and called for the total elimination of economic regulation.[53] By then, too, Alfred Kahn and his staff economists at the CAB had learned the limitations to partial, piecemeal deregulation: "The reason I concluded finally that the CAB should be abolished was my conviction that no government administrator was competent to determine the proper structure of the airline industry."[54] In October 1978, Congress passed the Airline Deregulation Act, which placed "maximum reliance on competitive market forces." The Civil Aeronautics Board would automatically certify entry, unless doing so damaged the public interest. Fares would be flexible within a wide zone of reasonableness, and mergers would be readily approved. If all went well, the Civil Aeronautics Board would cease to exist by 1985.[55]

212; Robert Crandall, "Speech in Detroit," 28 May 1975, in Robert Crandall Papers at American Airlines, Dallas, Texas.

[51] McCraw, *Prophets of Regulation*, chap. 7.

[52] See especially, Civil Aeronautics Board, Docket 30277, *Chicago-Midway Low Fare Route Proceeding*, 12 July 1978; and *CAB Order No. 38-7-40*, 74.

[53] Robert Crandall, "Airline Regulation: Sense and Nonsense," Remarks before the Rotary Club of Tulsa, 12 July 1978; also, Alfred Kahn, "A Funny Thing Happened on the Way to Cincinnati," before the American Association of Airport Executives, Cincinnati, Ohio, 22 May 1978.

[54] Alfred Kahn, "The Uneasy Marriage of Regulation and Competition," *Telematics* 5 (Sept. 1984): 16. At the time, however, few advocates of deregulation had recognized the need for stricter antitrust enforcement. By the time of this article, though, Kahn would warn that "the prevention of unfair competition is the proper job of the antitrust laws, not economic regulatory commissions."

[55] Certain regulatory functions involving customer services (baggage complaints, bumping, and smoking), interline ticketing, and joint fares would devolve upon the Department of

Signing of the Airline Deregulation Act, 1978 · President Jimmy Carter is second from the right, Alfred Kahn is at the far left. (Photograph reproduced from Thomas K. McCraw, *Prophets of Regulation* [Cambridge, Mass., 1984], facing p. 153.)

American Airlines and the Strategic Adjustment to Deregulation

The first year of airline deregulation "was one of the most difficult and tumultuous years of our history," commented Bob Crandall. "As an industry, we seemed bent on giving away the store."[56] And 1980 proved worse still. All but two of the major carriers lost money, with American Airlines' first-half losses of $120 million the worst in the industry. Passenger traffic slumped because of the recession, and the price of jet fuel doubled as a result of the second oil shock.[57] Intense competition for key routes, with wild discounting of fares, caught the industry and its regulators by surprise. The coincidence of deregu-

---

Transportation. U.S. Congress, House, Committee on Public Works, *Legislative History of the Airline Deregulation Act of 1978*, 96th Cong., 1st sess., 1978.

[56] Robert L. Crandall, "Opening Remarks, System Marketing Management Meeting," 2 April 1980, quoted in Richard Vietor, *American Airlines (A)* (Boston: HBS Case Services, Case No. 9–385–182, 1985), 1.

[57] Again, difficult macroeconomic conditions coincided with important changes within the industry. The second oil shock drove jet fuel prices from 40 to 90 cents a gallon—or to about 25 percent of operating costs. With inflation at 10.1 percent, wages per employee reached $26,691. As GNP growth turned negative (0.7 percent), airline traffic fell 4 percent. (American's traffic dropped 15 percent from a 1979 level inflated by United's strike.)

lation and severe macroeconomic shocks probably telescoped, and certainly aggravated, the process of structural adjustment.

The major carriers were totally unprepared. Although the Deregulation Act had proposed an orderly phase-out of regulation, reallocation of routes and fare competition swept past the board's half-hearted attempts at stabilization. A sort of reverse tarbaby effect set in, as competitive rivalry spread throughout the market.[58] By the spring of 1980, carriers were virtually free to determine the routes they served and the prices they charged.[59]

New entry by low-cost, no-frills, point-to-point carriers contributed to the shock. Former intrastates, charters, commuters, and start-ups sensed tremendous opportunities to make money on low-density, ill-served routes as well as on high-density, overpriced ones. With low overhead, nonunion labor, depreciated aircraft, leased facilities, and few extraneous services, these companies—PSA, Air Cal, Southwest, Capitol and World, and eventually Midway, New York Air, and People Express—put intense competitive pressure on the established carriers.[60]

When World Airways offered a transcontinental fare (New York–Los Angeles) of $108, the major carriers followed. Eastern tried to enter the market with a $99 fare, and fares soon plummeted to $88. Pricing madness next spread to the "peripheral transcon" markets of Boston, Washington, and Philadelphia.[61] Hastily, the major airlines began dropping unprofitable routes and entering the potentially profitable markets of their competitors. Braniff, for example, challenged American in the southwest, and Delta attacked American's market in Dallas from the east. Such unrestricted competition forced a dilution of yields (effective revenue per passenger mile), pushing break-even load factors higher. Of all the major carriers, American's was the highest.[62]

Accelerated "hubbing" was the first clear strategic response by the major carriers. The practice of concentrating connecting flights at a particular airport had been used to a limited extent since the 1960s.

---

[58] The economist James McKie used the "tarbaby" metaphor to describe the spread of economic regulation across market segments and functions; James McKie, "Regulation and the Free Market: The Problems of Boundaries," *Bell Journal of Economics* 1 (1970): 6–26.

[59] Office of Economic Analysis, Civil Aeronautics Board, *Competition and the Airlines: An Evaluation of Deregulation* (Washington, D.C., 1982), 22.

[60] Ibid., 108.

[61] Thomas Plaskett (vice-president of marketing, American Airlines), "Address to American Airlines Marketing Meeting," Spring 1981, 31.

[62] Salomon Brothers, *Industry Analysis*, 31 May 1983, 6.

Both Delta and Eastern had developed a hub at Atlanta, United at Chicago, American at Dallas, and Allegheny (now US AIR) at Pittsburgh. But hitherto regulation had severely limited the use of a hub-and-spoke route structure as an operating strategy.[63] Only after receiving route flexibility could the majors contemplate the potential economies of scale and scope that the hub-and-spoke system had to offer.[64]

But fleet composition, at least in the short run, was a major constraint on route restructuring. As Crandall explained in 1980, "the established carriers bought their airplanes years ago expecting to operate them over a stable and franchised route system. . . . Critical decisions about which airplanes to buy, and in what numbers, were based on marketing assumptions that seemed reasonable at the time. They could not—and did not—anticipate the free-for-all we have today."[65] Thus, the four-engine Boeing 707s, designed for transcontinental service in the mid-1950s when oil was cheap and load factors high, had become uneconomical by 1980. On most domestic routes, so had the 747s and even the older model 727s. Although a new generation of aircraft (Boeing 767s and 757s) was nearing the start of production, few of the major carriers could afford the price, nearly $25 million a plane.

Here, then, was the most fundamental market-structuring impact of regulation. Four decades of CAB control had penetrated to the operational core of the regulated firms. Fleet composition and route structure, the essential plant and operating method of the airline business, had become artifacts of public policy. Moreover, most other aspects of the business—work rules and crew assignments, terminal and gate investments, organization of maintenance, and all critical marketing activities—were shaped to fit the routes and fleet. Managers who realized this, and who could implement effective changes quickly, had an immense competitive advantage. But few did.

In terms of strategy, organizational structure, and performance, American Airlines, starting as the second largest but least efficient of incumbent domestic carriers, made the most thoroughgoing and successful adjustment to deregulation. Its reaction provides an especially clear contrast for examining the effects of regulatory change on business practice. Conversely, its size and revealed market power show how

---

[63] Morrison and Winston, *Economic Effects of Airline Deregulation*, 7; and Levine, "Airline Competition in Deregulated Markets," 413.

[64] CAB, Office of Economic Analysis, *Competition and the Airlines*, 49.

[65] Robert L. Crandall, "Remarks Before the 33rd Annual Conference of Airport Operators Council International," Mexico City, 30 Sept. 1980, 8.

Boeing 727 · Originally put into service in early 1964, the 727s had become uneconomical to fly on many domestic routes by the early 1980s. (Photograph reproduced courtesy of the Boeing Company.)

effective strategy, like regulation, can shape market structure to create sustainable profits.

American Airlines was not prepared for deregulation. Its break-even load factor was the industry's highest. Its labor costs were higher than the industry average and its productivity growth lower. Its fleet was the least fuel efficient, and its route structure the industry's most fragmented.[66] During the period in which regulation broke down (1968–74), American's management had made several serious errors: over-expansion into hotel properties, acquisition of too many wide-bodied aircraft, cutbacks in the development of computerized reservation systems, a failed merger attempt, and illegal campaign contributions. When chairman George Spater resigned in 1974, he left behind serious organizational problems and ruined morale.[67]

For the job of restoration, American's board chose Albert Casey, president of the Times Mirror Company. Casey, a rough-and-tumble, gregarious Boston Irishman with a self-deprecating sense of humor, specialized in finance but knew nothing about airlines. He found a top-heavy organization with inadequate management systems. Cost controls, planning, marketing, and the piece-parts of operations were thoroughly fragmented. The budgetary system, Casey recalled, "was a disaster." The new chairman quickly discovered that "Bob [Crandall] knew more about the company than anybody else," even though

[66] American Airlines, "Market Activity Report, 1980"; and Merrill Lynch, *Airline Industry Annual Financial Statistics*, December 1982.
[67] Serling, *Eagle: The Story of American Airlines*.

Alfred Casey, C. R. Smith, and Robert Crandall · Cyrus Smith (center) was head of American Airlines from 1934 to 1968. When his successor George Spater resigned in 1974, the board brought in Albert Casey (left), who in turn named Robert Crandall (right) president. (Photograph reprinted courtesy of American Airlines.)

he'd only been there one year. Crandall, who had held finance positions at Eastman Kodak and Hallmark Cards, was also experienced in managing information systems. Together, Casey and Crandall "got down and ripped the airline apart," creating cost controls and a centralized budgeting system.[68]

Both executives also encouraged the modernization and expansion of SABRE—American's computerized reservation system. This huge, real-time computer network, first developed in the mid-1960s to keep track of the growing volume of reservations, had become a vital component of American's operations even before deregulation.[69] Several of the major carriers had developed similar systems, and at least two of them—United's and TWA's—were comparable to American's. Then in 1975, American started committing resources to develop new features for SABRE and test marketing its terminals in travel agencies—the industry's fastest growing distribution channel. In 1976, as United prepared to expand its system (APOLLO), American

[68] Albert Casey, retired CEO, American Airlines, interview with author, 1 April 1987.
[69] Duncan Copeland, "Information Technology for First-Mover Advantage: The U.S. Airline Experience" (D.B.A. diss., Harvard Business School, 1990).

scooped the market with a large-scale program to sign up travel agents for SABRE. Now, recognizing SABRE as a strategic (rather than an operational) component of competitive advantage, American invested heavily.[70]

Between 1975 and 1979, Casey eliminated some managerial deadwood, sold the Americana Hotel chain, centralized maintenance, training, and computer operations, and moved American's corporate headquarters out of New York City to the Dallas–Fort Worth Airport. Still, in June 1980, when he appointed Crandall president and chief operating officer, the company was staggering under the brunt of competition.

Crandall moved quickly to staunch American's losses. In a matter of weeks, his management team developed a five-part plan to restructure American Airlines, creating a smaller, but more efficient company with a long-term goal of remaining a full-service national airline.[71] The plan was implemented immediately.

First, they grounded the fifty-three 707s. These aircraft—about one-fifth of American's capacity—were losing money every time they took off. This decision—to shrink the airline—was a drastic step that threatened an irretrievable loss of market share. Other difficult decisions were to cancel its order for 757s, which American could not afford, and to convert its underutilized 747s to freighters.

With fewer aircraft, American could eliminate a large number of direct, point-to-point, nonstop flights that were losing money without necessarily reducing the number of city-pairs served. Route flexibility provided a unique opportunity for American to restructure routes in a hub-and-spoke pattern, optimizing aircraft utilization, cost reduction, and market retention. American's planners assessed city availability, airport gates, weather conditions, traffic patterns, demographic trends, and competitors' systems. Above all, they studied the economies of scale and scope.

American had already concentrated 142 daily departures (29 percent of its system total) at the huge Dallas–Fort Worth Airport. These flights were grouped in a series of connecting "complexes" (the nearly simultaneous arrival and departure of multiple aircraft), the largest of which used nineteen gates. A similar, but smaller, hub operation had developed at Chicago's O'Hare Airport. The scale advantages in these arrangements derived from the concentration of labor resources

---

[70] Duncan Copeland, "Evolution of Airline Reservation Systems: 1945–1985," working paper, Harvard Business School, Boston, Mass., 1988).

[71] American Airlines, "Profit Improvement Plan" (a slide presentation), 1980.

Boeing 747 · Passengers are shown here alighting from Pan American's inaugural 747 flight, from London to New York, on 22 January 1970; American was flying 747s by March. Designed to carry 350–450 passengers, the Boeing 747 was 80 percent larger than the Douglas DC–8. By the time deregulation occurred in 1978, that capacity was so underutilized that American president Bob Crandall mandated the conversion of many 747s to freighters. (Photograph reproduced from Davies, *Airlines of the United States*, p. 573.)

and costly ground equipment (for example, aircraft pushers, baggage haulers, service vehicles, and maintenance equipment) at a single point, increasing their utilization and spreading those costs across more arrivals and departures (and passengers). Economies of scope were even greater. By using the hub to serve two groups of city markets on either side of it, an airline could provide service to many more city pairs and could offer more frequent service with fewer aircraft and flight crews. Thus, a hub connecting twenty cities to the east and twenty more to the west could provide one-stop service to 440 city pairs. At that level, an increment of one flight added forty-three more markets.[72]

On the revenue side, effective "complexing" was a critical part of this operating strategy. By scheduling large complexes, with one-hour stopovers, airlines could gather traffic from diffuse sources, substitute one-stop for nonstop service, retain customers end-to-end, and increase load factor on previously thin routes. Delta, with its regional hub at Atlanta, provided a model. Figure 3, which reflects American's initial analysis of hubs, illustrates both the cost and revenue advantages of large hubs and large complexes. The left side of the chart shows that for a relatively small increase in personnel, a huge number of additional city-pair markets could be served (through the geometric impact of hubbing one additional flight); similarly, the right side shows the

[72] Wesley G. Kaldahl, "Address to a Lenders Meeting," 4 May 1982.

Figure 3

How Complexes Realize
Economies of Scale

How Complexes Realize
Economies of Scale
1030 Complex in DFW:
Revenue and Expense

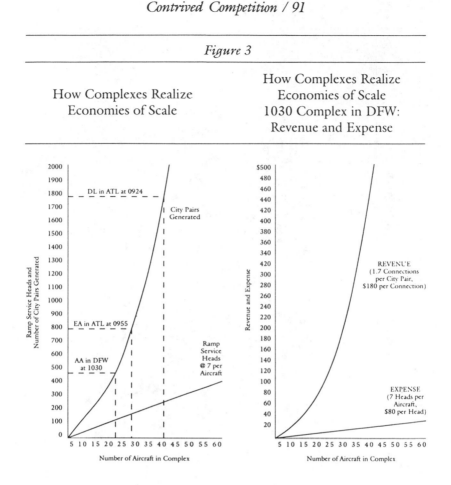

disproportionate gain in revenue (by adding connections to prevent loss of customers to connecting carriers) to expense.

Once these economics were clear, the other issues easily fell into place. American would focus 50 percent of its traffic at the Dallas–Fort Worth (DFW) "Superplex." The number of transcontinental non-stop flights was reduced; dozens of miscellaneous routes, Northeast business routes, and routes to Mexico were discontinued. But through DFW, twenty-two new destinations would be served within a year, increasing city-pair combinations from 655 to 1,519 and daily departures to 213.[73] By 1984 the number of daily departures would reach 300 in eleven daily connecting complexes, of which the largest used thirty-five gates (see Figures 4 and 5). This level of concentration was

[73] American Airlines, "The Dallas/Ft. Worth Connecting Complex," 20 Jan. 1982.

Figure 4

Cities Served by American Airlines Through the DFW Hub, 1980

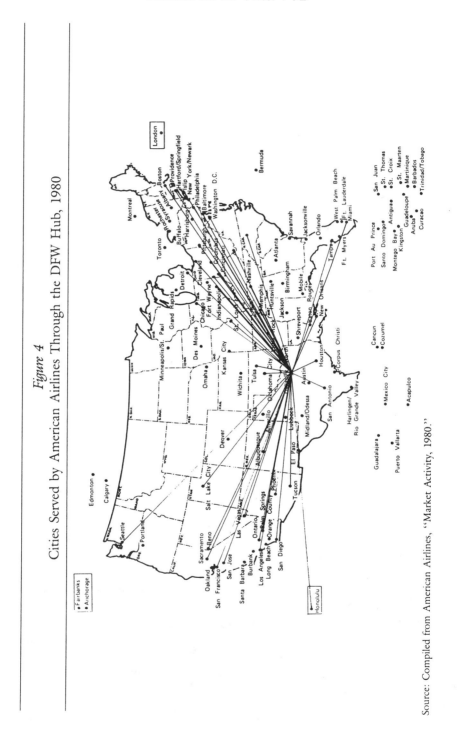

Source: Compiled from American Airlines, "Market Activity, 1980."

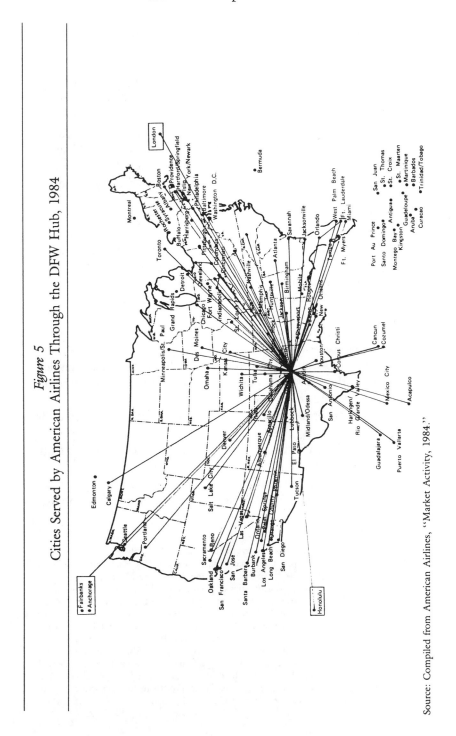

Figure 5

Cities Served by American Airlines Through the DFW Hub, 1984

Source: Compiled from American Airlines, "Market Activity, 1984."

nearly matched at O'Hare, with 224 daily departures serving sixty-five cities.[74]

With a smaller fleet and a more efficient route structure, American needed fewer employees. Crandall announced layoffs and early retirements, reducing personnel from 41,000 to 35,500 by the end of 1981. Labor productivity in every job classification was reviewed and improved to the extent allowed by labor contracts. Miscellaneous costs, especially for fuel, were attacked on every front. New flying procedures were adopted; aircraft were modified and even repainted to reduce drag. Seating density was increased everywhere and weight reduced.

Despite these efforts, American could not hope to compete on cost alone. Differentiation, with a full range of services targeted toward business travelers, was American's only prior competitive advantage. Thus, the last part of the plan was a marketing strategy that applied American's traditional strengths to its emerging hub-and-spoke network. Service, traffic control, and distribution were its critical components.[75]

Service, relatively unscathed by cost-cutting, would be maintained at existing levels for reservations, ticketing, baggage handling, in-flight amenities, and, above all, on-time departures. To hold business travelers on the system, the hub connections had to work efficiently, with little more than an hour between flights.

Pricing to maximize revenue yield and to fill seats would be implemented through SABRE. Peak-load and promotional pricing would need sufficient restrictions to prevent business travelers from crossing over from premium fares to discount categories, and enough flexibility to avoid selling too many discount seats and thus preempting premium customers.[76] Before long, American's reservation sys-

---

[74] Wesley G. Kaldahl, "Presentation to Airline Analysts," 2 July 1985, 7.

[75] Thomas G. Plaskett, vice-president, marketing, American Airlines, interview with the author, Aug. 1984; and Plaskett, "American Airlines Marketing Meeting," 24.

[76] Discount pricing across broad categories of passengers, which was sometimes forced by the "no-frills" discount carriers, was devastating to the profitability of high-cost carriers like American. In the spring of 1982, before American's strategy was fully implemented, Braniff suddenly shifted strategies after its rapid expansion as a full-service carrier proved unsustainable. Howard Putnam, who had been the president of Southwest Airlines, tried to save Braniff with a low-fare strategy—especially on routes in the Southwest and Midwest where it competed with American. In a moment of poor judgment, Robert Crandall allegedly telephoned Putnam and urged him to end the price war by raising prices 30 percent. Putnam made a tape recording of the conversation and gave it to the Justice Department. Crandall eventually settled the resulting suit by a consent decree, in which he agreed not to discuss pricing with other airline executives; *Business Week*, 5 Aug. 1985, 92.

tem could manage this more complex fare structure, allocating seats on each flight to five different classes of fares and shifting allocations daily.

SABRE also gave American an advantage, perhaps even an unfair advantage, in distribution channels. The great complexity of route and pricing options made travel agencies an appealing channel for perplexed travelers; it also made computerized reservation systems a necessity for travel agents. Crandall saw this, and he pushed SABRE to expand as fast as possible; the system had captured 27 percent of the travel agency market by 1983. Competitors complained that United's and American's reservation systems were programmed with a bias toward the owners' flights.[77] By the time the bias was removed in 1983, American's SABRE had become the industry's biggest and most profitable distribution system, as well as an awesome source of market and strategic data.

To cap the marketing plan, American devised a scheme to create brand loyalty and to bond its frequent flyers to the hub. With SABRE delivering the necessary automated record-keeping, American rolled out its AAdvantage program in the spring of 1981. AAdvantage gave passengers mileage credits for flying American, which could be accumulated and exchanged for free seats. By inventing the frequent flyer program, American seized a first-mover advantage, capturing 6.3 million subscribers, whose loyalty, given the cumulative nature of awards, strengthened over time.

With this short-run plan under way and showing results by the end of 1981, Crandall's management team turned to the longer-term issues of competing in an unregulated environment: labor productivity and costs, fleet modernization, and expansion.

Top management undertook a massive, three-year program of employee education on the impact and implications of competition.[78] Then, in 1983, it negotiated new contracts with American's unions that substantially relaxed work rules (especially for temporary workers and job cross-overs) and inaugurated a drastically lower "B" wage scale for newly hired employees.[79] In return, the company guaran-

---

[77] *United Airlines v. Civil Aeronautics Board*, 766 F.2d 1107, 1109 (7th Cir. 1985).

[78] Robert L. Crandall, interview with the author, August 1984; and interview with Judith Leff, September 1987; also, C. A Pasciuto, vice-president of employee relations, American Airlines, "Remarks Before Western Railroad Association," 28 April 1983.

[79] The "two-tier pay scale," as American takes pains to explain, is not a phrase coined by the company. Indeed, management did not initially see the "B" rate as a separate wage system. Rather, it was a front-end adjustment to lower costs of new employees. The same applied to flight attendants; it was a temporary measure, scheduled to reconverge with the

teed job security and profit sharing.[80]

With this "two-tier" wage system in place, American was ready to expand. In spring 1984, American ordered sixty-seven MD Super 80s, with an option to buy one hundred more at the same price. This stretch version of an older McDonnell-Douglas design, with two fuel-efficient engines and a two-pilot cockpit, could deliver 32 percent lower operating costs. With 142 seats (compared to 115 seats in a 727–100), it was the right size for most of American's hub-and-spoke routes.[81] McDonnell-Douglas, moreover, agreed to very favorable financing terms.

Now in a position to compete effectively, and with earnings of $500 million (exceeding those of all other carriers), American moved to complete its expansion. In 1985 Crandall announced American's re-entry into the East with two new hubs—at Nashville and at Raleigh-Durham. Both cities were growing rapidly and would provide American with a north-south route structure that straddled the hubs of two major competitors—Delta and Piedmont.[82] Eventually, American planned to use these hubs as its gateways into Europe.[83]

Market Structure and Industry Performance, 1978–1988

Four strategic patterns, or competitive types, were evident in the deregulated environment. None, however, was as successful as American's.

Building on their prior advantages, three other carriers besides American—United, Delta, and TWA—eventually developed full-service,

---

"A" scale after several years, and disappear altogether after nine years. With the pilots, American made a commitment to recall more than 500 already on furlough, but at 15 percent less than they were making before, for five years. American's management hoped that these temporary differentials would make American more competitive until its operating costs came down and its low-cost competitors accrued their own seniority and overhead costs. From the union's perspective, this temporary concession was the least unattractive means of protecting oldtimers from the cutbacks and benefit losses that deregulation made inevitable.

[80] American Airlines, "The Plan for Achieving Union Productivity Improvements," early 1982; and, "A Blueprint for the Future . . . ," American Airlines' Proposal to the Transport Workers Union, 1982.

[81] American Airlines, "Fleet and Route Planning Issues," mid-1984.

[82] American Airlines, "American's Planned North/South Hubs," Presentation to the Board of Directors, 17 July 1985.

[83] American did enter Europe in 1987, and it continued to expand as rapidly as it could acquire routes. But the new small hubs did not prove to be useful as gateways; Bridget O'Brian, "American Air Expands into Three Continents, Flexing Its U.S. Muscle," *Wall Street Journal*, 8 June 1990, 1, A4.

price-differentiated, hub-and-spoke trunk systems. United tried unsuccessfully to integrate into travel-related businesses before refocusing on airline operations to take advantage of its dominant size. Both Delta and TWA decided to acquire regionals (Western and Ozark) to gain the scale and hub strengthening deemed necessary to compete with American and United.

A second pattern, of full-price, hub-and-spoke regionals, proved transitory. Four large regional carriers—Western at Salt Lake City, Republic at Detroit and Minneapolis, US AIR at Pittsburgh, and Piedmont at Charlotte—strengthened their hubs to preempt competitive entry.[84] But when the national carriers eventually expanded and brought to bear their scope advantages, this "fortress" strategy proved to be transitional; all four regionals subsequently merged with nationals.[85]

A low-cost, limited service, low-fare strategy was pursued by several new entrants, by two failing trunks, and by one previously intrastate carrier. People Express was the most important, but eventually unsuccessful, new entrant using this strategy. Continental and Braniff were major carriers, which, after bankruptcy, rebuilt their operations as low-cost, discount carriers. Continental, a subsidiary of Texas Air, pursued a distinctive strategy of voiding labor contracts and benefit obligations through bankruptcy. By 1989, Texas Air had acquired People Express, Frontier, and Eastern, and was trying to rationalize operations and service a debt of about $6.5 billion.[86] Only Southwest, with long experience with no-frills, low-cost service, had remained profitable, and even grown, by making this strategic choice.

A fourth competitive strategy was adopted by commuter airlines hustling to survive in smaller, low-density markets. Initially, this was a viable business, with appropriate aircraft, sensible schedules, and low-cost labor. But the major airlines needed to control and integrate traffic fed from smaller communities into their hub operations. The commuters, meanwhile, needed gate space and services where they connected at the major airports. Joint marketing tie-ins between the major carriers and commuters therefore seemed to serve both interests. Eventually, these evolved into "code-sharing" arrangements (co-listing

[84] Bailey and Williams, "Sources of Rent in the Deregulated Airline Industry," 173–202.

[85] US AIR and Piedmont combined, and then acquired Pacific Southwest Air, to form a new national carrier by 1989. Half a dozen other small regional carriers did remain independent, serving small geographic niches in which the national carriers were not interested. These include Air Wisconsin, Alaska Air, Aloha, American West, Jet America, and Midway.

[86] M. Weinberg, *Continental Airlines (A)* (Boston: HBS Case Services No. 9–385–006, 1984); and, "House of Mirrors," *Wall Street Journal*, 7 April 1988, 1.

flights on computerized reservation systems), shared aircraft colors, capital infusions, and new names. By 1988, tie-ins had given the eight largest carriers effective control of forty-eight of the fifty largest commuters.[87] Foreclosure of entry was one of the consequences.

All of these strategic responses to deregulation, and the structural adjustments that accompanied them, had an obvious impact on overall industry structure. Figure 6 shows the wave of mergers that occurred between 1981 and 1988. The eight largest surviving carriers were among those certified by the CAB in 1938. Rationalization of industry structure did raise Big Four concentration to 61 percent—higher than in 1978, but less than in 1934.[88] Concentration levels were especially high at the major hubs and may have begun creating uncompetitive pricing. But for travelers flying between non-hub cities, concentration was less important, since airlines competed through different hubs.

The effects of deregulation on market structure and performance were also dramatic, although not so clearcut. Several exogenous events, including the second oil shock, the air traffic controllers' (PATCO) strike in 1981, and the 1982–83 recession, also shaped the patterns of adjustment. Yet with this qualification in mind, we can observe significant changes in important market characteristics: 1) entry and exit conditions; 2) price level and pricing mechanisms; 3) segmentation; 4) distribution channels; 5) cost structure; 6) operations; 7) demand; 8) service levels (and safety); and 9) industry profitability.

Entry into the industry and into individual city-pair markets clearly opened up as soon as the CAB lowered its barriers. As Table 3 indicates, several start-ups entered the business during the first few years of deregulation. Relatively low minimum efficient scale, small capital costs, and nonunion wages made this possible. Initially, economists, especially those associated with the new "contestability theory," thought that the airline industry without regulation would be a model contestable market. By this, they meant that entry (and exit) would be relatively easy and without cost, since there were few sunk costs (especially for entry into an individual city-pair market). If so, then the very threat of entry would hold fares down near marginal costs,

---

[87] Clinton V. Oster, Jr., and Don H. Pickrell, "Marketing Alliances and Competitive Strategy in the Airline Industry," *Logistics and Transportation Review* 22 (1986): 371–87; also, "Major U.S. Airlines Rapidly Gain Control Over Regional Lines," *Wall Street Journal*, 17 Feb. 1988.

[88] "Texas Air's Hard Bargainer," *New York Times*, 16 Sept. 1986.

Figure 6
Consolidation of Pre-Deregulation Trunk and Local Airlines

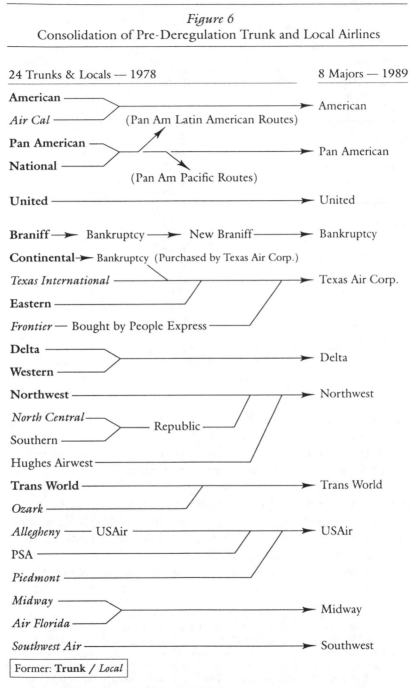

24 Trunks & Locals — 1978   8 Majors — 1989

American

Air Cal   (Pan Am Latin American Routes)   American

Pan American

National   (Pan Am Pacific Routes)   Pan American

United   United

Braniff ➤ Bankruptcy ➤ New Braniff ➤ Bankruptcy

Continental ➤ Bankruptcy (Purchased by Texas Air Corp.)

Texas International   Texas Air Corp.

Eastern

Frontier — Bought by People Express

Delta

Western   Delta

Northwest   Northwest

North Central

Southern   Republic

Hughes Airwest

Trans World   Trans World

Ozark

Allegheny — USAir   USAir

PSA

Piedmont

Midway

Air Florida   Midway

Southwest Air   Southwest

Former: **Trunk** / *Local*

Source: *Air Transport World*, June 1987, 64-65.

Table 3
New Entrant Airlines, 1979–1988

Entrant	Entry	Exit[a]
Midway Airlines	1979	
New York Air	1980	1986
People Express	1981	1986
Jet America	1981	1986
Muse Air	1981	1985
Pacific Express	1982	1984
Northeastern International	1982	1984
Hawaii Express	1982	1984
Best Airlines	1982	1984
Sunworld	1983	1988
American West	1983	
Air One	1983	1984
Regent Air	1983	1983
Frontier Horizon	1984	1986
Air Atlanta	1984	1987
Florida Express	1984	1987
Presidential Air	1985	1987
Transtar	1985	1987

[a]Most of these companies have gone bankrupt. A few, including New York Air, People Express, and Muse Air, have been acquired and/or consolidated on the verge of bankruptcy.

Source: DOT, *Air Carrier Monthly Traffic Statistics, 1986, 1987*, and *Air Transport World*, June 1987, 64–65.

even in a markets that were not structurally competitive in a traditional sense but that were "contestable."[89]

As Table 3 also shows, however, few of these entrants survived to 1988. The market did not prove to be frictionless, because incumbent firms derived competitive advantages from their specialized assets (such as loyal employees, route planners and marketers, training facilities, and reservation systems), and from their strategic choices. By building economies of scale and scope to lower unit costs, by segmenting markets with strategic pricing, and by developing control of distribution channels, the incumbent firms created competitive advantages and eventually foreclosed entry.[90] "For a while it was easy,"

[89] Elizabeth E. Bailey and John C. Panzar, "The Contestability of Airline Markets during the Transition to Deregulation," *Law and Contemporary Problems* 44 (Winter 1981): 809–22; and William J. Baumol, John C. Panzar, and Robert D. Willig, *Contestable Markets and the Theory of Industry Structure* (New York, 1982).

[90] Bailey, Graham, and Kaplan, *Deregulating the Airlines*; also, for a good review of the revisionist literature, see Dipendra Sinha, "The Theory of Contestable Markets and U.S. Airline Deregulation: A Survey," *Logistics and Transportation Review* 22 (1987): 405–19.

an American executive commented in 1983, "to blow United and American out of the market based on cost. But it isn't that easy any more."[91]

Deregulation allowed an immediate reduction of prices and a continuing fragmentation of pricing structure. Here too, the early pricing responses seemed to support the logic of contestability. Even monopolists lowered their fares.[92] Eventually, though, prices stabilized in the least competitive markets, and then increased. Price structure, meanwhile, fragmented into a wide range of special packages, discounts, and incentive deals. The proportion of passengers using discount fares had risen from 37 percent in 1977 to 91 percent in 1987.[93] Yield management became the sine qua non of airline marketing. This development should not have been surprising, in view of airline economics (lumpy bundles of seats with diverse marginal costs) and a history of similar, albeit constrained, pricing practices.[94]

Among the most striking outcomes of airline deregulation was the development and new strategic importance of distribution channels (methods of selling tickets). Under regulation, distribution channels were unimportant and unsophisticated. But with the transition to competition, customer access and control suddenly became critical for sellers, while the fluidity of adjusting markets caused extreme informational problems for buyers. Computerized reservation systems, with the ability to add a travel agency at a relatively small incremental cost and huge economies of scale (and scope), quickly became a competitive bottleneck, of which first movers took tremendous advantage. By 1988, American (SABRE) and United (APOLLO) controlled 70 percent of the travel agency channel, leaving competing systems (TWA, Delta, and Eastern) with too small a base and other carriers in abject dependency.[95]

Cost reduction was a more predictable result of deregulation. The most dramatic and politicized aspect of this process was the decreasing of labor costs. Elimination of work rules, increases in "hard" hours

---

[91] Don Carty, quoted in "A pact that will help American become a low-cost airline," *Business Week*, 28 Nov. 1983, 41.

[92] Meyer and Oster, Jr., *Deregulation and the Future of Intercity Passenger Travel*, 110.

[93] "Assessing the Effects of Airline Deregulation," *New York Times*, 20 March 1988.

[94] See Cherington, *Airline Price Policy*, 186–289.

[95] By 1985, travel agents accounted for 57 percent of all airline tickets sold; *United Airlines v. Aeronautics Board*, 766 F.2d 1107, 1109 (7th Cir. 1985); also, Civil Aeronautics Board, *Investigation into the Competitive Marketing of Air Transportation*, Order 82–12–85 (Washington, D.C., 1984), and U.S. Congress, Senate, Committee on Commerce, Subcommittee on Aviation, *Computer Reservation Systems*, 99th Cong., 1st sess., 19 March 1985.

for flight crews, and wage givebacks all contributed to lower costs.[96] Like American, every major carrier eventually moved to reduce costs across the entire range of operations—fuel, overhead, fleet, and route structure—as well as labor. One estimate put the overall cost reduction at 30 percent (from 4.5 to 3.3 cents per passenger mile) between 1981 and 1987.[97]

Perhaps the most important change in market structure was the fundamental redesign of operations. The hub-and-spoke route structure, combined with "complexing," was a major innovation over the predominantly point-to-point, nonstop operations encouraged by regulation. Besides the economies of scale and scope previously discussed, the full development of hub operations, combined with feeder tie-ins, created powerful barriers to entry by potential competitors.[98] Complexing also aggravated air-traffic congestion and placed a tremendous premium on gates and landing "slots." These scarce commodities, according to economists, had become bottleneck facilities that interfered with competition.[99]

Degradation of service quality could arguably be attributed to deregulation's success, since total demand for air transportation had doubled since 1978.[100] The higher traffic volume, without a concomitant improvement in air-traffic control systems or airport capacity, caused all sorts of operating problems, especially delays, although safety, according to several studies, had not suffered.[101] Yet some service degra-

---

[96] James Blumestock and Evelyn Thomchick, "Deregulation and Airline Labor Relations," *Logistics and Transportation Review* 22 (1986): 389–403; also, Meyer and Oster, *Deregulation and the Future of Intercity Passenger Travel*, 83–107. However, a study by Canadian economists indicates that "since deregulation, the growth rate of compensation in the U.S. airline industry exceeds that of the transport/utility sector of the economy and nearly matches that of the U.S. business sector"; Andriulaitis, et al., *Deregulation and Airline Employment*, 27, 31–32.

[97] *New York Times*, 20 March 1988.

[98] Bailey and Williams, "Sources of Rent," and David K. Massey, "Hub Strategies," *Airline Executive*, June 1987, 37–41. In commenting on this point, however, Meyer suggested that the prospect of point-to-point hub overflights with appropriate new aircraft, like 757s, 767s, and 737–300s, may partially undermine hub dominance.

[99] Proposed solutions, such as sale or auction of slots, were second-best, since dominant firms had the deepest pockets. Not surprisingly, Robert Crandall was a vocal advocate of a market for peak-hour slots. Lawrence T. Phillips, "Structural Change in the Airline Industry: Carrier Concentration at Large Hub Airports and its Implications for Competitive Behavior," *Transportation Journal* 25 (Winter 1985): 18–28; and Robert Crandall, interview, March 1987.

[100] Revenue-passenger miles grew 7.6 percent annually between 1968 and 1978, and 8.7 percent from 1978 to 1987; Merrill Lynch, *Airline Industry,* Nov. 1985, and Department of Transportation, *Air Carrier Monthly Traffic Statistics*, June 1987.

[101] In 1986, the number of federal controllers was down to 22,000, from 27,000 before the PATCO strike in 1981. By 1987, the number of departures handled per controller had

dation did reflect the deregulated carriers' freedom of strategic choice. One major change was the sharp reduction of nonstop, point-to-point service. Frequency of flights, on the other hand, improved 14 percent overall between 1977 and 1984, and 20 to 30 percent in major cities.[102] Consumer complaints about lost baggage, crowding in reservation and ticketing services, overbooking and bumping, and inflight services increased dramatically for all airlines, but with a sizable differential across companies.

Overall measures of industry performance changed dramatically. Load factor, a basic measure of capacity utilization and the industry's perennial problem under regulation, had risen significantly since the early 1970s (see Figure 7). Labor productivity, in terms of available seat miles, had also improved by 3.8 percent annually since 1978.[103] On the other hand, financial results were dismal. Several major carriers experienced persistent losses, and four (Continental, Braniff, Frontier, and People) failed altogether. A few firms were reasonably profitable—most notably American and US AIR—but the average was very low. Total net income for the major carriers over the nine years since deregulation was about $750 million, on sales of $313 billion. Return on equity, which had averaged 1.3 percent from 1970 to 1977, fell to 0.1 percent.[104]

Contrived Competition

The evolution of domestic airline regulation, and then deregulation, can best be understood as a *market-structuring process*. It was initiated to prevent price competition from limiting the growth of large systems. Between the 1930s and the late 1970s, it shaped most of the market's important characteristics—entry, exit, pricing, distribution, route structure, and fleet. In this sense, the market became an artifact of policy that bore little resemblance to any natural economic or tech-

---

risen by 52 percent. While the incidence of near-collisions had increased, most other safety measures had improved because of continuing advances in avionics; see, Federal Trade Commission, Bureau of Economics, *The Deregulated Airline Industry: A Review of the Evidence* (Washington, D.C., Jan. 1988), 76–77.

[102] FTC, *The Deregulated Airline Industry*, 61–83; also, Morrison and Winston, *The Economics of Airline Deregulation*, 25–47.

[103] Congressional Budget Office, *Policies for the Deregulated Airline Industry* (Washington, D.C., 1988), 4.

[104] Alfred Kahn, "Airline Deregulation—A Mixed Bag, But a Clear Success Nevertheless," *Transportation Law Journal* 16 (1988): 248–49 and footnote 58.

Figure 7
Domestic Trunk Load Factors, 1950–1987

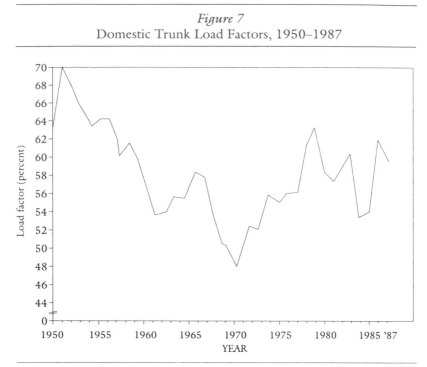

Sources: E. E. Bailey, D. R. Graham, and D. P. Kaplan, *Deregulating the Airlines* (Cambridge, Mass, 1985), 204-5; and Department of Transportation, *Air Carrier Monthly Traffic Statistics*, 1986 and 1987.

nological factors. This process, moreover, did not stop at the boundary of the firm. Regulation shaped the organizational resources of each airline, down to its operational core. This is clear in the case of American Airlines and is true, I think, for most companies in other regulated industries. Once regulation began to fail, or was perceived to fail, interest groups coalesced to provide the political pressure necessary for regulatory reform. Finally, deregulation allowed competition to reshape airline markets in dramatic new patterns.

By examining airline regulation from start to finish, in historical perspective, we can see these developments as a kind of dialectic between decentralized competitive forces and centralized administrative control. To understand and generalize on the causes and consequences of changing regulatory policy in the American context—to explain broad patterns of origination, effect, failure, and reform—we need to examine multiple factors and to accept complex relationships. The whole history of airline regulation, as well as that in other regulated industries, discredits monocausal theories from any individual academic discipline.

To explain the onset of economic regulation for airlines, and its subsequent removal, we need to look at five factors, or change drivers, that were evident in this history and that also apply to other regulated sectors: 1) changes in basic economic and political conditions; 2) technological developments; 3) new ideas about regulation's appropriateness and regulatory methods; 4) political entrepreneurship; and 5) regulatory failure.

The Great Depression was a sudden, seemingly inexplicable change in basic economic conditions that prompted a change in underlying political values and attitudes toward the role of government. Deflation and stagnation threatened to destroy the incipient passenger-airline business just as technological innovation (the DC–3 and other long-range, large-bodied aircraft) made passenger travel possible. Postal subsidies, meanwhile, and the existing form of federal regulation were inducing an unsustainable industry structure in which excess competition and below-cost entry were encouraged. Industry leaders, bureaucrats, and some legislators consequently came to believe that price and entry regulation by government was necessary to foster stable economic growth. And finally, Edgar Gorrell of the Air Transport Association mobilized the necessary political coalition to bring about the regulatory legislation.

Beginning in the late 1960s, the same factors were again at work. Basic macroeconomic conditions changed, from high real growth and low inflation to low growth and high inflation. Political values that traditionally supported regulation were eroded by the weak economic (and regulatory) performance and by extraordinary events in which government management appeared to fail. Technology contributed wide-bodied jets just when additional capacity was least needed. Regulators failed to address the accumulating problems effectively, resorting to irrational rate-of-return proceedings, capacity cartels, and a freeze on new route authorizations. Academic commentators had developed a regulatory critique, which gradually permeated the political establishment. And finally, in the mid-1970s, political entrepreneurs (Kennedy, Breyer, and Kahn) seized on the issue, helped crystallize an interest-group coalition that sought regulatory reform, and precipitated legislative change.

These same generic change drivers, though in different proportions, can account for the imposition and reform of economic regulation in most other areas of the American economy—in surface transportation, financial services, fossil fuels, and power generation. In all of these sectors, industry economics and technology underwent significant change in the early 1930s and the late 1960s. In both periods, existing forms of government intervention proved inadequate, and political coalitions emerged to bring about change.[105]

Historians and political scientists have focused on the causes of policy change, but they have often ignored the consequences of regulation for market structure, industry organization, and the behavior of the firm. In this article, I have tried to show how regulation shaped the airline industry according to government's evolving definition of the public interest, the methods and procedures of CAB regulation, and the continuing interaction of regulators and the firms in the industry. Thus, between 1938 and the late 1960s, the airline business developed as a network of point-to-point, nonstop routes (with aircraft fleets to match), with restricted entry and limited service competition, undifferentiated pricing, limited channels of distribution, and an inflated cost structure.

It is important and useful to see regulation in this light—as a market-shaping force—for several reasons. The responses of the firms and the market are, after all, the consequences of government intervention. If they seem to benefit the public interest, then they justify the regulation. If, however, they serve only a narrow, self-interested group—such as the regulated carriers or organized labor in this case—or if they impose significant inefficiencies or costs on the broader society, or if they create overwhelming asymmetries within the market, they will not remain economically or politically sustainable. Policy reform by legislators, adjustment by regulators, and effective management of the regulated firms all require a careful understanding of how regulation is shaping the market over time, and how those effects interact with technological developments and with the broader macroeconomic context.

The final aspect of regulation that this analysis of airlines tries to illuminate is its relationship to the internal workings of the business firms that constitute the supply side of the market. A firm, as Oliver Williamson has suggested, is a set of transactions, or (potential) market relationships, collected together within an organization. Thus, the boundary between firm and market is, at most, semitransparent.[106]

---

[105] For a comparison across several industries, see Richard Vietor, "Regulation and Competition in America, 1920s–1980s," in *Governments, Industries and Markets*, ed. Martin Chick (London, 1990), 10–35.

[106] Oliver E. Williamson, *The Economic Institutions of Capitalism* (New York, 1985).

As regulation shapes markets, it shapes the inner workings of firms—their investment decisions and asset mix, the operating systems (route structure, in this case), pricing and distribution, and managerial and professional skills. At the onset of deregulation, American Airlines' route structure, marketing system, fleet, and costs were the product of regulation.

But of course, business organizations like American Airlines are much more than a set of transactions. They are human institutions, composed, as William Lazonick puts it, of "organizational resources."[107] These are not merely the specialized assets that economists think of, but primarily the collective skills of managers, professionals, and workers, together with operating and competitive knowledge imbedded throughout the organization—for example, in institutional arrangements, software, training programs, labor relationships, and traditions. In the airline industry, these resources were shaped by regulation, and they were initially ill-suited to unrestricted competition. Robert Crandall saw this; he understood the industry's underlying economics, recognized American's strengths and its weaknesses, and hastened to adapt his firm to the new circumstances. The history of American Airlines' response to deregulation shows how these organizational resources could be used to build a competitive advantage before other firms responded, and then used to redefine airline markets into oligopolistic patterns that economists had not anticipated.[108]

Taken as a whole, then, the airlines' regulatory experience—and I believe that of other regulated industries as well—provides a historical model of how public policy changes, of how it affects markets, and of how business firms respond strategically, also shaping market outcomes. In the airlines, however, we can see the interaction of regulation with competition more clearly than in regulated industries like electric power or telecommunications, where natural monopolies prevailed. We might conclude from this history that regulated competition, at least in the American political and legal context, was a flawed concept. The idea that certain market characteristics could be shaped by government without affecting management's other prerogatives or inducing a distorted strategic response reflected a kind of hubris.

---

[107] William Lazonick, *Competitive Advantage on the Shop Floor* (Cambridge, Mass., 1990), and *Business Organization and the Myth of the Market Economy* (forthcoming).

[108] This point is acknowledged, and thoughtfully discussed, in Michael Levine, "Airline Competition," 393–417.

Unintended consequences abounded, eventually forcing structural adjustments, changes in policy, or both.

More than a decade after it began, airline deregulation is less than a total success. There are competitive bottlenecks (with gates, landing slots, and reservation systems), oligopolistic patterns of competition (for example, rising prices at dominant hubs), traffic congestion, and service problems. But costs are also lower and route structures more efficient; newer, safer aircraft are being financed with earned profits, and passengers generally have widespread choices of carriers and of pricing and service packages. Economies of scale and scope are better realized.

Competition scarcely appears more "perfect" in the airline industry than regulation; the problems are just different.

Amer. Stud. **10**, 3, 329-340 *Printed in Great Britain*

The Politics of American Broadcasting : Public Purposes and Private Interests

by ROBERT J. WILLIAMS
University of Durham

I

Public regulation of broadcasting in the United States effectively began during the First World War. The history of such regulation, from its beginning to the present, is essentially a catalogue of governmental attempts to keep pace with extremely rapid technological and commercial developments. Thus the regulation of broadcasting should be viewed more as a series of empirical adjustments to changing circumstances and conditions than as expressing a coherent philosophy or theory of administration. But, in their attempts to deal pragmatically with abuses in the broadcasting industry, regulators found themselves evolving principles and standards which served to define and clarify the relationship between the government and the broadcasting interests. The purpose of this paper is to examine this relationship and to account for the gulf which has developed between the ' theory ' and the practice of broadcast regulation.

The existence of a gap between the theory and practice of regulation in other areas of governmental activity has been thoroughly discussed.[1] In this view, regulatory agencies have been taken over, or captured, by the very interests they are supposed to regulate. This situation is most often explained by reference to the independent status of the agencies. It is the isolation of the agencies and their consequent lack of political support which is thought to make them peculiarly susceptible to pressure from organized interests. This article attempts to demonstrate that such explanations are essentially simplistic, and suggests that the political and regulatory realities of broadcasting are rather more complex than is generally imagined.

While the United States is one of the few countries which possesses a broadcasting system dominated by private enterprise, it is insufficiently appreciated that the story was nearly very different. Until the First World War, radio regulation was more or less limited to an attempt at identifying

---

[1] The classic work in this field is M. H. Bernstein, *Regulating Business by Independent Commission* (Princeton U.P., 1955). For a detailed critique of Bernstein's position see my article ' Politics and the Ecology of Regulation ', *Public Administration* (Autumn, 1976).

radio operators and to dividing the radio spectrum by function – that is, to keep ship, amateur, military and government transmissions apart.[2] But in common with other aspects of American life, the development of broadcasting was greatly affected by the impact of the First World War.

Nearly all radio stations in operation were taken under government control and run by the navy or the army. Such a takeover was provided for by a clause in the 1912 Act which stated that 'in time of war or public peril' the President might close or seize any radio apparatus. Government control acted as a catalyst to technological innovation in that exclusive patent rights were suspended for the duration. Thus it was the federal government that broke the frustrating deadlock of patent struggles which had threatened the future progress of the industry. It was the government which achieved the standardization of radio apparatus and which generally promoted and hastened the development of broadcasting. In a very real sense, broadcasting in America owed much of its initial development to government finance and navy administration.

It was a distinct possibility that the military monopoly would continue into peacetime and that the navy would 'continue the splendid work it carried on during the war.'[3] The nautical environment of radio meant that legislative proposals were referred to the House Committee on Merchant Marine and Fisheries. A bill providing for a continued navy control was introduced in 1918 and was enthusiastically supported by the Secretary of the Navy, who was a close friend of President Wilson, and by the State Department.

The bill was defeated and America was saved from 'socialised radio', but the defeat should not be attributed to the power of the vested interests in the broadcasting industry or the machinations of their spokesmen in Congress. While the activities of these groups is a familiar part of the contemporary scene, they had not in these early days acquired sufficient political 'muscle' to get their own way. The defeat is partly explained in terms of inter-service rivalry, in that the army was loathe to accept the idea of radio being controlled by the navy. Some historians also suggest that the defeat may well have had something to do with the repudiation of militarism which quickly set in after the armistice.[4]

However, the important issues were institutional and ideological: institutional in the sense that Congress was reluctant to grant general and arbitrary powers to the executive; ideological in that in Congress and elsewhere there

---

[2] Public Law, No. 264, 62nd Congress, 1912.

[3] Josephus Daniels, Secretary of the Navy, quoted by E. Barnouw, *A Tower in Babel* (vol. 1 of a *History of Broadcasting in the United States* (Oxford U.P., 1966), p. 53.

[4] *Ibid.*, p. 53.

was dismay and fear at the prospect of monopoly control of radio. This reflected in part the cluster of values and attitudes represented in American hostility to most forms of government intervention and control, in beliefs concerning the value of variety and diversity, in individualism and, above all, in the virtues of competition. Such values had already found legislative expression in the Sherman and Clayton Acts which were passed before the First World War.

The politics of broadcasting since this period have repeatedly centred on the same issues; who should regulate broadcasting and what are the proper limits of governmental intrusion into private activities? Institutional jealousies, ideological beliefs, and economic interests have all played their part in determining the nature and effectiveness of regulation.

Unlike the British experience, the case for a monopoly in broadcasting was never accepted. Congressman Greene's statement that 'it was not necessary for one person to own all the air in order to breathe'[5] struck a sympathetic chord inside and outside Congress. If government were not to have a major role in the future running of radio, it, at least, took steps to avoid a resumption of earlier patent struggles by sponsoring a merger which created the Radio Corporation of America in 1919. This was essentially an alliance of major companies with a government representative, Rear Admiral Bullard, sitting on the Board. But it would be a mistake to assume that the composition and character of the industry has not changed since the pioneering days. In the 1920s it was the manufacturers of radio equipment and not people who made or transmitted programmes who constituted the broadcasting interests. The potential of advertising on radio was not recognised immediately and programming was seen largely as a means of selling more radio receivers.

Freed from direct or effective supervision, the 1920s saw an anarchic boom in radio broadcasting. The number of radio stations increased rapidly and the search for a relatively clear signal became more and more difficult. In the absence of any effective controls the Secretary of Commerce, Herbert Hoover, convened a series of radio conferences and was largely guided by them in his broadcasting policies. Far from resisting government intervention, the representatives of the industry called for greater regulation which could accomplish an orderly re-allocation of stations. Hoover was both pleased and correct to assert that 'this is one of the few instances where the country is unanimous in its desire for more regulation'.[6]

---

[5] Government Control of Radio Communications, House of Representatives hearings, 65th Congress, 3rd Sess., 1918, p. 11.

[6] Radio Broadcast, May 1922; selected extracts contained in *The Memoirs of Herbert Hoover, 1920–33* (Hollis and Carter, 1952), pp. 139–48.

The vagueness of the 1912 Radio Law meant that there was no clear legislative authority which Hoover could use as the basis for action. Congress was unwilling to allow Hoover to become a virtual Czar of radio and was unable to get to grips with the problem itself. But the simple and overriding technical fact of life was that the broadcasting spectrum could not accommodate all those who wished to broadcast. To allow anybody a licence would have meant interference for everybody. The price of clear reception on one station was to prohibit the claims of another. Hoover was increasingly forced to deny licence applications and, in addition, he devised and enforced restrictions on transmitter power and hours of transmission.

Disappointed applicants and broadcasters frustrated by Hoover's restrictions turned, not to Congress, but to the courts for the redress of their grievances. Hoover remained unmoved and in 1925 he insisted that ' freedom cannot mean a licence to every person or corporation who wishes to broadcast his name or his wares '.[7] Broadcasting was not to be run in accordance with the wishes of private interests but rather he declared ' the ether is a public medium, and its use must be for the public benefit '.[8] Thus as early as 1925 the first principle of broadcast regulation had been elaborated. Subsequent administrations and Congresses have all paid lipservice to the idea propounded by Hoover that broadcasting could not be used simply to further private interests.

Hoover's attempts to regulate without explicit legislative authority were undermined in a series of court decisions[9] which found that the Secretary of Commerce had no power to make any regulations regarding radio licences. The collapse of regulation resulted in ' A mad scramble to get on the air and a broadcast of bedlam resulted '.[10]

The situation in broadcasting had now become intolerable and ' the demand for regulation was now imperative since the very existence of the industry was threatened '.[11] In 1926, representatives of the broadcasting industry and other groups applied pressure on Congress in a series of hearings on the industry and it was out of these hearings that the legislation establishing the first Federal Radio Commission emerged. An independent regulatory commission was the chosen vehicle of control because of the perennial Congressional fear of adding to the power of the executive.

[7] Quoted in W. B. Emery, *Broadcasting and Government* (Michigan U.P., 1971), p. 29.
[8] *Ibid.*, p. 29.
[9] *Hoover v. Intercity Radio Inc.*, 286 Fed. 1003 (1923). *United States v. Zenith Radio Corporation*, 12 Fed. (2nd) 616 (1926).
[10] E. P. Herring, *Public Administration and the Public Interest* (McGraw Hill, 1936), p. 160.
[11] *Ibid.*, p. 160.

II

The first regulatory commission to be responsible for radio could not have got off to a worse start. Congress failed to pass the deficiency appropriation bill of 1927 and consequently left the commission without any financial resources or staff, while the commissioners that were nominated to serve in that year had either not been confirmed by the Senate or had demonstrated a peculiarly high mortality rate. Despite these early tribulations, the Radio Act of 1927 marked a watershed in the relationship between government and broadcasters. It established a number of fundamental regulatory principles which have been further developed and refined in subsequent legislation.

The most important principle embodied in the Act was that the radio spectrum belonged to the public and that therefore a broadcaster acquired no ownership or property rights to a particular frequency, just because he had been permitted to broadcast on that wavelength. Moreover, it was established that no one had a right to a broadcast licence and that the commission was obliged to consider before granting or renewing a licence whether the public interest would be served by such a conferral. The perennial difficulty of the regulatory authorities has been to determine the compatibility of public purposes and private interests.

Once the largely technical problem of an efficient allocation of frequencies had been accomplished, the regulatory body turned its attention first to the non-technical qualifications of potential licensees and then by implication to the kind of programming transmitted. The Federal Communications Commission, which replaced the Radio Commission in 1934, was entrusted with the power to deny an application to broadcast on the grounds that it does not serve the 'public interest, convenience or necessity'.[12] These key words became the focus of a longstanding debate on the proper limits of government control and regulation of broadcasting. The problem was compounded by another section of the 1934 Communications Act which held that the commission had no power of censorship and no right to interfere with free speech.[13]

Given its mandate, the FCC has had to establish both the need for a service and criteria for distinguishing between those who wish to provide it. While the problem of what constituted 'need' for a broadcast service vexed the commission for a number of years, it ultimately decided that 'need' was demonstrated by a 'request from a qualified applicant for a technically feasible service'. For many years the FCC persistently refused to consider the adverse effect a new station might have on existing licensees, but by the

12 Communications Act, 1934, s. 303.
13 *Ibid.*, s. 326.

1950s the power of the broadcasting lobby had grown sufficiently to force a change in policy.[14]

The vast numbers of radio and television stations now in existence have rendered the 'need' issue somewhat academic as there are virtually no more opportunities to provide new services. But the doctrine has had a significant residual influence on the regulation of cable television. As we shall see, the FCC has been particularly sensitive to the potentially damaging economic effects of this new technology on conventional broadcasting services.

Having ascertained 'need' the regulatory body evolved criteria for choosing between applicants. How these criteria were developed and applied is a fascinating story in itself, but for present purposes the question is largely irrelevant in that the expansion of broadcasting to current levels makes the introduction of a new station increasingly rare. In recent times the commission has been largely concerned with whether or not a licence should be renewed. Controversy has occurred when the commission has strayed from ascertaining the applicant's citizenship, character, financial status and technical resources to the sensitive area of programming. In its programming and licensing policies the commission has repeatedly stated that its principal goal is the furtherance of the public interest. Implicit in its declared programming standards is the conviction that broadcasters transmit 'worthwhile'[15] programmes as well as pander to majority tastes and interests.

The theory of broadcast regulation is then not difficult to discover. The airwaves are assumed to be in the public domain and to be used in the public interest. Broadcasters may be allowed exclusive use of channels and frequencies but only for limited periods and only so long as the privilege is not abused for purely private interests. Broadcasters are under an obligation to provide a public service and are not allowed to employ exclusively commercial criteria in their programming schedules. In essence then private gain or advantage must be secondary to the 'public interest, convenience or necessity'.

The practice of regulation has been very different. Within generous limits broadcasters are pretty much free to pursue their private interests without fear of government controls. The licence to broadcast has been elevated from a limited and revocable privilege to the status of an absolute and eternal property right. A lucrative market in broadcast licences has developed which makes nonsense both of the elaborate procedures employed to allocate licences initially, and of the whole concept of public accountability in broadcasting. The renewal or transfer of a licence should be seen for what it really

---

[14] *FCC* v. *Carroll Broadcasting Company*, 258 F.2nd 440 (D.C. Cir. 1958).

[15] H. G. Irion, former Chief Hearing Examiner of the FCC, 'Criteria for Evaluating Competing Applicants', *Minnesota Law Review*, **43** (1959), 480.

is, the granting of a valuable commodity. Whatever the public intentions involved in licence allocation, they are now perceived to be highly profitable and marketable assets. Licences are renewed automatically, rarely suspended or revoked, and transfers of licences are regarded as a normal part of business practice.

If the theory of licensing is incompatible with its practice, the same is true of the programming aspect of regulation. Despite periodic mutterings about the public service responsibilities of licensees, the vast bulk of programming was aptly characterized by a former FCC Chairman as ' a vast wasteland '.[16] Thus in the two major areas of licensing and programming there is an apparently stark conflict between declared public purposes and the unfettered pursuit of private interests.

The pronounced incongruence between the theory and practice of broadcasting is not susceptible to any monocausal explanation. Those who seek to explain the failure of regulation purely in terms of the capacity of powerful vested interests to manipulate the political system for their own economic ends, are simplifying to the point of distortion. It would be foolish to underestimate the influence of such economic forces, but, as we shall see, other factors have made the regulatory process more complex and less susceptible to simplistic explanation.

One obvious factor, which is partly responsible for the gulf between the theory and practice of regulation, is the continuing difficulty experienced by regulatory authorities in adapting to innovation and new technologies within the broadcasting industry. The pace and direction of change has proved too fast and unpredictable for consistent or coherent regulation. No sooner had the FCC come to terms with AM radio than it was faced with FM radio, VHF television, UHF television and more recently cable and subscription television. Rapid technological change places enormous pressures on administrators to change their policies and even their philosophies.

Thus, in many important policy areas, the theory of broadcast regulation is outmoded and even obsolete. The FCC attempts to regulate broadcasting by controlling individual radio and television stations, but most programming and much advertising is put out by the networks which are largely free from commission control. Similarly, the FCC evolved policies regarding the importance of balanced and diverse programming schedules in the days when there were a relatively few broadcasters. In the present situation, with over five thousand radio and several hundred television stations, the need for broadcasters to be all things to all men is much reduced.

When discussing the strength of economic interests in influencing broad-

---

[16] N. Minow, *Equal Time; the Private Broadcaster and the Public Interest* (Atheneum, 1964), p. 55.

casting policies, it is well to be clear which particular interests are paramount at any one time. It is at least doubtful whether manufacturers of broadcasting equipment, the major networks, leading advertisers and local station owners could be said to have identical or even similar economic interests. It is even more difficult to subsume the important differences within the television industry into one economic interest as an extra ingredient for the political cauldron. The bitter battle over cable television has demonstrated that the broadcasting interests are not monolithic and that explanations which emphasize the economic and political power of the broadcasting industry are, at least, in need of careful specification and qualification. The FCC's approach to the problems generated by cable television demonstrates an attempt to reach compromise settlements acceptable to all parties. This is a clear case not of industry capture of a political body but of a regulatory authority endeavouring to reconcile apparently incompatible elements within the regulated industry.

It is easy to see why the theory of industry capture has achieved widespread acceptance. It is highly plausible and partially accurate. The argument has particular force when it focuses on the comfortable relationship which exists between some broadcasting interests and many influential members of Congress. In an era when television and radio have supplanted more traditional means of electioneering, it would indeed be strange if elected politicians were to be indifferent to the views of such potentially powerful interests. Every member of Congress is dependent on the co-operation and goodwill of the broadcasting media in his state. Furthermore, Congressmen are prone to regard the allocation of broadcast licences as coming under the provisions of senatorial courtesy.

The organization responsible for the regulation of broadcasting, the Federal Communications Commission, has a small staff and a low budget. It is highly susceptible to the least amount of Congressional pressure. Given the peculiar distribution of power within Congress, it only requires the efforts of a small number of Congressmen in key positions to make life intolerable for the commission. One consequence of this situation is that 'Agencies seldom take steps under their rule-making power which do not have some support from Congress. In view of his almost autocratic powers the committee chairman's views are likely to be given extraordinary weight'.[17] Any attempt by the FCC to expand its rule-making authority in areas sensitive to Congressional interests may invite a crushing response. One attempt by the FCC to restrict the amount of advertising allowed was held invalid and was described by a Congressional committee as 'an out-

---

[17] W. Cary, *Politics and the Regulatory Agencies* (McGraw Hill, 1967), p. 53.

standing example of a regulatory agency arrogating to itself the right to legislate '.[18]

The failure of the FCC to relate the theory to the practice of broadcast regulation is largely explicable in terms of the profusion of obstacles and handicaps it has to overcome. Perhaps the most persuasive reason for the failure of regulation to achieve declared public purposes is that the objectives themselves are either vacuous or extremely vague.

The basic criterion used in all broadcast regulation is that of the public interest, but there has been a great reluctance to specify in a concrete fashion what this might mean. It is assumed that it represents something wider, more comprehensive, more enduring or even more worthwhile than the naked pursuit of self-interest. Congress discharges its responsibilities in passing the statutes creating the regulatory authorities, but such statutes are nearly always vague and ill-defined. The objectives of broadcast regulation are then far from clear and the standard of the public interest has proved a singularly unhelpful guide to action. Consequently, broadcast regulation is characterized by a marked lack of purpose and a minimum of legislative guidance. Such arrangements are favoured by Congress, because they allow Congress to retain great flexibility in shaping the nature and extent of regulatory activity.

The weakness of regulatory bodies may suggest not evidence of capture by vested economic interests but a general lack of legislative or political guidance. The FCC has demonstrated on countless occasions a lack of confidence in its own activities. It is constantly aware that, should it arouse hostility from any sector of the broadcasting industry, then the likely consequence will be legislative or judicial retribution. Thus, the commission has, in all its policies, edged forward slowly and tentatively rather like a man crossing a minefield. It ventured slowly into the area of programme regulation, conscious that it was moving into the sacred field of the First Amendment freedoms. On the question of cable television, it debated for many years as to whether it held jurisdiction over it. The commission hedged, vacillated and generally delayed until Congress was forced to give a lead.

The FCC is expected to approach major policy issues without legislative guidance but with the threat of a Congressional veto if it puts a foot wrong. The consequence is that it is reluctant and slow to formulate policies appropriate to a rapidly changing environment while its capacity to apply coherently and consistently any policies it does evolve is severely reduced. A number of basic defects in broadcast regulation can be traced to the vagueness of the regulatory mandate and its crippling effects on policy making. A policy vacuum, in turn, is likely to lead to unequal treatment of like cases, to

[18] *Ibid.*, p. 47.

uncertainty caused by such regulatory inconsistency, and to extensive and elaborate legal procedures, since each case is, in essence, a new law.

III

The picture which emerges from the foregoing analysis of the FCC is of a regulatory tortoise, slow, cautious and myopic; a creature at home in a familiar environment and unable and unwilling to venture far afield or to cope with unexpected change. It welcomes the routine and predictable and fears the new and the uncertain. It is a small, weak and undernourished creature scarcely able to support itself in the political jungle. It knows when to be deferential to the large carnivores and is careful not to impinge on their territory without invitation. Faced with threats and intimidation, it is likely to retreat into its shell or to go into hibernation in the hope that the problem will either go away or resolve itself. But it would be wrong to attribute this entire behaviour pattern to the activities of the relevant economic interests. Their influence is only one of the many elements which constitute the regulatory environment.

The complexities inherent in the regulatory task have at least as much to do with the so-called failure of regulation as the most comprehensive of 'capture' theories. Despite the severe handicaps and obstacles it faces, it is revealing that the FCC has, on occasion, displayed remarkable independence and courage. The alleged capture of the FCC by the broadcasting interests fails to account for many of the recent actions of the commission. The perspective of those who see regulation as ineffective is not often shared by broadcasters themselves for 'TV stations which have lost their licence, or newspaper owners forced to divest themselves of TV ownership or networks faced with a half-hour reduction in prime-time programming are not likely to think of themselves as playing the role of captor with respect to the FCC'.[19] This is not to deny the success of the broadcasting interest in securing regulatory policies generally favourable to their objectives but rather suggests that the channels of influence are not one way. Broadcasting policies are not so much dictated by the economic interests but more the product of a process of interaction between regulator and regulated.

Clearly, in a free enterprise economy, there are limits to the ability of public authorities to compel powerful economic groups to act against their own interests. The politics of broadcasting must necessarily consist of an accommodation between the clearly understood, tangible goals of private enterprise and the more nebulous and general responsibilities of regulatory bodies. The enormous and rapid growth of broadcasting into a multi-

[19] J. Q. Wilson, 'The Dead Hand of Regulation', *The Public Interest*, 25 (1971), p. 47.

billion dollar industry in a period of about twenty-five years has politicized the environment of regulation. In theory, the FCC holds a life and death power over investments worth hundreds of millions of dollars. The enormousness of this responsibility has the understandable effect of making the commission rather hesitant about exercizing its powers. Only on rare occasions can the transgressions of broadcasters be so grave as to justify the use of the ultimate weapon, revocation of licence. But the fact that the FCC exercizes this power only rarely does not imply that broadcasters are insensitive to its strictures or rebukes. The existence of this Damocletian threat frequently has a sobering effect on the more intemperate broadcaster.

The politics of broadcasting are not susceptible to facile generalization. It resembles a struggle between a cat and a mouse, in that the large powerful economic interests constantly strive to exert their superiority over the smaller, weaker regulatory authority. But, as in the cartoons, the cat does not always win and the mouse may prove to be a painful irritant. Naturally, the mouse rarely dares to face the cat in open combat, and so it is in broadcast regulation.

It is clearly undeniable that the broadcasting interests, in common with other large, wealthy, well-organized economic groups in American society, exercise considerable influence over the policies related to their spheres of activity. If we add to this general reservoir of influence and access the undoubted leverage obtained from what might be termed the electoral connexion, the political 'muscle' of the broadcasters is impressive. This is a practical, or empirical judgement, not an ethical or moral position. The influence of broadcasters is a political fact of life which may be used to support or to refute incompatible understandings of American politics.

The role of economic interests in the politics of broadcasting is clearly considerable but whether one approves or disapproves of it depends on the particular ideological position adopted. Those who support vigorous public control of private enterprise tend to view any consensus between regulators and regulated as evidence that private profit has triumphed over the public interest. Earlier it was argued that a common fallacy in regulatory discussions is to assume an identity of interest amongst the regulated; the second part of this fallacy is the assumption that the interests of the regulated are always and necessarily incompatible with the public interest. The logic of the critics' position is that any decision by the FCC which is seen to favour the broadcasting interests must, almost by definition, be evidence that the commission is acting contrary to the public interest. This is clearly nonsense and surely the important point is not whether the FCC serves the ends of the broadcasting industry but whether these are legitimate and justifiable ends.

The public interest is a porous concept which is prone to conflicting interpretations. Assuming that, in one sense, the question of the proper goals of broadcast regulation is an ideological matter incapable of demonstration, then the question becomes an institutional one. Instead of asking what are the goals of regulation, we should ask who is responsible for defining them. It seems uncontroversial to assume that this is properly a Congressional responsibility and, if no clear expression of what it regards as desirable has been forthcoming, it is hardly surprising that the FCC has been reluctant to arrogate that right to itself.

There is then no incongruity between the theory and practice of regulation, because, by any yardstick, the FCC generally regulates in the way Congress has directed it. If the effect of such regulation is to foster private interests, it can only be because Congress regards existing policies as compatible with the public interest. In the absence of a large, well-organized and politically influential opposition to current broadcasting policies, the FCC has demonstrated a consistent and understandable concern for its own survival. The politics of broadcasting then conform to the consensual image of American politics in that the absence of fundamental conflicts over ends permits orderly resolution of disputes over means.

This analysis has shown that the pattern of broadcast regulation is determined by a complex interaction of many different factors, forces and groups. It has tried to indicate the nature of the political and other constraints which shape the behaviour of the FCC and which require the rejection of facile, if plausible, accounts of its activities. The FCC, although operating in a politically sensitive area, is not to be regarded as a unique entity, but rather as representative of the more general tensions and unresolved problems of political and public accountability in American government.[20]

---

[20] A version of this paper was presented at a Conference on American Politics in the University of Essex in January 1976.

ACKNOWLEDGMENTS

Barton, Frank L. and Byron Nupp. "Regulation and Economic Performance in Transportation." *George Washington Law Review* 31 (1962): 186–97. Courtesy of Yale University Law Library.

Bromley, Willard S. "The Making of Forest Policy in Pulp and Paper Trade Associations, 1878–1986." *Journal of Forest History* 30 (1986): 192–96. Reprinted with the permission of the Forest History Society. Courtesy of the Forest History Society.

Christainsen, Gregory B. and Robert H. Haveman. "Public Regulations and the Slowdown in Productivity Growth." *American Economic Review* 71 (1981): 320–25. Reprinted with the permission of the American Economic Association. Courtesy of Yale University Law Library.

Clary, David A. "What Price Sustained Yield? The Forest Service, Community Stability, and Timber Monopoly under the 1944 Sustained-Yield Act." *Journal of Forest History* 31 (1987): 4–18. Reprinted with the permission of the Forest History Society. Courtesy of the Forest History Society.

Cleveland, Paul A. "Domestic Trunk Air Transportation: From Regulatory Control to Deregulation." *Essays in Economic and Business History* 7 (1989): 176–89. Reprinted with the permission of the University of Southern California, Department of History. Courtesy of the University of Southern California, Department of History.

Coburn, Leonard L. "Eighty Years of U.S. Petroleum Pipeline Regulation." *Journal of Transport History* 9 (1988): 149–69. Reprinted with the permission of Manchester University Press. Courtesy of Yale University Seeley G. Mudd Library.

Dye, Thomas R. "Oligarchic Tendencies in National Policy-Making: The Role of the Private Policy-Planning Organizations." *Journal of Politics* 40 (1978): 309–31. Reprinted from the *Journal of Politics*, by permission of the author and the University of Texas Press. Courtesy of Yale University Sterling Memorial Library.

Fix, Michael and George C. Eads. "The Prospects for Regulatory Reform: The Legacy of Reagan's First Term." *Yale Journal on Regulation* 2 (1985): 293–318. Copyright 1985 by the *Yale Journal on Regulation*, Box 401A Yale Station, New Haven, CT 06520. Reprinted from Vol. 2 by permission. All rights reserved. Courtesy of Yale University Law Library.

Kahn, Alfred E. "Deregulation: Looking Backward and Looking Forward." Yale Journal on Regulation 7 (1990): 325–54. Copyright 1990 by the Yale Journal *on Regulation*, Box 401A Yale Station, New Haven, CT 06520. Reprinted from Vol. 7 by permission. All rights reserved. Courtesy of Yale University Law Library.

Kaserman, David L., L. Roy Kavanaugh, and Richard C. Tepel. "To Which Fiddle Does the Regulator Dance? Some Empirical Evidence." *Review of Industrial Organization* 1 (1984): 246–58. Reprinted with the permission of the author. Courtesy of the author.

McQuaid, Kim. "Big Business and Public Policy in Contemporary United States." *Quarterly Review of Economics and Finance* 20 (1980): 57–68. Reprinted with the permission of the University of Illinois at Urbana-Champaign, Bureau of Economic and Business Research. Courtesy of Yale University Sterling Memorial Library.

Morton, Alexander Lyall. "Emerging Structural Changes in Transport and Public Utilities: Northeast Railroads: Restructured or Nationalized?" *American Economic Review* 65 (1975): 284–88. Reprinted with the permission of the American Economic Association. Courtesy of Yale University Law Library.

Peterson, R.D. "The CAB's Struggle to Establish Price and Route Rivalry in World Air Transport." *American Journal of Economics and Sociology* 49 (1990): 65–80. Reprinted with the permission of the *American Journal of Economics and Sociology*. Courtesy of Yale University Sterling Memorial Library.

Petracca, Mark P. "Federal Advisory Committees, Interest Groups, and the Administrative State." *Congress and the Presidency* 13 (1986): 83–114. Reprinted with the permission of *Congress and the Presidency*. Courtesy of Yale University Sterling Memorial Library.

Plotkin, Sidney. "Corporate Power & Political Resistance: The Case of the Energy Mobilization Board." *Polity* 18 (1985): 115–37. Reprinted with the permission of the Northeastern Political Science Association. Courtesy of Yale University Sterling Memorial Library.

Reich, Robert B. "Bailout: A Comparative Study in Law and Industrial Structure." *Yale Journal on Regulation* 2 (1985): 163–224. Copyright 1985 by the *Yale Journal on Regulation*, Box 401A Yale Station, New Haven, CT 06520. Reprinted from Vol. 2 by permission. All rights reserved. Courtesy of Yale University Law Library.

Siegmund, Fred. "Competition and Performance in the Airline Industry." *Policy Studies Review* 9 (1990): 649–63. Reprinted with the permission of Transaction Publishers. Courtesy of Yale University Social Science Library.

Vietor, Richard H.K. "Contrived Competition: Airline Regulation and Deregulation, 1925–1988." *Business History Review* 64 (1990): 61–108. Reprinted with the permission of the Harvard Business School. Courtesy of Yale University Sterling Memorial Library.

Williams, Robert J. "The Politics of American Broadcasting: Public Purposes and Private Interests." *Journal of American Studies* 10 (1976): 329–40. Copyright Cambridge University Press 1976. Reprinted with the permission of Cambridge University Press. Courtesy of Yale University Sterling Memorial Library.